SUPERGIRL

VOLUME 3: GHOSTS OF KRYPTON

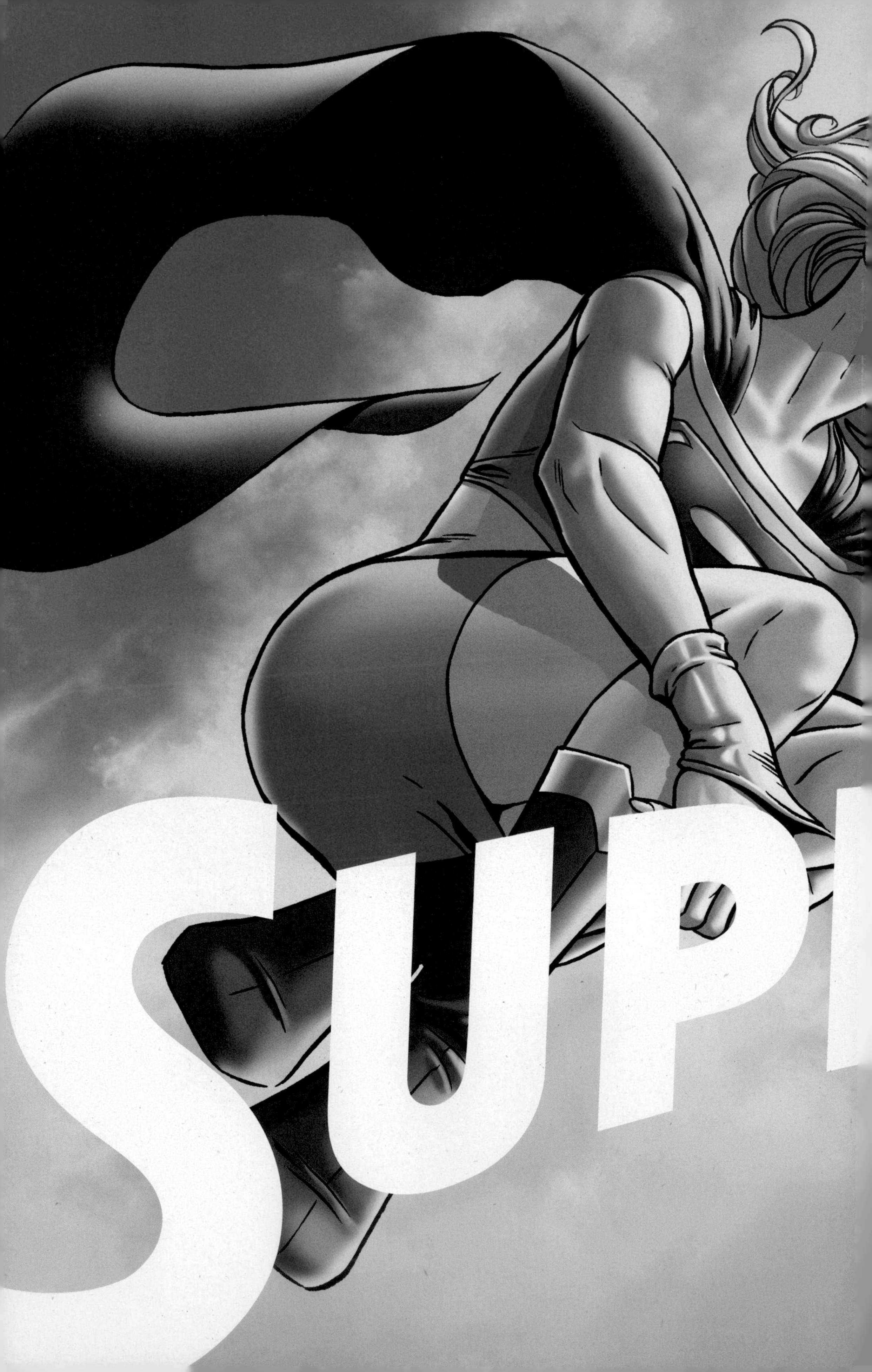
SUP

ERGIRL

VOLUME 3: GHOSTS OF KRYPTON

SUPERGIRL BASED ON CHARACTERS CREATED BY JERRY SIEGEL AND JOE SHUSTER
SUPERMAN CREATED BY JERRY SIEGEL AND JOE SHUSTER
By special arrangement with the Jerry Siegel family

Collection cover by DREW JOHNSON, RAY SNYDER
and SHANNON BLANCHARD

Matt Idelson Editor – Original Series
Nachie Castro, Tom Palmer Jr. Associate Editors – Original Series
Jeb Woodard Group Editor – Collected Editions
Erika Rothberg Editor – Collected Edition
Steve Cook Design Director – Books
Louis Prandi Publication Design

Bob Harras Senior VP – Editor-in-Chief, DC Comics

Diane Nelson President
Dan DiDio Publisher
Jim Lee Publisher
Geoff Johns President & Chief Creative Officer
Amit Desai Executive VP – Business & Marketing Strategy,
Direct to Consumer & Global Franchise Management
Sam Ades Senior VP – Direct to Consumer
Bobbie Chase VP – Talent Development
Mark Chiarello Senior VP – Art, Design & Collected Editions
John Cunningham Senior VP – Sales & Trade Marketing
Anne DePies Senior VP – Business Strategy, Finance & Administration
Don Falletti VP – Manufacturing Operations
Lawrence Ganem VP – Editorial Administration & Talent Relations
Alison Gill Senior VP – Manufacturing & Operations
Hank Kanalz Senior VP – Editorial Strategy & Administration
Jay Kogan VP – Legal Affairs
Thomas Loftus VP – Business Affairs
Jack Mahan VP – Business Affairs
Nick J. Napolitano VP – Manufacturing Administration
Eddie Scannell VP – Consumer Marketing
Courtney Simmons Senior VP – Publicity & Communications
Jim (Ski) Sokolowski VP – Comic Book Specialty Sales & Trade Marketing
Nancy Spears VP – Mass, Book, Digital Sales & Trade Marketing

SUPERGIRL VOL. 3: GHOSTS OF KRYPTON

DC Comics, 2900 West Alameda Ave., Burbank, CA 91505
Printed by Solisco Printers, Scott, QC, Canada. 4/28/17. First Printing.
ISBN: 978-1-4012-7079-7

Library of Congress Cataloging-in-Publication Data is available.

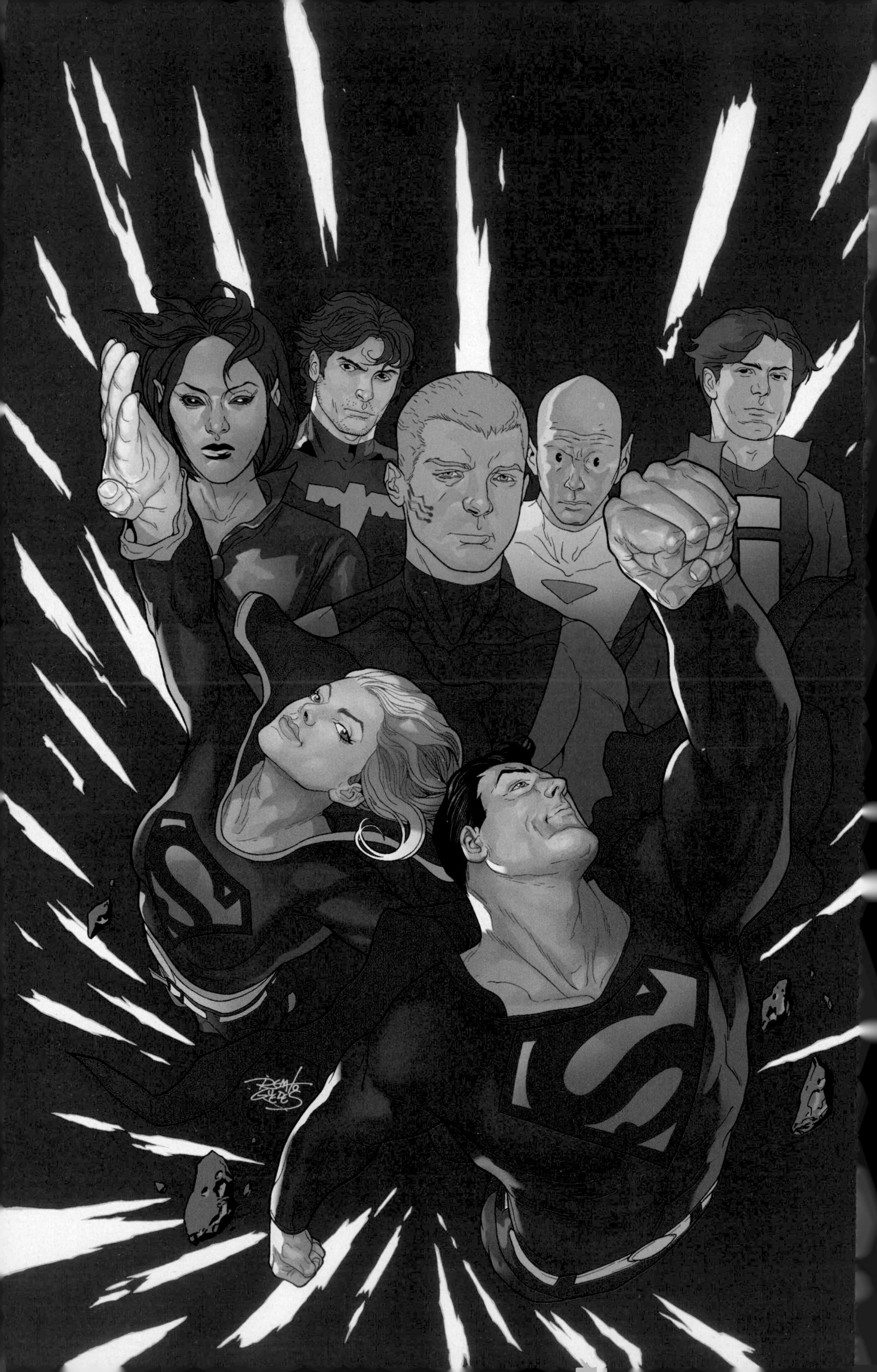

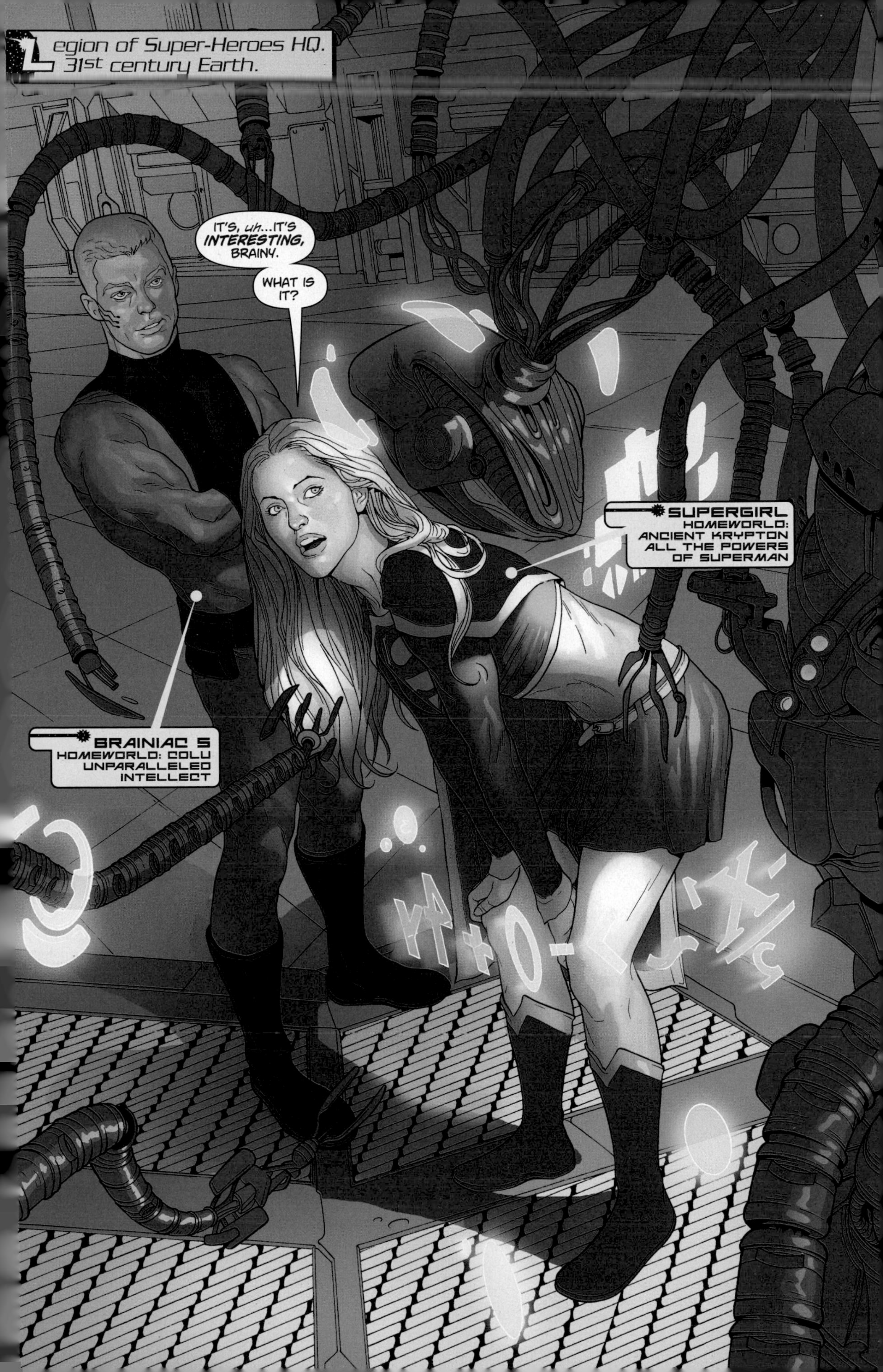
Legion of Super-Heroes HQ. 31st century Earth.
IT'S, uh...IT'S INTERESTING, BRAINY.
WHAT IS IT?
SUPERGIRL HOMEWORLD: ANCIENT KRYPTON ALL THE POWERS OF SUPERMAN
BRAINIAC 5 HOMEWORLD: COLU UNPARALLELED INTELLECT

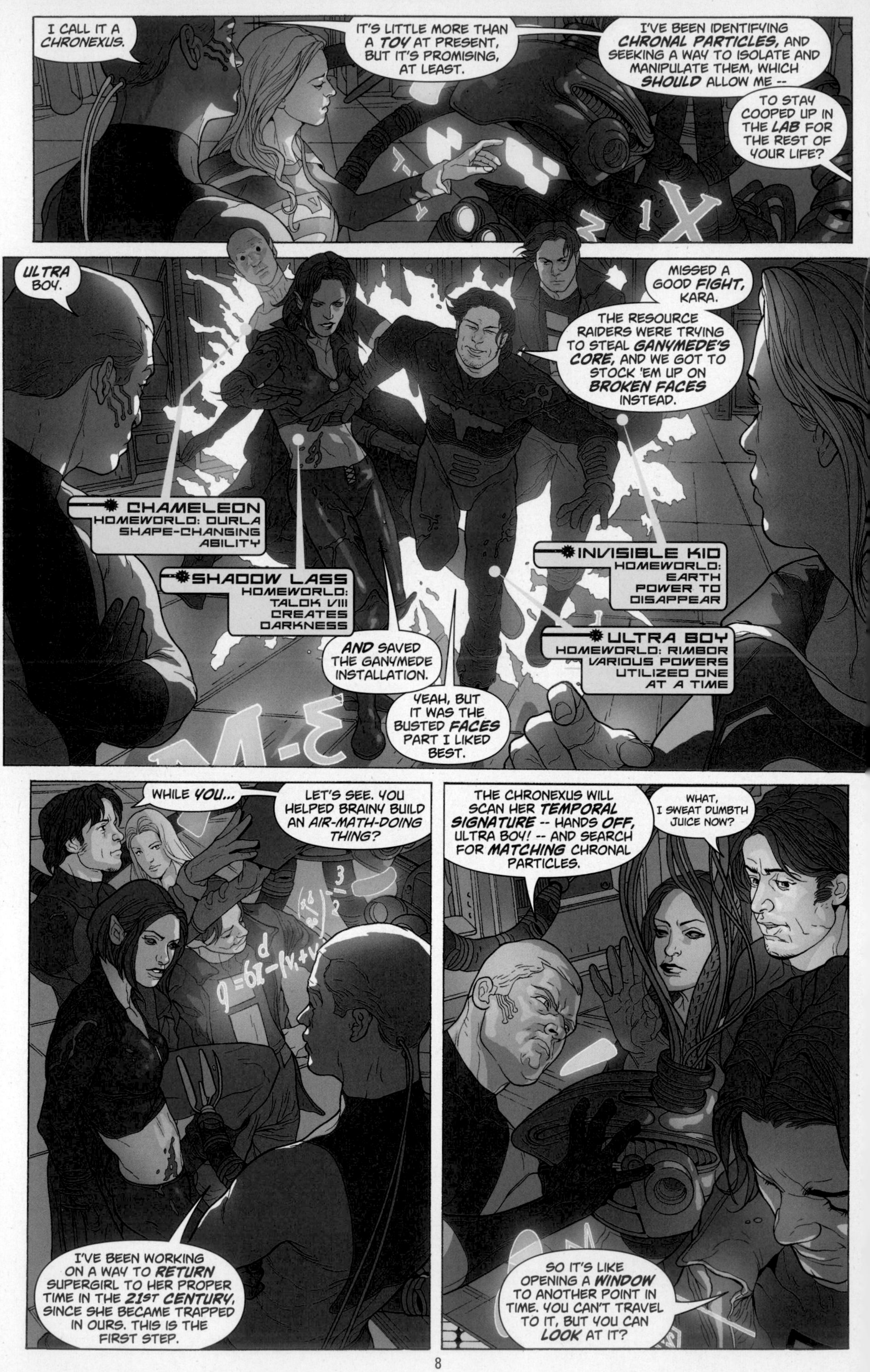
I CALL IT A CHRONEXUS.
IT'S LITTLE MORE THAN A TOY AT PRESENT, BUT IT'S PROMISING, AT LEAST.
I'VE BEEN IDENTIFYING CHRONAL PARTICLES, AND SEEKING A WAY TO ISOLATE AND MANIPULATE THEM, WHICH SHOULD ALLOW ME --
TO STAY COOPED UP IN THE LAB FOR THE REST OF YOUR LIFE?
ULTRA BOY.
MISSED A GOOD FIGHT, KARA.
THE RESOURCE RAIDERS WERE TRYING TO STEAL GANYMEDE'S CORE, AND WE GOT TO STOCK 'EM UP ON BROKEN FACES INSTEAD.
CHAMELEON
HOMEWORLD: DURLA
SHAPE-CHANGING ABILITY
SHADOW LASS
HOMEWORLD: TALOK VIII
CREATES DARKNESS
INVISIBLE KID
HOMEWORLD: EARTH
POWER TO DISAPPEAR
ULTRA BOY
HOMEWORLD: RIMBOR
VARIOUS POWERS UTILIZED ONE AT A TIME
AND SAVED THE GANYMEDE INSTALLATION.
YEAH, BUT IT WAS THE BUSTED FACES PART I LIKED BEST.
WHILE YOU...
LET'S SEE. YOU HELPED BRAINY BUILD AN AIR-MATH-DOING THING?
I'VE BEEN WORKING ON A WAY TO RETURN SUPERGIRL TO HER PROPER TIME IN THE 21ST CENTURY, SINCE SHE BECAME TRAPPED IN OURS. THIS IS THE FIRST STEP.
THE CHRONEXUS WILL SCAN HER TEMPORAL SIGNATURE -- HANDS OFF, ULTRA BOY! -- AND SEARCH FOR MATCHING CHRONAL PARTICLES.
WHAT, I SWEAT DUMBTH JUICE NOW?
SO IT'S LIKE OPENING A WINDOW TO ANOTHER POINT IN TIME. YOU CAN'T TRAVEL TO IT, BUT YOU CAN LOOK AT IT?

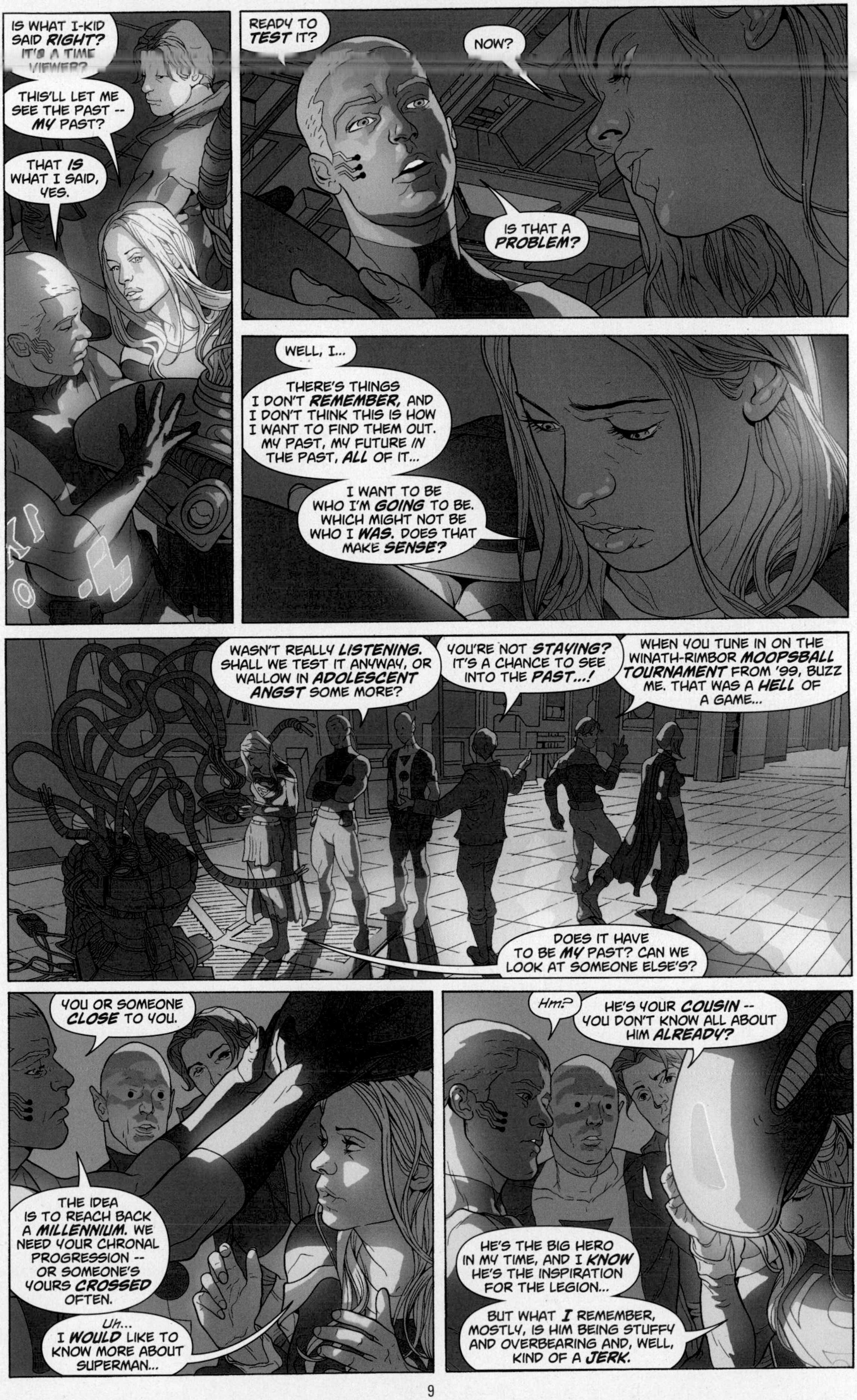
IS WHAT I-KID SAID RIGHT? IT'S A TIME VIEWER?
THIS'LL LET ME SEE THE PAST -- MY PAST?
THAT IS WHAT I SAID, YES.
READY TO TEST IT?
NOW?
IS THAT A PROBLEM?
WELL, I...
THERE'S THINGS I DON'T REMEMBER, AND I DON'T THINK THIS IS HOW I WANT TO FIND THEM OUT. MY PAST, MY FUTURE IN THE PAST, ALL OF IT...
I WANT TO BE WHO I'M GOING TO BE. WHICH MIGHT NOT BE WHO I WAS. DOES THAT MAKE SENSE?
WASN'T REALLY LISTENING. SHALL WE TEST IT ANYWAY, OR WALLOW IN ADOLESCENT ANGST SOME MORE?
YOU'RE NOT STAYING? IT'S A CHANCE TO SEE INTO THE PAST...!
WHEN YOU TUNE IN ON THE WINATH-RIMBOR MOOPSBALL TOURNAMENT FROM '99, BUZZ ME. THAT WAS A HELL OF A GAME...
DOES IT HAVE TO BE MY PAST? CAN WE LOOK AT SOMEONE ELSE'S?
YOU OR SOMEONE CLOSE TO YOU.
THE IDEA IS TO REACH BACK A MILLENNIUM. WE NEED YOUR CHRONAL PROGRESSION -- OR SOMEONE'S YOURS CROSSED OFTEN.
Uh... I WOULD LIKE TO KNOW MORE ABOUT SUPERMAN...
Hm?
HE'S YOUR COUSIN -- YOU DON'T KNOW ALL ABOUT HIM ALREADY?
HE'S THE BIG HERO IN MY TIME, AND I KNOW HE'S THE INSPIRATION FOR THE LEGION...
BUT WHAT I REMEMBER, MOSTLY, IS HIM BEING STUFFY AND OVERBEARING AND, WELL, KIND OF A JERK.

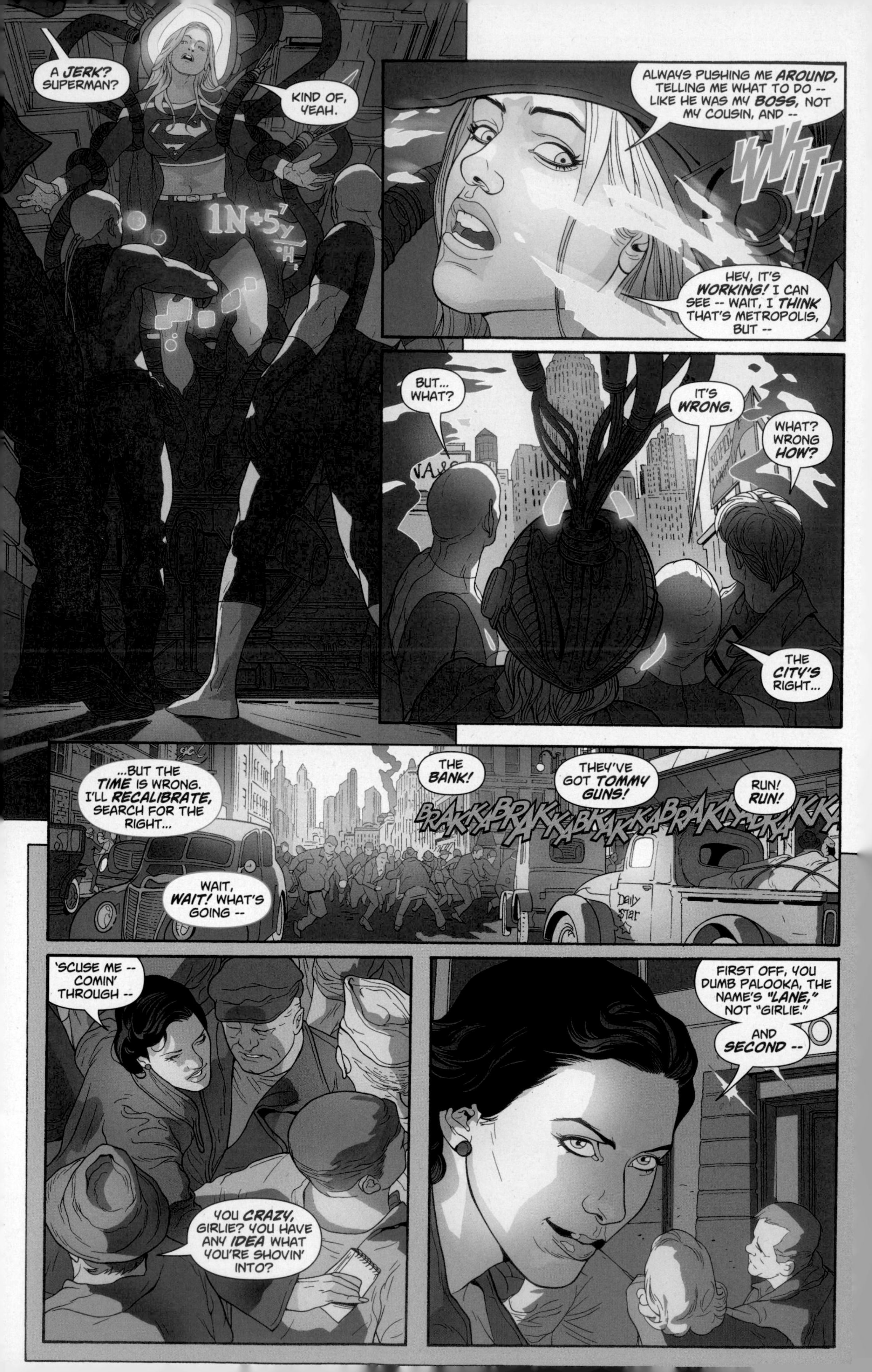
A JERK? SUPERMAN?
KIND OF, YEAH.
ALWAYS PUSHING ME AROUND, TELLING ME WHAT TO DO -- LIKE HE WAS MY BOSS, NOT MY COUSIN, AND --
VVVTTT
HEY, IT'S WORKING! I CAN SEE -- WAIT, I THINK THAT'S METROPOLIS, BUT --
BUT... WHAT?
IT'S WRONG.
WHAT? WRONG HOW?
THE CITY'S RIGHT...
...BUT THE TIME IS WRONG. I'LL RECALIBRATE, SEARCH FOR THE RIGHT...
THE BANK!
THEY'VE GOT TOMMY GUNS!
RUN! RUN!
BRAKKABRAKKABRAKKABRAKKABRAKKABRAKK
WAIT, WAIT! WHAT'S GOING --
Daily Star
'SCUSE ME -- COMIN' THROUGH --
YOU CRAZY, GIRLIE? YOU HAVE ANY IDEA WHAT YOU'RE SHOVIN' INTO?
FIRST OFF, YOU DUMB PALOOKA, THE NAME'S "LANE," NOT "GIRLIE."
AND SECOND --

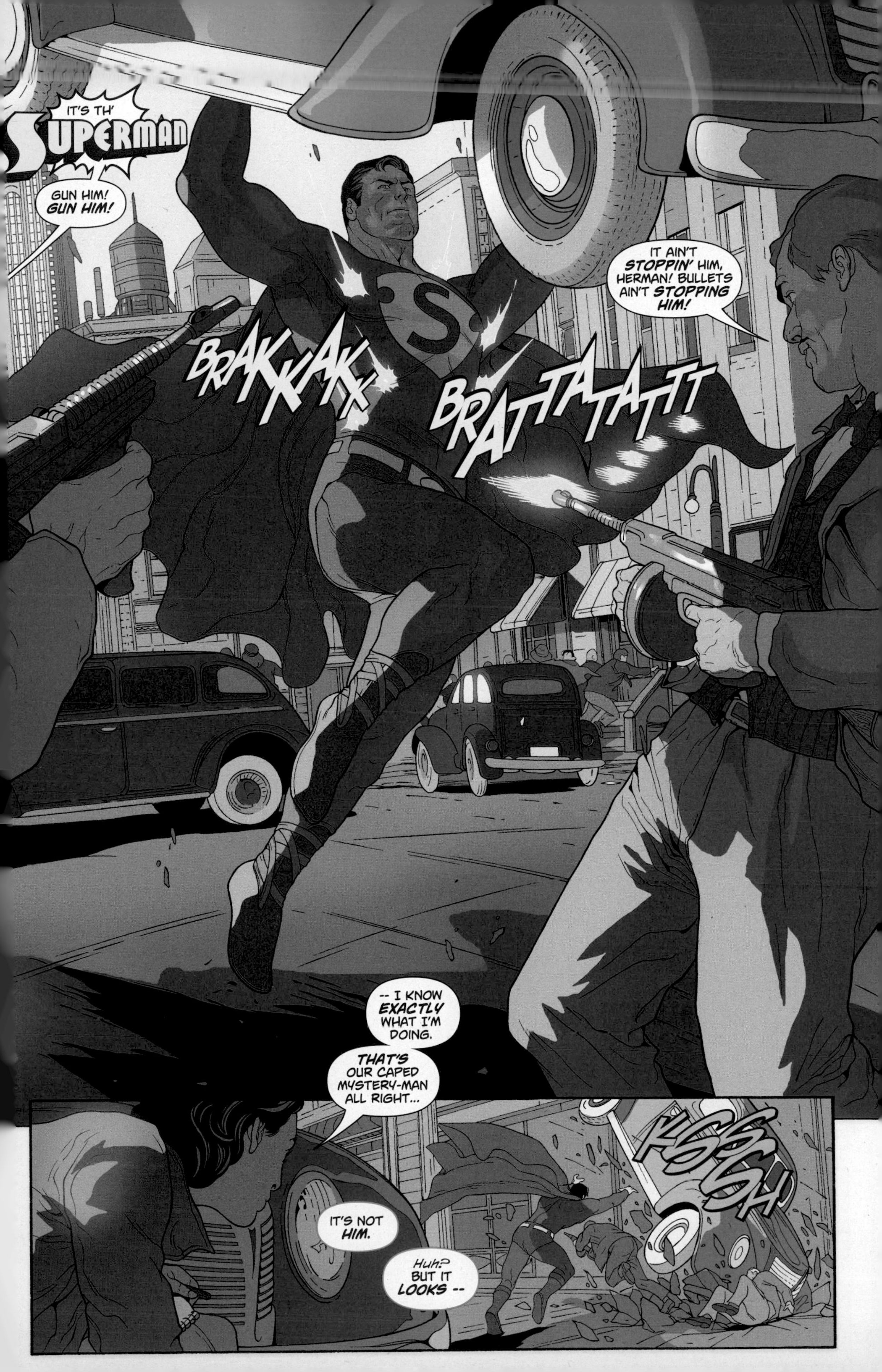
IT'S TH' SUPERMAN
GUN HIM! GUN HIM!
IT AIN'T STOPPIN' HIM, HERMAN! BULLETS AIN'T STOPPING HIM!
BRAKKAKK
BRATTTATATTT
-- I KNOW EXACTLY WHAT I'M DOING.
THAT'S OUR CAPED MYSTERY-MAN ALL RIGHT...
IT'S NOT HIM.
Huh? BUT IT LOOKS --
KSSSH

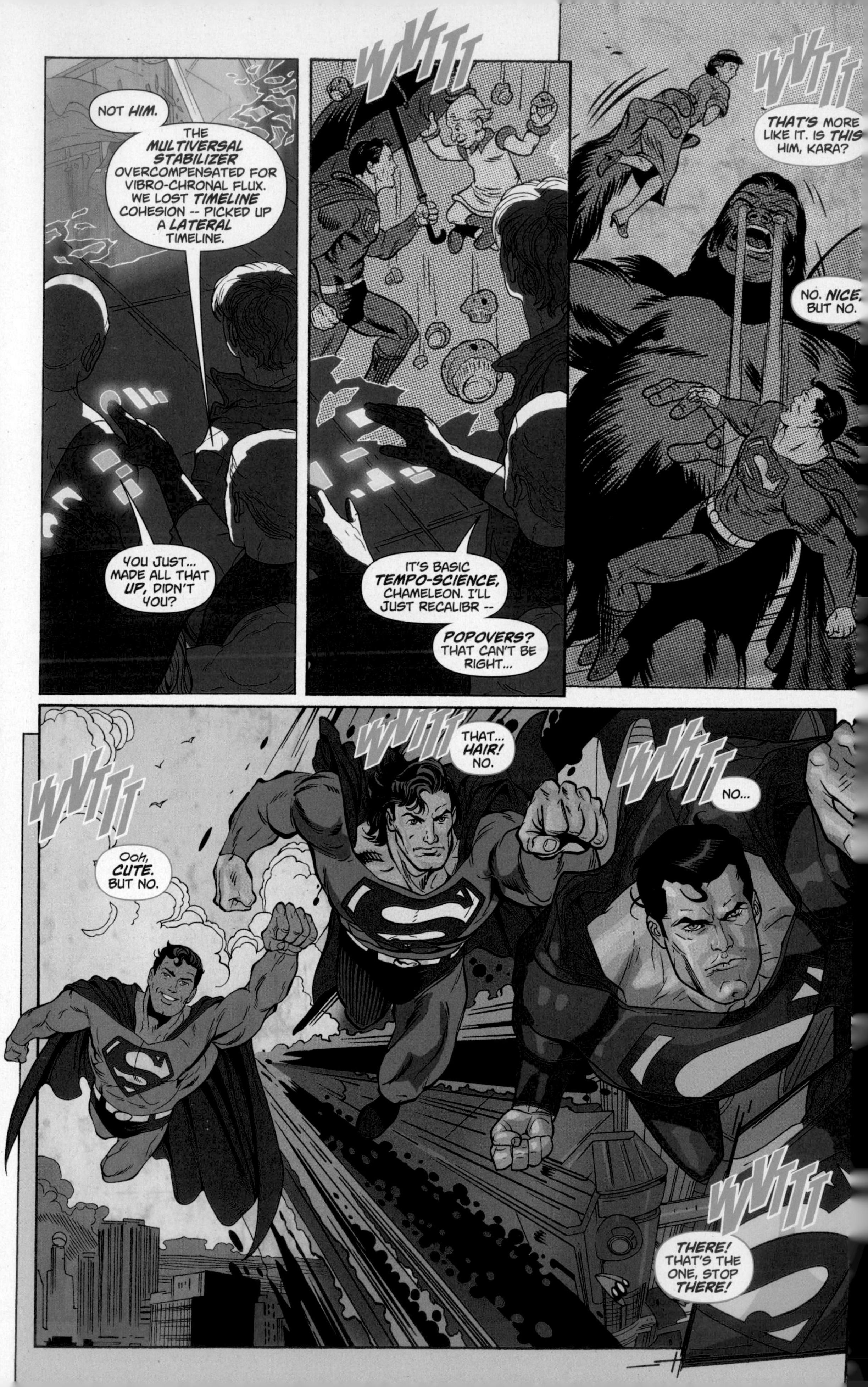
NOT HIM.
THE MULTIVERSAL STABILIZER OVERCOMPENSATED FOR VIBRO-CHRONAL FLUX. WE LOST TIMELINE COHESION -- PICKED UP A LATERAL TIMELINE.
YOU JUST... MADE ALL THAT UP, DIDN'T YOU?
WVVTTT
IT'S BASIC TEMPO-SCIENCE, CHAMELEON. I'LL JUST RECALIBR --
POPOVERS? THAT CAN'T BE RIGHT...
WVVTTT
THAT'S MORE LIKE IT. IS THIS HIM, KARA?
NO. NICE, BUT NO.
WVVTTT
Ooh, CUTE. BUT NO.
WVVTTT
THAT... HAIR! NO.
WVVTTT
NO...
WVVTTT
THERE! THAT'S THE ONE, STOP THERE!

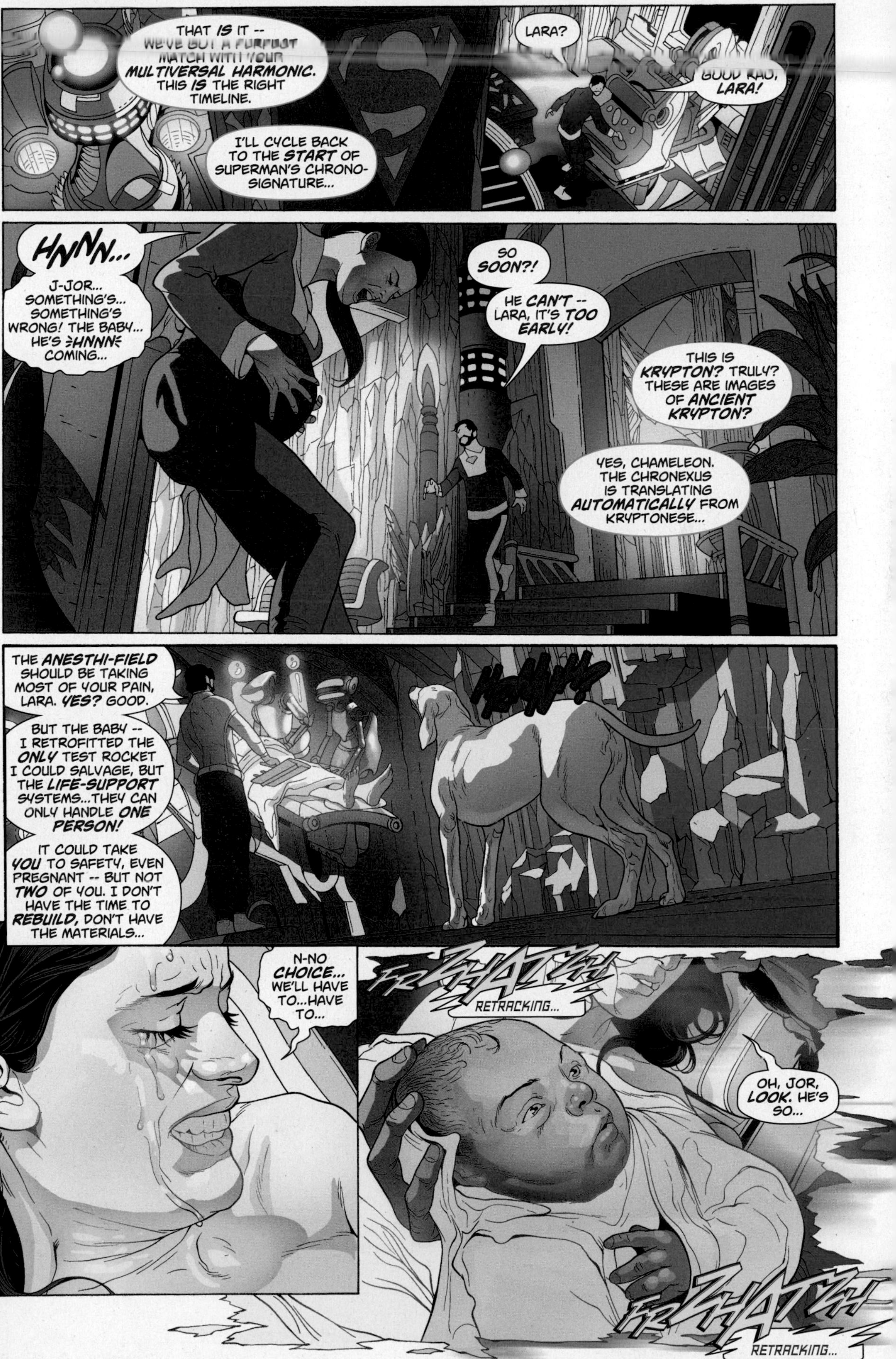
THAT IS IT -- WE'VE GOT A PERFECT MATCH WITH YOUR MULTIVERSAL HARMONIC. THIS IS THE RIGHT TIMELINE.
I'LL CYCLE BACK TO THE START OF SUPERMAN'S CHRONO-SIGNATURE...
LARA?
GOOD RAO, LARA!
HNNN...
J-JOR... SOMETHING'S... SOMETHING'S WRONG! THE BABY... HE'S HNNN COMING...
SO SOON?!
HE CAN'T -- LARA, IT'S TOO EARLY!
THIS IS KRYPTON? TRULY? THESE ARE IMAGES OF ANCIENT KRYPTON?
YES, CHAMELEON. THE CHRONEXUS IS TRANSLATING AUTOMATICALLY FROM KRYPTONESE...
THE ANESTHI-FIELD SHOULD BE TAKING MOST OF YOUR PAIN, LARA. YES? GOOD.
BUT THE BABY -- I RETROFITTED THE ONLY TEST ROCKET I COULD SALVAGE, BUT THE LIFE-SUPPORT SYSTEMS...THEY CAN ONLY HANDLE ONE PERSON!
IT COULD TAKE YOU TO SAFETY, EVEN PREGNANT -- BUT NOT TWO OF YOU. I DON'T HAVE THE TIME TO REBUILD, DON'T HAVE THE MATERIALS...
N-NO CHOICE... WE'LL HAVE TO...HAVE TO...
FRZHATCH
RETRACKING...
OH, JOR, LOOK. HE'S SO...
FRZHATCH
RETRACKING...

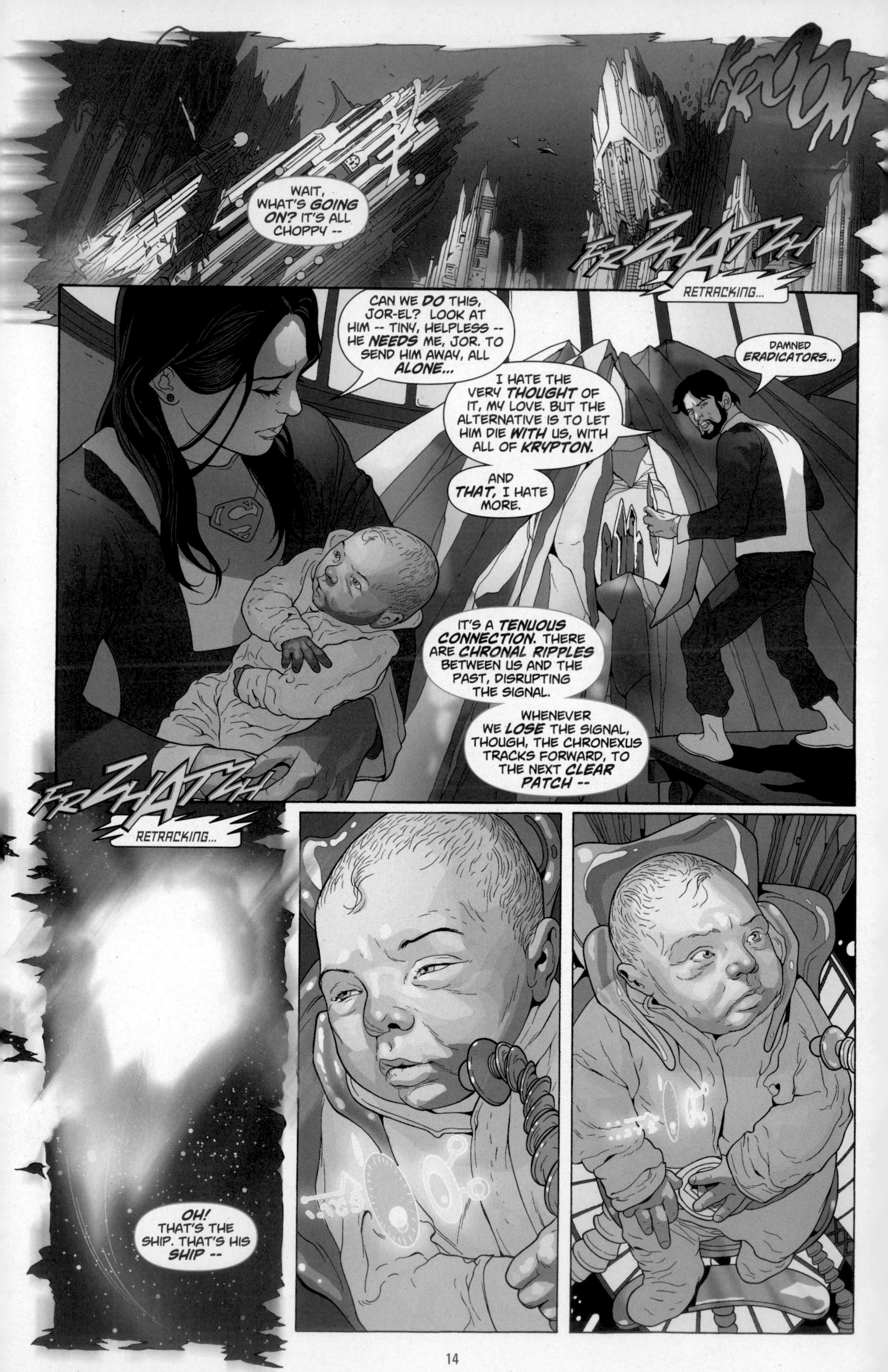
KROOM
WAIT, WHAT'S GOING ON? IT'S ALL CHOPPY --
FRZHATZH
RETRACKING...
CAN WE DO THIS, JOR-EL? LOOK AT HIM -- TINY, HELPLESS -- HE NEEDS ME, JOR. TO SEND HIM AWAY, ALL ALONE...
DAMNED ERADICATORS...
I HATE THE VERY THOUGHT OF IT, MY LOVE. BUT THE ALTERNATIVE IS TO LET HIM DIE WITH US, WITH ALL OF KRYPTON.
AND THAT, I HATE MORE.
IT'S A TENUOUS CONNECTION. THERE ARE CHRONAL RIPPLES BETWEEN US AND THE PAST, DISRUPTING THE SIGNAL.
WHENEVER WE LOSE THE SIGNAL, THOUGH, THE CHRONEXUS TRACKS FORWARD, TO THE NEXT CLEAR PATCH --
FRZHATZH
RETRACKING...
OH! THAT'S THE SHIP. THAT'S HIS SHIP --

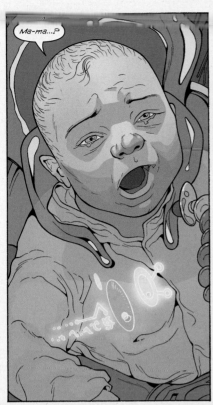

Ma-ma...?

SUBJECT REGAINING CONSCIOUSNESS.

CONTRA-INDICATED. INITIATING SOMNO-RAYS.

SOMNO-RAYS ACTIVE. INDUCING HIBERNI-LEVEL SLEEP...

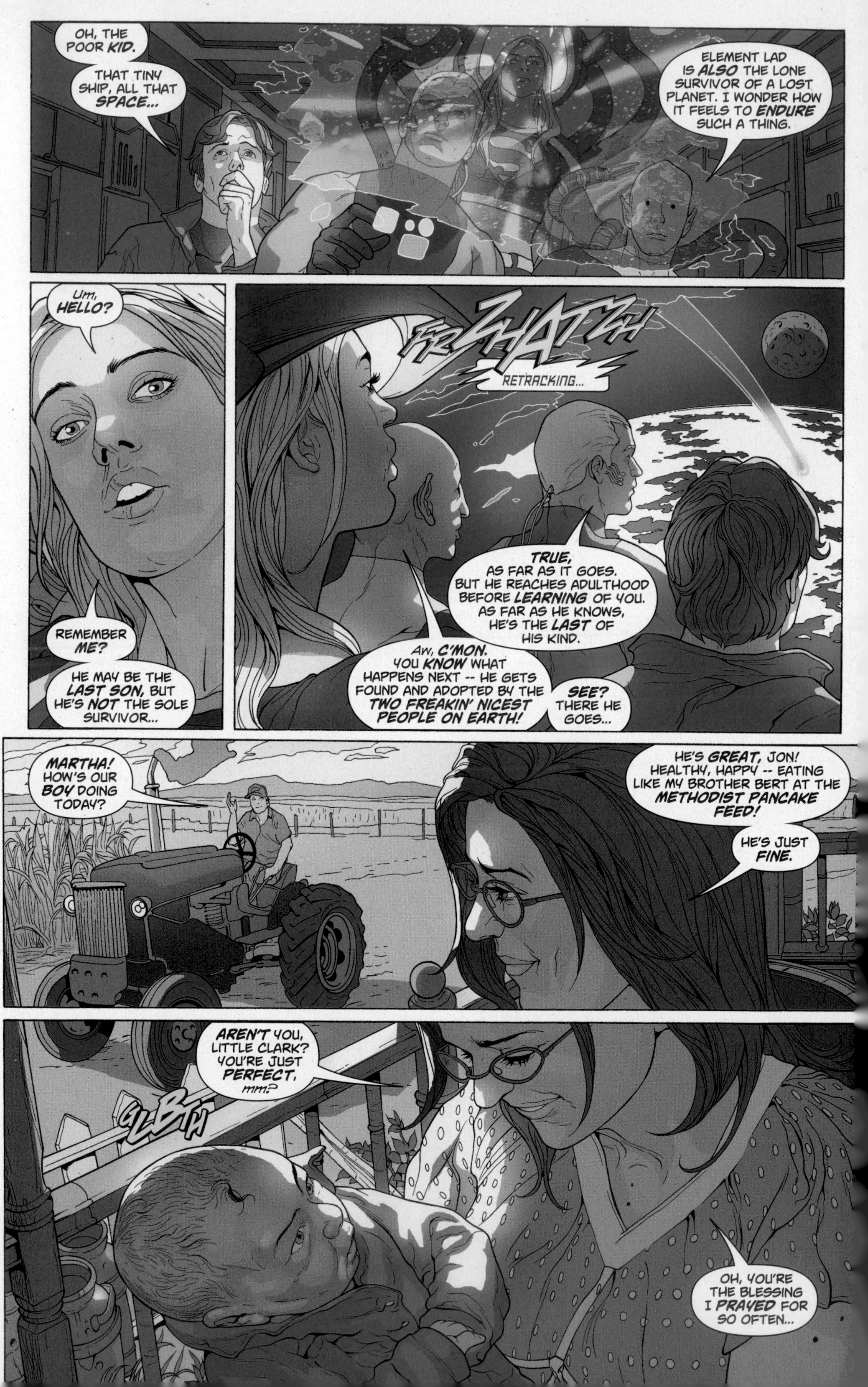
OH, THE POOR KID.
THAT TINY SHIP, ALL THAT SPACE...
ELEMENT LAD IS ALSO THE LONE SURVIVOR OF A LOST PLANET. I WONDER HOW IT FEELS TO ENDURE SUCH A THING.
Um, HELLO?
REMEMBER ME?
HE MAY BE THE LAST SON, BUT HE'S NOT THE SOLE SURVIVOR...
FRZHATCH
RETRACKING...
TRUE, AS FAR AS IT GOES. BUT HE REACHES ADULTHOOD BEFORE LEARNING OF YOU. AS FAR AS HE KNOWS, HE'S THE LAST OF HIS KIND.
Aw, C'MON. YOU KNOW WHAT HAPPENS NEXT -- HE GETS FOUND AND ADOPTED BY THE TWO FREAKIN' NICEST PEOPLE ON EARTH!
SEE? THERE HE GOES...
MARTHA! HOW'S OUR BOY DOING TODAY?
HE'S GREAT, JON! HEALTHY, HAPPY -- EATING LIKE MY BROTHER BERT AT THE METHODIST PANCAKE FEED!
HE'S JUST FINE.
AREN'T YOU, LITTLE CLARK? YOU'RE JUST PERFECT, mm?
GLBTH
OH, YOU'RE THE BLESSING I PRAYED FOR SO OFTEN...

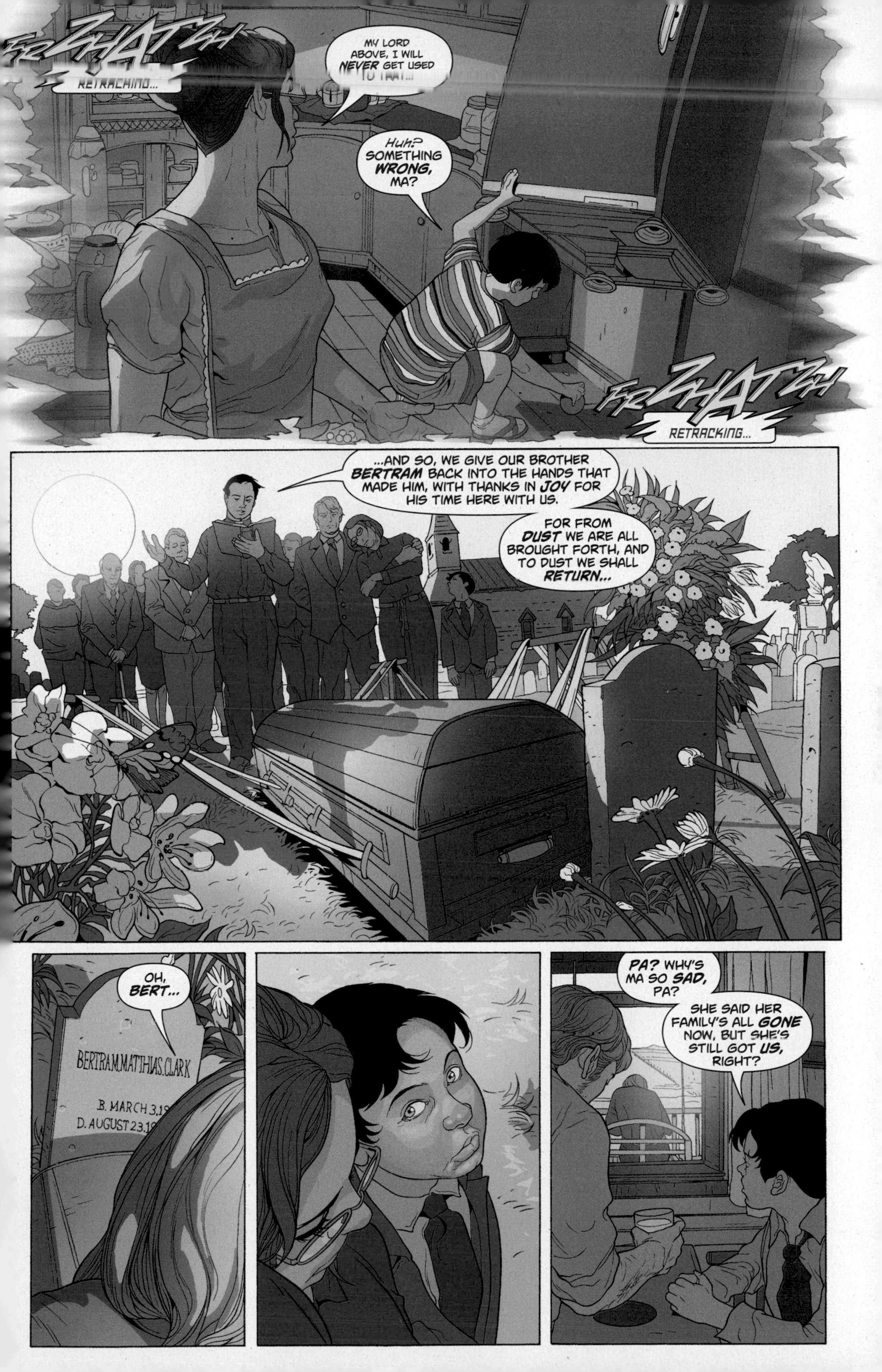
FRZHATZZH
RETRACKING...
MY LORD ABOVE, I WILL NEVER GET USED TO THAT...
Huh? SOMETHING WRONG, MA?
FRZHATZZH
RETRACKING...
...AND SO, WE GIVE OUR BROTHER BERTRAM BACK INTO THE HANDS THAT MADE HIM, WITH THANKS IN JOY FOR HIS TIME HERE WITH US.
FOR FROM DUST WE ARE ALL BROUGHT FORTH, AND TO DUST WE SHALL RETURN...
OH, BERT...
BERTRAM.MATTHIAS.CLARK
PA? WHY'S MA SO SAD, PA?
SHE SAID HER FAMILY'S ALL GONE NOW, BUT SHE'S STILL GOT US, RIGHT?

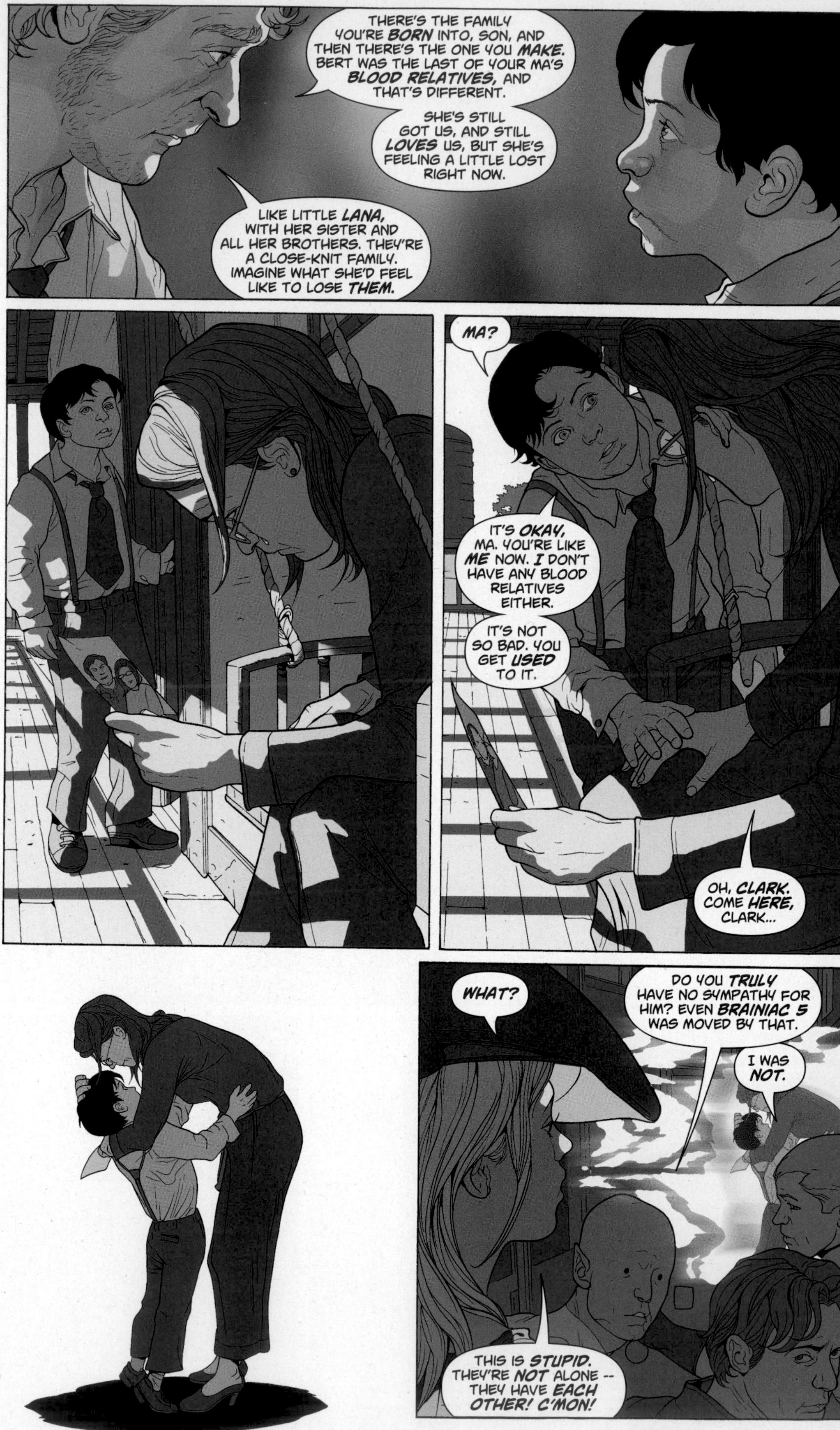

THERE'S THE FAMILY YOU'RE BORN INTO, SON, AND THEN THERE'S THE ONE YOU MAKE. BERT WAS THE LAST OF YOUR MA'S BLOOD RELATIVES, AND THAT'S DIFFERENT.
SHE'S STILL GOT US, AND STILL LOVES US, BUT SHE'S FEELING A LITTLE LOST RIGHT NOW.
LIKE LITTLE LANA, WITH HER SISTER AND ALL HER BROTHERS. THEY'RE A CLOSE-KNIT FAMILY. IMAGINE WHAT SHE'D FEEL LIKE TO LOSE THEM.
MA?
IT'S OKAY, MA. YOU'RE LIKE ME NOW. I DON'T HAVE ANY BLOOD RELATIVES EITHER.
IT'S NOT SO BAD. YOU GET USED TO IT.
OH, CLARK. COME HERE, CLARK...
WHAT?
DO YOU TRULY HAVE NO SYMPATHY FOR HIM? EVEN BRAINIAC 5 WAS MOVED BY THAT.
I WAS NOT.
THIS IS STUPID. THEY'RE NOT ALONE -- THEY HAVE EACH OTHER! C'MON!

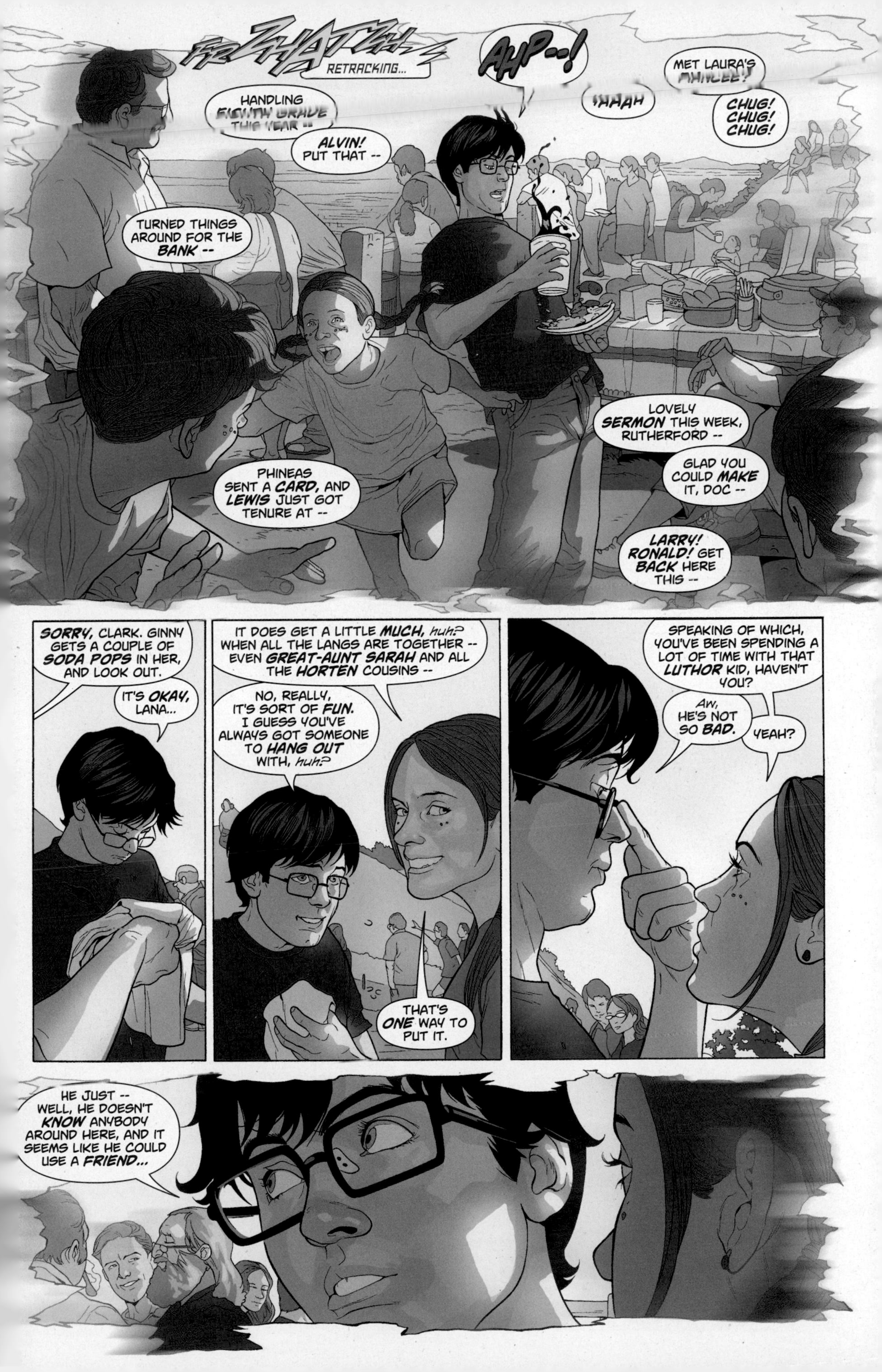
FRZHATCH
RETRACKING...
HANDLING
AHP--!
MET LAURA'S
CHUG! CHUG! CHUG!
ALVIN! PUT THAT --
TURNED THINGS AROUND FOR THE BANK --
LOVELY SERMON THIS WEEK, RUTHERFORD --
GLAD YOU COULD MAKE IT, DOC --
PHINEAS SENT A CARD, AND LEWIS JUST GOT TENURE AT --
LARRY! RONALD! GET BACK HERE THIS --
SORRY, CLARK. GINNY GETS A COUPLE OF SODA POPS IN HER, AND LOOK OUT.
IT'S OKAY, LANA...
IT DOES GET A LITTLE MUCH, huh? WHEN ALL THE LANGS ARE TOGETHER -- EVEN GREAT-AUNT SARAH AND ALL THE HORTEN COUSINS --
NO, REALLY, IT'S SORT OF FUN. I GUESS YOU'VE ALWAYS GOT SOMEONE TO HANG OUT WITH, huh?
THAT'S ONE WAY TO PUT IT.
SPEAKING OF WHICH, YOU'VE BEEN SPENDING A LOT OF TIME WITH THAT LUTHOR KID, HAVEN'T YOU?
Aw, HE'S NOT SO BAD.
YEAH?
HE JUST -- WELL, HE DOESN'T KNOW ANYBODY AROUND HERE, AND IT SEEMS LIKE HE COULD USE A FRIEND...

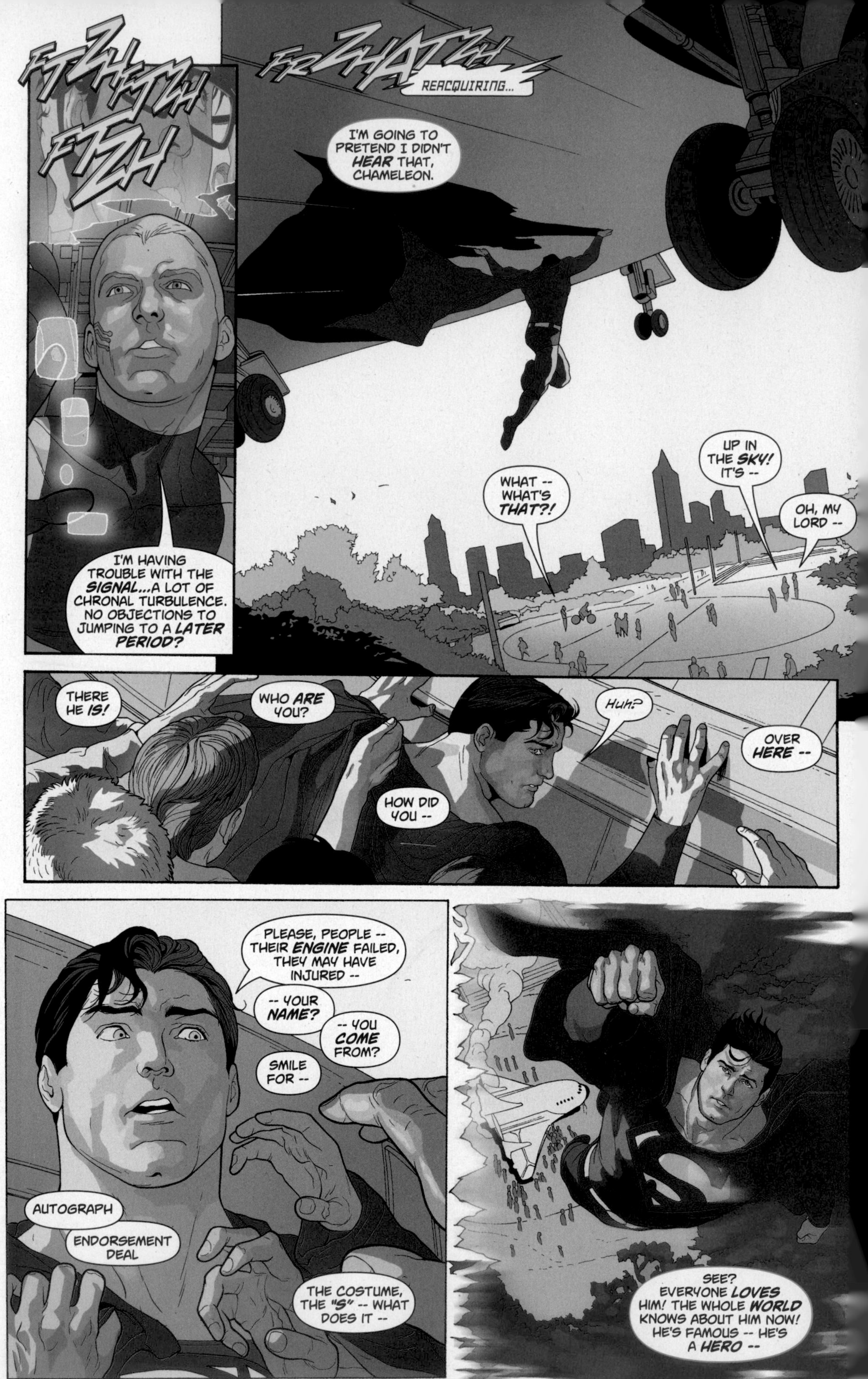
FTZHFTZH FTZH
FRZHATZH
REACQUIRING...
I'M GOING TO PRETEND I DIDN'T HEAR THAT, CHAMELEON.
I'M HAVING TROUBLE WITH THE SIGNAL... A LOT OF CHRONAL TURBULENCE. NO OBJECTIONS TO JUMPING TO A LATER PERIOD?
WHAT -- WHAT'S THAT?!
UP IN THE SKY! IT'S --
OH, MY LORD --
THERE HE IS!
WHO ARE YOU?
HOW DID YOU --
Huh?
OVER HERE --
PLEASE, PEOPLE -- THEIR ENGINE FAILED, THEY MAY HAVE INJURED --
-- YOUR NAME?
-- YOU COME FROM?
SMILE FOR --
AUTOGRAPH
ENDORSEMENT DEAL
THE COSTUME, THE "S" -- WHAT DOES IT --
SEE? EVERYONE LOVES HIM! THE WHOLE WORLD KNOWS ABOUT HIM NOW! HE'S FAMOUS -- HE'S A HERO --

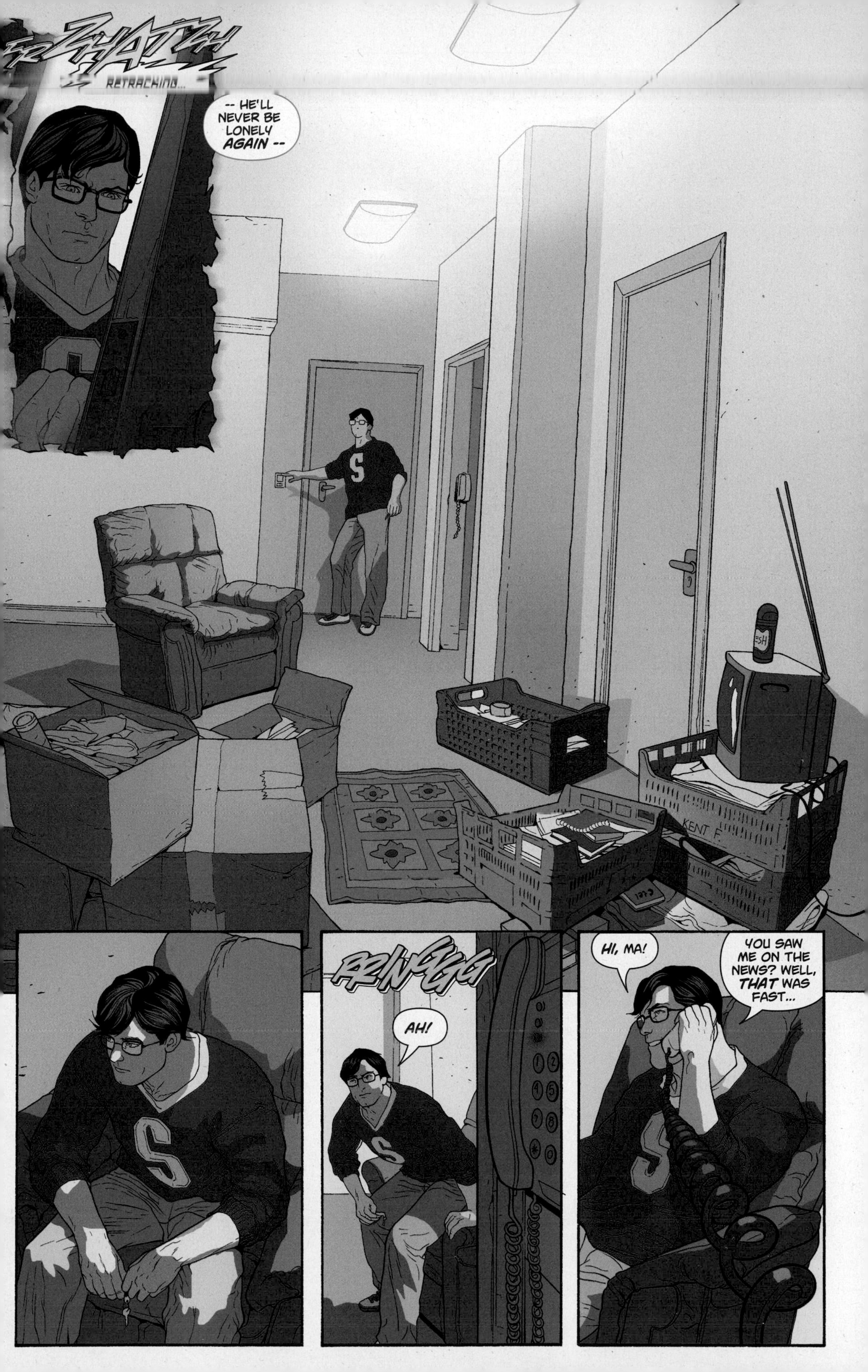
FRZHATCH
RETRACKING...
-- HE'LL NEVER BE LONELY AGAIN --
KENT F.
RRINGGG
AH!
HI, MA!
YOU SAW ME ON THE NEWS? WELL, THAT WAS FAST...

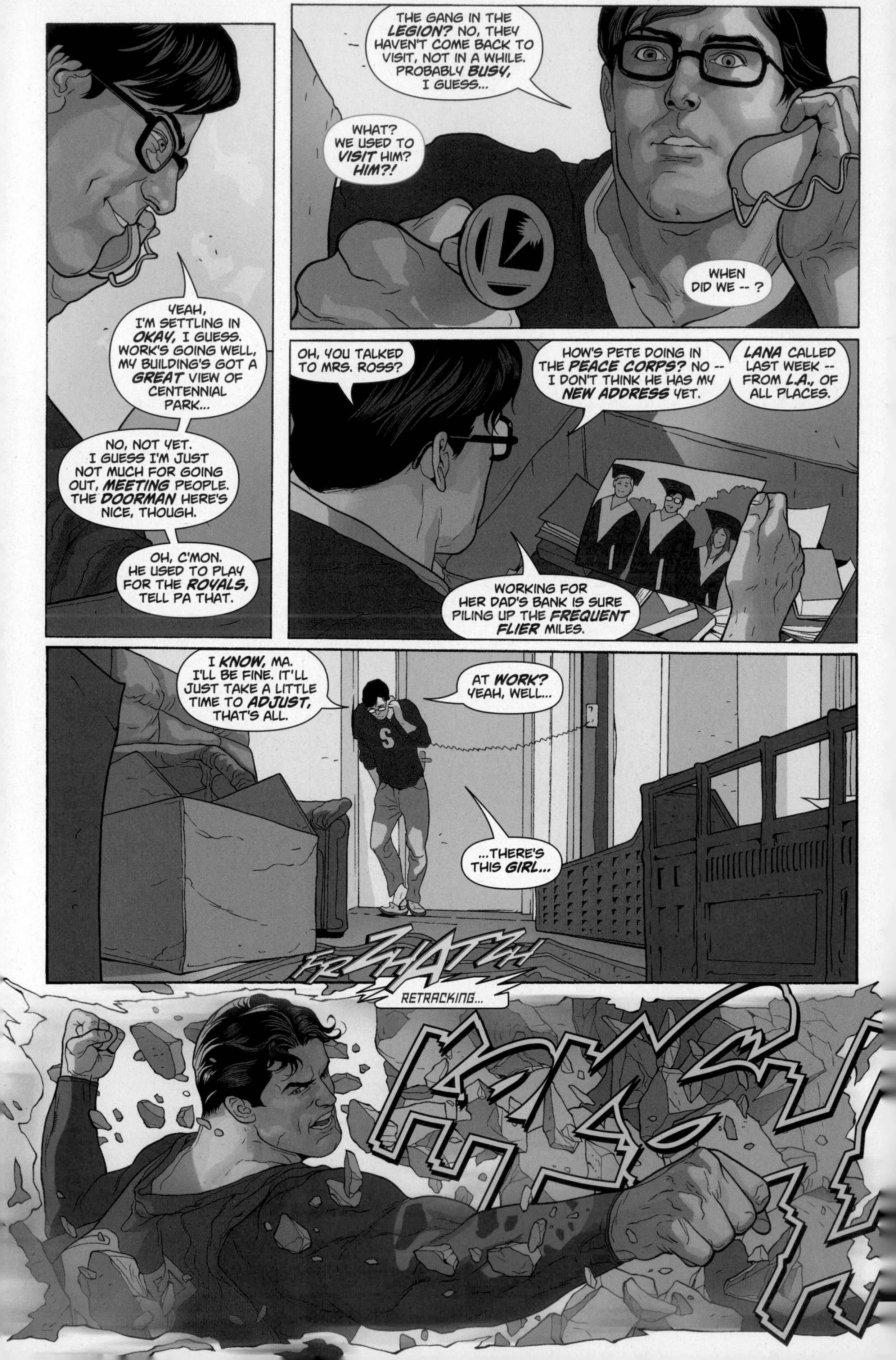

THE GANG IN THE LEGION? NO, THEY HAVEN'T COME BACK TO VISIT, NOT IN A WHILE. PROBABLY BUSY, I GUESS...
WHAT? WE USED TO VISIT HIM? HIM?!
WHEN DID WE -- ?
YEAH, I'M SETTLING IN OKAY, I GUESS. WORK'S GOING WELL, MY BUILDING'S GOT A GREAT VIEW OF CENTENNIAL PARK...
NO, NOT YET. I GUESS I'M JUST NOT MUCH FOR GOING OUT, MEETING PEOPLE. THE DOORMAN HERE'S NICE, THOUGH.
OH, C'MON. HE USED TO PLAY FOR THE ROYALS, TELL PA THAT.
OH, YOU TALKED TO MRS. ROSS?
HOW'S PETE DOING IN THE PEACE CORPS? NO -- I DON'T THINK HE HAS MY NEW ADDRESS YET.
LANA CALLED LAST WEEK -- FROM L.A., OF ALL PLACES.
WORKING FOR HER DAD'S BANK IS SURE PILING UP THE FREQUENT FLIER MILES.
I KNOW, MA. I'LL BE FINE. IT'LL JUST TAKE A LITTLE TIME TO ADJUST, THAT'S ALL.
AT WORK? YEAH, WELL...
...THERE'S THIS GIRL...
FRZHATZH
RETRACKING...

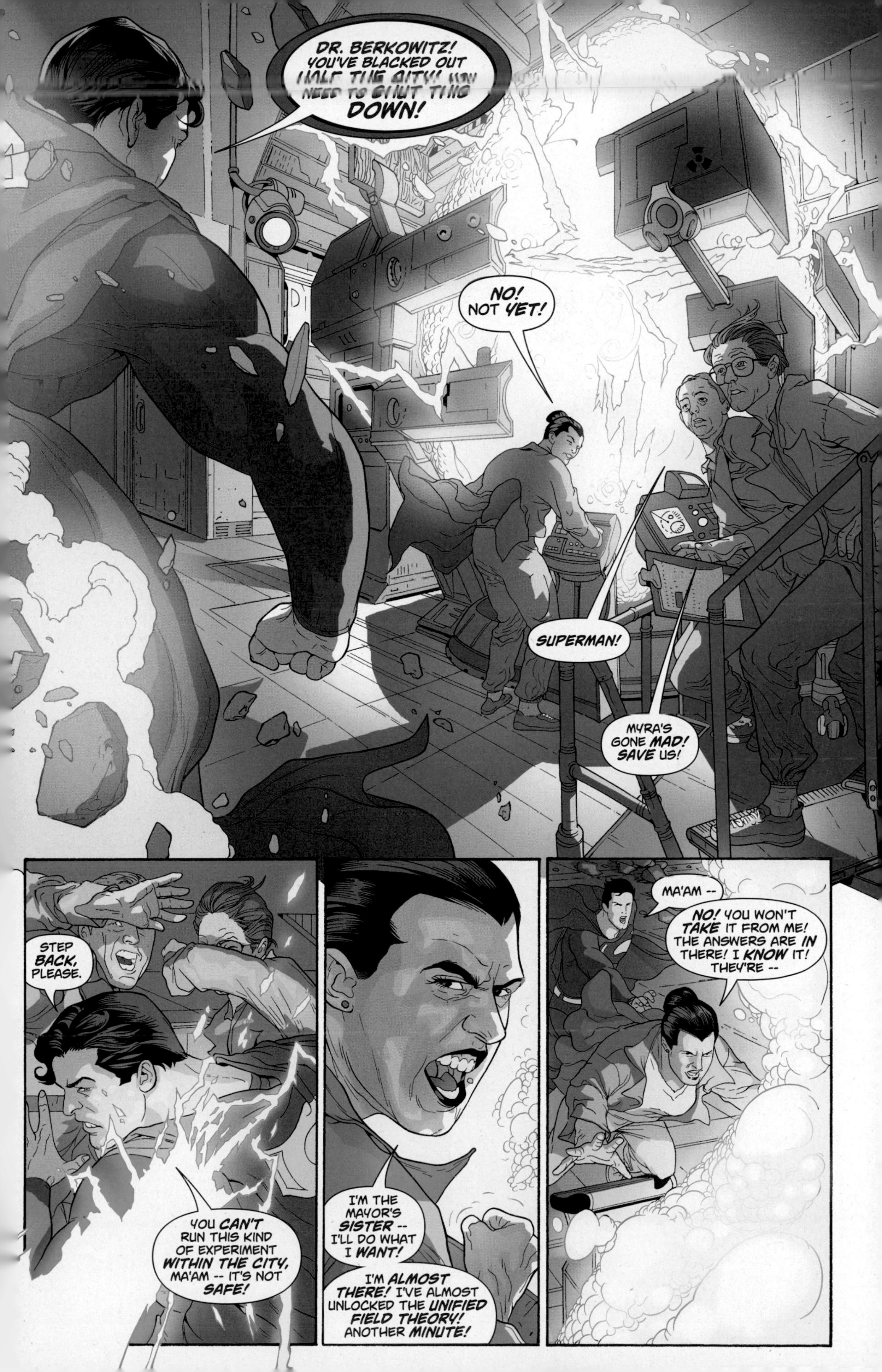
DR. BERKOWITZ! YOU'VE BLACKED OUT
DOWN!
NO! NOT YET!
SUPERMAN!
MYRA'S GONE MAD! SAVE US!
STEP BACK, PLEASE.
YOU CAN'T RUN THIS KIND OF EXPERIMENT WITHIN THE CITY, MA'AM -- IT'S NOT SAFE!
I'M THE MAYOR'S SISTER -- I'LL DO WHAT I WANT!
I'M ALMOST THERE! I'VE ALMOST UNLOCKED THE UNIFIED FIELD THEORY! ANOTHER MINUTE!
MA'AM --
NO! YOU WON'T TAKE IT FROM ME! THE ANSWERS ARE IN THERE! I KNOW IT! THEY'RE --

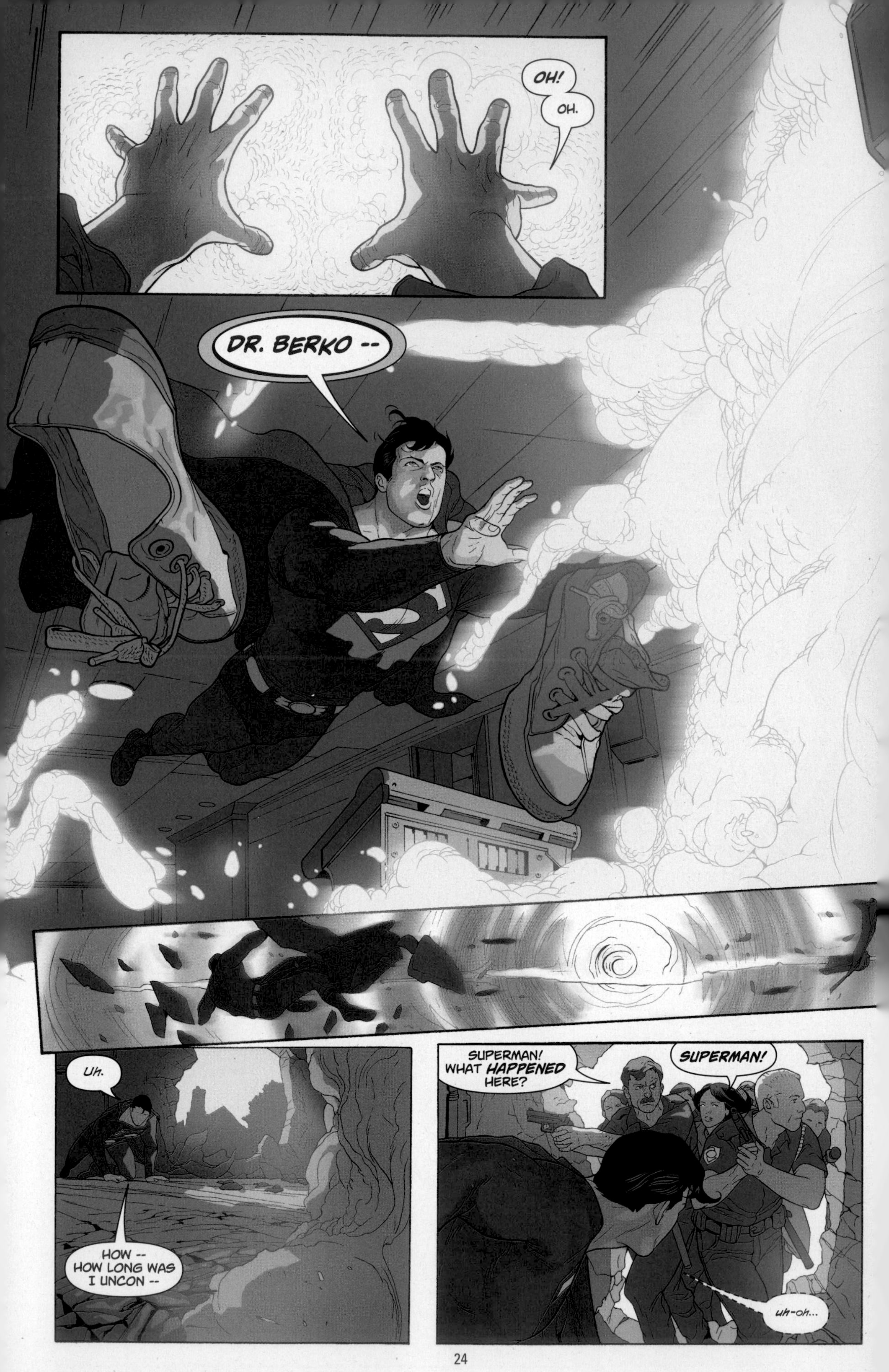
OH!
OH.
DR. BERKO --
Uh.
HOW -- HOW LONG WAS I UNCON --
SUPERMAN! WHAT HAPPENED HERE?
SUPERMAN!
uh-oh...

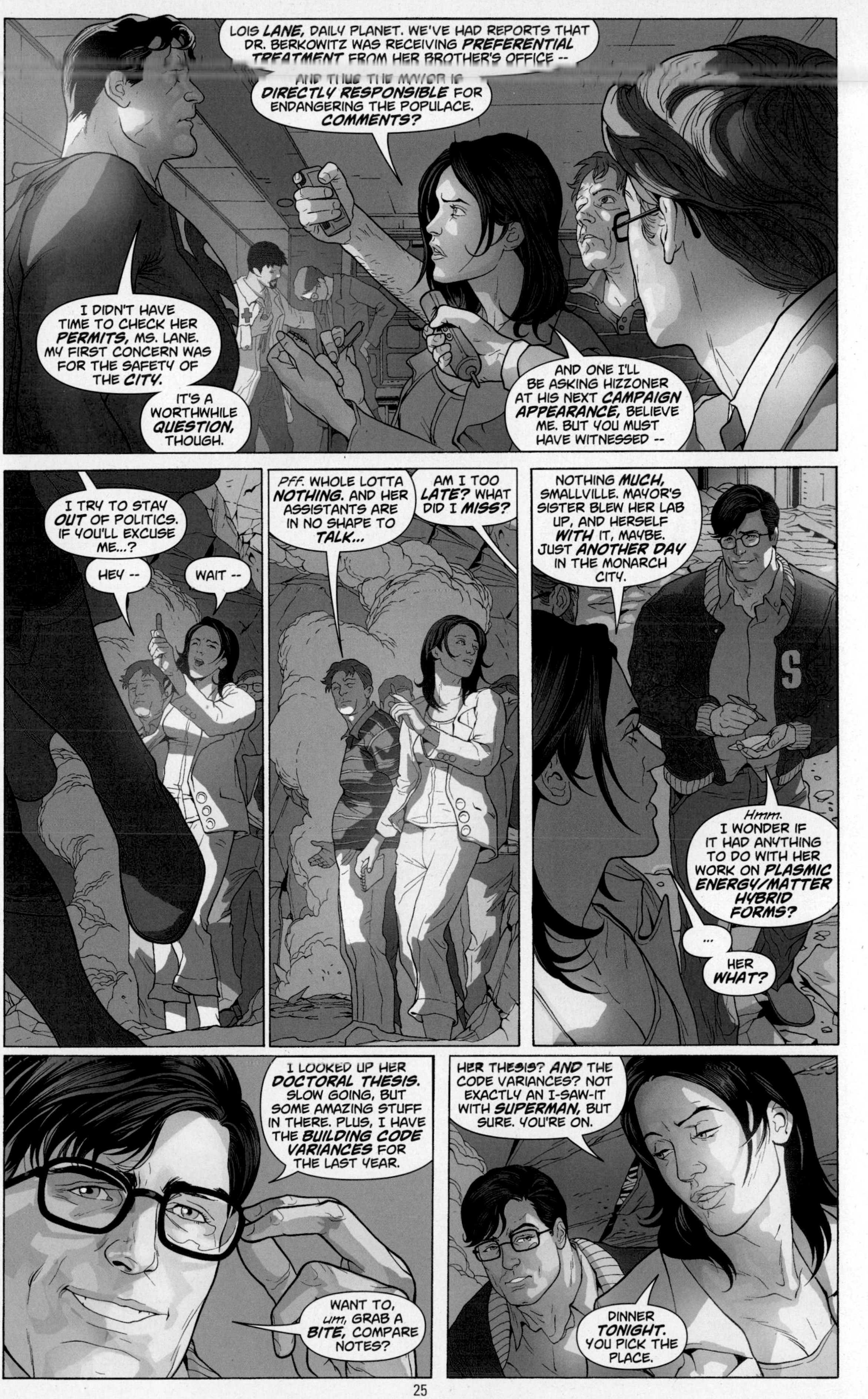
LOIS LANE, DAILY PLANET. WE'VE HAD REPORTS THAT DR. BERKOWITZ WAS RECEIVING PREFERENTIAL TREATMENT FROM HER BROTHER'S OFFICE --
AND THUS THE MAYOR IS DIRECTLY RESPONSIBLE FOR ENDANGERING THE POPULACE. COMMENTS?
I DIDN'T HAVE TIME TO CHECK HER PERMITS, MS. LANE. MY FIRST CONCERN WAS FOR THE SAFETY OF THE CITY.
IT'S A WORTHWHILE QUESTION, THOUGH.
AND ONE I'LL BE ASKING HIZZONER AT HIS NEXT CAMPAIGN APPEARANCE, BELIEVE ME. BUT YOU MUST HAVE WITNESSED --
I TRY TO STAY OUT OF POLITICS. IF YOU'LL EXCUSE ME...?
HEY --
WAIT --
Pff. WHOLE LOTTA NOTHING. AND HER ASSISTANTS ARE IN NO SHAPE TO TALK...
AM I TOO LATE? WHAT DID I MISS?
NOTHING MUCH, SMALLVILLE. MAYOR'S SISTER BLEW HER LAB UP, AND HERSELF WITH IT, MAYBE. JUST ANOTHER DAY IN THE MONARCH CITY.
Hmm. I WONDER IF IT HAD ANYTHING TO DO WITH HER WORK ON PLASMIC ENERGY/MATTER HYBRID FORMS?
...
HER WHAT?
I LOOKED UP HER DOCTORAL THESIS. SLOW GOING, BUT SOME AMAZING STUFF IN THERE. PLUS, I HAVE THE BUILDING CODE VARIANCES FOR THE LAST YEAR.
WANT TO, um, GRAB A BITE, COMPARE NOTES?
HER THESIS? AND THE CODE VARIANCES? NOT EXACTLY AN I-SAW-IT WITH SUPERMAN, BUT SURE. YOU'RE ON.
DINNER TONIGHT. YOU PICK THE PLACE.

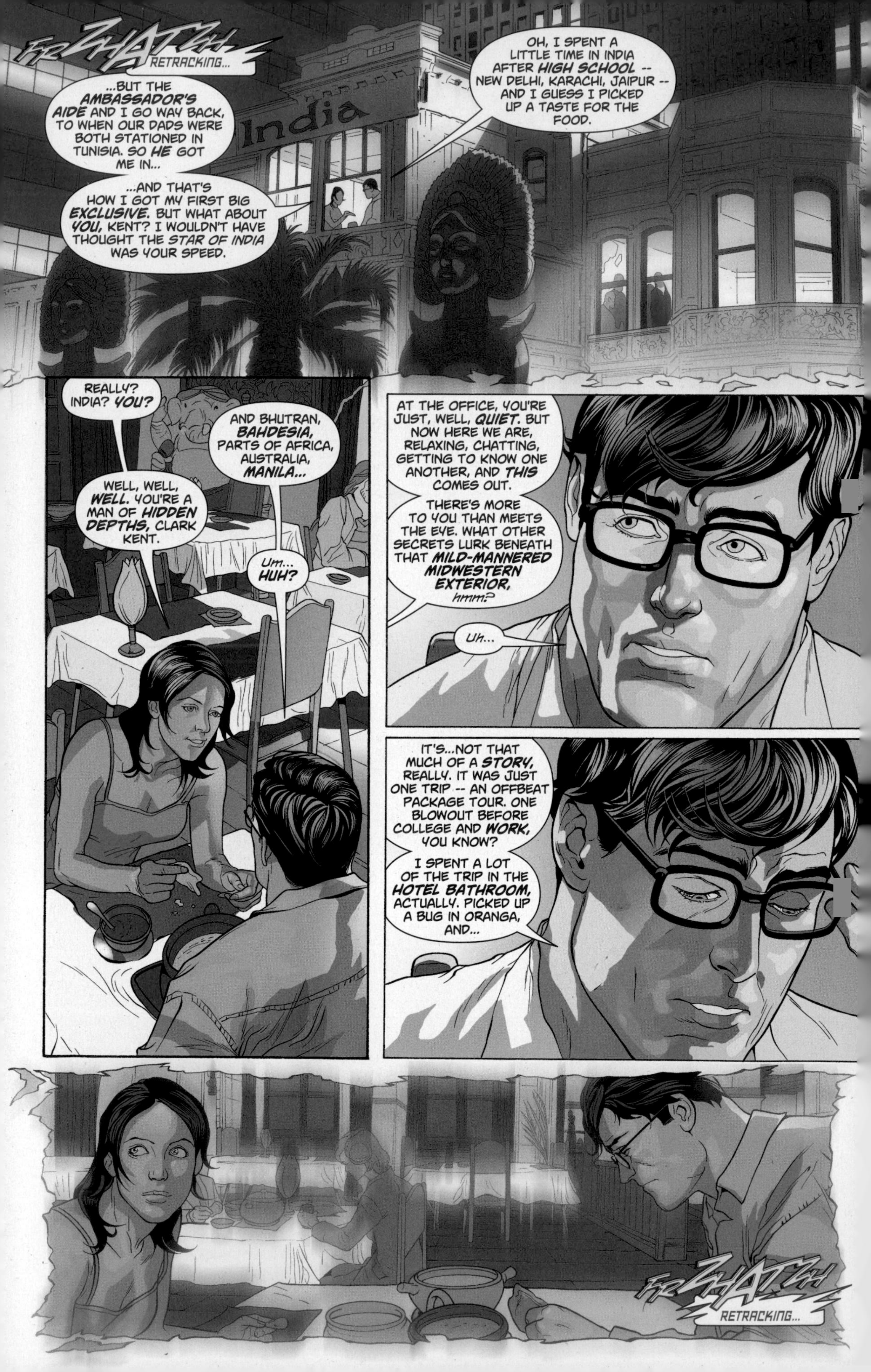
FRZHATZH
RETRACKING...
...BUT THE AMBASSADOR'S AIDE AND I GO WAY BACK, TO WHEN OUR DADS WERE BOTH STATIONED IN TUNISIA. SO HE GOT ME IN...
...AND THAT'S HOW I GOT MY FIRST BIG EXCLUSIVE. BUT WHAT ABOUT YOU, KENT? I WOULDN'T HAVE THOUGHT THE STAR OF INDIA WAS YOUR SPEED.
India
OH, I SPENT A LITTLE TIME IN INDIA AFTER HIGH SCHOOL -- NEW DELHI, KARACHI, JAIPUR -- AND I GUESS I PICKED UP A TASTE FOR THE FOOD.
REALLY? INDIA? YOU?
AND BHUTRAN, BAHDESIA, PARTS OF AFRICA, AUSTRALIA, MANILA...
WELL, WELL, WELL. YOU'RE A MAN OF HIDDEN DEPTHS, CLARK KENT.
Um... HUH?
AT THE OFFICE, YOU'RE JUST, WELL, QUIET. BUT NOW HERE WE ARE, RELAXING, CHATTING, GETTING TO KNOW ONE ANOTHER, AND THIS COMES OUT.
THERE'S MORE TO YOU THAN MEETS THE EYE. WHAT OTHER SECRETS LURK BENEATH THAT MILD-MANNERED MIDWESTERN EXTERIOR, hmm?
Uh...
IT'S...NOT THAT MUCH OF A STORY, REALLY. IT WAS JUST ONE TRIP -- AN OFFBEAT PACKAGE TOUR. ONE BLOWOUT BEFORE COLLEGE AND WORK, YOU KNOW?
I SPENT A LOT OF THE TRIP IN THE HOTEL BATHROOM, ACTUALLY. PICKED UP A BUG IN ORANGA, AND...
FRZHATZH
RETRACKING...

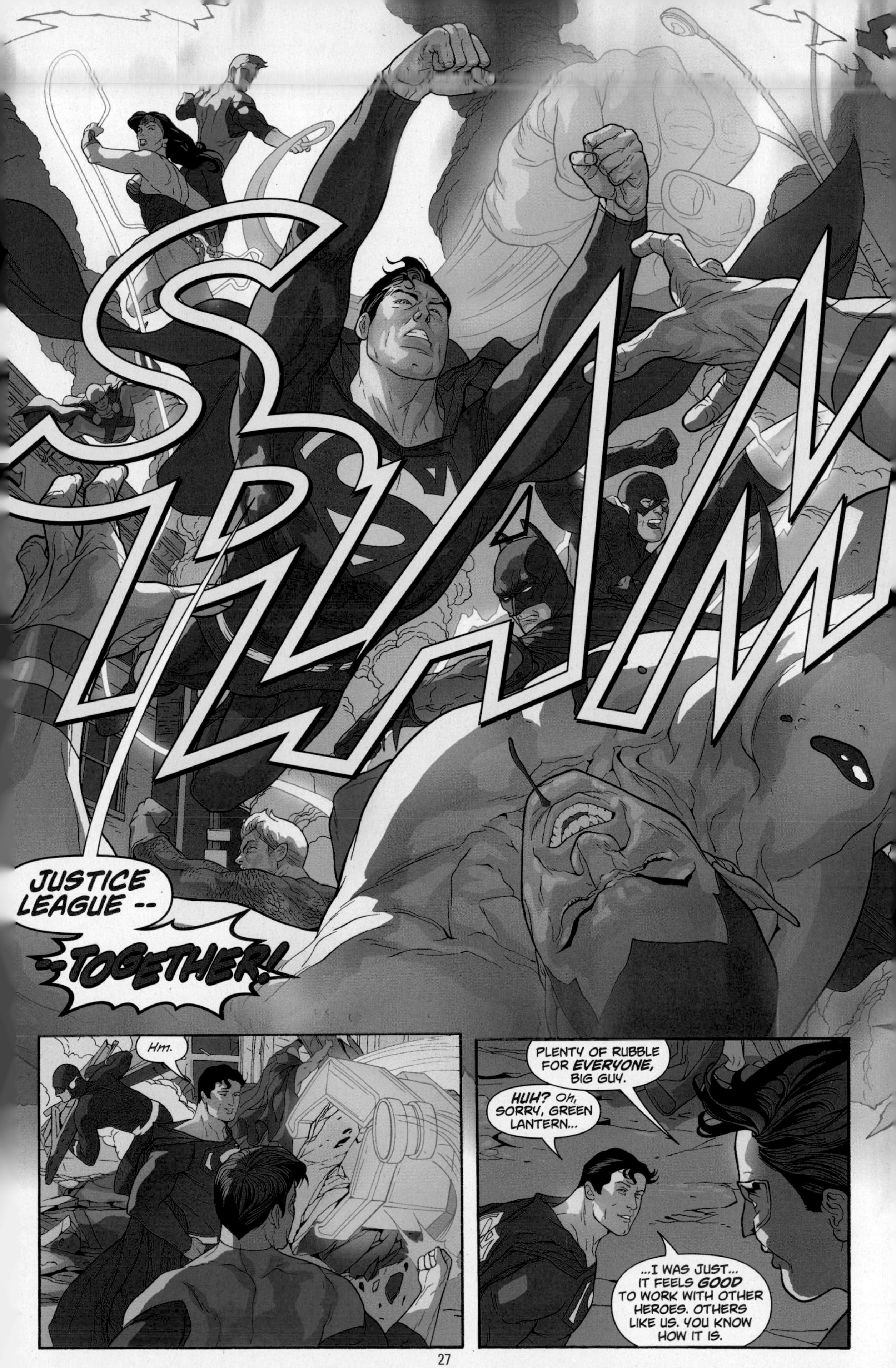
SPLAM
JUSTICE LEAGUE --
-- TOGETHER!
Hm.
PLENTY OF RUBBLE FOR EVERYONE, BIG GUY.
HUH? Oh, SORRY, GREEN LANTERN...
...I WAS JUST... IT FEELS GOOD TO WORK WITH OTHER HEROES. OTHERS LIKE US. YOU KNOW HOW IT IS.

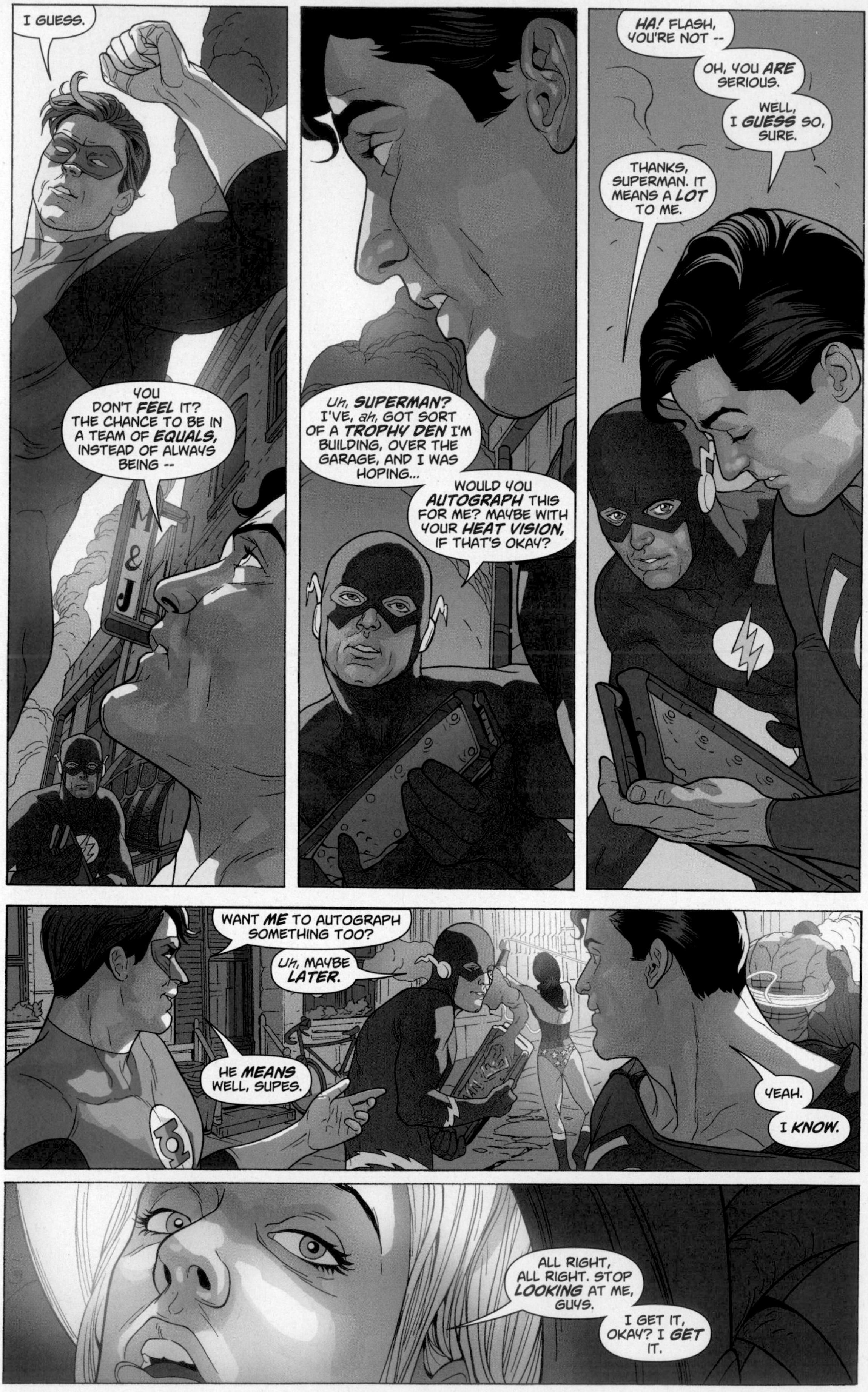
I GUESS.
YOU DON'T FEEL IT? THE CHANCE TO BE IN A TEAM OF EQUALS, INSTEAD OF ALWAYS BEING --
Uh, SUPERMAN? I'VE, ah, GOT SORT OF A TROPHY DEN I'M BUILDING, OVER THE GARAGE, AND I WAS HOPING...
WOULD YOU AUTOGRAPH THIS FOR ME? MAYBE WITH YOUR HEAT VISION, IF THAT'S OKAY?
HA! FLASH, YOU'RE NOT --
OH, YOU ARE SERIOUS.
WELL, I GUESS SO, SURE.
THANKS, SUPERMAN. IT MEANS A LOT TO ME.
WANT ME TO AUTOGRAPH SOMETHING TOO?
Uh, MAYBE LATER.
HE MEANS WELL, SUPES.
YEAH.
I KNOW.
M & J
ALL RIGHT, ALL RIGHT. STOP LOOKING AT ME, GUYS.
I GET IT, OKAY? I GET IT.

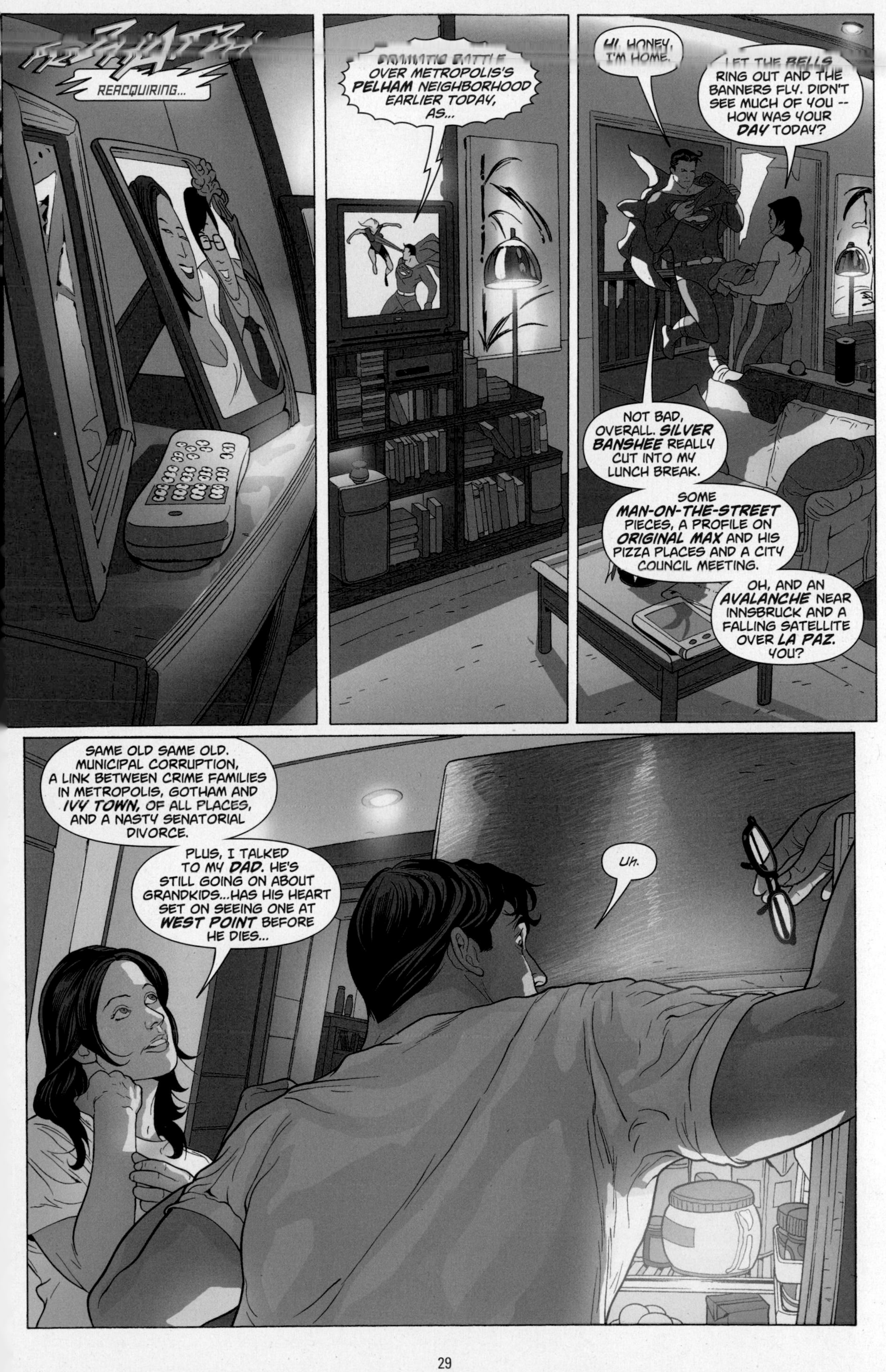

REACQUIRING...
OVER METROPOLIS'S PELHAM NEIGHBORHOOD EARLIER TODAY, AS...
HI, HONEY, I'M HOME.
LET THE BELLS RING OUT AND THE BANNERS FLY. DIDN'T SEE MUCH OF YOU -- HOW WAS YOUR DAY TODAY?
NOT BAD, OVERALL. SILVER BANSHEE REALLY CUT INTO MY LUNCH BREAK.
SOME MAN-ON-THE-STREET PIECES, A PROFILE ON ORIGINAL MAX AND HIS PIZZA PLACES AND A CITY COUNCIL MEETING.
OH, AND AN AVALANCHE NEAR INNSBRUCK AND A FALLING SATELLITE OVER LA PAZ. YOU?
SAME OLD SAME OLD. MUNICIPAL CORRUPTION, A LINK BETWEEN CRIME FAMILIES IN METROPOLIS, GOTHAM AND IVY TOWN, OF ALL PLACES, AND A NASTY SENATORIAL DIVORCE.
PLUS, I TALKED TO MY DAD. HE'S STILL GOING ON ABOUT GRANDKIDS...HAS HIS HEART SET ON SEEING ONE AT WEST POINT BEFORE HE DIES...
Uh.

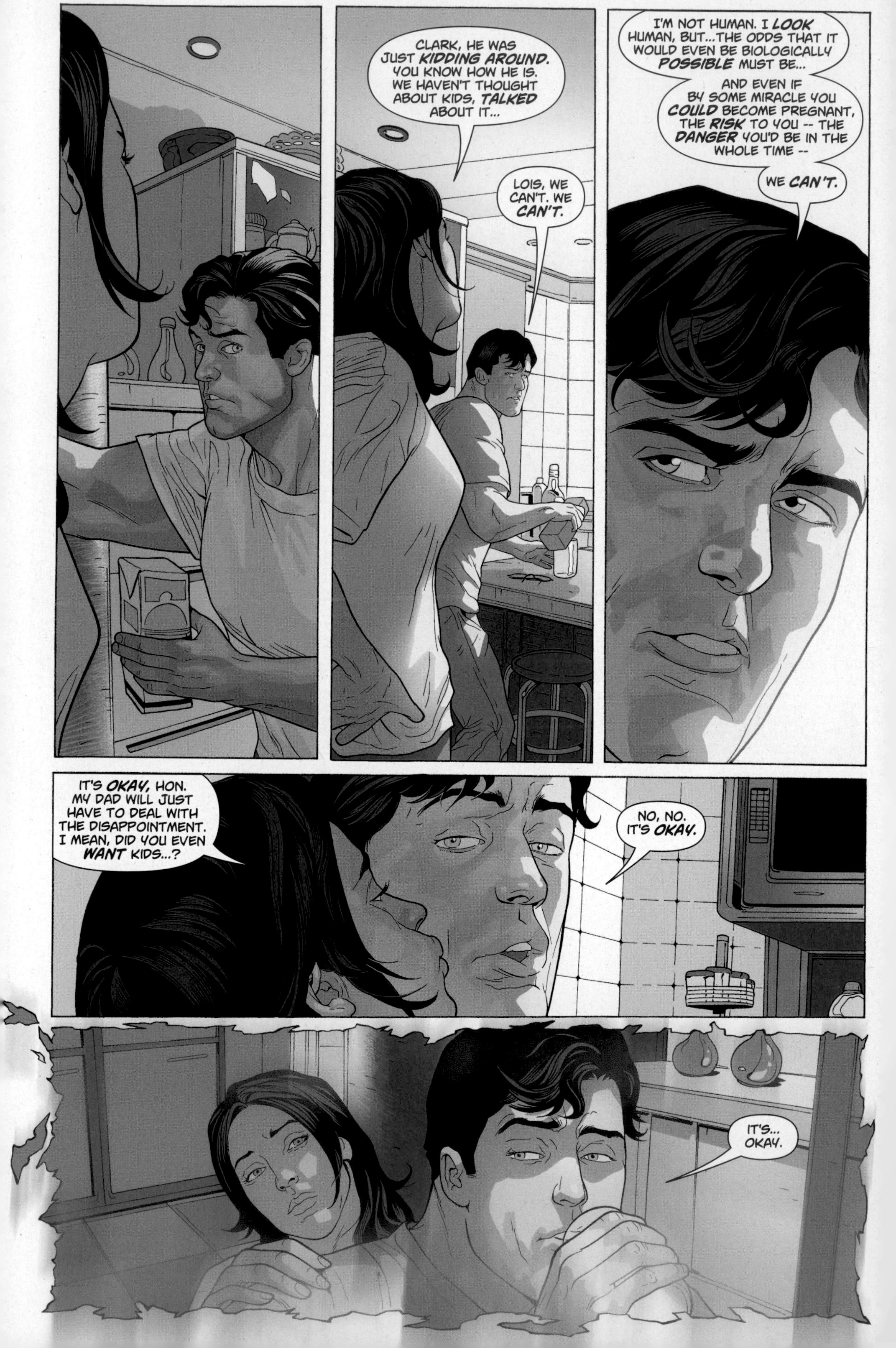
CLARK, HE WAS JUST KIDDING AROUND. YOU KNOW HOW HE IS. WE HAVEN'T THOUGHT ABOUT KIDS, TALKED ABOUT IT...
LOIS, WE CAN'T. WE CAN'T.
I'M NOT HUMAN. I LOOK HUMAN, BUT...THE ODDS THAT IT WOULD EVEN BE BIOLOGICALLY POSSIBLE MUST BE...
AND EVEN IF BY SOME MIRACLE YOU COULD BECOME PREGNANT, THE RISK TO YOU -- THE DANGER YOU'D BE IN THE WHOLE TIME --
WE CAN'T.
IT'S OKAY, HON. MY DAD WILL JUST HAVE TO DEAL WITH THE DISAPPOINTMENT. I MEAN, DID YOU EVEN WANT KIDS...?
NO, NO. IT'S OKAY.
IT'S... OKAY.

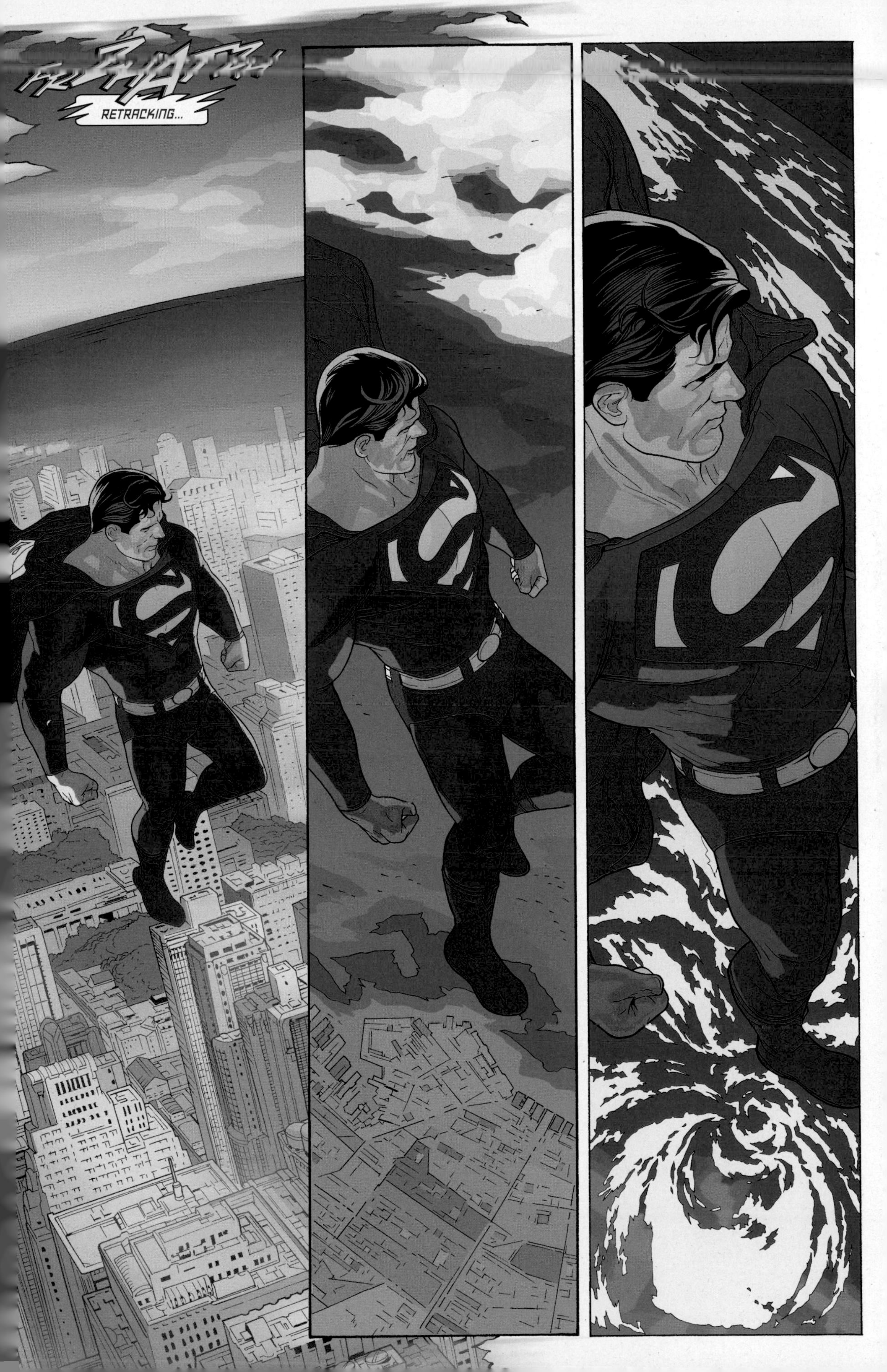
RETRACKING...

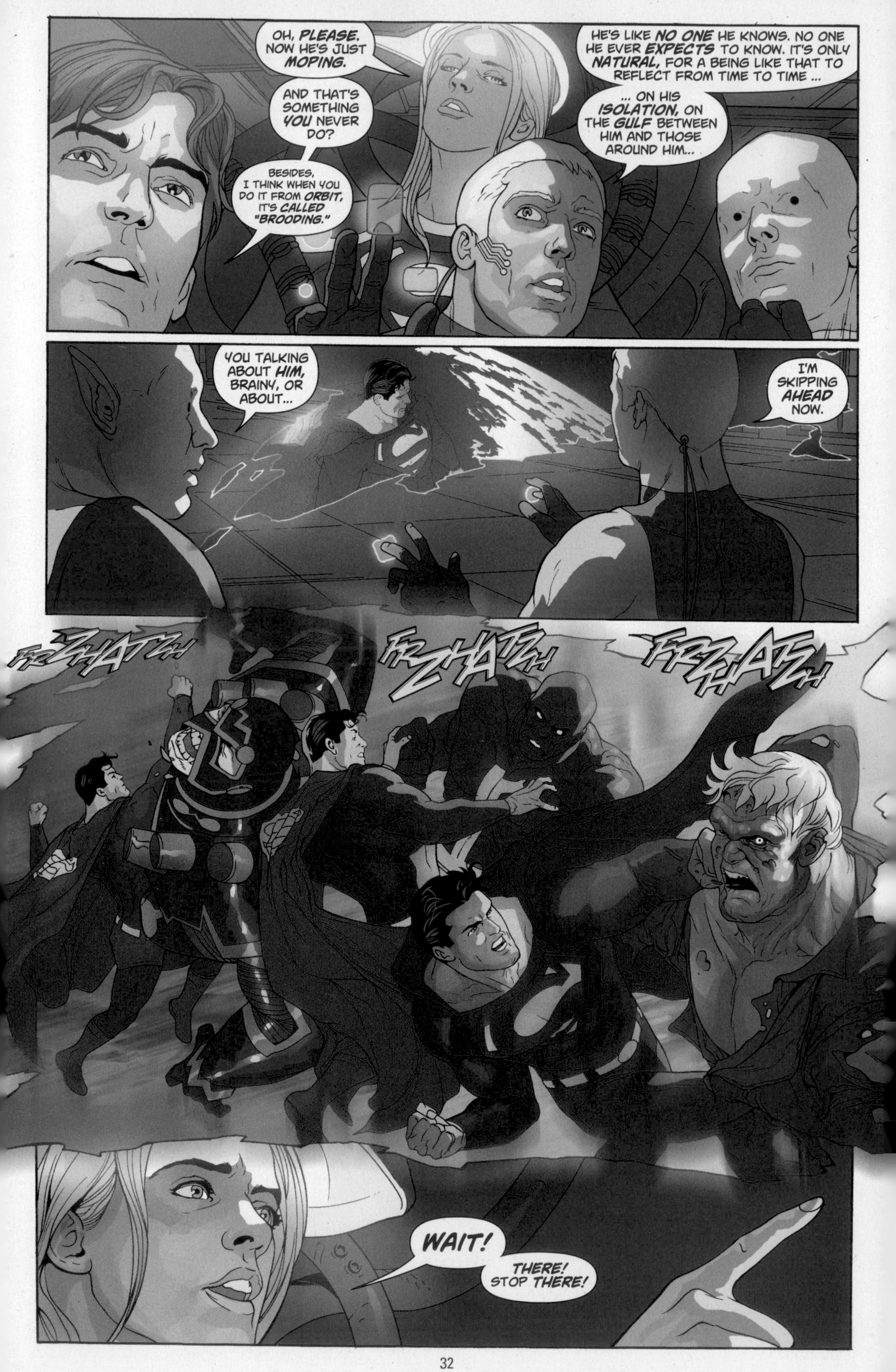
OH, PLEASE. NOW HE'S JUST MOPING.
AND THAT'S SOMETHING YOU NEVER DO?
BESIDES, I THINK WHEN YOU DO IT FROM ORBIT, IT'S CALLED "BROODING."
HE'S LIKE NO ONE HE KNOWS. NO ONE HE EVER EXPECTS TO KNOW. IT'S ONLY NATURAL, FOR A BEING LIKE THAT TO REFLECT FROM TIME TO TIME ...
... ON HIS ISOLATION, ON THE GULF BETWEEN HIM AND THOSE AROUND HIM...
YOU TALKING ABOUT HIM, BRAINY, OR ABOUT...
I'M SKIPPING AHEAD NOW.
FRZHATZH
FRZHATZH
FRZHATZH
WAIT!
THERE! STOP THERE!

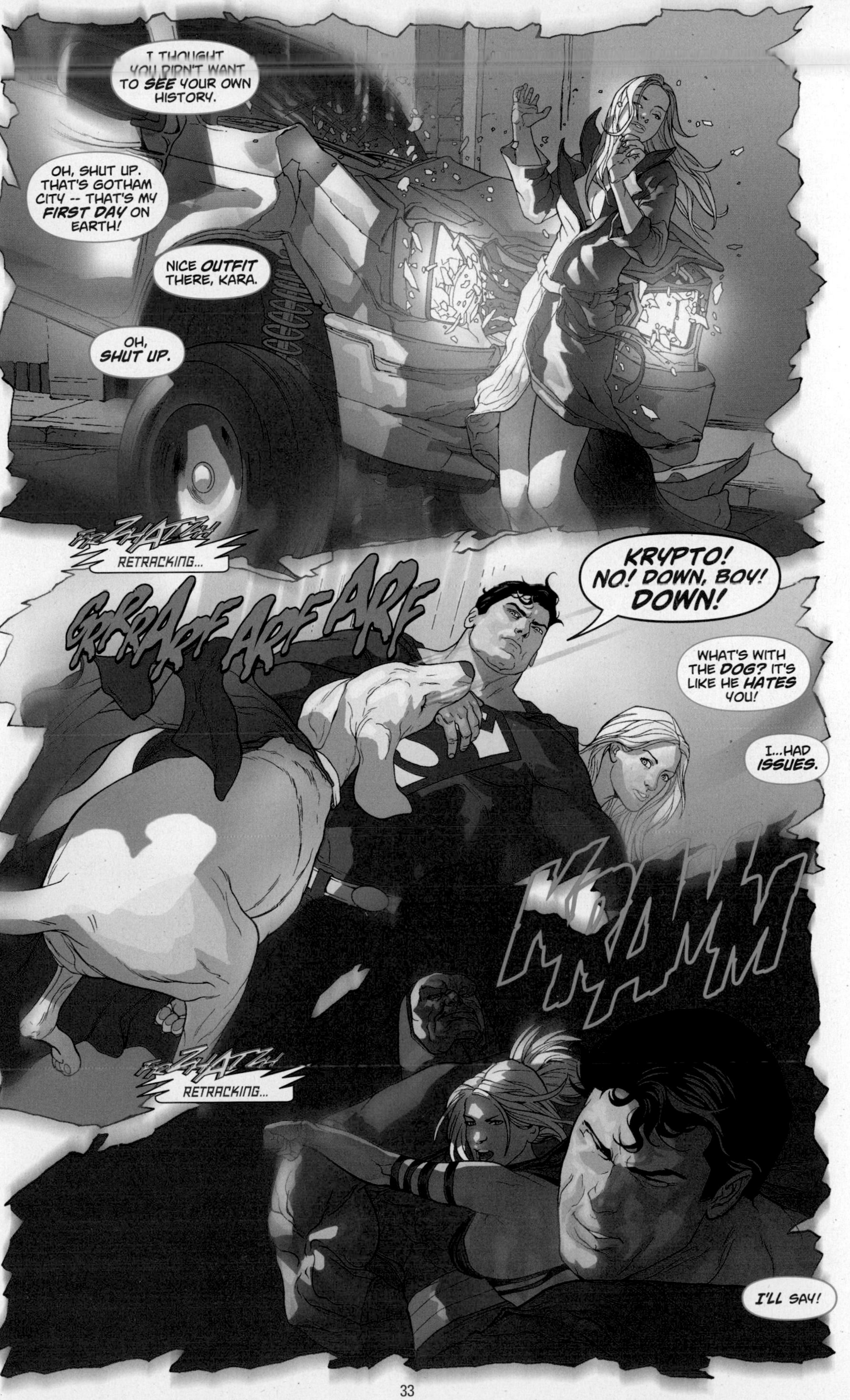

I THOUGHT YOU DIDN'T WANT TO SEE YOUR OWN HISTORY.
OH, SHUT UP. THAT'S GOTHAM CITY -- THAT'S MY FIRST DAY ON EARTH!
NICE OUTFIT THERE, KARA.
OH, SHUT UP.
RETRACKING...
GRRRARF ARF ARF
KRYPTO! NO! DOWN, BOY! DOWN!
WHAT'S WITH THE DOG? IT'S LIKE HE HATES YOU!
I...HAD ISSUES.
KRAMM
RETRACKING...
I'LL SAY!

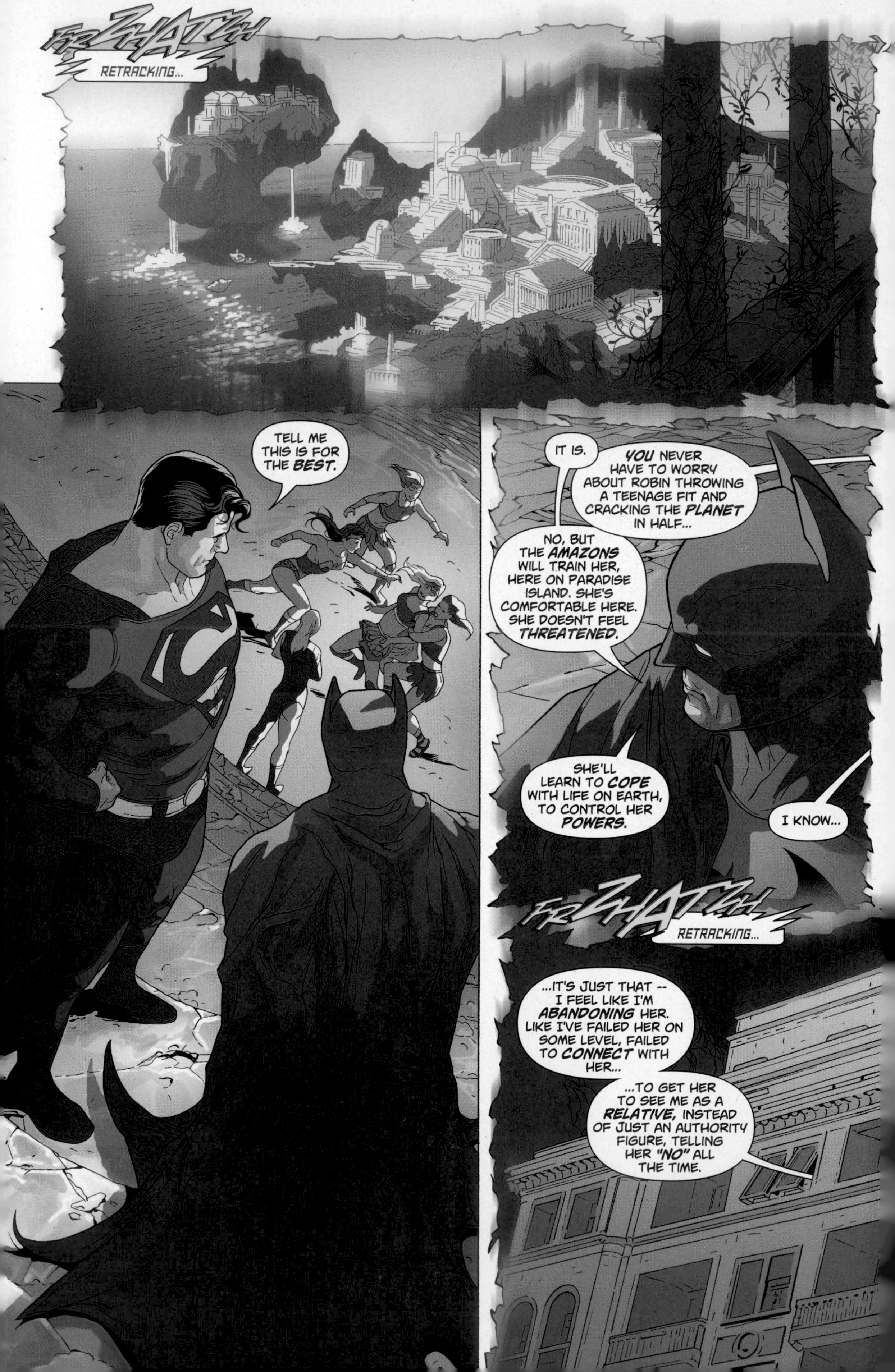
FRZHATCH
RETRACKING...
TELL ME THIS IS FOR THE BEST.
IT IS.
YOU NEVER HAVE TO WORRY ABOUT ROBIN THROWING A TEENAGE FIT AND CRACKING THE PLANET IN HALF...
NO, BUT THE AMAZONS WILL TRAIN HER, HERE ON PARADISE ISLAND. SHE'S COMFORTABLE HERE. SHE DOESN'T FEEL THREATENED.
SHE'LL LEARN TO COPE WITH LIFE ON EARTH, TO CONTROL HER POWERS.
I KNOW...
FRZHATCH
RETRACKING...
...IT'S JUST THAT -- I FEEL LIKE I'M ABANDONING HER. LIKE I'VE FAILED HER ON SOME LEVEL, FAILED TO CONNECT WITH HER...
...TO GET HER TO SEE ME AS A RELATIVE, INSTEAD OF JUST AN AUTHORITY FIGURE, TELLING HER "NO" ALL THE TIME.

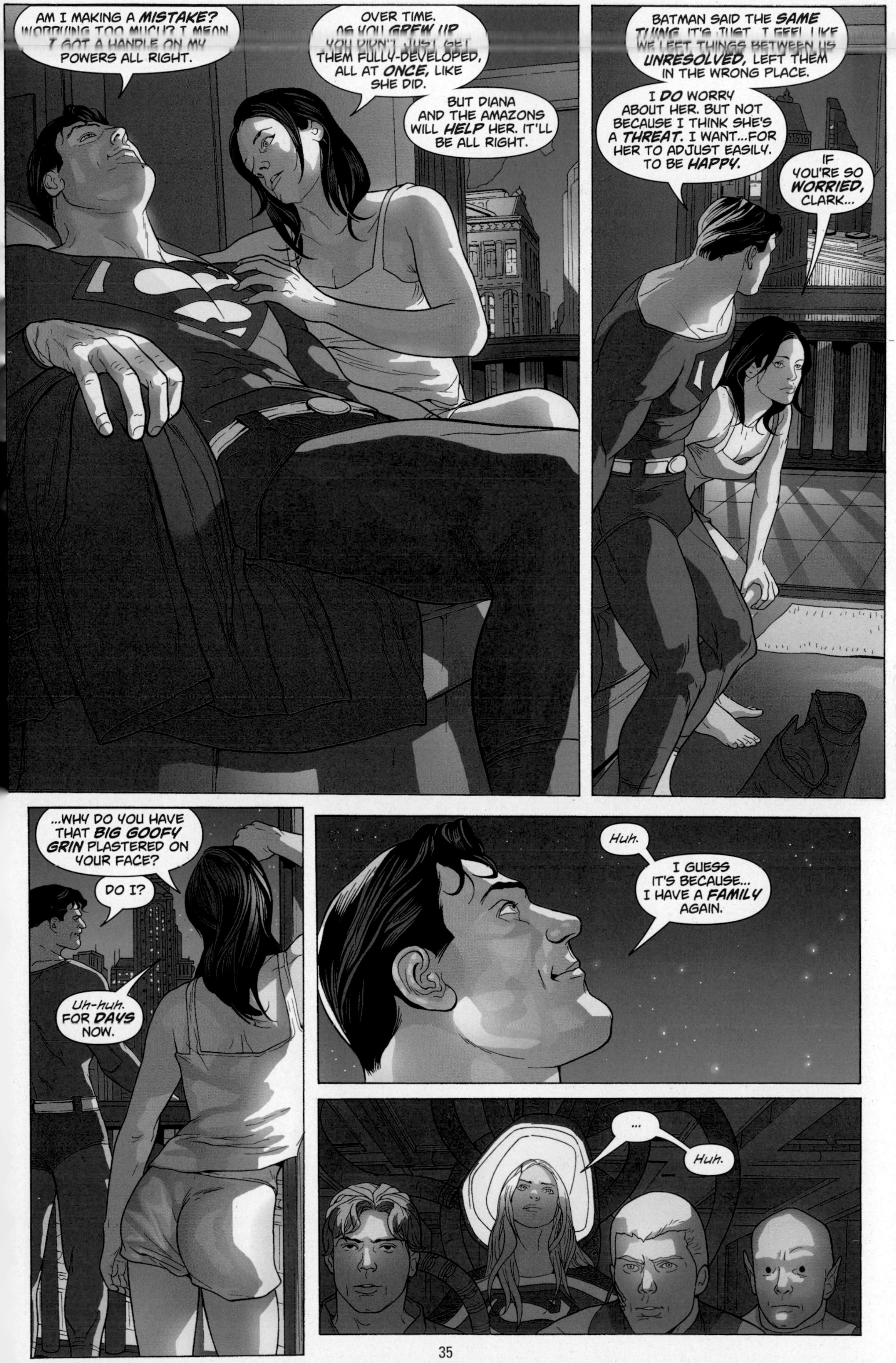
AM I MAKING A MISTAKE? WORRYING TOO MUCH? I MEAN I GOT A HANDLE ON MY POWERS ALL RIGHT.
OVER TIME. AS YOU GREW UP. YOU DIDN'T JUST GET THEM FULLY-DEVELOPED, ALL AT ONCE, LIKE SHE DID.
BUT DIANA AND THE AMAZONS WILL HELP HER. IT'LL BE ALL RIGHT.
BATMAN SAID THE SAME THING. IT'S JUST...I FEEL LIKE WE LEFT THINGS BETWEEN US UNRESOLVED, LEFT THEM IN THE WRONG PLACE.
I DO WORRY ABOUT HER. BUT NOT BECAUSE I THINK SHE'S A THREAT. I WANT...FOR HER TO ADJUST EASILY. TO BE HAPPY.
IF YOU'RE SO WORRIED, CLARK...
...WHY DO YOU HAVE THAT BIG GOOFY GRIN PLASTERED ON YOUR FACE?
DO I?
Uh-huh. FOR DAYS NOW.
Huh.
I GUESS IT'S BECAUSE... I HAVE A FAMILY AGAIN.
...
Huh.

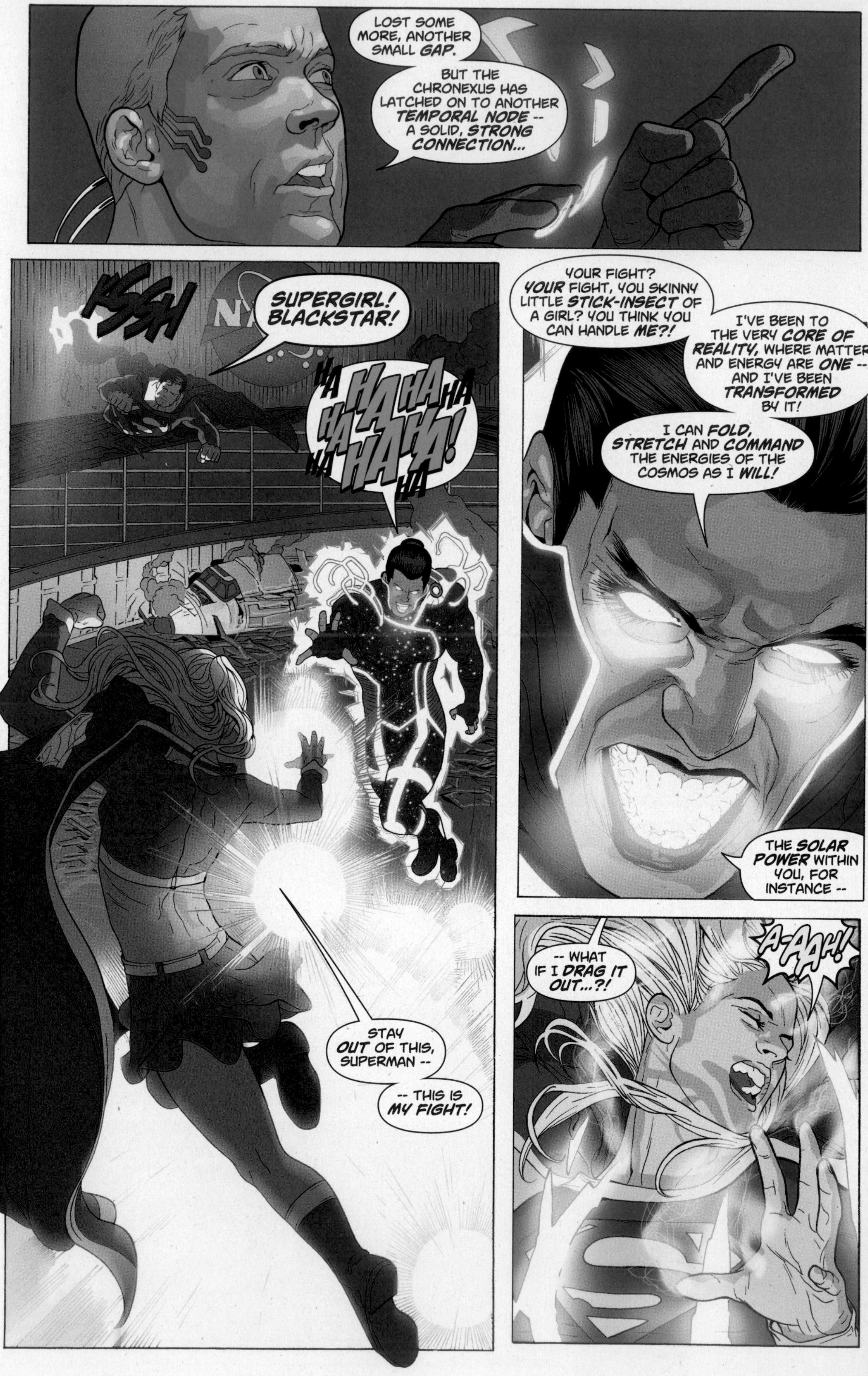

LOST SOME MORE, ANOTHER SMALL GAP.
BUT THE CHRONEXUS HAS LATCHED ON TO ANOTHER TEMPORAL NODE -- A SOLID, STRONG CONNECTION...
KSSH
SUPERGIRL! BLACKSTAR!
HA HA HAHA HA HA HA HAHA! HA
STAY OUT OF THIS, SUPERMAN --
-- THIS IS MY FIGHT!
YOUR FIGHT? YOUR FIGHT, YOU SKINNY LITTLE STICK-INSECT OF A GIRL? YOU THINK YOU CAN HANDLE ME?!
I'VE BEEN TO THE VERY CORE OF REALITY, WHERE MATTER AND ENERGY ARE ONE -- AND I'VE BEEN TRANSFORMED BY IT!
I CAN FOLD, STRETCH AND COMMAND THE ENERGIES OF THE COSMOS AS I WILL!
THE SOLAR POWER WITHIN YOU, FOR INSTANCE --
-- WHAT IF I DRAG IT OUT...?!
A-AAH!

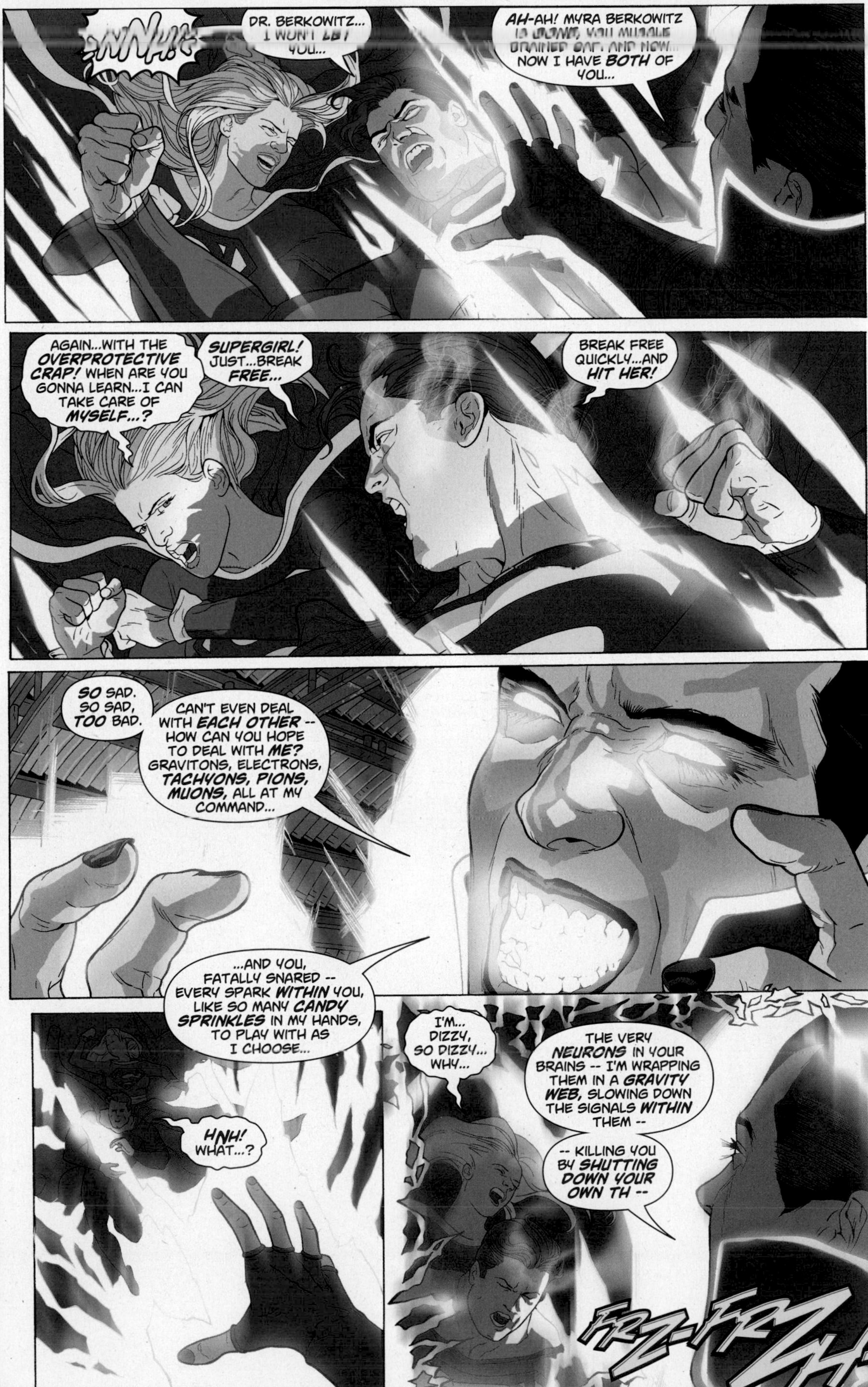

DR. BERKOWITZ... I WON'T LET YOU...
AH-AH! MYRA BERKOWITZ
NOW I HAVE BOTH OF YOU...
AGAIN...WITH THE OVERPROTECTIVE CRAP! WHEN ARE YOU GONNA LEARN...I CAN TAKE CARE OF MYSELF...?
SUPERGIRL! JUST...BREAK FREE...
BREAK FREE QUICKLY...AND HIT HER!
SO SAD. SO SAD, TOO BAD.
CAN'T EVEN DEAL WITH EACH OTHER -- HOW CAN YOU HOPE TO DEAL WITH ME? GRAVITONS, ELECTRONS, TACHYONS, PIONS, MUONS, ALL AT MY COMMAND...
...AND YOU, FATALLY SNARED -- EVERY SPARK WITHIN YOU, LIKE SO MANY CANDY SPRINKLES IN MY HANDS, TO PLAY WITH AS I CHOOSE...
HNH! WHAT...?
I'M... DIZZY, SO DIZZY... WHY...
THE VERY NEURONS IN YOUR BRAINS -- I'M WRAPPING THEM IN A GRAVITY WEB, SLOWING DOWN THE SIGNALS WITHIN THEM --
-- KILLING YOU BY SHUTTING DOWN YOUR OWN TH --
FRZ-FRZH-

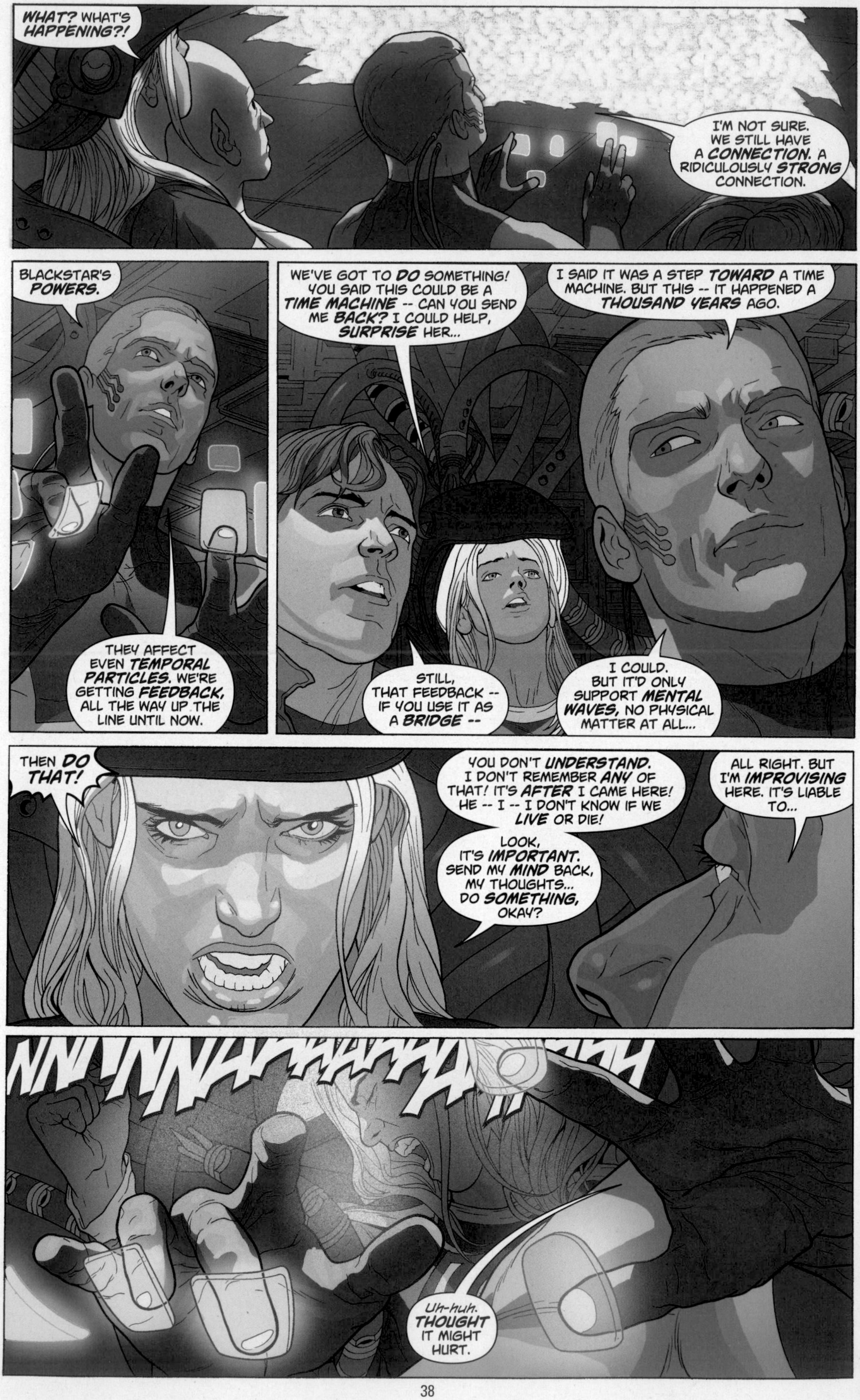
WHAT? WHAT'S HAPPENING?!
I'M NOT SURE. WE STILL HAVE A CONNECTION. A RIDICULOUSLY STRONG CONNECTION.
BLACKSTAR'S POWERS.
THEY AFFECT EVEN TEMPORAL PARTICLES. WE'RE GETTING FEEDBACK, ALL THE WAY UP THE LINE UNTIL NOW.
WE'VE GOT TO DO SOMETHING! YOU SAID THIS COULD BE A TIME MACHINE -- CAN YOU SEND ME BACK? I COULD HELP, SURPRISE HER...
I SAID IT WAS A STEP TOWARD A TIME MACHINE. BUT THIS -- IT HAPPENED A THOUSAND YEARS AGO.
STILL, THAT FEEDBACK -- IF YOU USE IT AS A BRIDGE --
I COULD. BUT IT'D ONLY SUPPORT MENTAL WAVES, NO PHYSICAL MATTER AT ALL...
THEN DO THAT!
YOU DON'T UNDERSTAND. I DON'T REMEMBER ANY OF THAT! IT'S AFTER I CAME HERE! HE -- I -- I DON'T KNOW IF WE LIVE OR DIE!
LOOK, IT'S IMPORTANT. SEND MY MIND BACK, MY THOUGHTS... DO SOMETHING, OKAY?
ALL RIGHT. BUT I'M IMPROVISING HERE. IT'S LIABLE TO...
NNNNNNAAAAAAAAHHHHH
Uh-huh. THOUGHT IT MIGHT HURT.

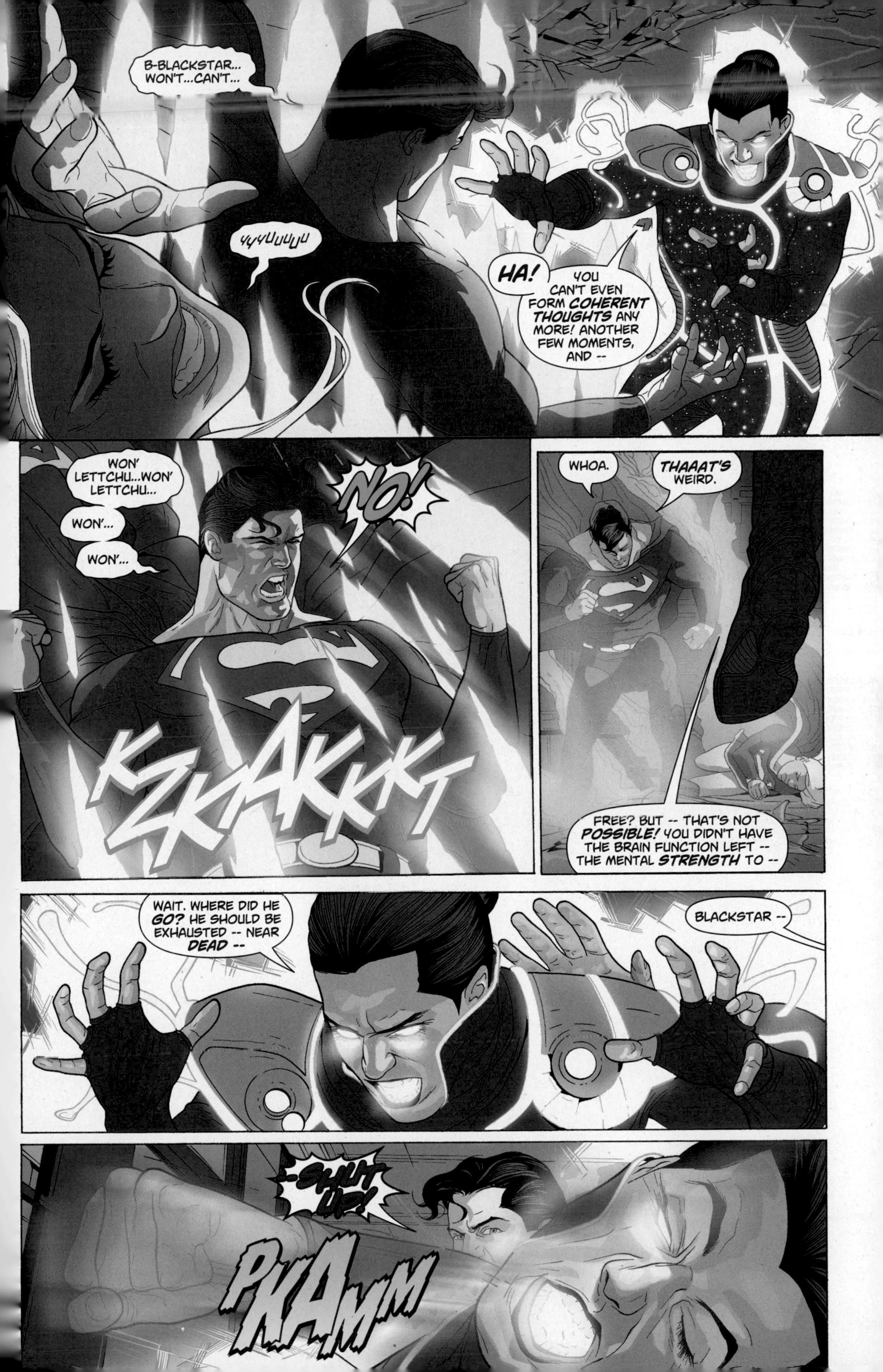
B-BLACKSTAR... WON'T...CAN'T...
YYYUUUUU
HA!
YOU CAN'T EVEN FORM COHERENT THOUGHTS ANY MORE! ANOTHER FEW MOMENTS, AND --
WON' LETTCHU...WON' LETTCHU...
WON'...
WON'...
NO!
KZKAKKT
WHOA.
THAAAT'S WEIRD.
FREE? BUT -- THAT'S NOT POSSIBLE! YOU DIDN'T HAVE THE BRAIN FUNCTION LEFT -- THE MENTAL STRENGTH TO --
WAIT. WHERE DID HE GO? HE SHOULD BE EXHAUSTED -- NEAR DEAD --
BLACKSTAR --
-SHUT UP!
PKAMM

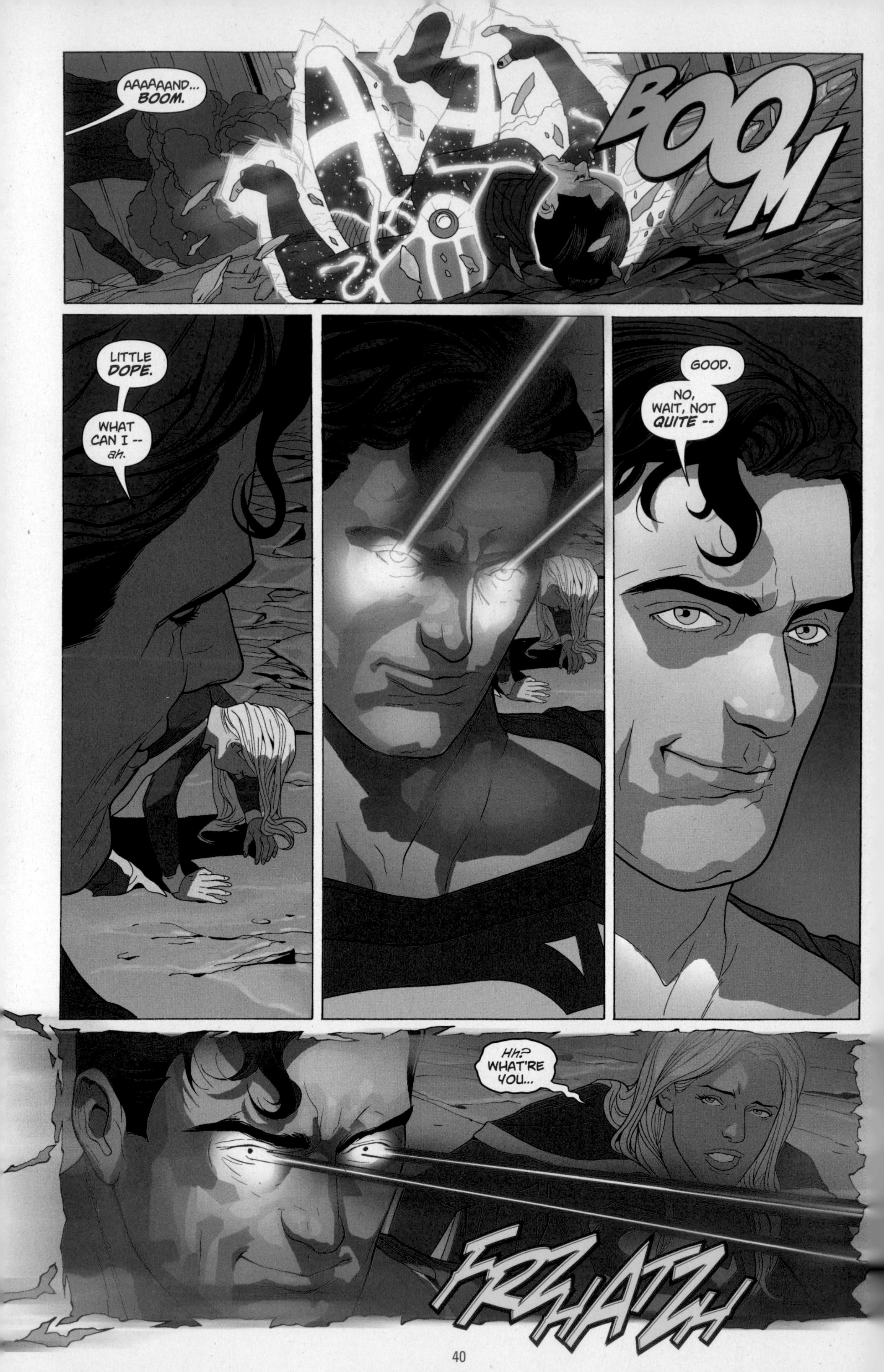
AAAAAAND... BOOM.
BOOM
LITTLE DOPE.
WHAT CAN I -- ah.
GOOD.
NO, WAIT, NOT QUITE --
Hh? WHAT'RE YOU...
FRZHATZH

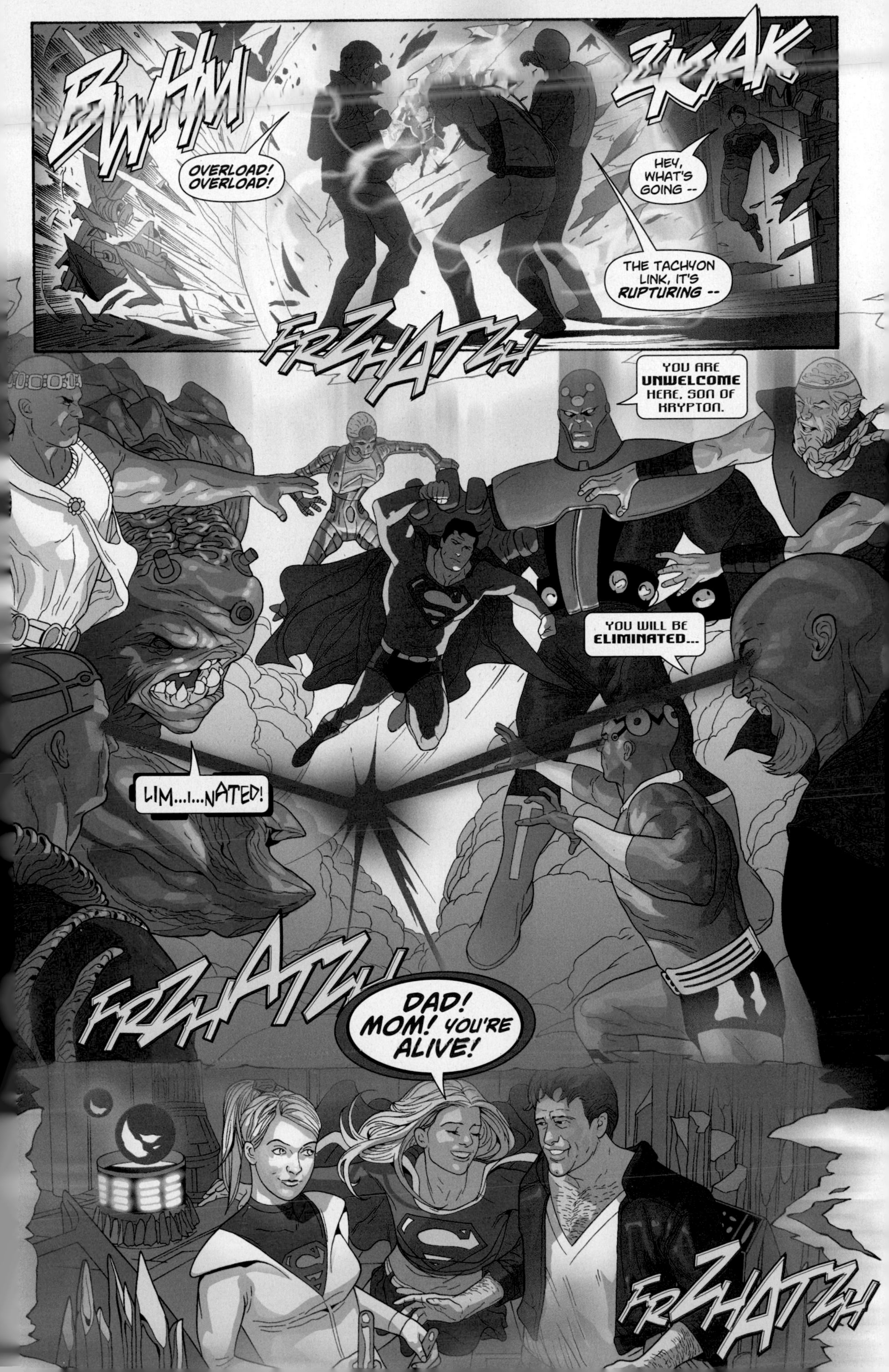
BWHM
OVERLOAD! OVERLOAD!
ZKAK
HEY, WHAT'S GOING --
THE TACHYON LINK, IT'S RUPTURING --
FRZHATZH
YOU ARE UNWELCOME HERE, SON OF KRYPTON.
YOU WILL BE ELIMINATED...
LIM...I...NATED!
FRZHATZH
DAD! MOM! YOU'RE ALIVE!
FRZHATZH

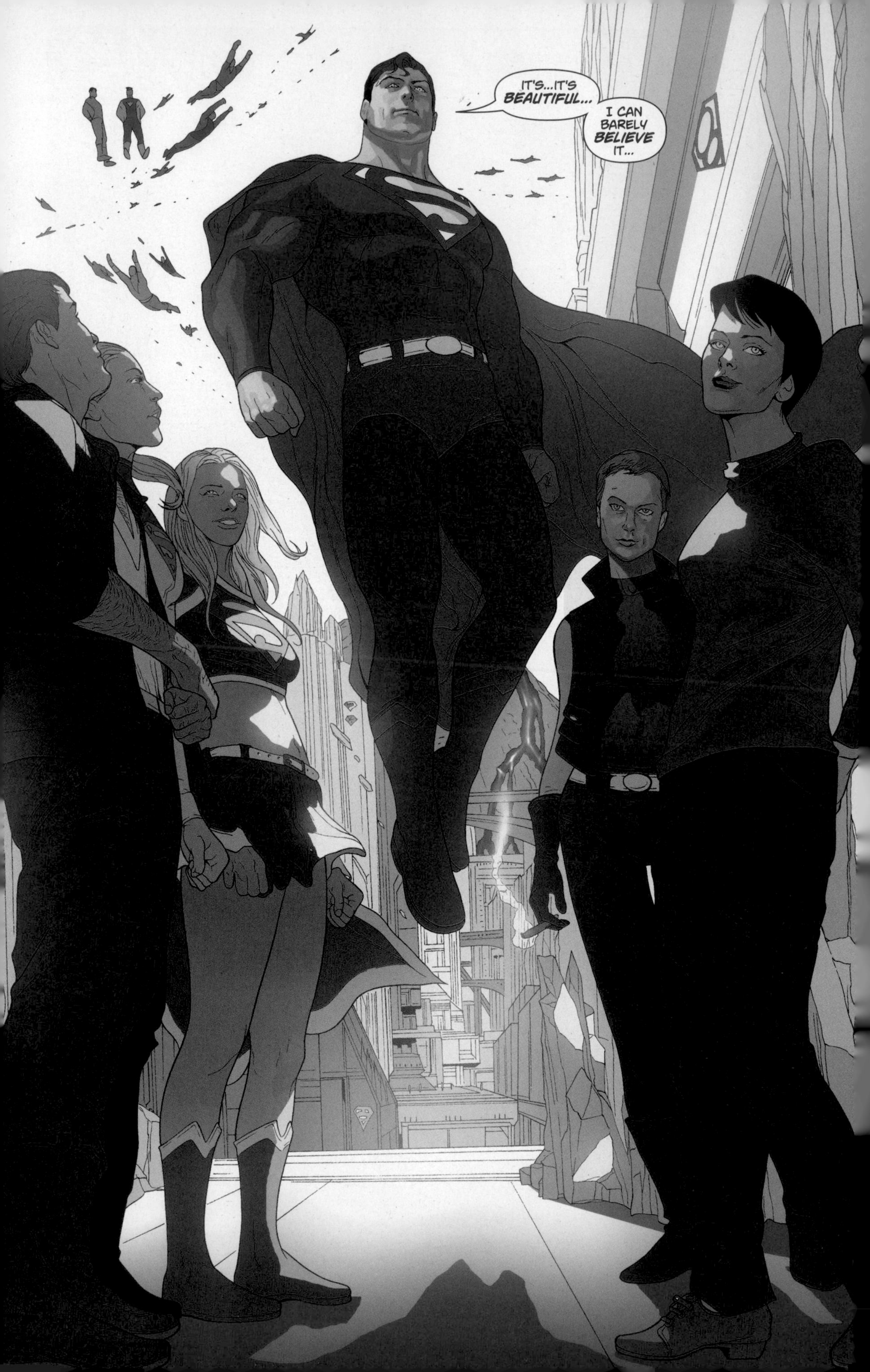
IT'S...IT'S **BEAUTIFUL...**
I CAN BARELY **BELIEVE** IT...

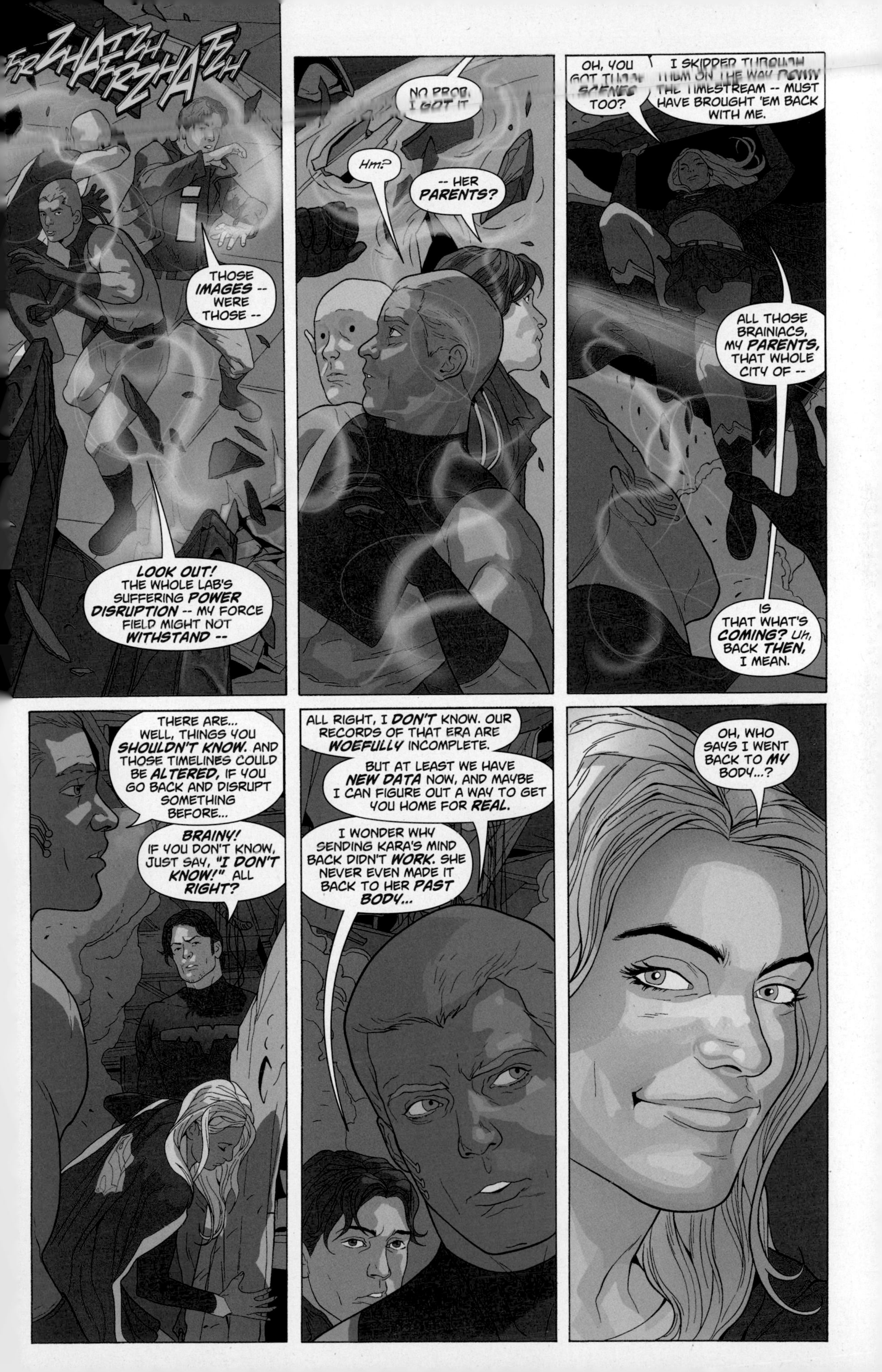
FRZHATZH FRZHATZH
THOSE IMAGES -- WERE THOSE --
LOOK OUT! THE WHOLE LAB'S SUFFERING POWER DISRUPTION -- MY FORCE FIELD MIGHT NOT WITHSTAND --
NO PROB. I GOT IT
Hm?
-- HER PARENTS?
OH, YOU GOT THOSE SCENES TOO?
I SKIPPED THROUGH THEM ON THE WAY DOWN THE TIMESTREAM -- MUST HAVE BROUGHT 'EM BACK WITH ME.
ALL THOSE BRAINIACS, MY PARENTS, THAT WHOLE CITY OF --
IS THAT WHAT'S COMING? Uh, BACK THEN, I MEAN.
THERE ARE... WELL, THINGS YOU SHOULDN'T KNOW. AND THOSE TIMELINES COULD BE ALTERED, IF YOU GO BACK AND DISRUPT SOMETHING BEFORE...
BRAINY! IF YOU DON'T KNOW, JUST SAY, "I DON'T KNOW!" ALL RIGHT?
ALL RIGHT, I DON'T KNOW. OUR RECORDS OF THAT ERA ARE WOEFULLY INCOMPLETE.
BUT AT LEAST WE HAVE NEW DATA NOW, AND MAYBE I CAN FIGURE OUT A WAY TO GET YOU HOME FOR REAL.
I WONDER WHY SENDING KARA'S MIND BACK DIDN'T WORK. SHE NEVER EVEN MADE IT BACK TO HER PAST BODY...
OH, WHO SAYS I WENT BACK TO MY BODY...?

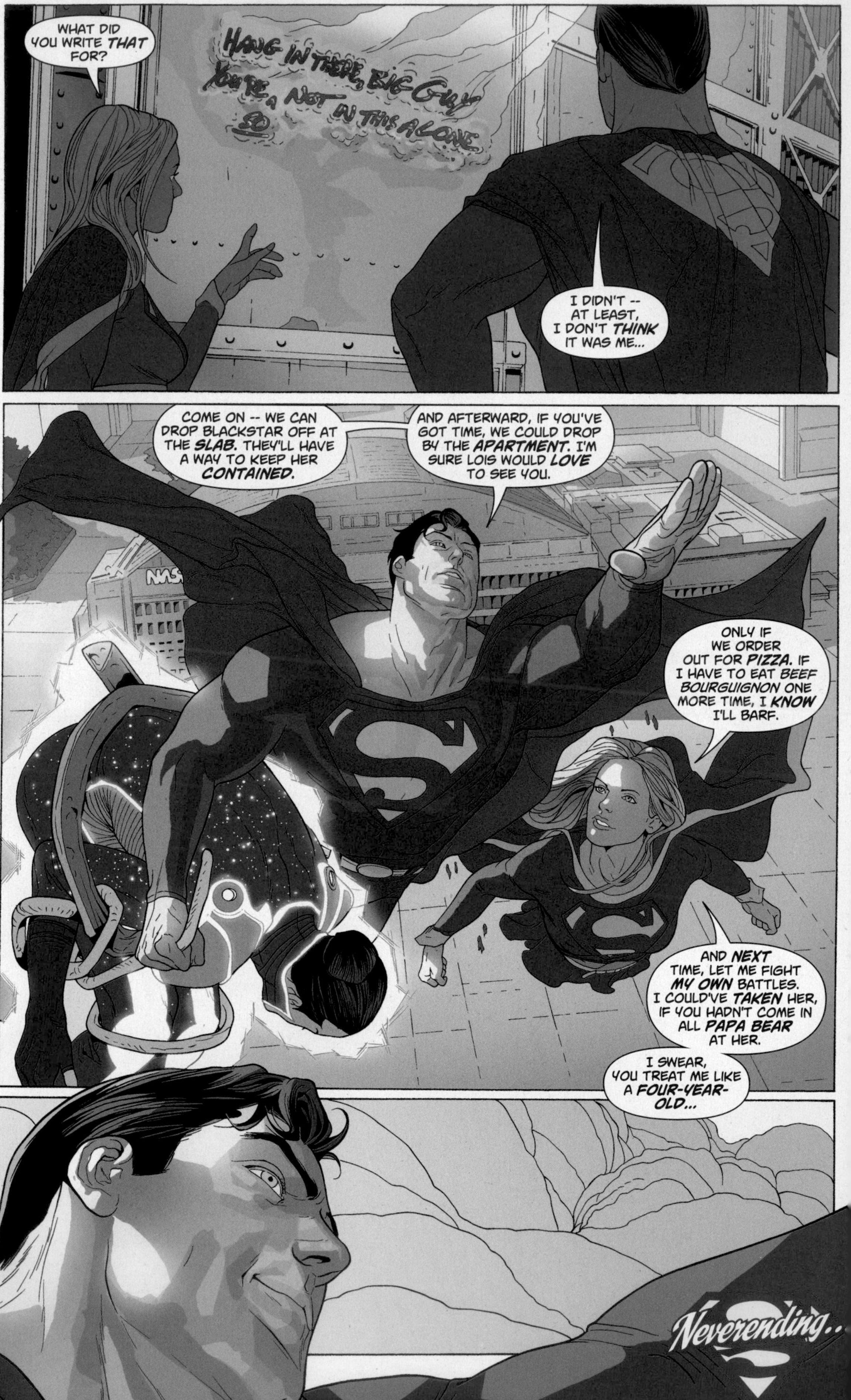
WHAT DID YOU WRITE THAT FOR?
HANG IN THERE, BIG GUY
YOU'RE NOT IN THIS ALONE.
SO
I DIDN'T -- AT LEAST, I DON'T THINK IT WAS ME...
COME ON -- WE CAN DROP BLACKSTAR OFF AT THE SLAB. THEY'LL HAVE A WAY TO KEEP HER CONTAINED.
AND AFTERWARD, IF YOU'VE GOT TIME, WE COULD DROP BY THE APARTMENT. I'M SURE LOIS WOULD LOVE TO SEE YOU.
ONLY IF WE ORDER OUT FOR PIZZA. IF I HAVE TO EAT BEEF BOURGUIGNON ONE MORE TIME, I KNOW I'LL BARF.
AND NEXT TIME, LET ME FIGHT MY OWN BATTLES. I COULD'VE TAKEN HER, IF YOU HADN'T COME IN ALL PAPA BEAR AT HER.
I SWEAR, YOU TREAT ME LIKE A FOUR-YEAR-OLD...
Neverending...

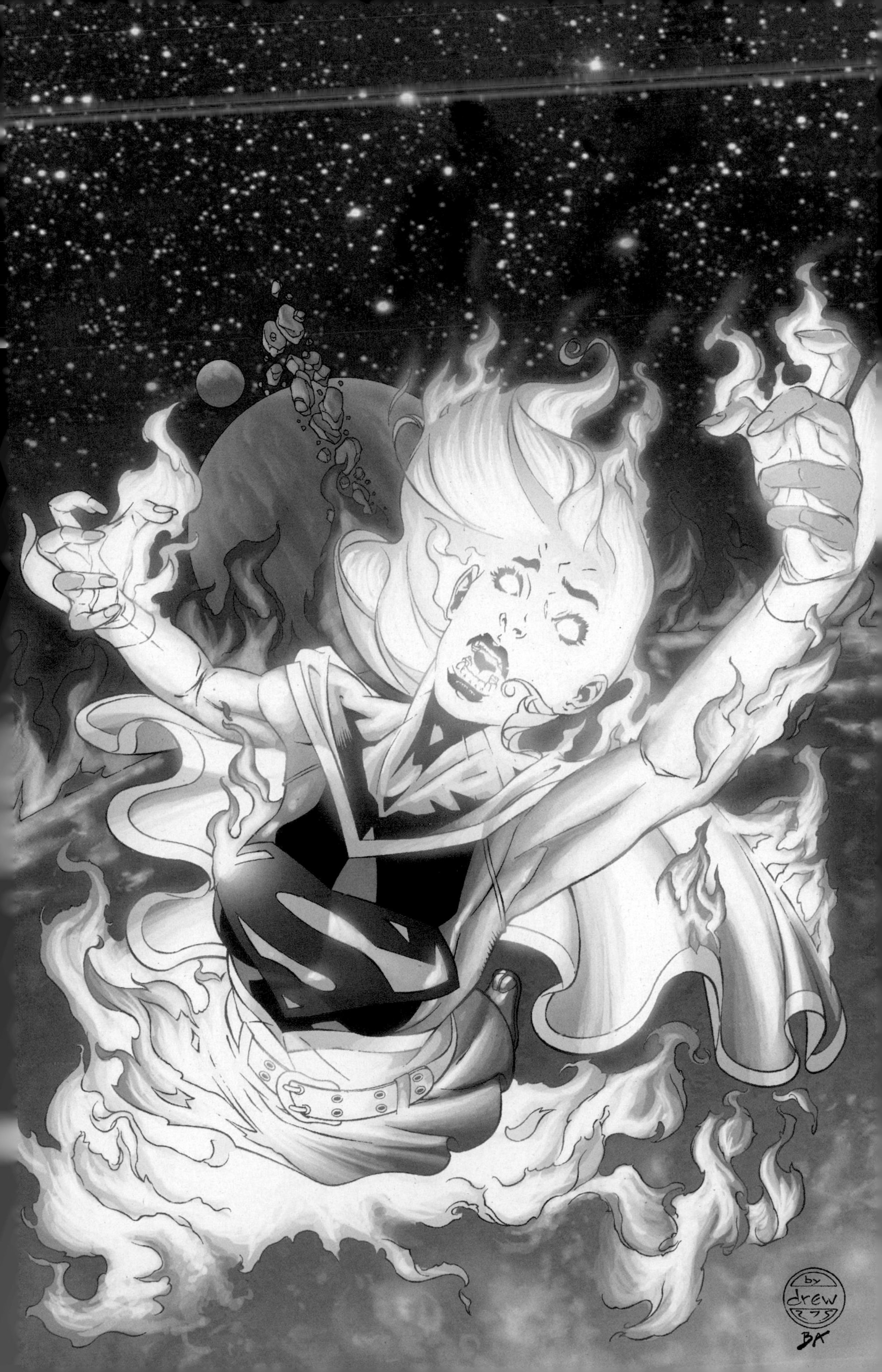
by
drew
2.7.5
BA

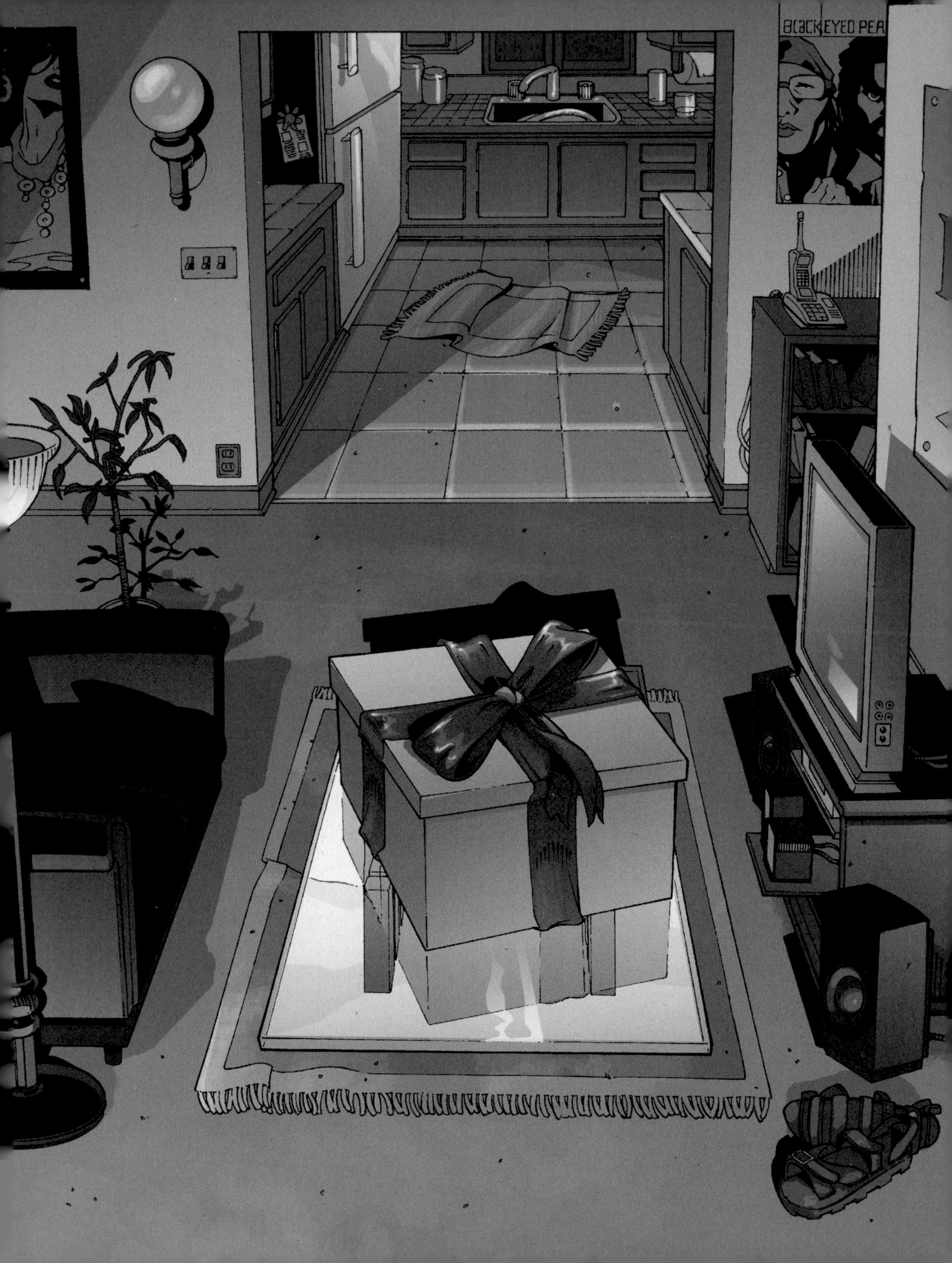
BLACKEYED PEA

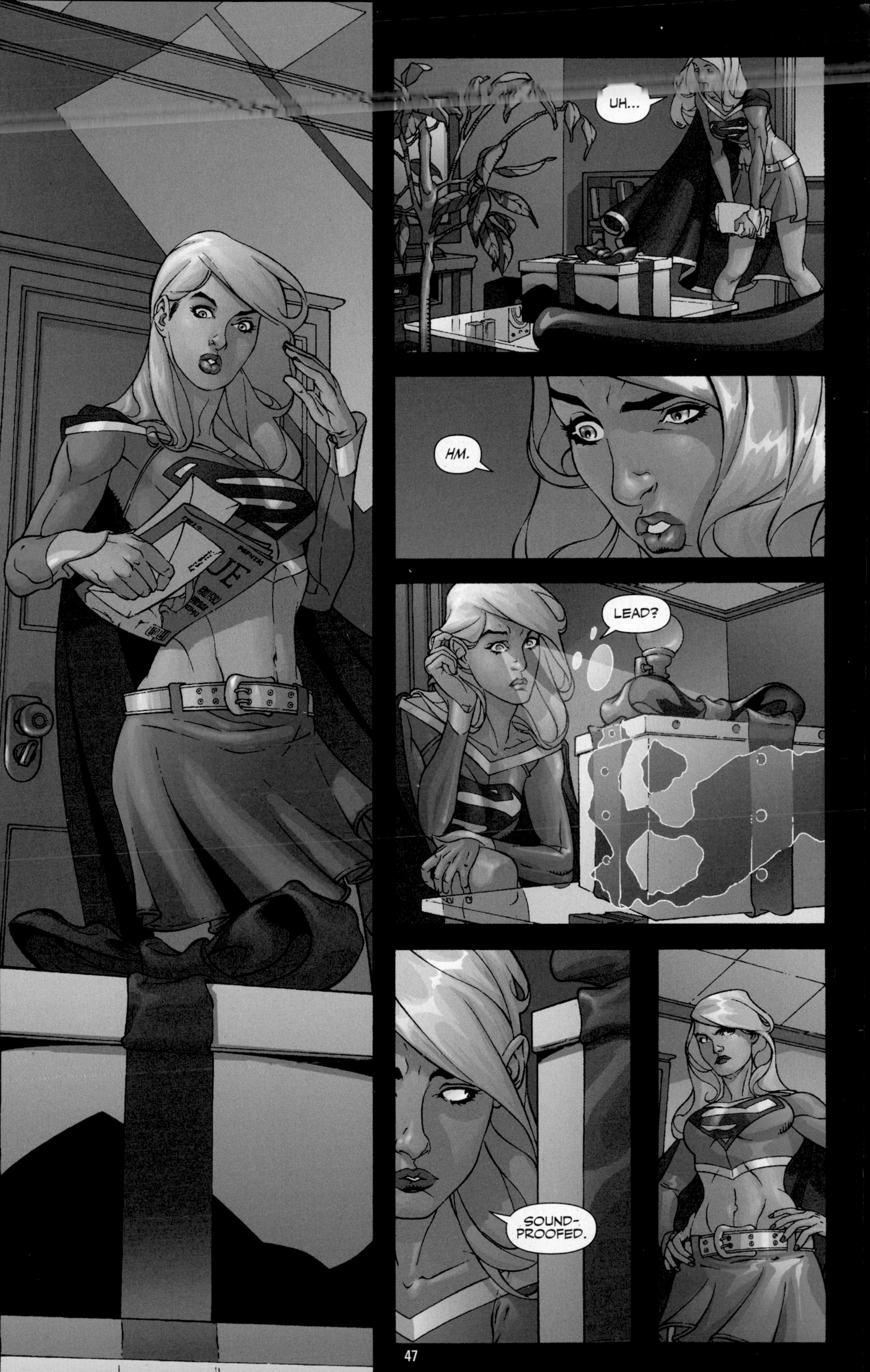
UH...
HM.
LEAD?
SOUND-PROOFED.

Mistake.

WHAT...?

BRiiiNG
BRiiiNG

HELLO?

YOU OPENED IT, DIDN'T YOU.

WHAT? I--

OH MY GOD. WHAT IS WRONG WITH YOU?

SOMEONE BYPASSES MY SECURITY SYSTEM, LEAVES YOU A PACKAGE SPECIFICALLY DESIGNED TO FOIL YOUR POWERS...AND YOU OPEN IT?

24 HOURS

EAST SIDE GOTHAM MOTEL

EASY NO-HASSLE PAY DAY LOAN

Action news NOW AT 10 P

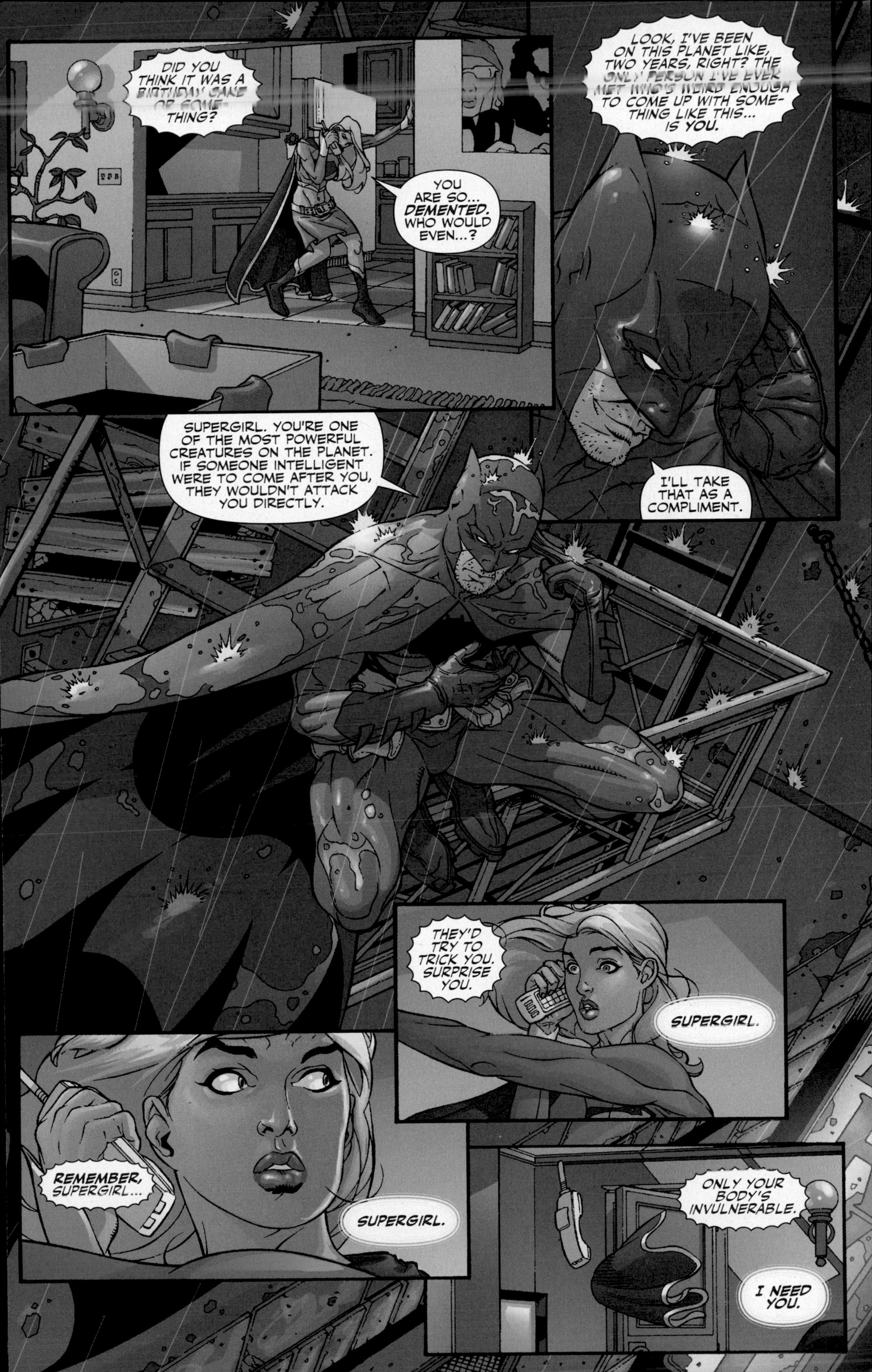
DID YOU THINK IT WAS A BIRTHDAY CAKE OR SOME-THING?
YOU ARE SO... DEMENTED. WHO WOULD EVEN...?
LOOK, I'VE BEEN ON THIS PLANET LIKE, TWO YEARS, RIGHT? THE ONLY PERSON I'VE EVER MET WHO'S WEIRD ENOUGH TO COME UP WITH SOME-THING LIKE THIS... IS YOU.
I'LL TAKE THAT AS A COMPLIMENT.
SUPERGIRL. YOU'RE ONE OF THE MOST POWERFUL CREATURES ON THE PLANET. IF SOMEONE INTELLIGENT WERE TO COME AFTER YOU, THEY WOULDN'T ATTACK YOU DIRECTLY.
THEY'D TRY TO TRICK YOU. SURPRISE YOU.
SUPERGIRL.
REMEMBER, SUPERGIRL...
SUPERGIRL.
ONLY YOUR BODY'S INVULNERABLE.
I NEED YOU.

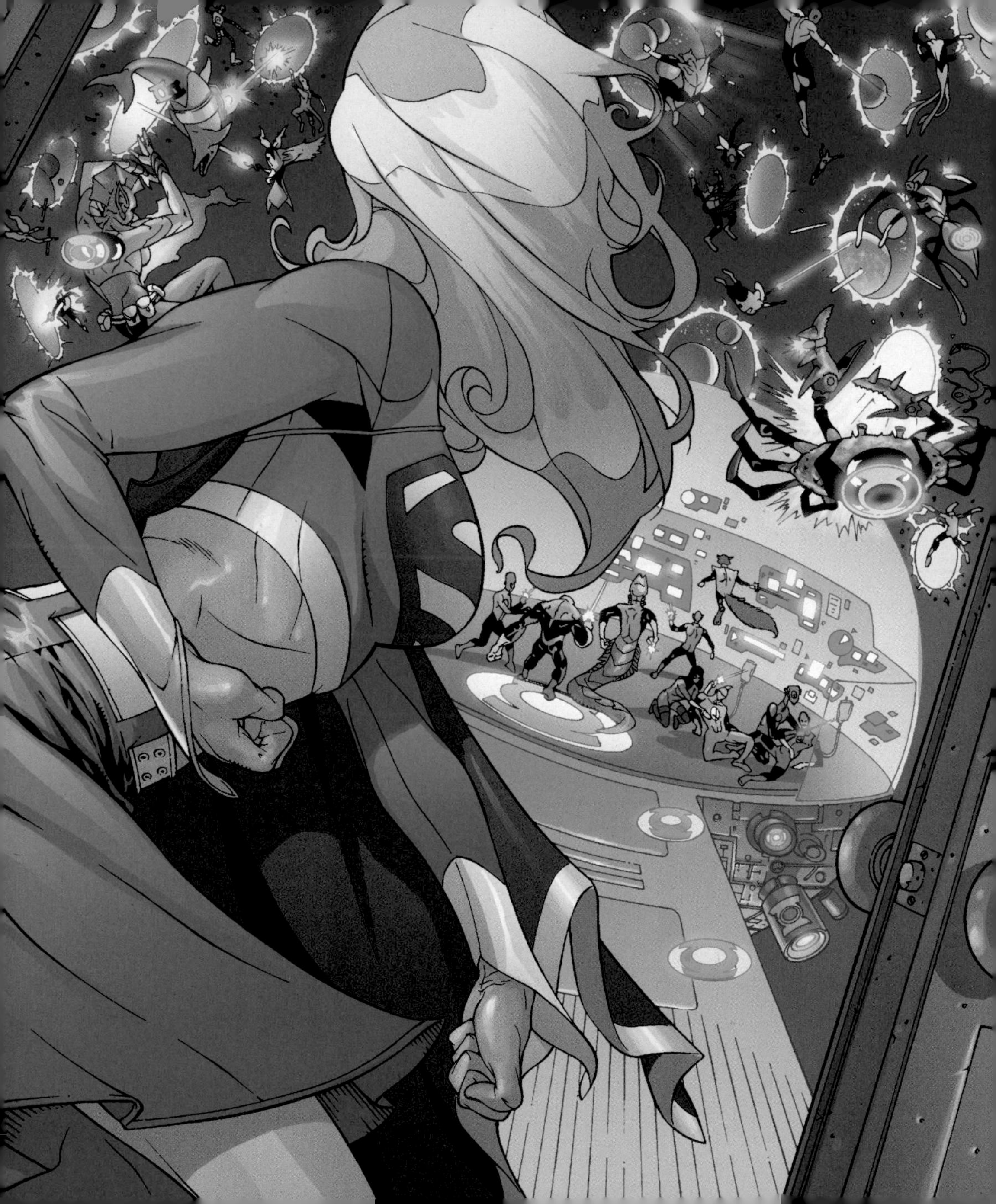

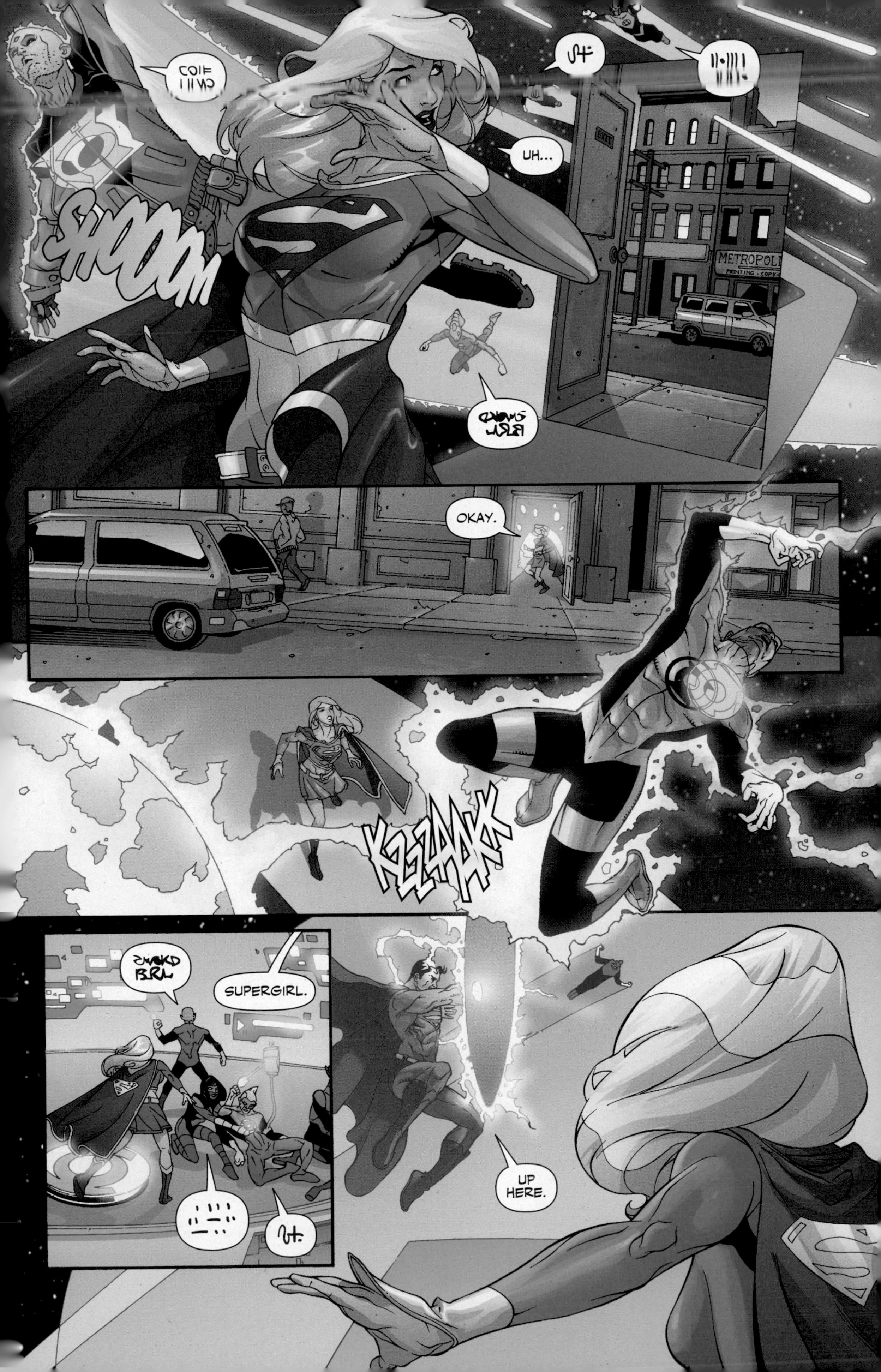
UH...
EXIT
METROPOLI
PRINTING · COPY
OKAY.
SUPERGIRL.
UP HERE.

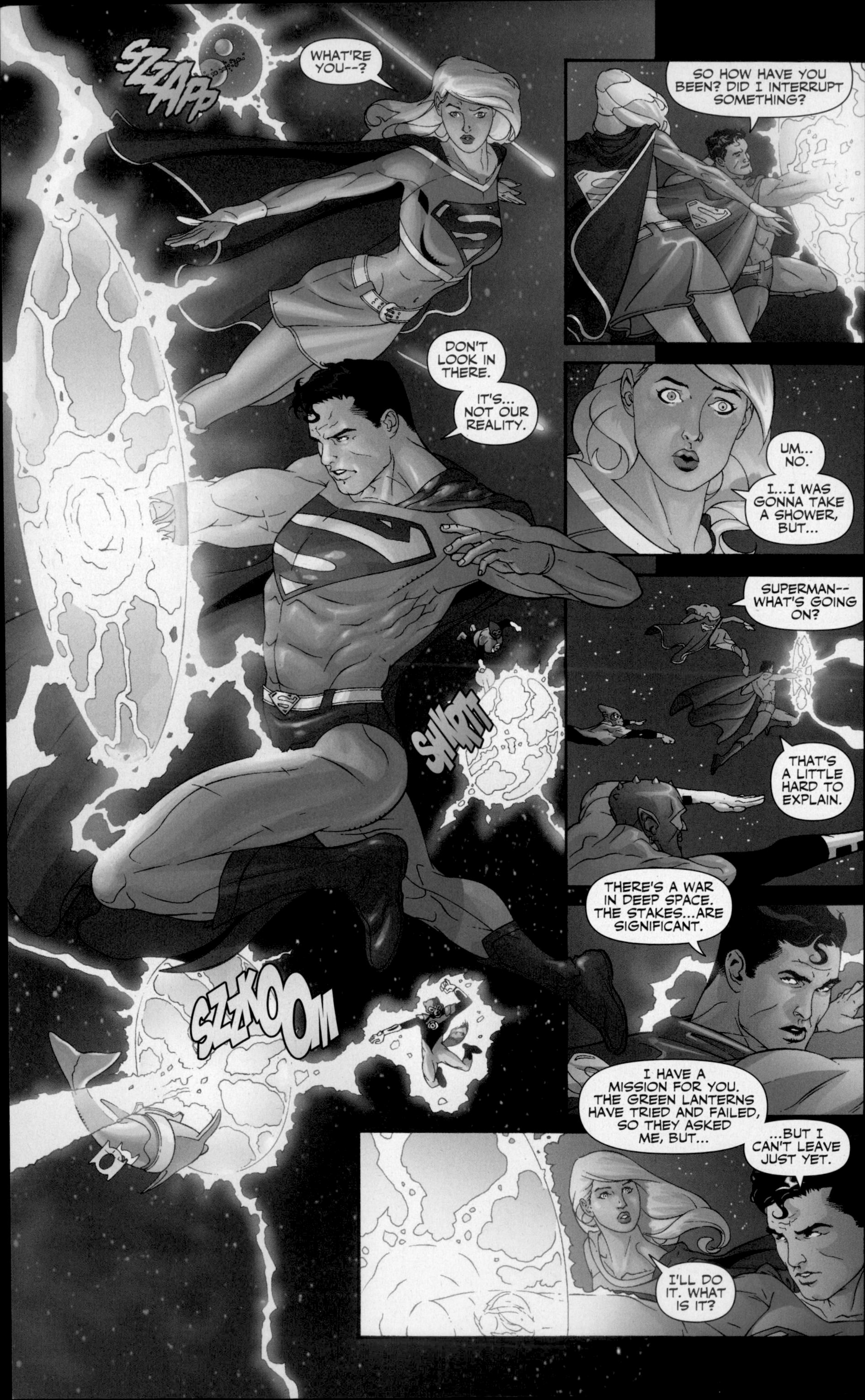
SZZAPP
WHAT'RE YOU--?
SO HOW HAVE YOU BEEN? DID I INTERRUPT SOMETHING?
DON'T LOOK IN THERE.
IT'S... NOT OUR REALITY.
UM... NO.
I...I WAS GONNA TAKE A SHOWER, BUT...
SHKRTT
SUPERMAN-- WHAT'S GOING ON?
THAT'S A LITTLE HARD TO EXPLAIN.
THERE'S A WAR IN DEEP SPACE. THE STAKES...ARE SIGNIFICANT.
SZZKOOM
I HAVE A MISSION FOR YOU. THE GREEN LANTERNS HAVE TRIED AND FAILED, SO THEY ASKED ME, BUT...
...BUT I CAN'T LEAVE JUST YET.
I'LL DO IT. WHAT IS IT?

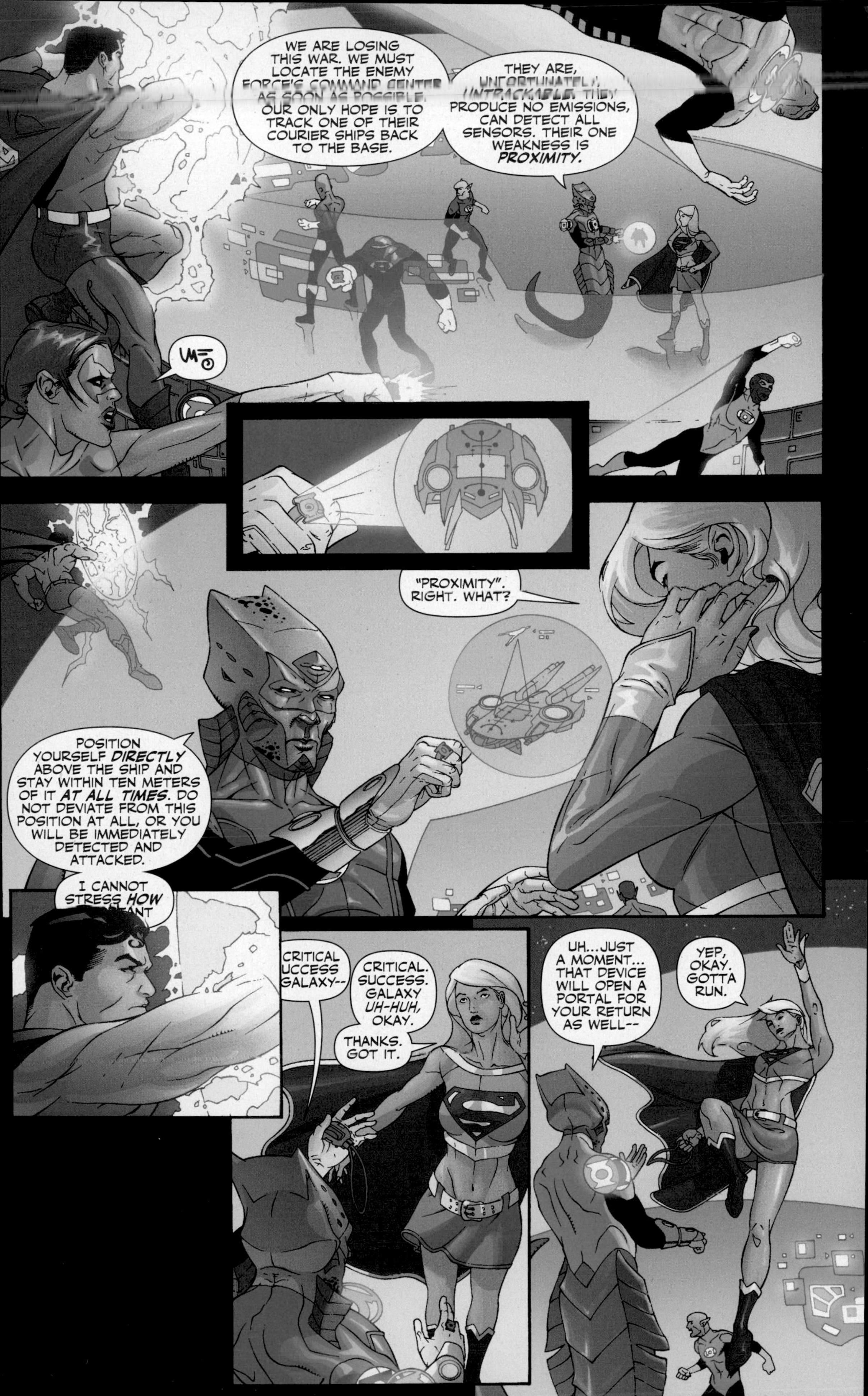
WE ARE LOSING THIS WAR. WE MUST LOCATE THE ENEMY FORCE'S COMMAND CENTER AS SOON AS POSSIBLE. OUR ONLY HOPE IS TO TRACK ONE OF THEIR COURIER SHIPS BACK TO THE BASE.
THEY ARE, UNFORTUNATELY, *UNTRACKABLE.* THEY PRODUCE NO EMISSIONS, CAN DETECT ALL SENSORS. THEIR ONE WEAKNESS IS ***PROXIMITY.***
"PROXIMITY". RIGHT. WHAT?
POSITION YOURSELF ***DIRECTLY*** ABOVE THE SHIP AND STAY WITHIN TEN METERS OF IT ***AT ALL TIMES***. DO NOT DEVIATE FROM THIS POSITION AT ALL, OR YOU WILL BE IMMEDIATELY DETECTED AND ATTACKED.
I CANNOT STRESS ***HOW***
CRITICAL SUCCESS GALAXY--
CRITICAL. SUCCESS. GALAXY ***UH-HUH,*** OKAY.
THANKS. GOT IT.
UH...JUST A MOMENT... THAT DEVICE WILL OPEN A PORTAL FOR YOUR RETURN AS WELL--
YEP, OKAY. GOTTA RUN.

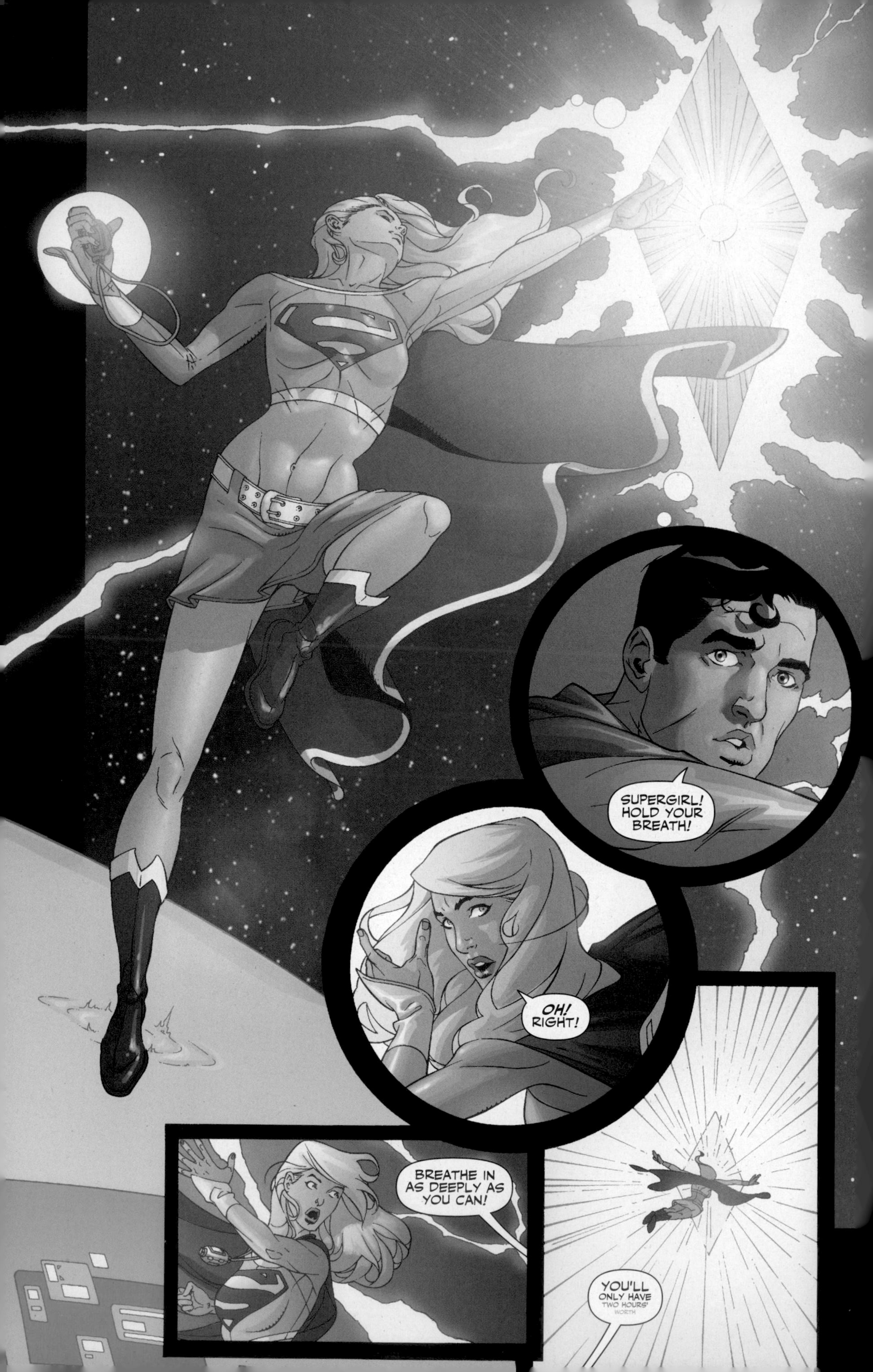
SUPERGIRL! HOLD YOUR BREATH!
OH! RIGHT!
BREATHE IN AS DEEPLY AS YOU CAN!
YOU'LL ONLY HAVE TWO HOURS' WORTH

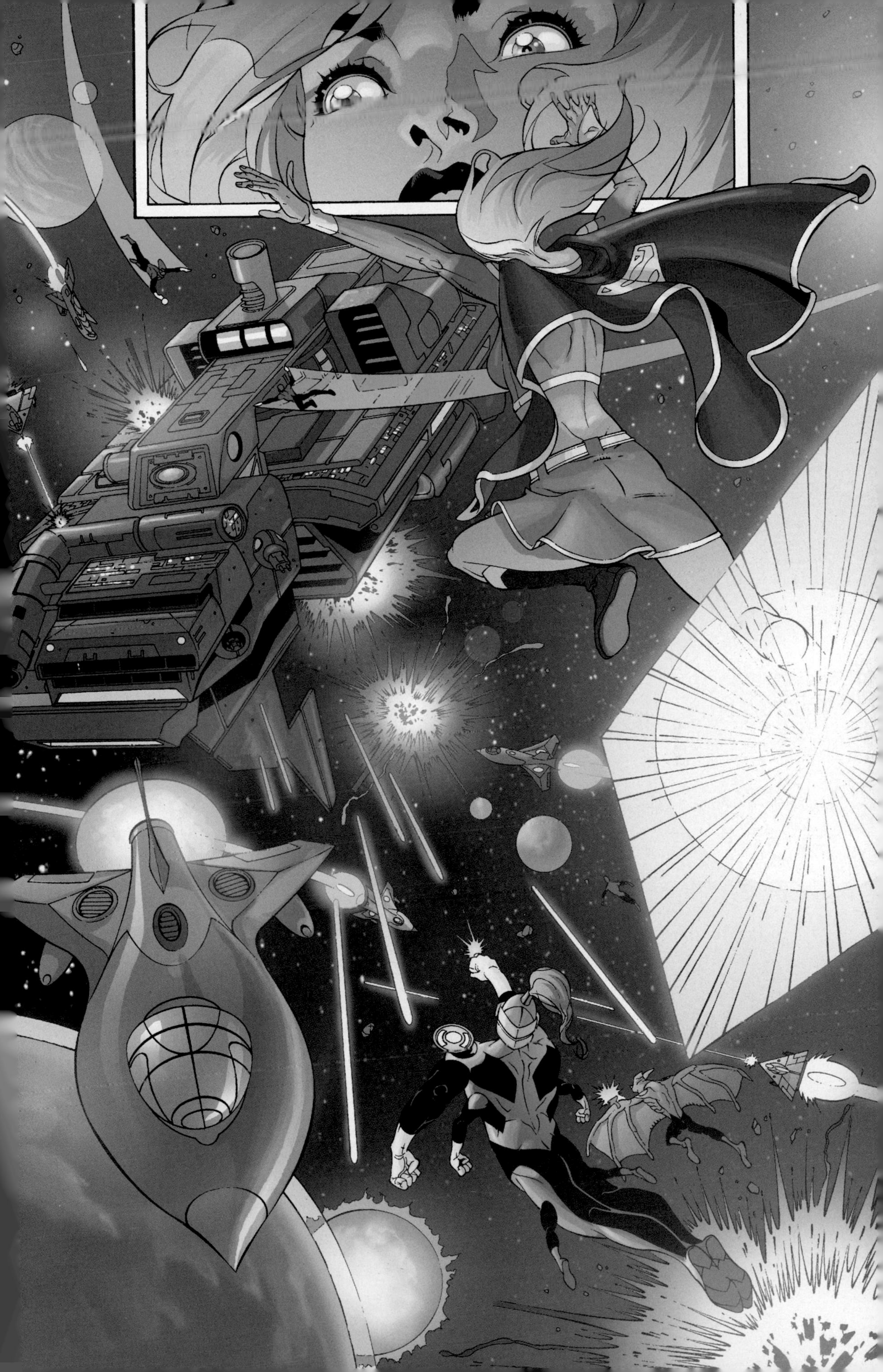

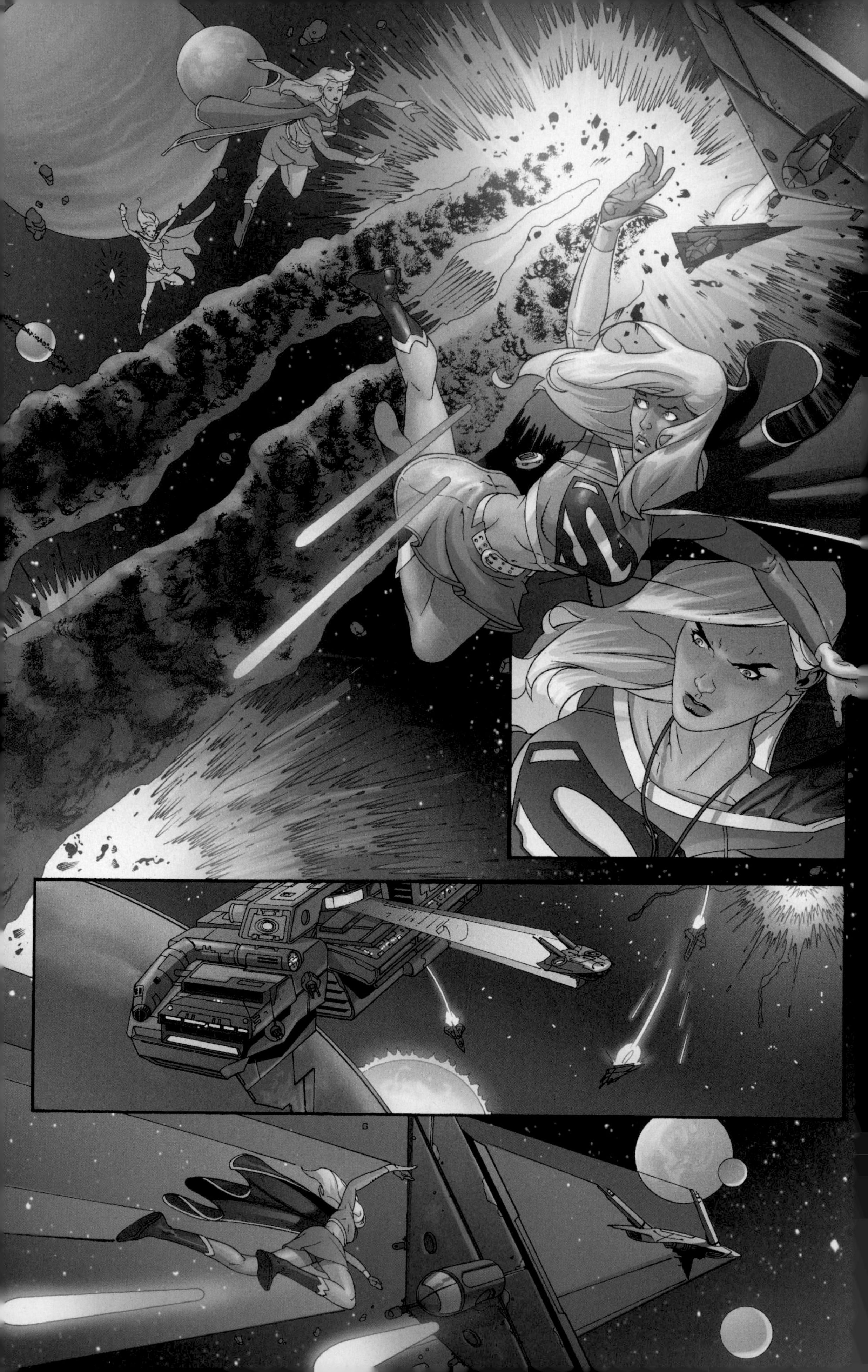

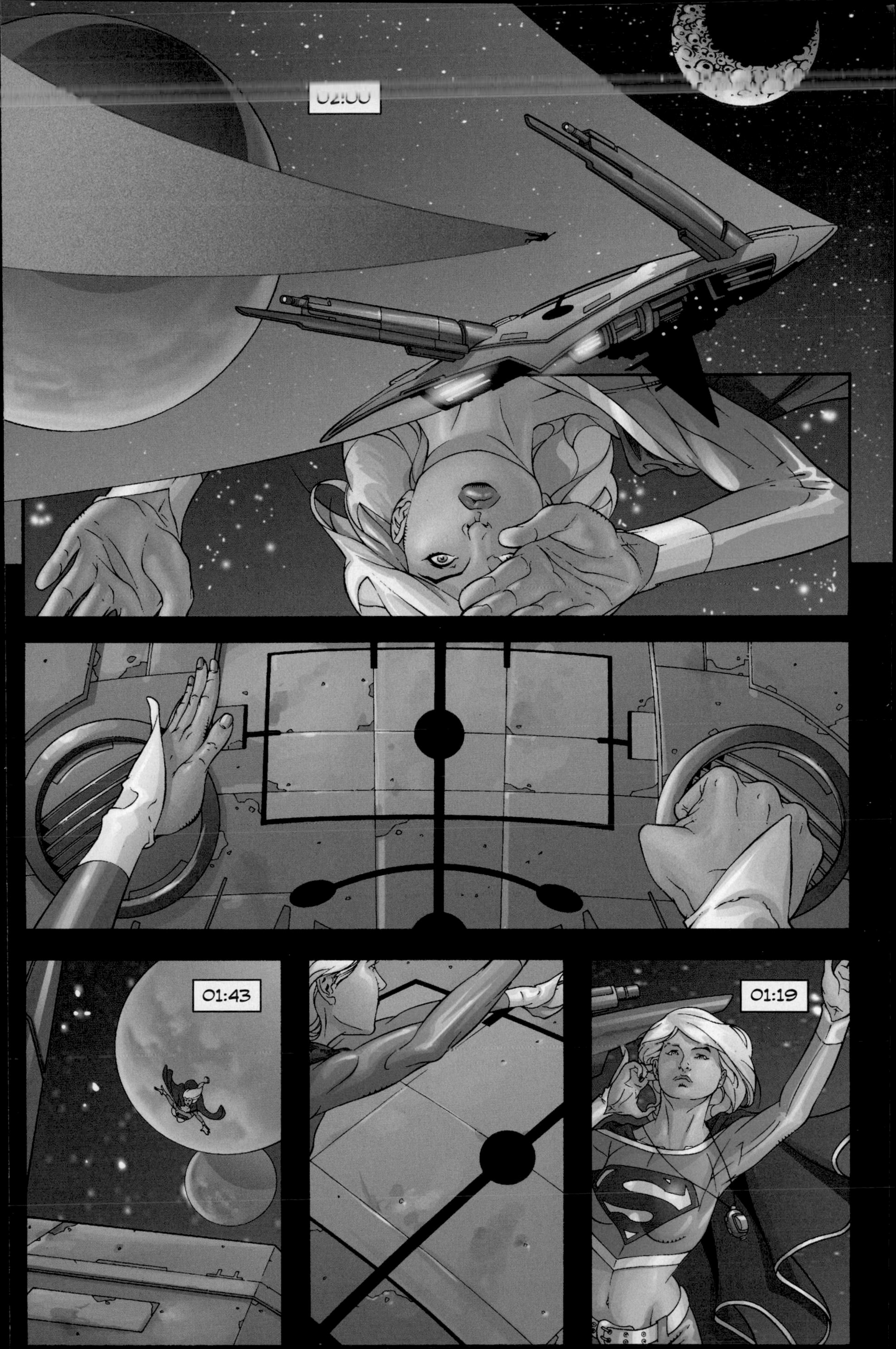
02:00
01:43
01:19

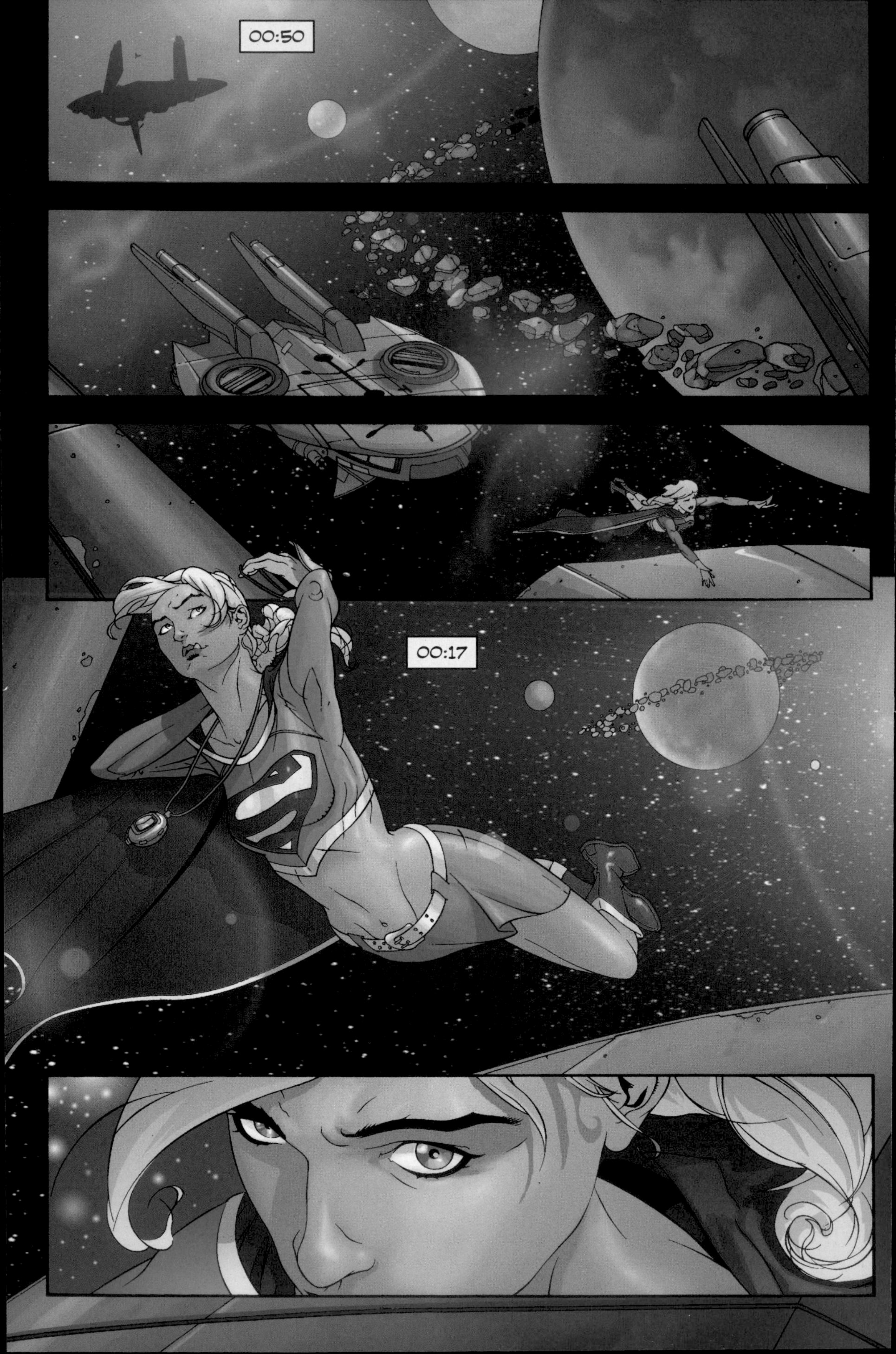

00:50
00:17

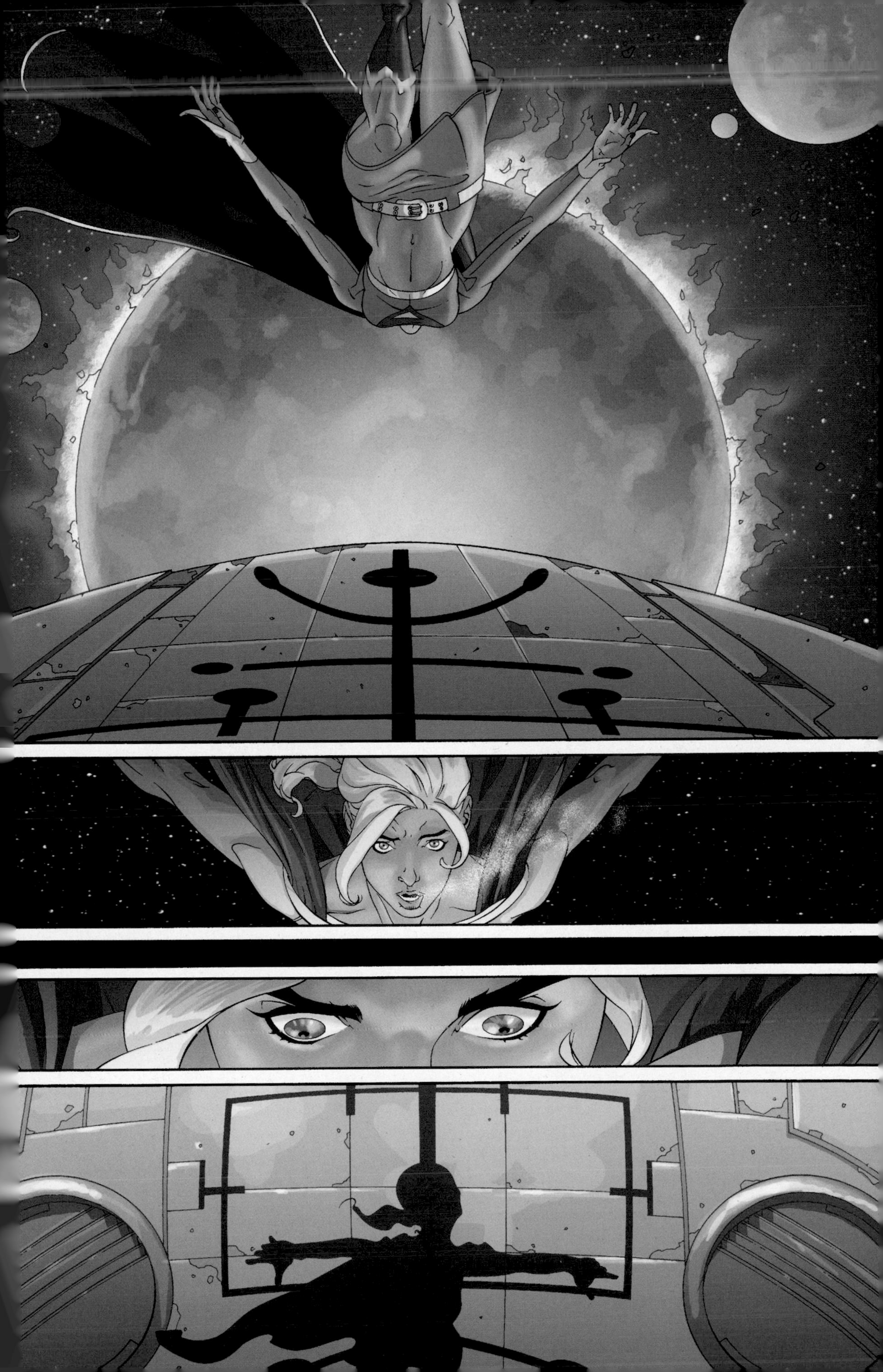

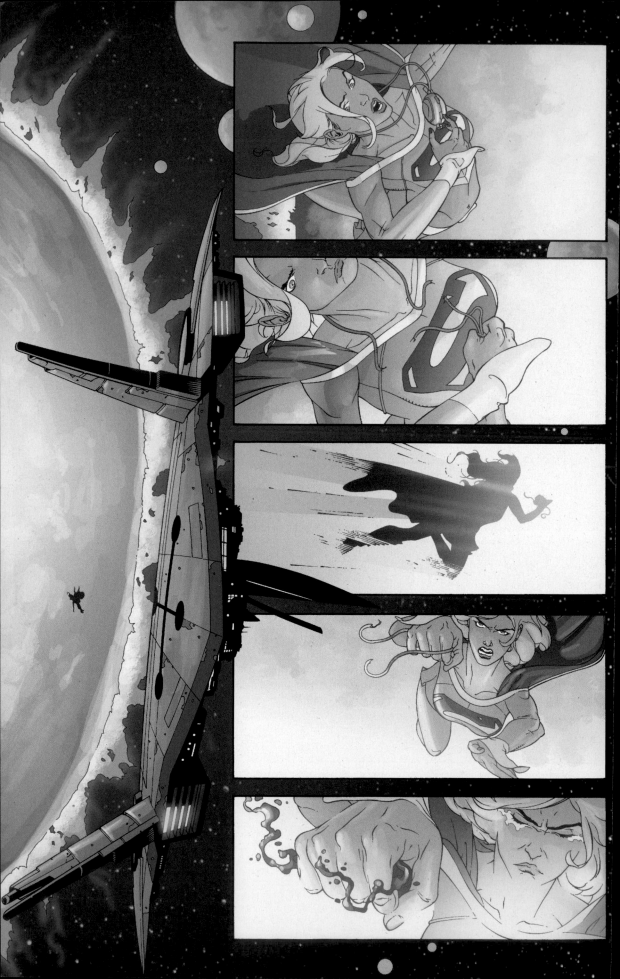

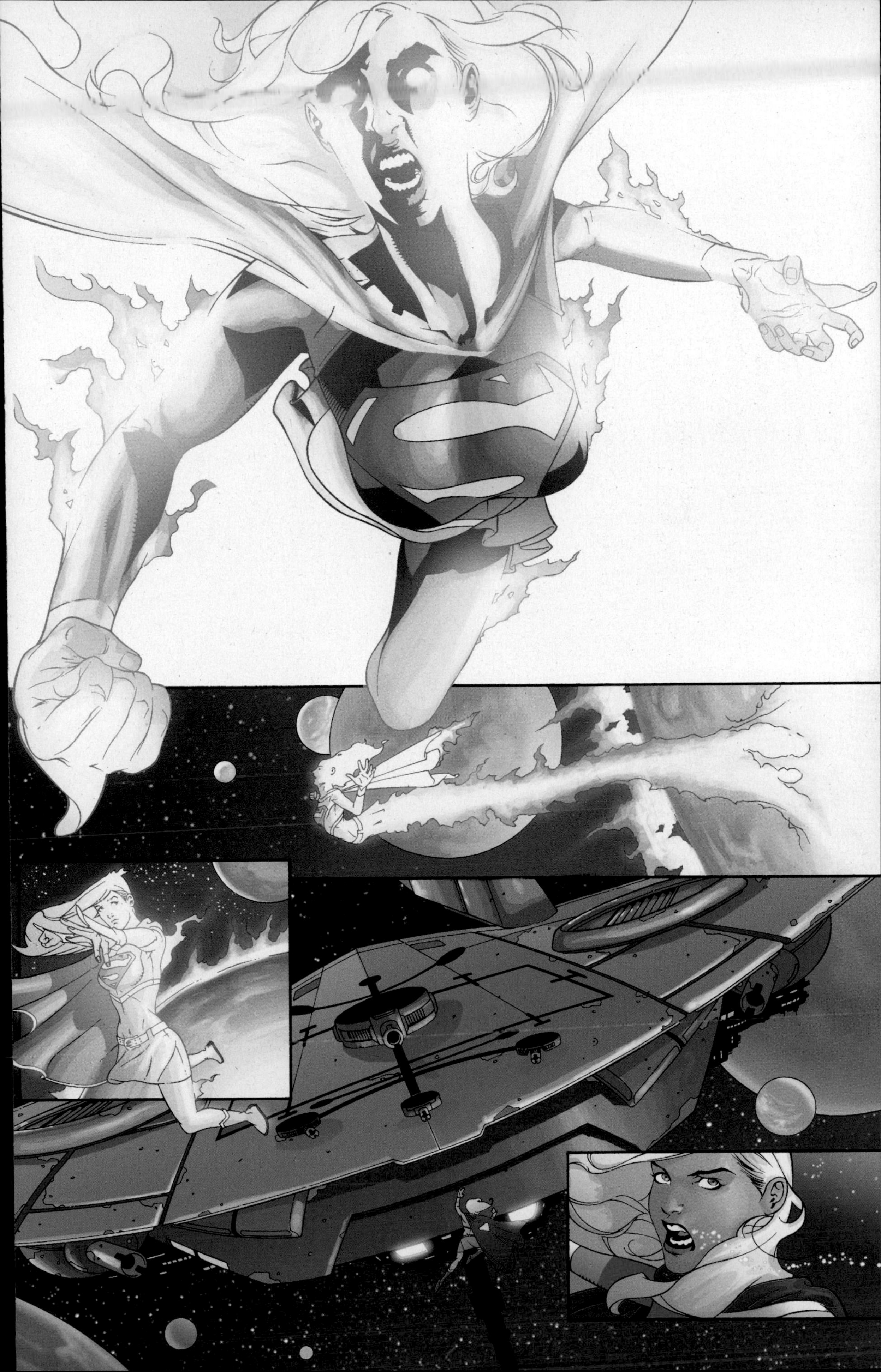

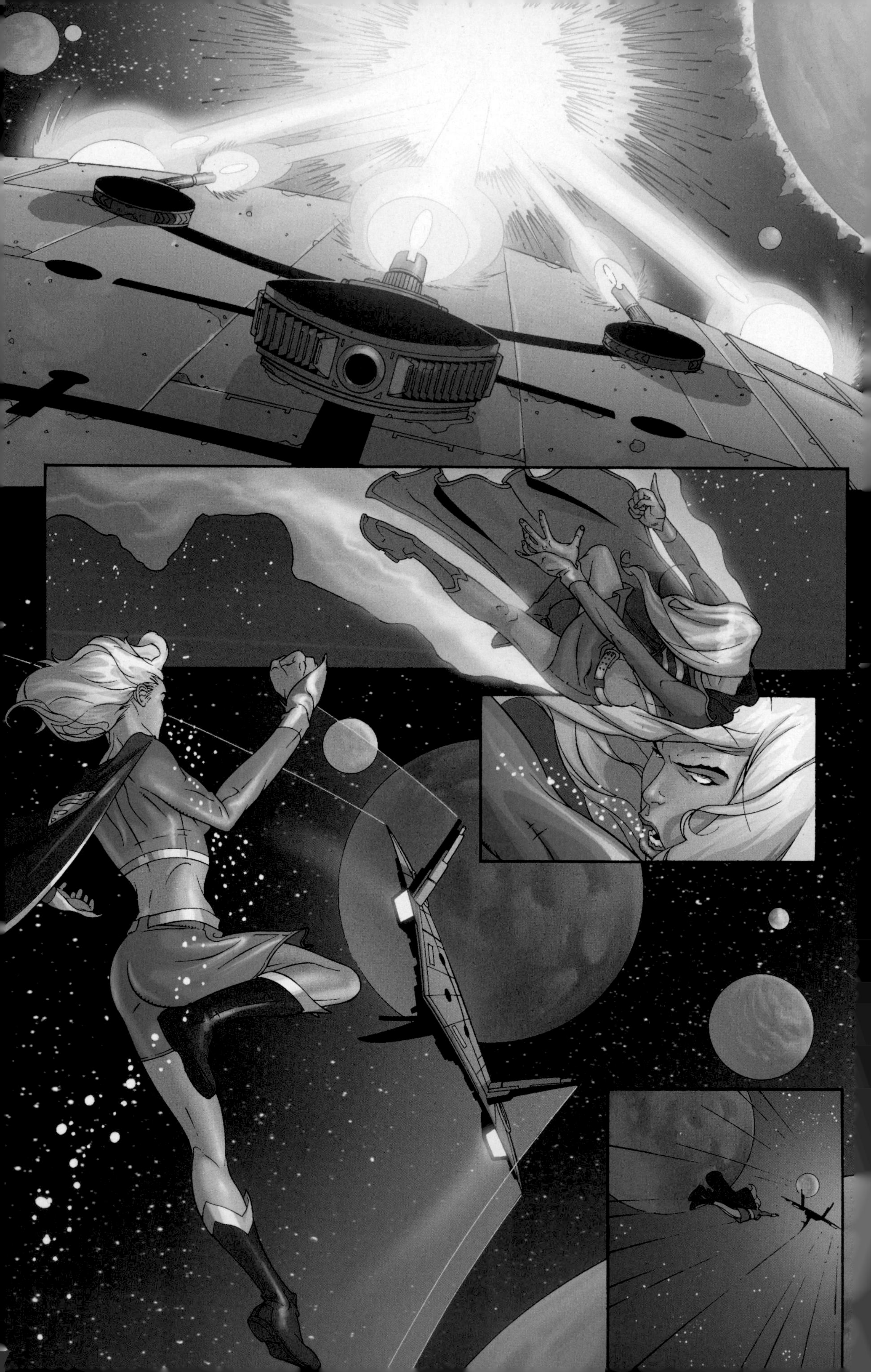

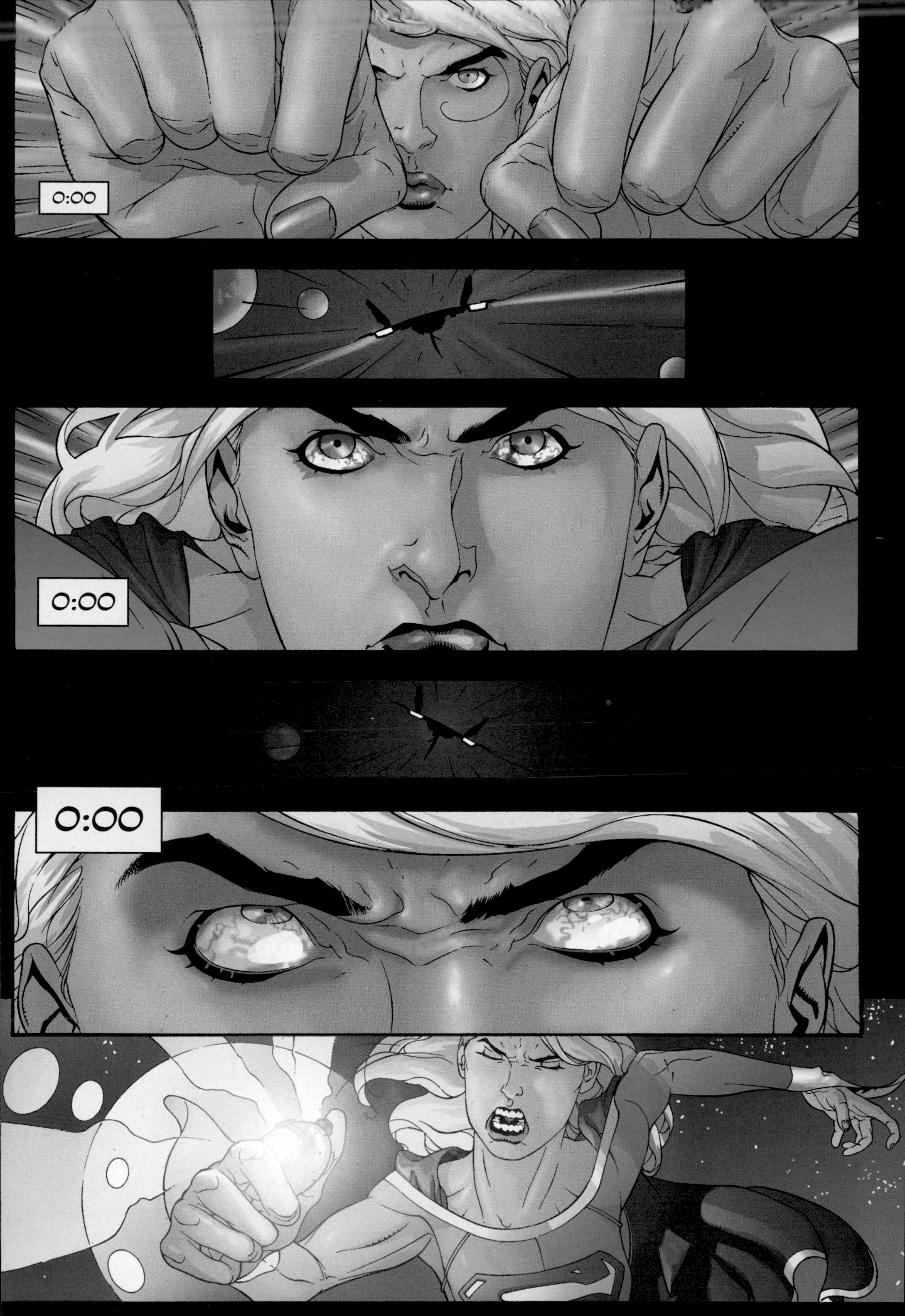
0:00
0:00
0:00

SHHBOOOOM

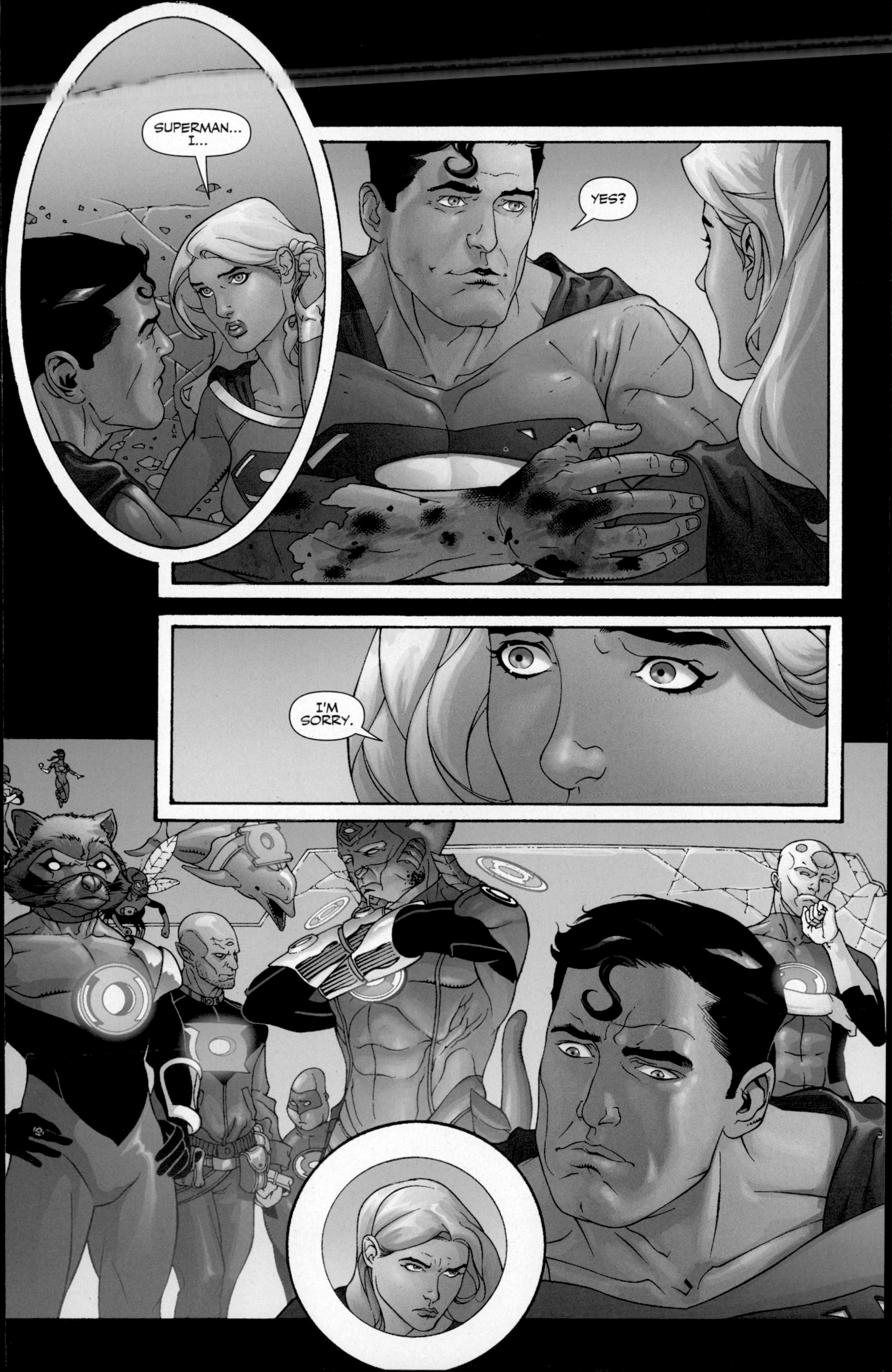
SUPERMAN... I...
YES?
I'M SORRY.

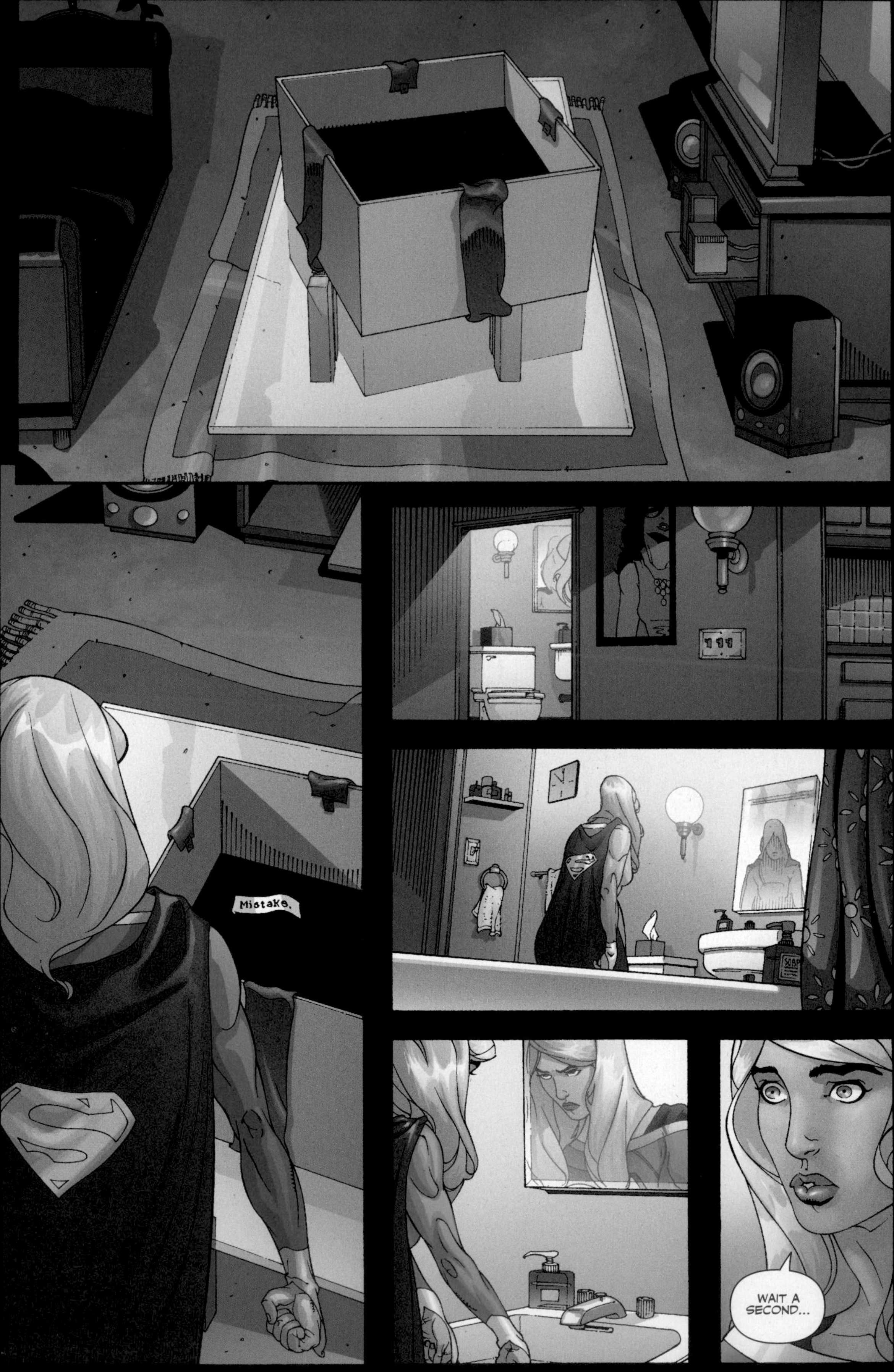

Mistake.
WAIT A SECOND...

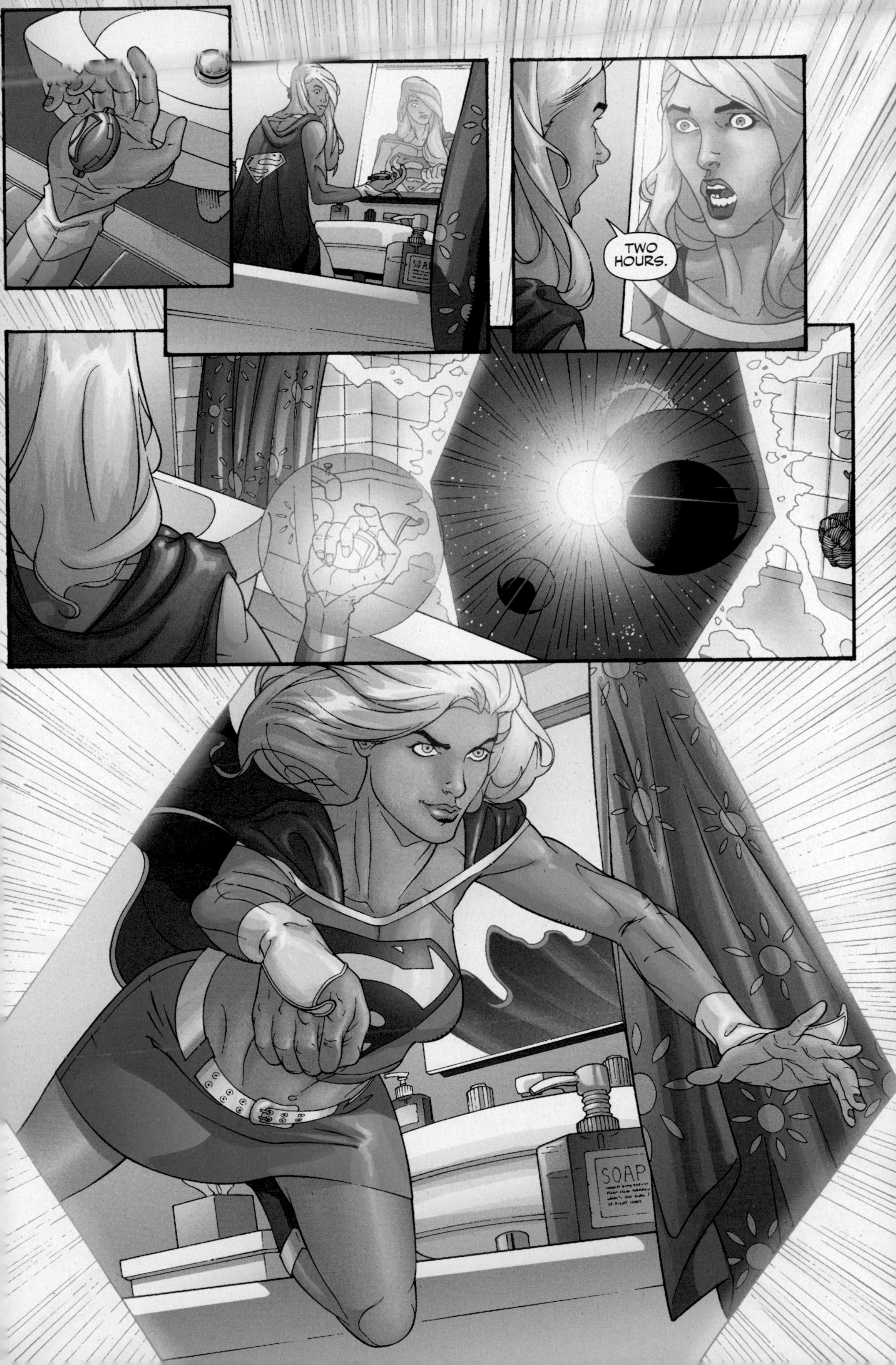
TWO HOURS.
SOAP

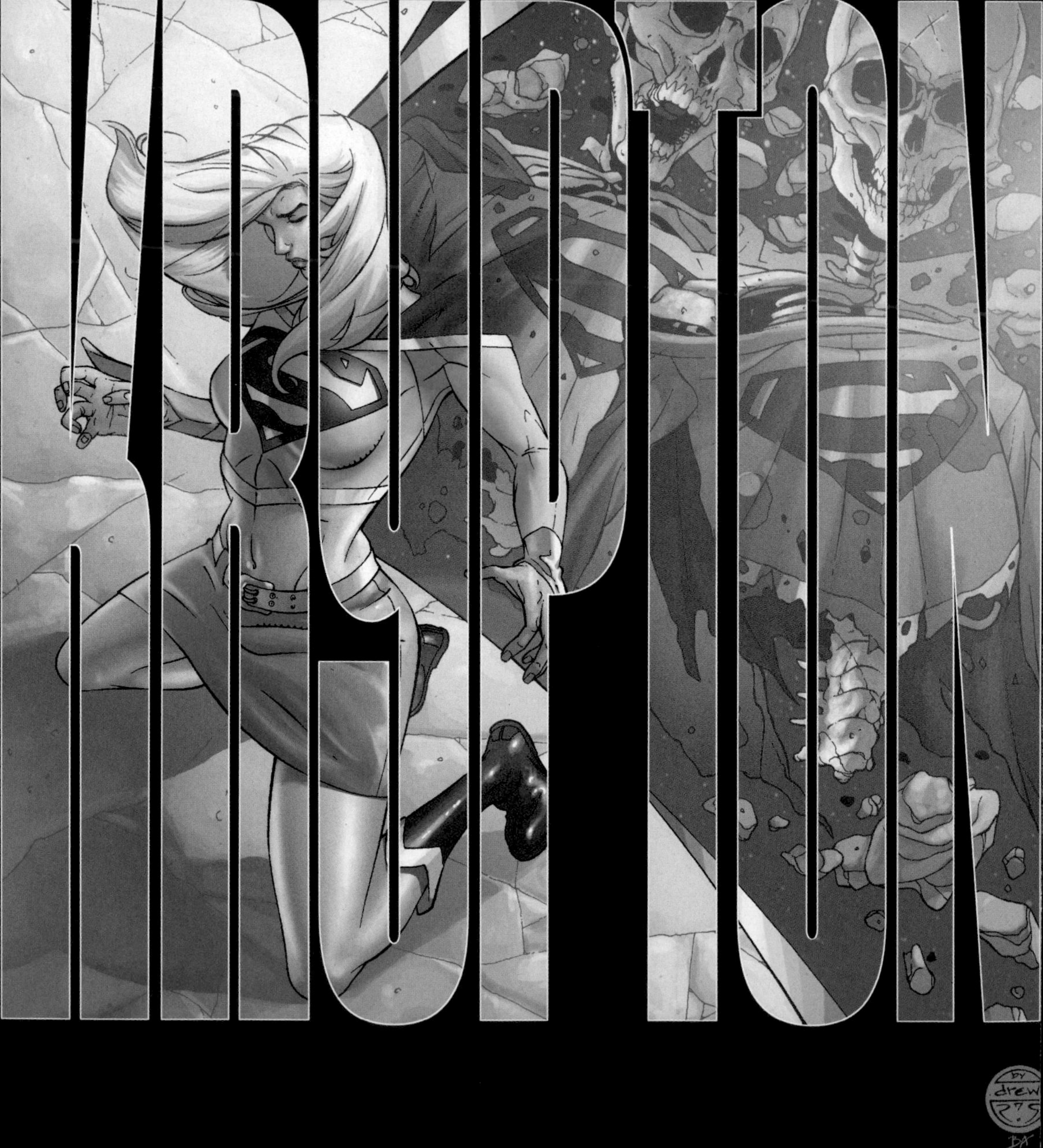
KRYPTON

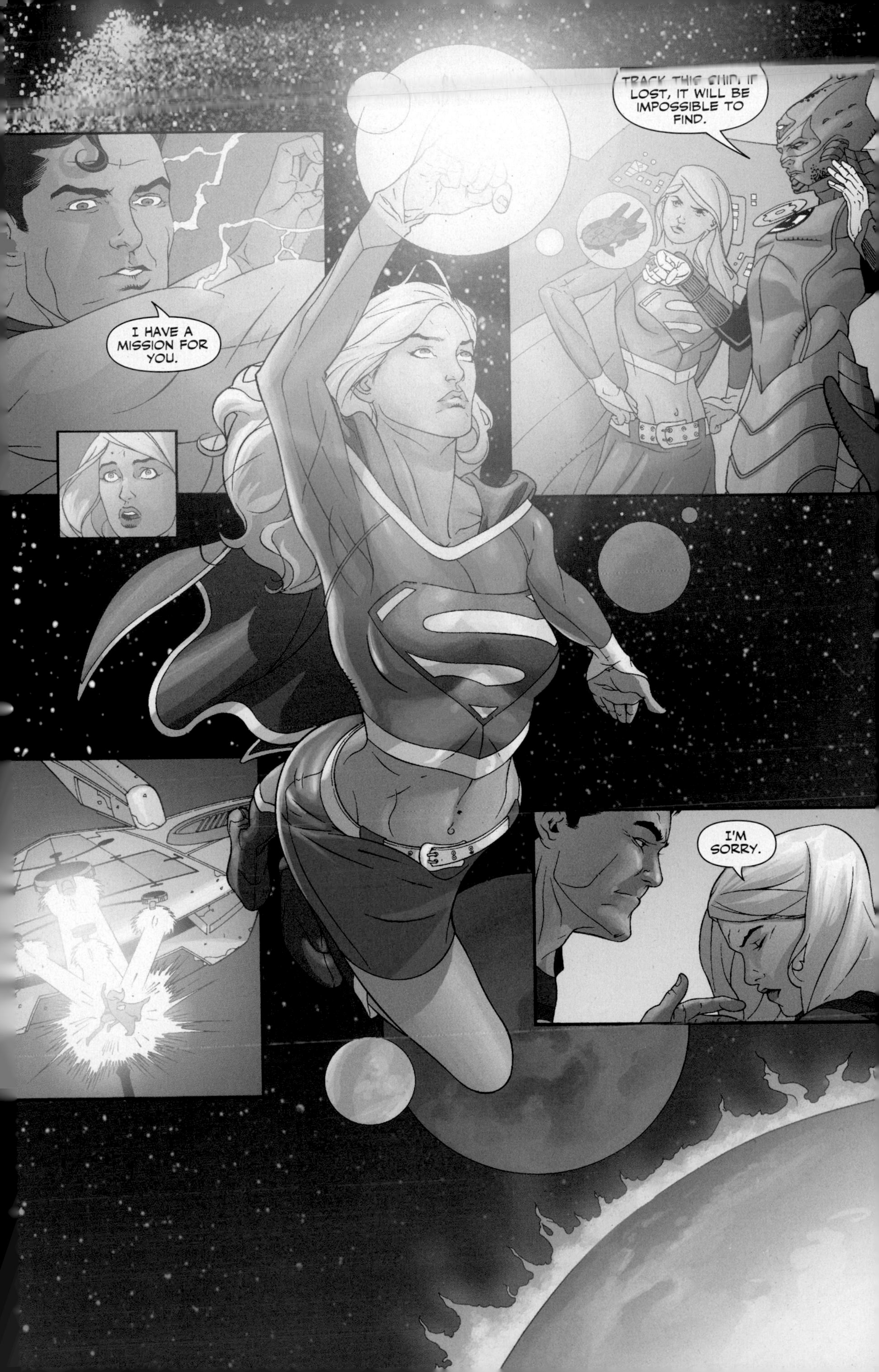
TRACK THIS SHIP. IF LOST, IT WILL BE IMPOSSIBLE TO FIND.
I HAVE A MISSION FOR YOU.
I'M SORRY.

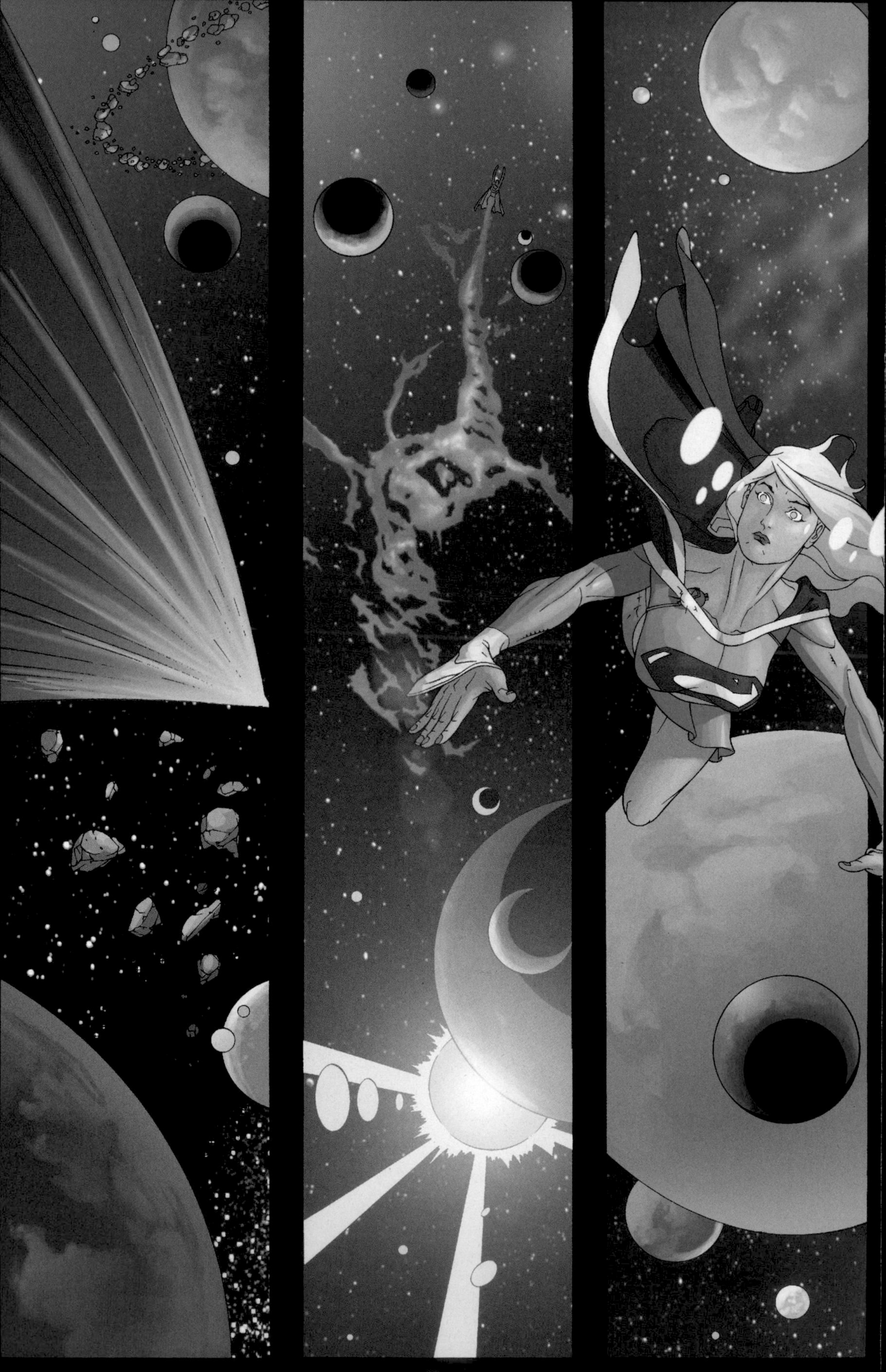

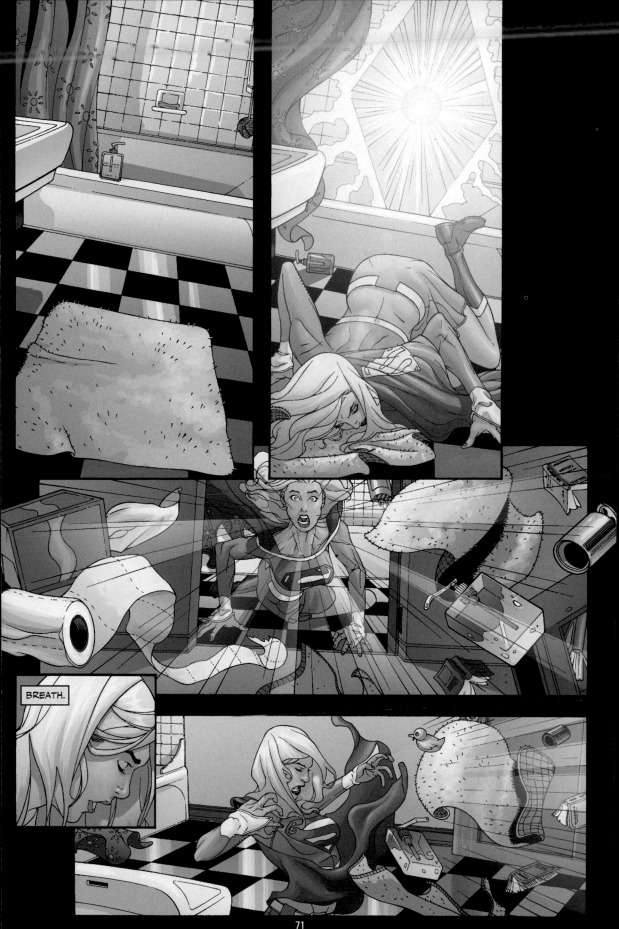

BREATH.

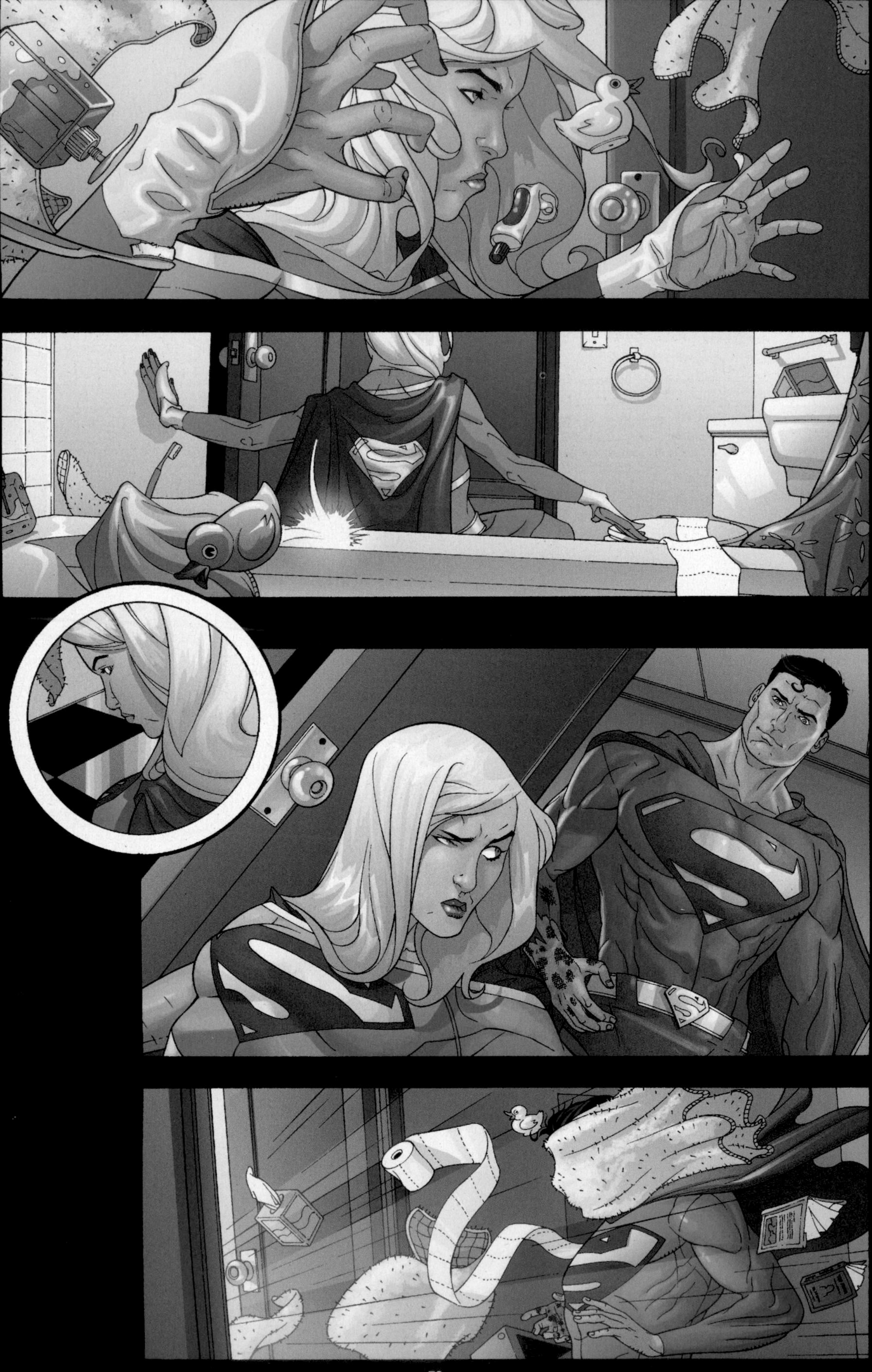

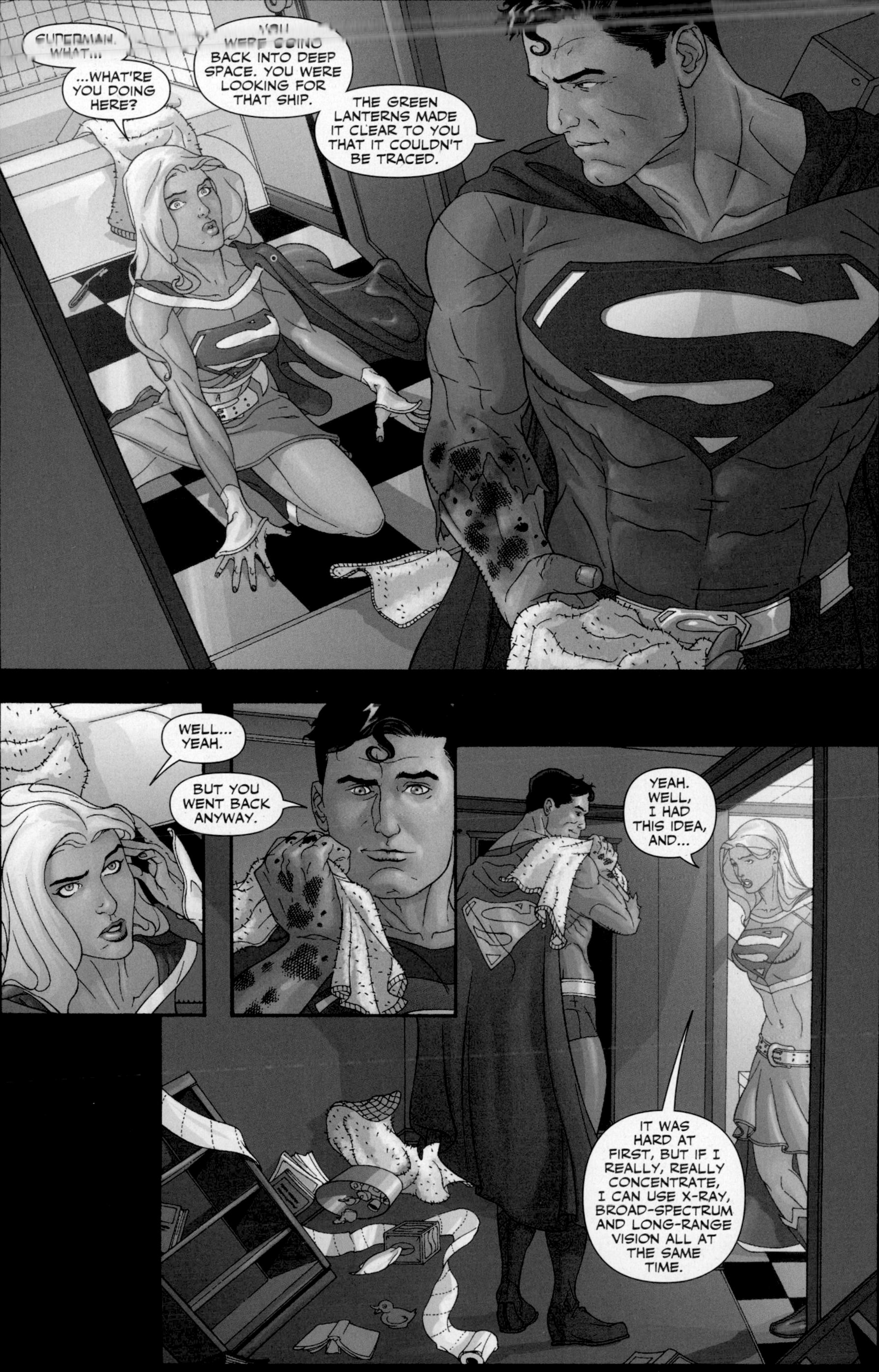

SUPERMAN. WHAT...
...WHAT'RE YOU DOING HERE?
YOU WERE GOING BACK INTO DEEP SPACE. YOU WERE LOOKING FOR THAT SHIP.
THE GREEN LANTERNS MADE IT CLEAR TO YOU THAT IT COULDN'T BE TRACED.
WELL... YEAH.
BUT YOU WENT BACK ANYWAY.
YEAH. WELL, I HAD THIS IDEA, AND...
IT WAS HARD AT FIRST, BUT IF I REALLY, REALLY CONCENTRATE, I CAN USE X-RAY, BROAD-SPECTRUM AND LONG-RANGE VISION ALL AT THE SAME TIME.

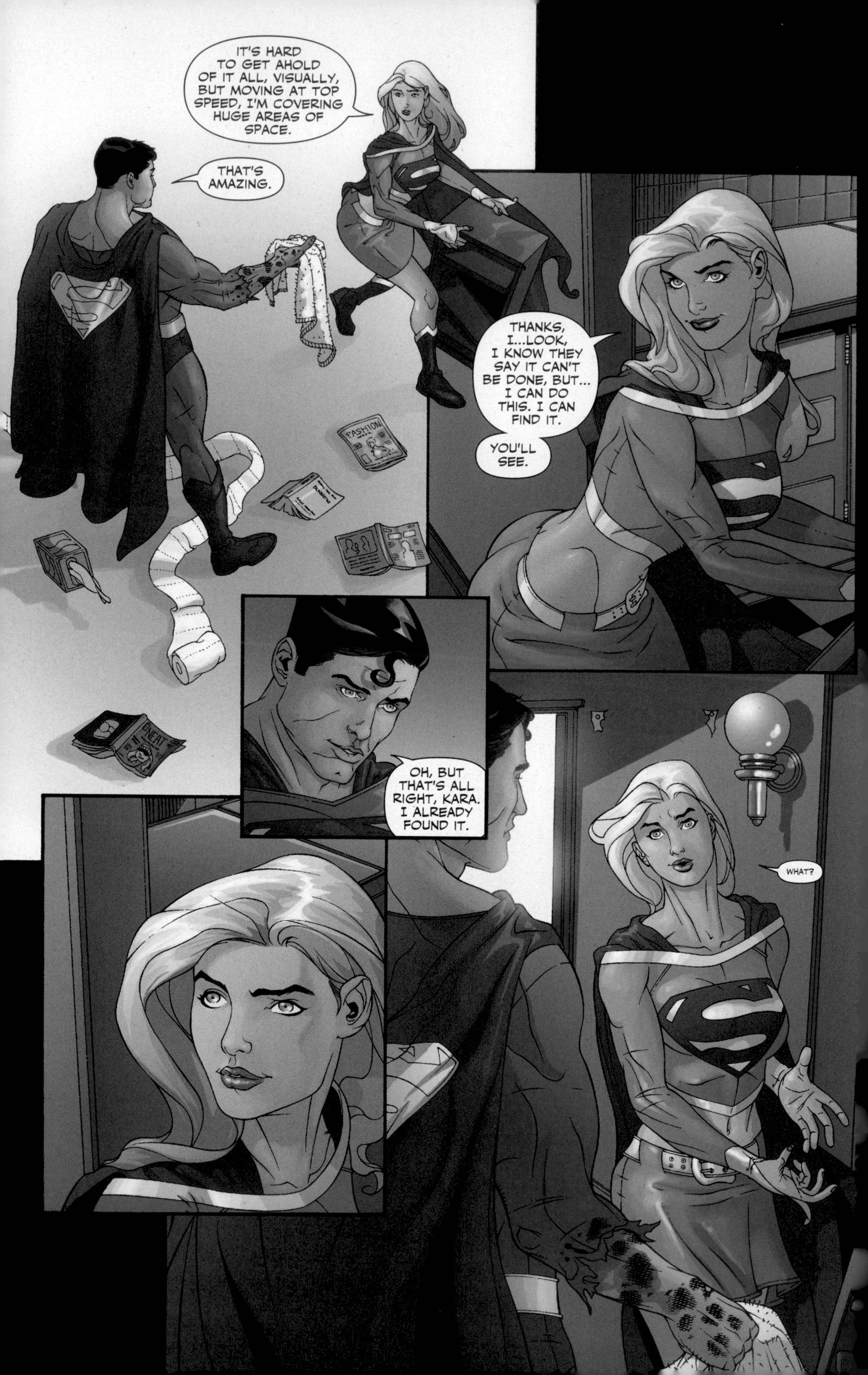
IT'S HARD TO GET AHOLD OF IT ALL, VISUALLY, BUT MOVING AT TOP SPEED, I'M COVERING HUGE AREAS OF SPACE.
THAT'S AMAZING.
THANKS, I...LOOK, I KNOW THEY SAY IT CAN'T BE DONE, BUT... I CAN DO THIS. I CAN FIND IT.
YOU'LL SEE.
OH, BUT THAT'S ALL RIGHT, KARA. I ALREADY FOUND IT.
WHAT?

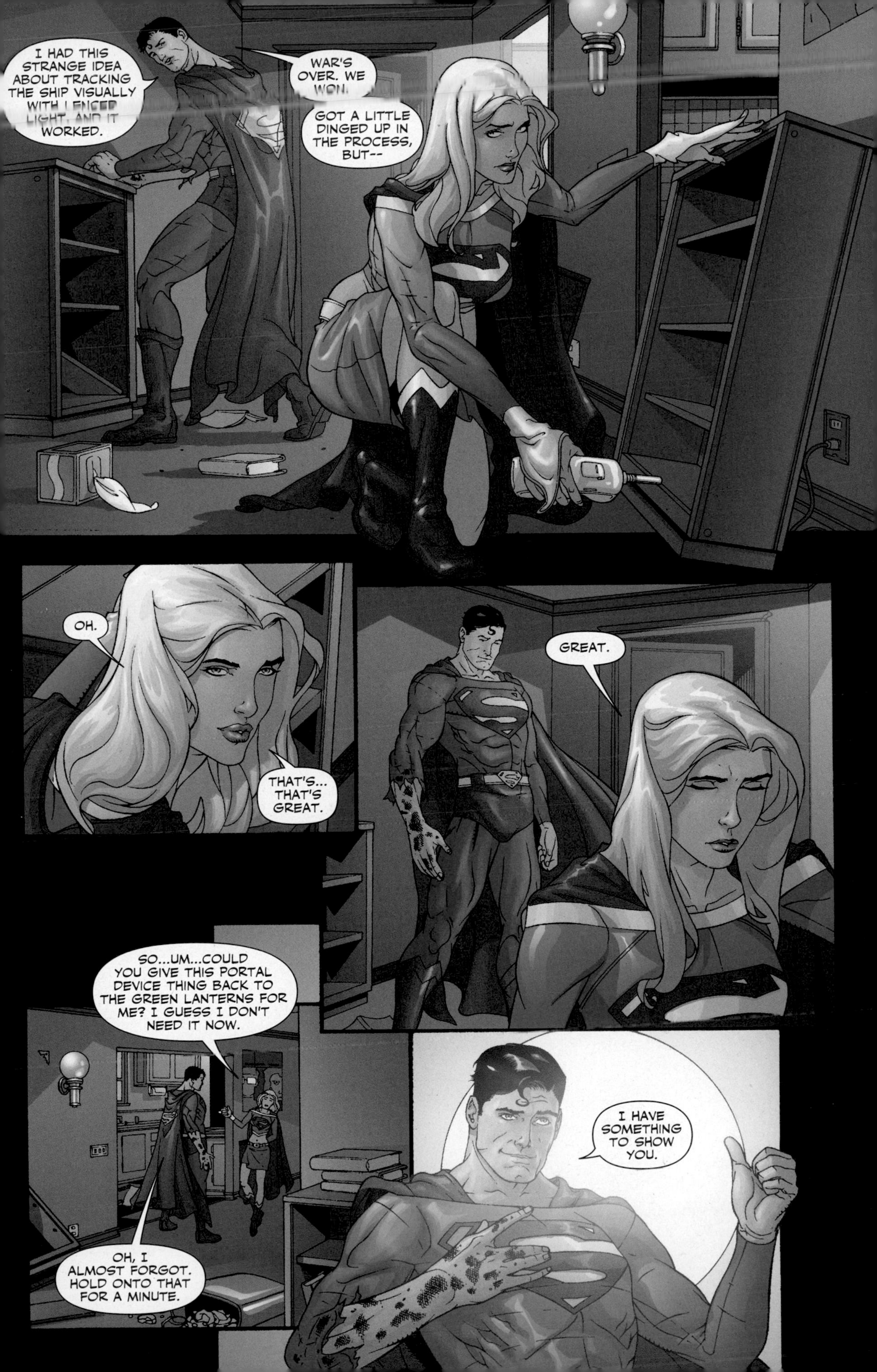
I HAD THIS STRANGE IDEA ABOUT TRACKING THE SHIP VISUALLY WITH LENSED LIGHT. AND IT WORKED.
WAR'S OVER. WE WON.
GOT A LITTLE DINGED UP IN THE PROCESS, BUT--
OH.
THAT'S... THAT'S GREAT.
GREAT.
SO...UM...COULD YOU GIVE THIS PORTAL DEVICE THING BACK TO THE GREEN LANTERNS FOR ME? I GUESS I DON'T NEED IT NOW.
OH, I ALMOST FORGOT. HOLD ONTO THAT FOR A MINUTE.
I HAVE SOMETHING TO SHOW YOU.

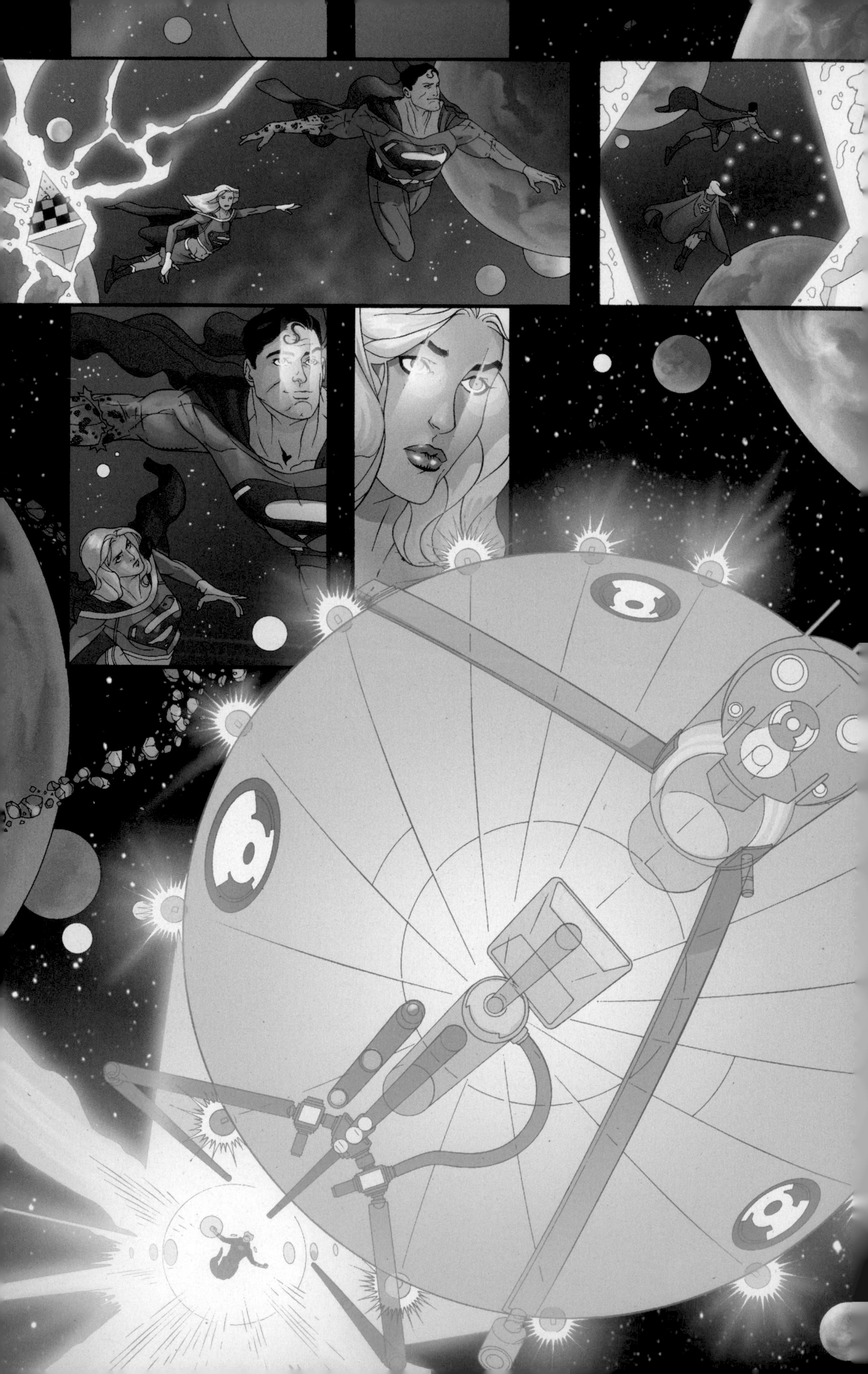

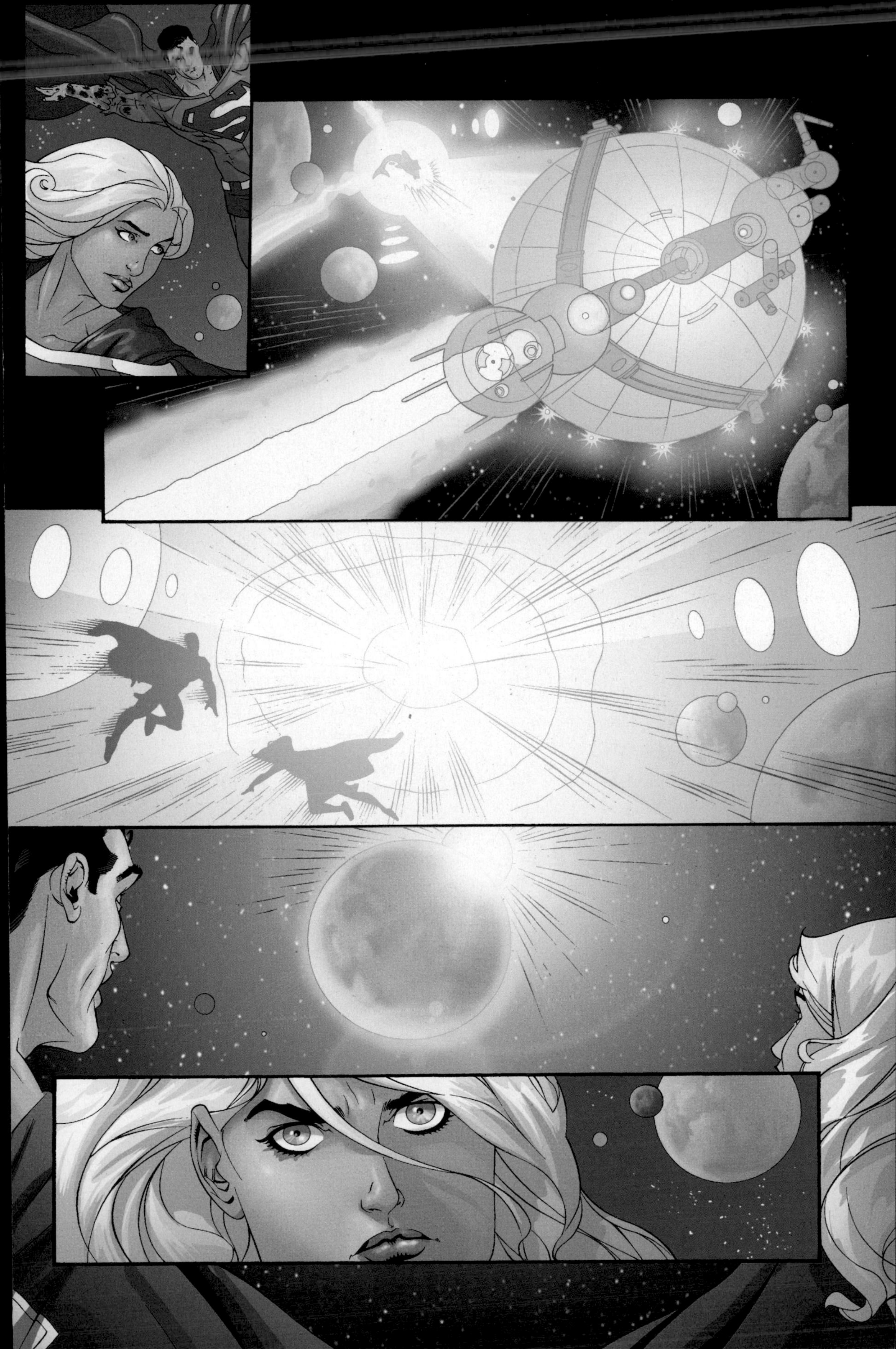

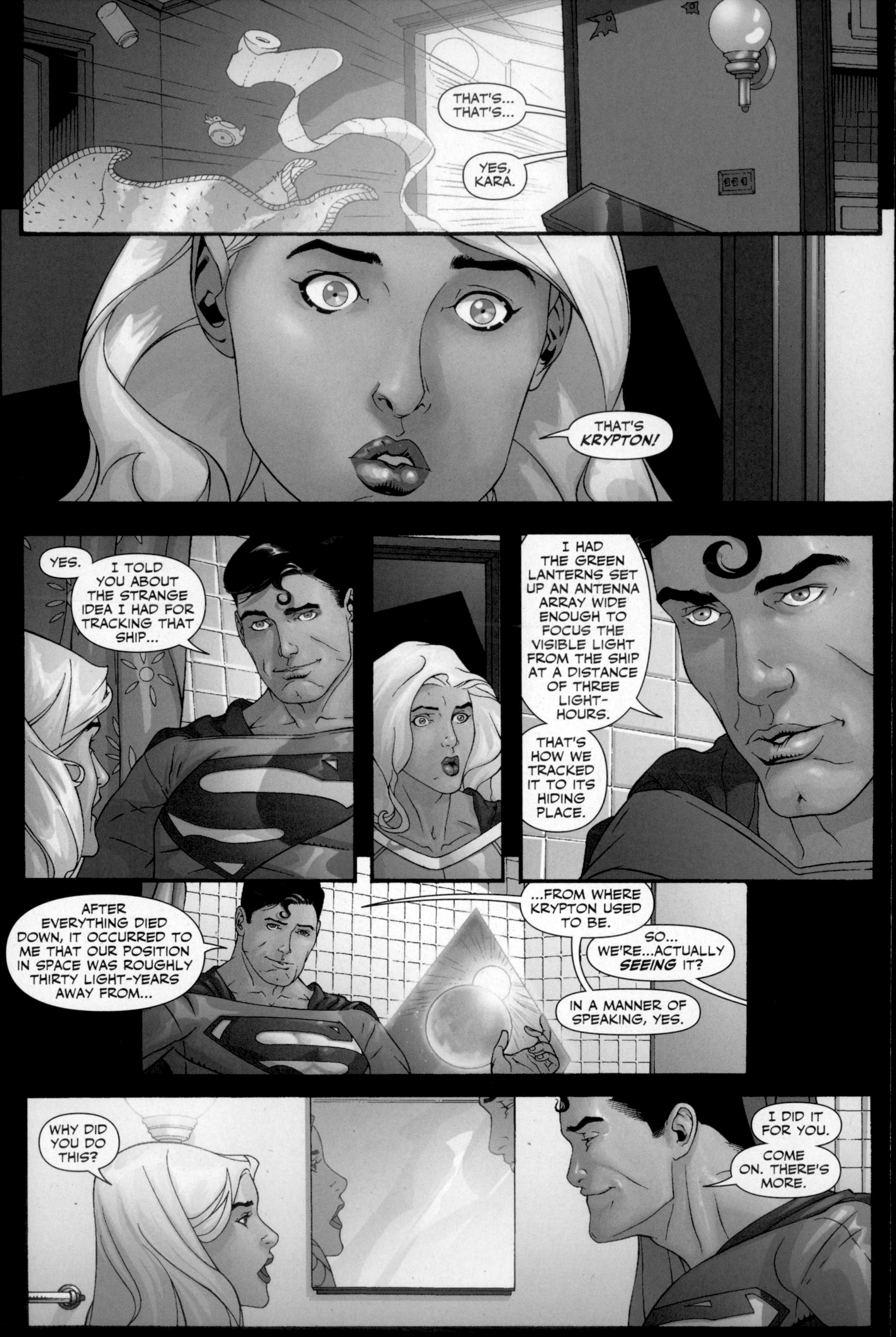

THAT'S... THAT'S...
YES, KARA.
THAT'S KRYPTON!
YES.
I TOLD YOU ABOUT THE STRANGE IDEA I HAD FOR TRACKING THAT SHIP...
I HAD THE GREEN LANTERNS SET UP AN ANTENNA ARRAY WIDE ENOUGH TO FOCUS THE VISIBLE LIGHT FROM THE SHIP AT A DISTANCE OF THREE LIGHT-HOURS.
THAT'S HOW WE TRACKED IT TO ITS HIDING PLACE.
AFTER EVERYTHING DIED DOWN, IT OCCURRED TO ME THAT OUR POSITION IN SPACE WAS ROUGHLY THIRTY LIGHT-YEARS AWAY FROM...
...FROM WHERE KRYPTON USED TO BE.
SO... WE'RE...ACTUALLY SEEING IT?
IN A MANNER OF SPEAKING, YES.
WHY DID YOU DO THIS?
I DID IT FOR YOU.
COME ON. THERE'S MORE.

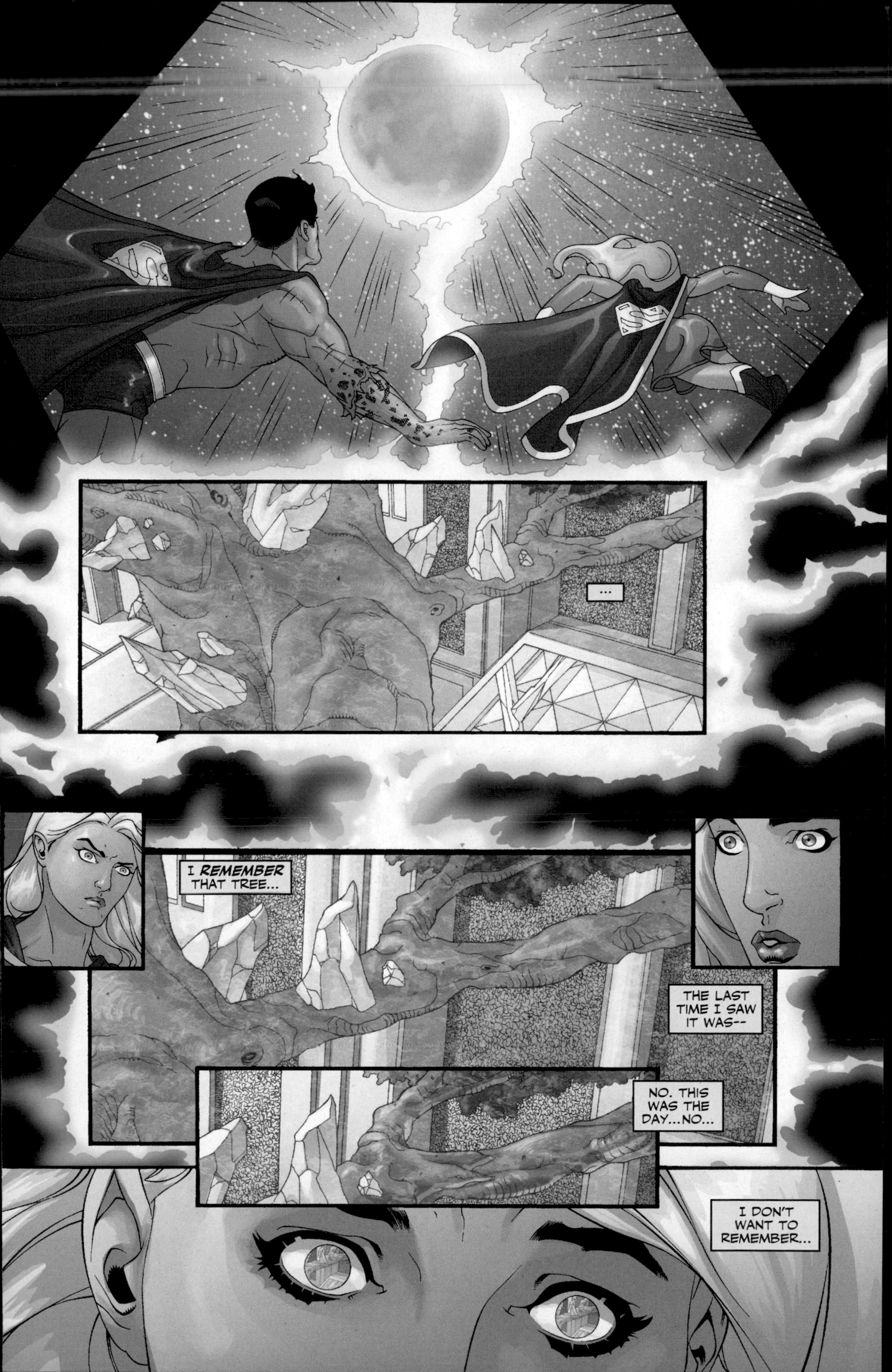
...
I REMEMBER THAT TREE...
THE LAST TIME I SAW IT WAS--
NO. THIS WAS THE DAY...NO...
I DON'T WANT TO REMEMBER...

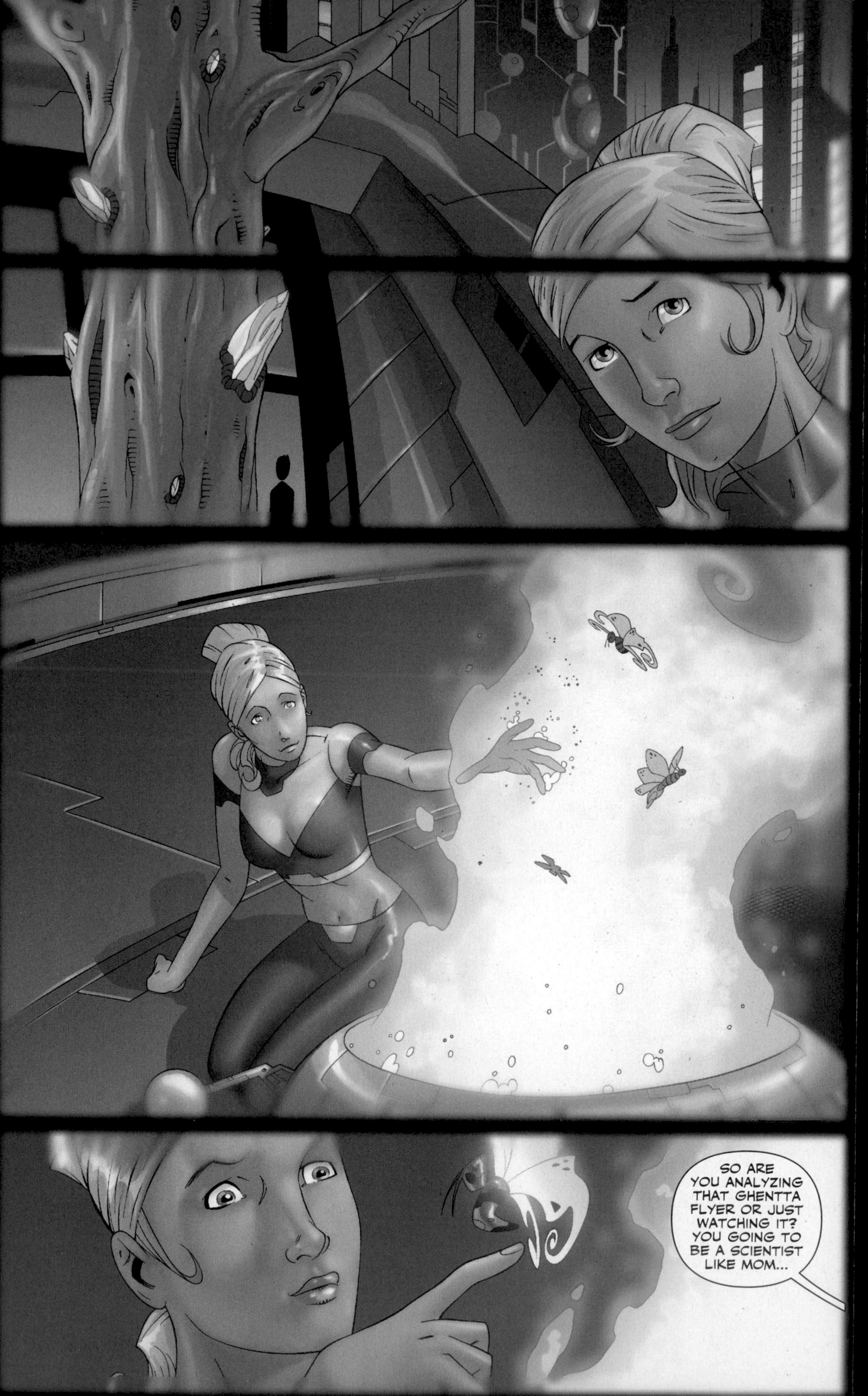
SO ARE YOU ANALYZING THAT GHENTTA FLYER OR JUST WATCHING IT? YOU GOING TO BE A SCIENTIST LIKE MOM...

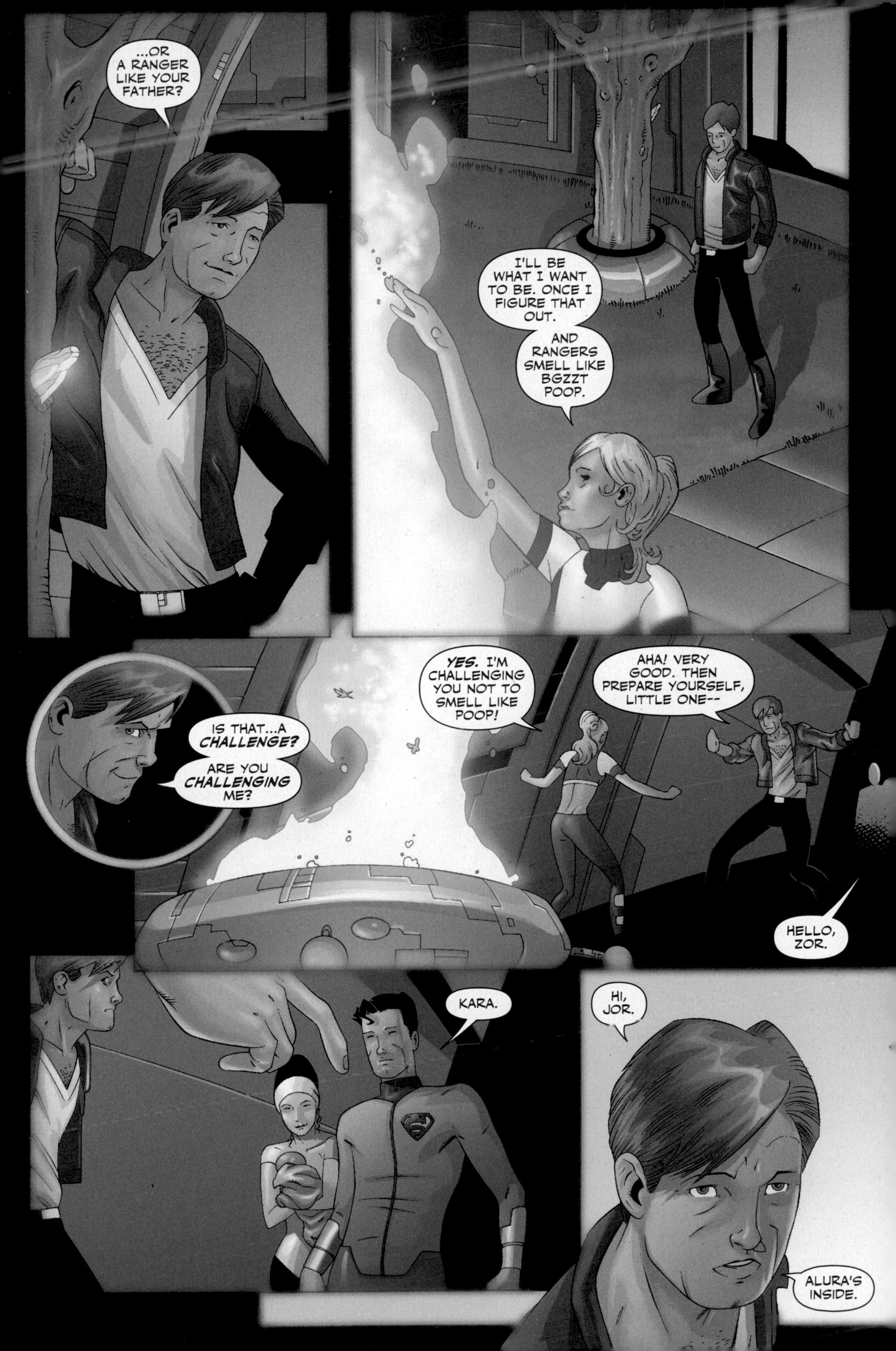
...OR A RANGER LIKE YOUR FATHER?
I'LL BE WHAT I WANT TO BE. ONCE I FIGURE THAT OUT.
AND RANGERS SMELL LIKE BGZZT POOP.
IS THAT...A CHALLENGE?
ARE YOU CHALLENGING ME?
YES. I'M CHALLENGING YOU NOT TO SMELL LIKE POOP!
AHA! VERY GOOD. THEN PREPARE YOURSELF, LITTLE ONE--
HELLO, ZOR.
KARA.
HI, JOR.
ALURA'S INSIDE.

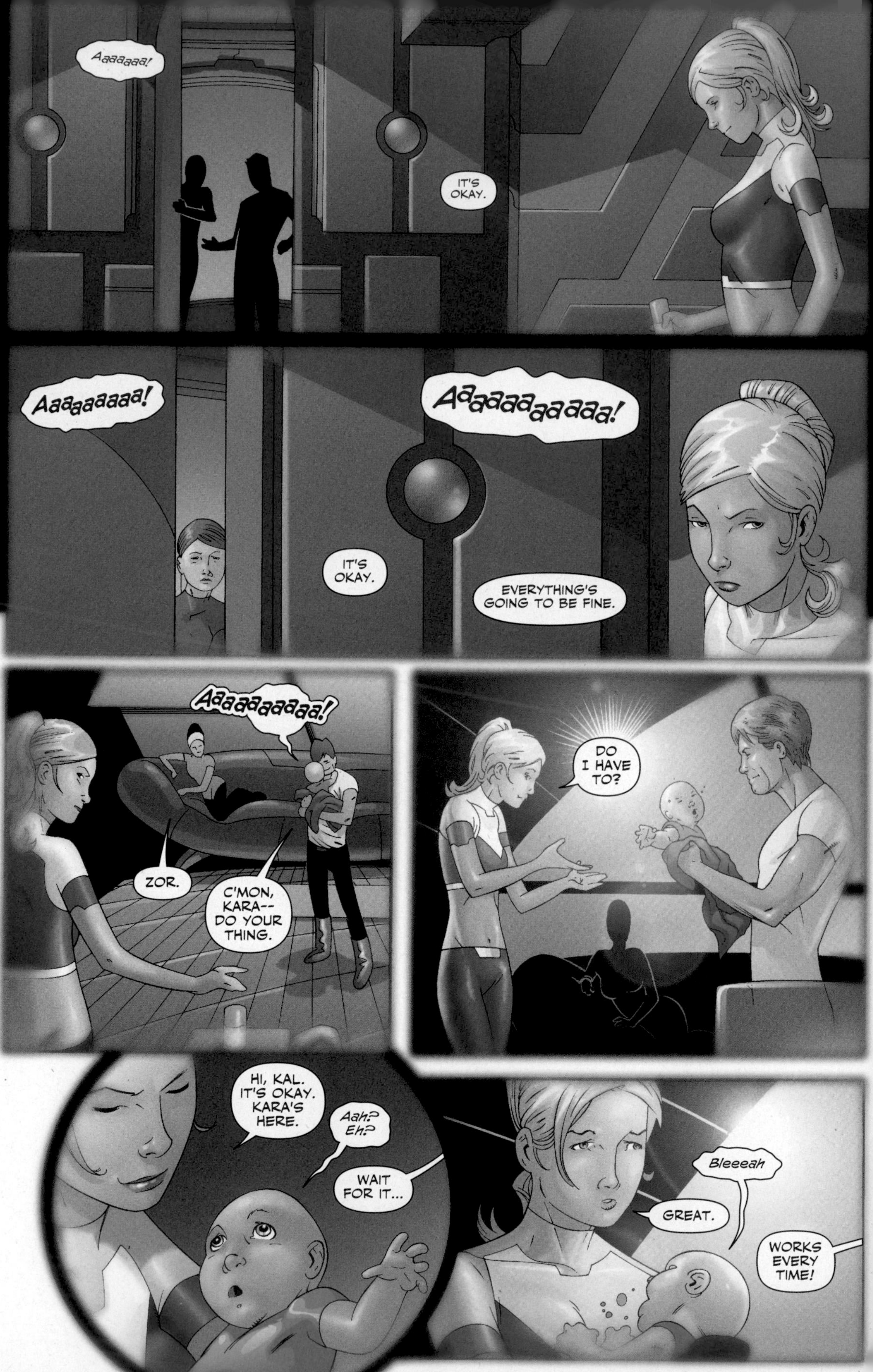
Aaaaaaa!
IT'S OKAY.
Aaaaaaaaa!
Aaaaaaaaaaaa!
IT'S OKAY.
EVERYTHING'S GOING TO BE FINE.
Aaaaaaaaaaa!
ZOR.
C'MON, KARA-- DO YOUR THING.
DO I HAVE TO?
HI, KAL. IT'S OKAY. KARA'S HERE.
Aah? Eh?
WAIT FOR IT...
Bleeeah
GREAT.
WORKS EVERY TIME!

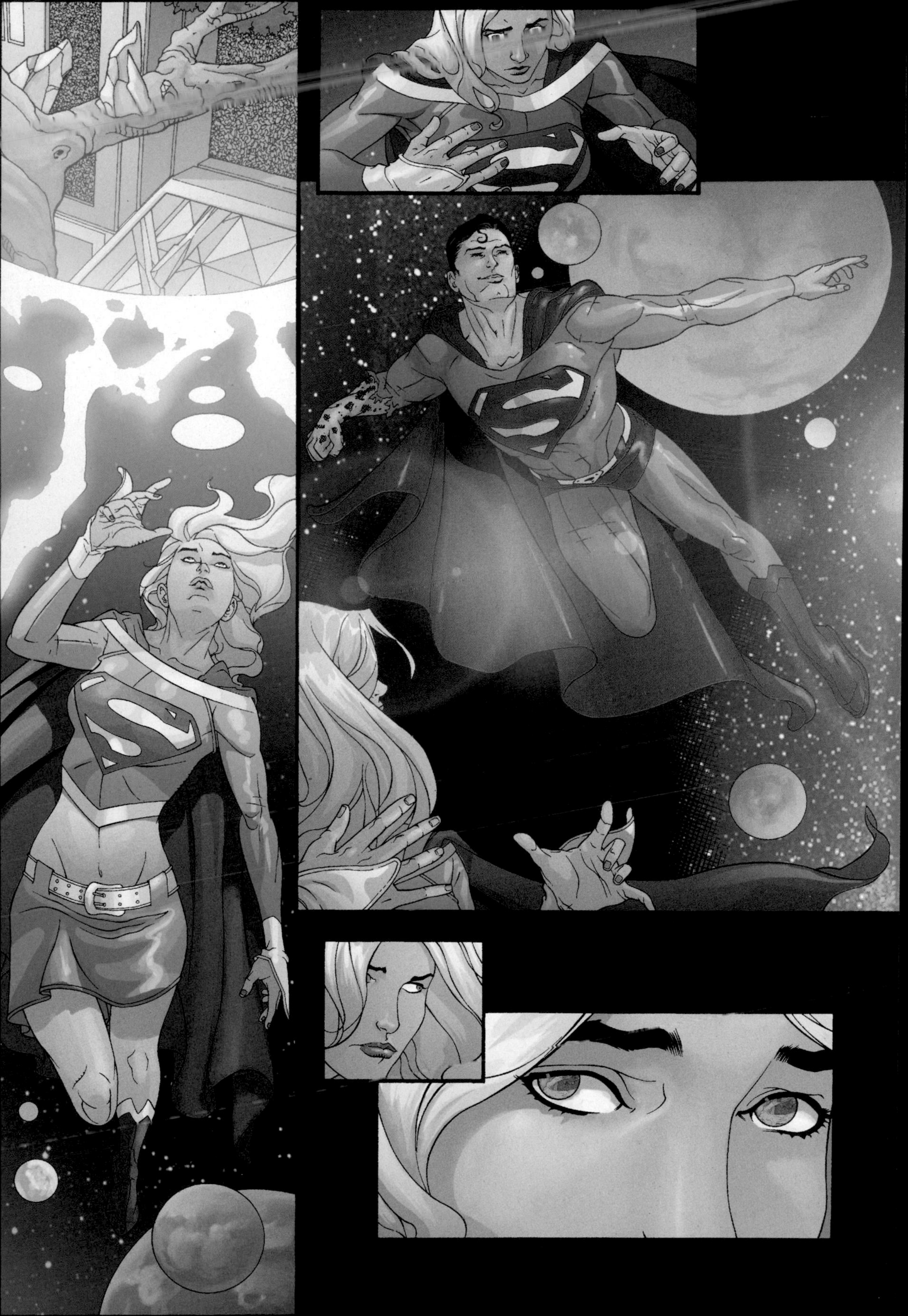

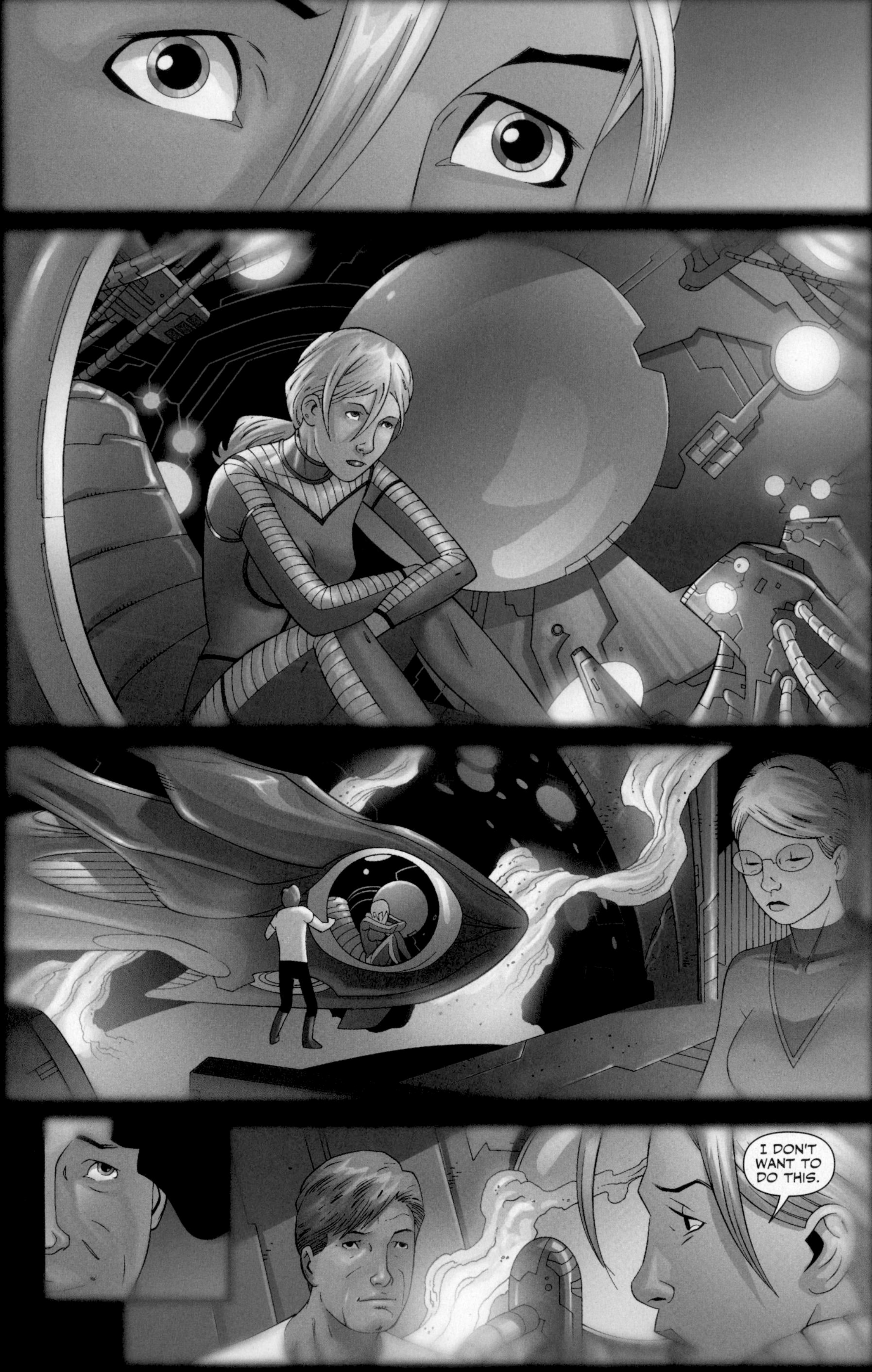
I DON'T WANT TO DO THIS.

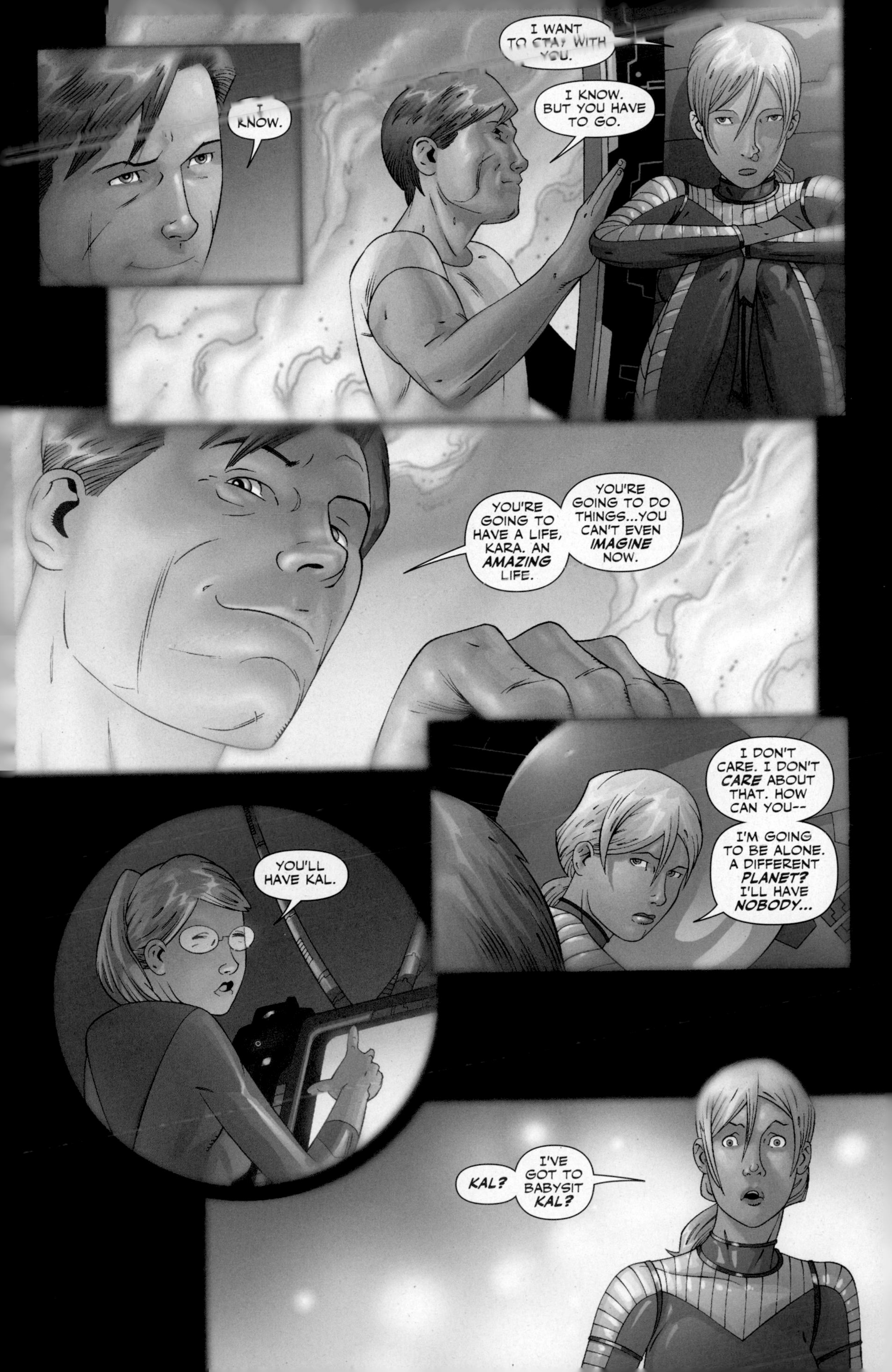

I WANT TO STAY WITH YOU.
I KNOW.
I KNOW. BUT YOU HAVE TO GO.
YOU'RE GOING TO HAVE A LIFE, KARA. AN AMAZING LIFE.
YOU'RE GOING TO DO THINGS...YOU CAN'T EVEN IMAGINE NOW.
I DON'T CARE. I DON'T CARE ABOUT THAT. HOW CAN YOU--
I'M GOING TO BE ALONE. A DIFFERENT PLANET? I'LL HAVE NOBODY...
YOU'LL HAVE KAL.
KAL?
I'VE GOT TO BABYSIT KAL?

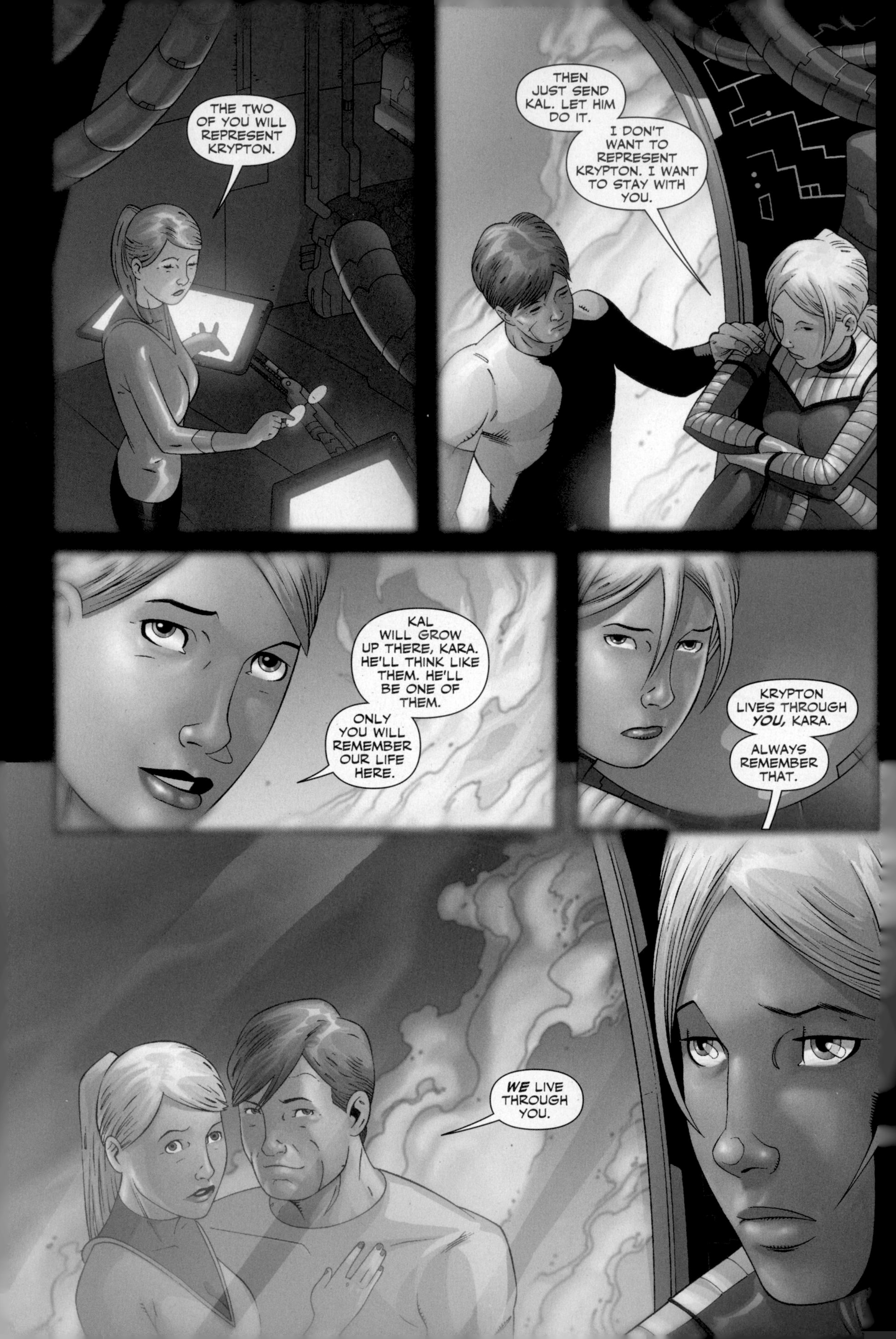
THE TWO OF YOU WILL REPRESENT KRYPTON.
THEN JUST SEND KAL. LET HIM DO IT.
I DON'T WANT TO REPRESENT KRYPTON. I WANT TO STAY WITH YOU.
KAL WILL GROW UP THERE, KARA. HE'LL THINK LIKE THEM. HE'LL BE ONE OF THEM.
ONLY YOU WILL REMEMBER OUR LIFE HERE.
KRYPTON LIVES THROUGH *YOU,* KARA.
ALWAYS REMEMBER THAT.
WE LIVE THROUGH YOU.

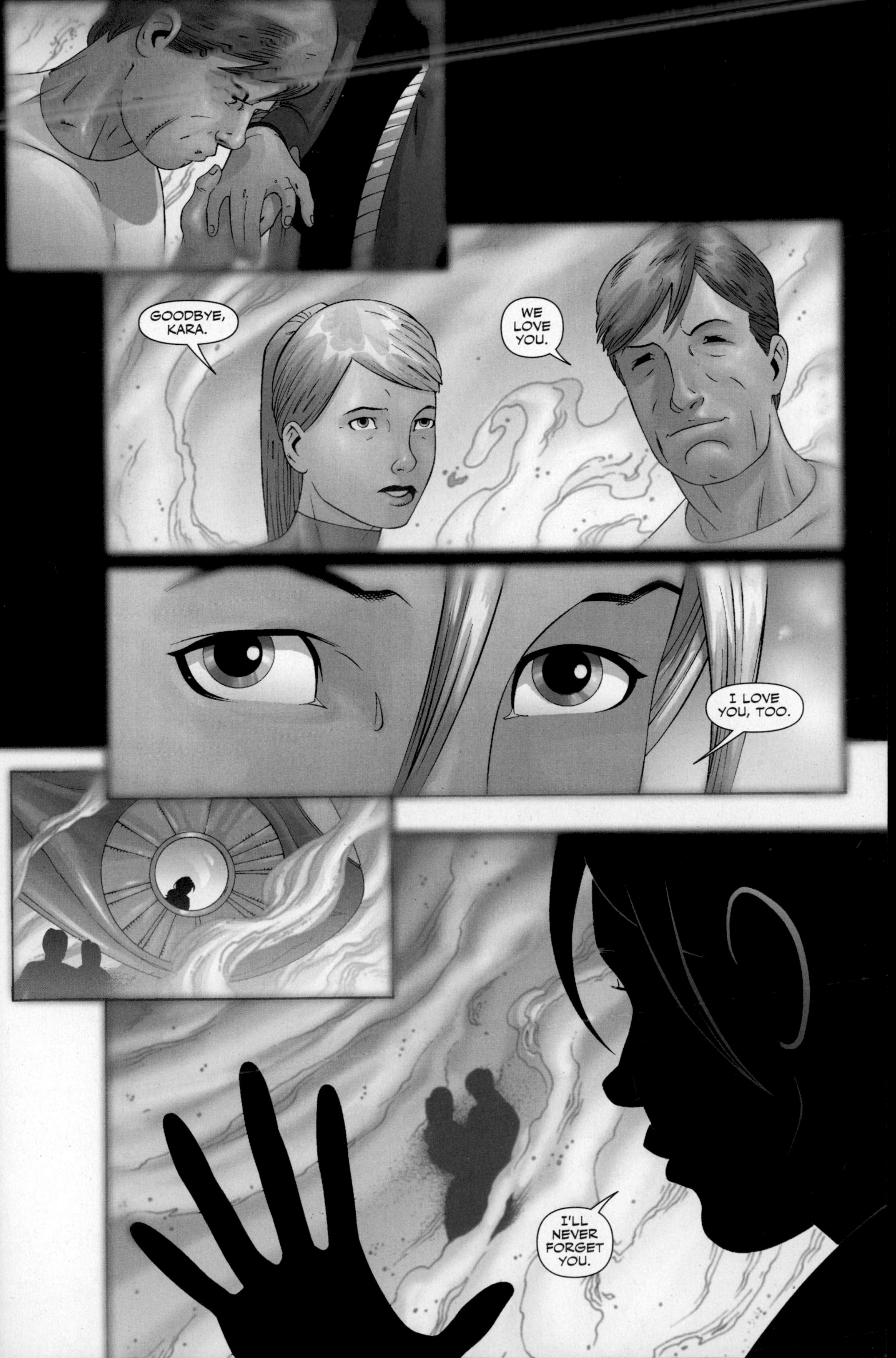
GOODBYE, KARA.
WE LOVE YOU.
I LOVE YOU, TOO.
I'LL NEVER FORGET YOU.

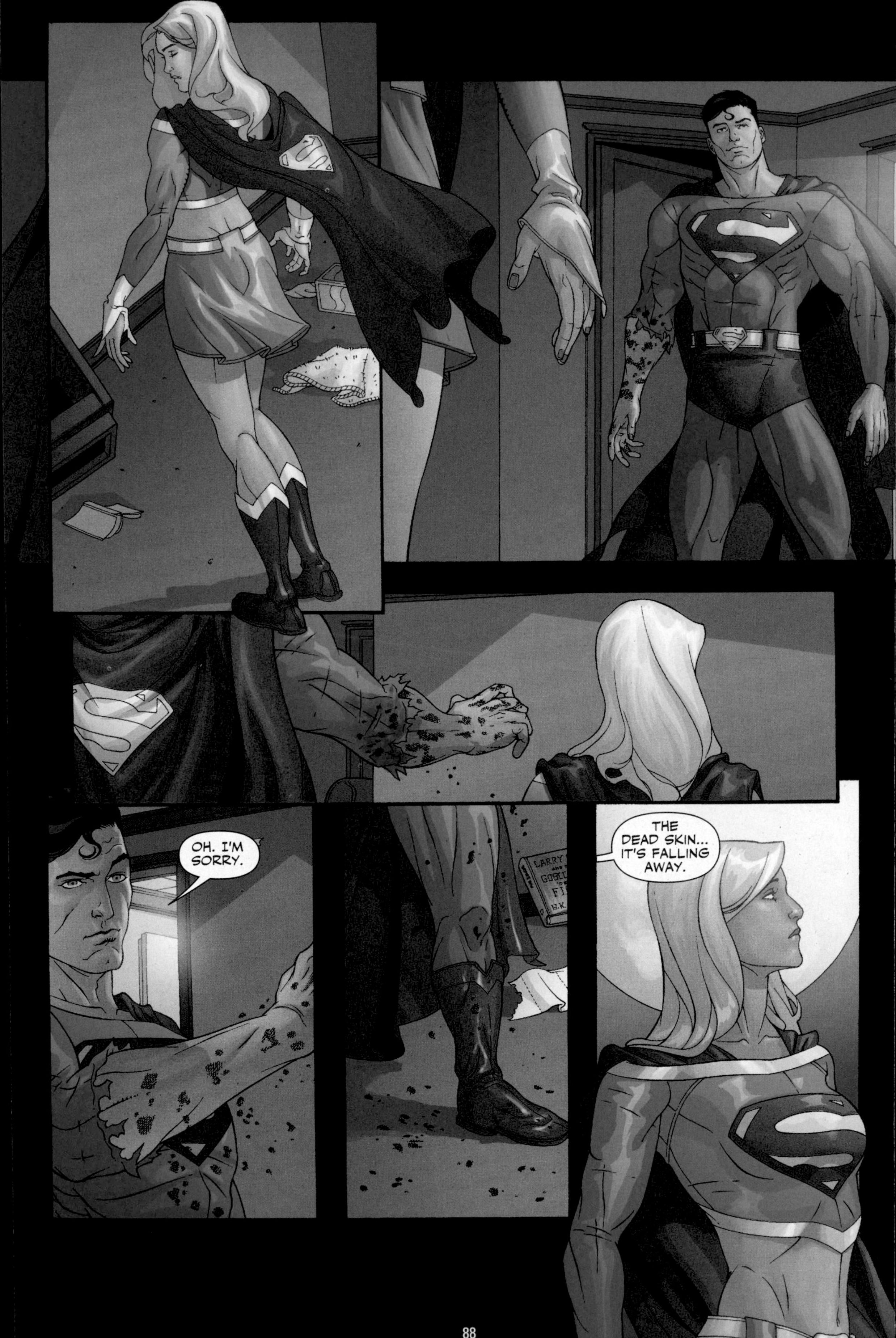
OH. I'M SORRY.
THE DEAD SKIN... IT'S FALLING AWAY.

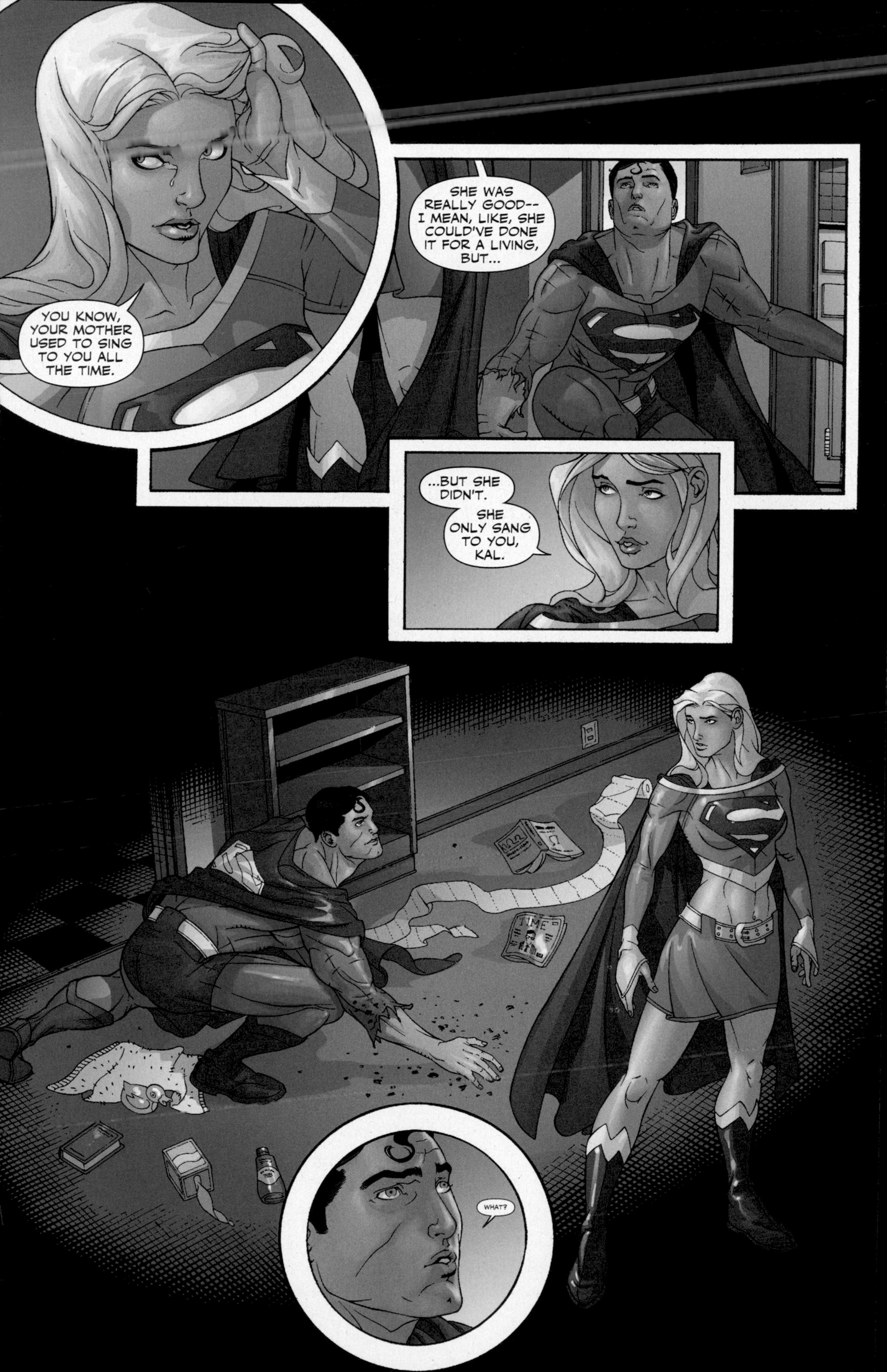
YOU KNOW, YOUR MOTHER USED TO SING TO YOU ALL THE TIME.
SHE WAS REALLY GOOD-- I MEAN, LIKE, SHE COULD'VE DONE IT FOR A LIVING, BUT...
...BUT SHE DIDN'T.
SHE ONLY SANG TO YOU, KAL.
WHAT?

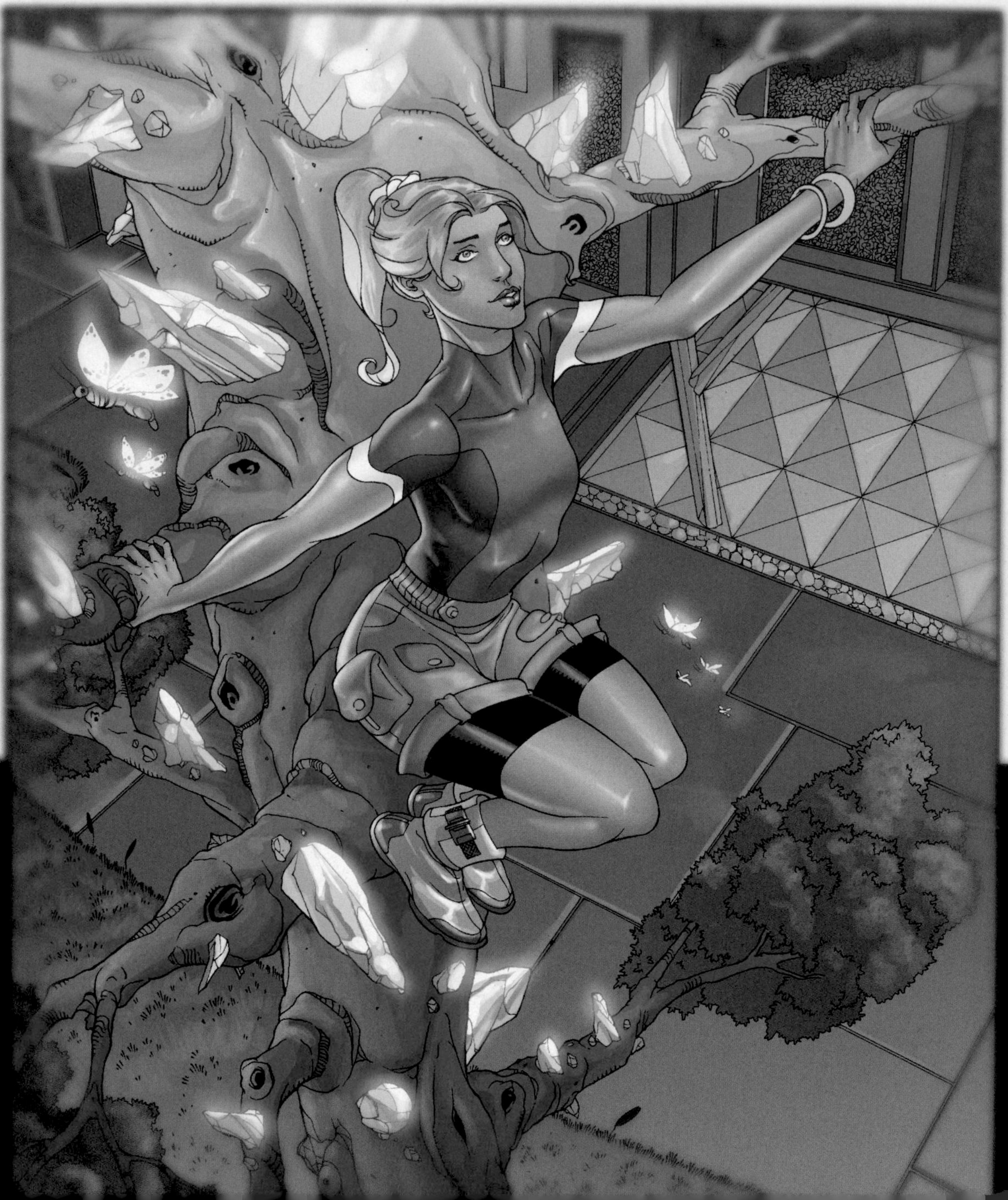

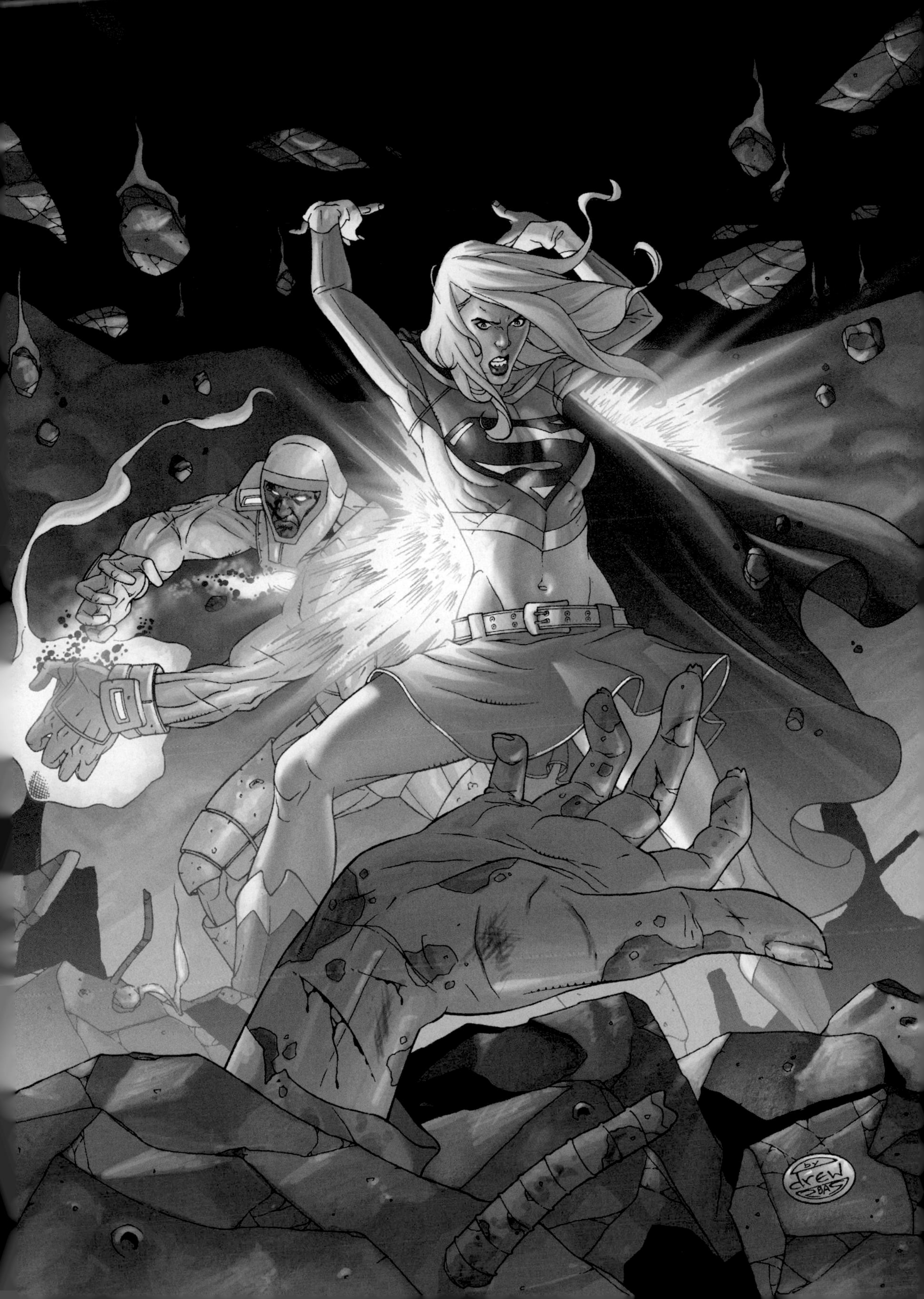

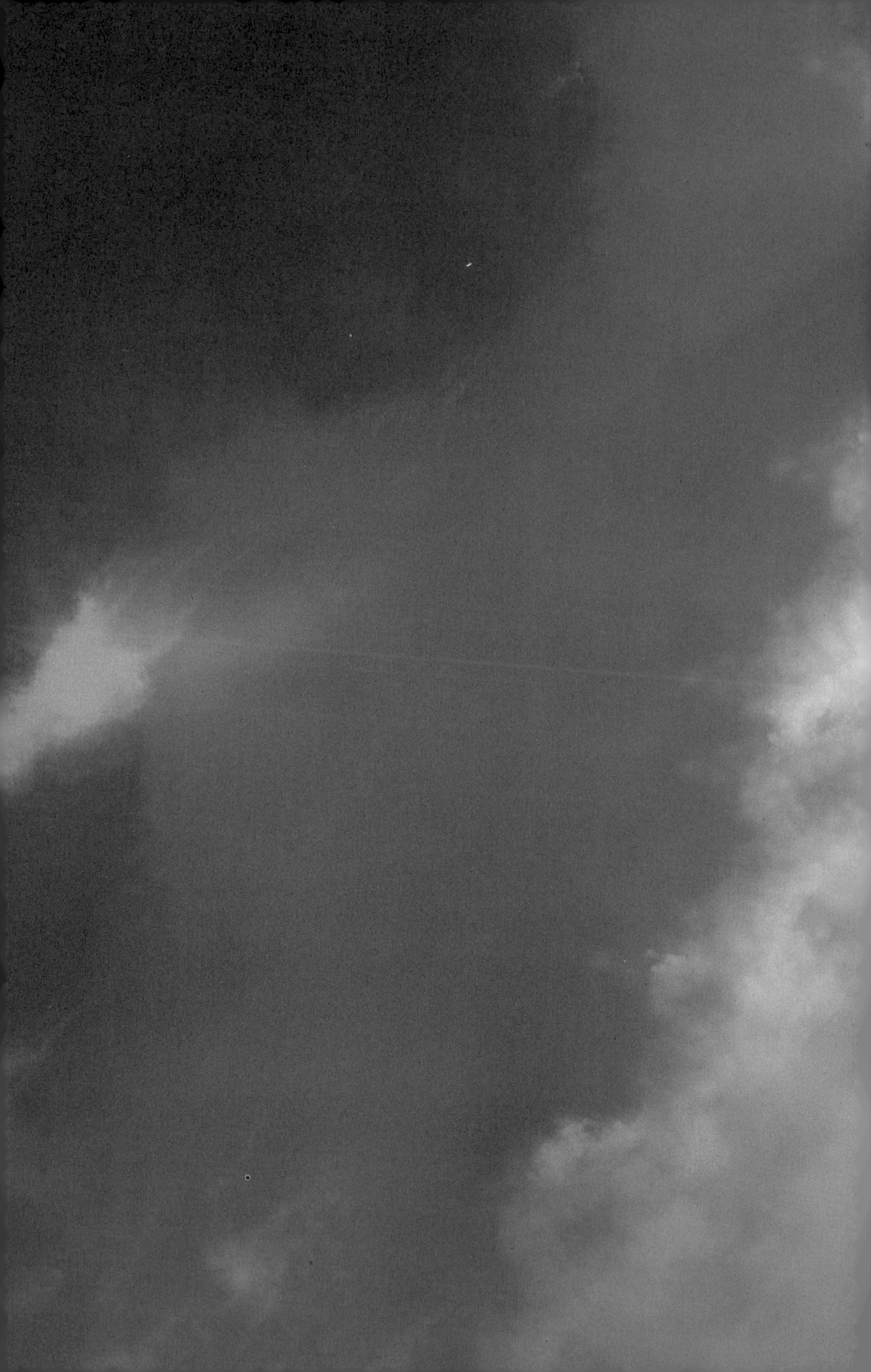

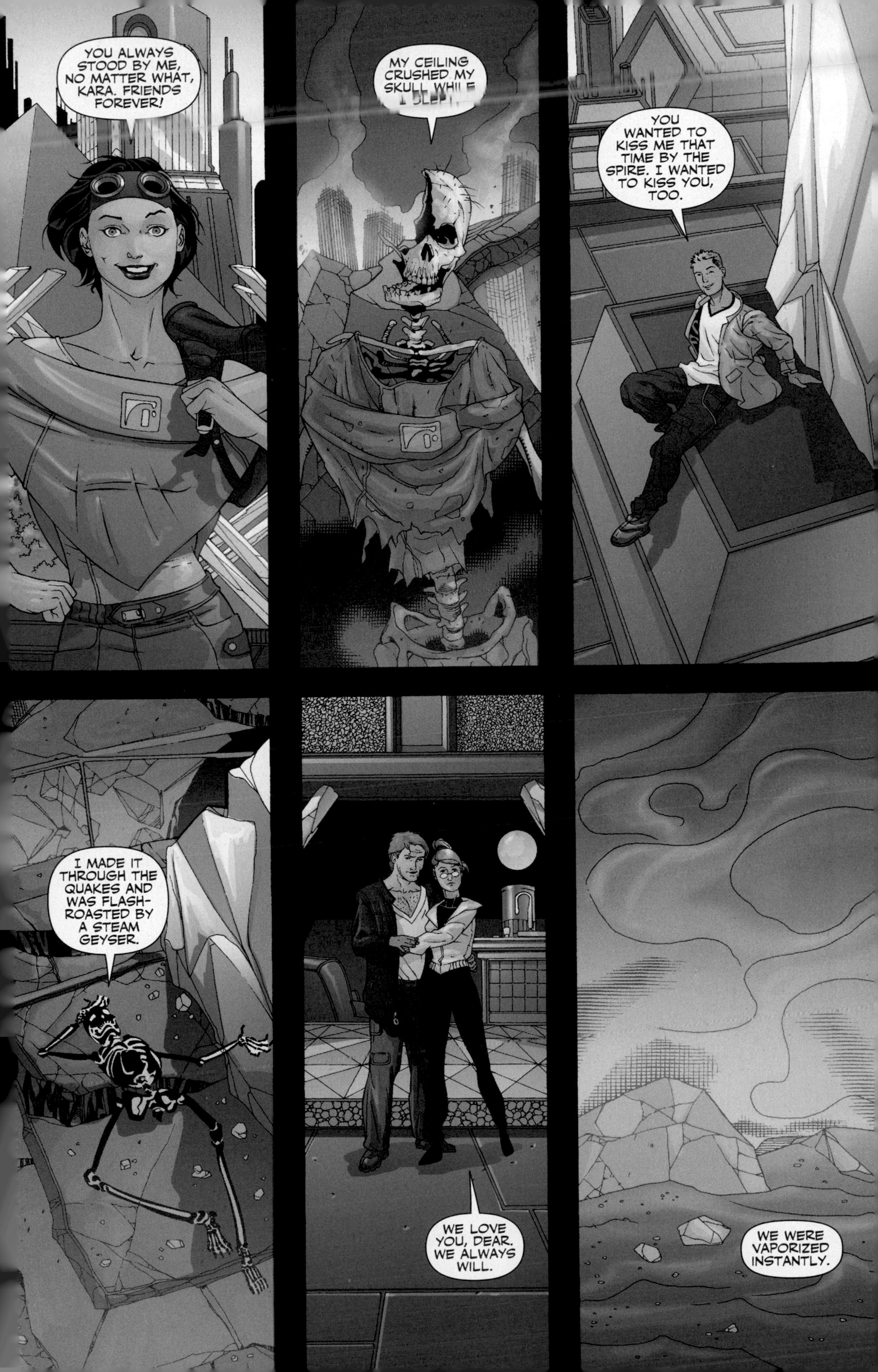
YOU ALWAYS STOOD BY ME, NO MATTER WHAT, KARA. FRIENDS FOREVER!
MY CEILING CRUSHED MY SKULL WHILE
YOU WANTED TO KISS ME THAT TIME BY THE SPIRE. I WANTED TO KISS YOU, TOO.
I MADE IT THROUGH THE QUAKES AND WAS FLASH-ROASTED BY A STEAM GEYSER.
WE LOVE YOU, DEAR. WE ALWAYS WILL.
WE WERE VAPORIZED INSTANTLY.

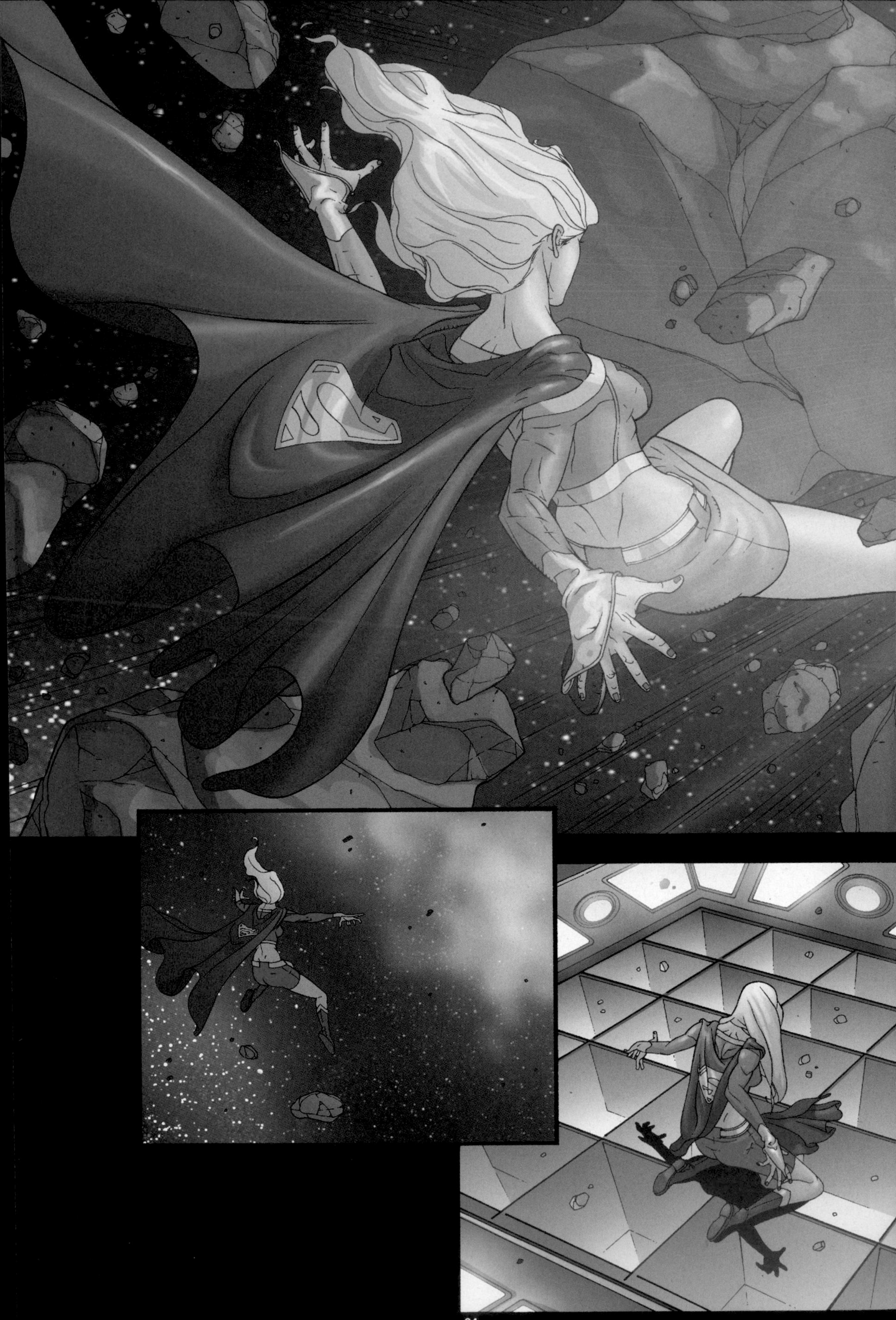

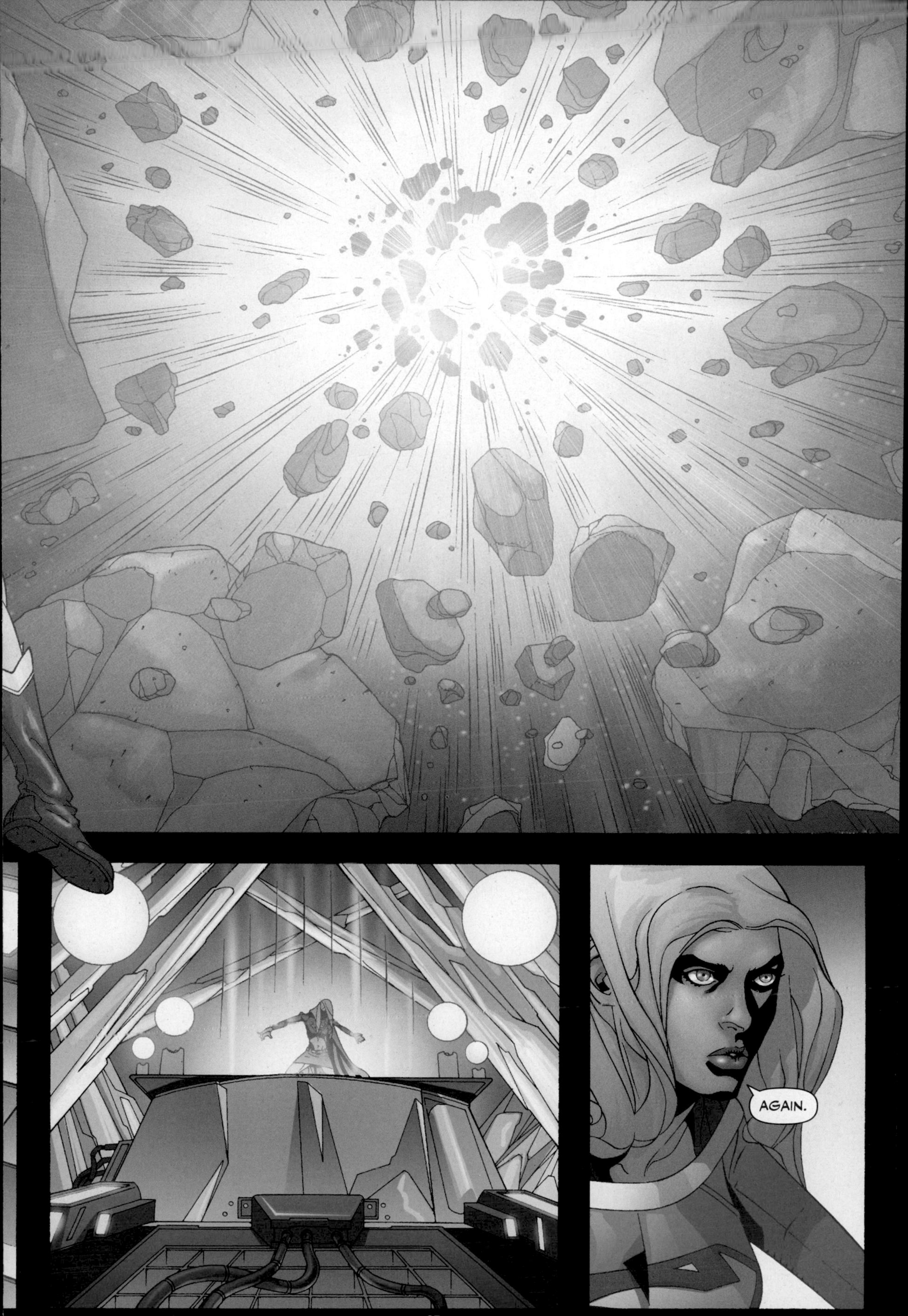
AGAIN.

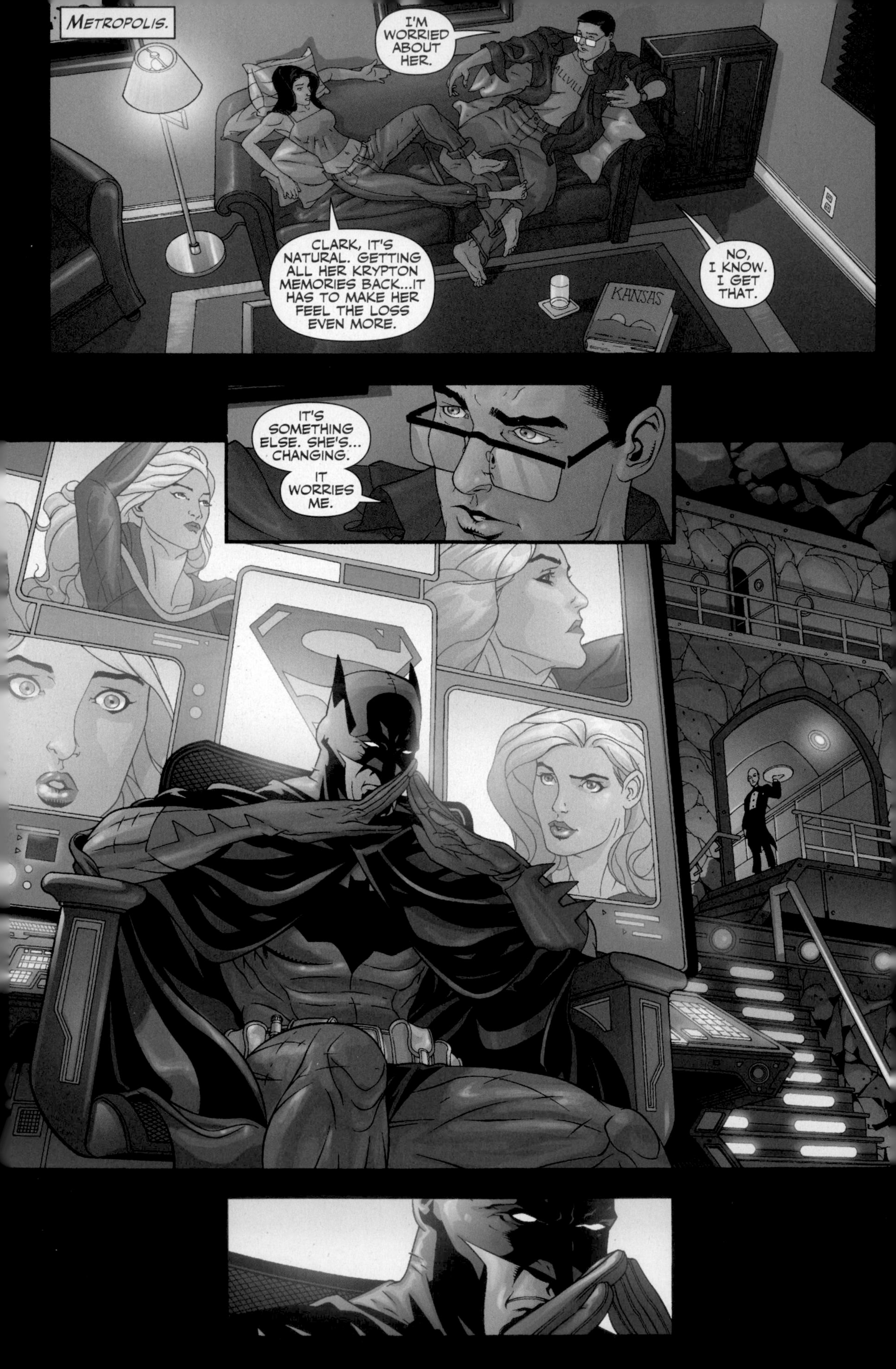
METROPOLIS.
I'M WORRIED ABOUT HER.
CLARK, IT'S NATURAL. GETTING ALL HER KRYPTON MEMORIES BACK...IT HAS TO MAKE HER FEEL THE LOSS EVEN MORE.
NO, I KNOW. I GET THAT.
KANSAS
IT'S SOMETHING ELSE. SHE'S... CHANGING.
IT WORRIES ME.

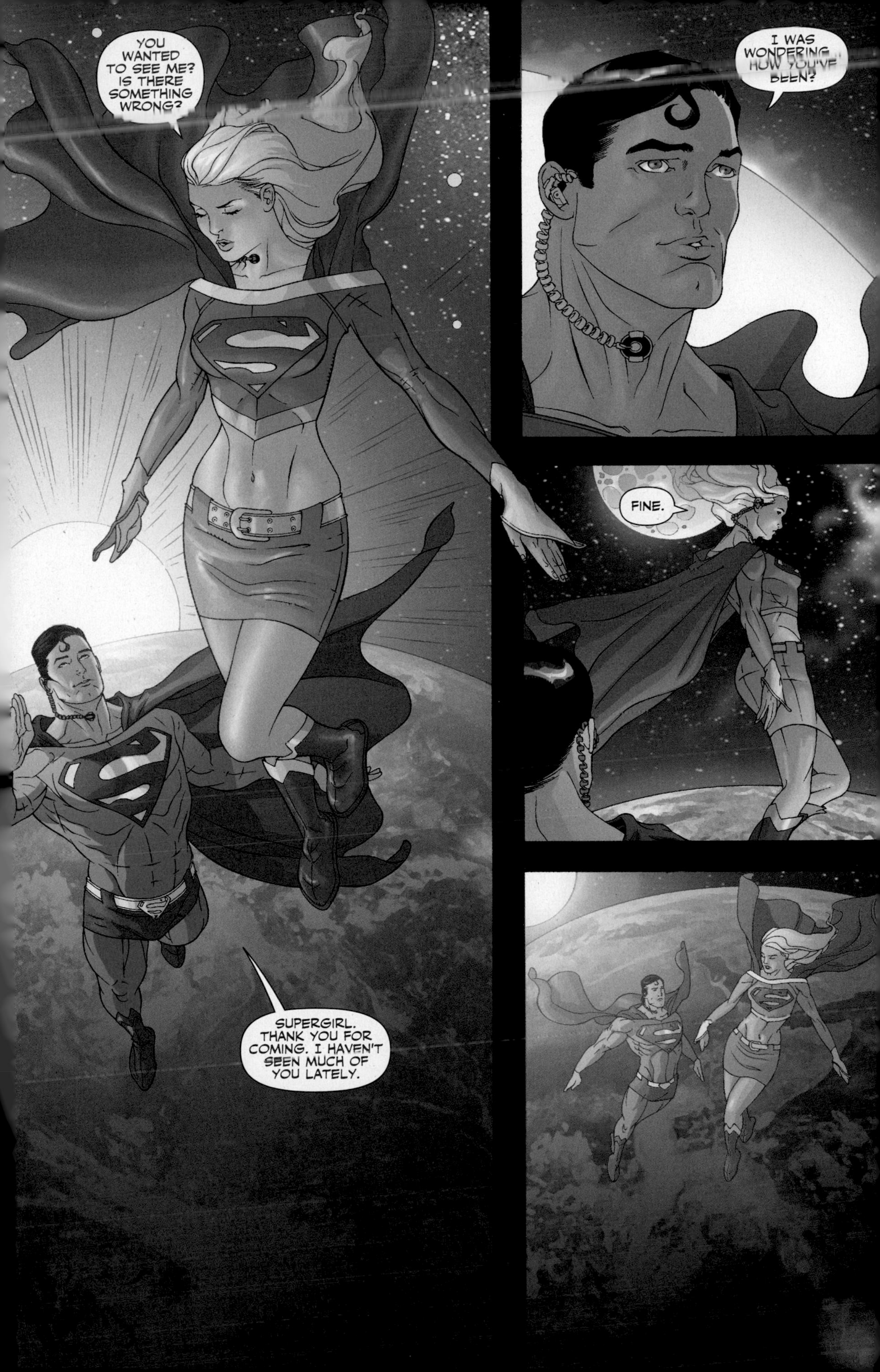
YOU WANTED TO SEE ME? IS THERE SOMETHING WRONG?
SUPERGIRL. THANK YOU FOR COMING. I HAVEN'T SEEN MUCH OF YOU LATELY.
I WAS WONDERING HOW YOU'VE BEEN?
FINE.

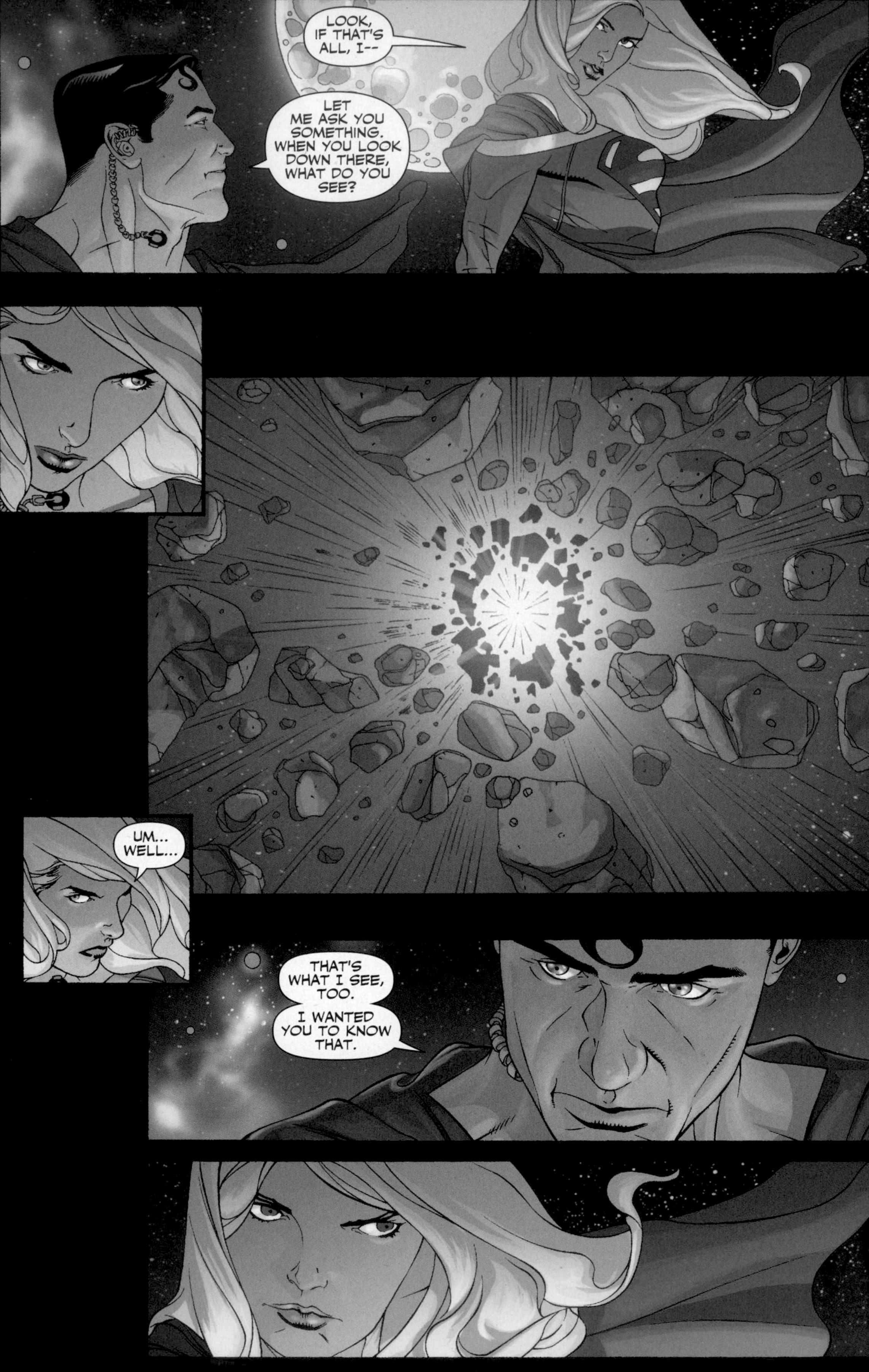
LOOK, IF THAT'S ALL, I--
LET ME ASK YOU SOMETHING. WHEN YOU LOOK DOWN THERE, WHAT DO YOU SEE?
UM... WELL...
THAT'S WHAT I SEE, TOO.
I WANTED YOU TO KNOW THAT.

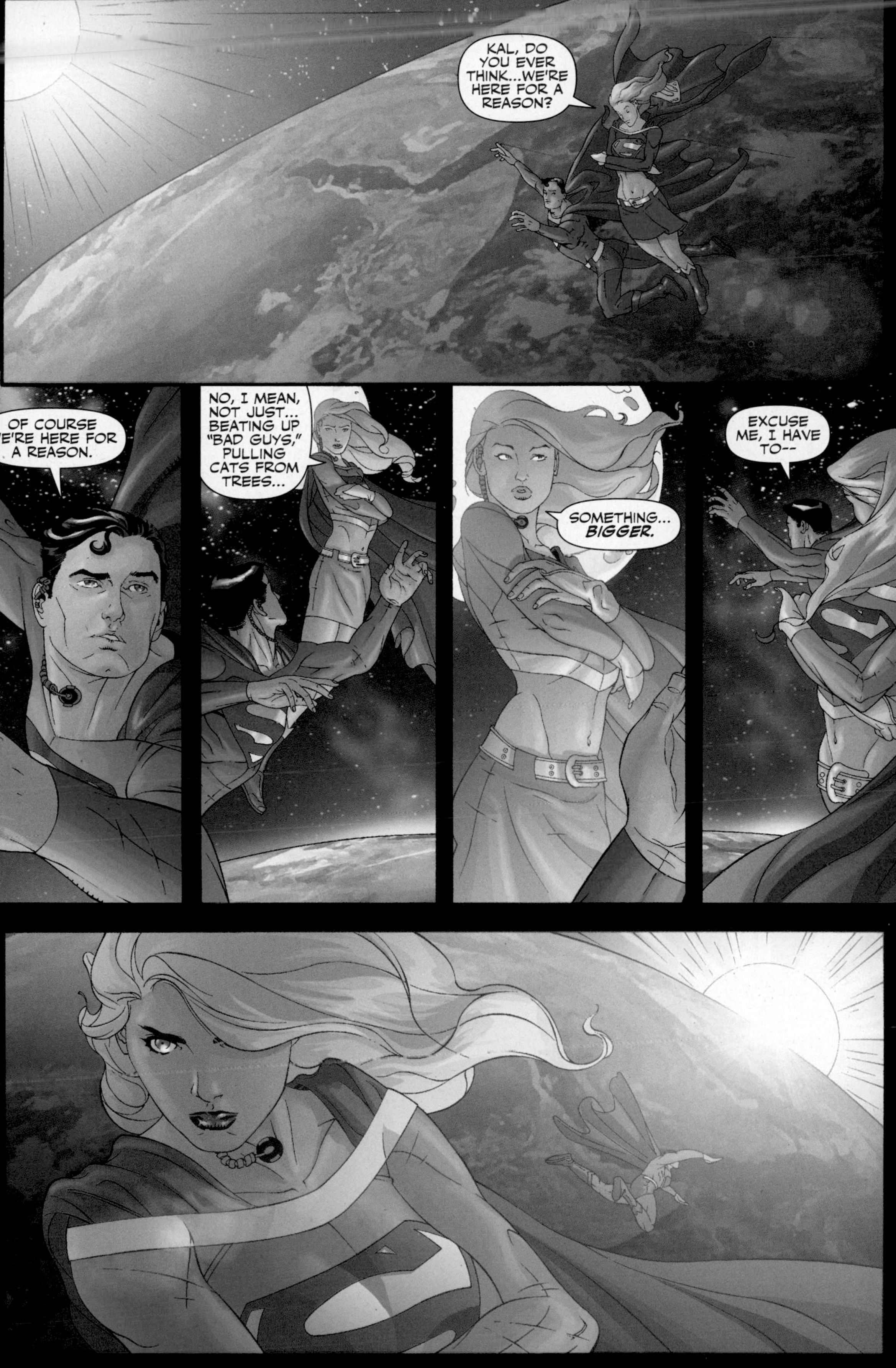
KAL, DO YOU EVER THINK...WE'RE HERE FOR A REASON?
OF COURSE WE'RE HERE FOR A REASON.
NO, I MEAN, NOT JUST... BEATING UP "BAD GUYS," PULLING CATS FROM TREES...
SOMETHING... BIGGER.
EXCUSE ME, I HAVE TO--

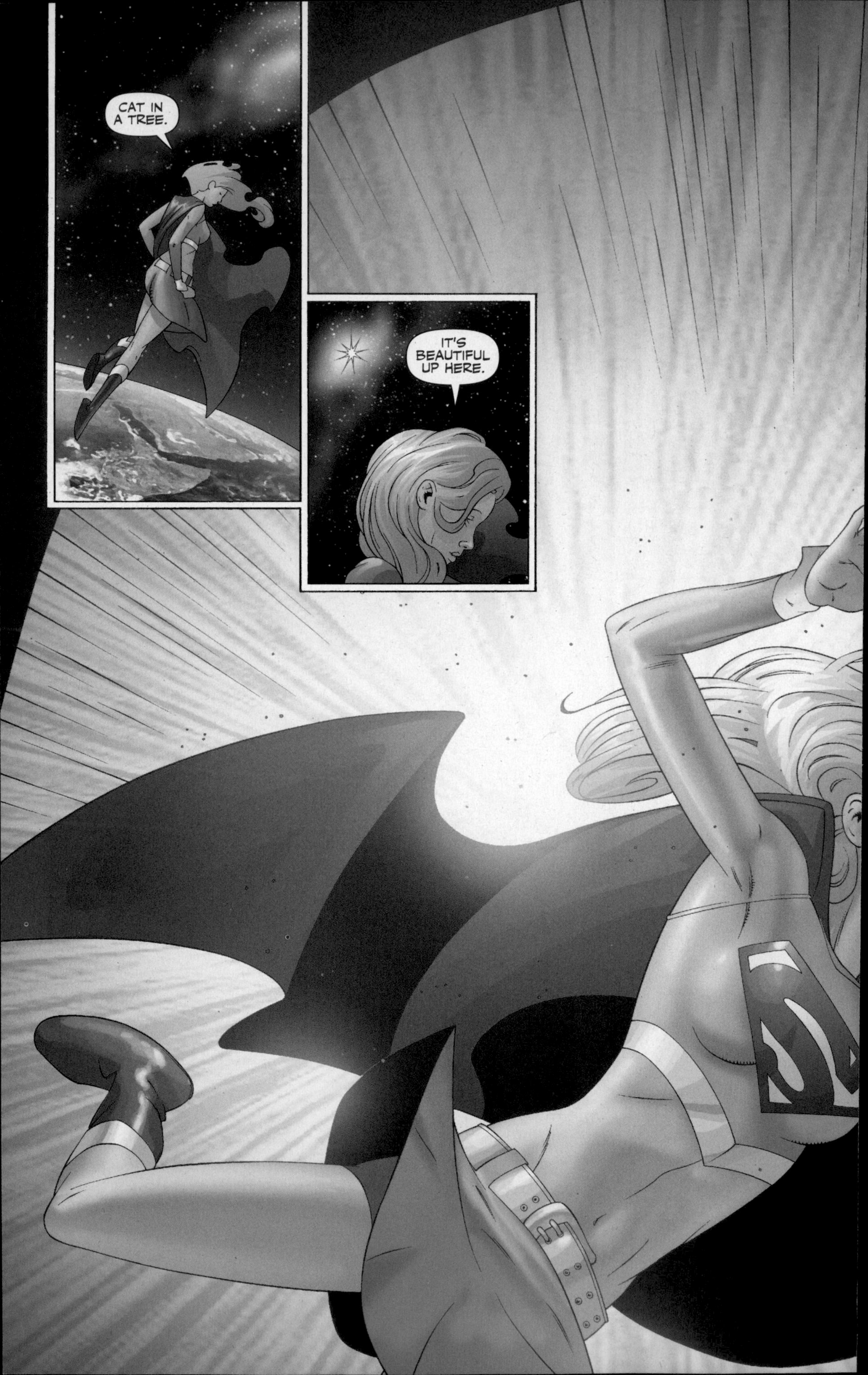
CAT IN A TREE.
IT'S BEAUTIFUL UP HERE.

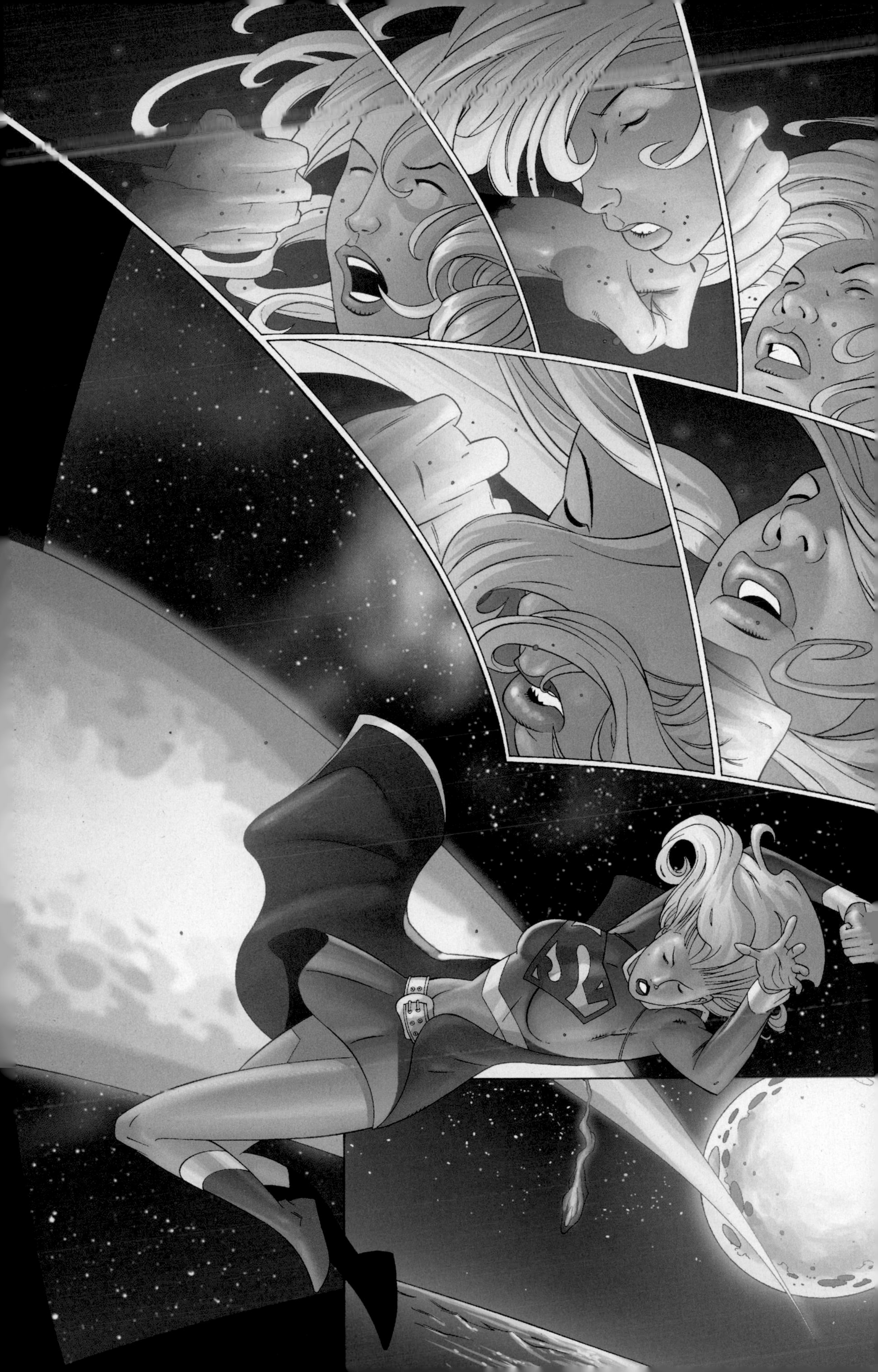

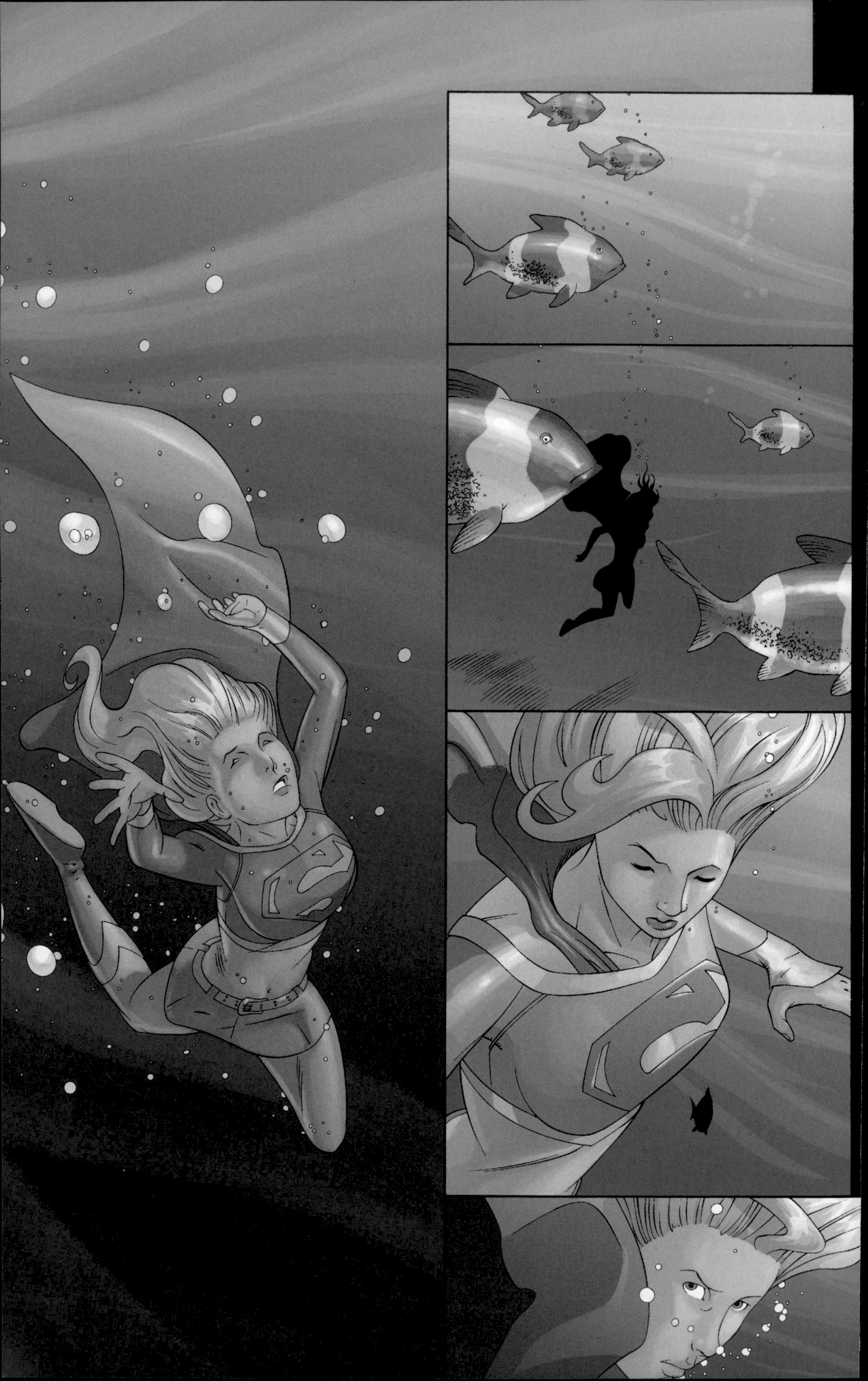

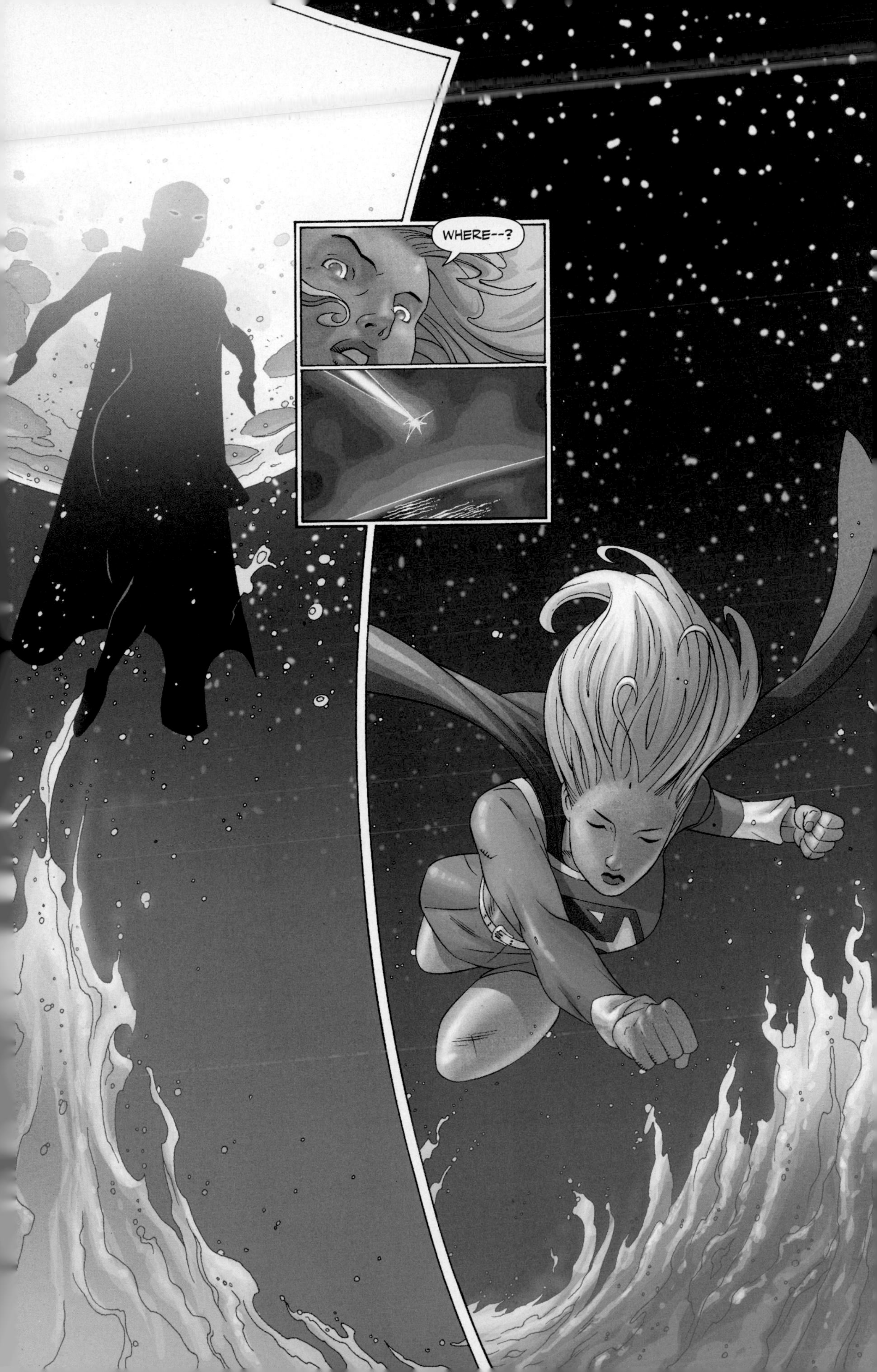
WHERE--?

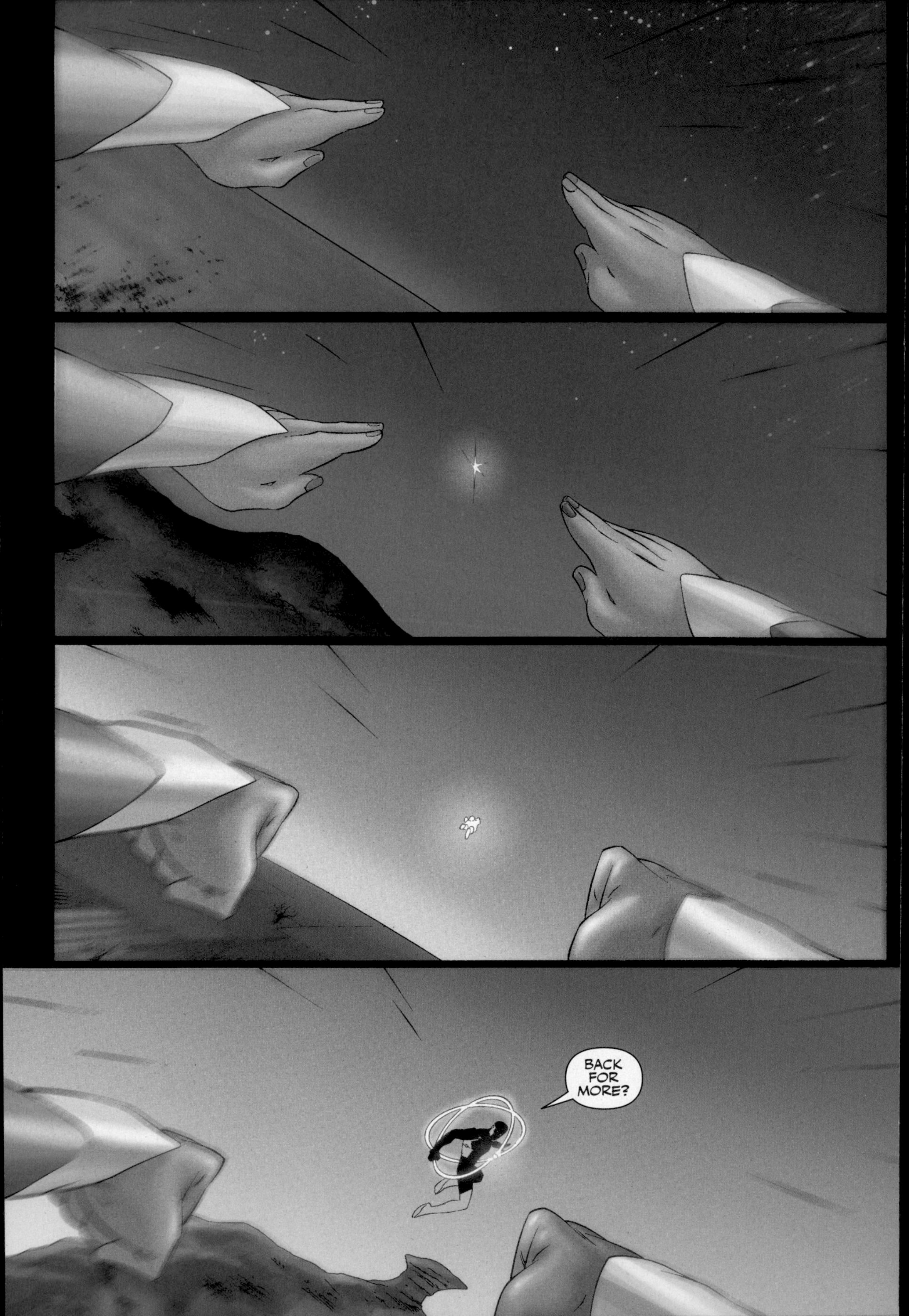
BACK FOR MORE?

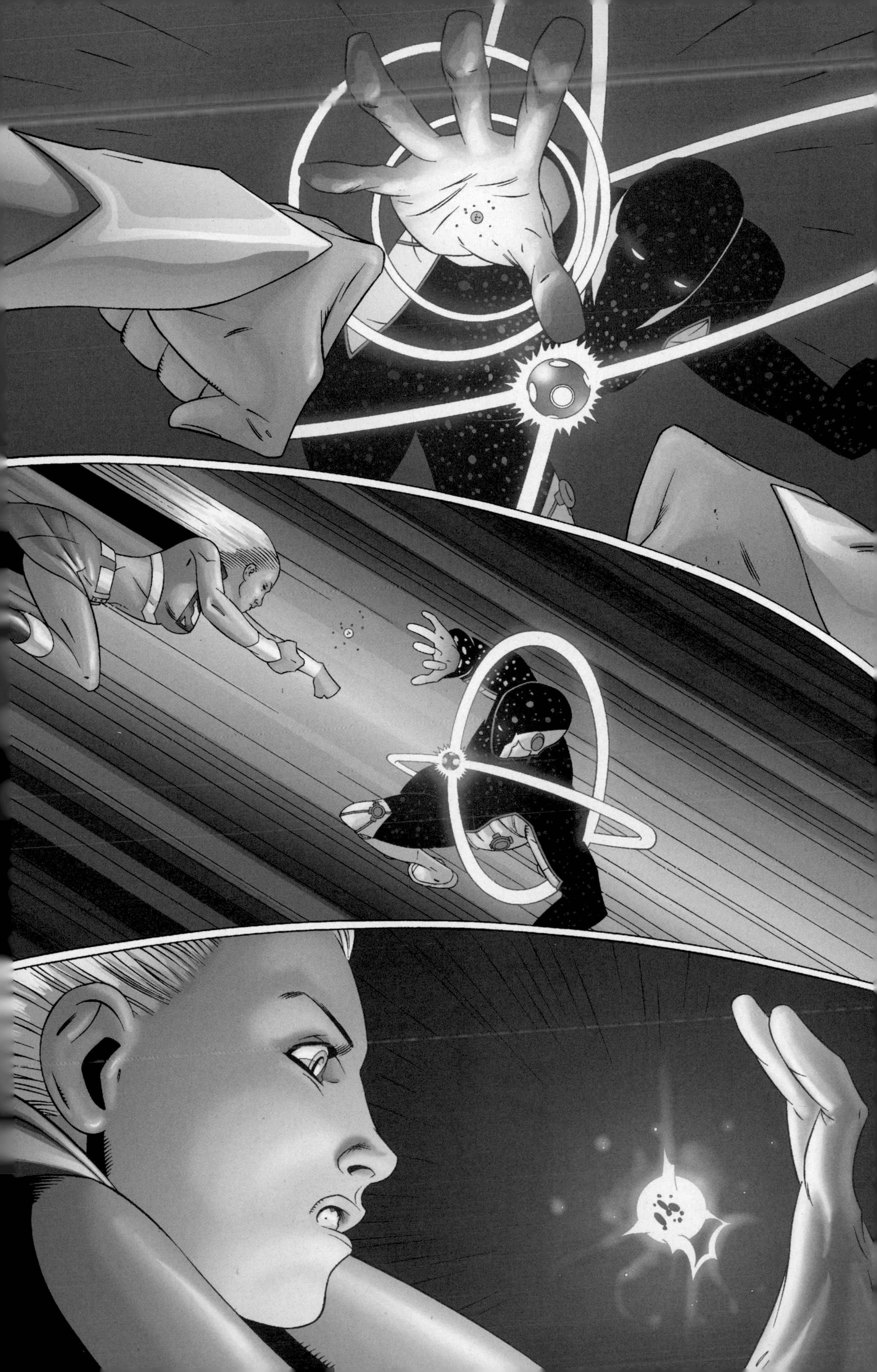

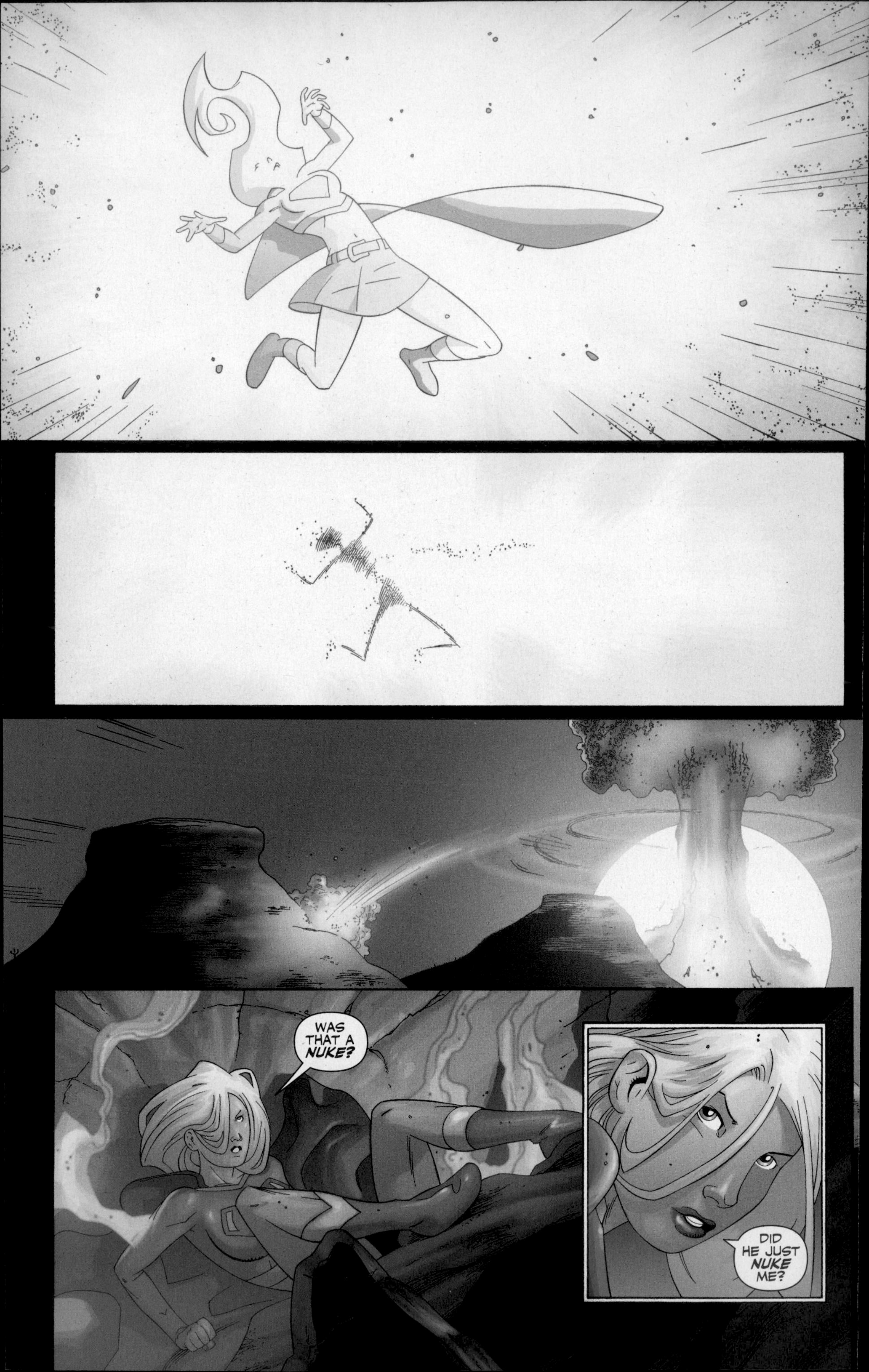
WAS THAT A NUKE?
DID HE JUST NUKE ME?

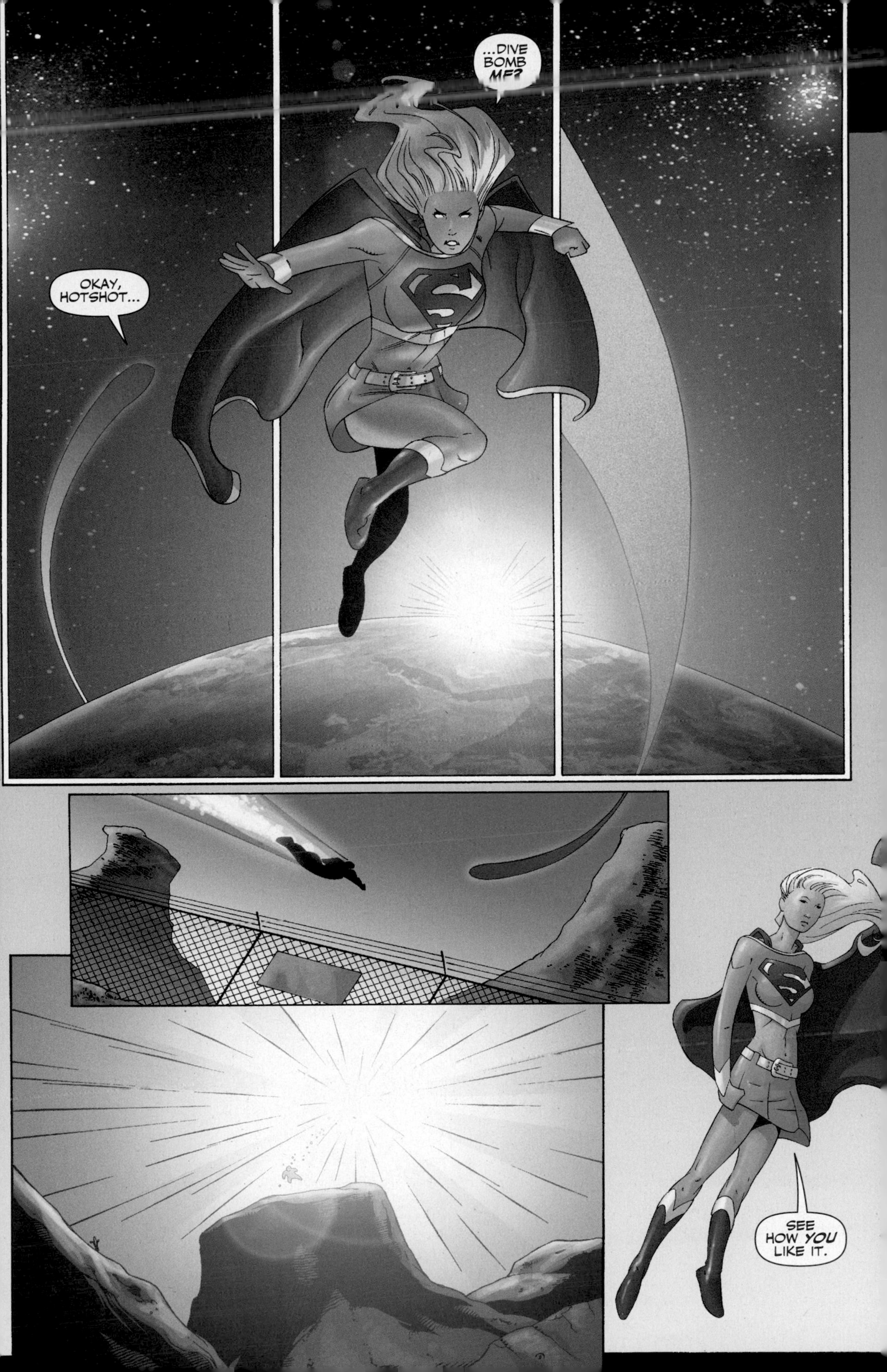
OKAY, HOTSHOT...
...DIVE BOMB ME?
SEE HOW YOU LIKE IT.

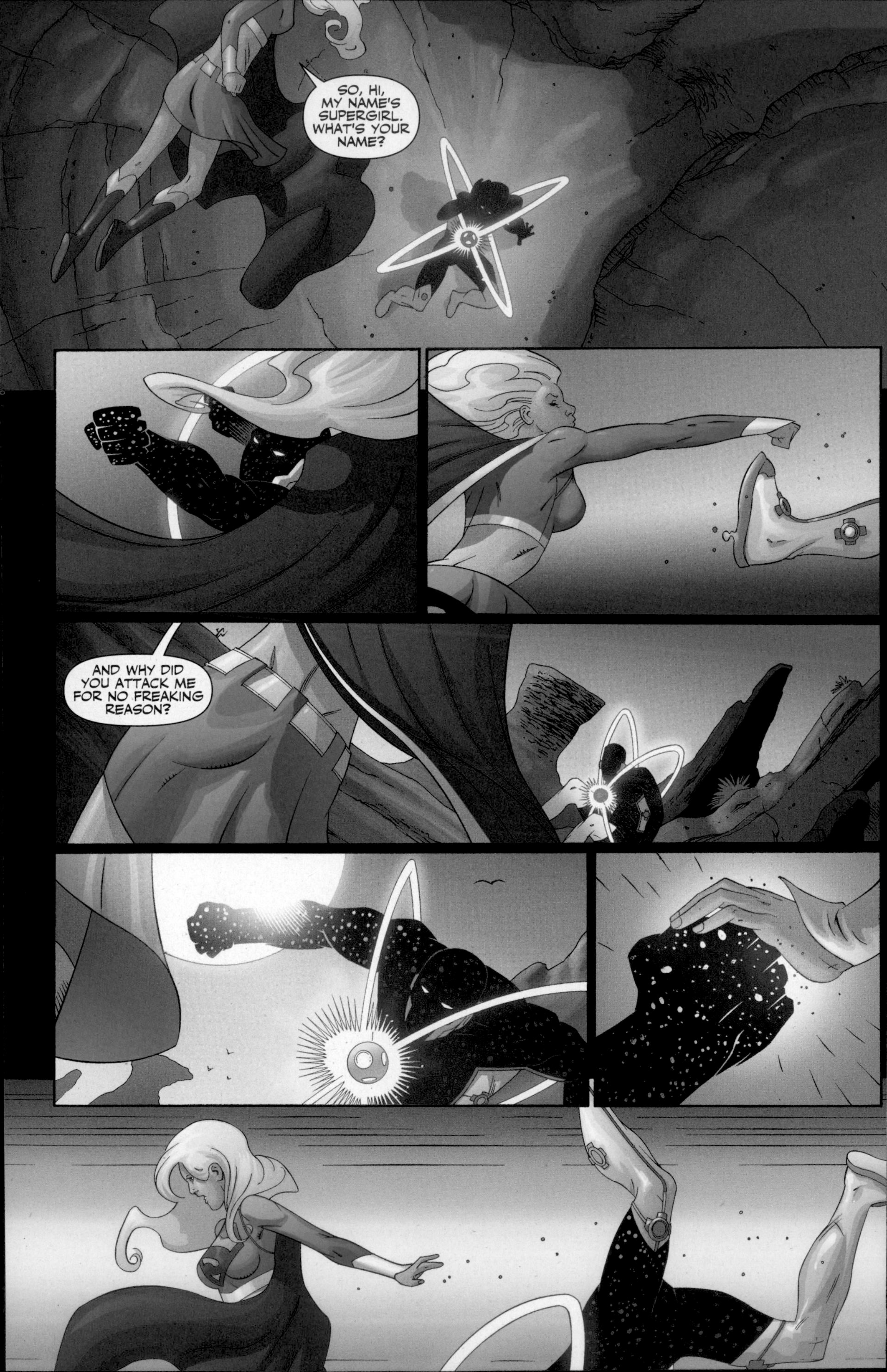
SO, HI, MY NAME'S SUPERGIRL. WHAT'S YOUR NAME?
AND WHY DID YOU ATTACK ME FOR NO FREAKING REASON?

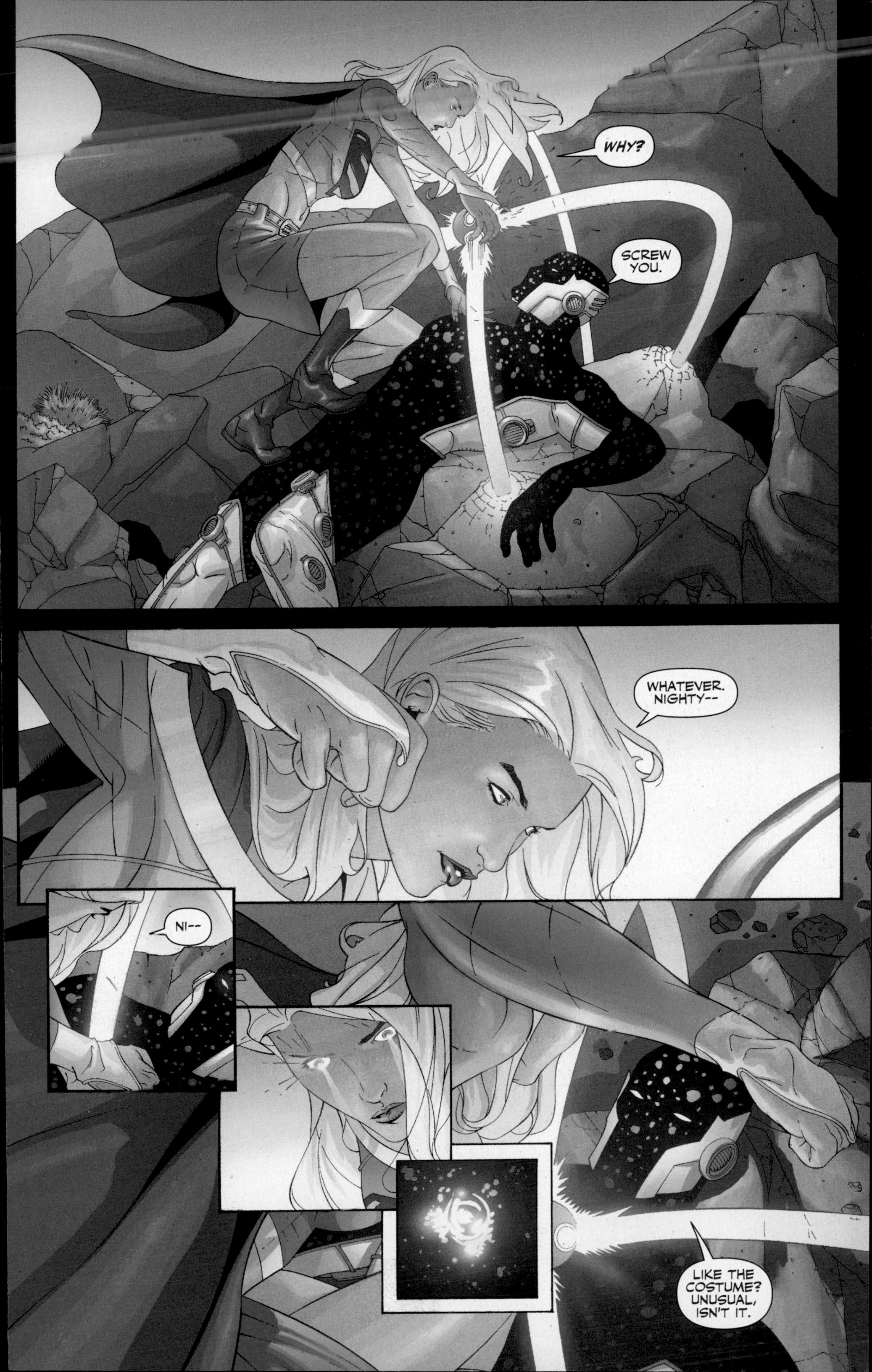
WHY?
SCREW YOU.
WHATEVER. NIGHTY--
NI--
LIKE THE COSTUME? UNUSUAL, ISN'T IT.

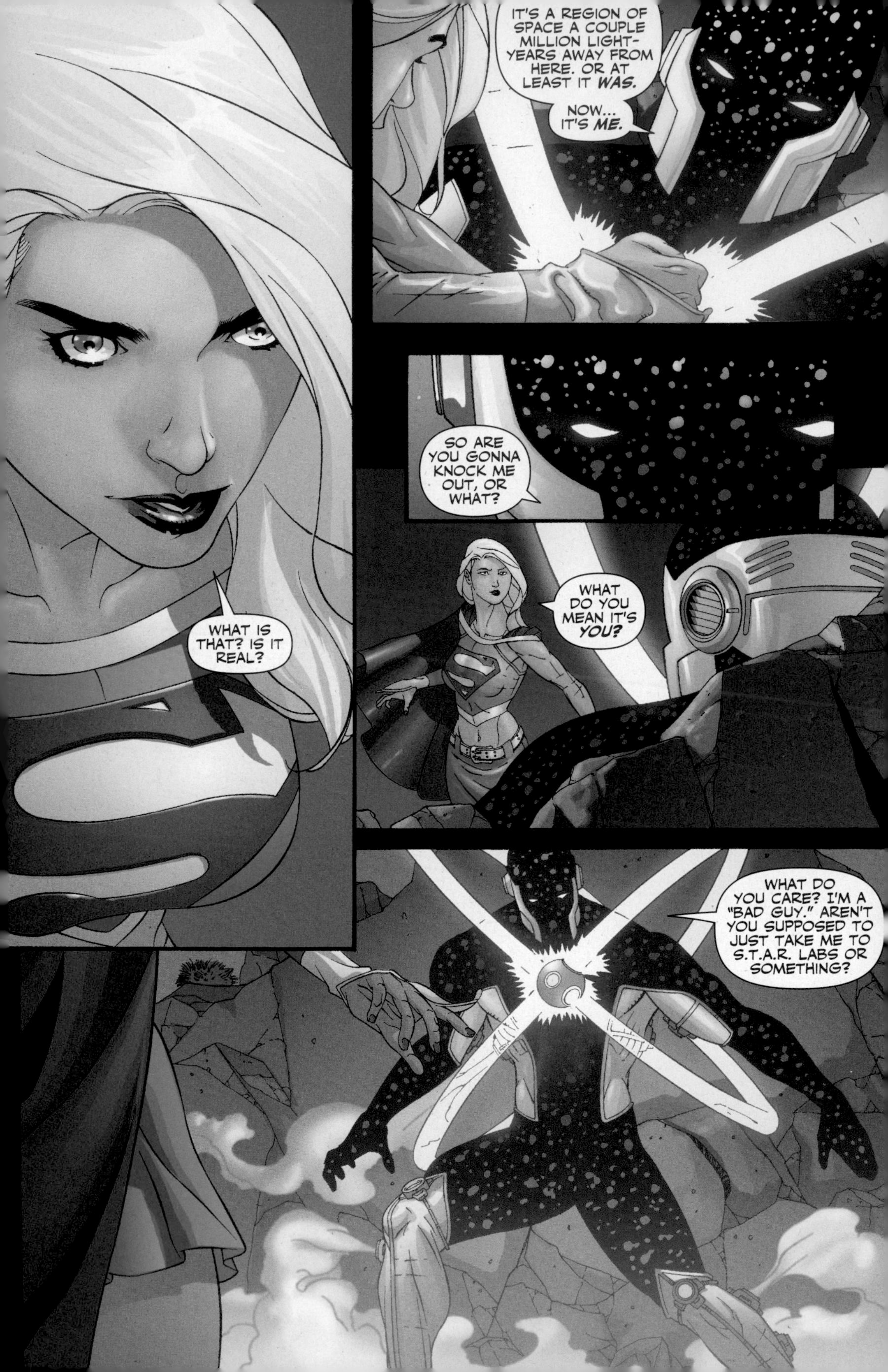
IT'S A REGION OF SPACE A COUPLE MILLION LIGHT-YEARS AWAY FROM HERE. OR AT LEAST IT *WAS.*
NOW... IT'S *ME.*
WHAT IS THAT? IS IT REAL?
SO ARE YOU GONNA KNOCK ME OUT, OR WHAT?
WHAT DO YOU MEAN IT'S *YOU?*
WHAT DO YOU CARE? I'M A "BAD GUY." AREN'T YOU SUPPOSED TO JUST TAKE ME TO S.T.A.R. LABS OR SOMETHING?

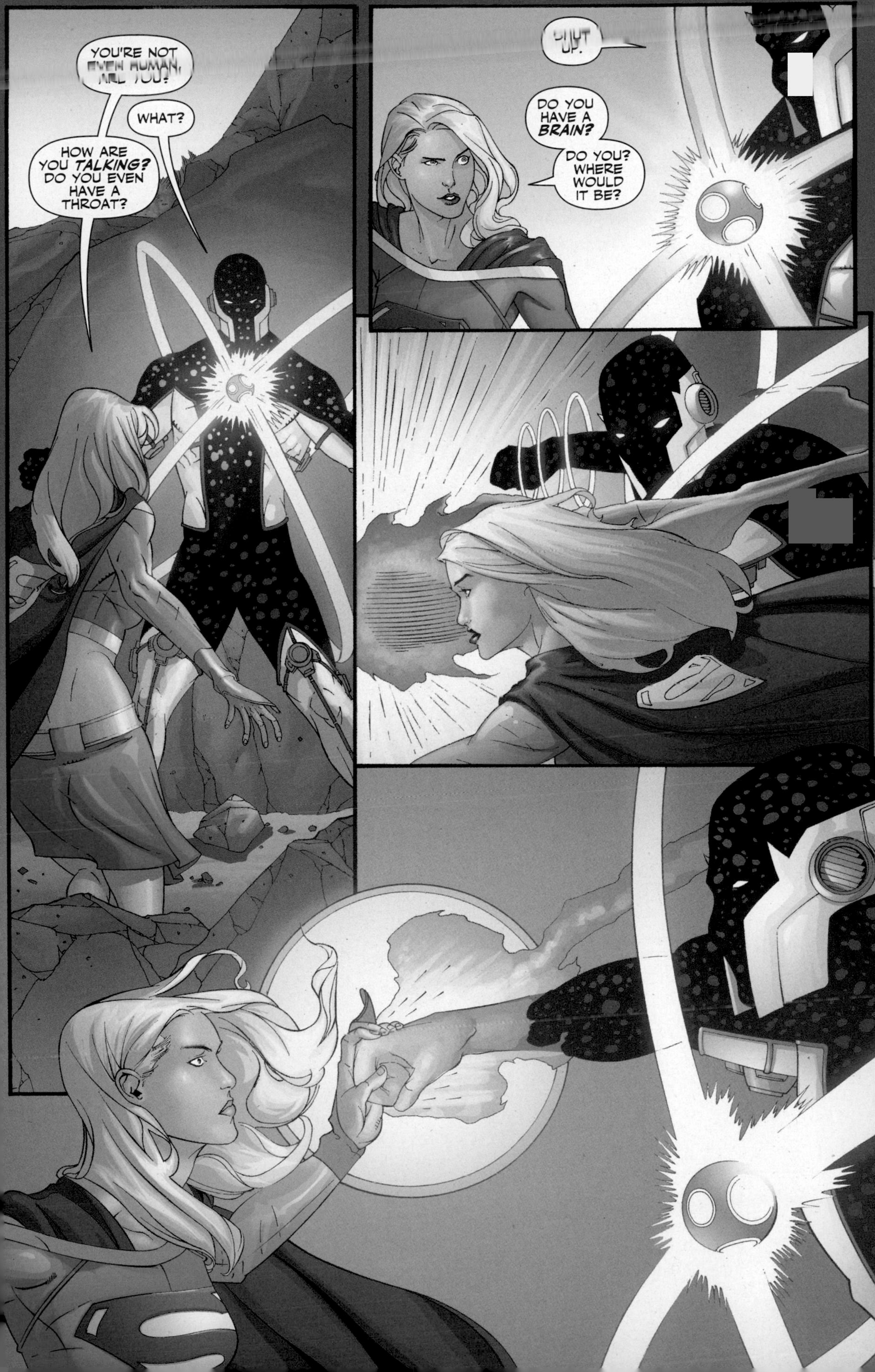
YOU'RE NOT
WHAT?
HOW ARE YOU *TALKING?* DO YOU EVEN HAVE A THROAT?
DO YOU HAVE A *BRAIN?*
DO YOU? WHERE WOULD IT BE?

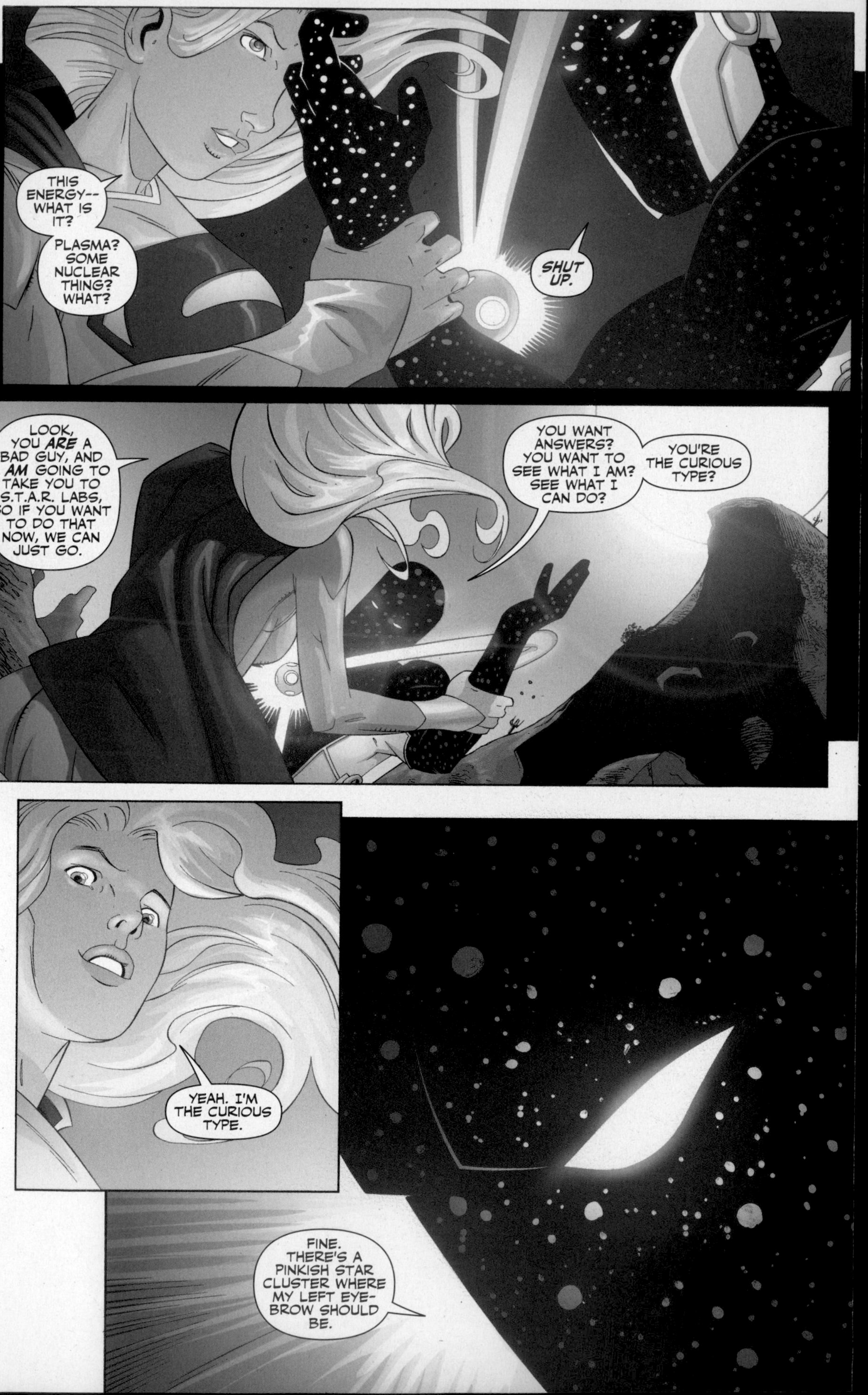
THIS ENERGY-- WHAT IS IT?
PLASMA? SOME NUCLEAR THING? WHAT?
SHUT UP.
LOOK, YOU ARE A BAD GUY, AND I AM GOING TO TAKE YOU TO S.T.A.R. LABS, SO IF YOU WANT TO DO THAT NOW, WE CAN JUST GO.
YOU WANT ANSWERS? YOU WANT TO SEE WHAT I AM? SEE WHAT I CAN DO?
YOU'RE THE CURIOUS TYPE?
YEAH. I'M THE CURIOUS TYPE.
FINE. THERE'S A PINKISH STAR CLUSTER WHERE MY LEFT EYE-BROW SHOULD BE.

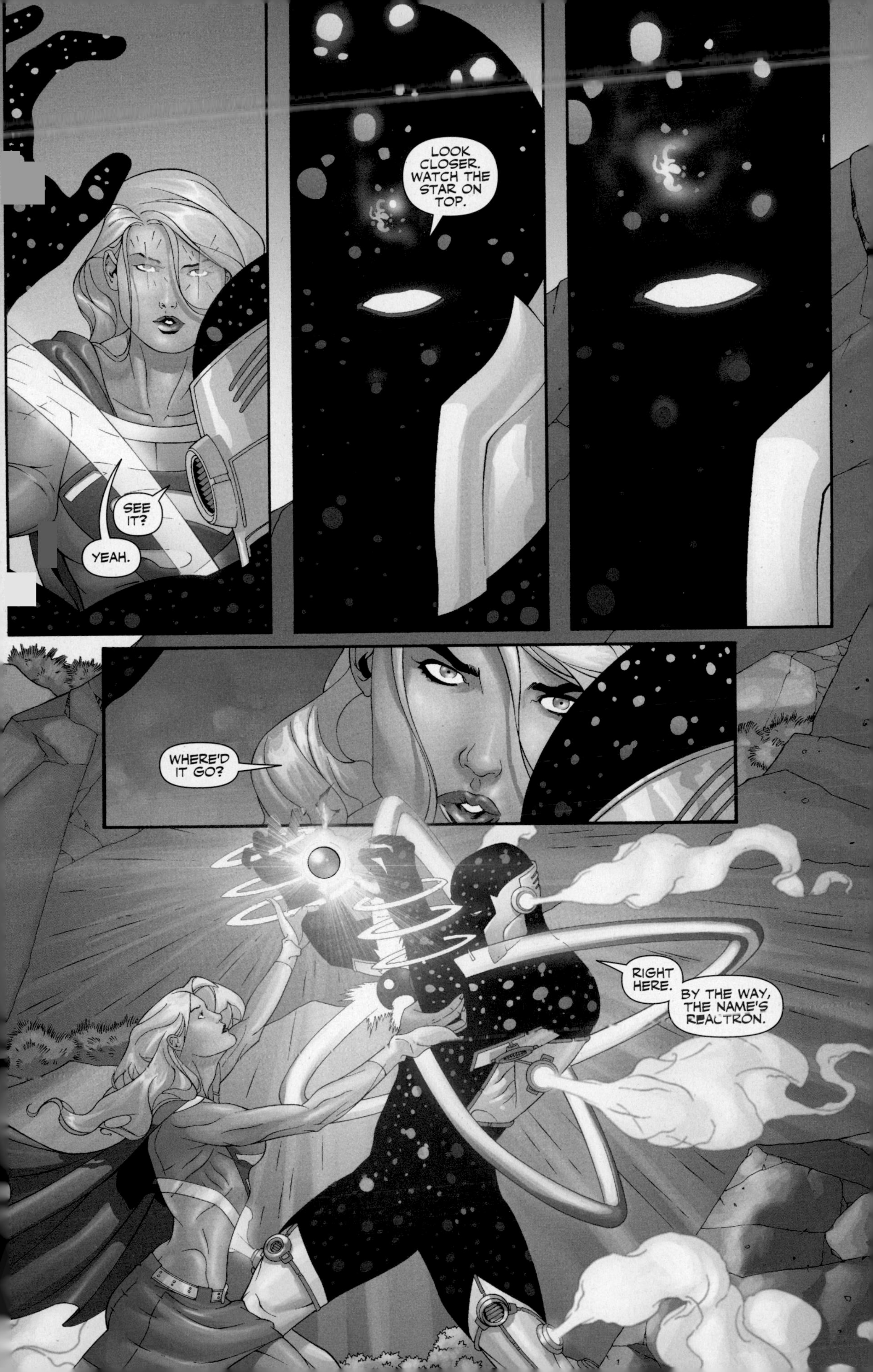
LOOK CLOSER. WATCH THE STAR ON TOP.
SEE IT?
YEAH.
WHERE'D IT GO?
RIGHT HERE.
BY THE WAY, THE NAME'S REACTRON.

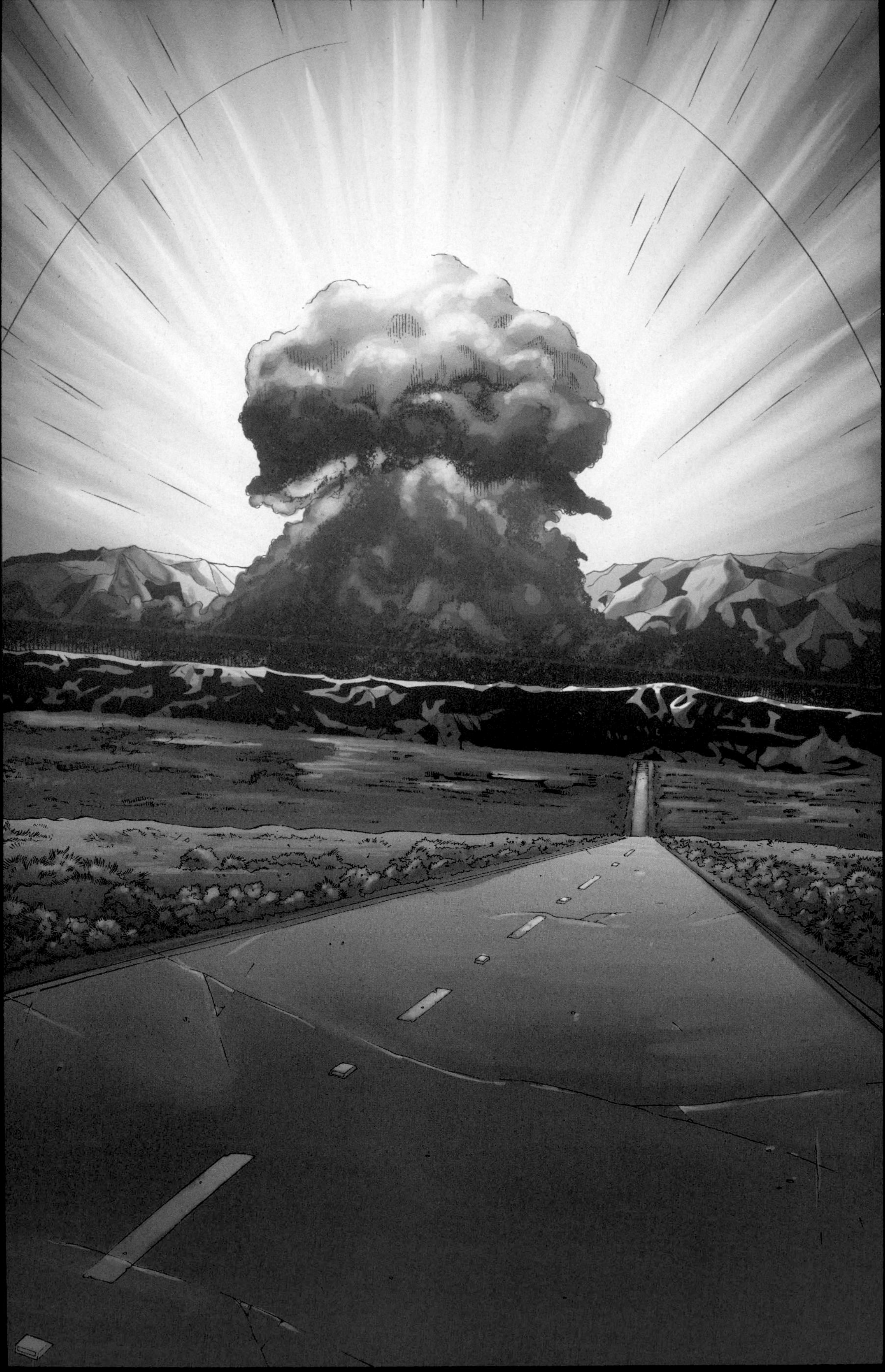

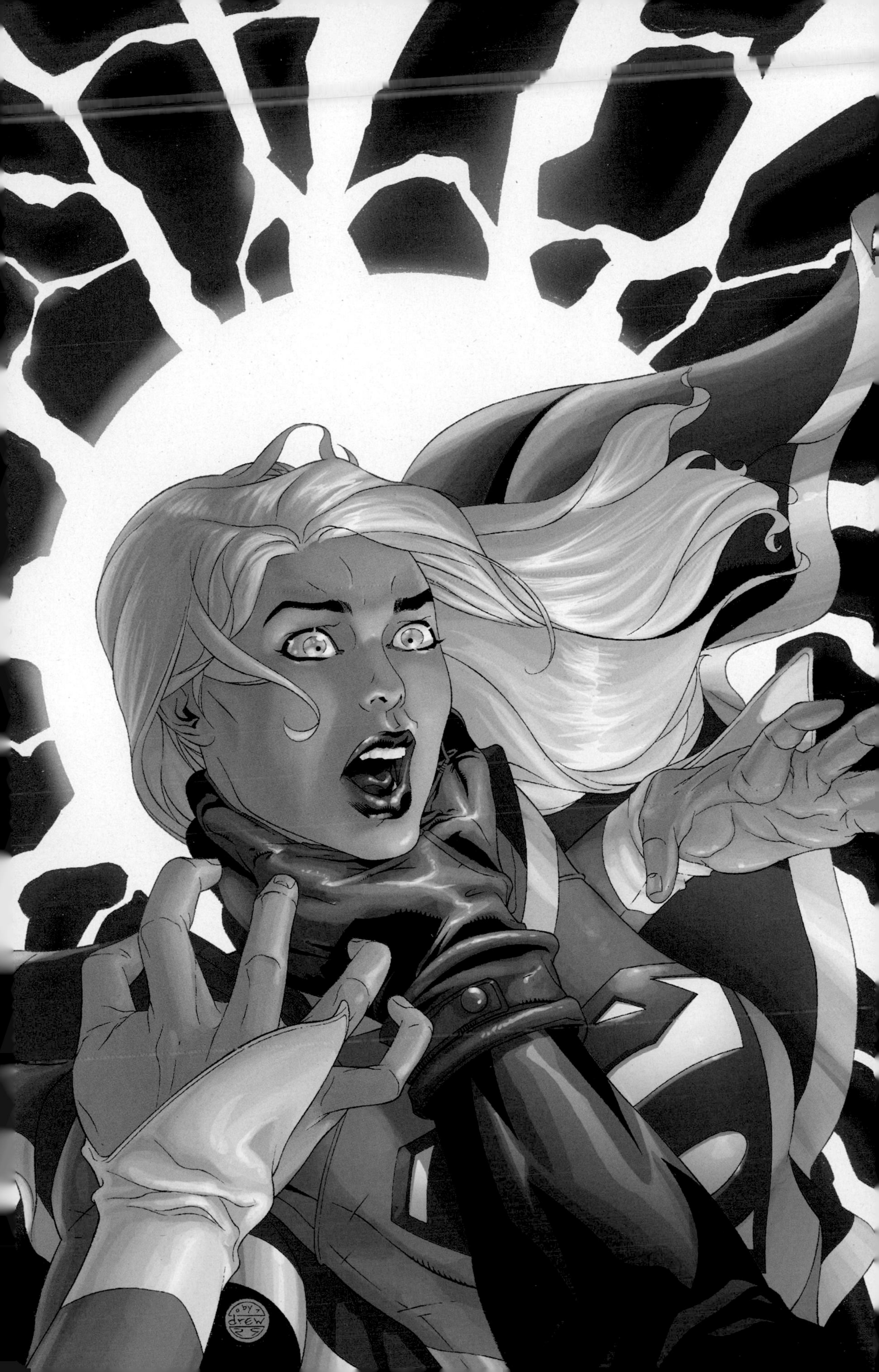

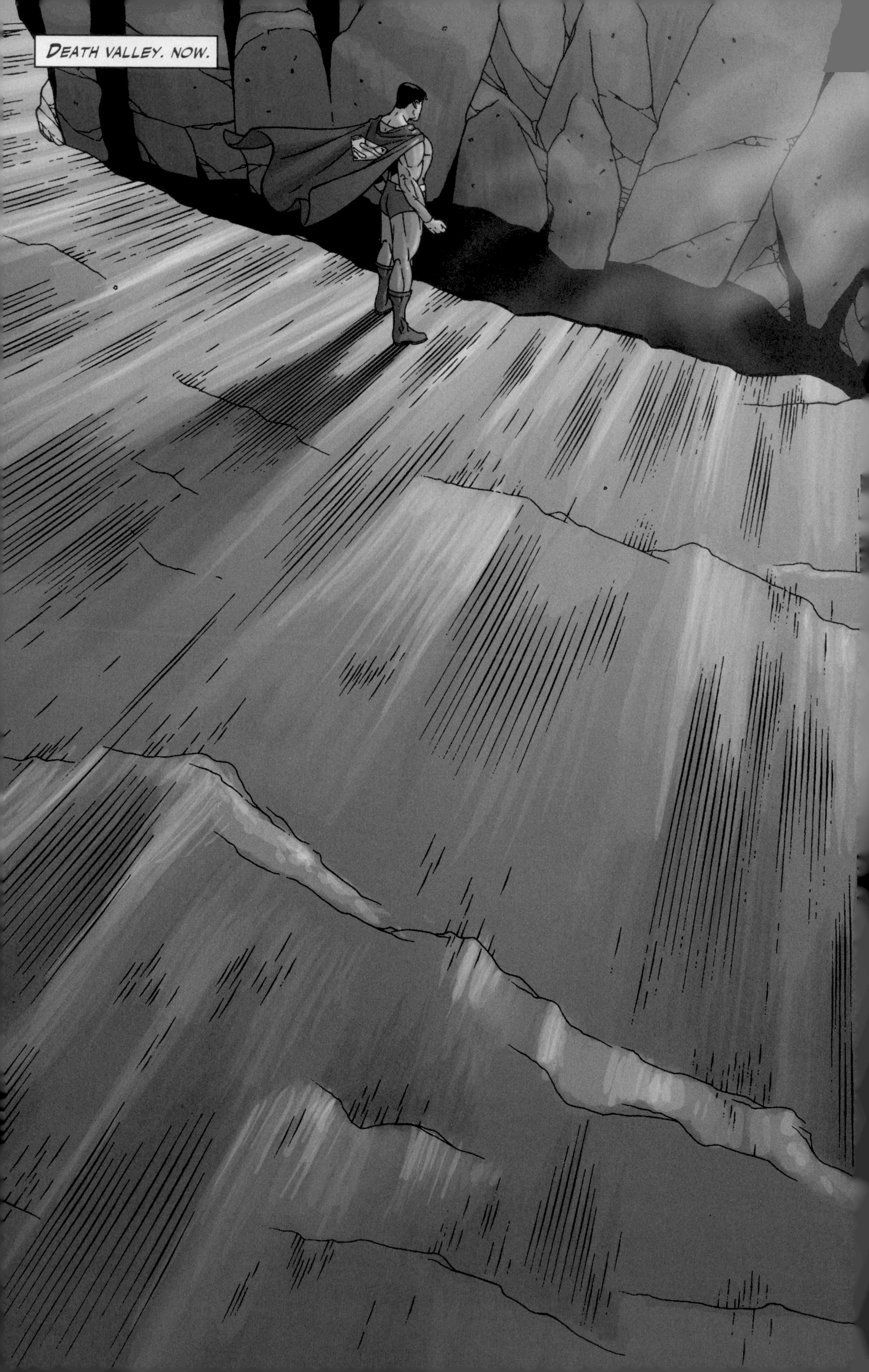
DEATH VALLEY. NOW.

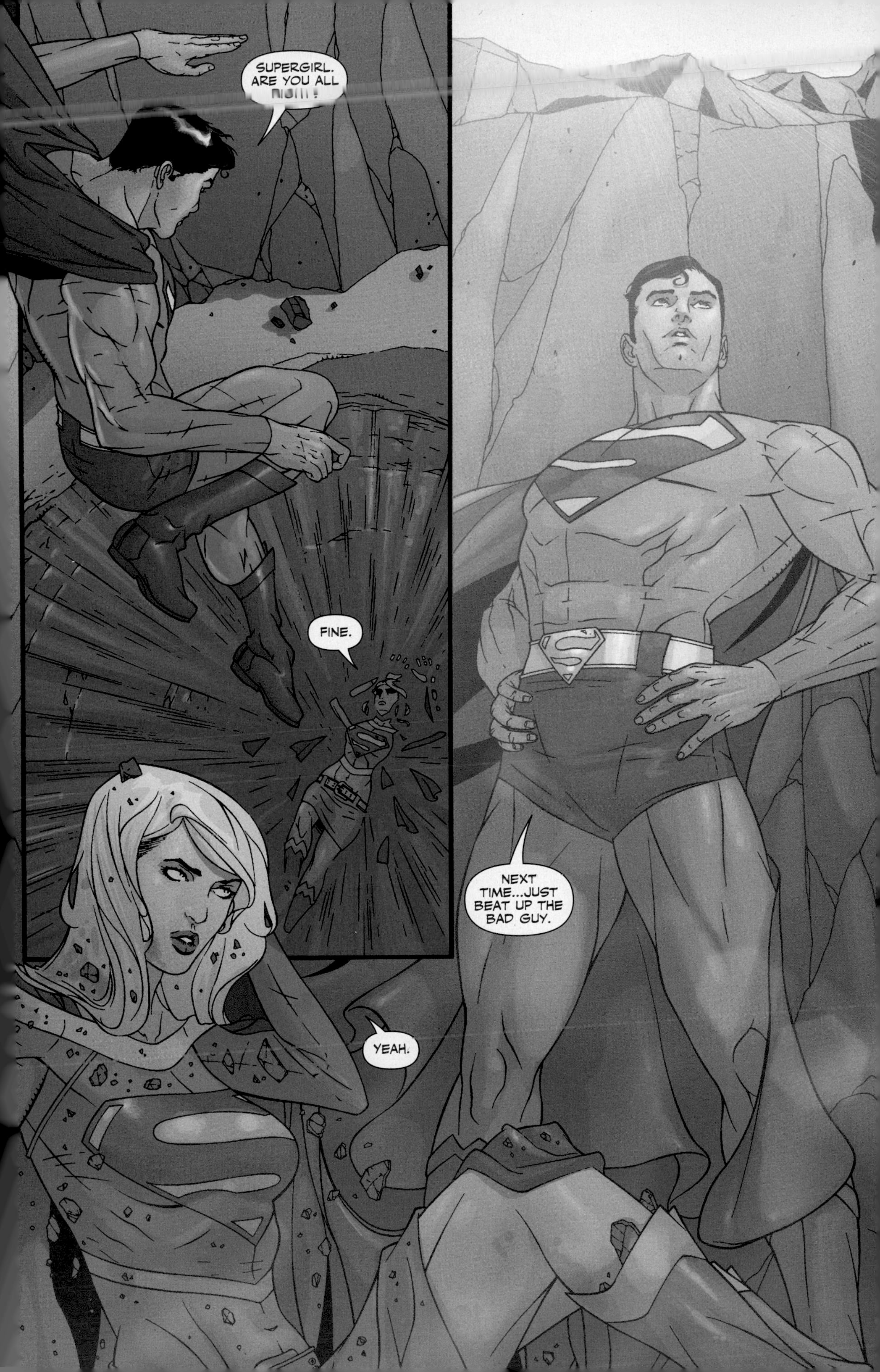
SUPERGIRL. ARE YOU ALL
FINE.
YEAH.
NEXT TIME...JUST BEAT UP THE BAD GUY.

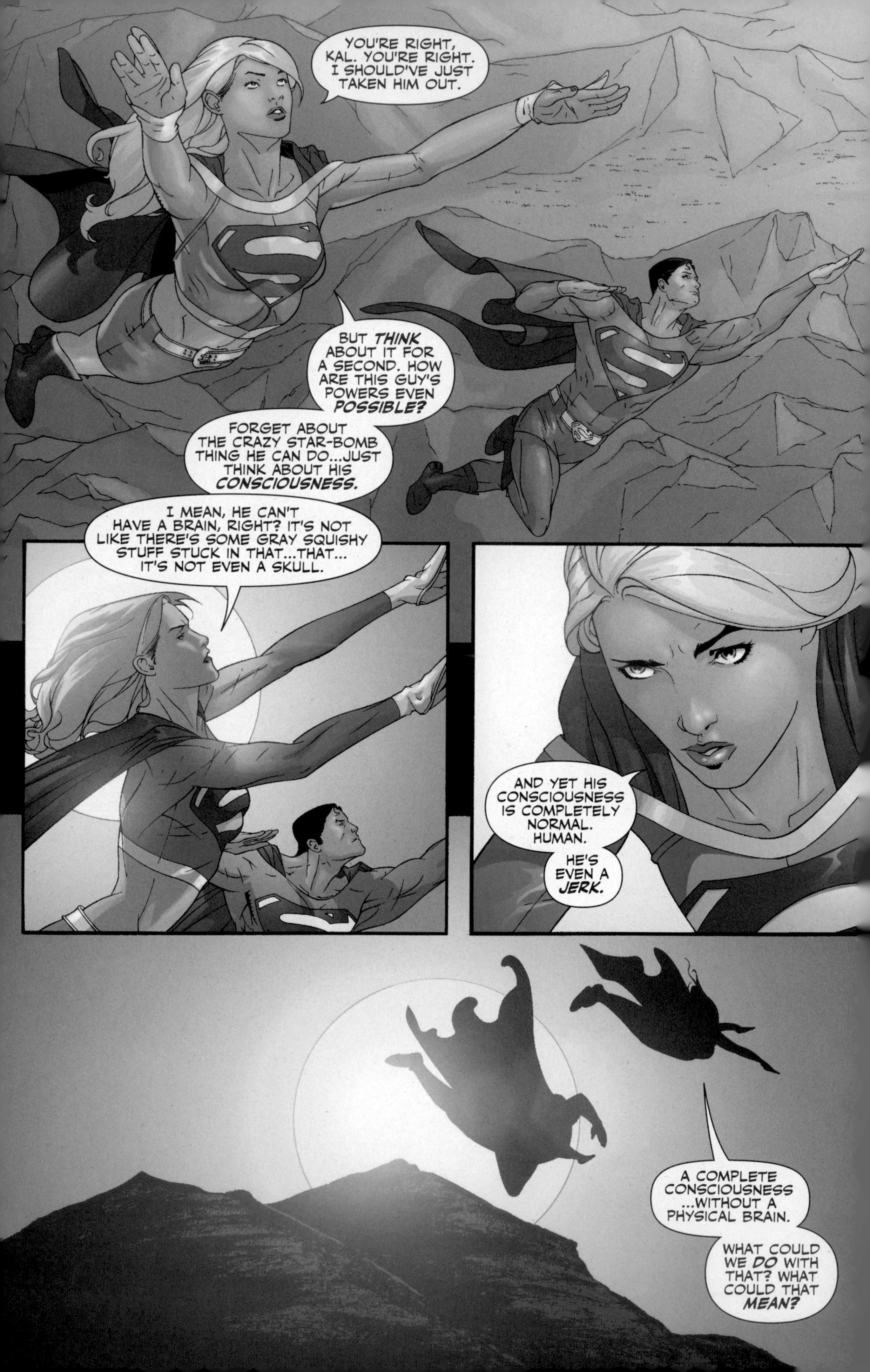
YOU'RE RIGHT, KAL. YOU'RE RIGHT. I SHOULD'VE JUST TAKEN HIM OUT.
BUT THINK ABOUT IT FOR A SECOND. HOW ARE THIS GUY'S POWERS EVEN POSSIBLE?
FORGET ABOUT THE CRAZY STAR-BOMB THING HE CAN DO...JUST THINK ABOUT HIS CONSCIOUSNESS.
I MEAN, HE CAN'T HAVE A BRAIN, RIGHT? IT'S NOT LIKE THERE'S SOME GRAY SQUISHY STUFF STUCK IN THAT...THAT... IT'S NOT EVEN A SKULL.
AND YET HIS CONSCIOUSNESS IS COMPLETELY NORMAL. HUMAN.
HE'S EVEN A JERK.
A COMPLETE CONSCIOUSNESS ...WITHOUT A PHYSICAL BRAIN.
WHAT COULD WE DO WITH THAT? WHAT COULD THAT MEAN?

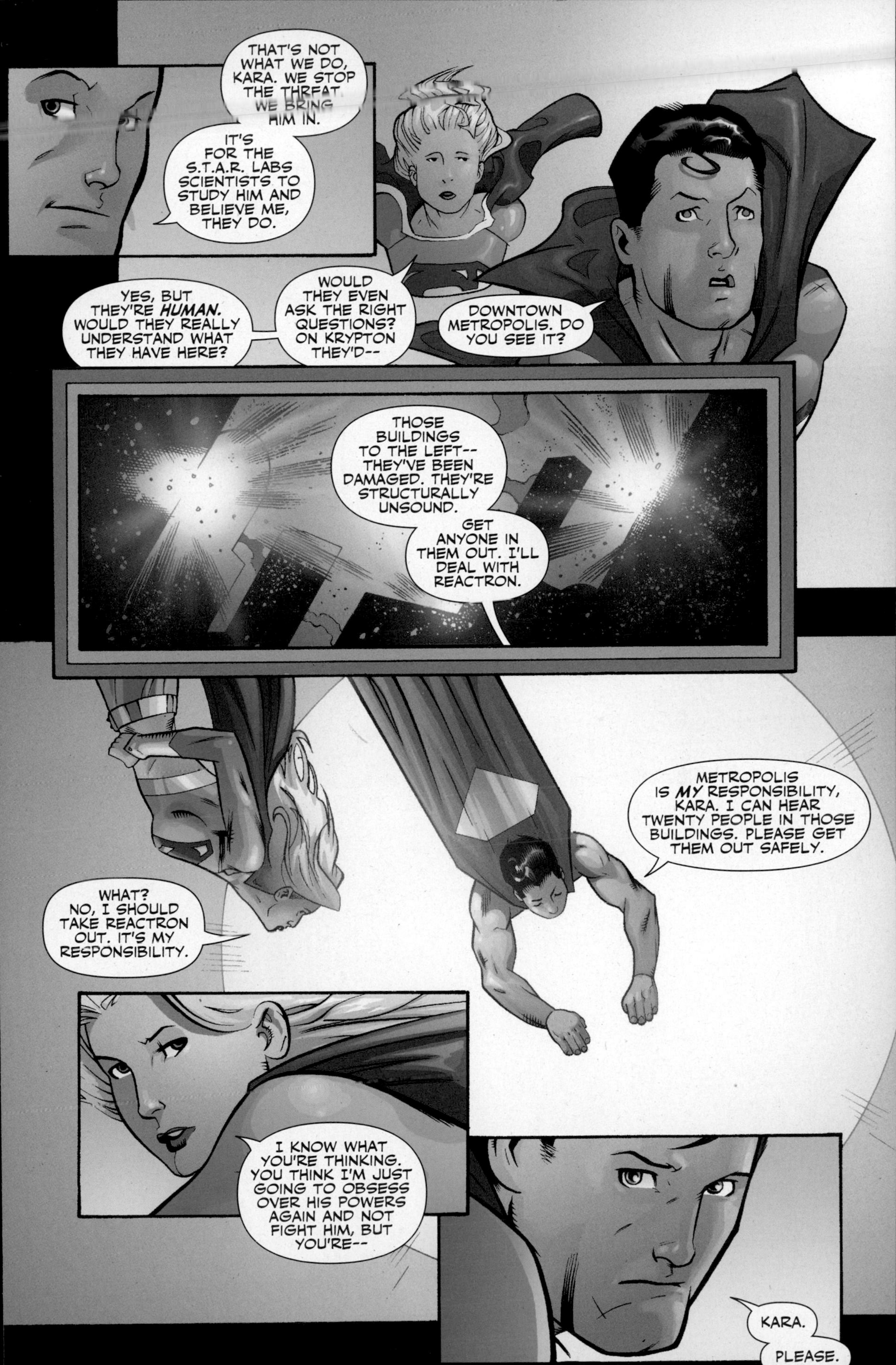

THAT'S NOT WHAT WE DO, KARA. WE STOP THE THREAT. WE BRING HIM IN.
IT'S FOR THE S.T.A.R. LABS SCIENTISTS TO STUDY HIM AND BELIEVE ME, THEY DO.
YES, BUT THEY'RE *HUMAN.* WOULD THEY REALLY UNDERSTAND WHAT THEY HAVE HERE?
WOULD THEY EVEN ASK THE RIGHT QUESTIONS? ON KRYPTON THEY'D--
DOWNTOWN METROPOLIS. DO YOU SEE IT?
THOSE BUILDINGS TO THE LEFT-- THEY'VE BEEN DAMAGED. THEY'RE STRUCTURALLY UNSOUND.
GET ANYONE IN THEM OUT. I'LL DEAL WITH REACTRON.
METROPOLIS IS *MY* RESPONSIBILITY, KARA. I CAN HEAR TWENTY PEOPLE IN THOSE BUILDINGS. PLEASE GET THEM OUT SAFELY.
WHAT? NO, I SHOULD TAKE REACTRON OUT. IT'S MY RESPONSIBILITY.
I KNOW WHAT YOU'RE THINKING. YOU THINK I'M JUST GOING TO OBSESS OVER HIS POWERS AGAIN AND NOT FIGHT HIM, BUT YOU'RE--
KARA.
PLEASE.

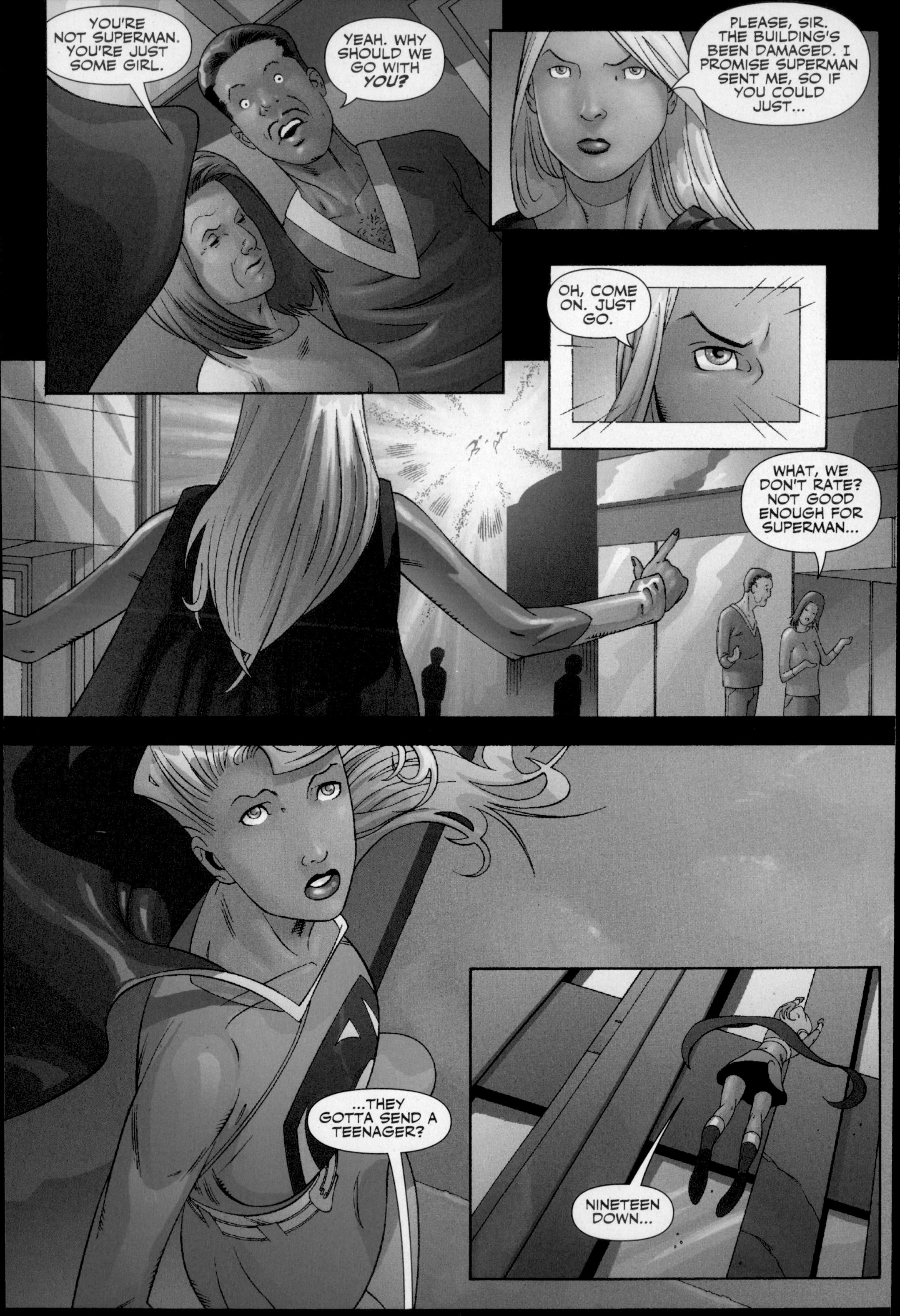
YOU'RE NOT SUPERMAN. YOU'RE JUST SOME GIRL.
YEAH. WHY SHOULD WE GO WITH *YOU?*
PLEASE, SIR. THE BUILDING'S BEEN DAMAGED. I PROMISE SUPERMAN SENT ME, SO IF YOU COULD JUST...
OH, COME ON. JUST GO.
WHAT, WE DON'T RATE? NOT GOOD ENOUGH FOR SUPERMAN...
...THEY GOTTA SEND A TEENAGER?
NINETEEN DOWN...

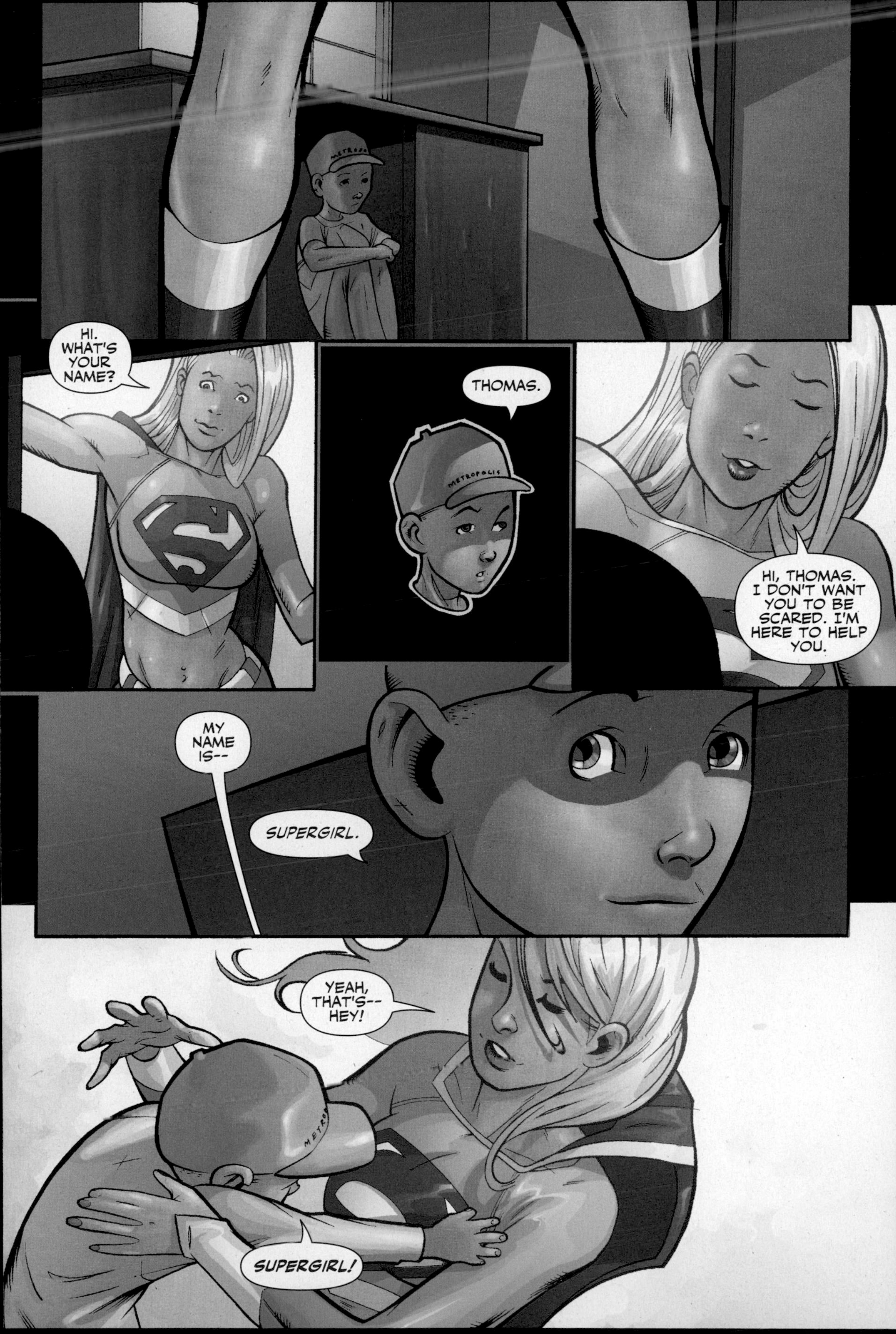
HI. WHAT'S YOUR NAME?
THOMAS.
HI, THOMAS. I DON'T WANT YOU TO BE SCARED. I'M HERE TO HELP YOU.
MY NAME IS--
SUPERGIRL.
YEAH, THAT'S-- HEY!
SUPERGIRL!

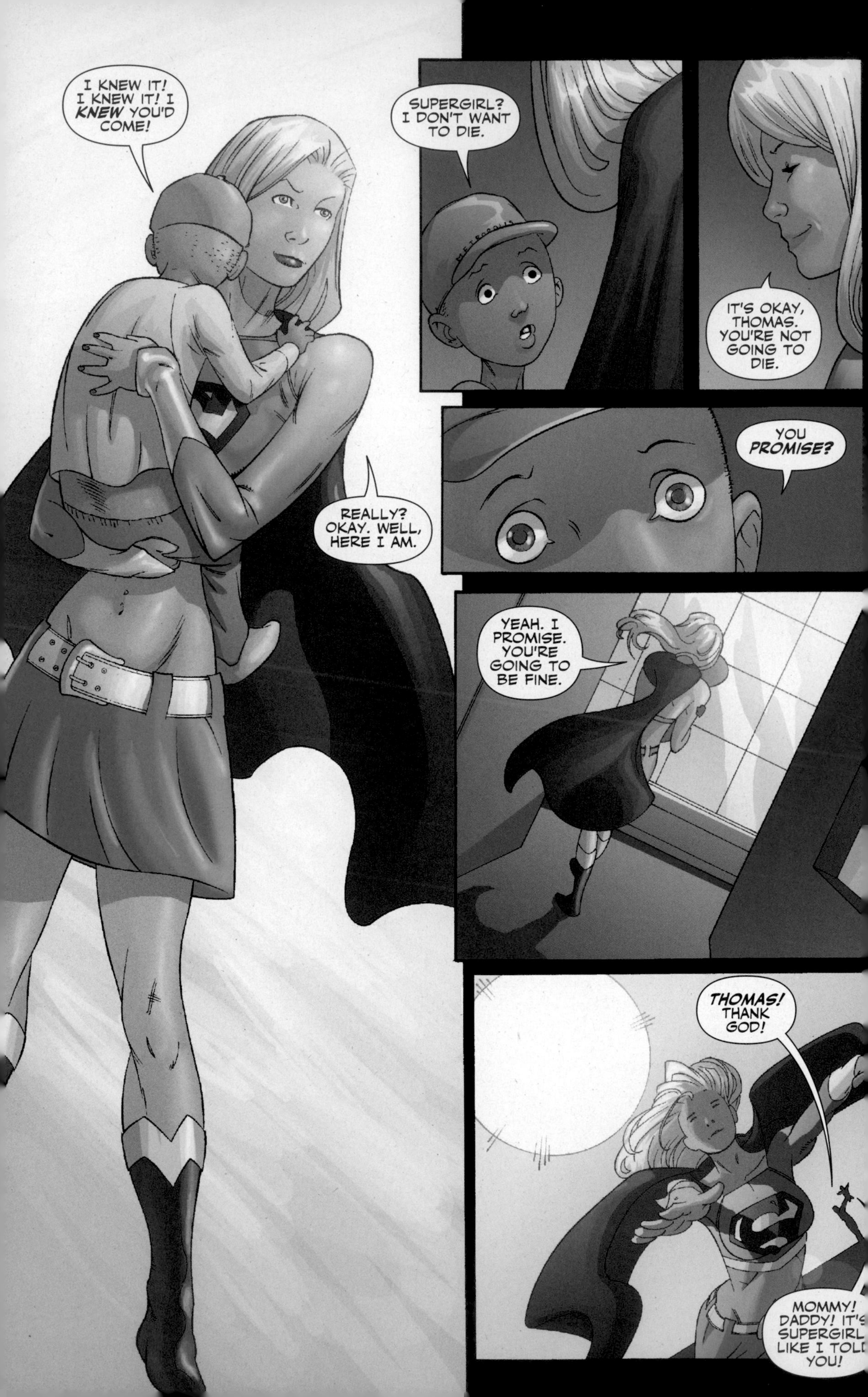
I KNEW IT! I KNEW IT! I KNEW YOU'D COME!
REALLY? OKAY. WELL, HERE I AM.
SUPERGIRL? I DON'T WANT TO DIE.
IT'S OKAY, THOMAS. YOU'RE NOT GOING TO DIE.
YOU PROMISE?
YEAH. I PROMISE. YOU'RE GOING TO BE FINE.
THOMAS! THANK GOD!
MOMMY! DADDY! IT'S SUPERGIRL LIKE I TOLD YOU!

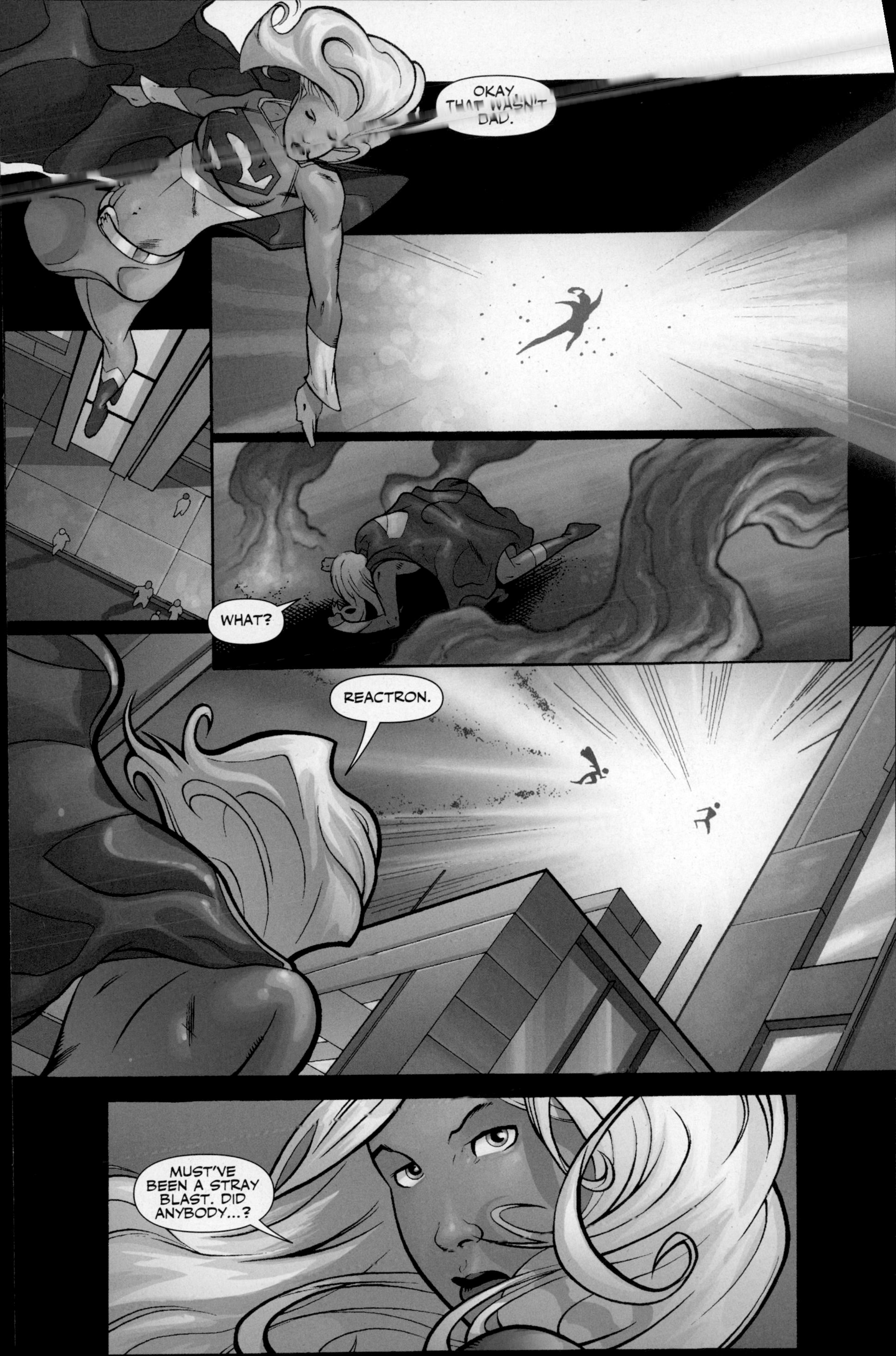

OKAY, THAT WASN'T DAD.
WHAT?
REACTRON.
MUST'VE BEEN A STRAY BLAST. DID ANYBODY...?

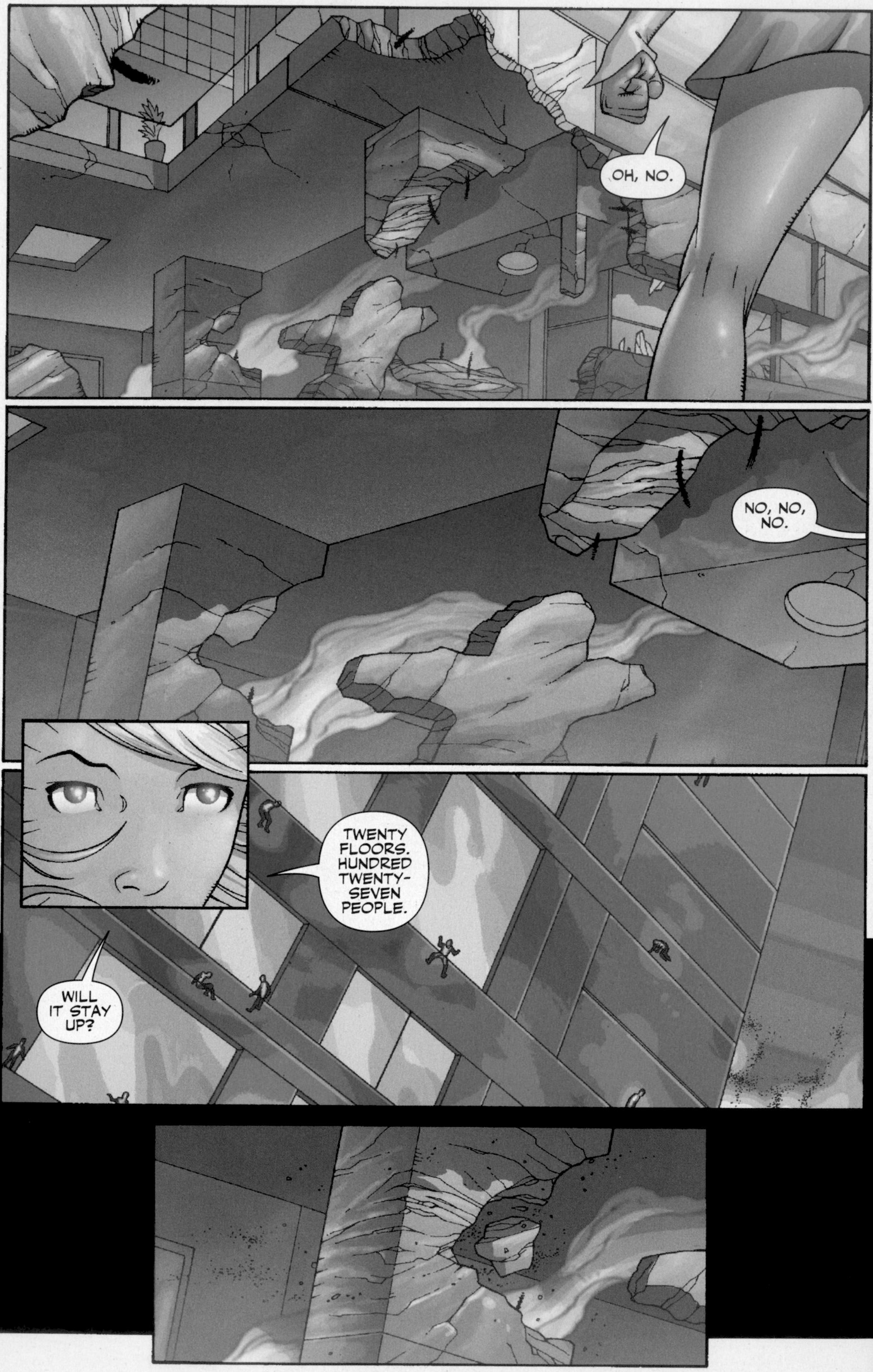
OH, NO.
NO, NO, NO.
TWENTY FLOORS. HUNDRED TWENTY-SEVEN PEOPLE.
WILL IT STAY UP?

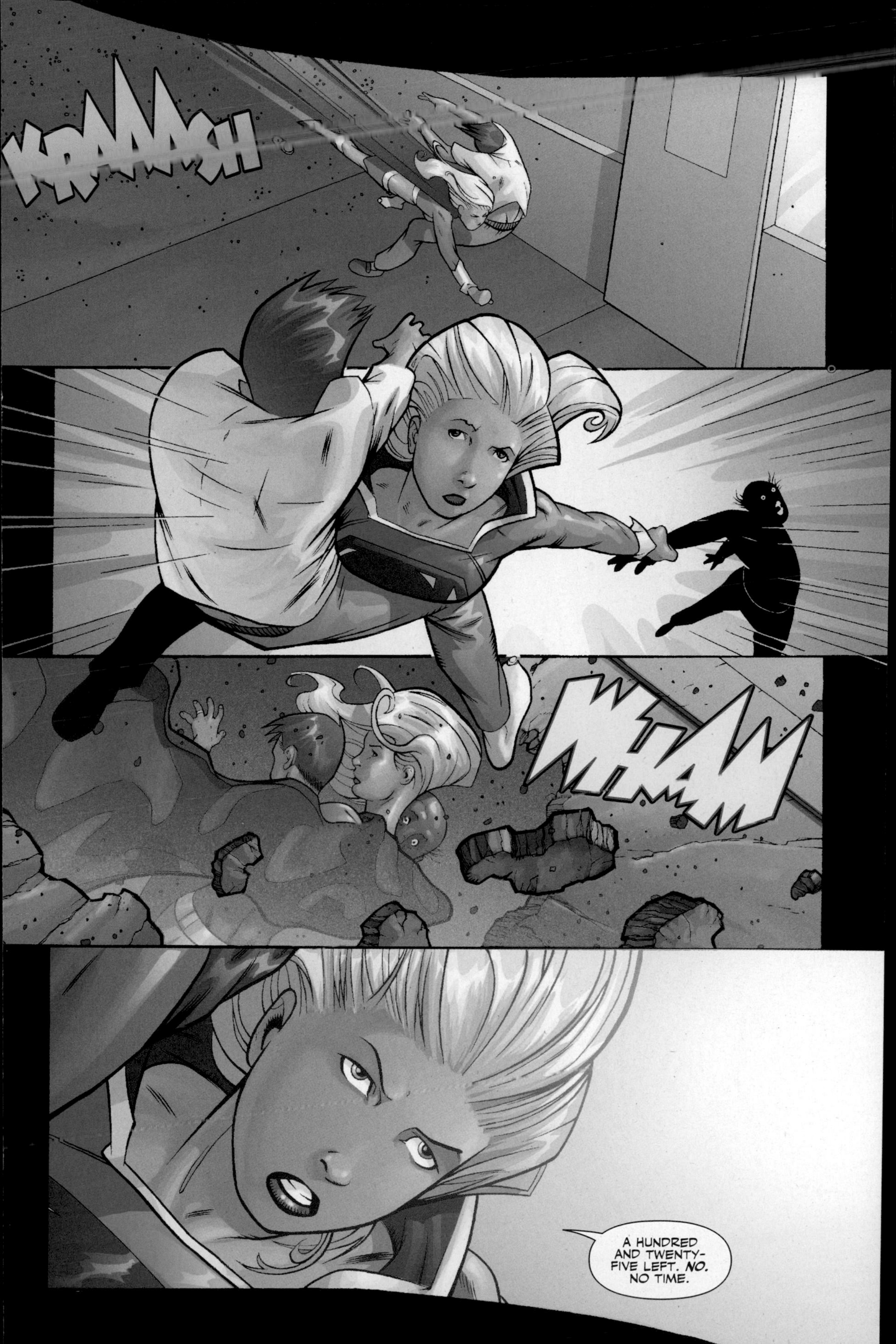
KRAAASH
WHAM
A HUNDRED AND TWENTY-FIVE LEFT. NO. NO TIME.

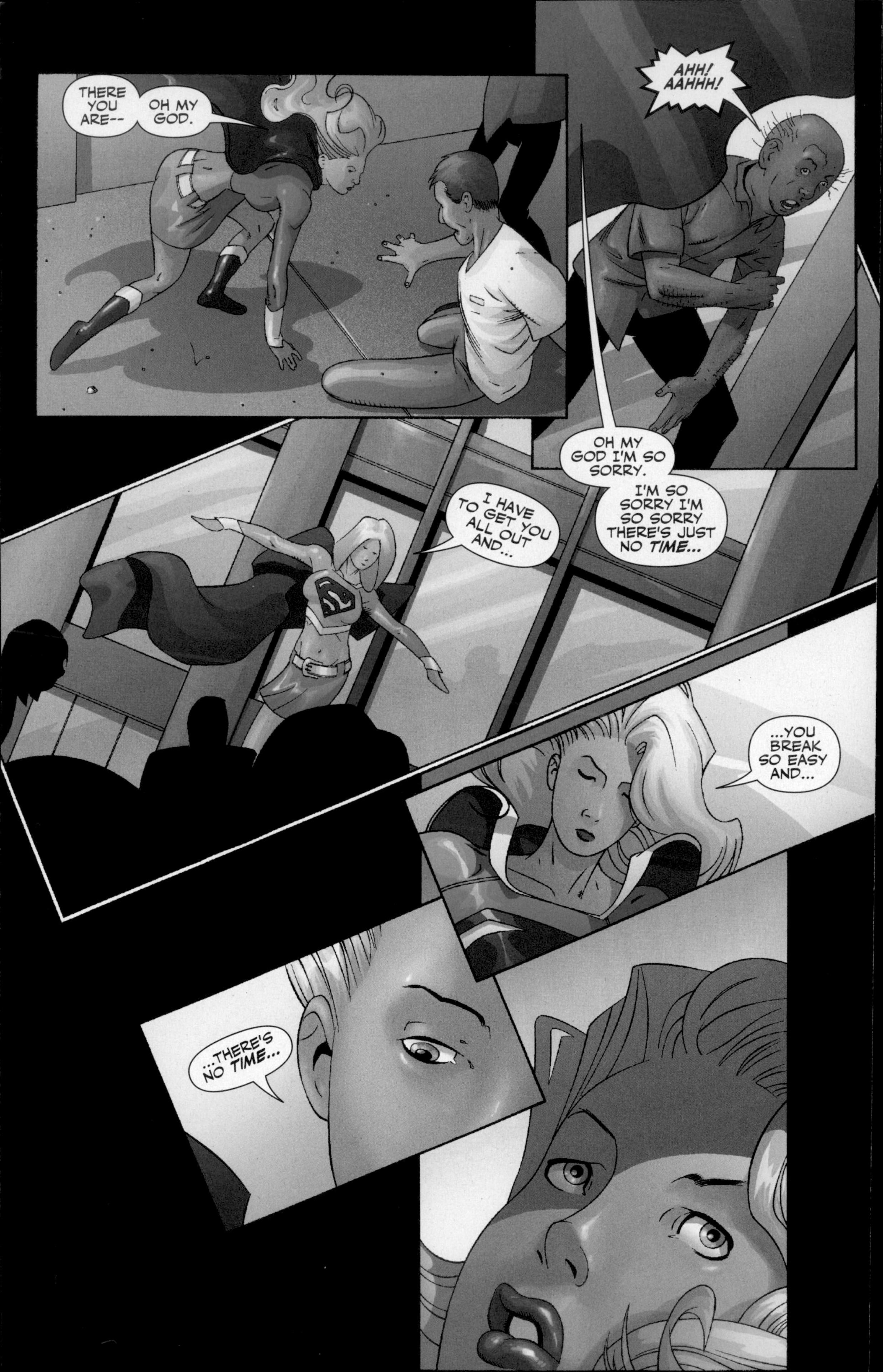
THERE YOU ARE--
OH MY GOD.
AHH! AAHHH!
OH MY GOD I'M SO SORRY.
I'M SO SORRY I'M SO SORRY THERE'S JUST NO *TIME*...
I HAVE TO GET YOU ALL OUT AND...
...YOU BREAK SO EASY AND...
...THERE'S NO *TIME*...

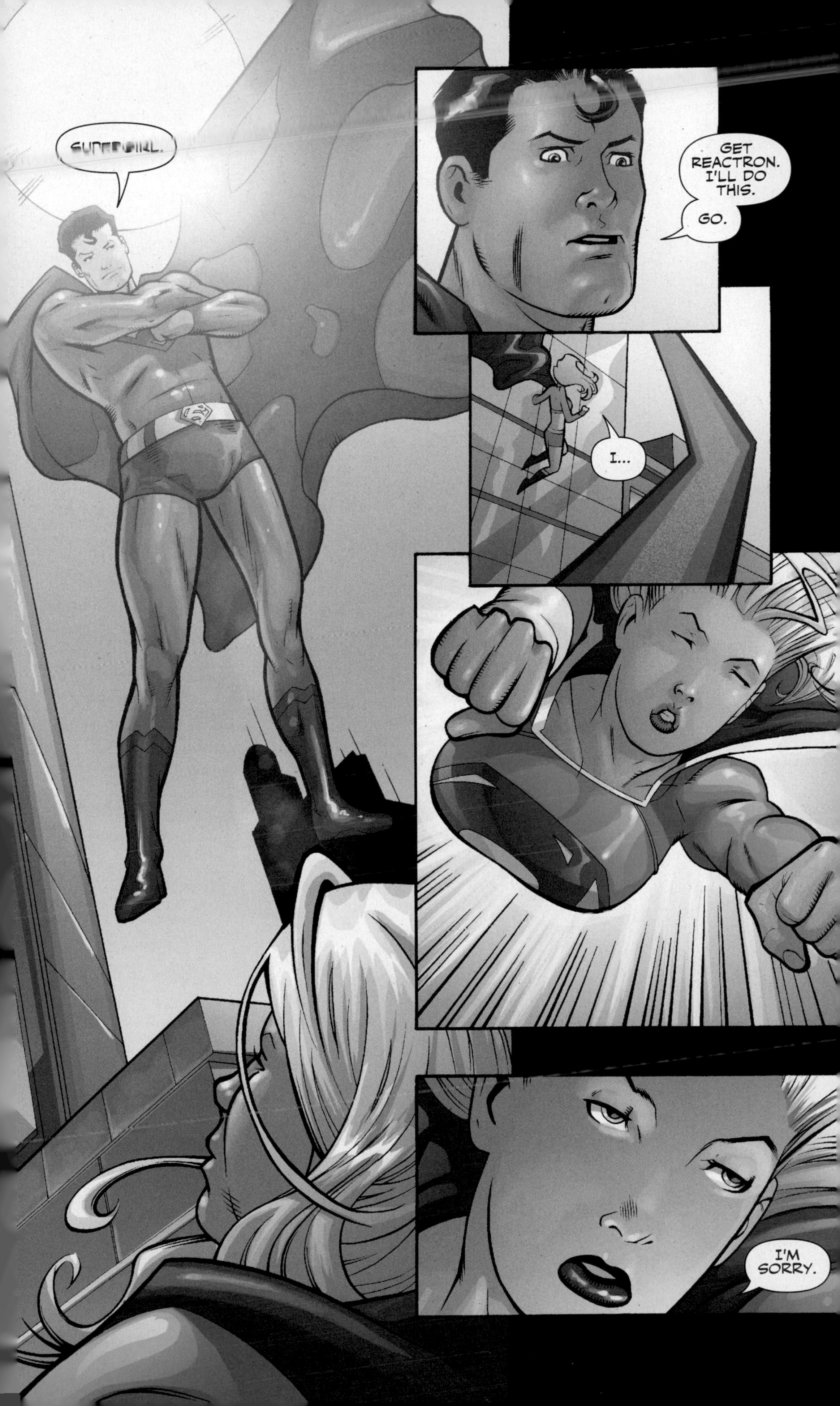
SUPERGIRL.
GET REACTRON. I'LL DO THIS.
GO.
I...
I'M SORRY.

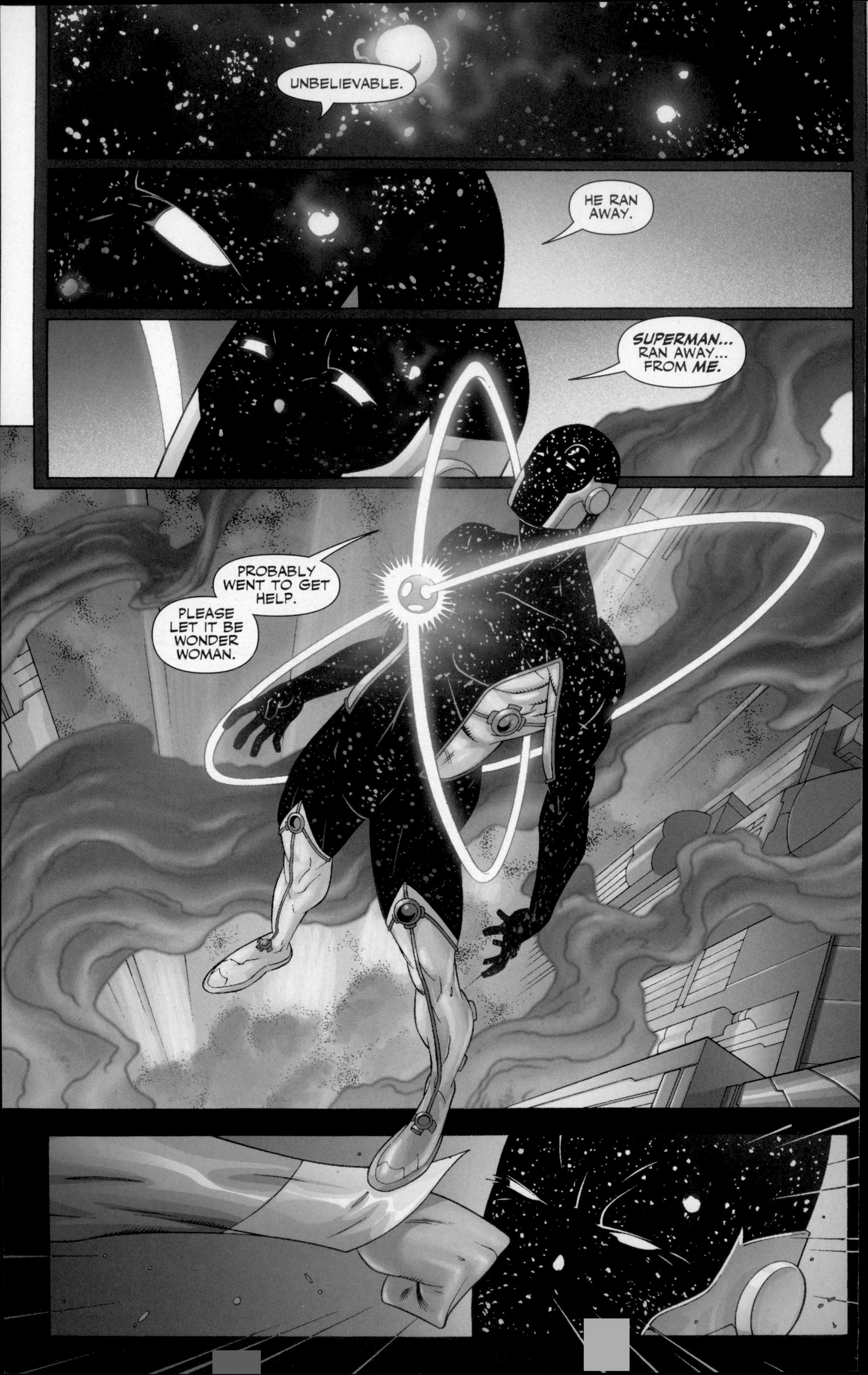
UNBELIEVABLE.
HE RAN AWAY.
SUPERMAN... RAN AWAY... FROM ME.
PROBABLY WENT TO GET HELP.
PLEASE LET IT BE WONDER WOMAN.

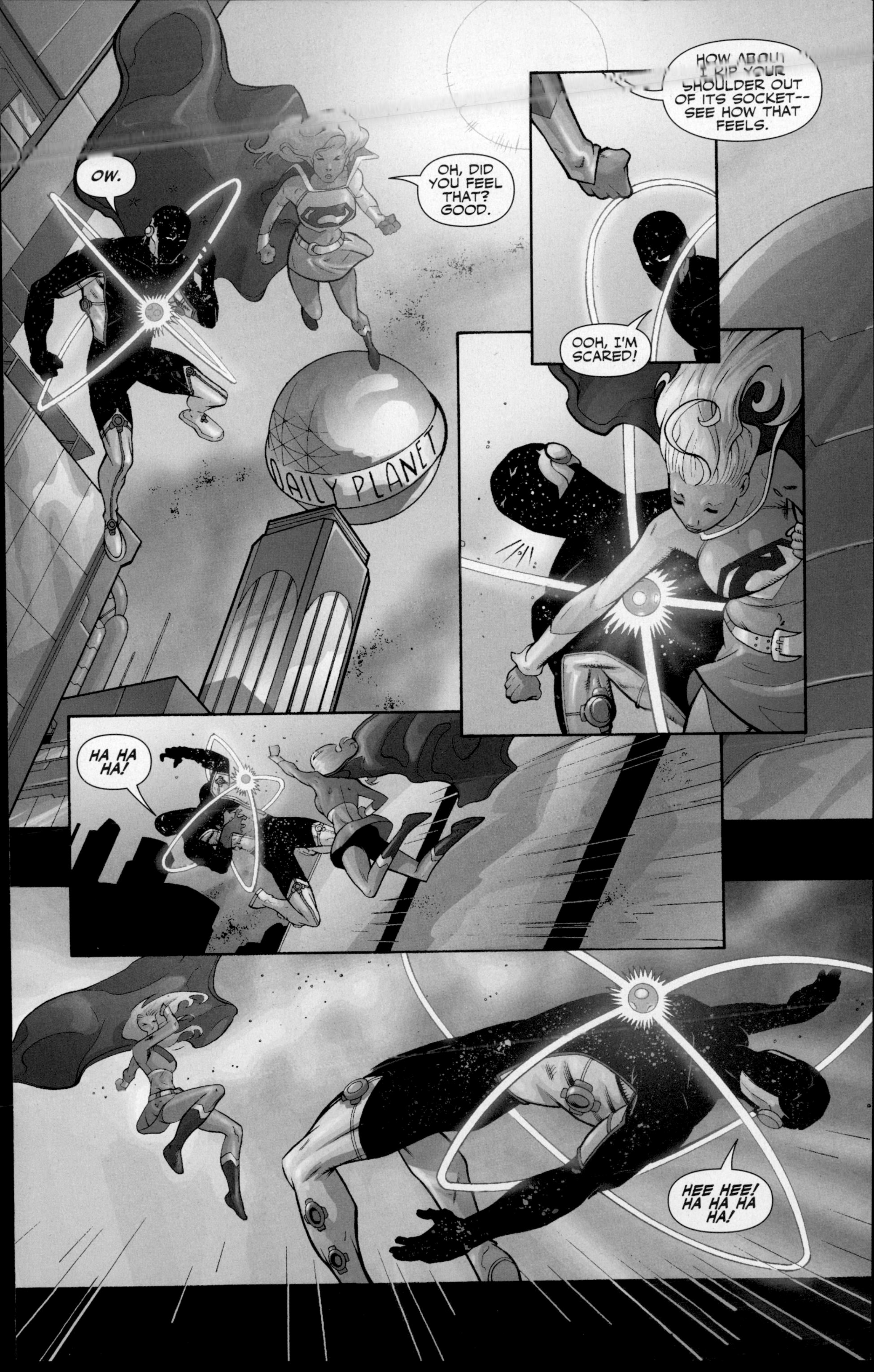
OW.
OH, DID YOU FEEL THAT? GOOD.
HOW ABOUT I RIP YOUR SHOULDER OUT OF ITS SOCKET-- SEE HOW THAT FEELS.
OOH, I'M SCARED!
DAILY PLANET
HA HA HA!
HEE HEE! HA HA HA HA!

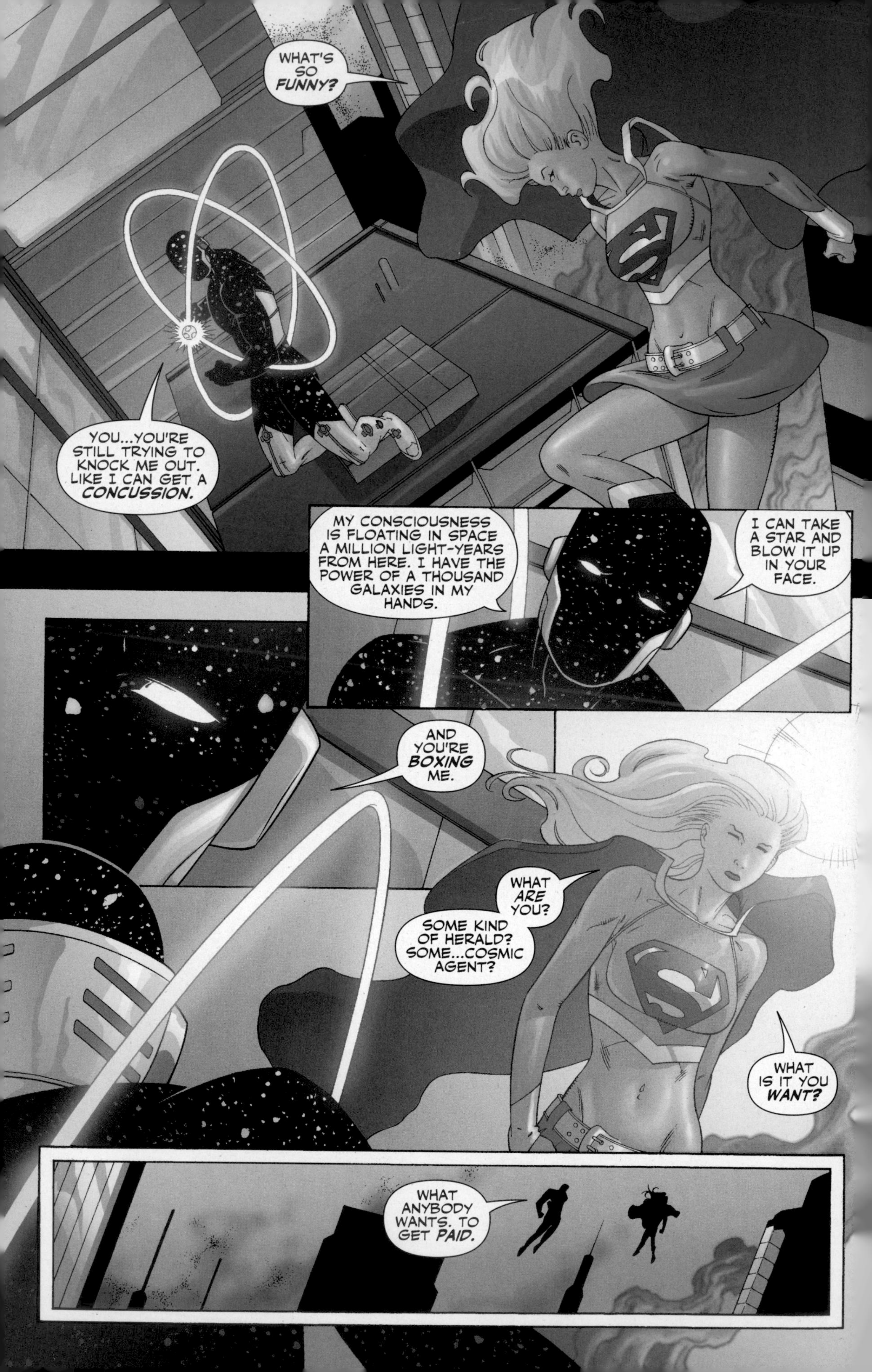
WHAT'S SO FUNNY?
YOU...YOU'RE STILL TRYING TO KNOCK ME OUT. LIKE I CAN GET A CONCUSSION.
MY CONSCIOUSNESS IS FLOATING IN SPACE A MILLION LIGHT-YEARS FROM HERE. I HAVE THE POWER OF A THOUSAND GALAXIES IN MY HANDS.
I CAN TAKE A STAR AND BLOW IT UP IN YOUR FACE.
AND YOU'RE BOXING ME.
WHAT ARE YOU?
SOME KIND OF HERALD? SOME...COSMIC AGENT?
WHAT IS IT YOU WANT?
WHAT ANYBODY WANTS. TO GET PAID.

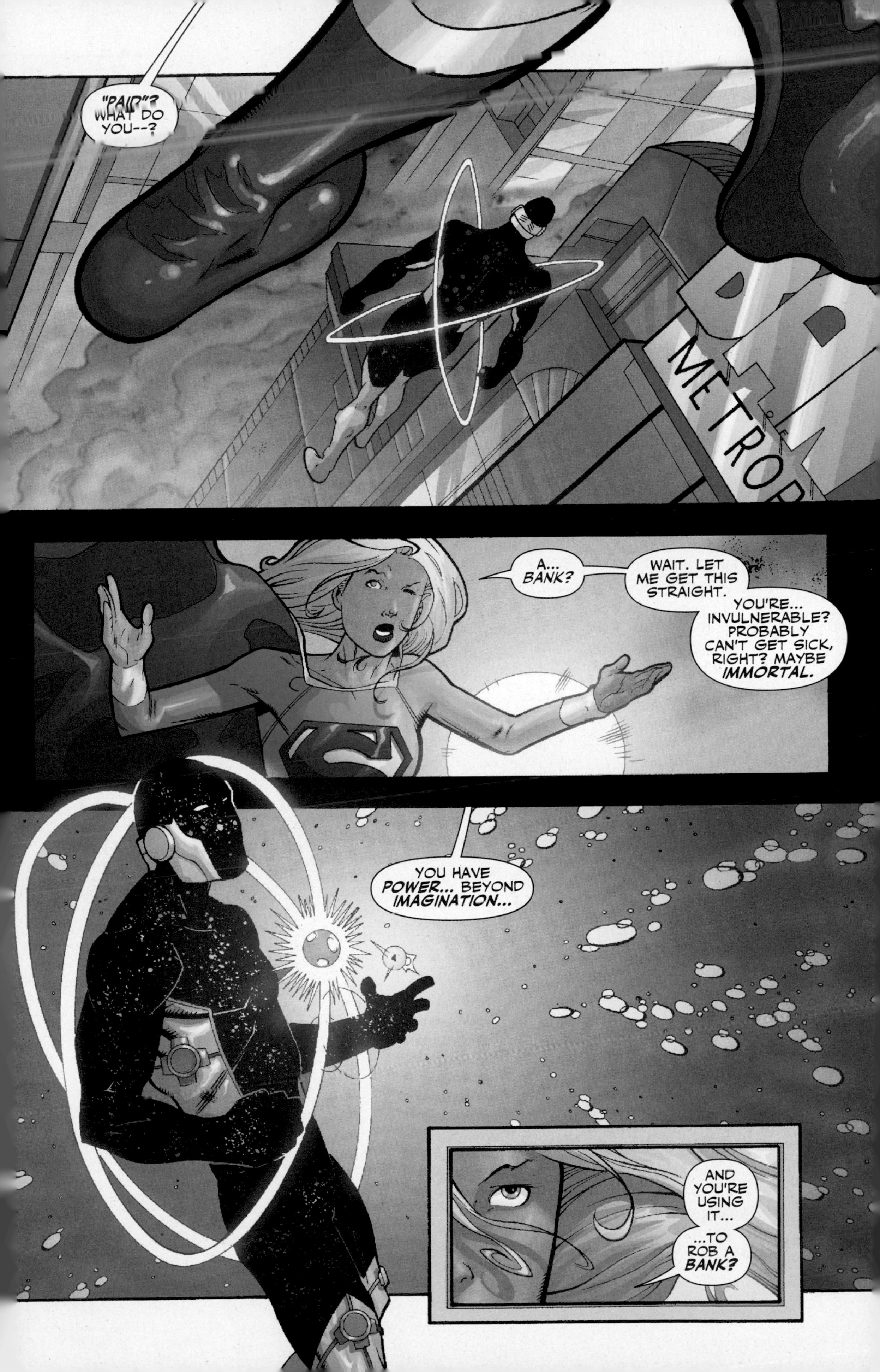

"PAIR"? WHAT DO YOU--?
METRO
A... BANK?
WAIT. LET ME GET THIS STRAIGHT.
YOU'RE... INVULNERABLE? PROBABLY CAN'T GET SICK, RIGHT? MAYBE IMMORTAL.
YOU HAVE POWER... BEYOND IMAGINATION...
AND YOU'RE USING IT...
...TO ROB A BANK?

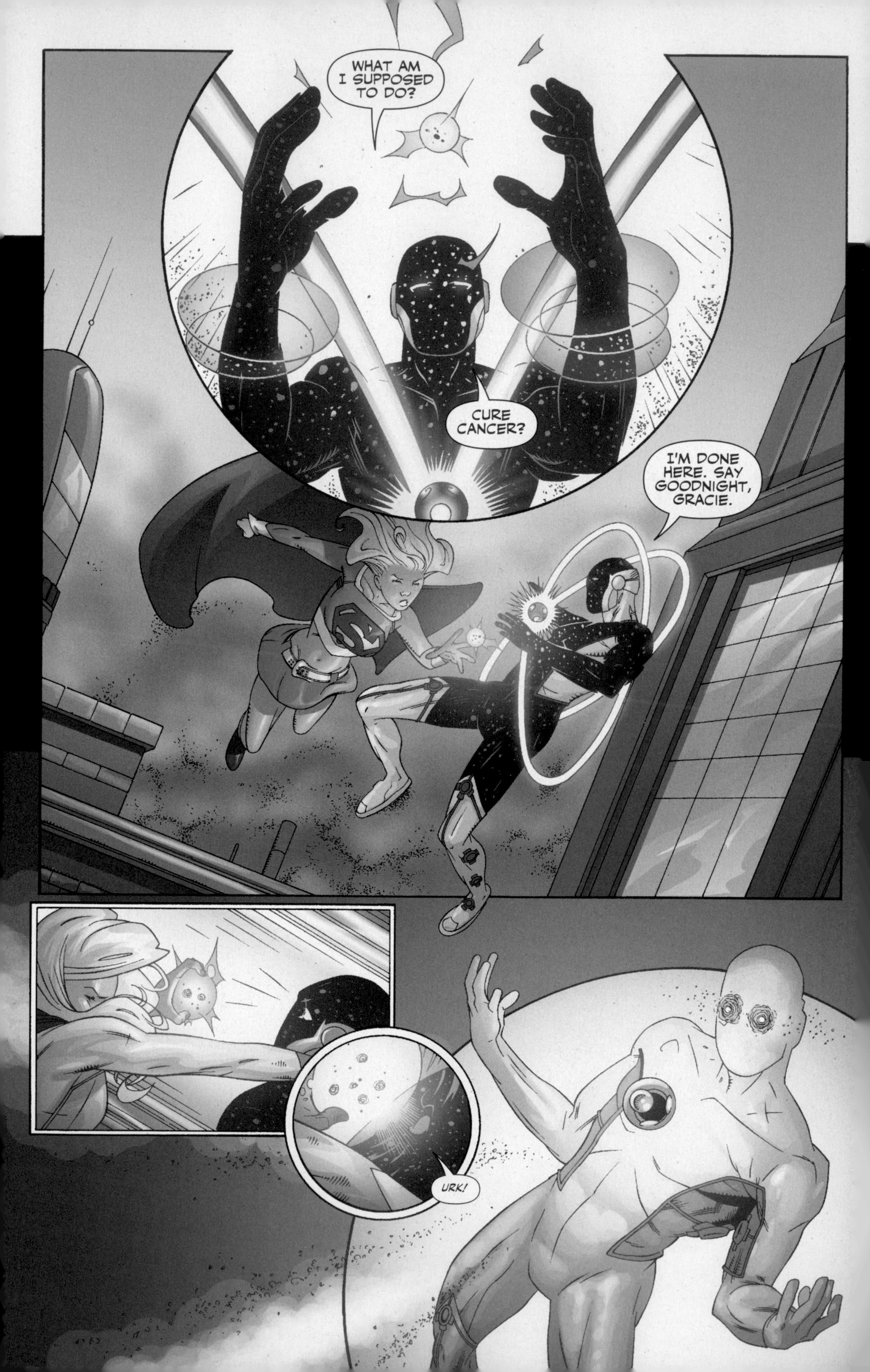
WHAT AM I SUPPOSED TO DO?
CURE CANCER?
I'M DONE HERE. SAY GOODNIGHT, GRACIE.
URK!

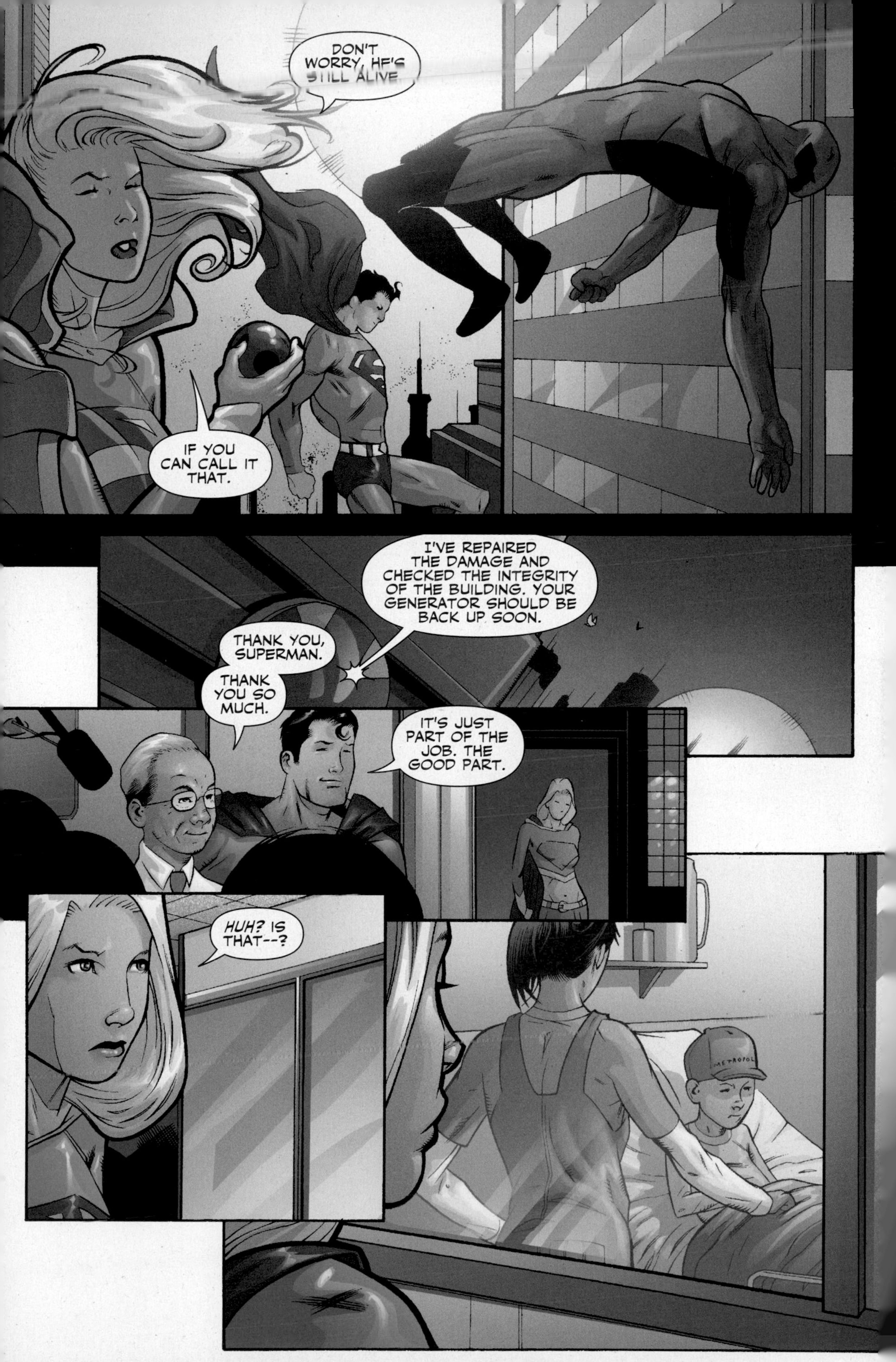
DON'T WORRY, HE'S STILL ALIVE
IF YOU CAN CALL IT THAT.
I'VE REPAIRED THE DAMAGE AND CHECKED THE INTEGRITY OF THE BUILDING. YOUR GENERATOR SHOULD BE BACK UP SOON.
THANK YOU, SUPERMAN.
THANK YOU SO MUCH.
IT'S JUST PART OF THE JOB. THE GOOD PART.
HUH? IS THAT--?

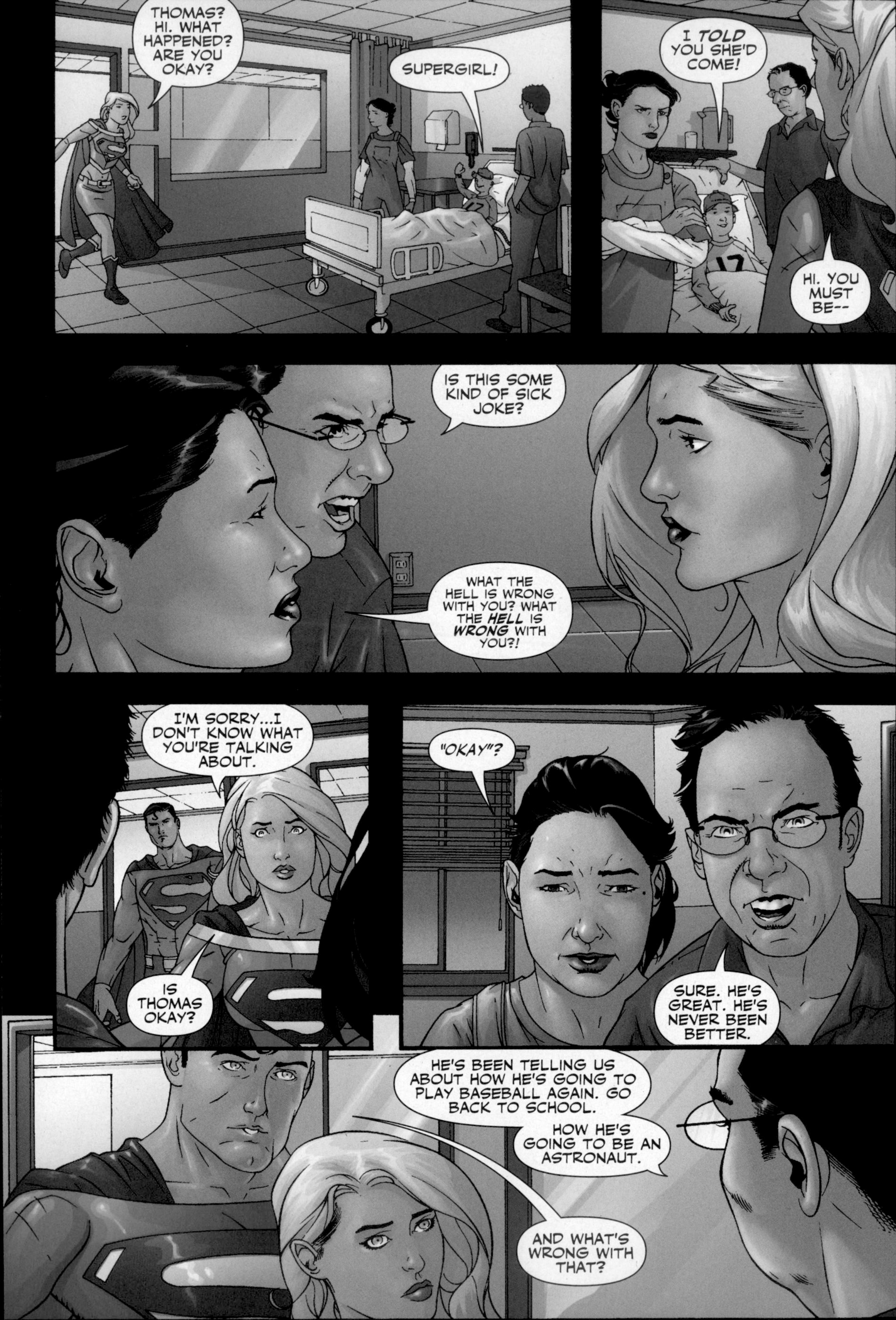
THOMAS? HI. WHAT HAPPENED? ARE YOU OKAY?
SUPERGIRL!
I TOLD YOU SHE'D COME!
HI. YOU MUST BE--
IS THIS SOME KIND OF SICK JOKE?
WHAT THE HELL IS WRONG WITH YOU? WHAT THE HELL IS WRONG WITH YOU?!
I'M SORRY...I DON'T KNOW WHAT YOU'RE TALKING ABOUT.
IS THOMAS OKAY?
"OKAY"?
SURE. HE'S GREAT. HE'S NEVER BEEN BETTER.
HE'S BEEN TELLING US ABOUT HOW HE'S GOING TO PLAY BASEBALL AGAIN. GO BACK TO SCHOOL.
HOW HE'S GOING TO BE AN ASTRONAUT.
AND WHAT'S WRONG WITH THAT?

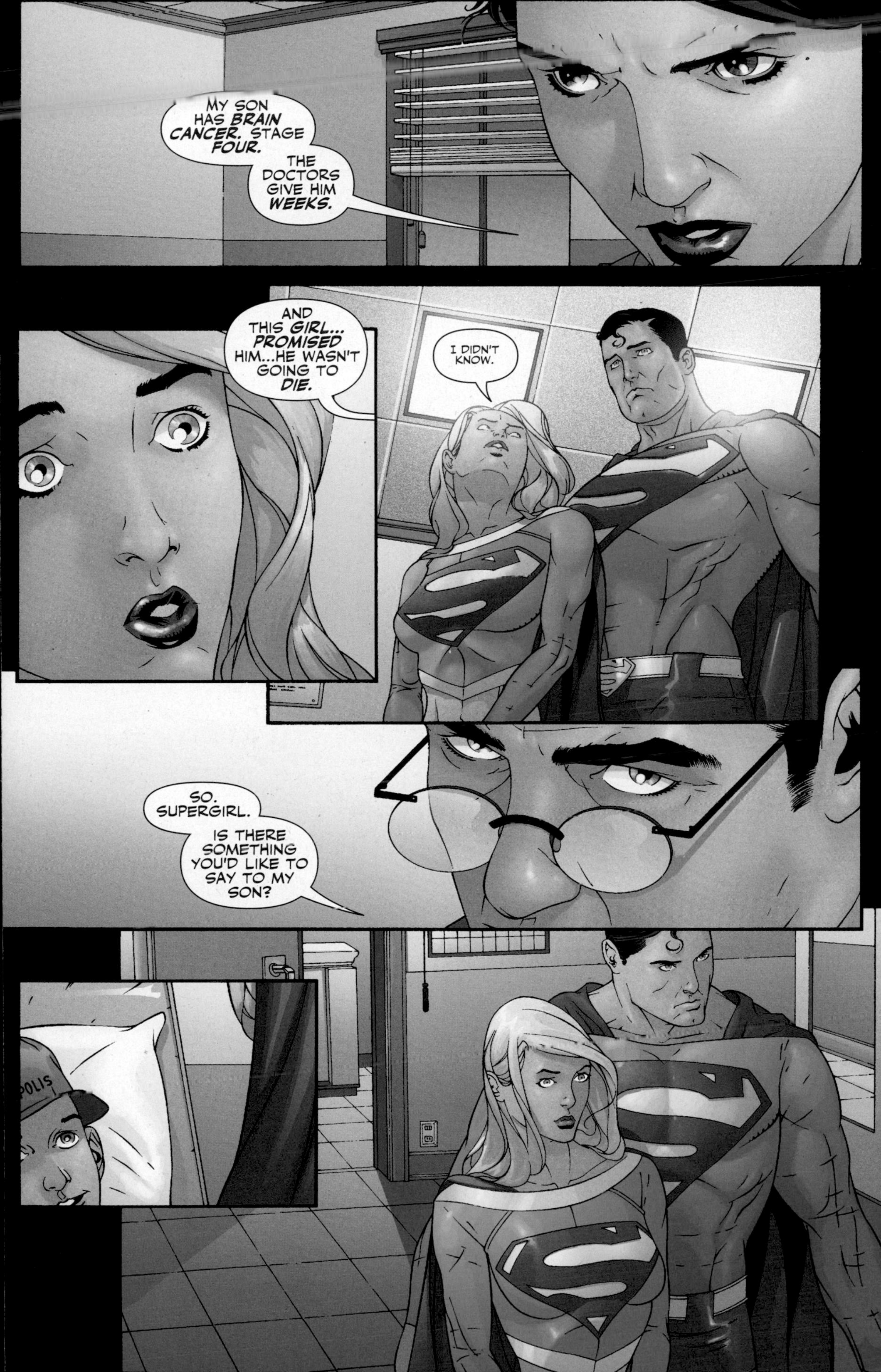

MY SON HAS BRAIN CANCER. STAGE FOUR.
THE DOCTORS GIVE HIM WEEKS.
AND THIS GIRL... PROMISED HIM...HE WASN'T GOING TO DIE.
I DIDN'T KNOW.
SO. SUPERGIRL.
IS THERE SOMETHING YOU'D LIKE TO SAY TO MY SON?
POLIS

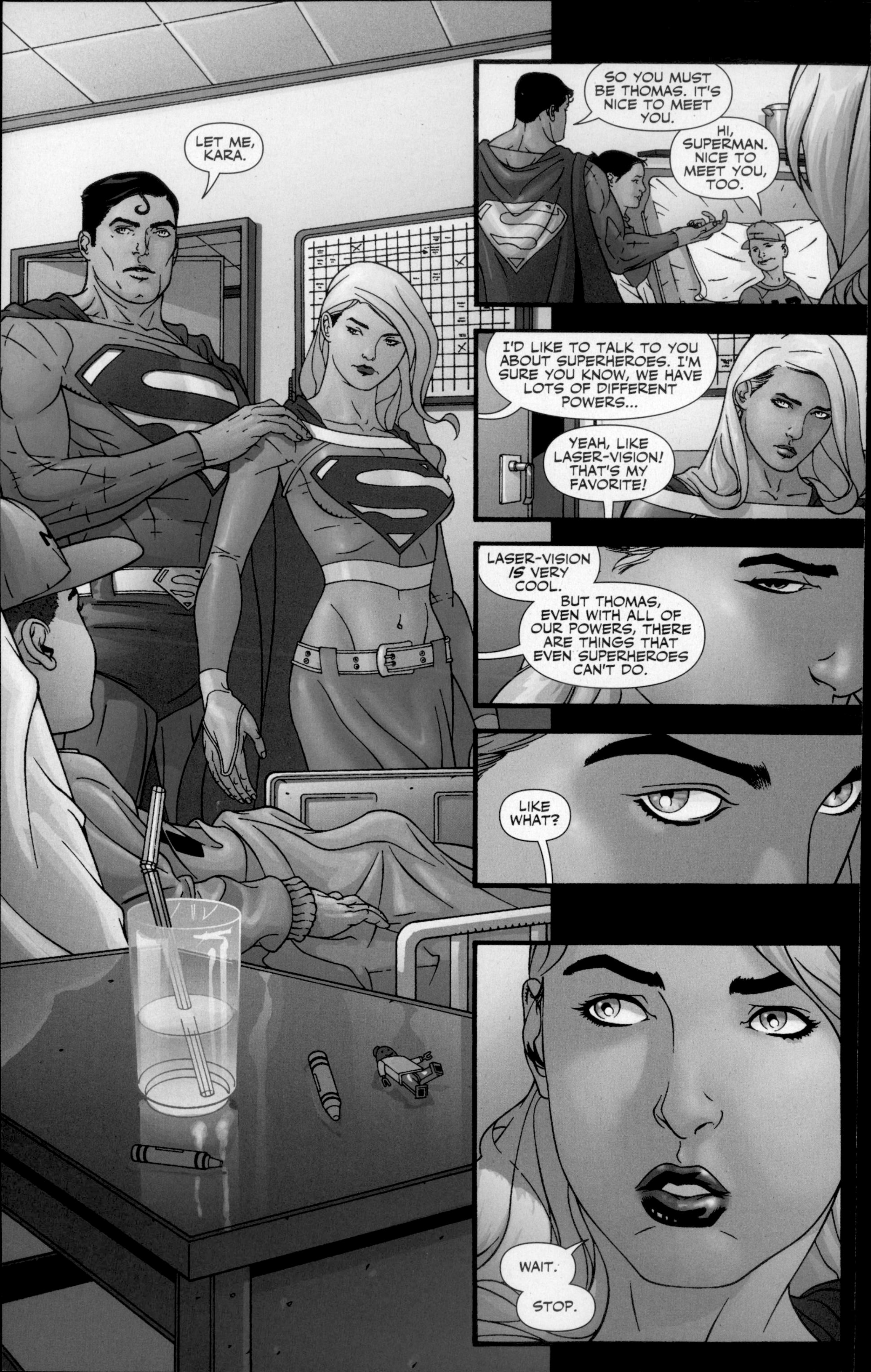
LET ME, KARA.
SO YOU MUST BE THOMAS. IT'S NICE TO MEET YOU.
HI, SUPERMAN. NICE TO MEET YOU, TOO.
I'D LIKE TO TALK TO YOU ABOUT SUPERHEROES. I'M SURE YOU KNOW, WE HAVE LOTS OF DIFFERENT POWERS...
YEAH, LIKE LASER-VISION! THAT'S MY FAVORITE!
LASER-VISION *IS* VERY COOL.
BUT THOMAS, EVEN WITH ALL OF OUR POWERS, THERE ARE THINGS THAT EVEN SUPERHEROES CAN'T DO.
LIKE WHAT?
WAIT.
STOP.

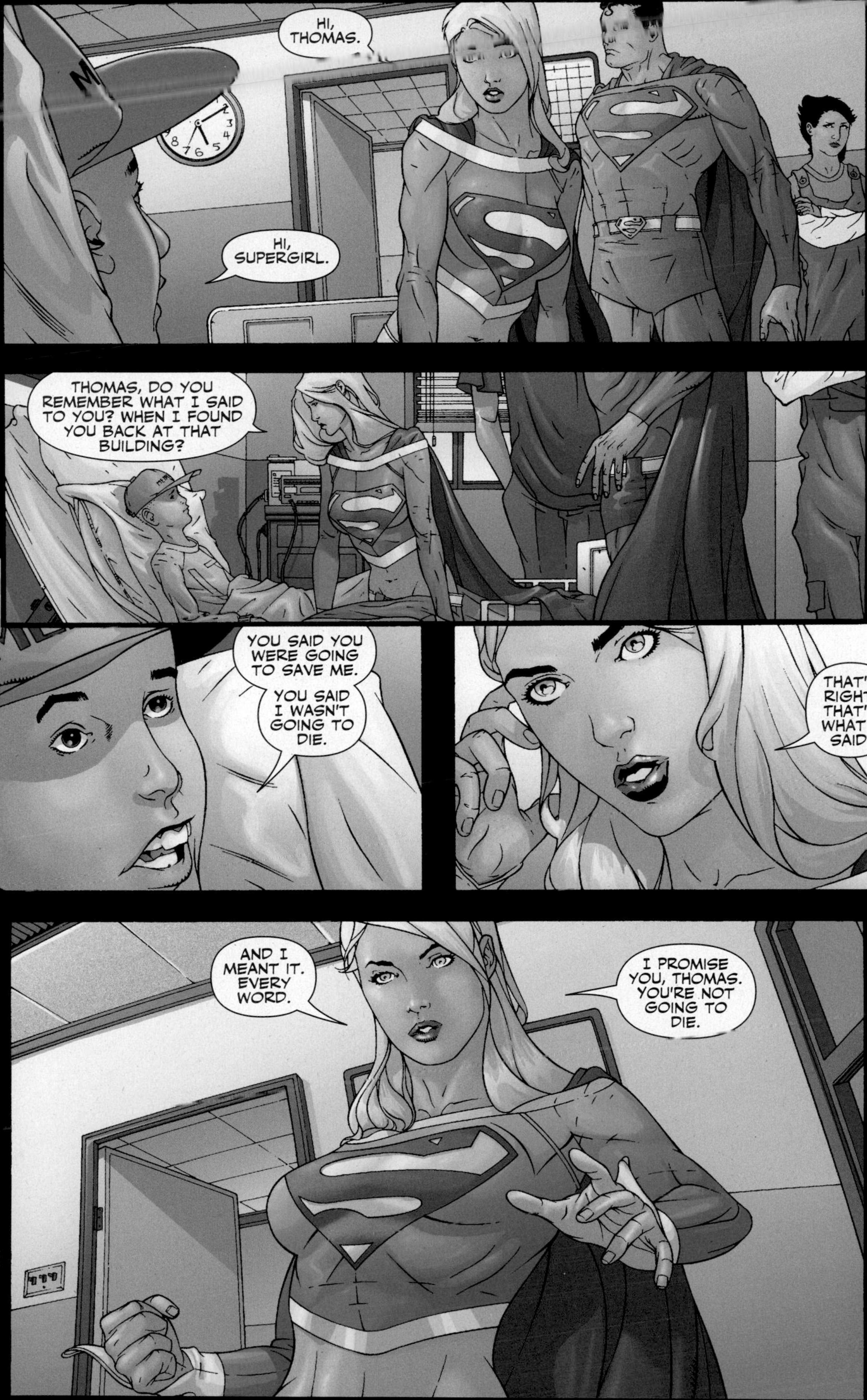
HI, THOMAS.
HI, SUPERGIRL.
THOMAS, DO YOU REMEMBER WHAT I SAID TO YOU? WHEN I FOUND YOU BACK AT THAT BUILDING?
YOU SAID YOU WERE GOING TO SAVE ME.
YOU SAID I WASN'T GOING TO DIE.
THAT'S RIGHT. THAT'S WHAT I SAID.
AND I MEANT IT. EVERY WORD.
I PROMISE YOU, THOMAS. YOU'RE NOT GOING TO DIE.

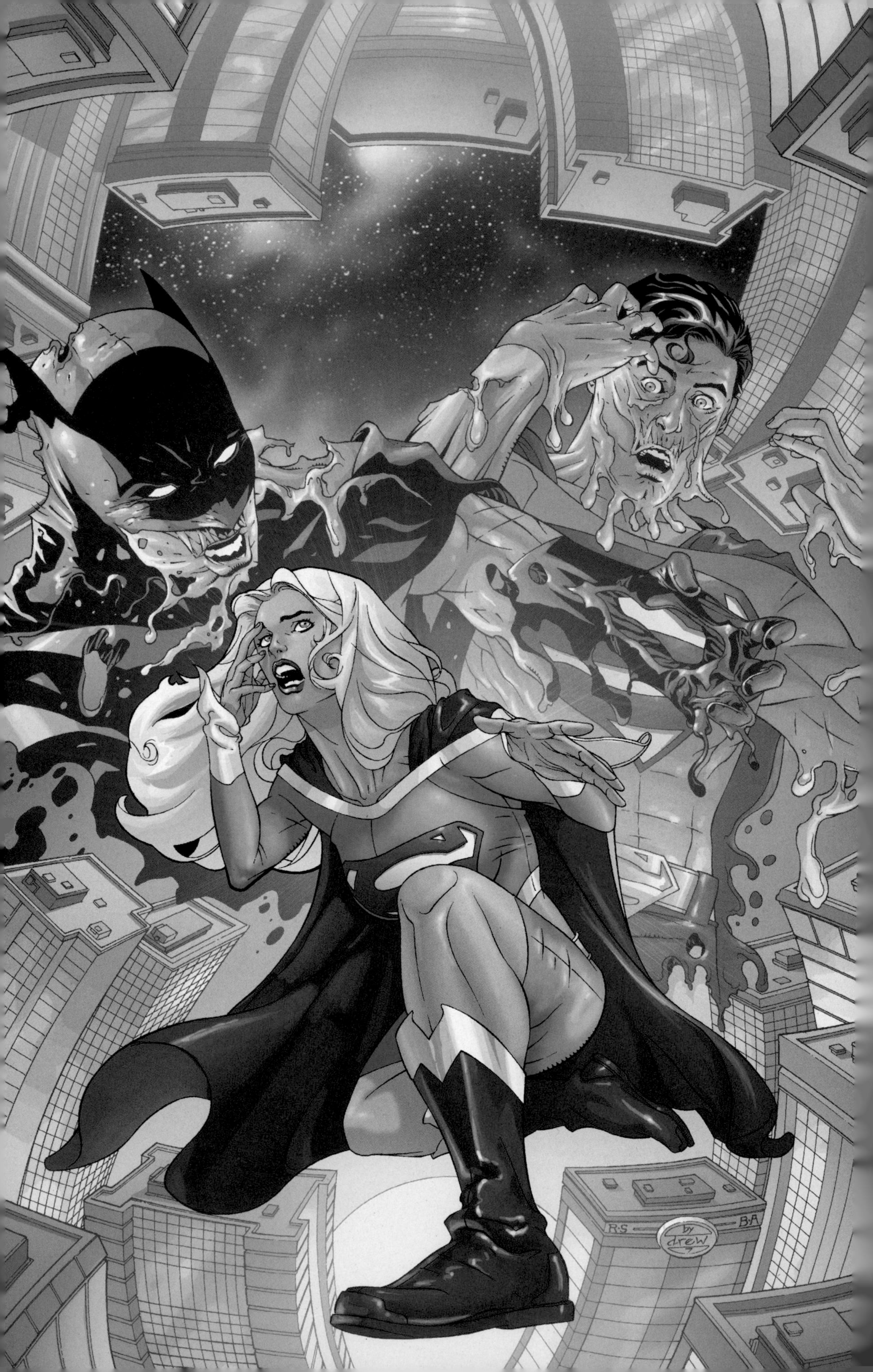

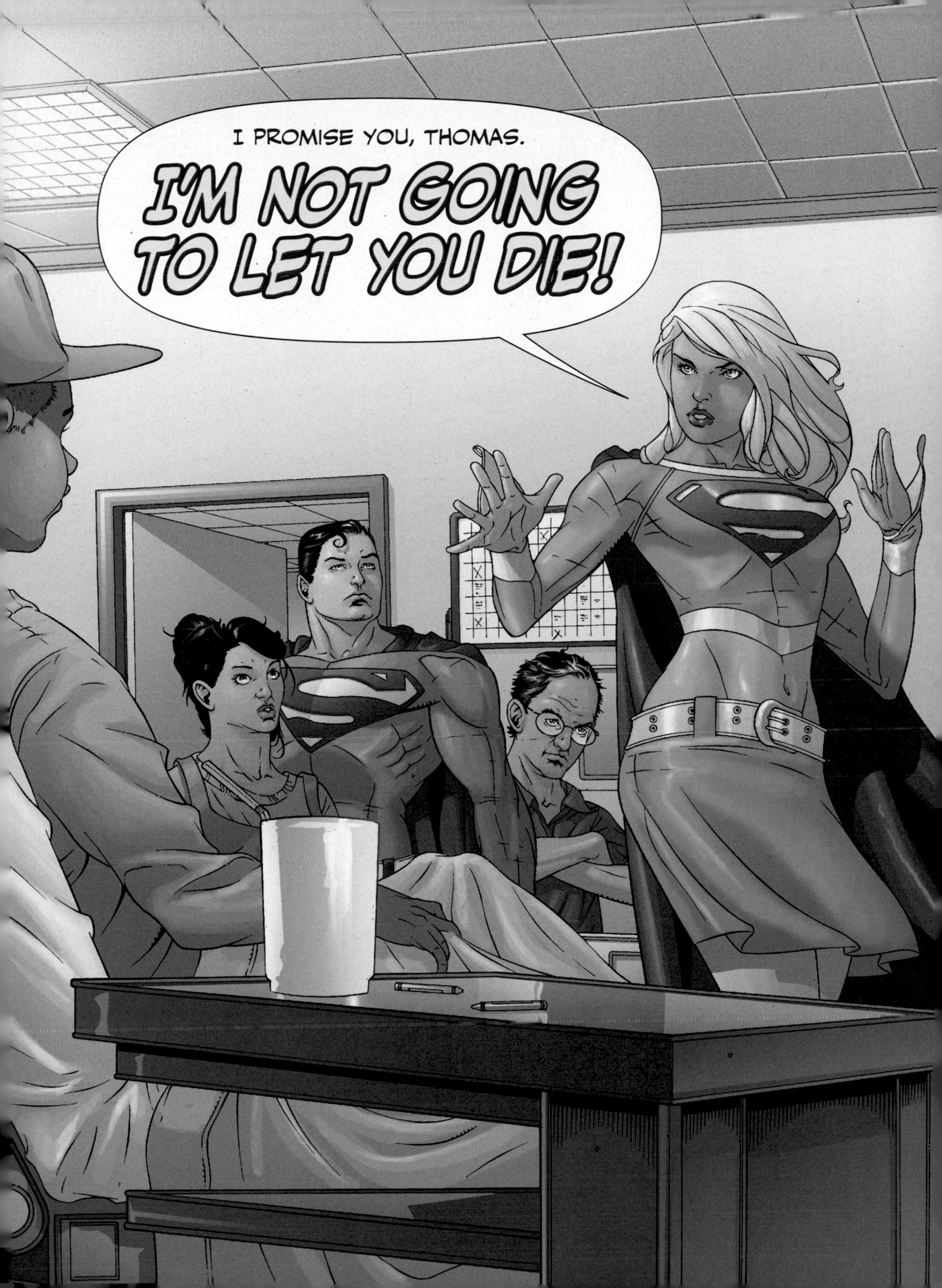
I PROMISE YOU, THOMAS.
I'M NOT GOING TO LET YOU DIE!

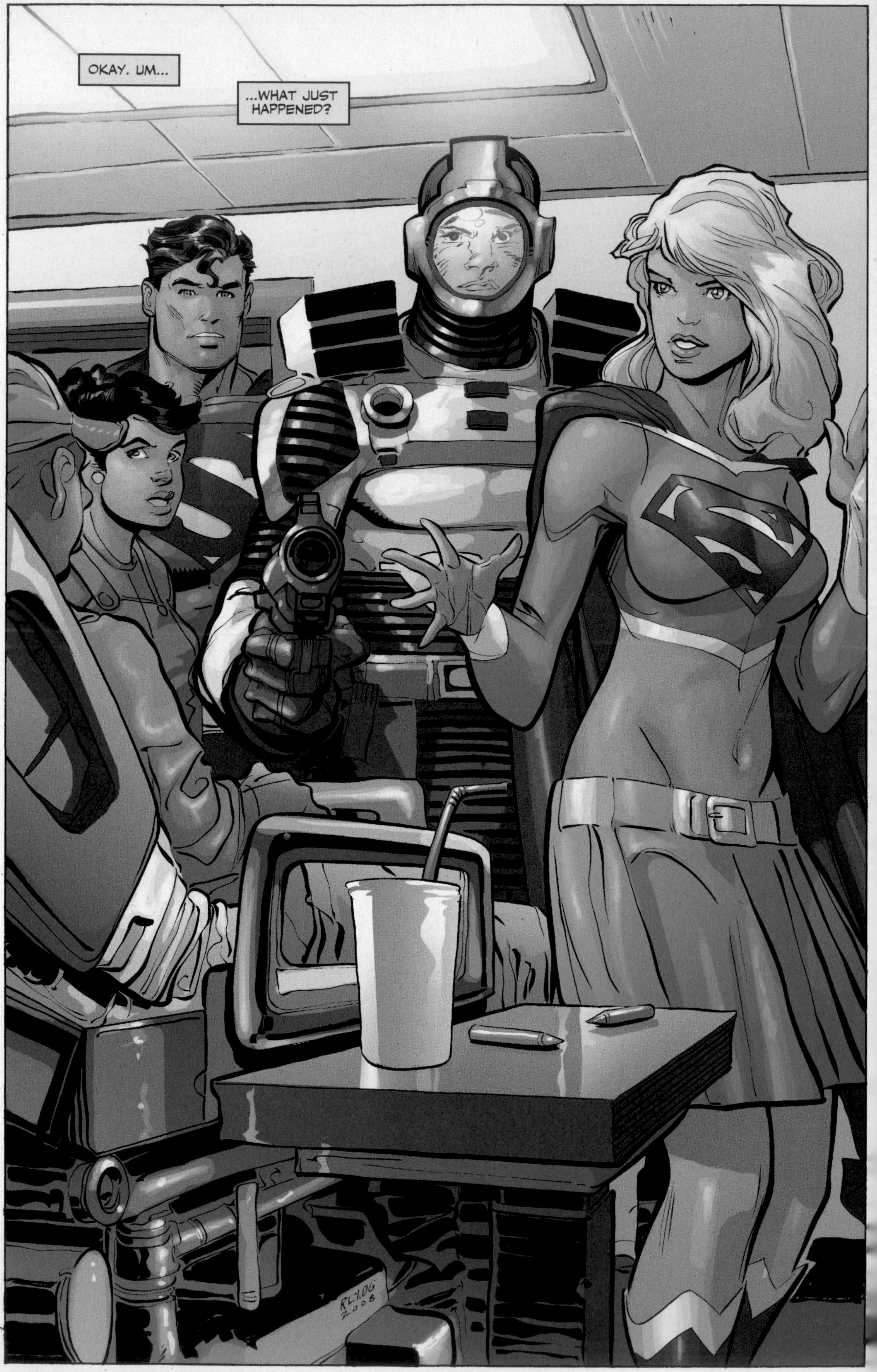
OKAY. UM...
...WHAT JUST HAPPENED?

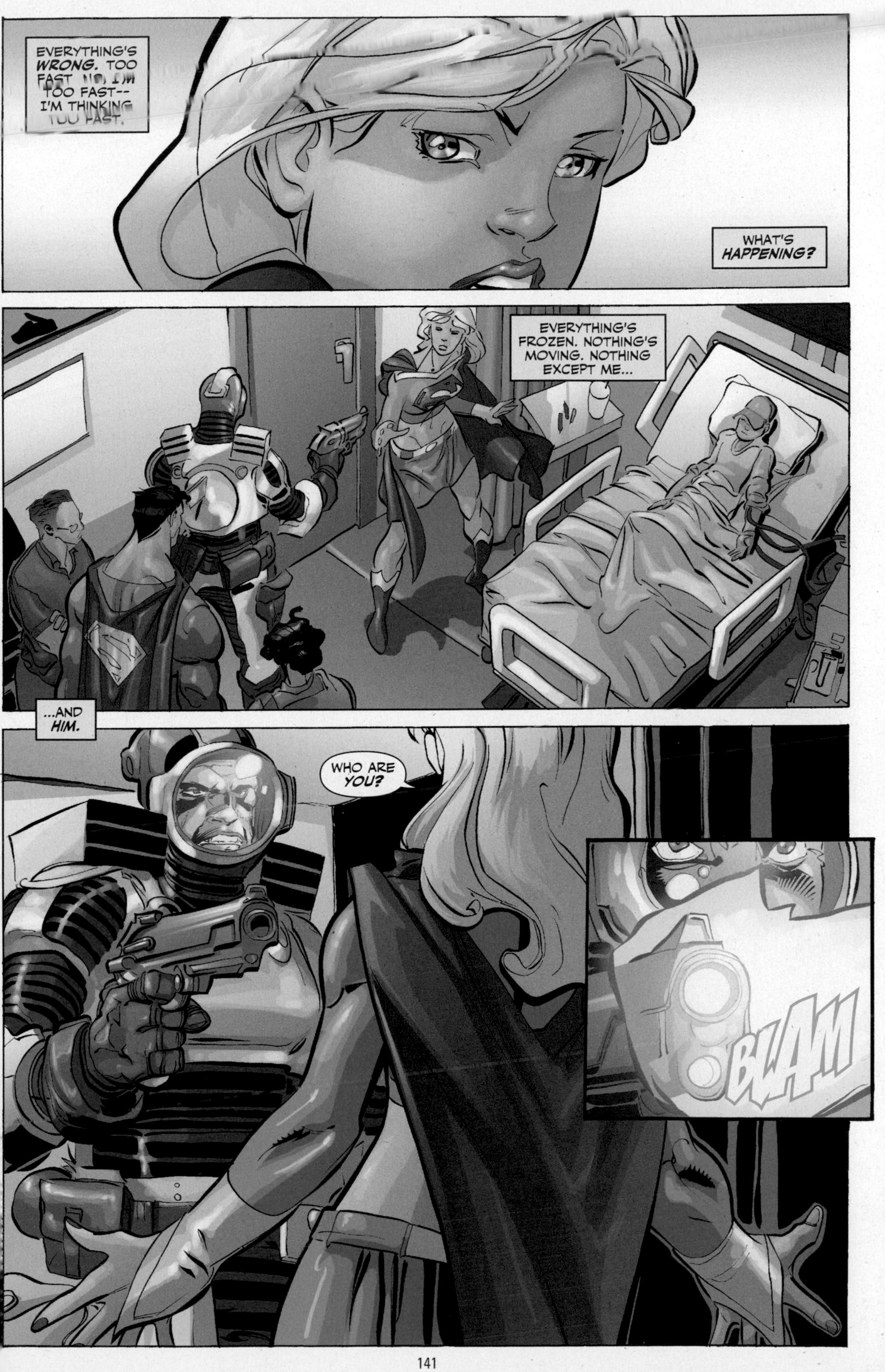
EVERYTHING'S WRONG. TOO FAST. NO, I'M TOO FAST-- I'M THINKING TOO FAST.
WHAT'S HAPPENING?
EVERYTHING'S FROZEN. NOTHING'S MOVING. NOTHING EXCEPT ME...
...AND HIM.
WHO ARE YOU?
BLAM

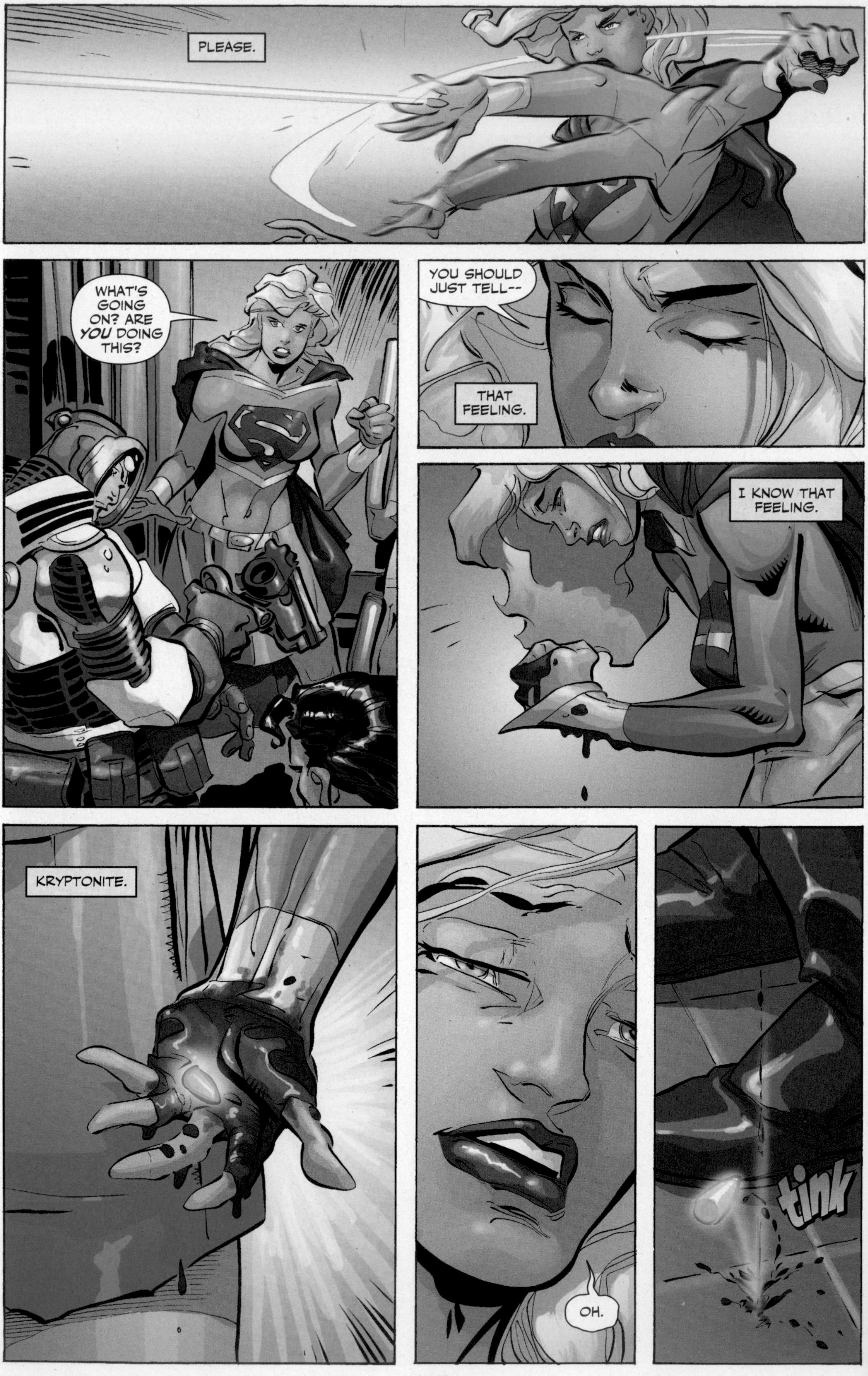
PLEASE.
WHAT'S GOING ON? ARE *YOU* DOING THIS?
YOU SHOULD JUST TELL--
THAT FEELING.
I KNOW THAT FEELING.
KRYPTONITE.
OH.
tink

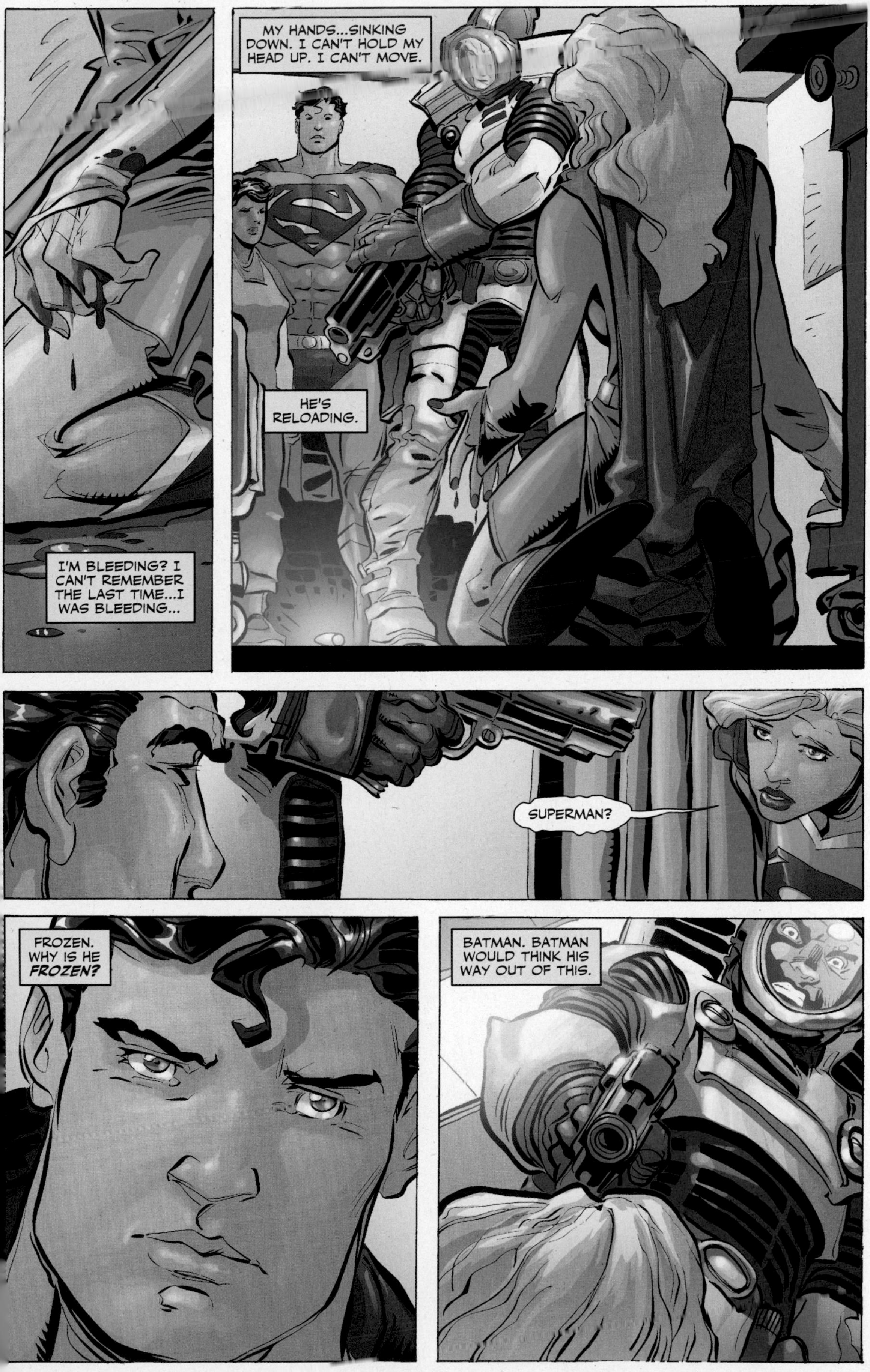

MY HANDS...SINKING DOWN. I CAN'T HOLD MY HEAD UP. I CAN'T MOVE.
HE'S RELOADING.
I'M BLEEDING? I CAN'T REMEMBER THE LAST TIME...I WAS BLEEDING...
SUPERMAN?
FROZEN. WHY IS HE *FROZEN?*
BATMAN. BATMAN WOULD THINK HIS WAY OUT OF THIS.

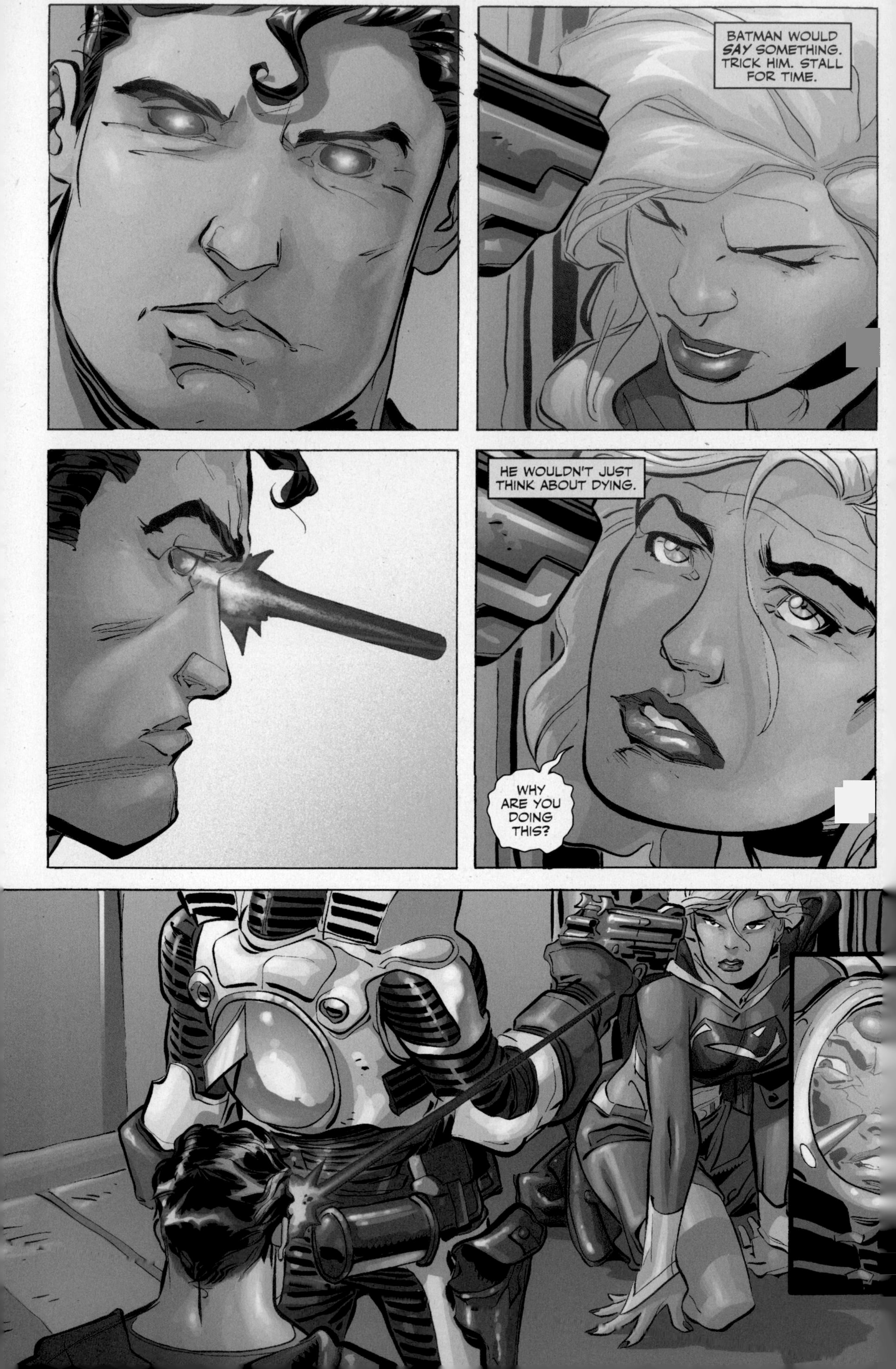
BATMAN WOULD SAY SOMETHING. TRICK HIM. STALL FOR TIME.
HE WOULDN'T JUST THINK ABOUT DYING.
WHY ARE YOU DOING THIS?

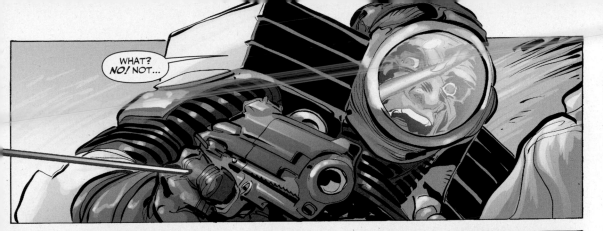

WHAT? *NO!* NOT...

...THE *SUIT*...

EVERYTHING SHIMMERS. EVERYTHING SHINES...

...AND THEN IT FOLDS...

...AND THEN WE'RE GONE.

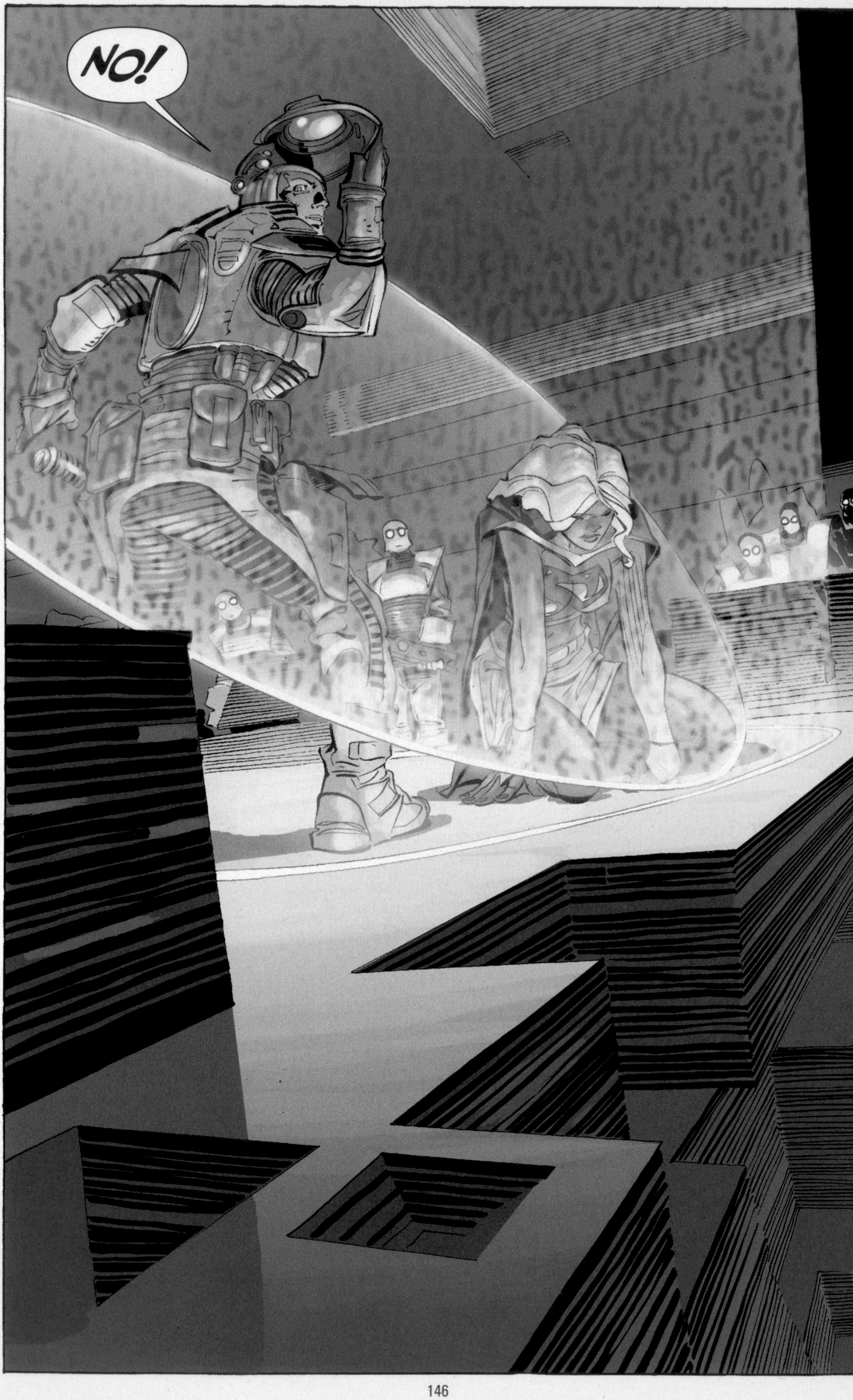
NO!

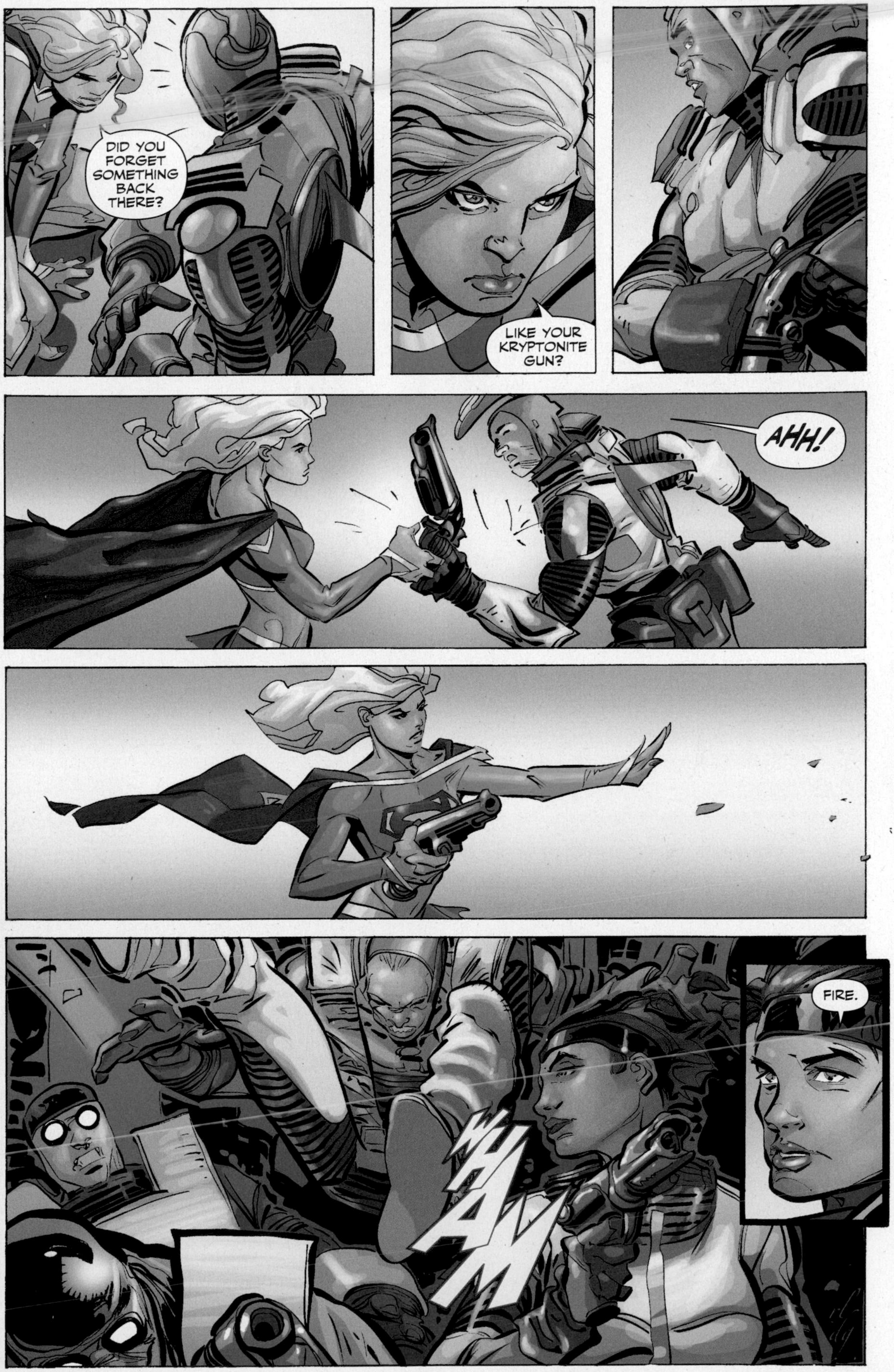
DID YOU FORGET SOMETHING BACK THERE?
LIKE YOUR KRYPTONITE GUN?
AHH!
FIRE.
WHAM

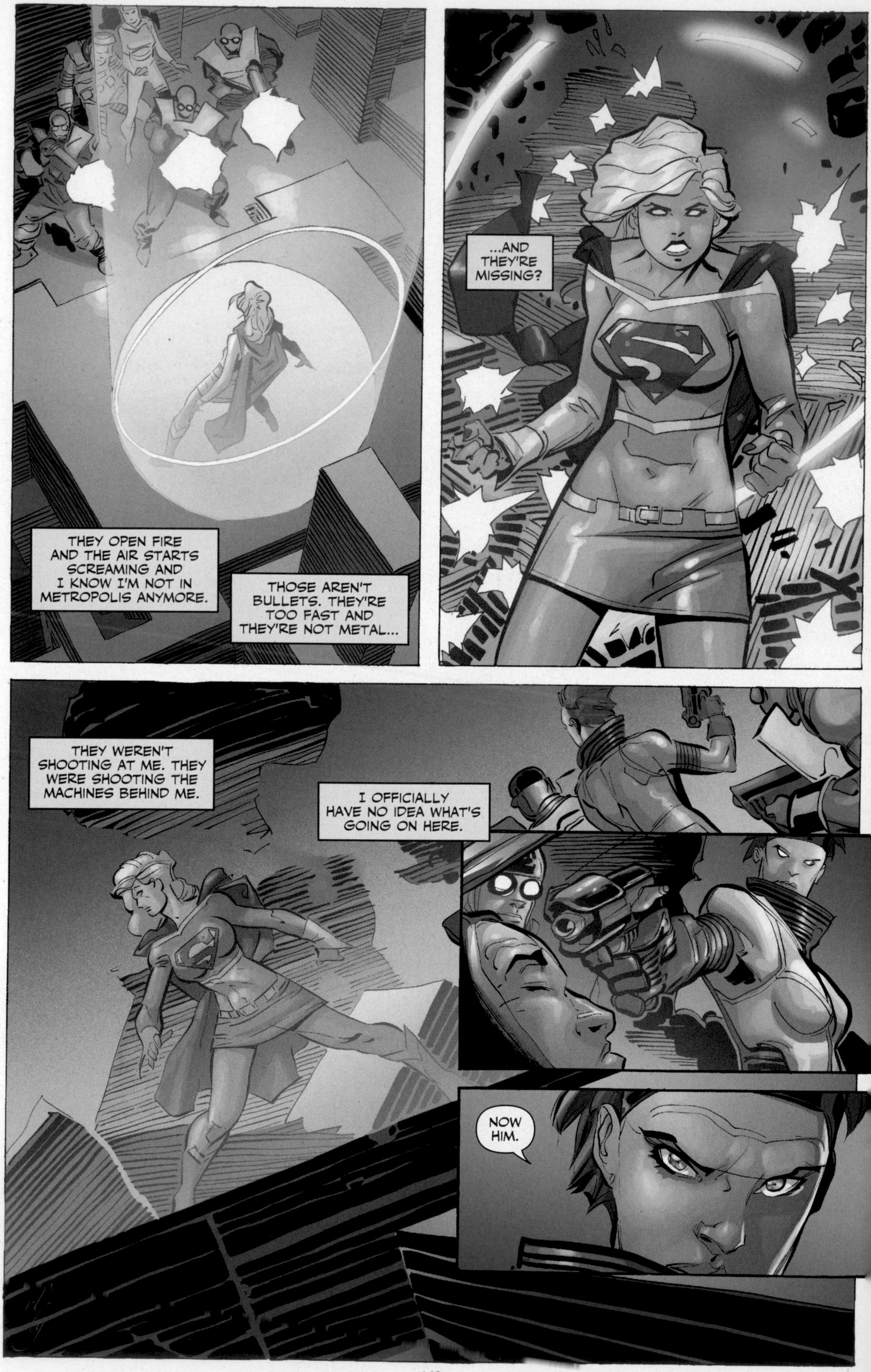
THEY OPEN FIRE AND THE AIR STARTS SCREAMING AND I KNOW I'M NOT IN METROPOLIS ANYMORE.
THOSE AREN'T BULLETS. THEY'RE TOO FAST AND THEY'RE NOT METAL...
...AND THEY'RE MISSING?
THEY WEREN'T SHOOTING AT ME. THEY WERE SHOOTING THE MACHINES BEHIND ME.
I OFFICIALLY HAVE NO IDEA WHAT'S GOING ON HERE.
NOW HIM.

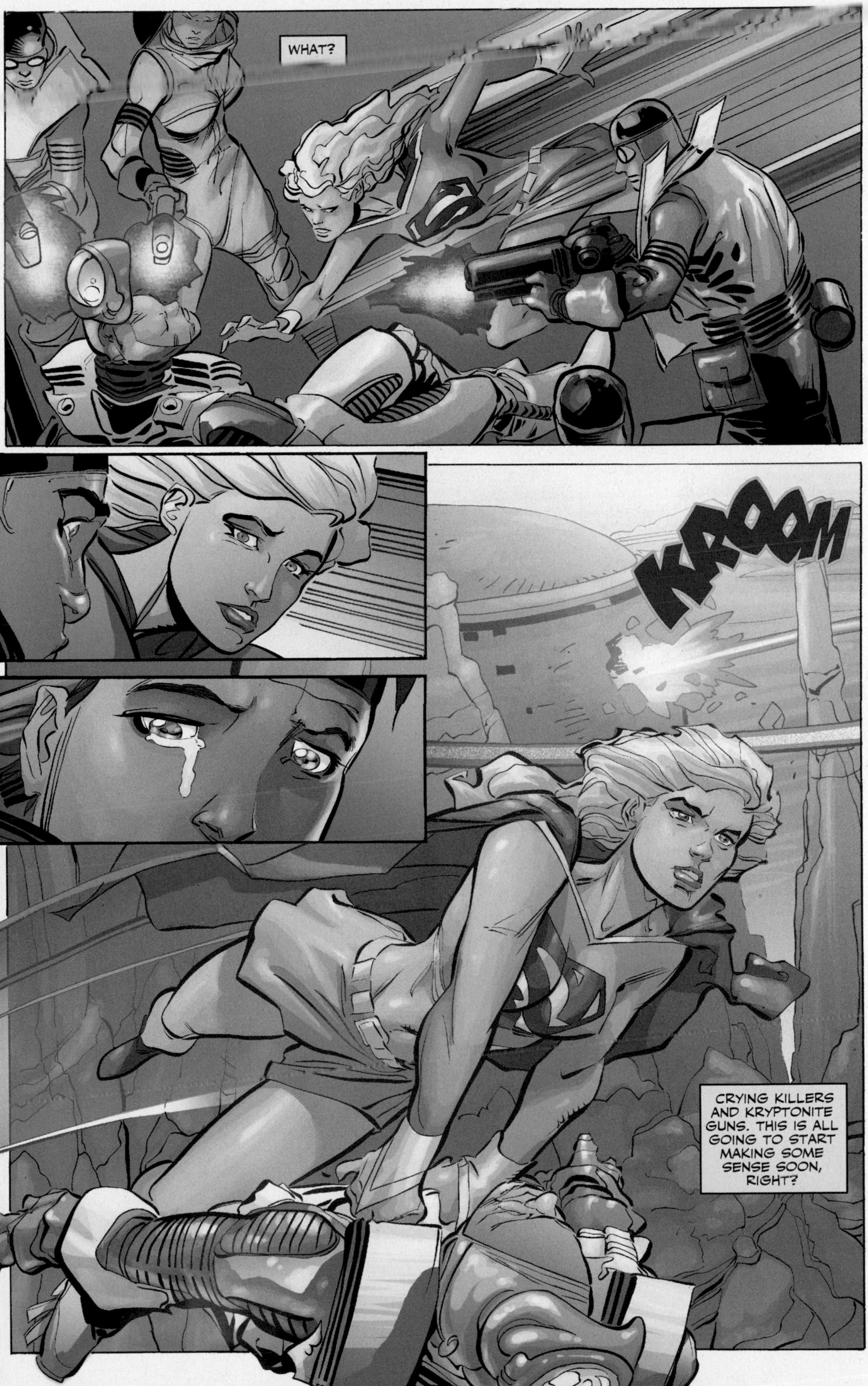
WHAT?
KROOM
CRYING KILLERS AND KRYPTONITE GUNS. THIS IS ALL GOING TO START MAKING SOME SENSE SOON, RIGHT?

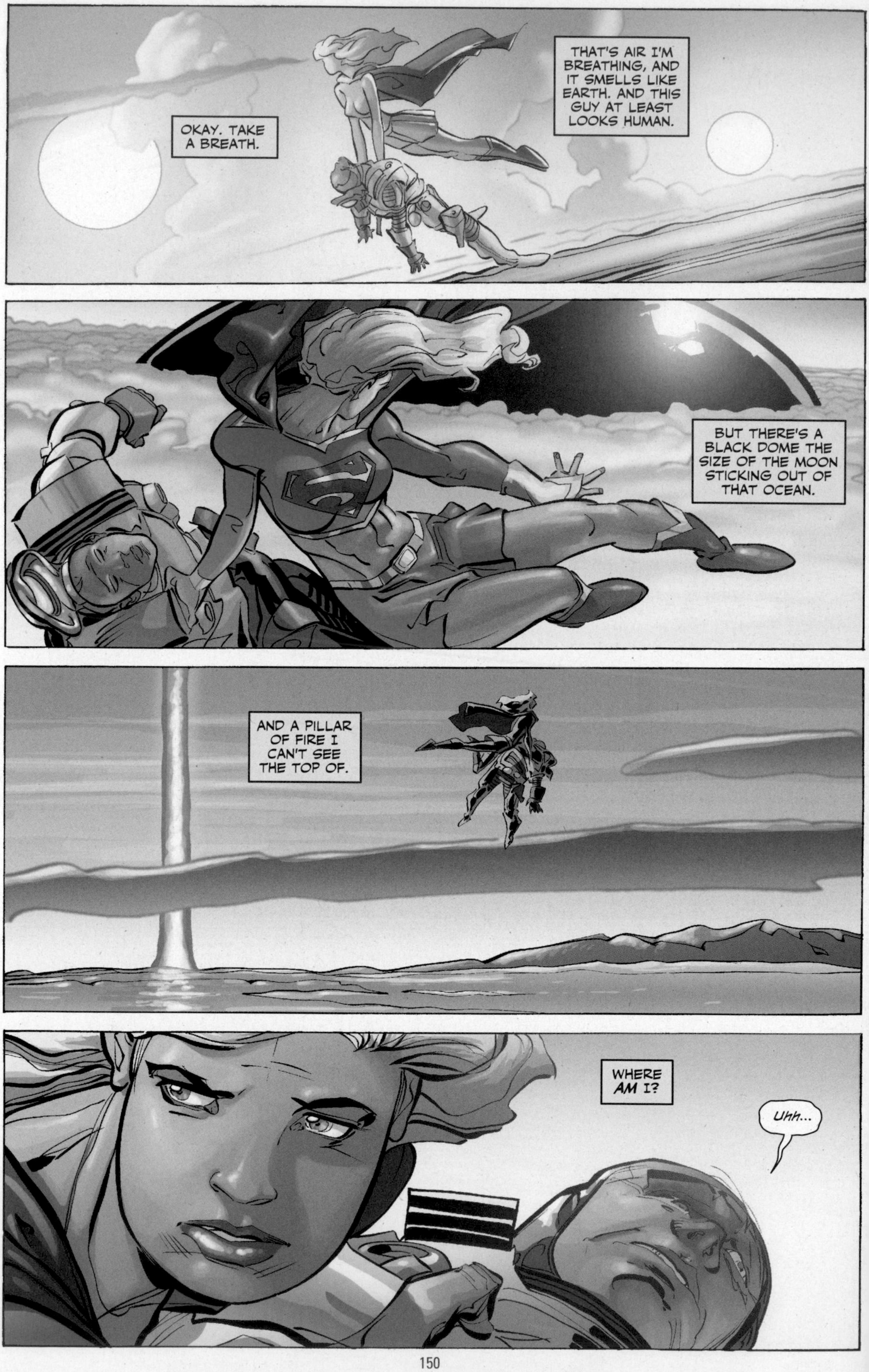
OKAY. TAKE A BREATH.
THAT'S AIR I'M BREATHING, AND IT SMELLS LIKE EARTH. AND THIS GUY AT LEAST LOOKS HUMAN.
BUT THERE'S A BLACK DOME THE SIZE OF THE MOON STICKING OUT OF THAT OCEAN.
AND A PILLAR OF FIRE I CAN'T SEE THE TOP OF.
WHERE *AM* I?
Uhh...

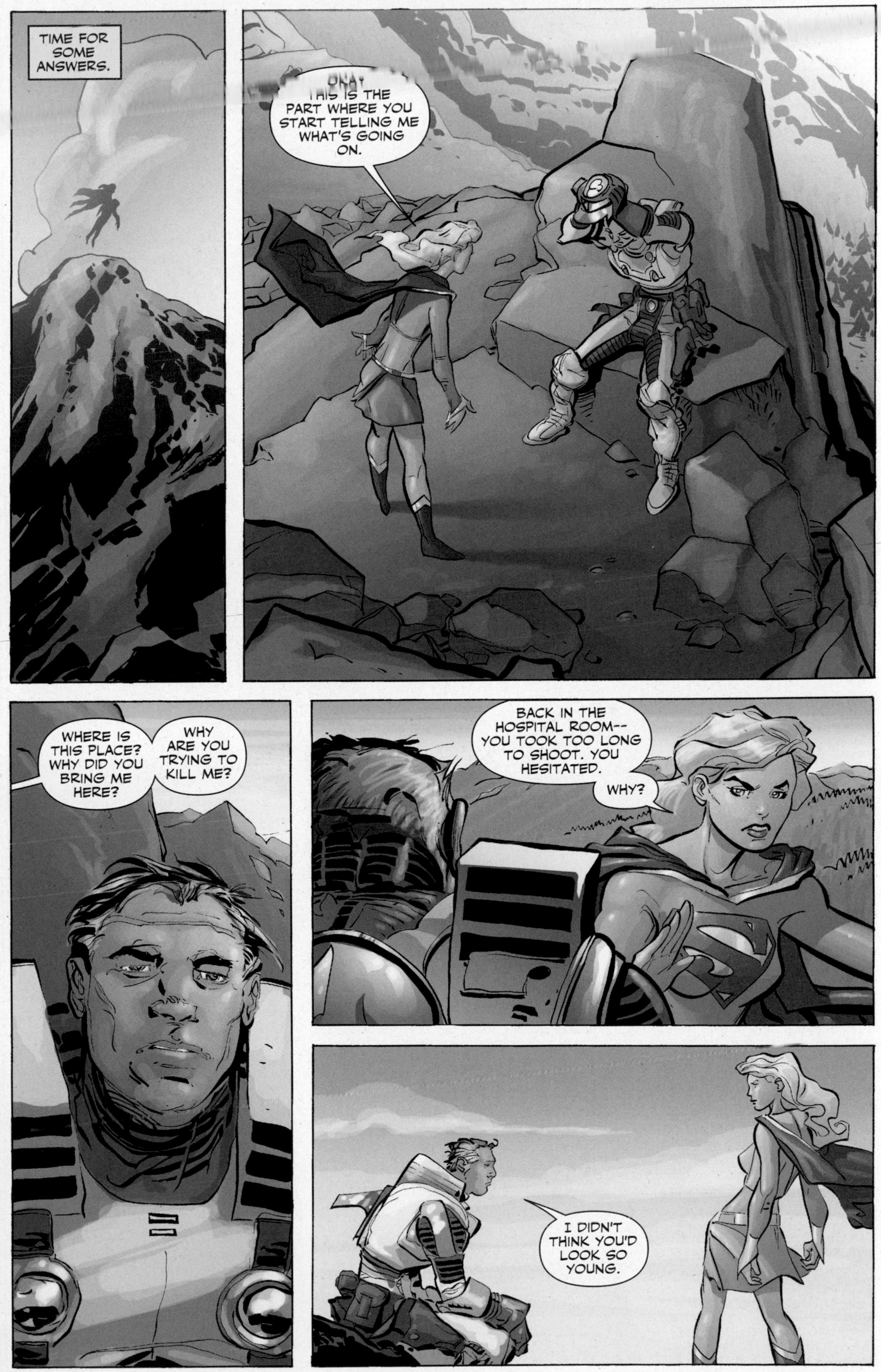
TIME FOR SOME ANSWERS.
THIS IS THE PART WHERE YOU START TELLING ME WHAT'S GOING ON.
WHERE IS THIS PLACE? WHY DID YOU BRING ME HERE?
WHY ARE YOU TRYING TO KILL ME?
BACK IN THE HOSPITAL ROOM-- YOU TOOK TOO LONG TO SHOOT. YOU HESITATED.
WHY?
I DIDN'T THINK YOU'D LOOK SO YOUNG.

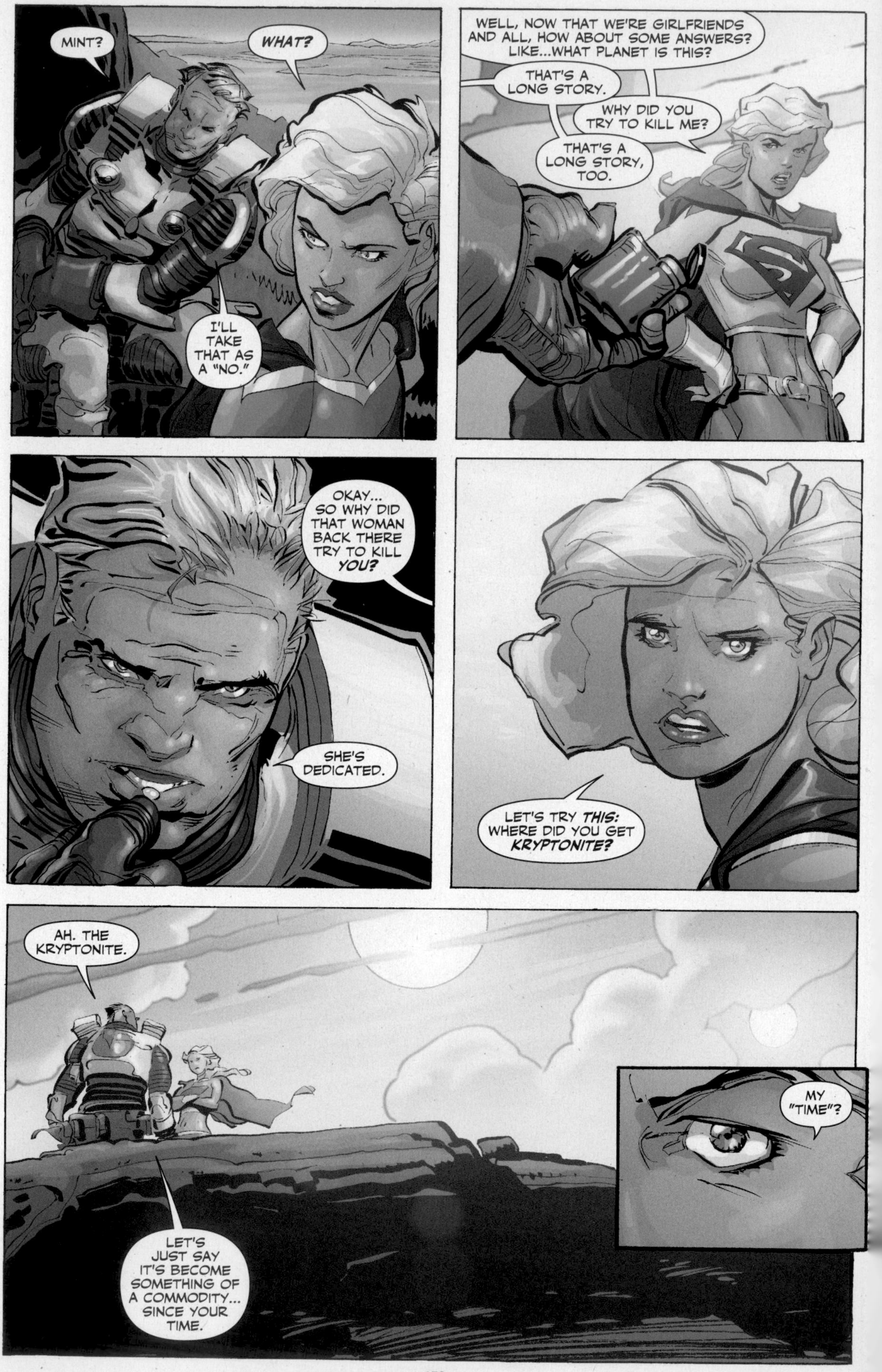
MINT?
WHAT?
I'LL TAKE THAT AS A "NO."
WELL, NOW THAT WE'RE GIRLFRIENDS AND ALL, HOW ABOUT SOME ANSWERS? LIKE...WHAT PLANET IS THIS?
THAT'S A LONG STORY.
WHY DID YOU TRY TO KILL ME?
THAT'S A LONG STORY, TOO.
OKAY... SO WHY DID THAT WOMAN BACK THERE TRY TO KILL YOU?
SHE'S DEDICATED.
LET'S TRY THIS: WHERE DID YOU GET KRYPTONITE?
AH. THE KRYPTONITE.
LET'S JUST SAY IT'S BECOME SOMETHING OF A COMMODITY... SINCE YOUR TIME.
MY "TIME"?

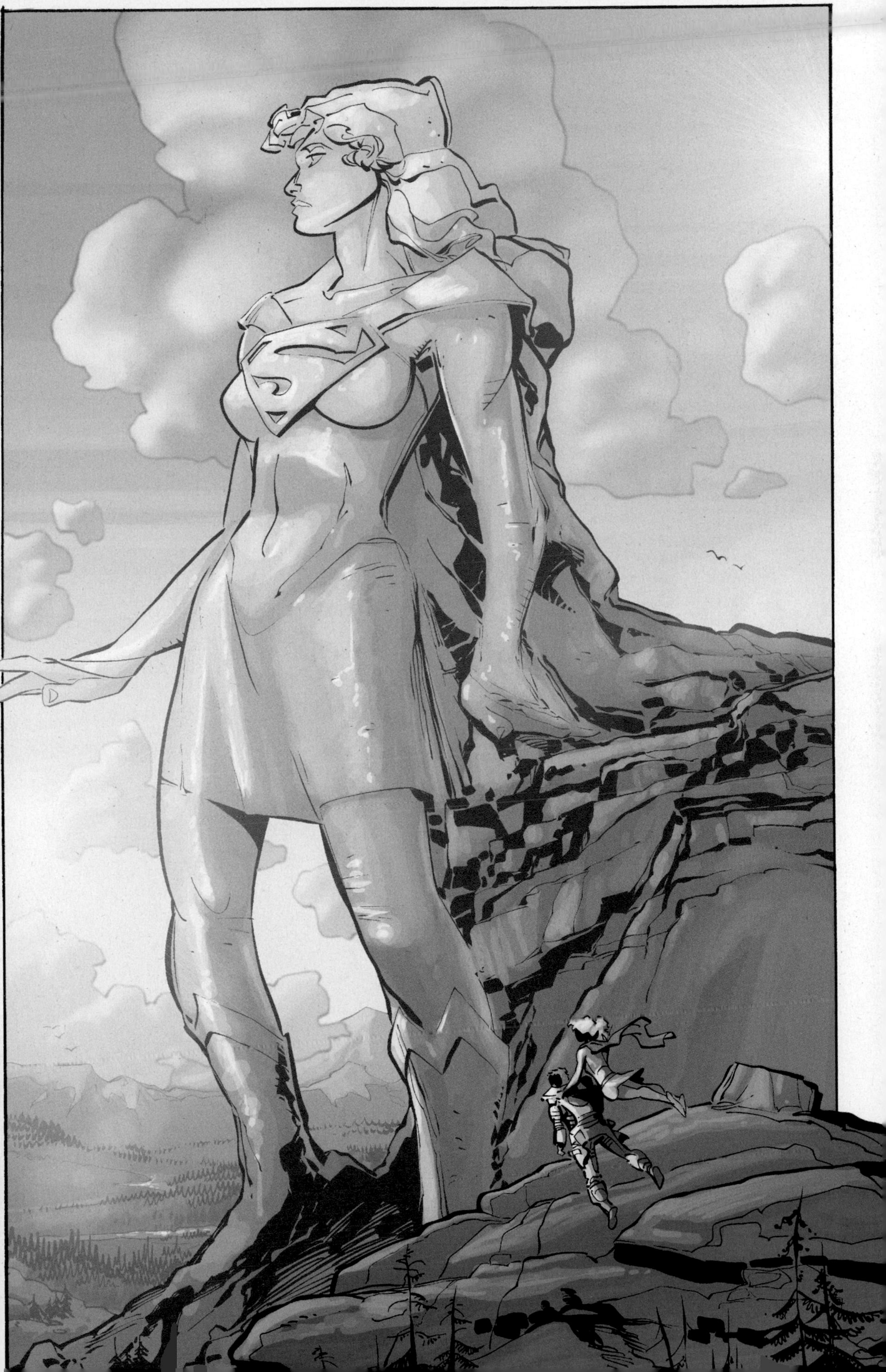

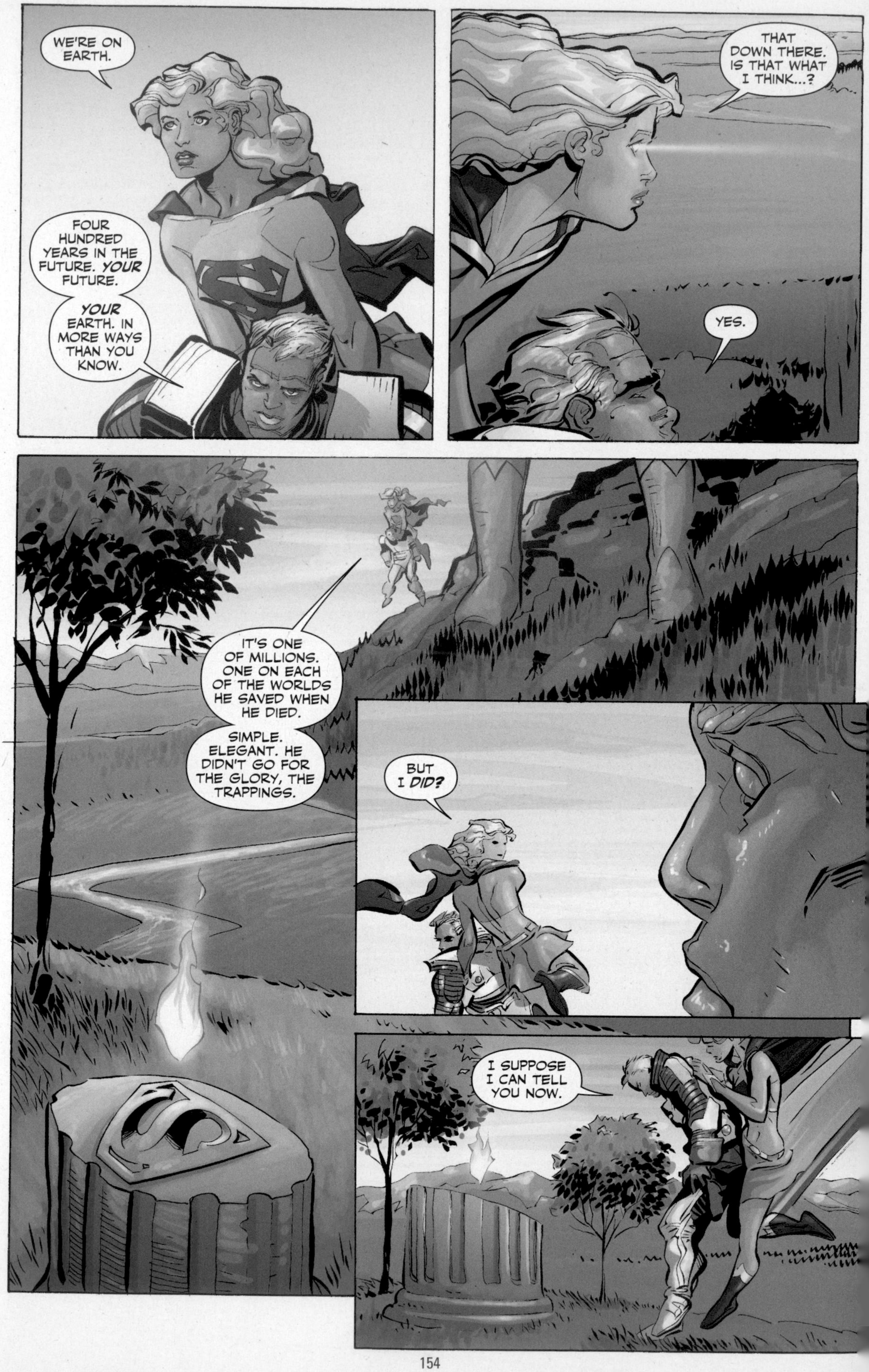
WE'RE ON EARTH.
FOUR HUNDRED YEARS IN THE FUTURE. *YOUR* FUTURE.
YOUR EARTH. IN MORE WAYS THAN YOU KNOW.
THAT DOWN THERE. IS THAT WHAT I THINK...?
YES.
IT'S ONE OF MILLIONS. ONE ON EACH OF THE WORLDS HE SAVED WHEN HE DIED.
SIMPLE. ELEGANT. HE DIDN'T GO FOR THE GLORY, THE TRAPPINGS.
BUT I *DID?*
I SUPPOSE I CAN TELL YOU NOW.

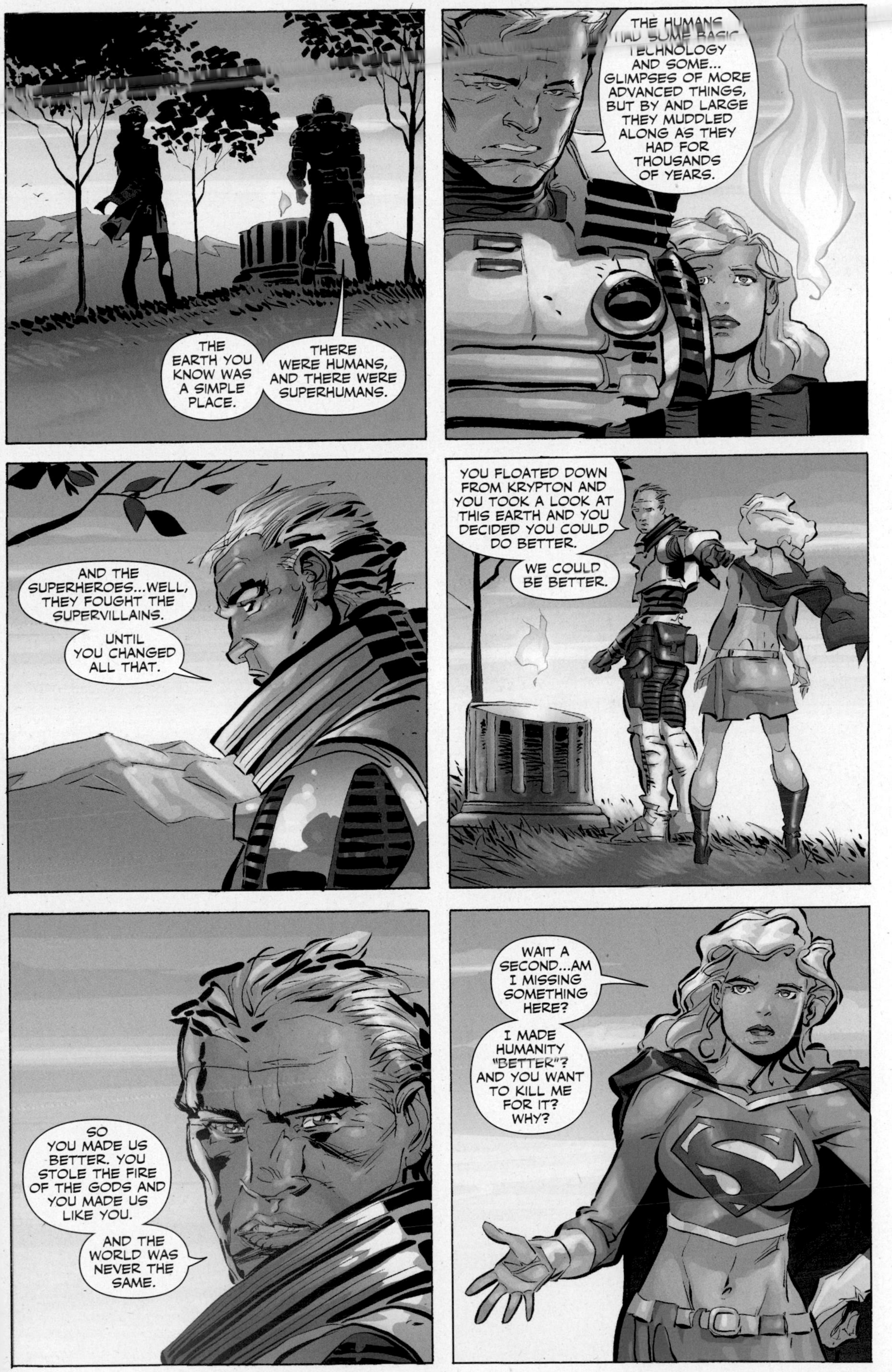
THE EARTH YOU KNOW WAS A SIMPLE PLACE.
THERE WERE HUMANS, AND THERE WERE SUPERHUMANS.
THE HUMANS HAD SOME BASIC TECHNOLOGY AND SOME... GLIMPSES OF MORE ADVANCED THINGS, BUT BY AND LARGE THEY MUDDLED ALONG AS THEY HAD FOR THOUSANDS OF YEARS.
AND THE SUPERHEROES...WELL, THEY FOUGHT THE SUPERVILLAINS.
UNTIL YOU CHANGED ALL THAT.
YOU FLOATED DOWN FROM KRYPTON AND YOU TOOK A LOOK AT THIS EARTH AND YOU DECIDED YOU COULD DO BETTER.
WE COULD BE BETTER.
SO YOU MADE US BETTER. YOU STOLE THE FIRE OF THE GODS AND YOU MADE US LIKE YOU.
AND THE WORLD WAS NEVER THE SAME.
WAIT A SECOND...AM I MISSING SOMETHING HERE?
I MADE HUMANITY "BETTER"? AND YOU WANT TO KILL ME FOR IT? WHY?

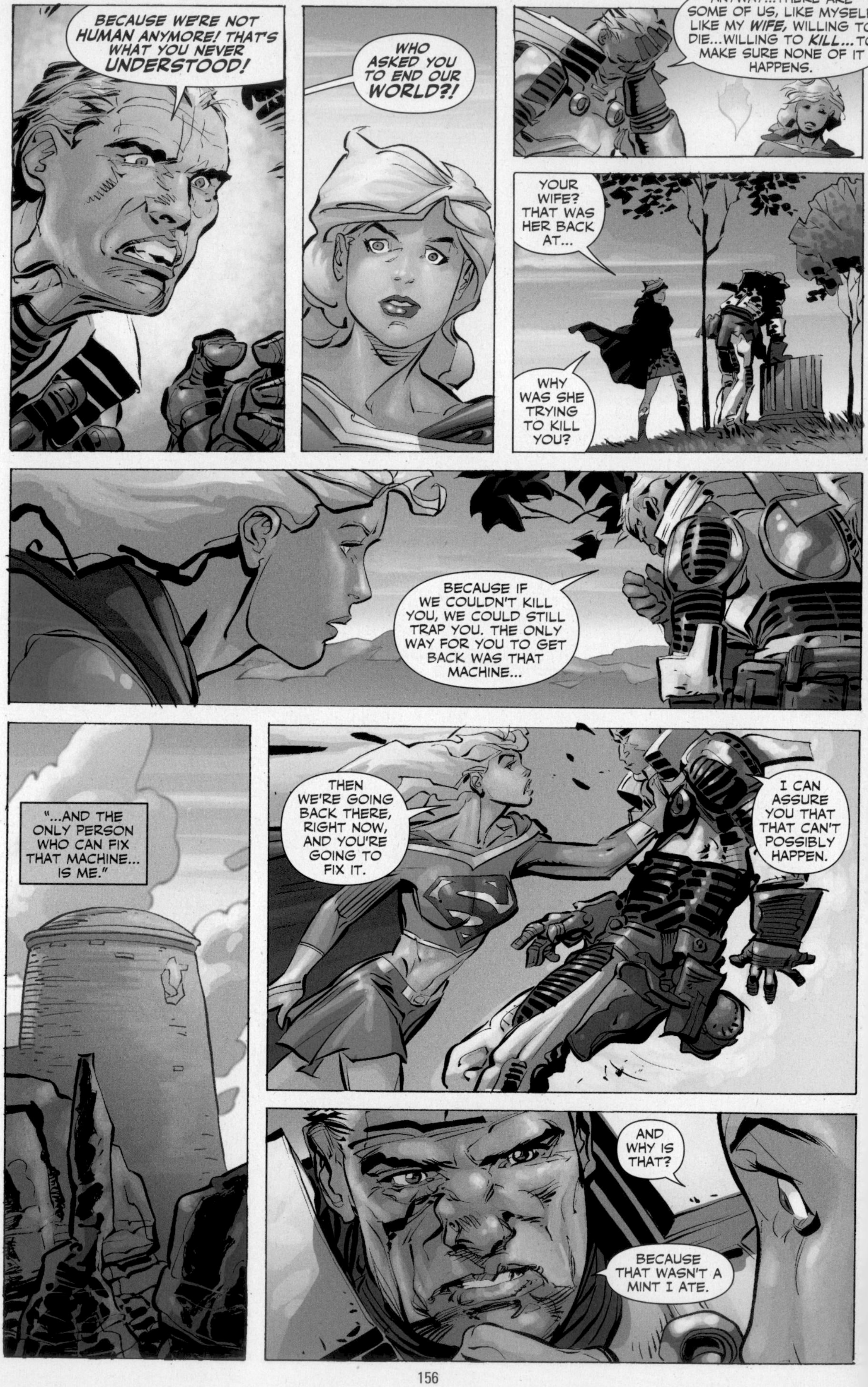
BECAUSE WE'RE NOT HUMAN ANYMORE! THAT'S WHAT YOU NEVER UNDERSTOOD!
WHO ASKED YOU TO END OUR WORLD?!
ANYWAY...THERE ARE SOME OF US, LIKE MYSELF, LIKE MY WIFE, WILLING TO DIE...WILLING TO KILL...TO MAKE SURE NONE OF IT HAPPENS.
YOUR WIFE? THAT WAS HER BACK AT...
WHY WAS SHE TRYING TO KILL YOU?
BECAUSE IF WE COULDN'T KILL YOU, WE COULD STILL TRAP YOU. THE ONLY WAY FOR YOU TO GET BACK WAS THAT MACHINE...
"...AND THE ONLY PERSON WHO CAN FIX THAT MACHINE... IS ME."
THEN WE'RE GOING BACK THERE, RIGHT NOW, AND YOU'RE GOING TO FIX IT.
I CAN ASSURE YOU THAT THAT CAN'T POSSIBLY HAPPEN.
AND WHY IS THAT?
BECAUSE THAT WASN'T A MINT I ATE.

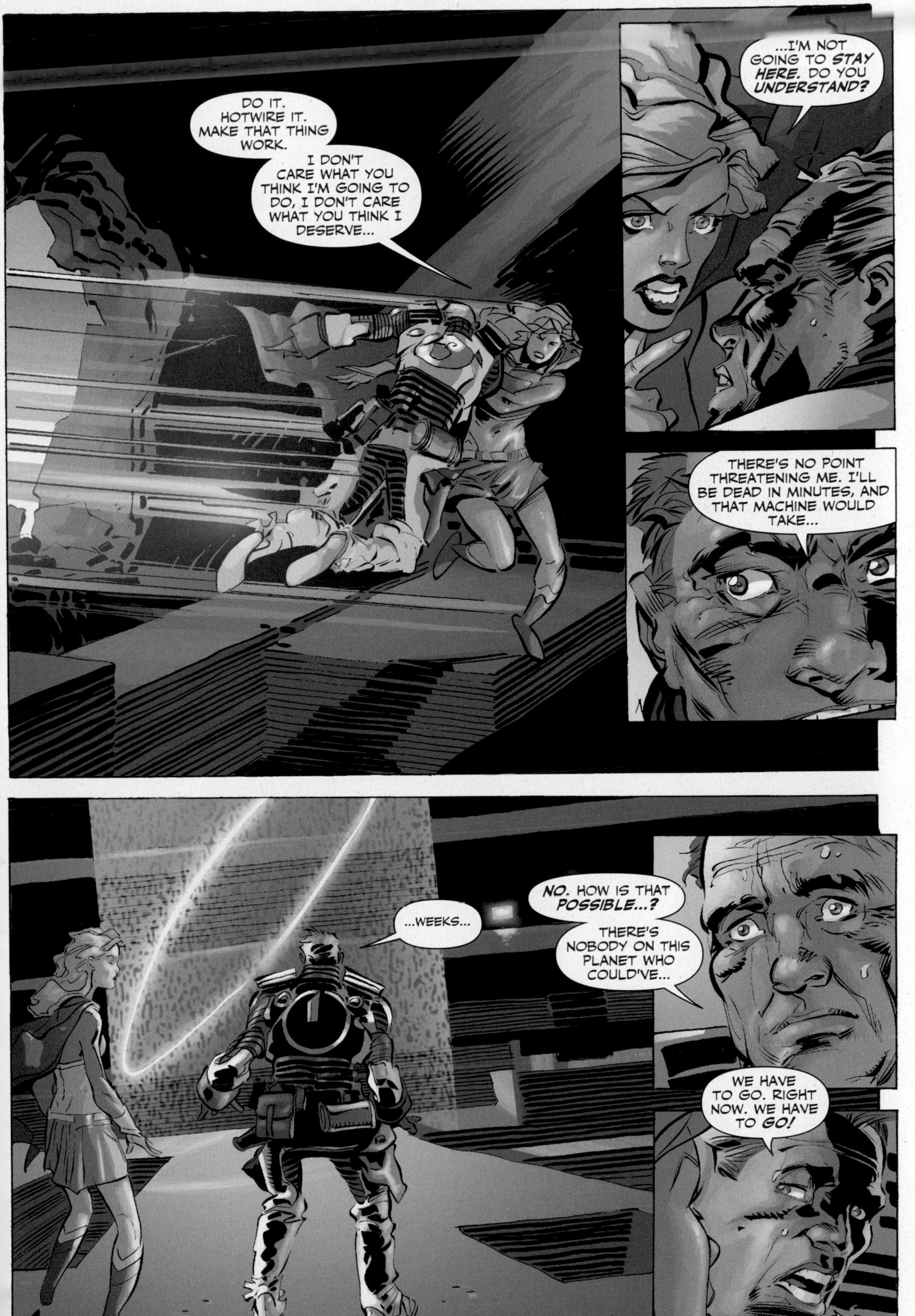
DO IT. HOTWIRE IT. MAKE THAT THING WORK.
I DON'T CARE WHAT YOU THINK I'M GOING TO DO, I DON'T CARE WHAT YOU THINK I DESERVE...
...I'M NOT GOING TO STAY HERE. DO YOU UNDERSTAND?
THERE'S NO POINT THREATENING ME. I'LL BE DEAD IN MINUTES, AND THAT MACHINE WOULD TAKE...
...WEEKS...
NO. HOW IS THAT POSSIBLE...?
THERE'S NOBODY ON THIS PLANET WHO COULD'VE...
WE HAVE TO GO. RIGHT NOW. WE HAVE TO GO!
THEY'RE ALREADY HERE!

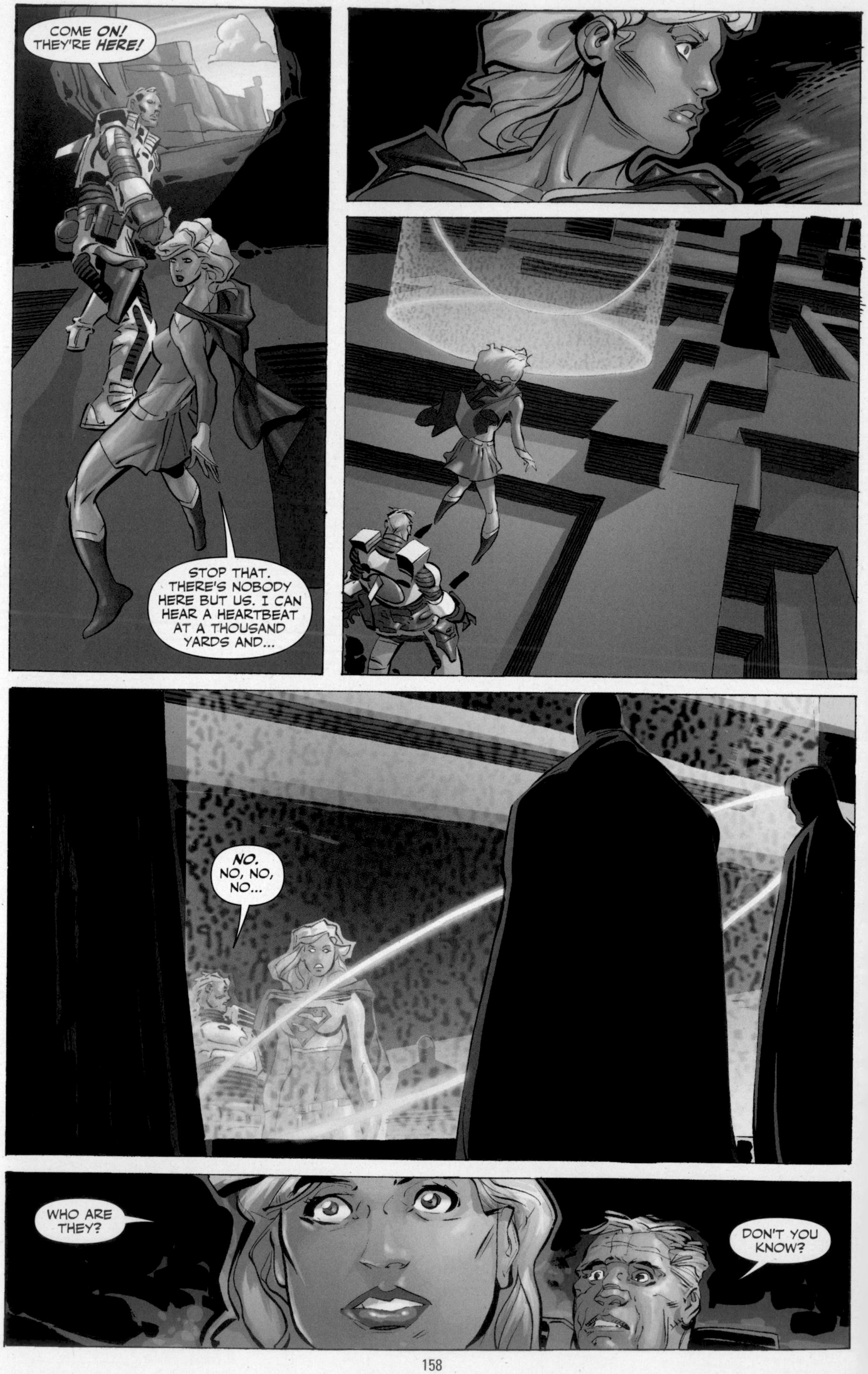
COME ON! THEY'RE HERE!
STOP THAT. THERE'S NOBODY HERE BUT US. I CAN HEAR A HEARTBEAT AT A THOUSAND YARDS AND...
NO. NO, NO, NO...
WHO ARE THEY?
DON'T YOU KNOW?

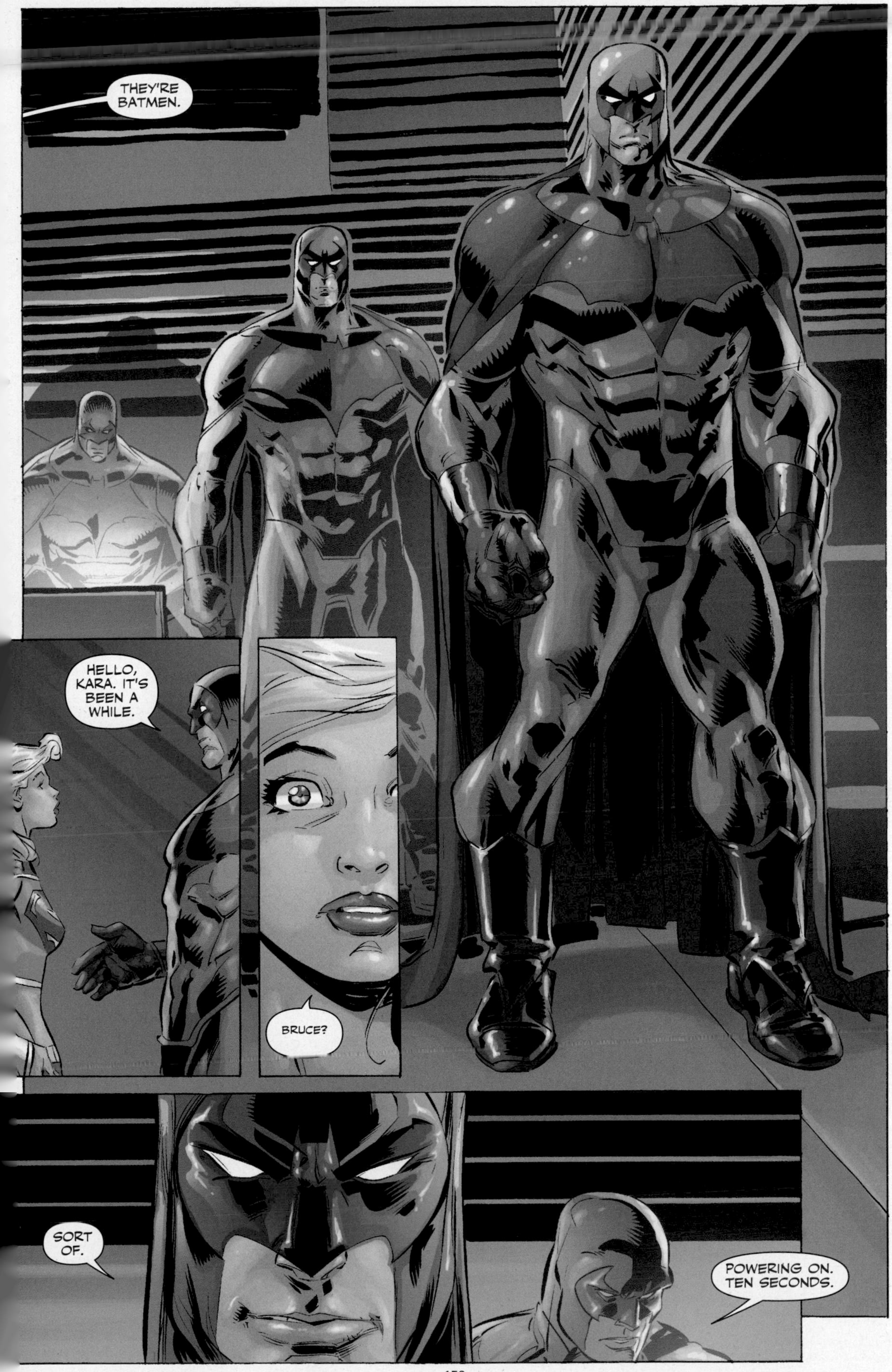
THEY'RE BATMEN.
HELLO, KARA. IT'S BEEN A WHILE.
BRUCE?
SORT OF.
POWERING ON. TEN SECONDS.

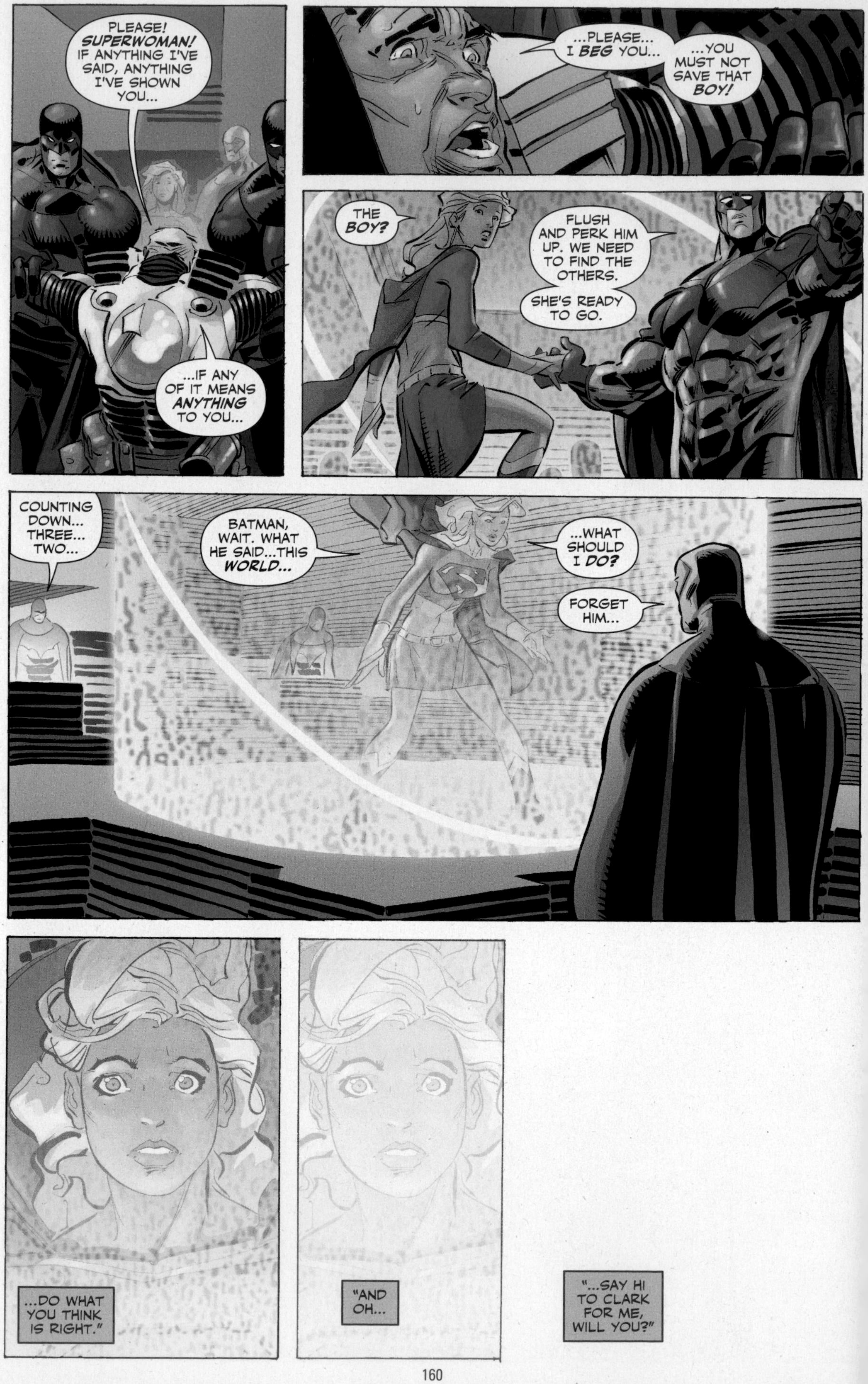
PLEASE! SUPERWOMAN! IF ANYTHING I'VE SAID, ANYTHING I'VE SHOWN YOU...
...IF ANY OF IT MEANS ANYTHING TO YOU...
...PLEASE... I BEG YOU...
...YOU MUST NOT SAVE THAT BOY!
THE BOY?
FLUSH AND PERK HIM UP. WE NEED TO FIND THE OTHERS.
SHE'S READY TO GO.
COUNTING DOWN... THREE... TWO...
BATMAN, WAIT. WHAT HE SAID...THIS WORLD...
...WHAT SHOULD I DO?
FORGET HIM...
...DO WHAT YOU THINK IS RIGHT."
"AND OH...
"...SAY HI TO CLARK FOR ME, WILL YOU?"

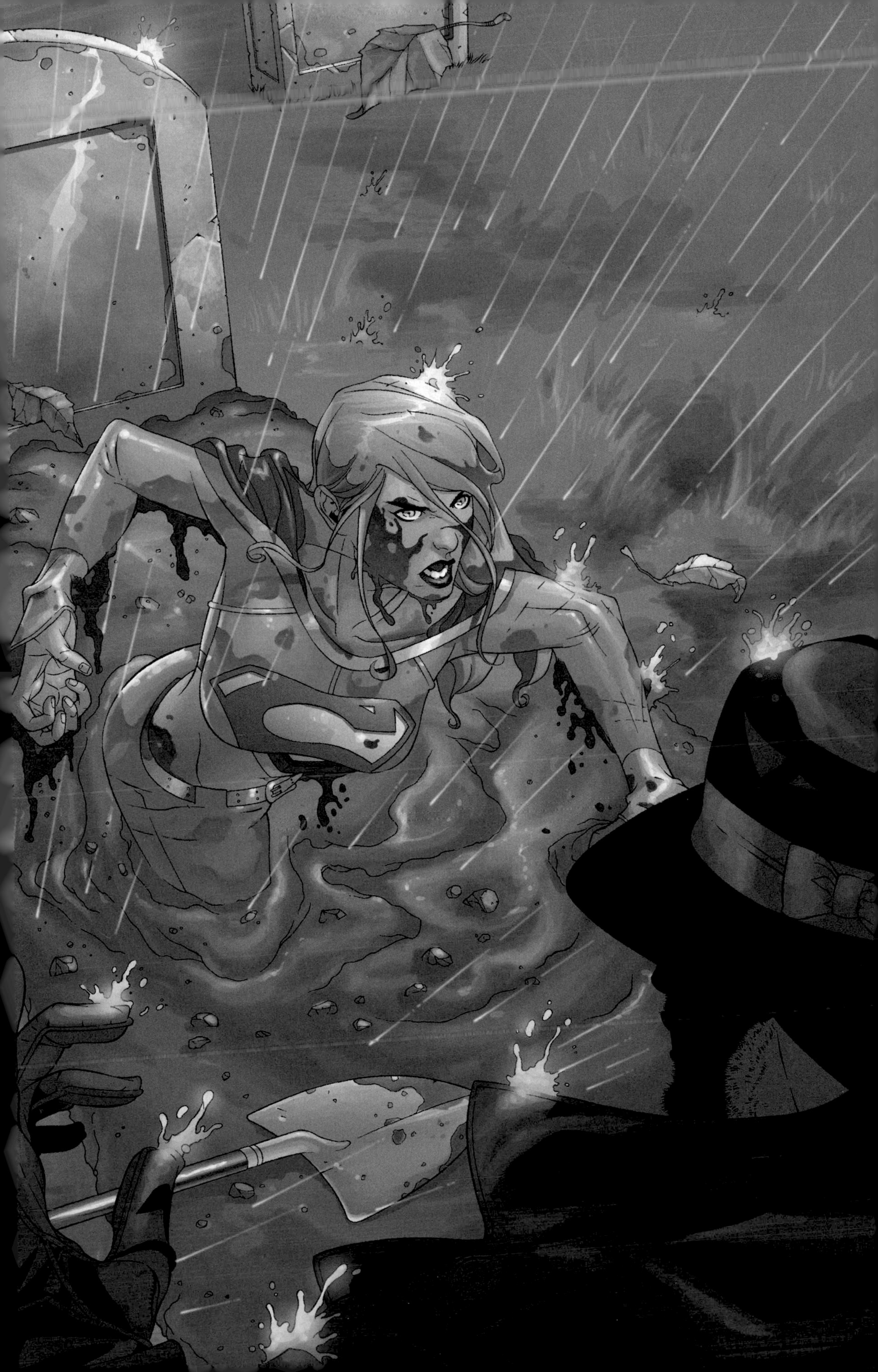

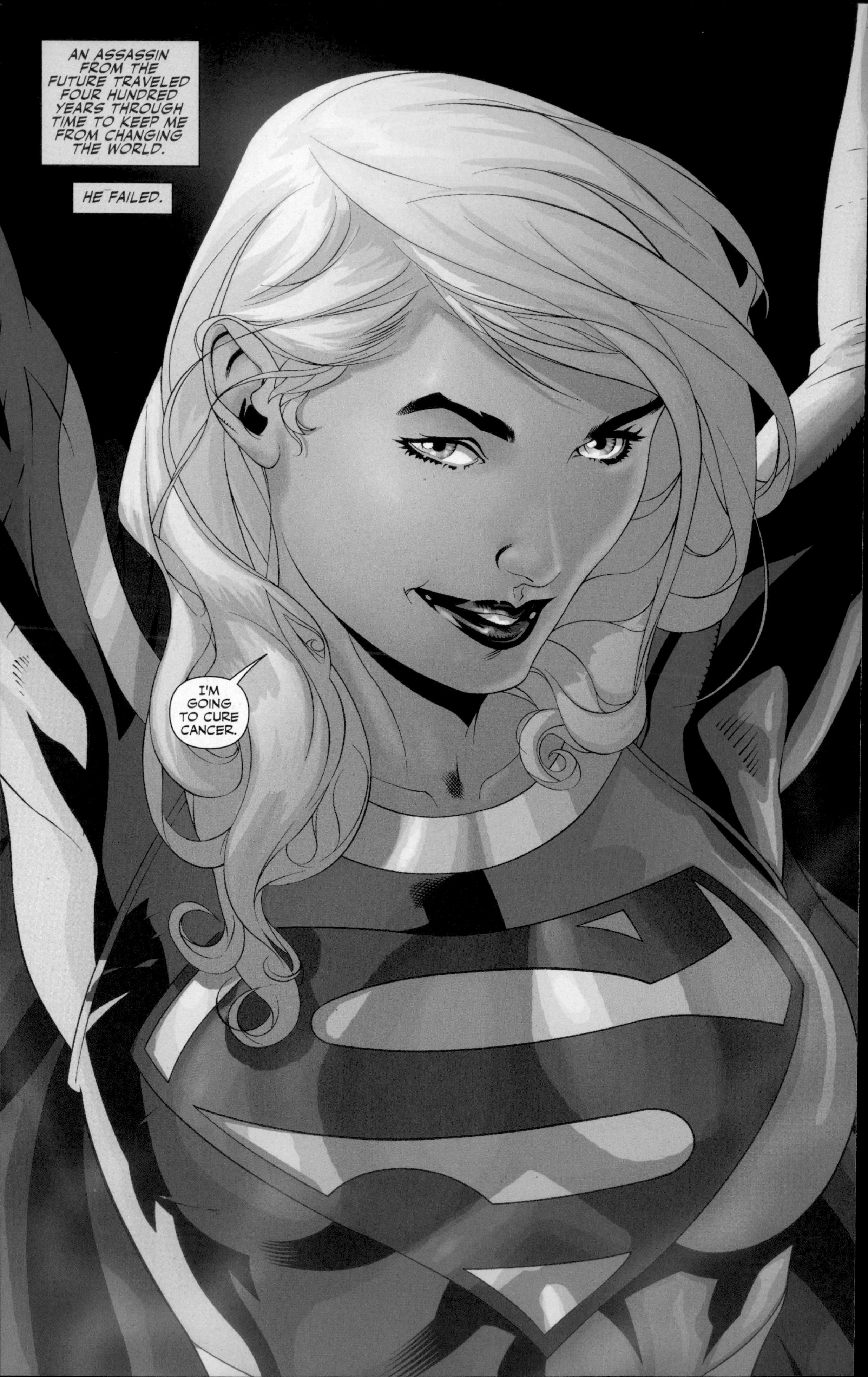
AN ASSASSIN FROM THE FUTURE TRAVELED FOUR HUNDRED YEARS THROUGH TIME TO KEEP ME FROM CHANGING THE WORLD.
HE FAILED.
I'M GOING TO CURE CANCER.

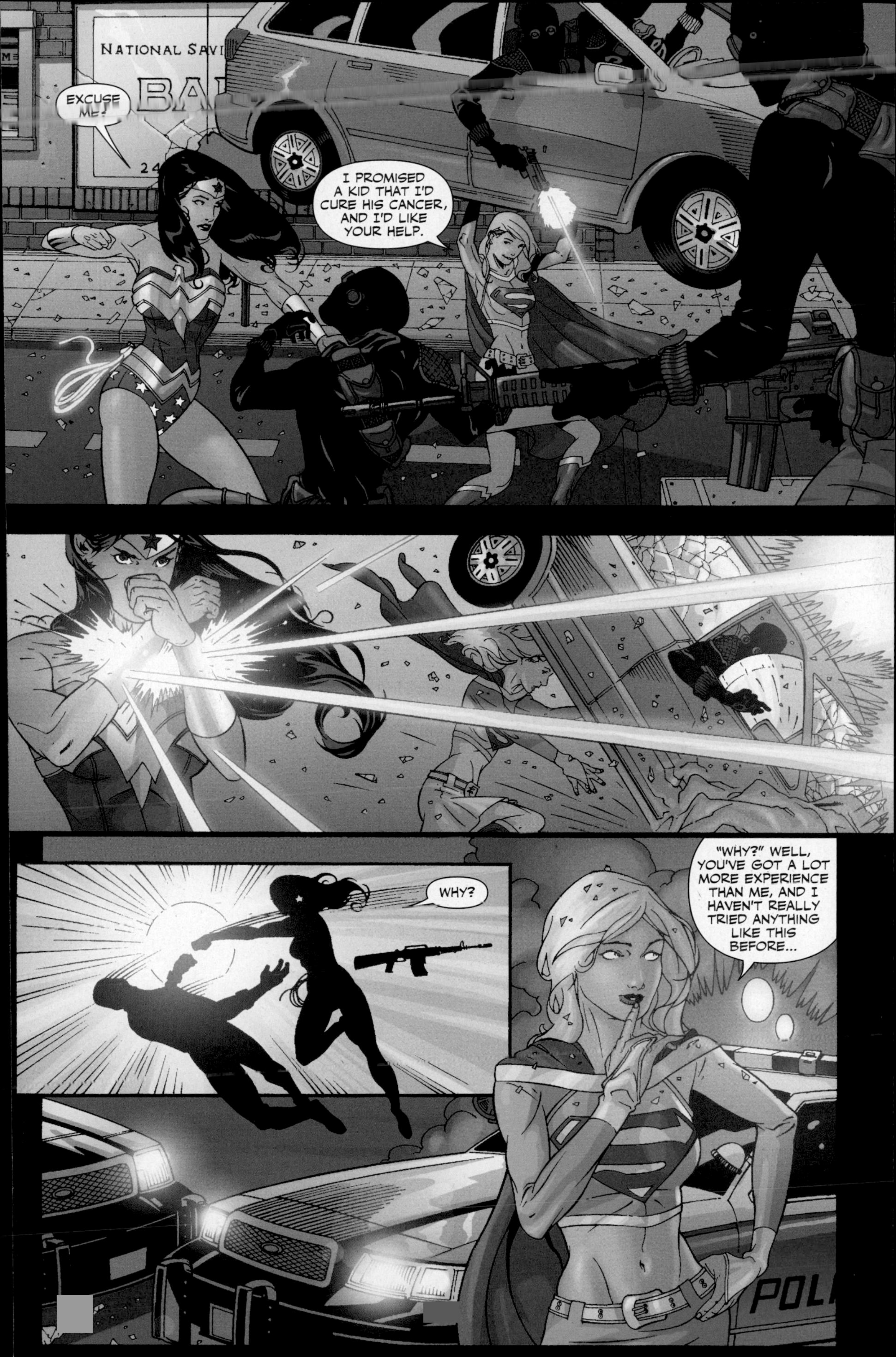
NATIONAL SAVI
EXCUSE ME!
I PROMISED A KID THAT I'D CURE HIS CANCER, AND I'D LIKE YOUR HELP.
WHY?
"WHY?" WELL, YOU'VE GOT A LOT MORE EXPERIENCE THAN ME, AND I HAVEN'T REALLY TRIED ANYTHING LIKE THIS BEFORE...
POLI

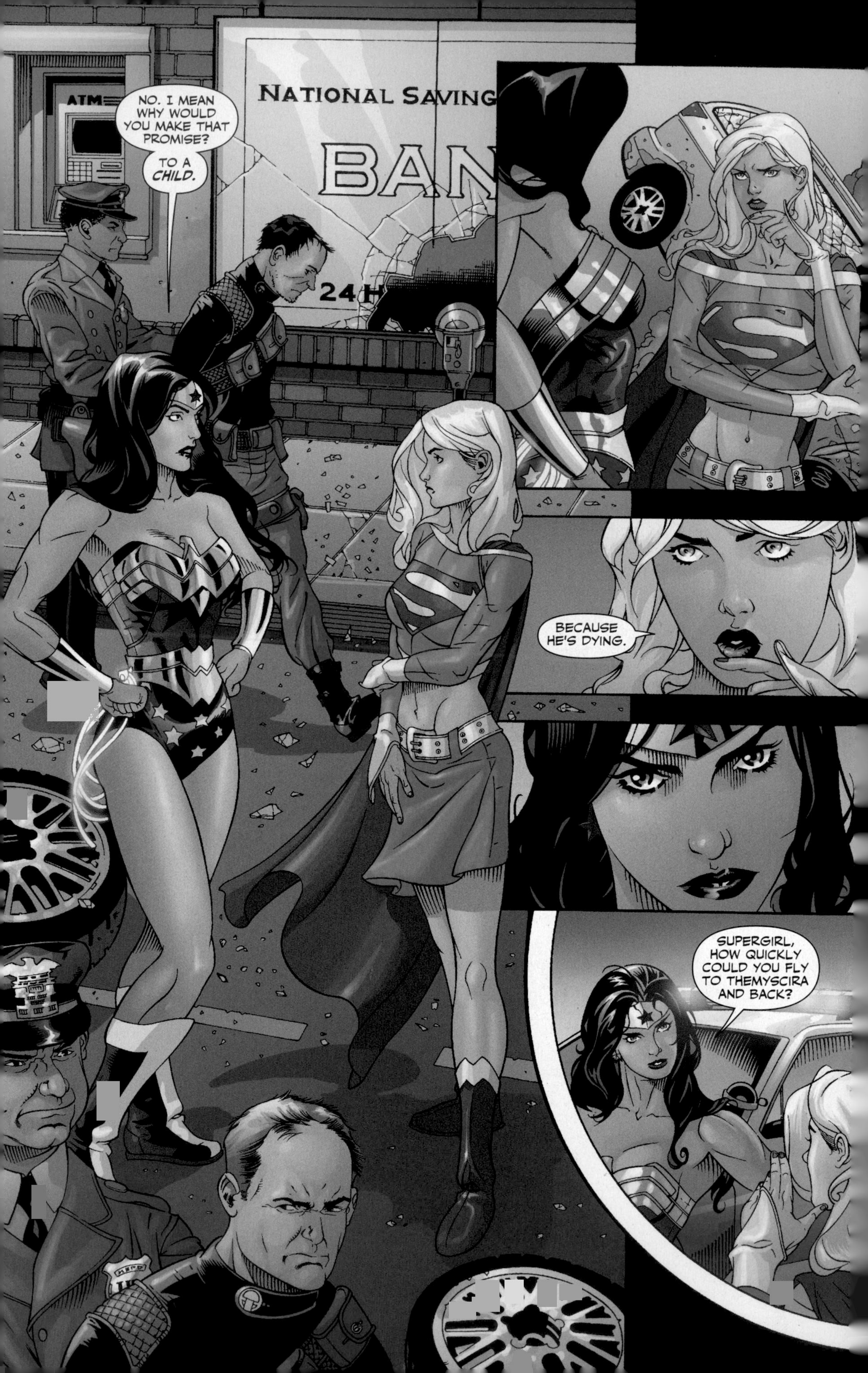

ATM
NATIONAL SAVING
BAN
24 H
NO. I MEAN WHY WOULD YOU MAKE THAT PROMISE?
TO A *CHILD.*
BECAUSE HE'S DYING.
SUPERGIRL, HOW QUICKLY COULD YOU FLY TO THEMYSCIRA AND BACK?

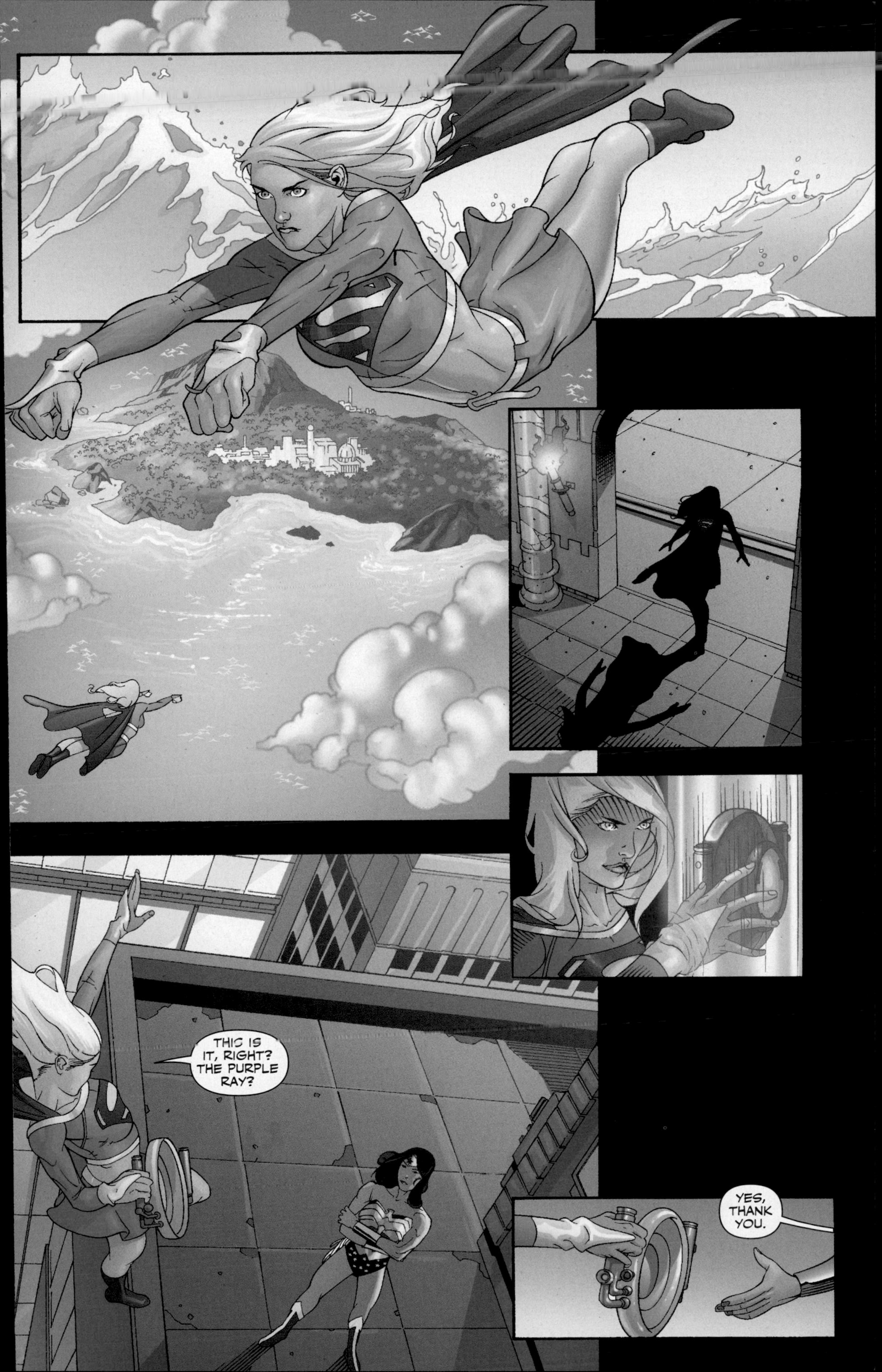
THIS IS IT, RIGHT? THE PURPLE RAY?
YES, THANK YOU.

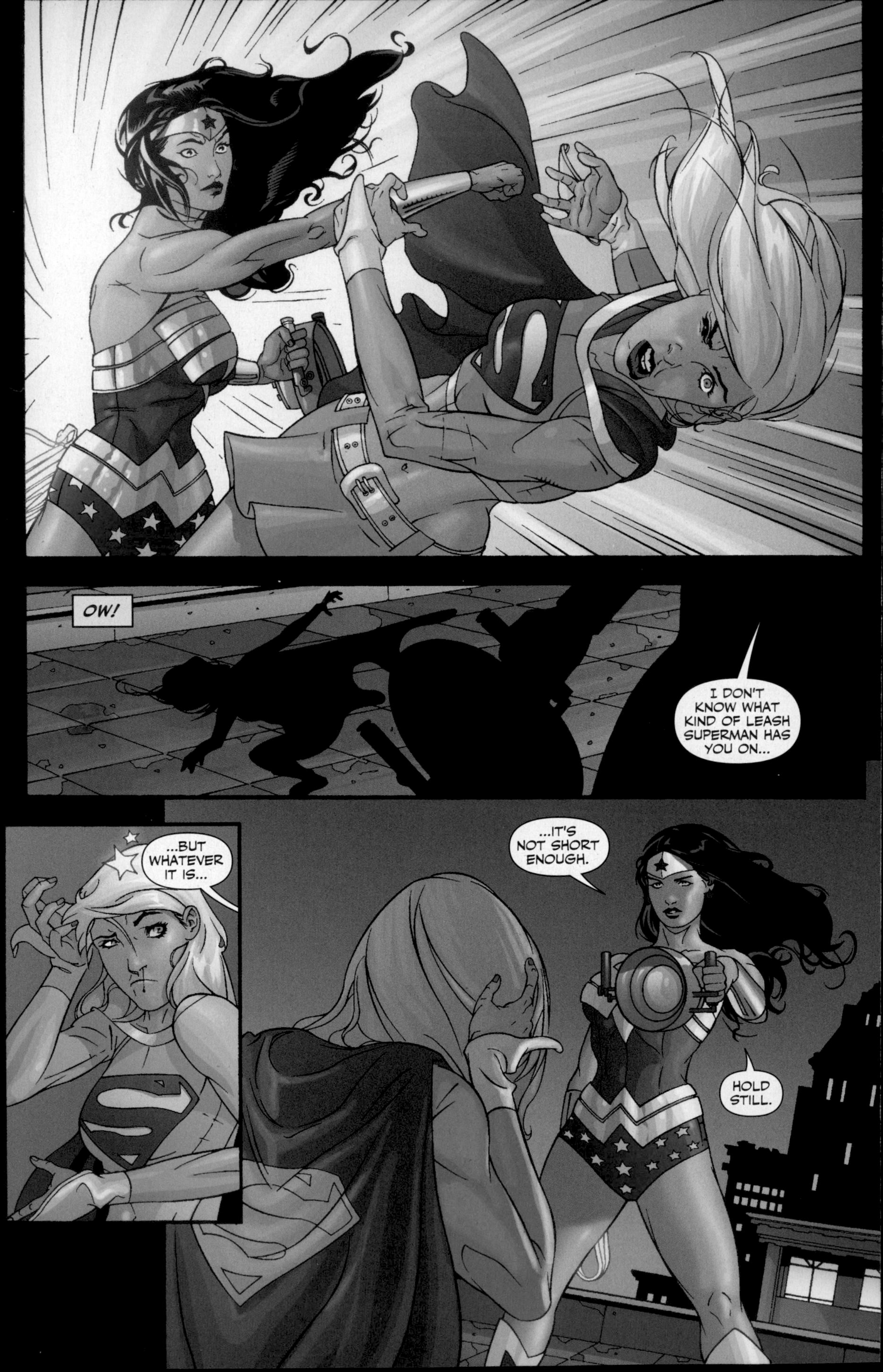

OW!
I DON'T KNOW WHAT KIND OF LEASH SUPERMAN HAS YOU ON...
...BUT WHATEVER IT IS...
...IT'S NOT SHORT ENOUGH.
HOLD STILL.

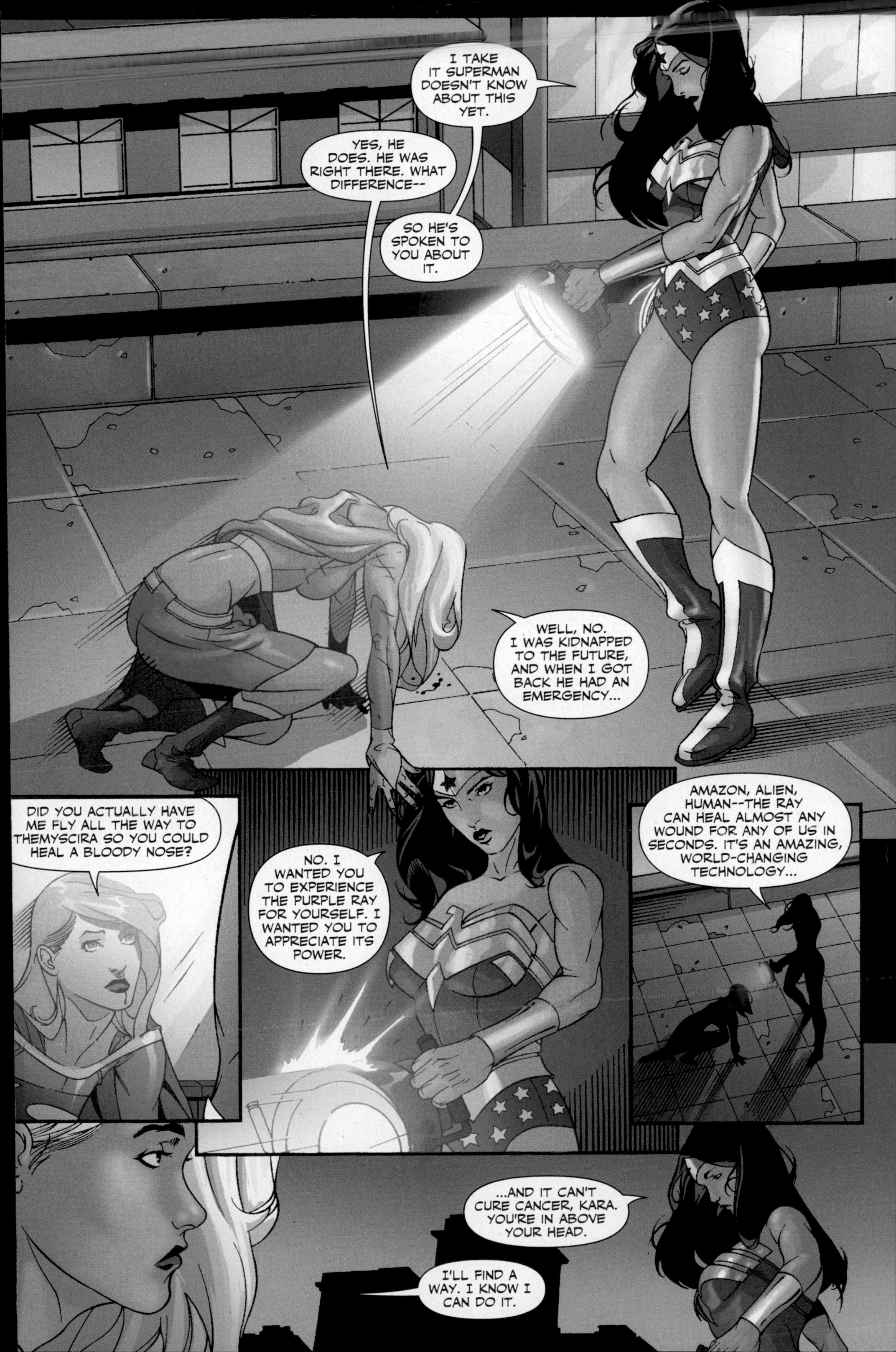
I TAKE IT SUPERMAN DOESN'T KNOW ABOUT THIS YET.
YES, HE DOES. HE WAS RIGHT THERE. WHAT DIFFERENCE--
SO HE'S SPOKEN TO YOU ABOUT IT.
WELL, NO. I WAS KIDNAPPED TO THE FUTURE, AND WHEN I GOT BACK HE HAD AN EMERGENCY...
DID YOU ACTUALLY HAVE ME FLY ALL THE WAY TO THEMYSCIRA SO YOU COULD HEAL A BLOODY NOSE?
NO. I WANTED YOU TO EXPERIENCE THE PURPLE RAY FOR YOURSELF. I WANTED YOU TO APPRECIATE ITS POWER.
AMAZON, ALIEN, HUMAN--THE RAY CAN HEAL ALMOST ANY WOUND FOR ANY OF US IN SECONDS. IT'S AN AMAZING, WORLD-CHANGING TECHNOLOGY...
...AND IT CAN'T CURE CANCER, KARA. YOU'RE IN ABOVE YOUR HEAD.
I'LL FIND A WAY. I KNOW I CAN DO IT.

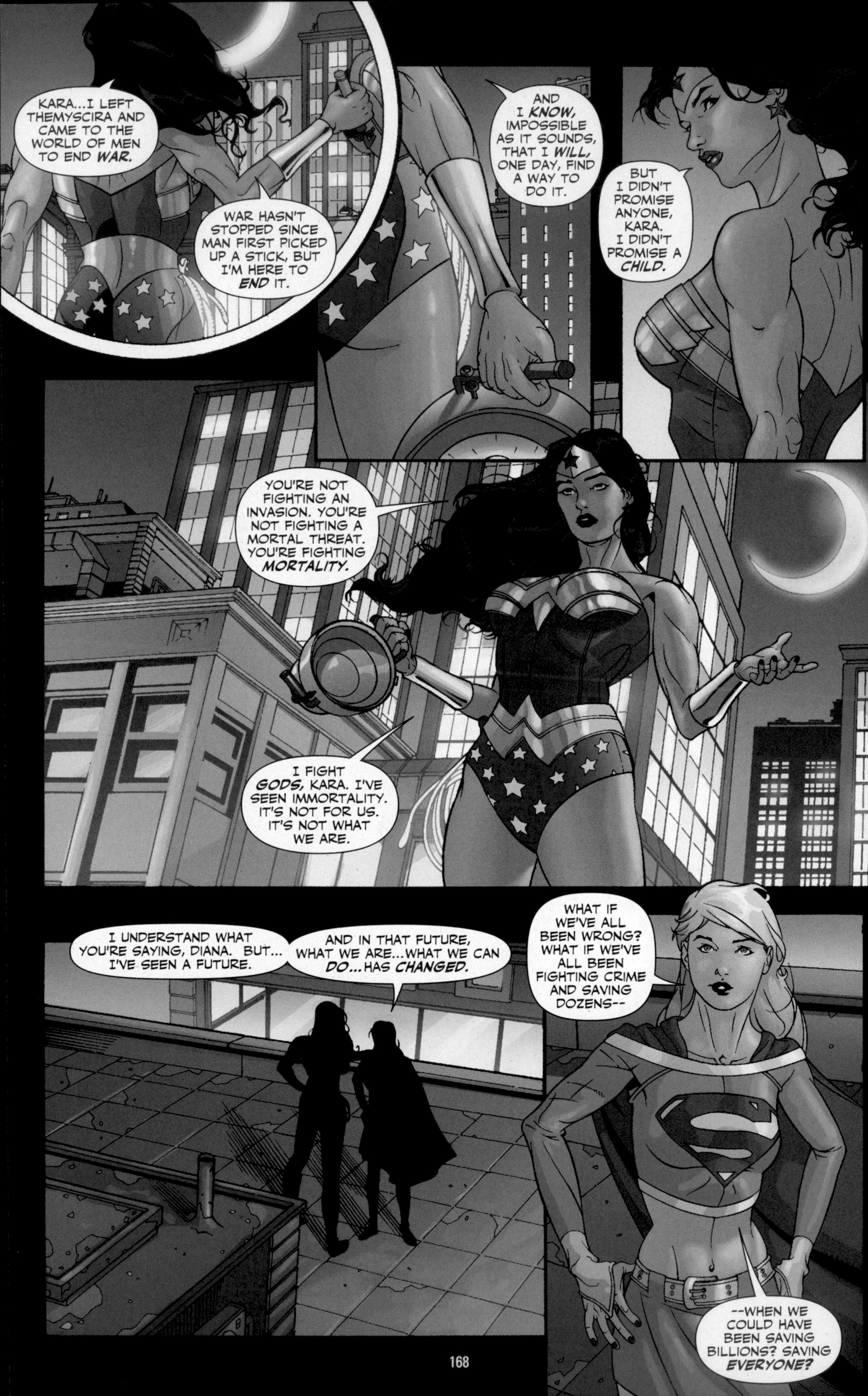
KARA...I LEFT THEMYSCIRA AND CAME TO THE WORLD OF MEN TO END WAR.
WAR HASN'T STOPPED SINCE MAN FIRST PICKED UP A STICK, BUT I'M HERE TO END IT.
AND I KNOW, IMPOSSIBLE AS IT SOUNDS, THAT I WILL, ONE DAY, FIND A WAY TO DO IT.
BUT I DIDN'T PROMISE ANYONE, KARA. I DIDN'T PROMISE A CHILD.
YOU'RE NOT FIGHTING AN INVASION. YOU'RE NOT FIGHTING A MORTAL THREAT. YOU'RE FIGHTING MORTALITY.
I FIGHT GODS, KARA. I'VE SEEN IMMORTALITY. IT'S NOT FOR US. IT'S NOT WHAT WE ARE.
I UNDERSTAND WHAT YOU'RE SAYING, DIANA. BUT... I'VE SEEN A FUTURE.
AND IN THAT FUTURE, WHAT WE ARE...WHAT WE CAN DO...HAS CHANGED.
WHAT IF WE'VE ALL BEEN WRONG? WHAT IF WE'VE ALL BEEN FIGHTING CRIME AND SAVING DOZENS--
--WHEN WE COULD HAVE BEEN SAVING BILLIONS? SAVING EVERYONE?

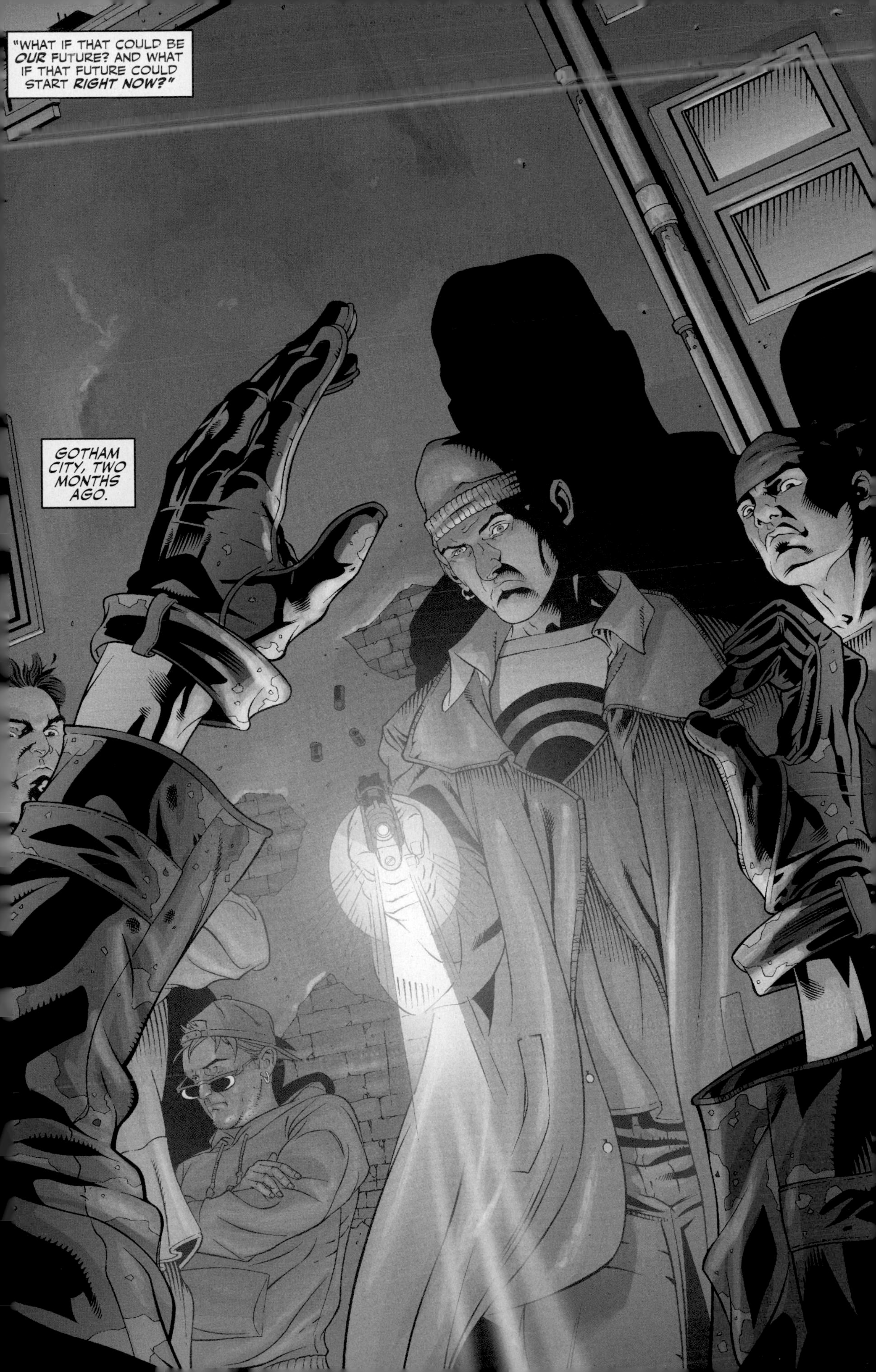
"WHAT IF THAT COULD BE OUR FUTURE? AND WHAT IF THAT FUTURE COULD START RIGHT NOW?"
GOTHAM CITY, TWO MONTHS AGO.

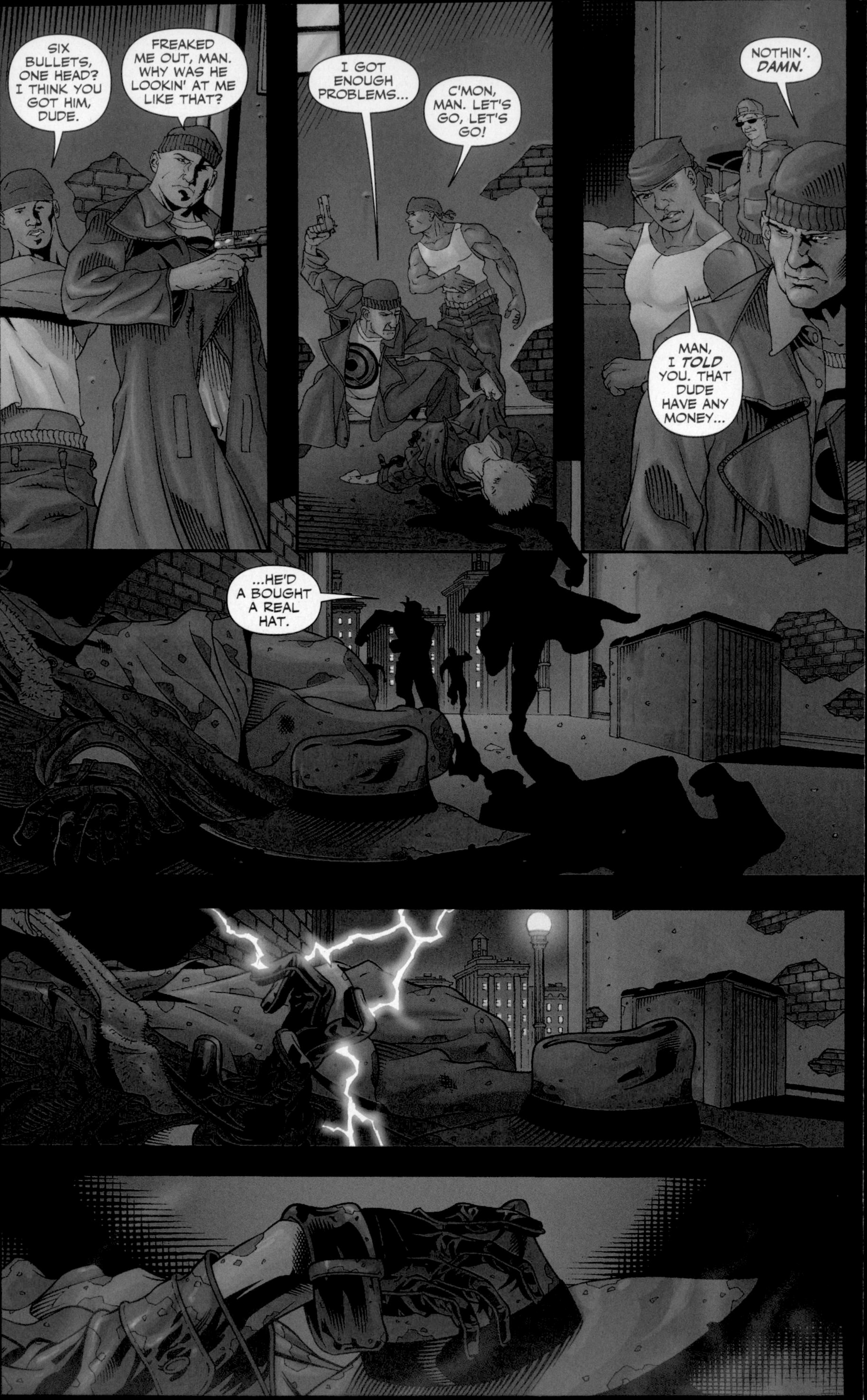
SIX BULLETS, ONE HEAD? I THINK YOU GOT HIM, DUDE.
FREAKED ME OUT, MAN. WHY WAS HE LOOKIN' AT ME LIKE THAT?
I GOT ENOUGH PROBLEMS...
C'MON, MAN. LET'S GO, LET'S GO!
NOTHIN'. DAMN.
MAN, I TOLD YOU. THAT DUDE HAVE ANY MONEY...
...HE'D A BOUGHT A REAL HAT.

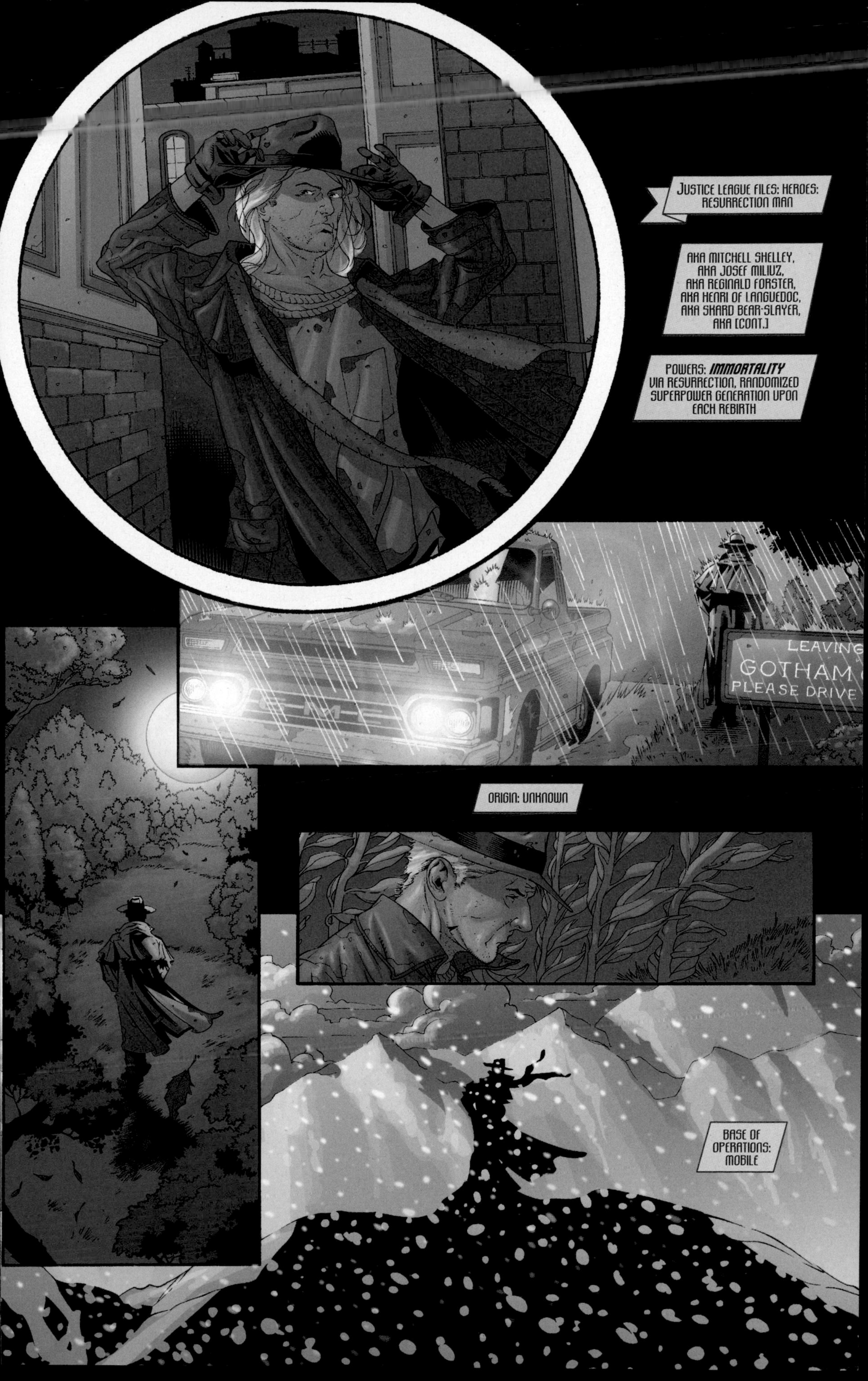
JUSTICE LEAGUE FILES: HEROES: RESURRECTION MAN
AKA MITCHELL SHELLEY, AKA JOSEF MILIUZ, AKA REGINALD FORSTER, AKA HENRI OF LANGUEDOC, AKA SKARD BEAR-SLAYER, AKA [CONT.]
POWERS: ***IMMORTALITY*** VIA RESURRECTION, RANDOMIZED SUPERPOWER GENERATION UPON EACH REBIRTH
LEAVING
GOTHAM
PLEASE DRIVE
ORIGIN: UNKNOWN
BASE OF OPERATIONS: MOBILE

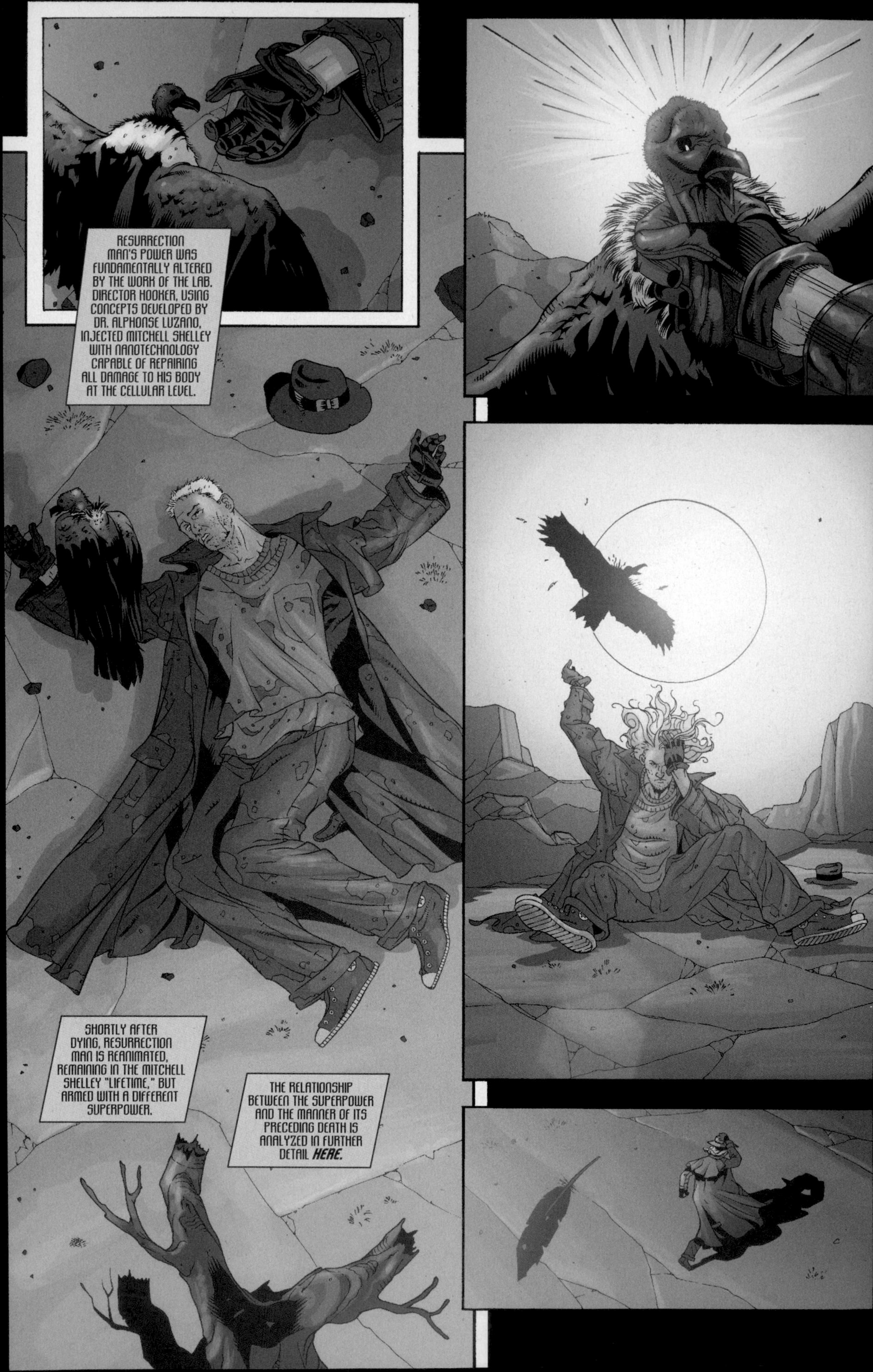
RESURRECTION MAN'S POWER WAS FUNDAMENTALLY ALTERED BY THE WORK OF THE LAB. DIRECTOR HOOKER, USING CONCEPTS DEVELOPED BY DR. ALPHONSE LUZANO, INJECTED MITCHELL SHELLEY WITH NANOTECHNOLOGY CAPABLE OF REPAIRING ALL DAMAGE TO HIS BODY AT THE CELLULAR LEVEL.
SHORTLY AFTER DYING, RESURRECTION MAN IS REANIMATED, REMAINING IN THE MITCHELL SHELLEY "LIFETIME," BUT ARMED WITH A DIFFERENT SUPERPOWER.
THE RELATIONSHIP BETWEEN THE SUPERPOWER AND THE MANNER OF ITS PRECEDING DEATH IS ANALYZED IN FURTHER DETAIL *HERE*.

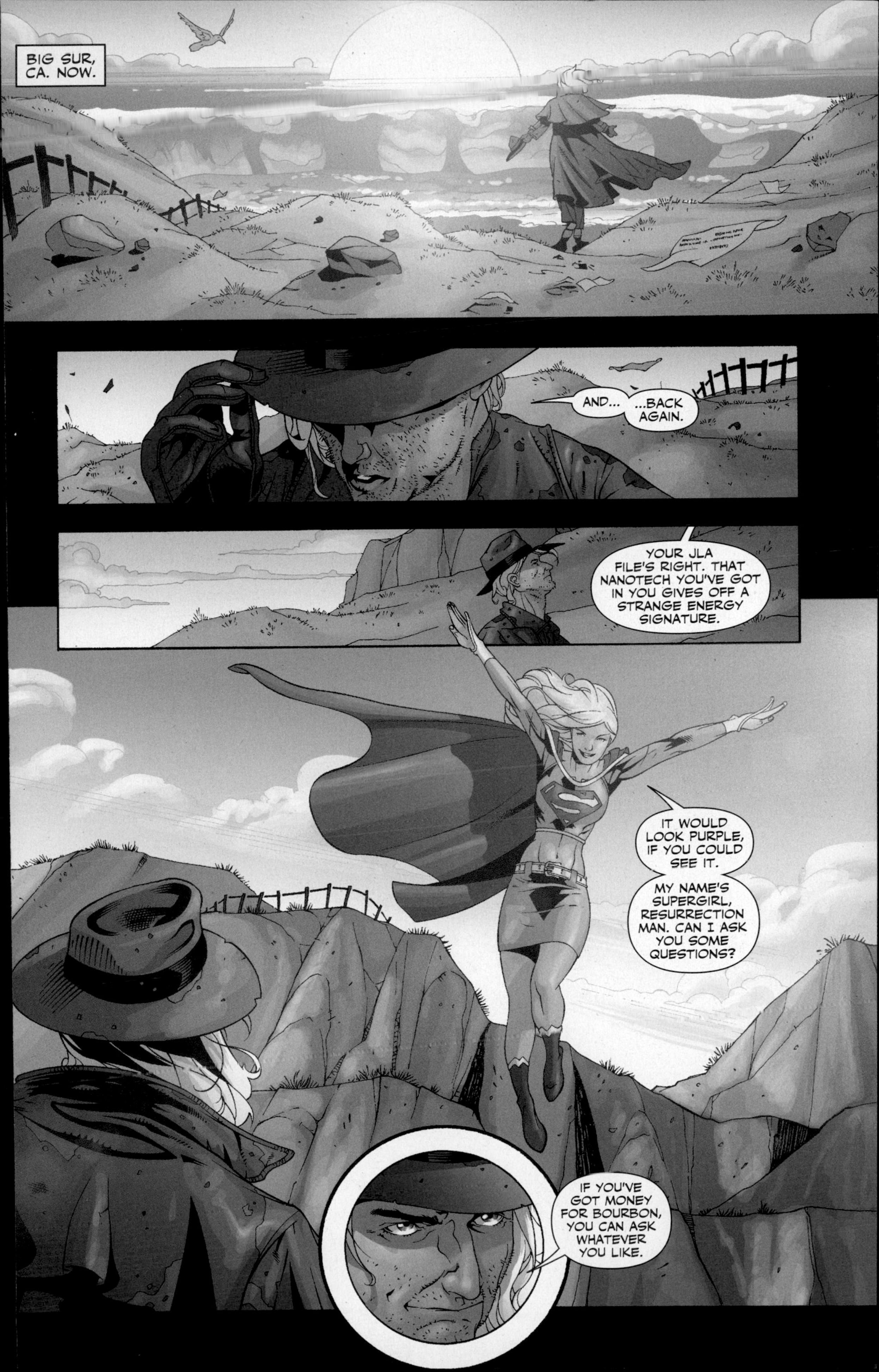
BIG SUR, CA. NOW.
AND...
...BACK AGAIN.
YOUR JLA FILE'S RIGHT. THAT NANOTECH YOU'VE GOT IN YOU GIVES OFF A STRANGE ENERGY SIGNATURE.
IT WOULD LOOK PURPLE, IF YOU COULD SEE IT.
MY NAME'S SUPERGIRL, RESURRECTION MAN. CAN I ASK YOU SOME QUESTIONS?
IF YOU'VE GOT MONEY FOR BOURBON, YOU CAN ASK WHATEVER YOU LIKE.

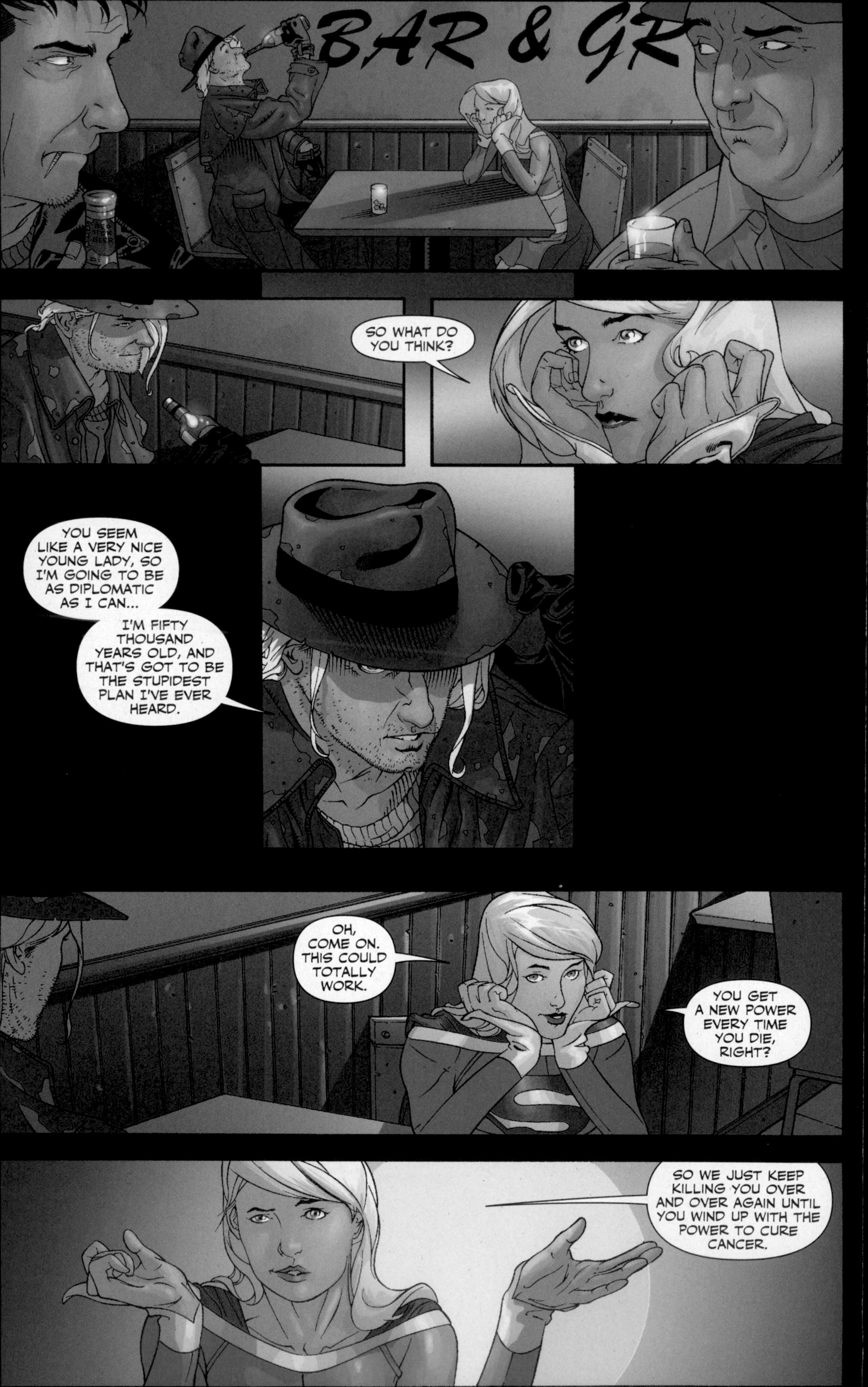
BAR & GR
SO WHAT DO YOU THINK?
YOU SEEM LIKE A VERY NICE YOUNG LADY, SO I'M GOING TO BE AS DIPLOMATIC AS I CAN...
I'M FIFTY THOUSAND YEARS OLD, AND THAT'S GOT TO BE THE STUPIDEST PLAN I'VE EVER HEARD.
OH, COME ON. THIS COULD TOTALLY WORK.
YOU GET A NEW POWER EVERY TIME YOU DIE, RIGHT?
SO WE JUST KEEP KILLING YOU OVER AND OVER AGAIN UNTIL YOU WIND UP WITH THE POWER TO CURE CANCER.

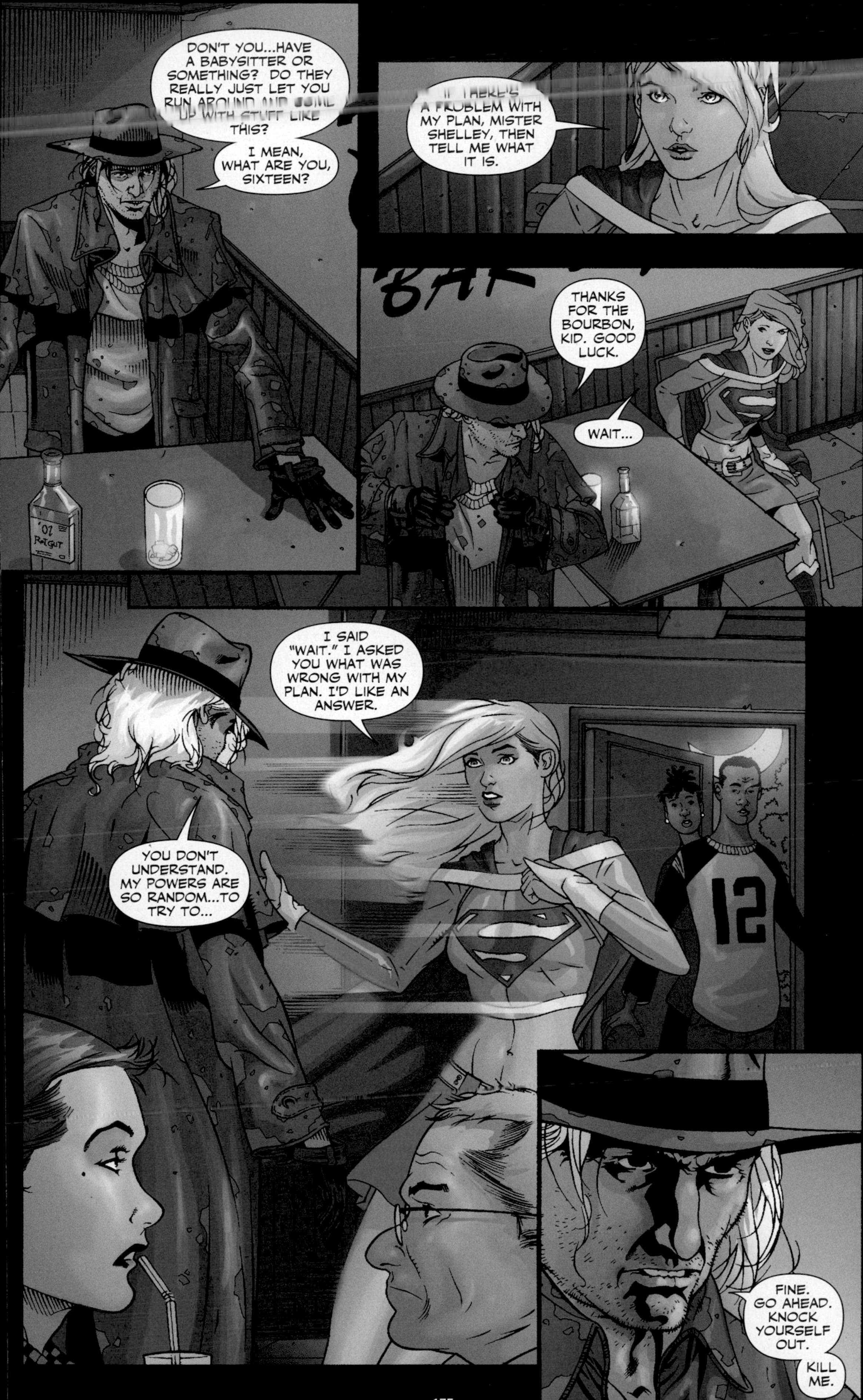
DON'T YOU...HAVE A BABYSITTER OR SOMETHING? DO THEY REALLY JUST LET YOU RUN AROUND AND UP WITH STUFF LIKE THIS?
I MEAN, WHAT ARE YOU, SIXTEEN?
IF THERE'S A PROBLEM WITH MY PLAN, MISTER SHELLEY, THEN TELL ME WHAT IT IS.
BAK
THANKS FOR THE BOURBON, KID. GOOD LUCK.
WAIT...
'02 ROTGUT
I SAID "WAIT." I ASKED YOU WHAT WAS WRONG WITH MY PLAN. I'D LIKE AN ANSWER.
YOU DON'T UNDERSTAND. MY POWERS ARE SO RANDOM...TO TRY TO...
12
FINE. GO AHEAD. KNOCK YOURSELF OUT.
KILL ME.

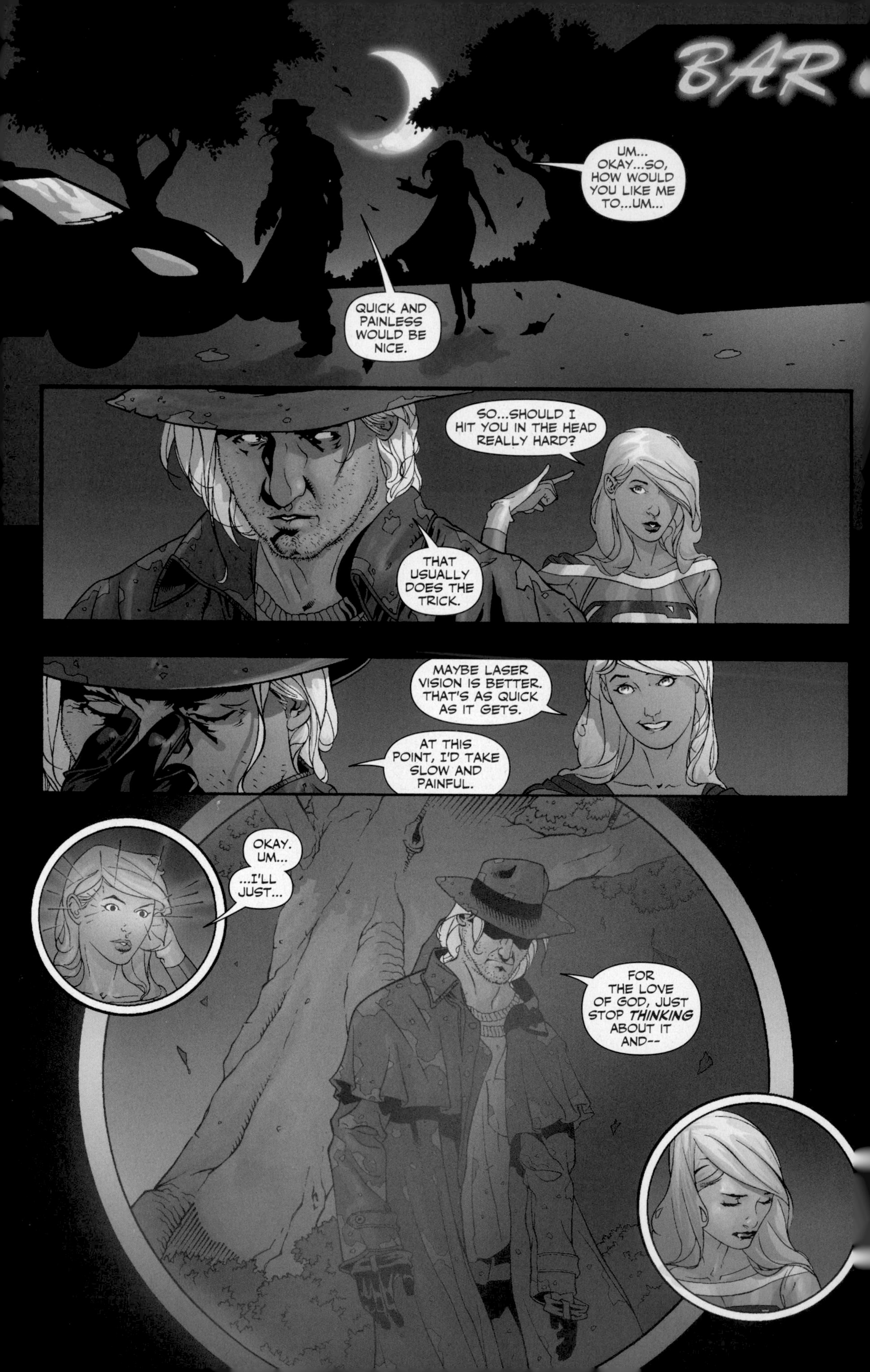
BAR
UM... OKAY...SO, HOW WOULD YOU LIKE ME TO...UM...
QUICK AND PAINLESS WOULD BE NICE.
SO...SHOULD I HIT YOU IN THE HEAD REALLY HARD?
THAT USUALLY DOES THE TRICK.
MAYBE LASER VISION IS BETTER. THAT'S AS QUICK AS IT GETS.
AT THIS POINT, I'D TAKE SLOW AND PAINFUL.
OKAY. UM... ...I'LL JUST...
FOR THE LOVE OF GOD, JUST STOP *THINKING* ABOUT IT AND--

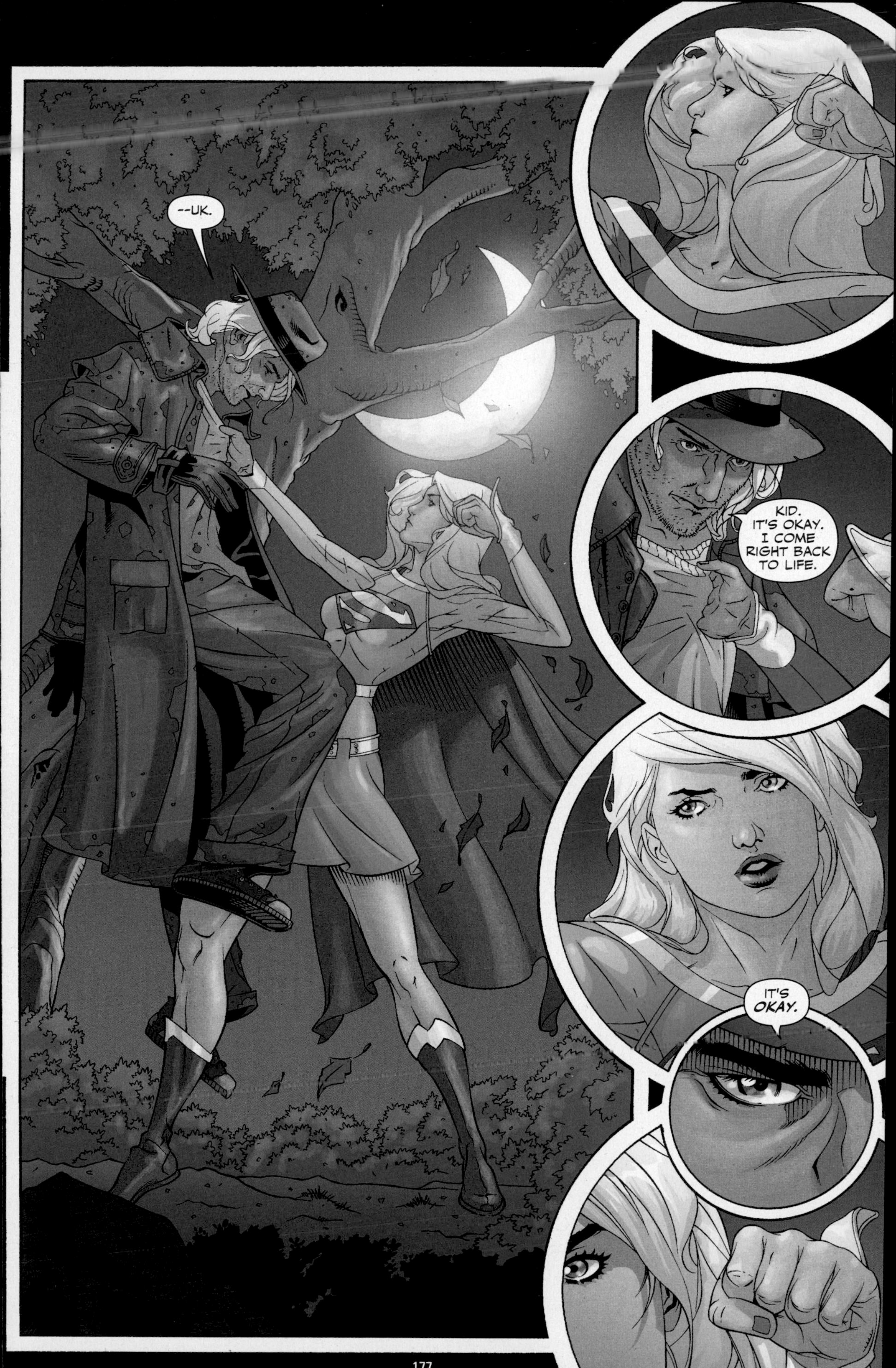
--UK.
KID. IT'S OKAY. I COME RIGHT BACK TO LIFE.
IT'S OKAY.

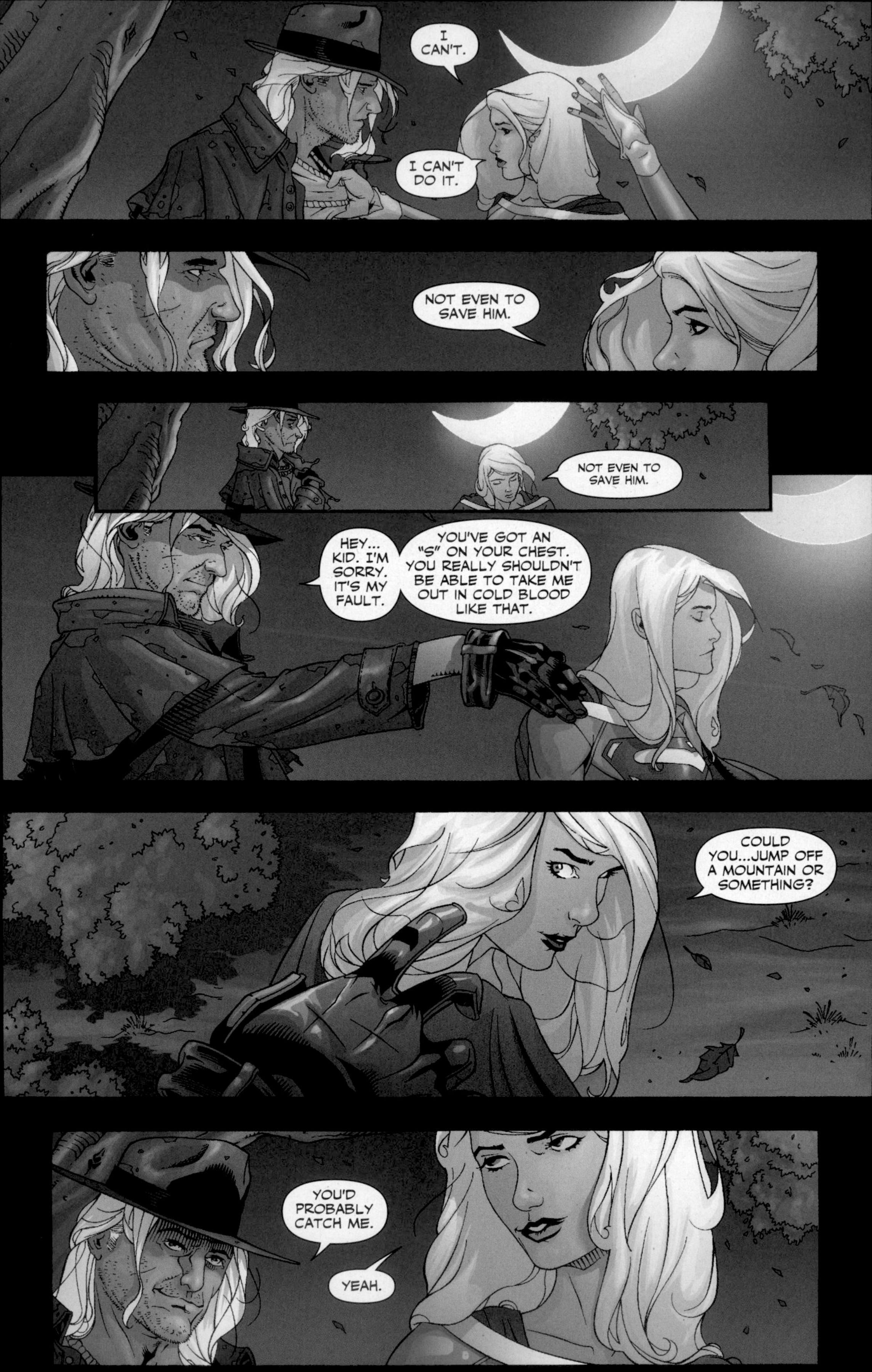
I CAN'T.
I CAN'T DO IT.
NOT EVEN TO SAVE HIM.
NOT EVEN TO SAVE HIM.
HEY... KID. I'M SORRY. IT'S MY FAULT.
YOU'VE GOT AN "S" ON YOUR CHEST. YOU REALLY SHOULDN'T BE ABLE TO TAKE ME OUT IN COLD BLOOD LIKE THAT.
COULD YOU...JUMP OFF A MOUNTAIN OR SOMETHING?
YOU'D PROBABLY CATCH ME.
YEAH.

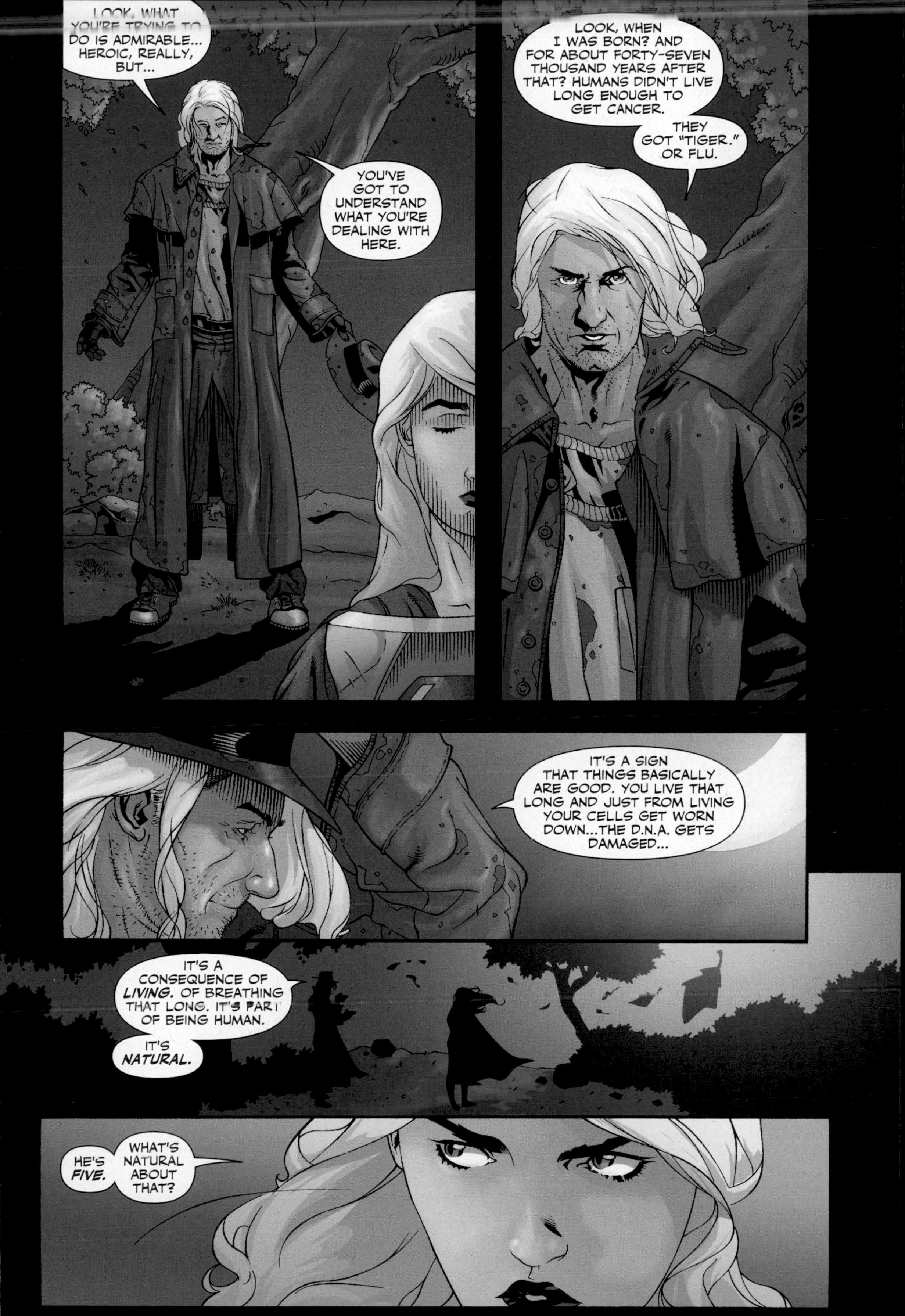
LOOK, WHAT YOU'RE TRYING TO DO IS ADMIRABLE... HEROIC, REALLY, BUT...
YOU'VE GOT TO UNDERSTAND WHAT YOU'RE DEALING WITH HERE.
LOOK, WHEN I WAS BORN? AND FOR ABOUT FORTY-SEVEN THOUSAND YEARS AFTER THAT? HUMANS DIDN'T LIVE LONG ENOUGH TO GET CANCER.
THEY GOT "TIGER." OR FLU.
IT'S A SIGN THAT THINGS BASICALLY ARE GOOD. YOU LIVE THAT LONG AND JUST FROM LIVING YOUR CELLS GET WORN DOWN...THE D.N.A. GETS DAMAGED...
IT'S A CONSEQUENCE OF *LIVING.* OF BREATHING THAT LONG. IT'S PART OF BEING HUMAN.
IT'S *NATURAL.*
HE'S *FIVE.*
WHAT'S NATURAL ABOUT THAT?

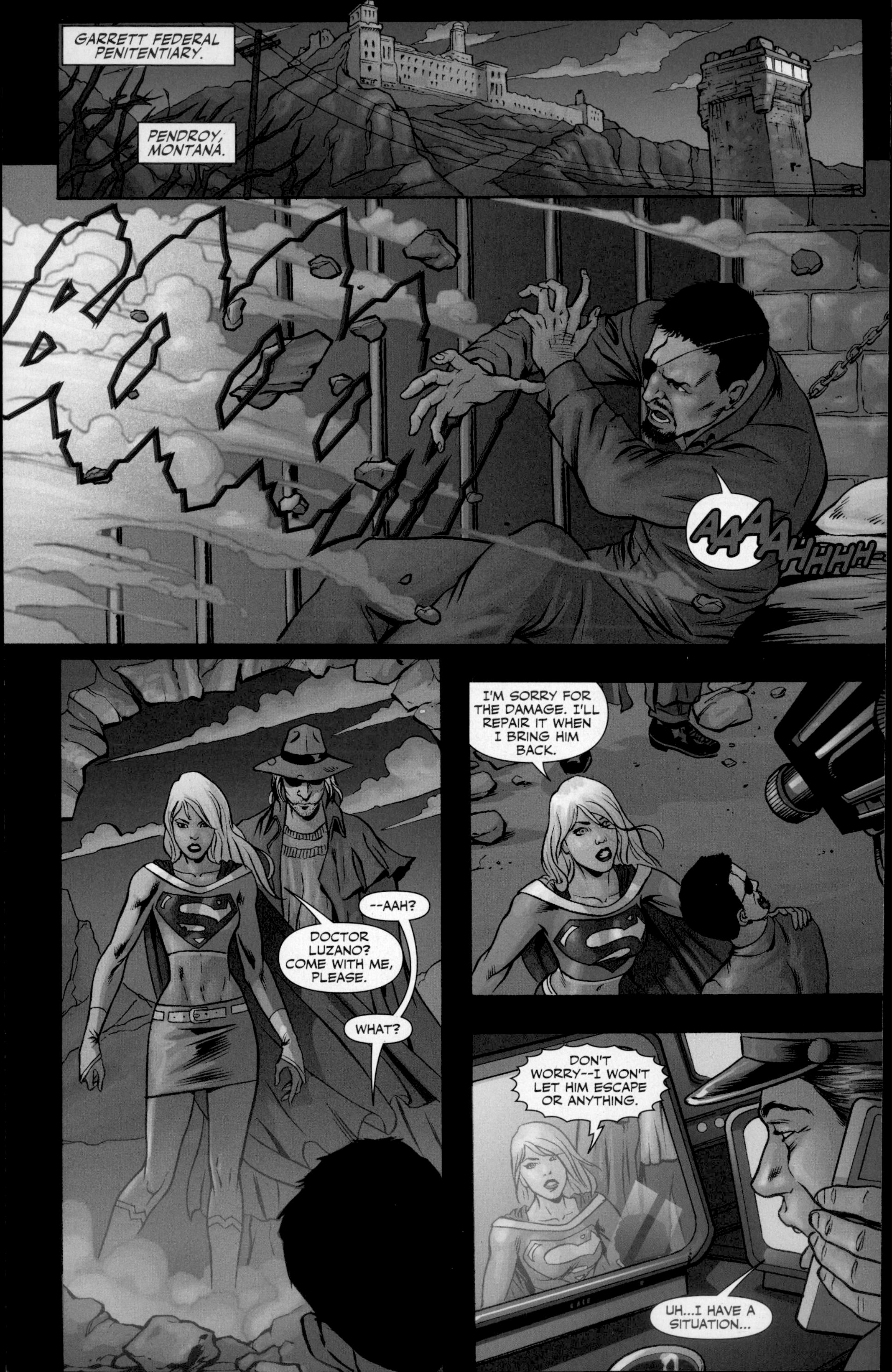

GARRETT FEDERAL PENITENTIARY.
PENDROY, MONTANA.
AAAAHHHH--
--AAH?
DOCTOR LUZANO? COME WITH ME, PLEASE.
WHAT?
I'M SORRY FOR THE DAMAGE. I'LL REPAIR IT WHEN I BRING HIM BACK.
DON'T WORRY--I WON'T LET HIM ESCAPE OR ANYTHING.
UH...I HAVE A SITUATION...

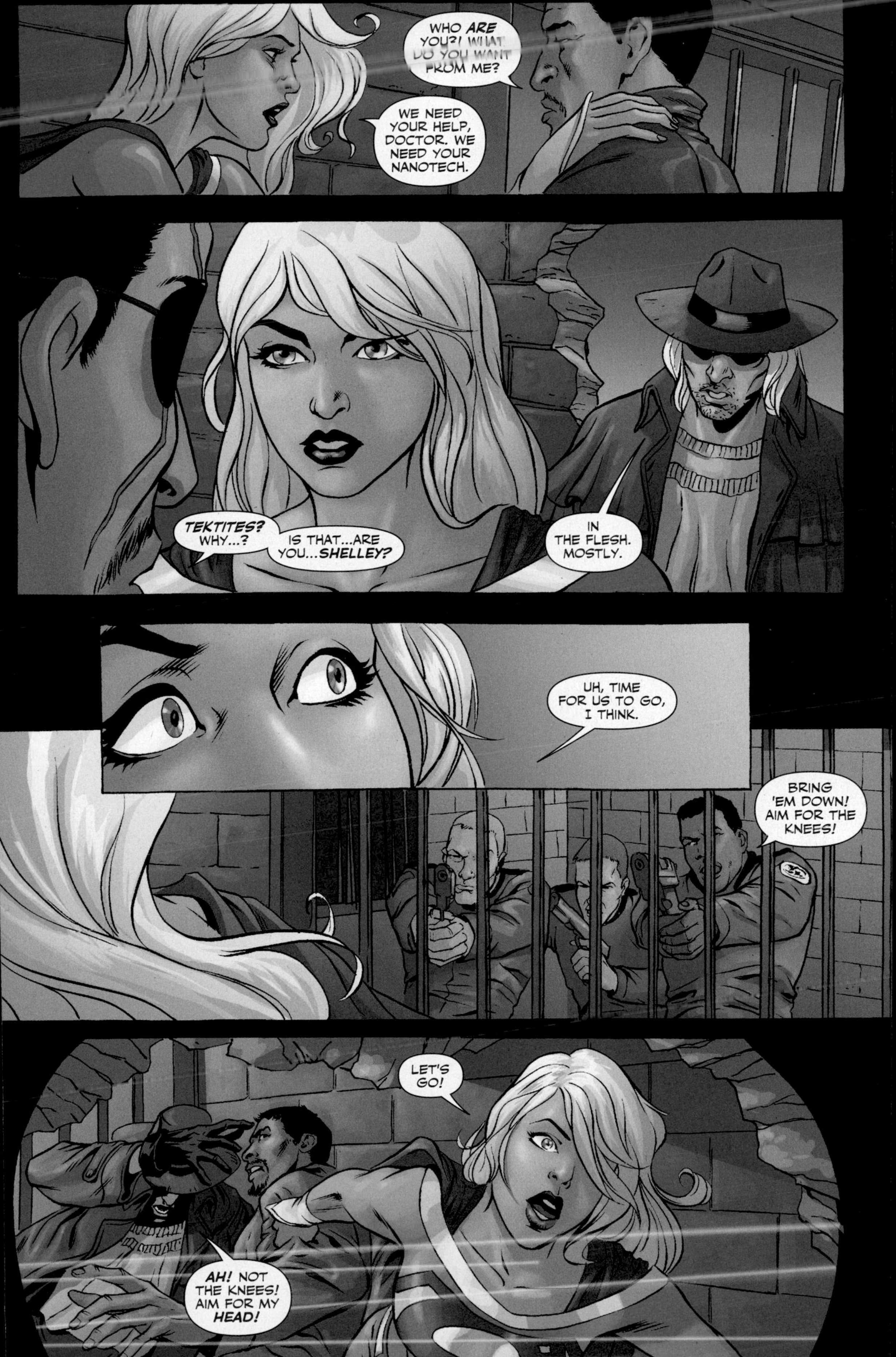
WHO **ARE** YOU?! WHAT DO YOU WANT FROM ME?
WE NEED YOUR HELP, DOCTOR. WE NEED YOUR NANOTECH.
TEKTITES? WHY...?
IS THAT...ARE YOU...***SHELLEY?***
IN THE FLESH. MOSTLY.
UH, TIME FOR US TO GO, I THINK.
BRING 'EM DOWN! AIM FOR THE KNEES!
LET'S GO!
AH! NOT THE KNEES! AIM FOR MY ***HEAD!***

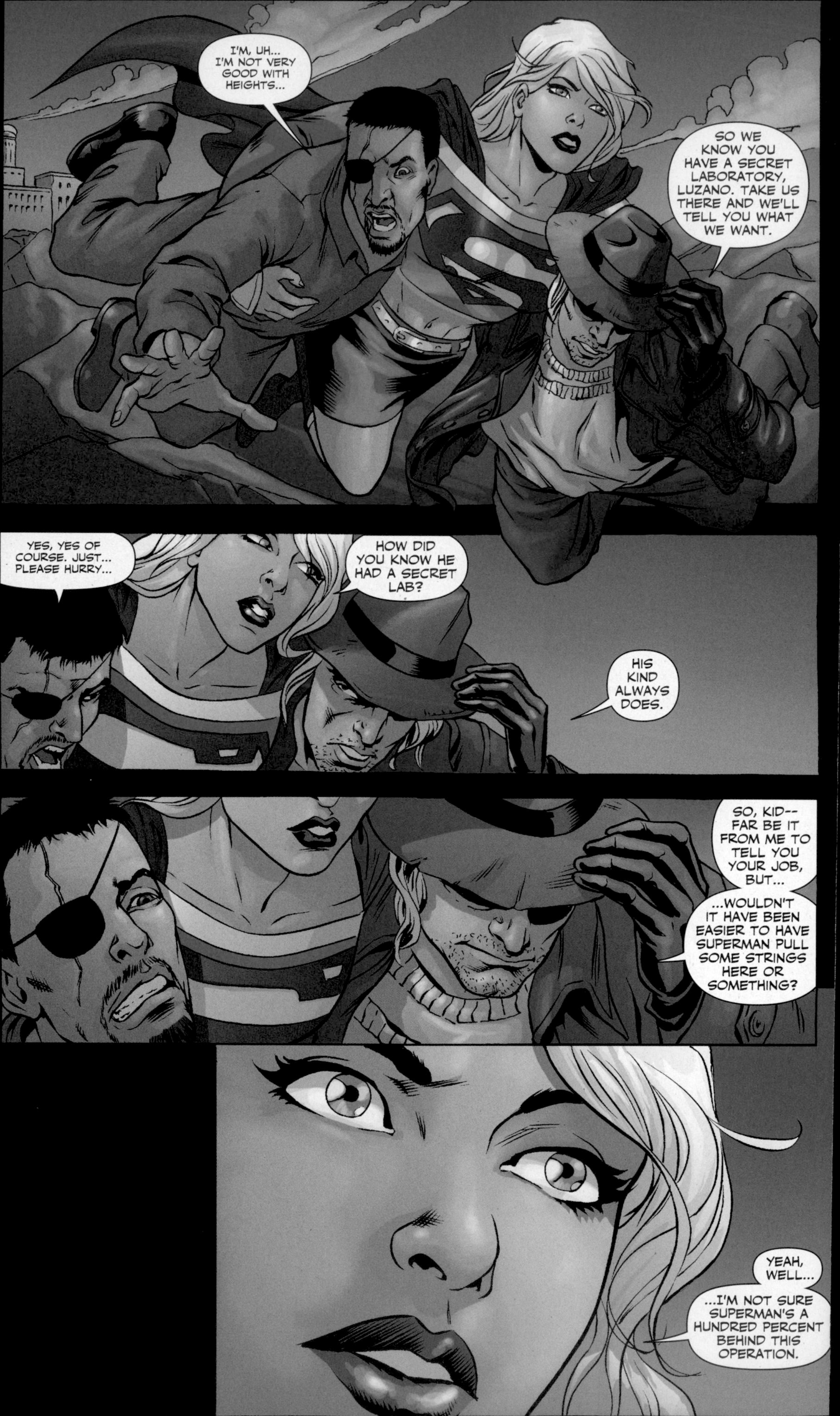
I'M, UH... I'M NOT VERY GOOD WITH HEIGHTS...
SO WE KNOW YOU HAVE A SECRET LABORATORY, LUZANO. TAKE US THERE AND WE'LL TELL YOU WHAT WE WANT.
YES, YES OF COURSE. JUST... PLEASE HURRY...
HOW DID YOU KNOW HE HAD A SECRET LAB?
HIS KIND ALWAYS DOES.
SO, KID-- FAR BE IT FROM ME TO TELL YOU YOUR JOB, BUT...
...WOULDN'T IT HAVE BEEN EASIER TO HAVE SUPERMAN PULL SOME STRINGS HERE OR SOMETHING?
YEAH, WELL...
...I'M NOT SURE SUPERMAN'S A HUNDRED PERCENT BEHIND THIS OPERATION.

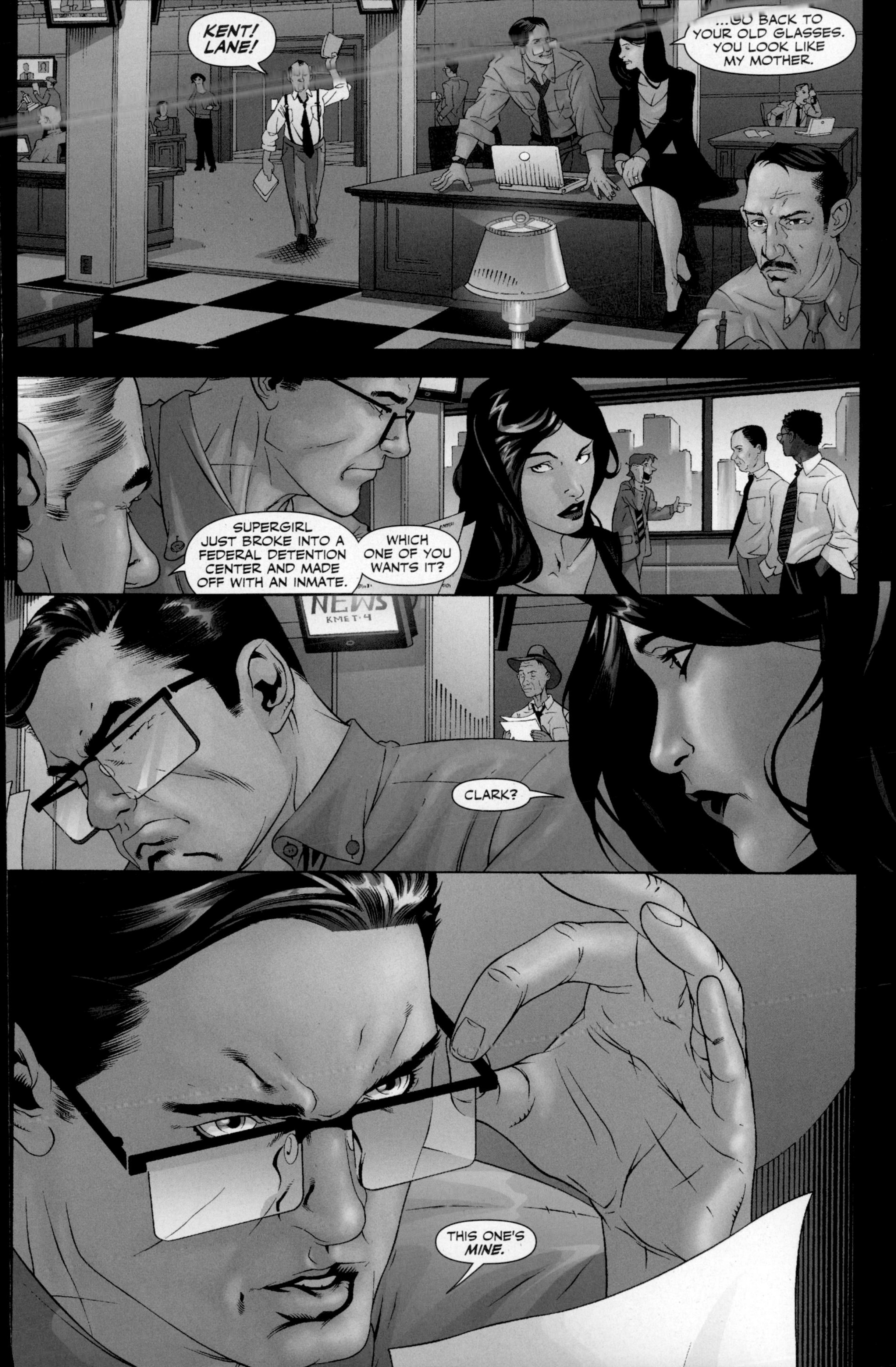
KENT! LANE!
...GO BACK TO YOUR OLD GLASSES. YOU LOOK LIKE MY MOTHER.
SUPERGIRL JUST BROKE INTO A FEDERAL DETENTION CENTER AND MADE OFF WITH AN INMATE.
WHICH ONE OF YOU WANTS IT?
NEWS
KMET·4
CLARK?
THIS ONE'S MINE.

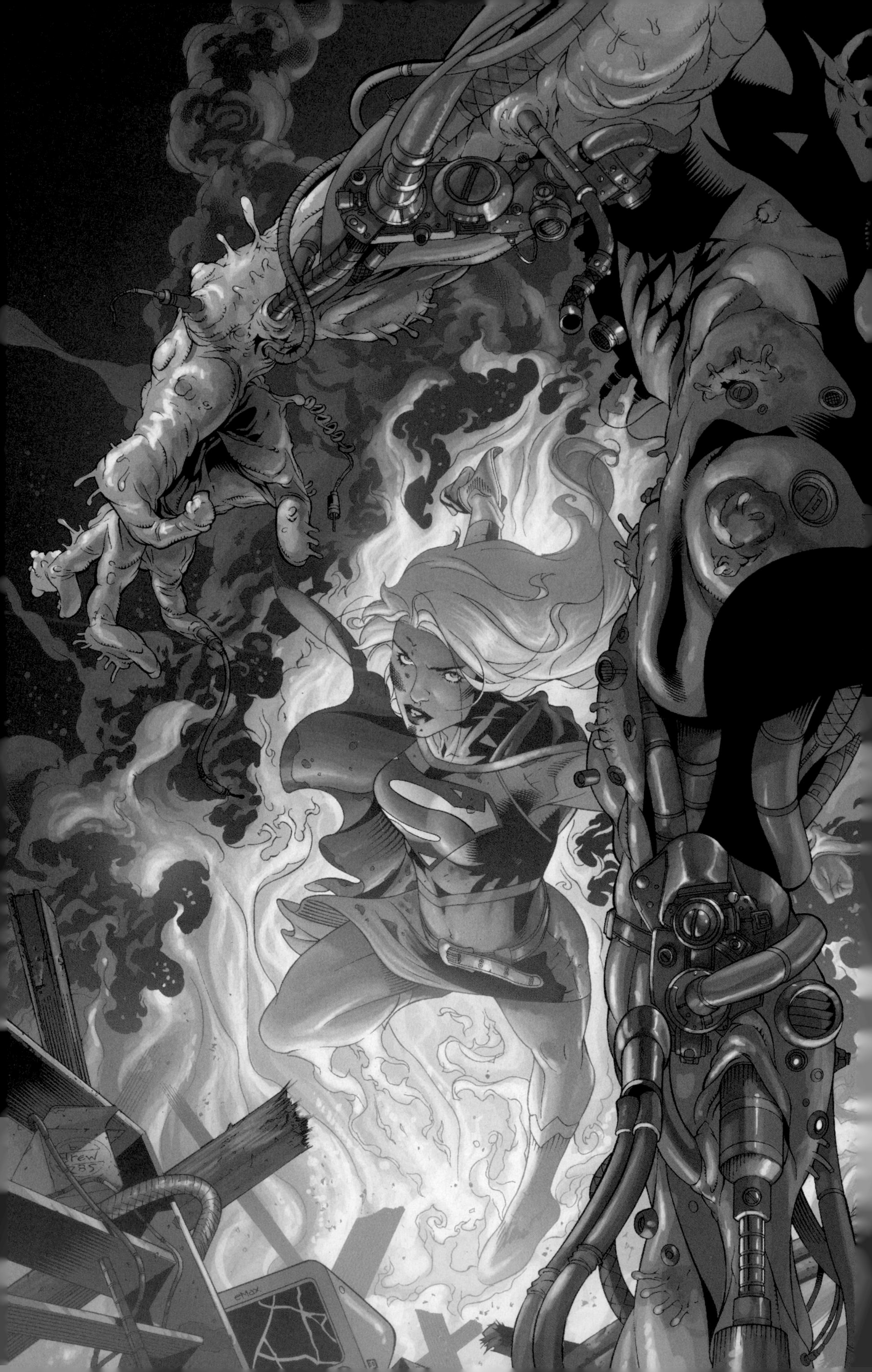

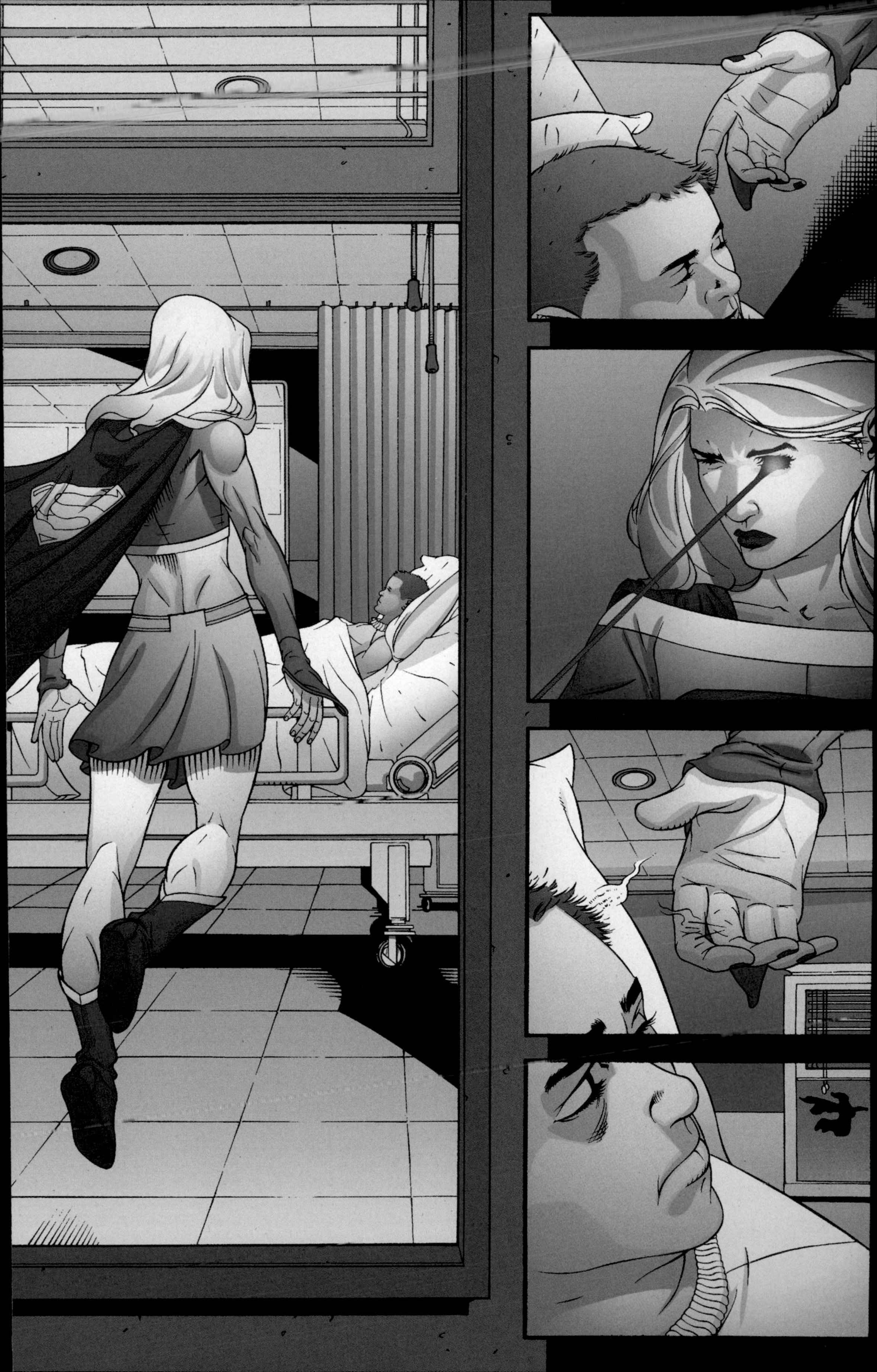

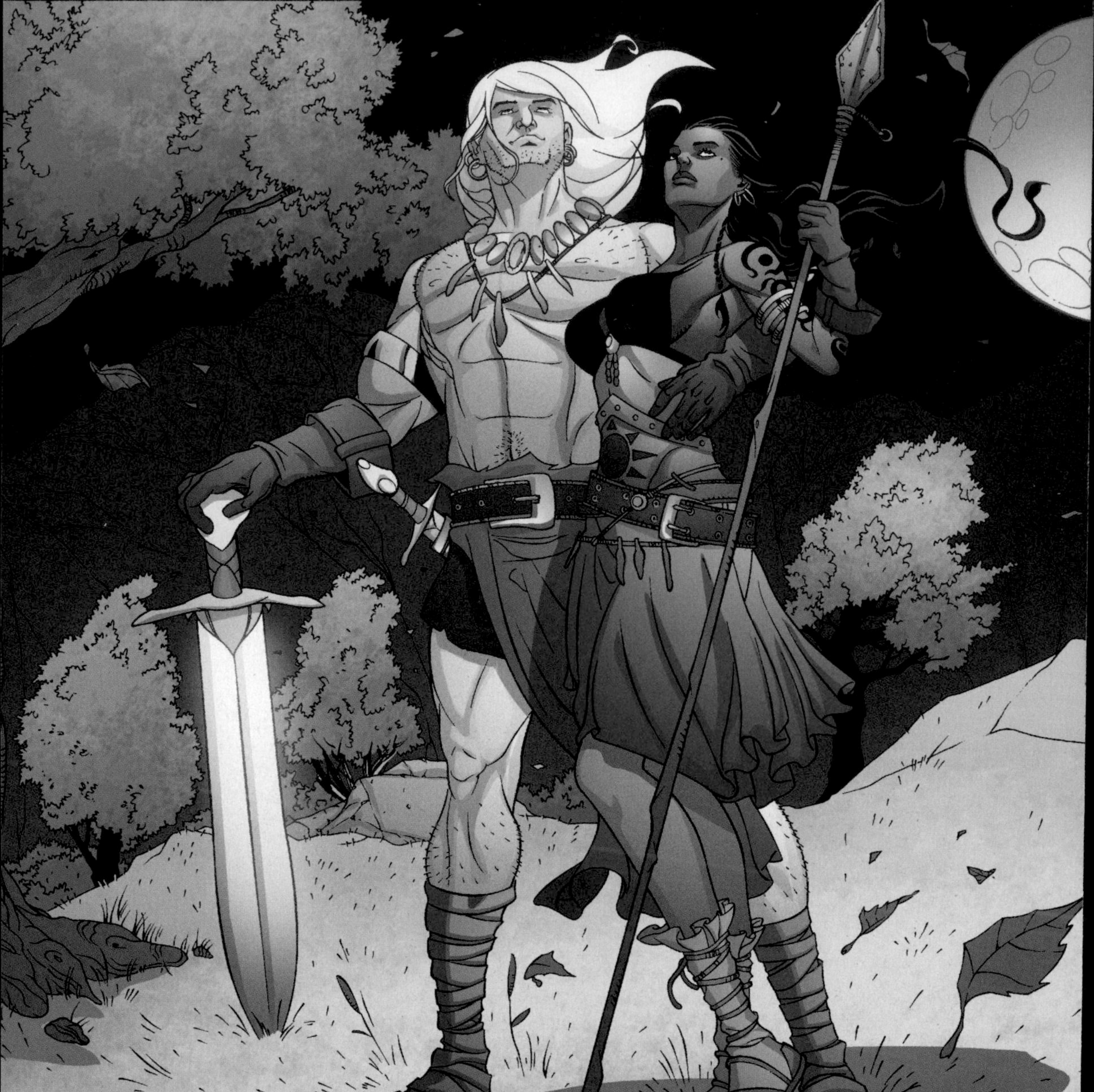

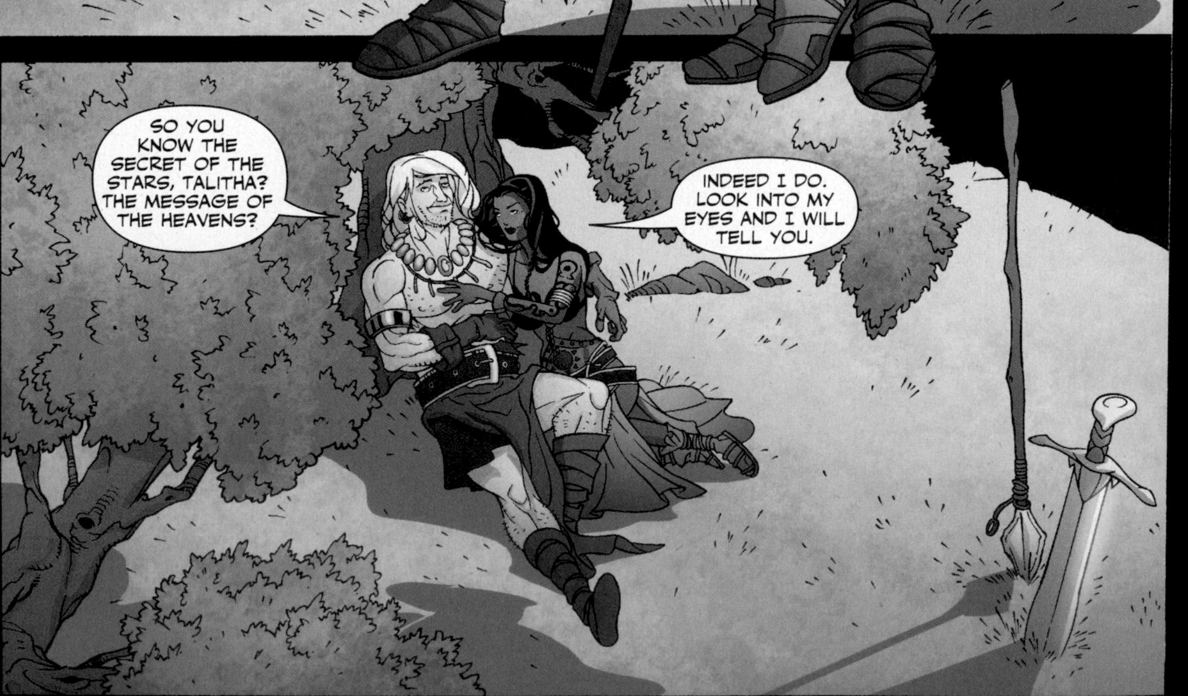
SO YOU KNOW THE SECRET OF THE STARS, TALITHA? THE MESSAGE OF THE HEAVENS?
INDEED I DO. LOOK INTO MY EYES AND I WILL TELL YOU.

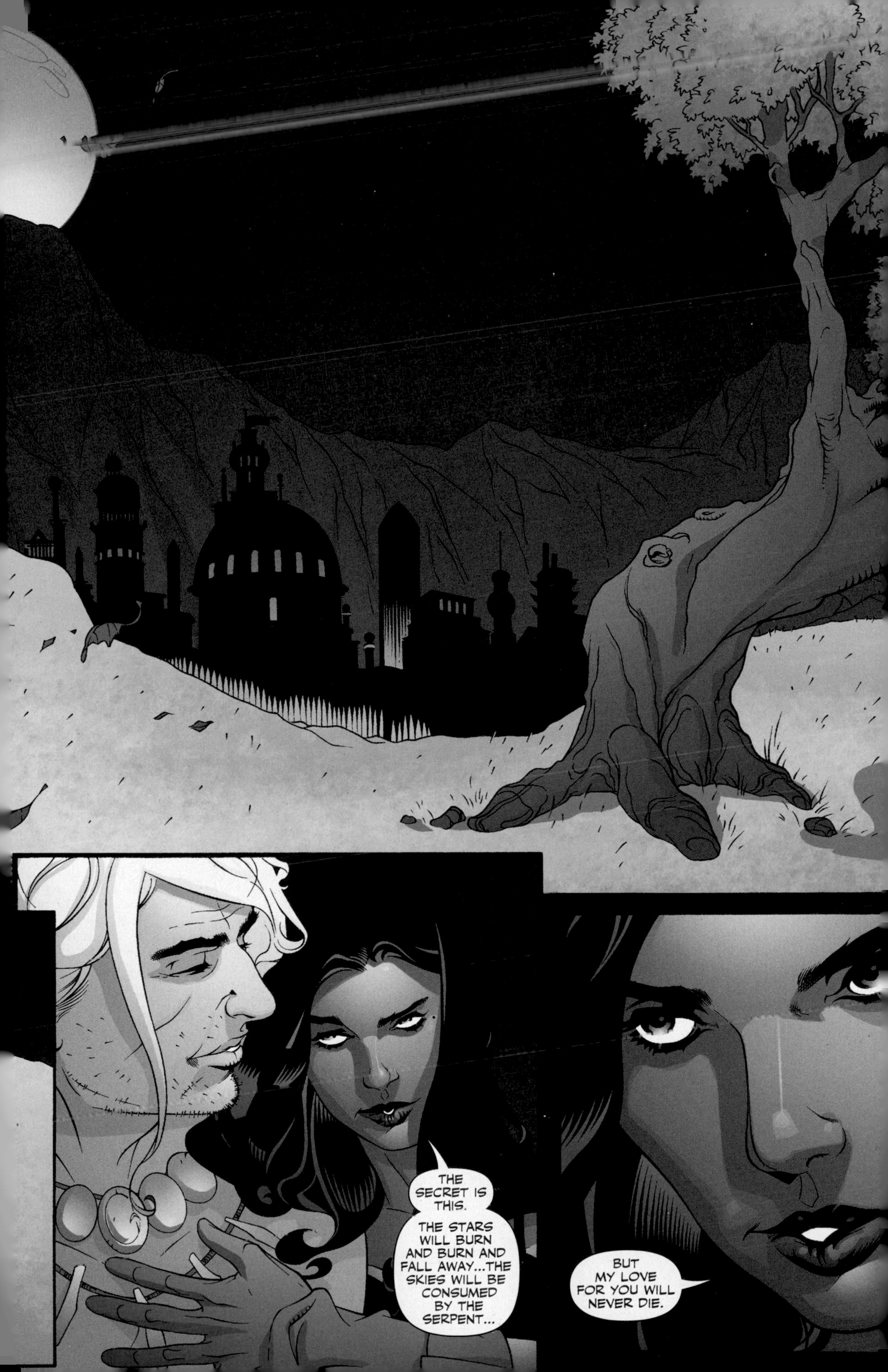
THE SECRET IS THIS.
THE STARS WILL BURN AND BURN AND FALL AWAY...THE SKIES WILL BE CONSUMED BY THE SERPENT...
BUT MY LOVE FOR YOU WILL NEVER DIE.

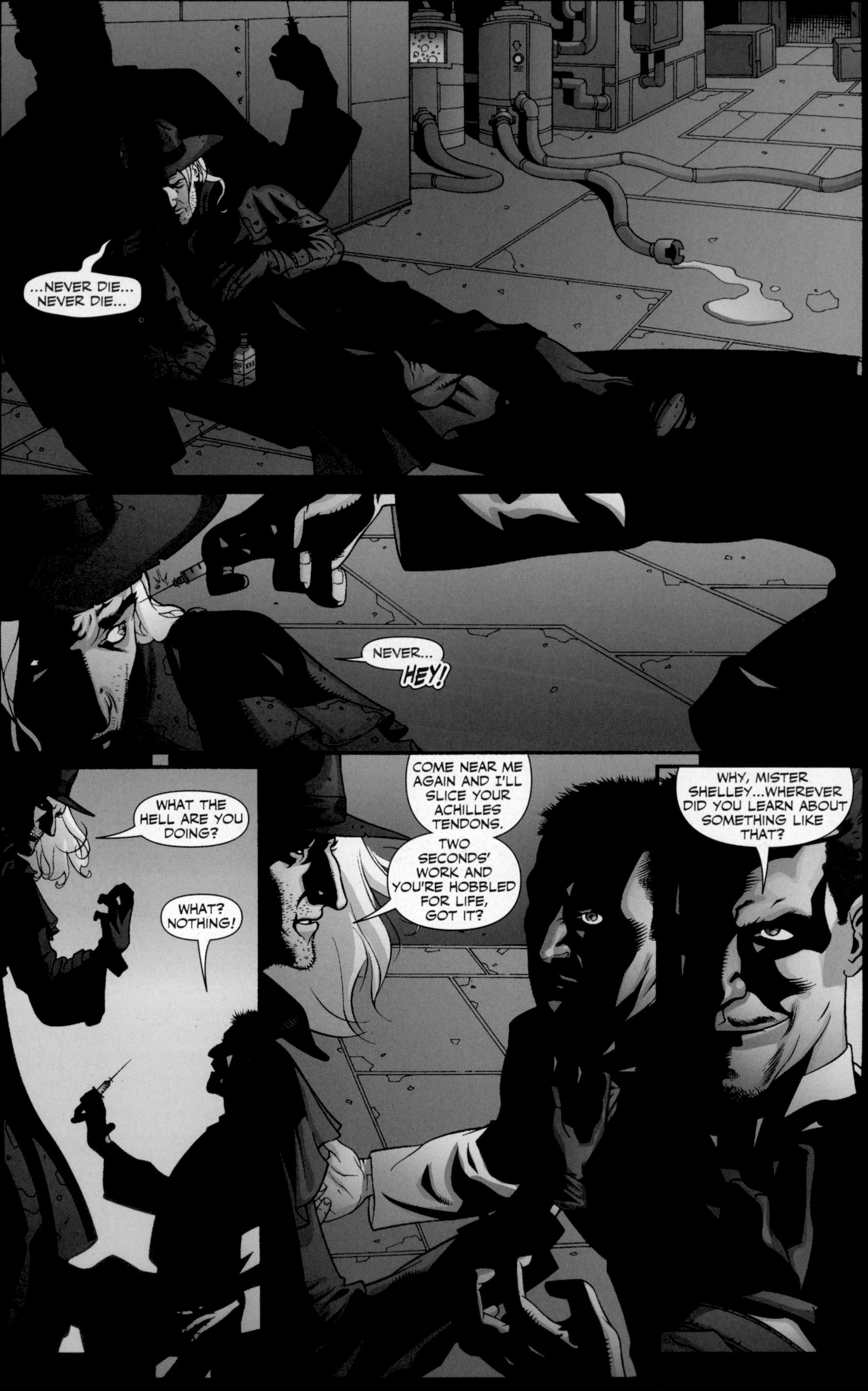
...NEVER DIE... NEVER DIE...
NEVER... HEY!
WHAT THE HELL ARE YOU DOING?
WHAT? NOTHING!
COME NEAR ME AGAIN AND I'LL SLICE YOUR ACHILLES TENDONS.
TWO SECONDS' WORK AND YOU'RE HOBBLED FOR LIFE, GOT IT?
WHY, MISTER SHELLEY...WHEREVER DID YOU LEARN ABOUT SOMETHING LIKE THAT?

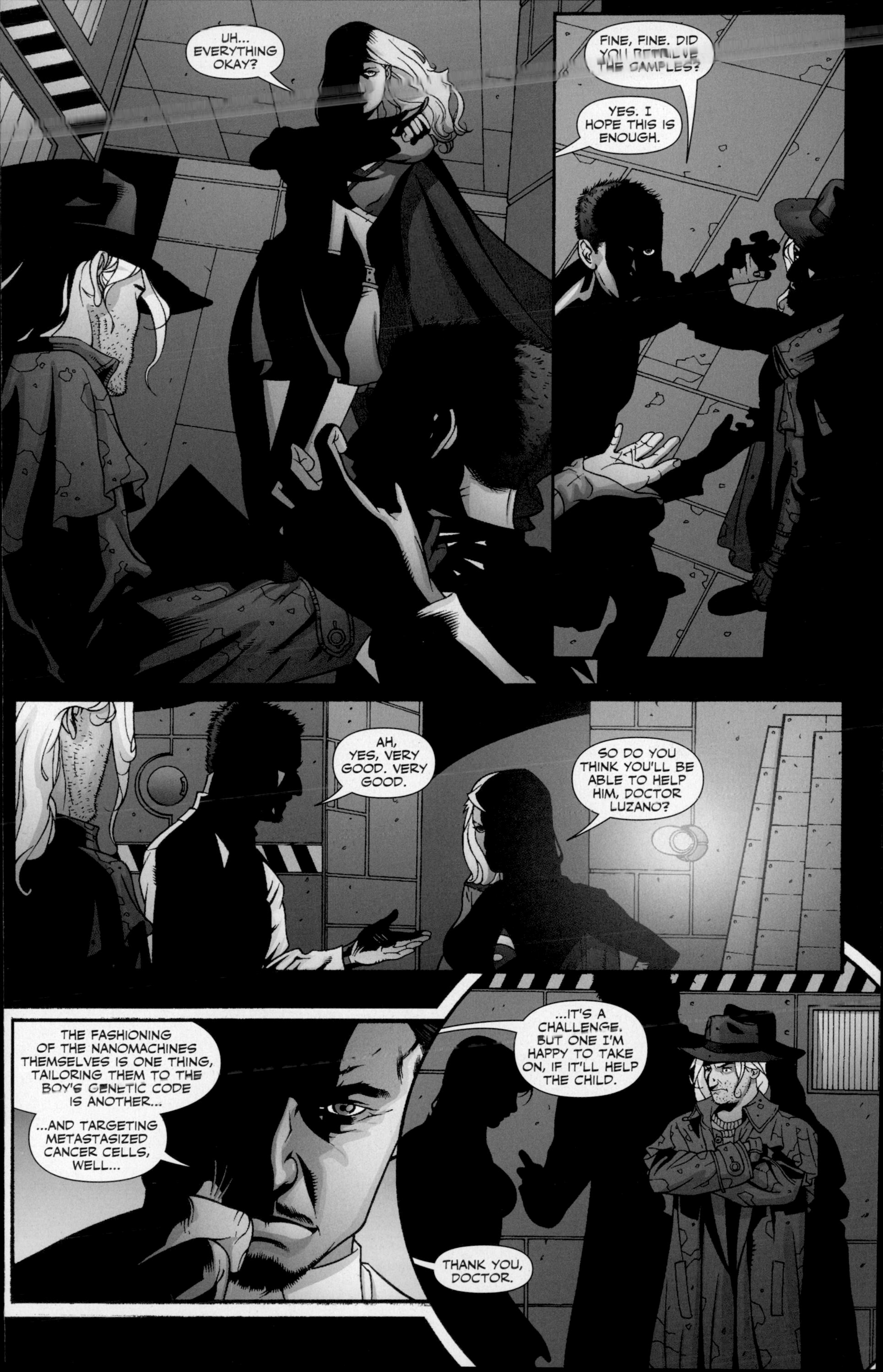
UH... EVERYTHING OKAY?
FINE, FINE. DID YOU RETRIEVE THE SAMPLES?
YES. I HOPE THIS IS ENOUGH.
AH, YES, VERY GOOD. VERY GOOD.
SO DO YOU THINK YOU'LL BE ABLE TO HELP HIM, DOCTOR LUZANO?
THE FASHIONING OF THE NANOMACHINES THEMSELVES IS ONE THING, TAILORING THEM TO THE BOY'S GENETIC CODE IS ANOTHER...
...AND TARGETING METASTASIZED CANCER CELLS, WELL...
...IT'S A CHALLENGE. BUT ONE I'M HAPPY TO TAKE ON, IF IT'LL HELP THE CHILD.
THANK YOU, DOCTOR.

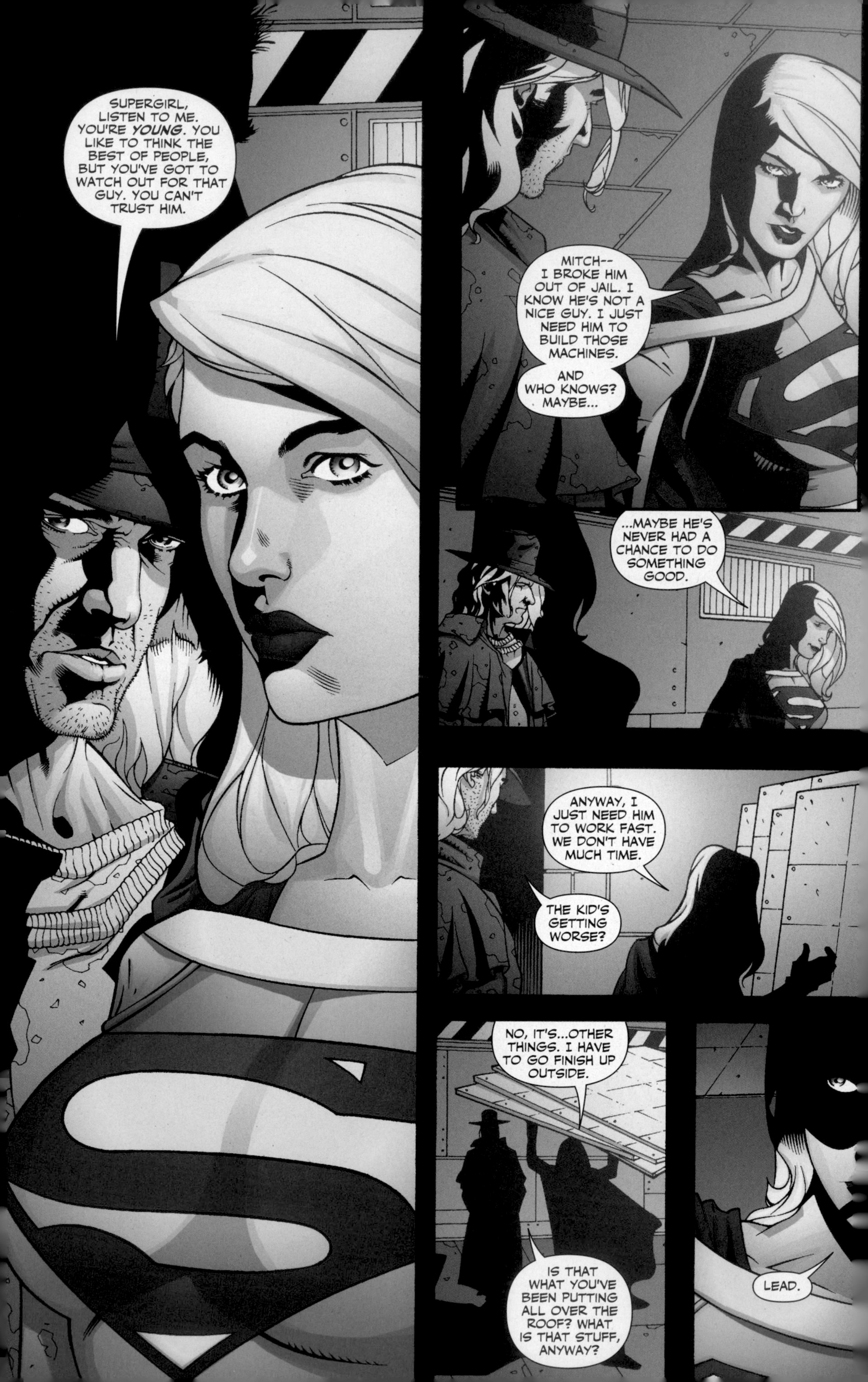
SUPERGIRL, LISTEN TO ME. YOU'RE YOUNG. YOU LIKE TO THINK THE BEST OF PEOPLE, BUT YOU'VE GOT TO WATCH OUT FOR THAT GUY. YOU CAN'T TRUST HIM.
MITCH-- I BROKE HIM OUT OF JAIL. I KNOW HE'S NOT A NICE GUY. I JUST NEED HIM TO BUILD THOSE MACHINES.
AND WHO KNOWS? MAYBE...
...MAYBE HE'S NEVER HAD A CHANCE TO DO SOMETHING GOOD.
ANYWAY, I JUST NEED HIM TO WORK FAST. WE DON'T HAVE MUCH TIME.
THE KID'S GETTING WORSE?
NO, IT'S...OTHER THINGS. I HAVE TO GO FINISH UP OUTSIDE.
IS THAT WHAT YOU'VE BEEN PUTTING ALL OVER THE ROOF? WHAT IS THAT STUFF, ANYWAY?
LEAD.

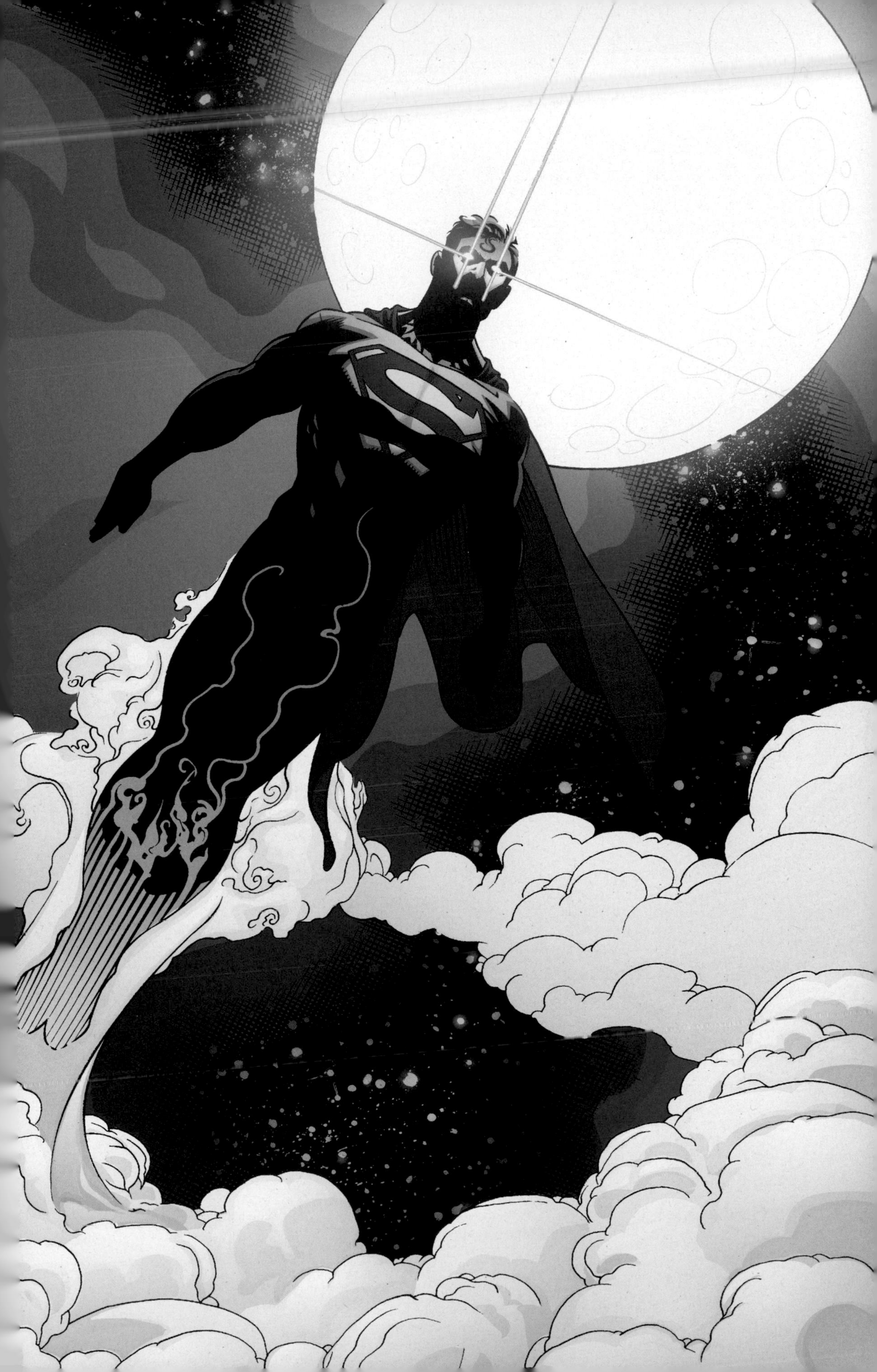

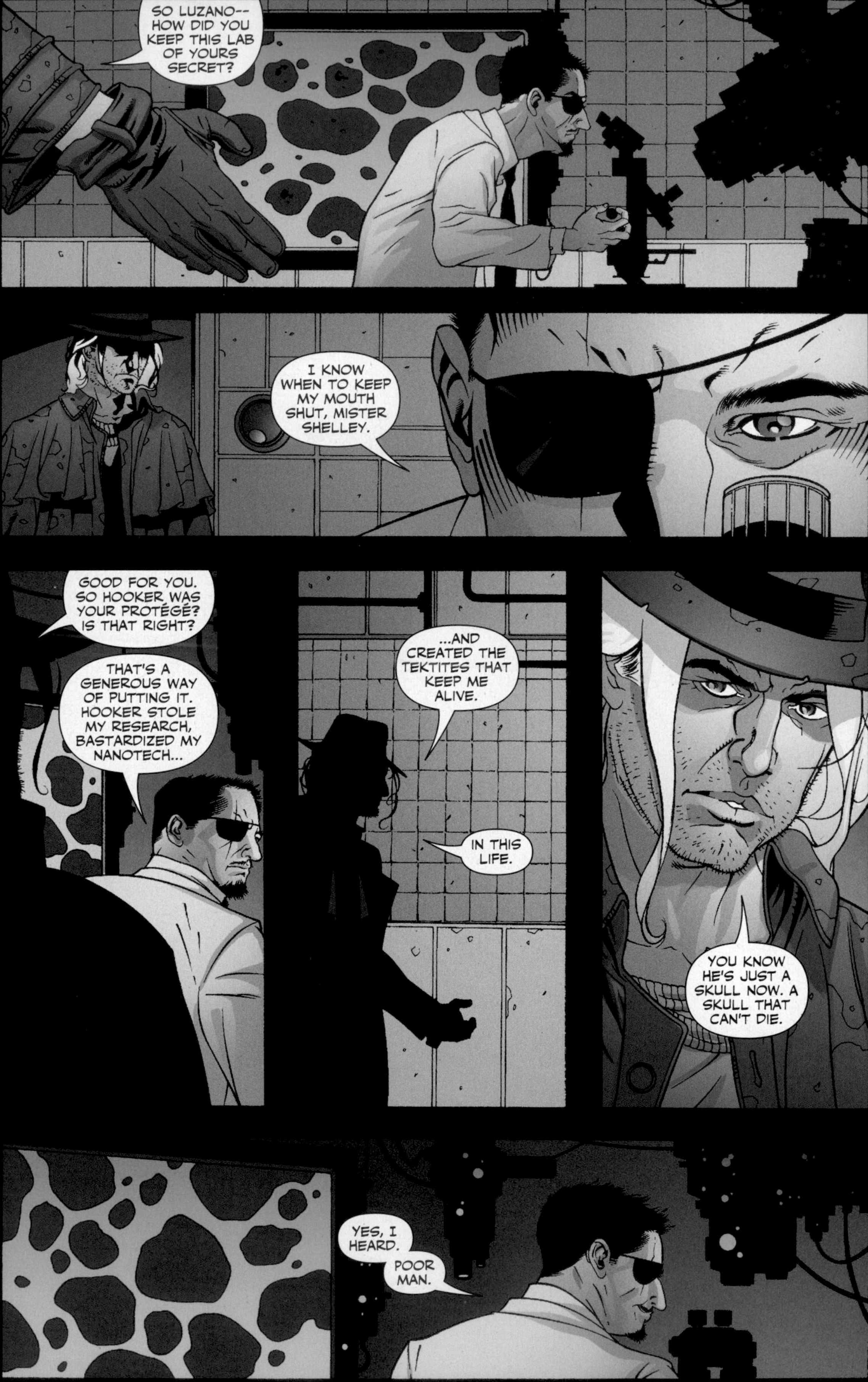
SO LUZANO-- HOW DID YOU KEEP THIS LAB OF YOURS SECRET?
I KNOW WHEN TO KEEP MY MOUTH SHUT, MISTER SHELLEY.
GOOD FOR YOU. SO HOOKER WAS YOUR PROTÉGÉ? IS THAT RIGHT?
THAT'S A GENEROUS WAY OF PUTTING IT. HOOKER STOLE MY RESEARCH, BASTARDIZED MY NANOTECH...
...AND CREATED THE TEKTITES THAT KEEP ME ALIVE.
IN THIS LIFE.
YOU KNOW HE'S JUST A SKULL NOW. A SKULL THAT CAN'T DIE.
YES, I HEARD.
POOR MAN.

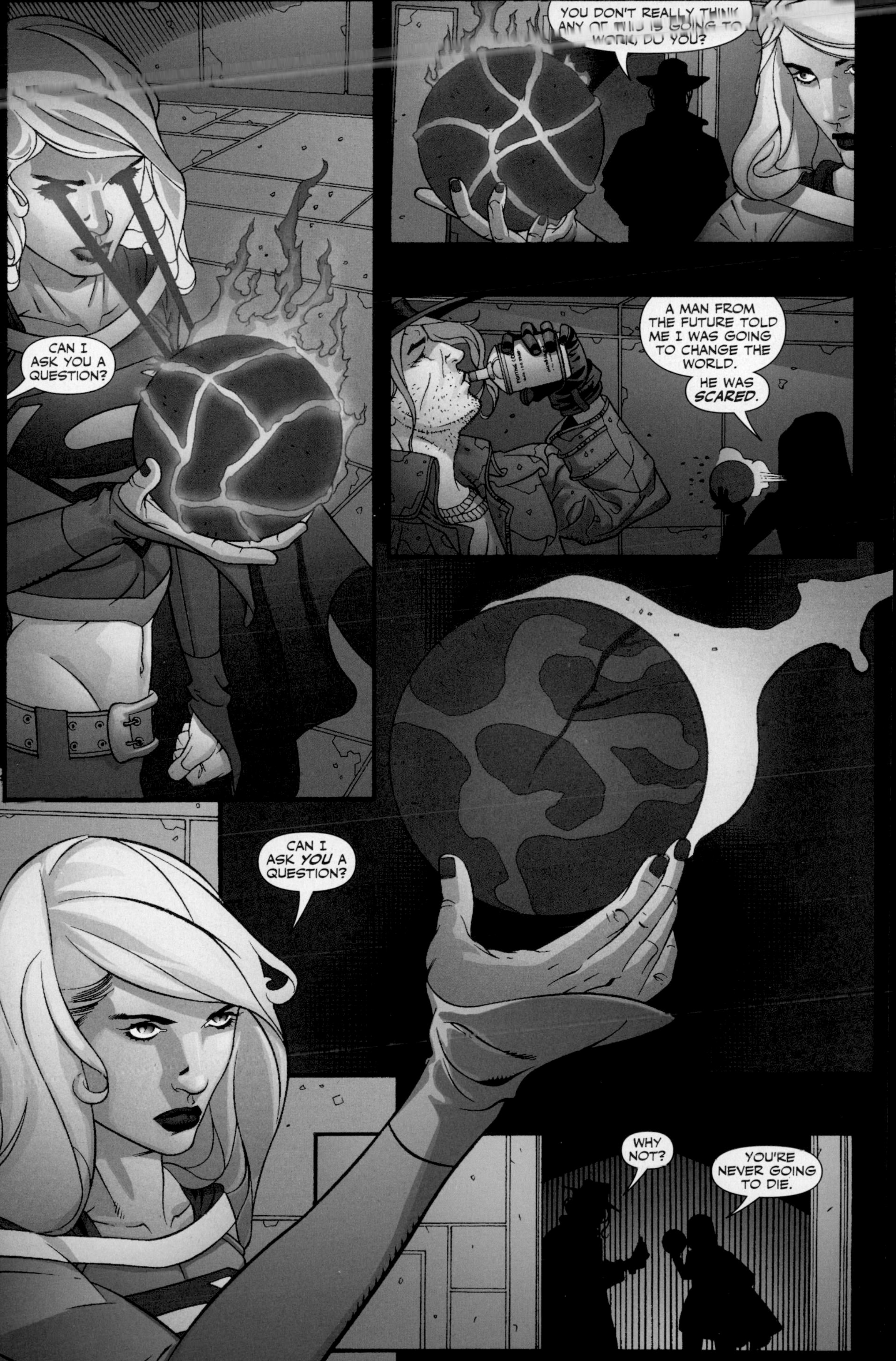
CAN I ASK YOU A QUESTION?
YOU DON'T REALLY THINK ANY OF THIS IS GOING TO WORK, DO YOU?
A MAN FROM THE FUTURE TOLD ME I WAS GOING TO CHANGE THE WORLD.
HE WAS *SCARED*.
CAN I ASK *YOU* A QUESTION?
WHY NOT?
YOU'RE NEVER GOING TO DIE.

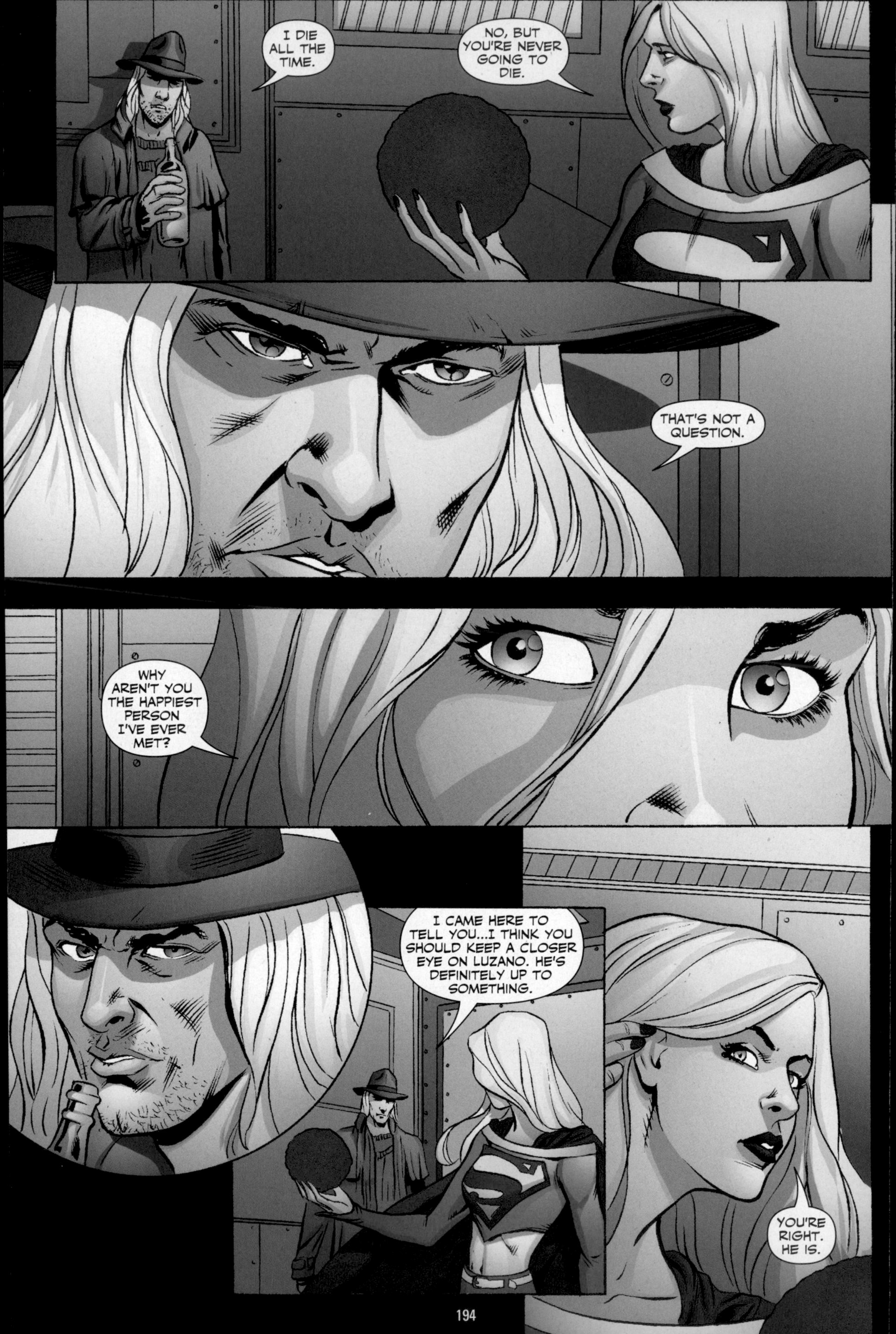
I DIE ALL THE TIME.
NO, BUT YOU'RE NEVER GOING TO DIE.
THAT'S NOT A QUESTION.
WHY AREN'T YOU THE HAPPIEST PERSON I'VE EVER MET?
I CAME HERE TO TELL YOU...I THINK YOU SHOULD KEEP A CLOSER EYE ON LUZANO. HE'S DEFINITELY UP TO SOMETHING.
YOU'RE RIGHT. HE IS.

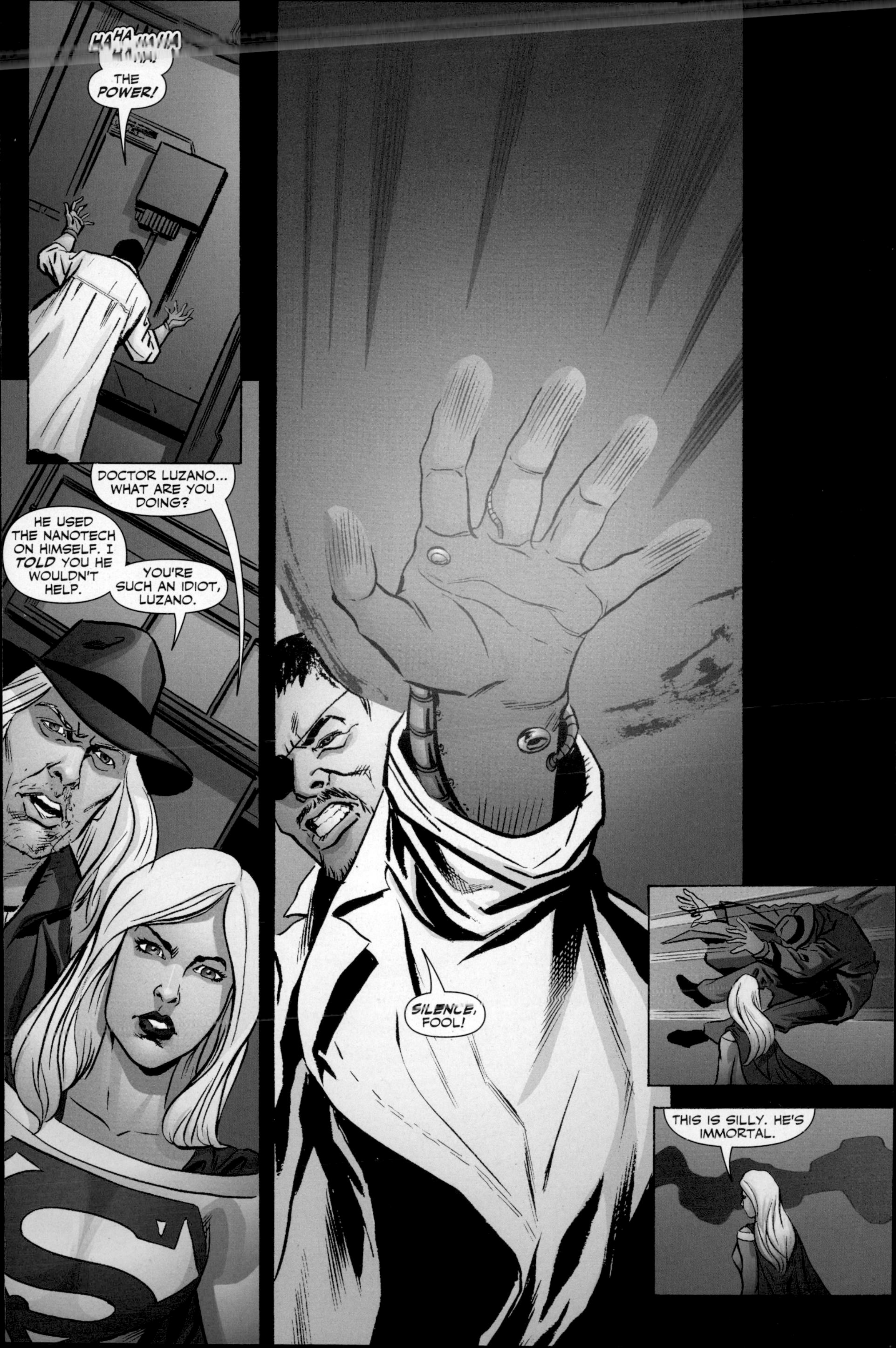
HAHA
THE POWER!
DOCTOR LUZANO... WHAT ARE YOU DOING?
HE USED THE NANOTECH ON HIMSELF. I TOLD YOU HE WOULDN'T HELP.
YOU'RE SUCH AN IDIOT, LUZANO.
SILENCE, FOOL!
THIS IS SILLY. HE'S IMMORTAL.

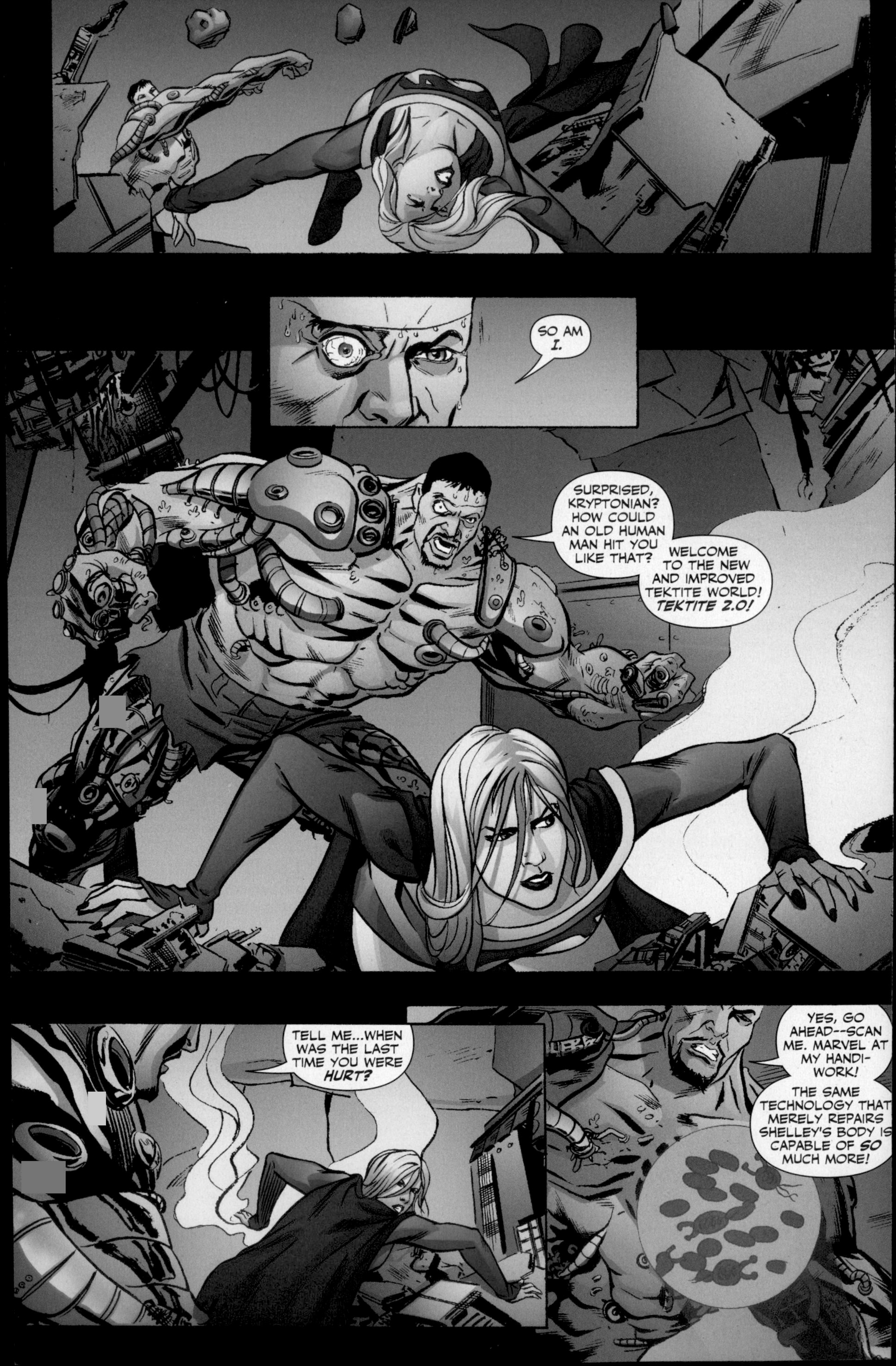
SO AM I.
SURPRISED, KRYPTONIAN? HOW COULD AN OLD HUMAN MAN HIT YOU LIKE THAT?
WELCOME TO THE NEW AND IMPROVED TEKTITE WORLD! TEKTITE 2.0!
TELL ME...WHEN WAS THE LAST TIME YOU WERE HURT?
YES, GO AHEAD--SCAN ME. MARVEL AT MY HANDI-WORK!
THE SAME TECHNOLOGY THAT MERELY REPAIRS SHELLEY'S BODY IS CAPABLE OF SO MUCH MORE!

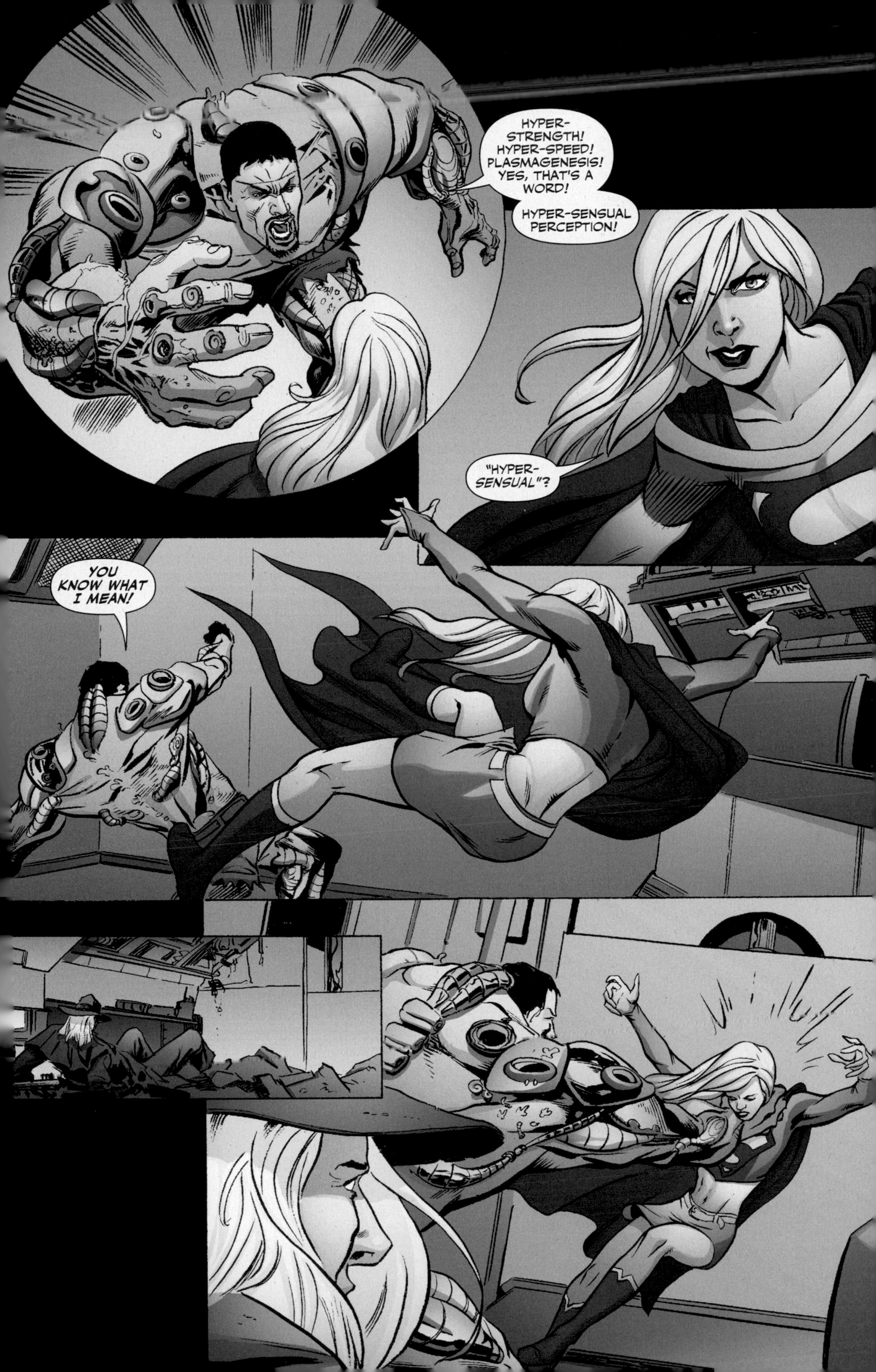
HYPER-STRENGTH! HYPER-SPEED! PLASMAGENESIS! YES, THAT'S A WORD!
HYPER-SENSUAL PERCEPTION!
"HYPER-SENSUAL"?
YOU KNOW WHAT I MEAN!

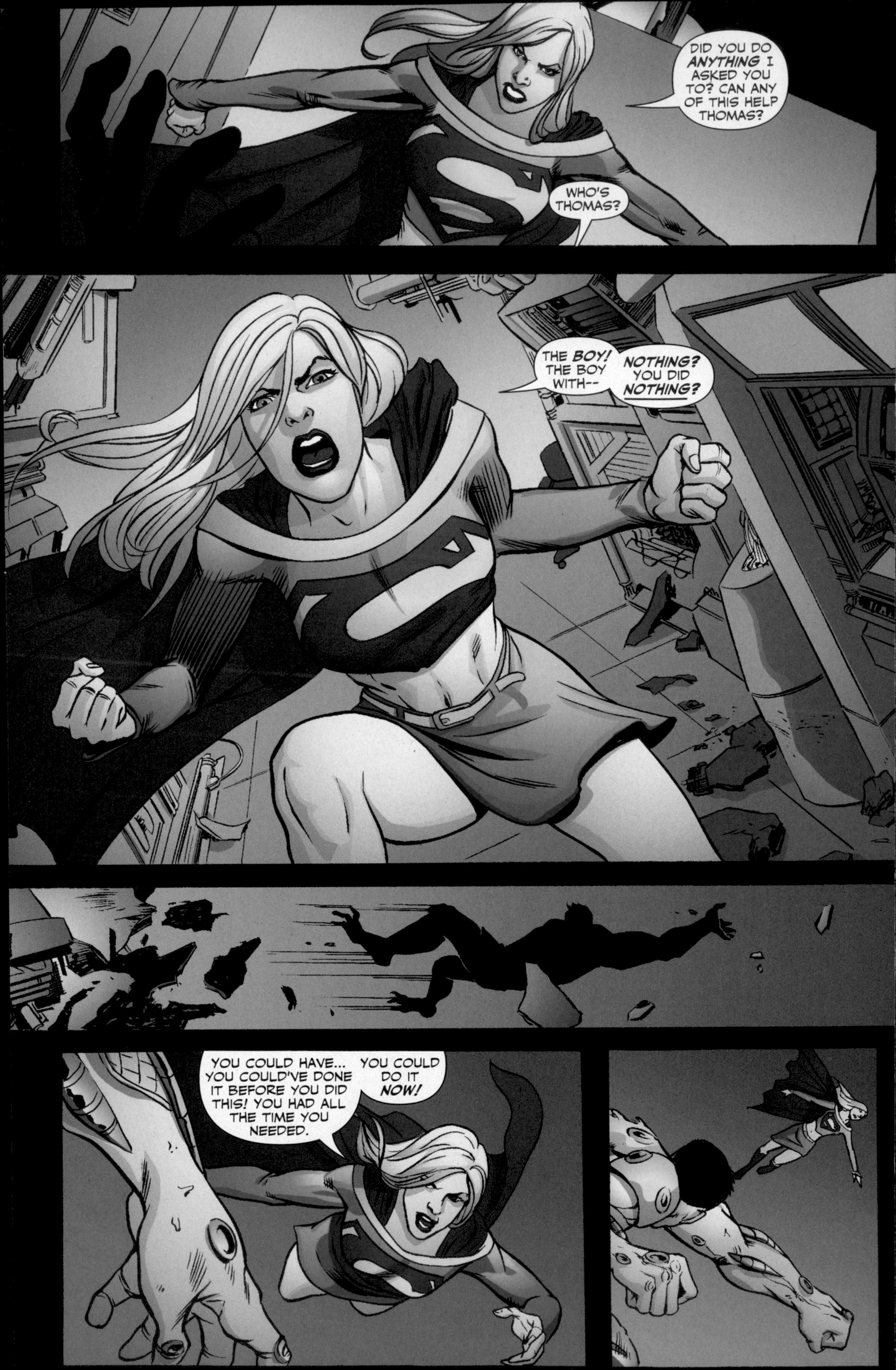
DID YOU DO ANYTHING I ASKED YOU TO? CAN ANY OF THIS HELP THOMAS?
WHO'S THOMAS?
THE BOY! THE BOY WITH--
NOTHING? YOU DID NOTHING?
YOU COULD HAVE... YOU COULD'VE DONE IT BEFORE YOU DID THIS! YOU HAD ALL THE TIME YOU NEEDED.
YOU COULD DO IT NOW!

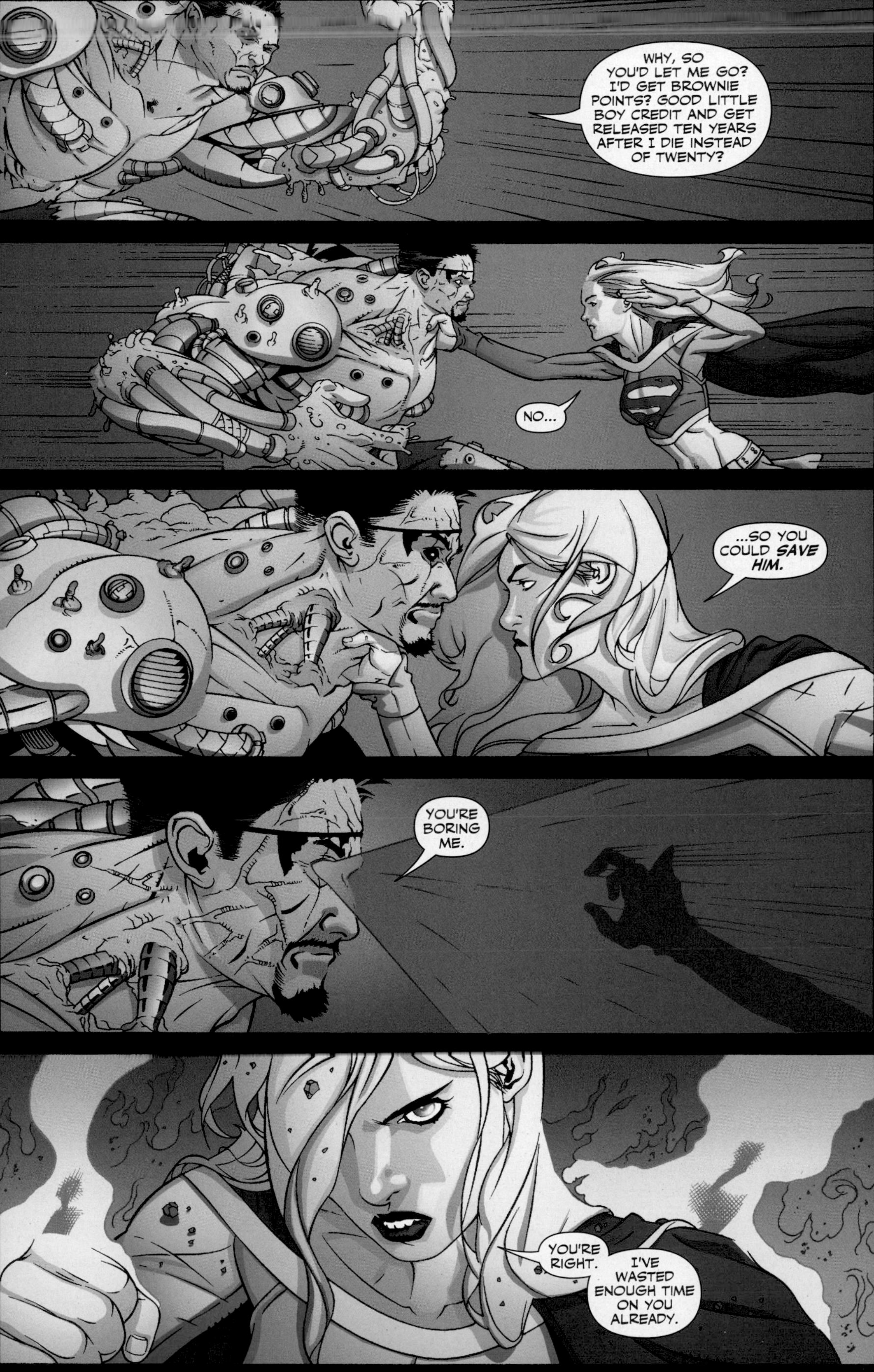
WHY, SO YOU'D LET ME GO? I'D GET BROWNIE POINTS? GOOD LITTLE BOY CREDIT AND GET RELEASED TEN YEARS AFTER I DIE INSTEAD OF TWENTY?
NO...
...SO YOU COULD *SAVE* HIM.
YOU'RE BORING ME.
YOU'RE RIGHT.
I'VE WASTED ENOUGH TIME ON YOU ALREADY.

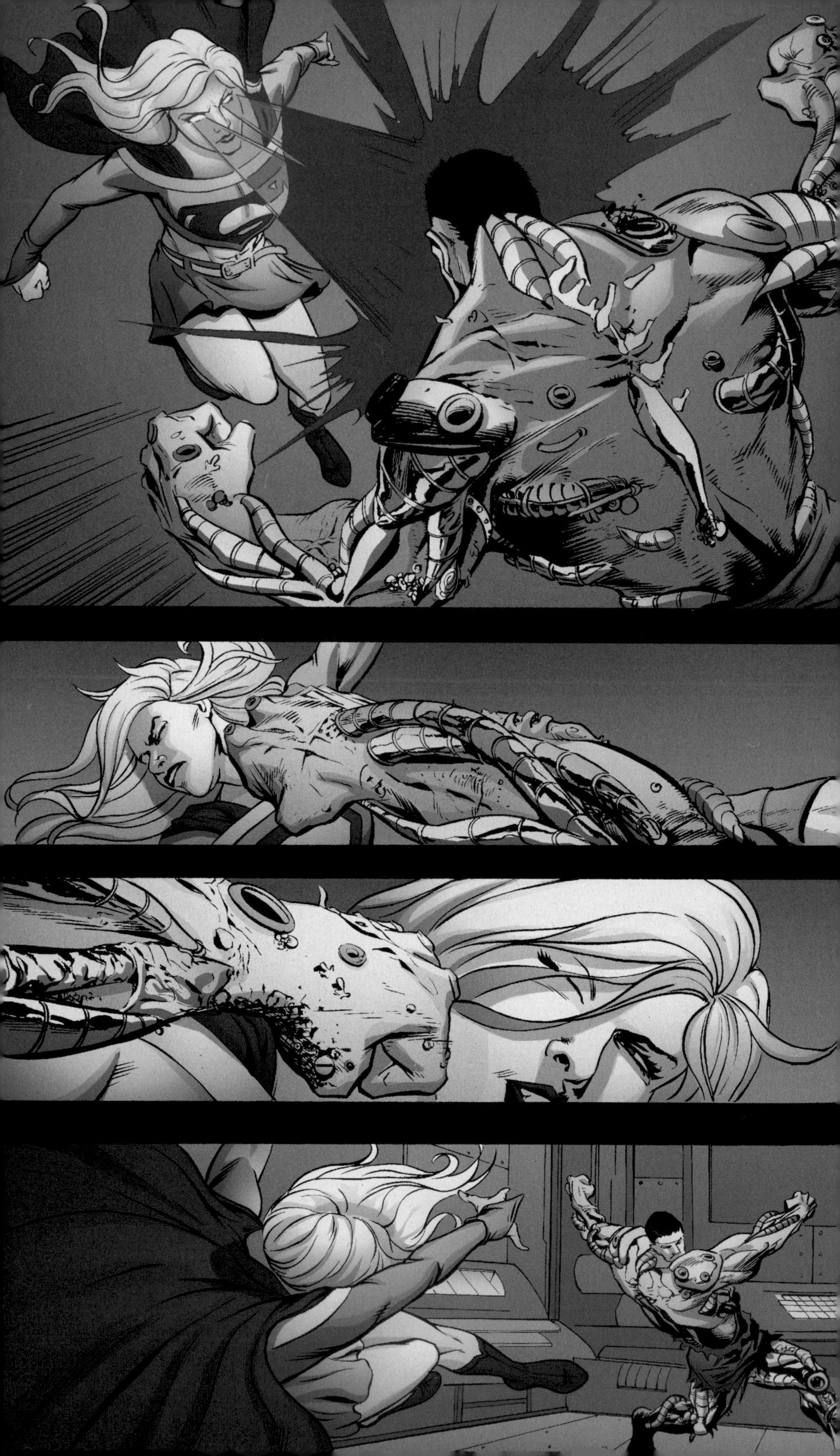

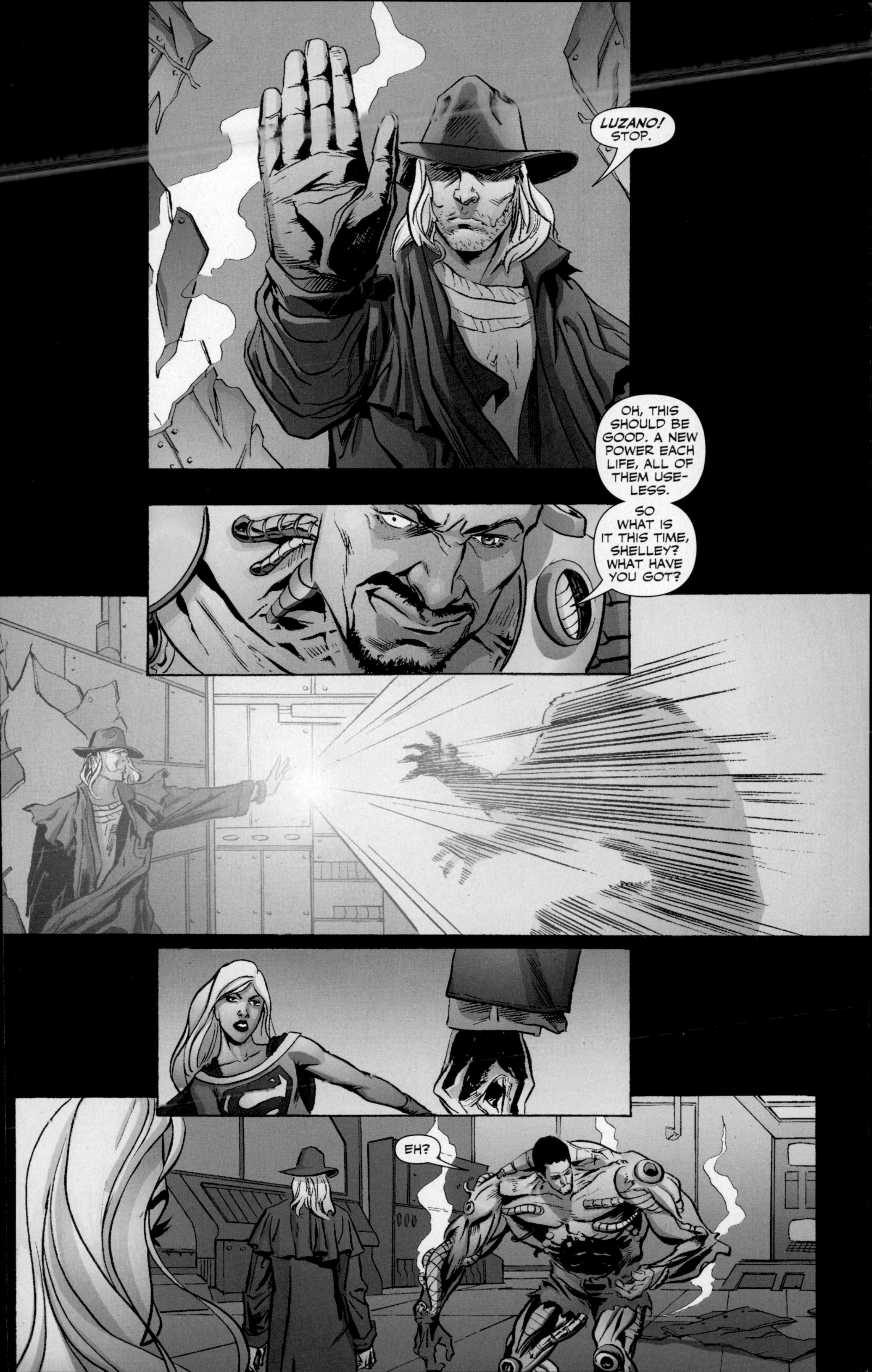
LUZANO! STOP.
OH, THIS SHOULD BE GOOD. A NEW POWER EACH LIFE, ALL OF THEM USE-LESS.
SO WHAT IS IT THIS TIME, SHELLEY? WHAT HAVE YOU GOT?
EH?

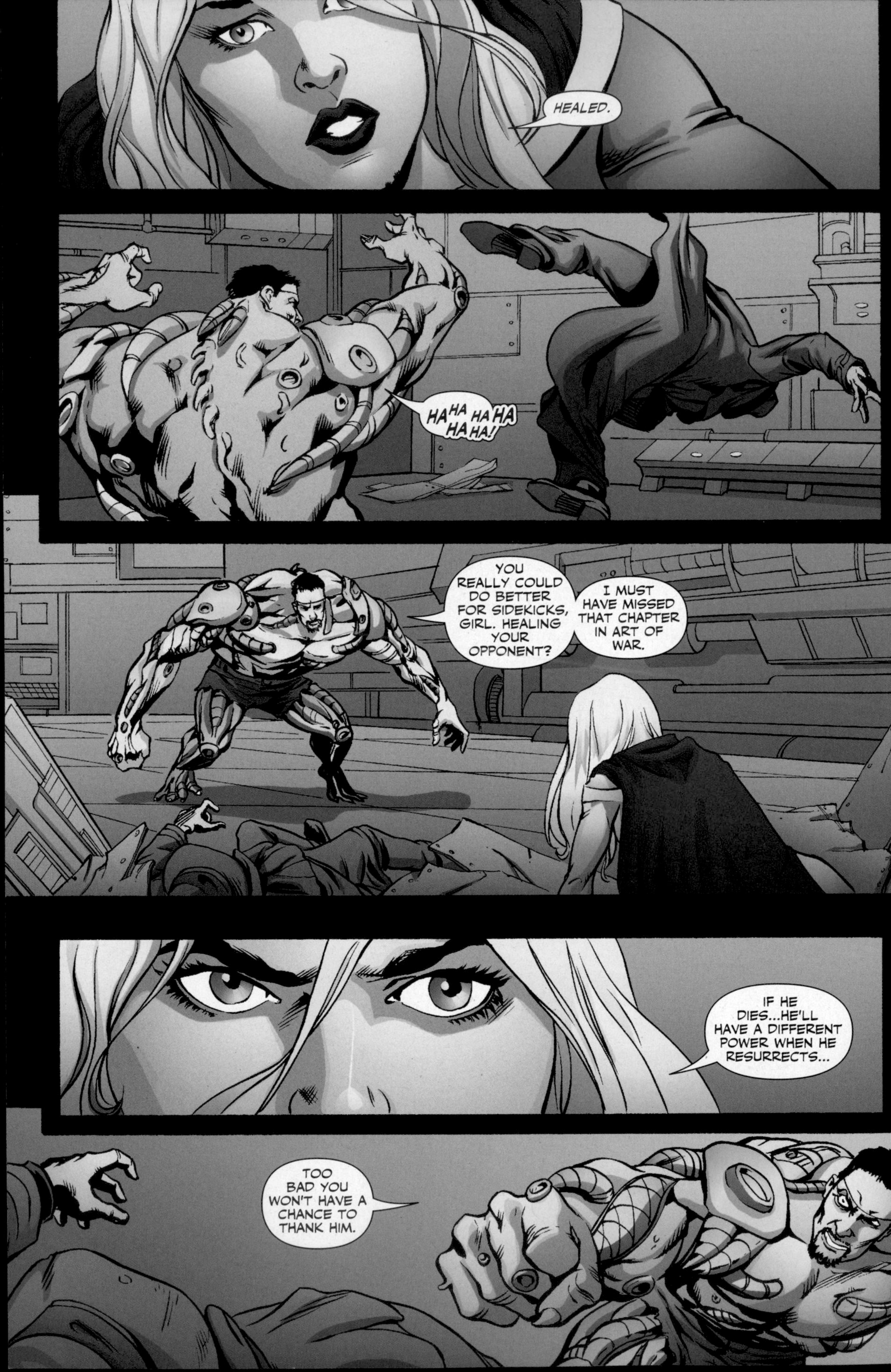
HEALED.
HAHA HAHA HAHA!
YOU REALLY COULD DO BETTER FOR SIDEKICKS, GIRL. HEALING YOUR OPPONENT?
I MUST HAVE MISSED THAT CHAPTER IN ART OF WAR.
IF HE DIES...HE'LL HAVE A DIFFERENT POWER WHEN HE RESURRECTS...
TOO BAD YOU WON'T HAVE A CHANCE TO THANK HIM.

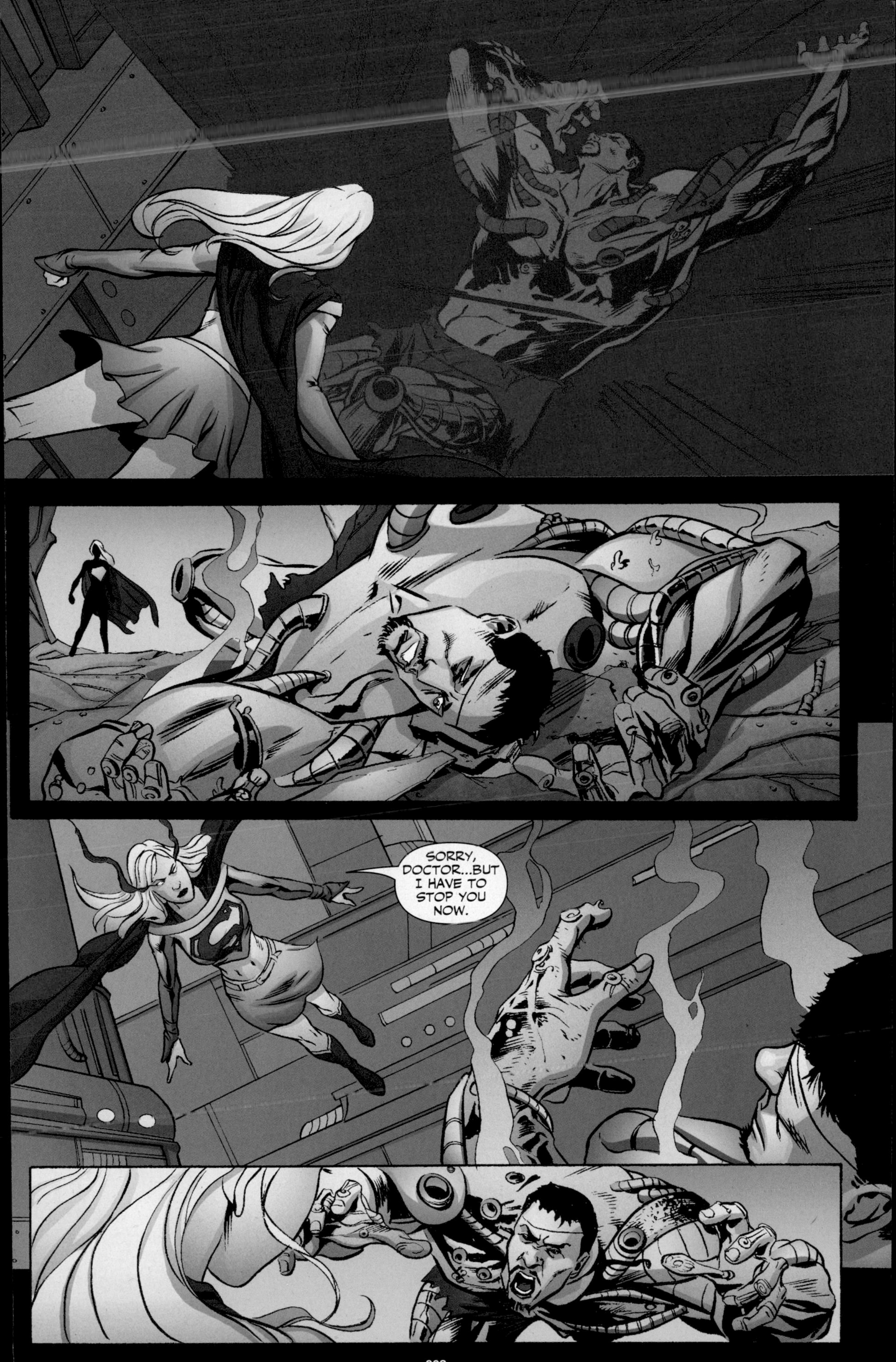
SORRY, DOCTOR...BUT I HAVE TO STOP YOU NOW.

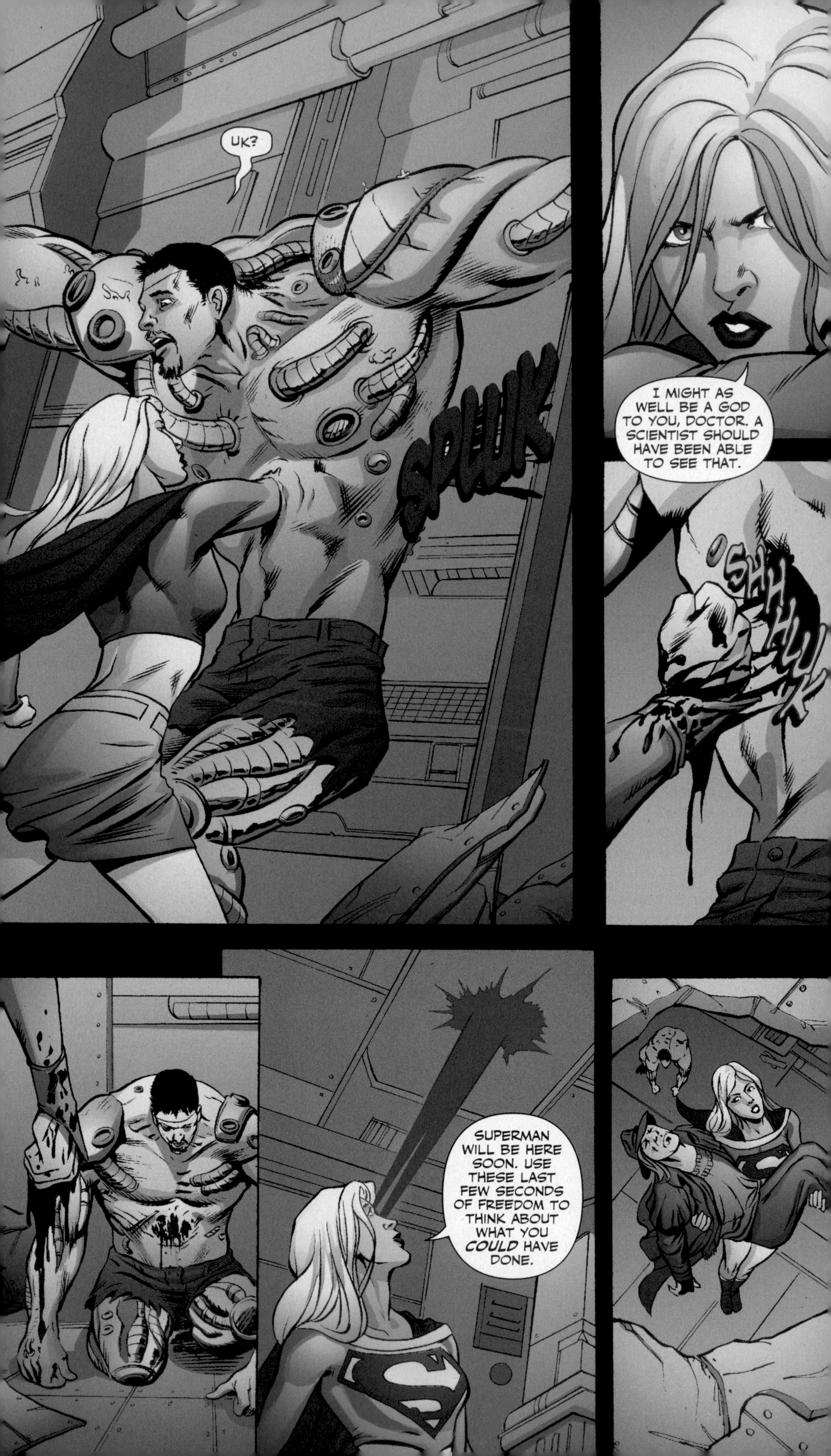
UK?
SPLUK
I MIGHT AS WELL BE A GOD TO YOU, DOCTOR. A SCIENTIST SHOULD HAVE BEEN ABLE TO SEE THAT.
SHHHUK
SUPERMAN WILL BE HERE SOON. USE THESE LAST FEW SECONDS OF FREEDOM TO THINK ABOUT WHAT YOU *COULD* HAVE DONE.

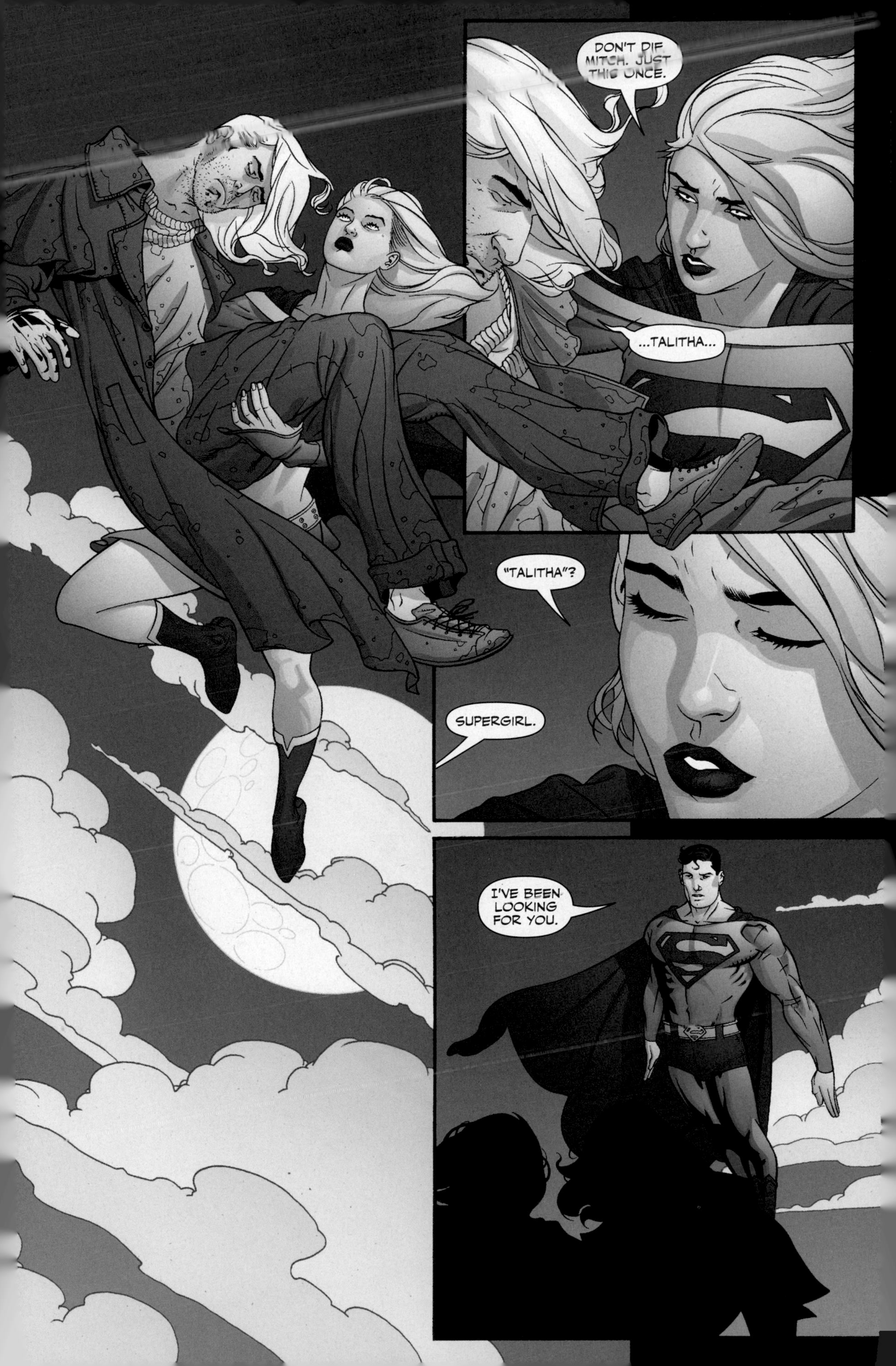
DON'T DIE MITCH. JUST THIS ONCE.
...TALITHA...
"TALITHA"?
SUPERGIRL.
I'VE BEEN LOOKING FOR YOU.

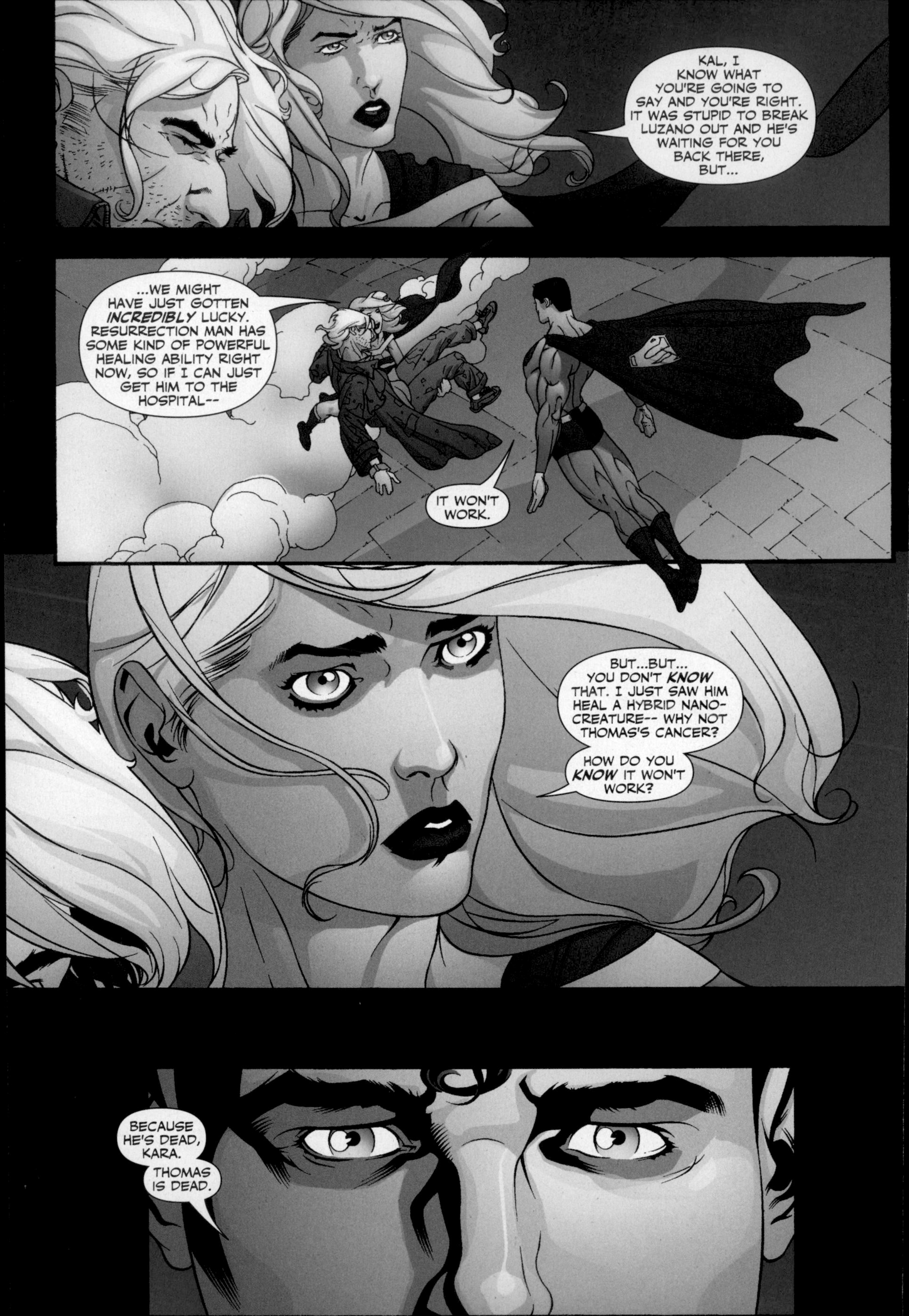
KAL, I KNOW WHAT YOU'RE GOING TO SAY AND YOU'RE RIGHT. IT WAS STUPID TO BREAK LUZANO OUT AND HE'S WAITING FOR YOU BACK THERE, BUT...
...WE MIGHT HAVE JUST GOTTEN *INCREDIBLY* LUCKY. RESURRECTION MAN HAS SOME KIND OF POWERFUL HEALING ABILITY RIGHT NOW, SO IF I CAN JUST GET HIM TO THE HOSPITAL--
IT WON'T WORK.
BUT...BUT... YOU DON'T *KNOW* THAT. I JUST SAW HIM HEAL A HYBRID NANO-CREATURE-- WHY NOT THOMAS'S CANCER?
HOW DO YOU *KNOW* IT WON'T WORK?
BECAUSE HE'S DEAD, KARA.
THOMAS IS DEAD.

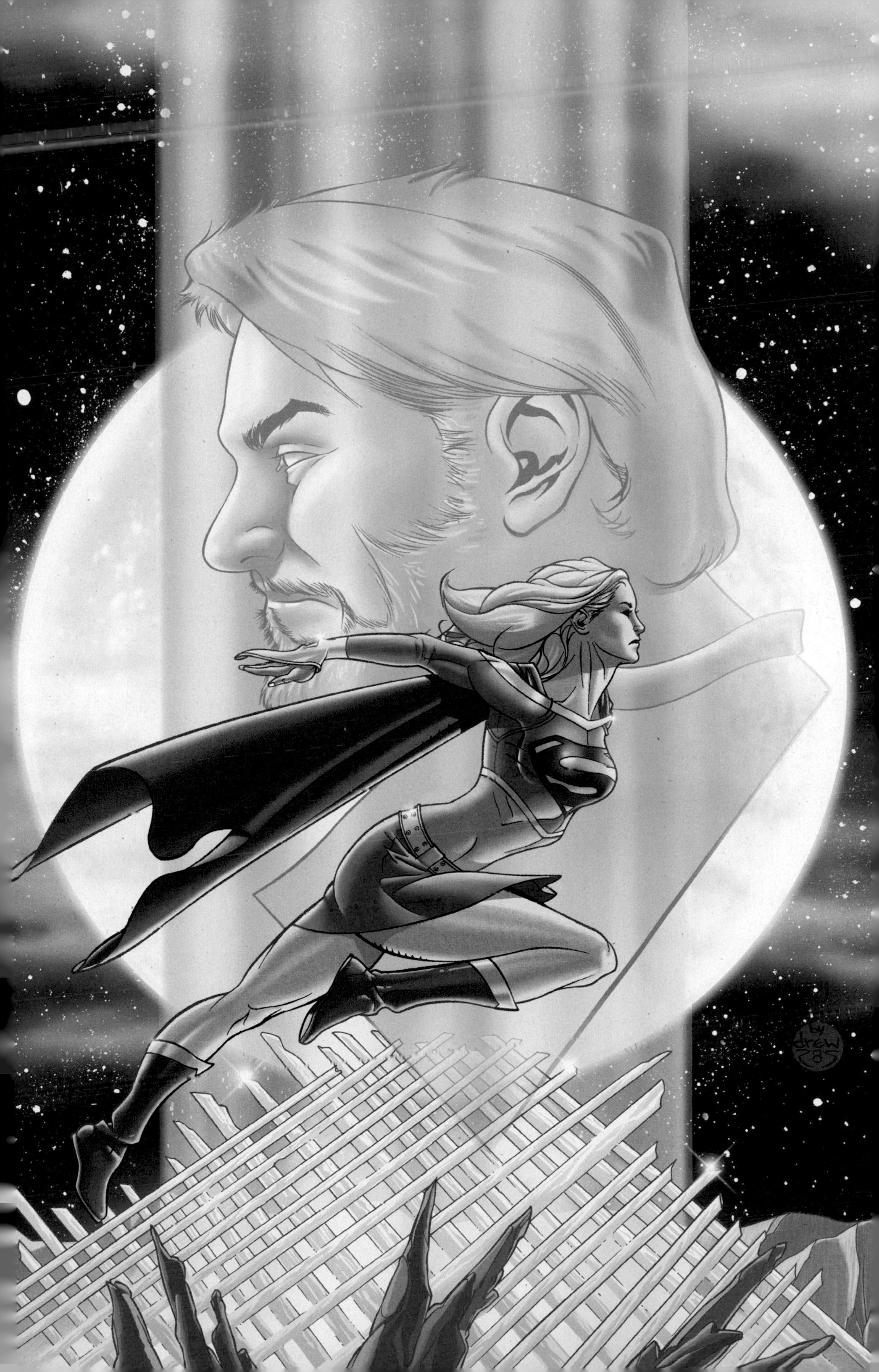

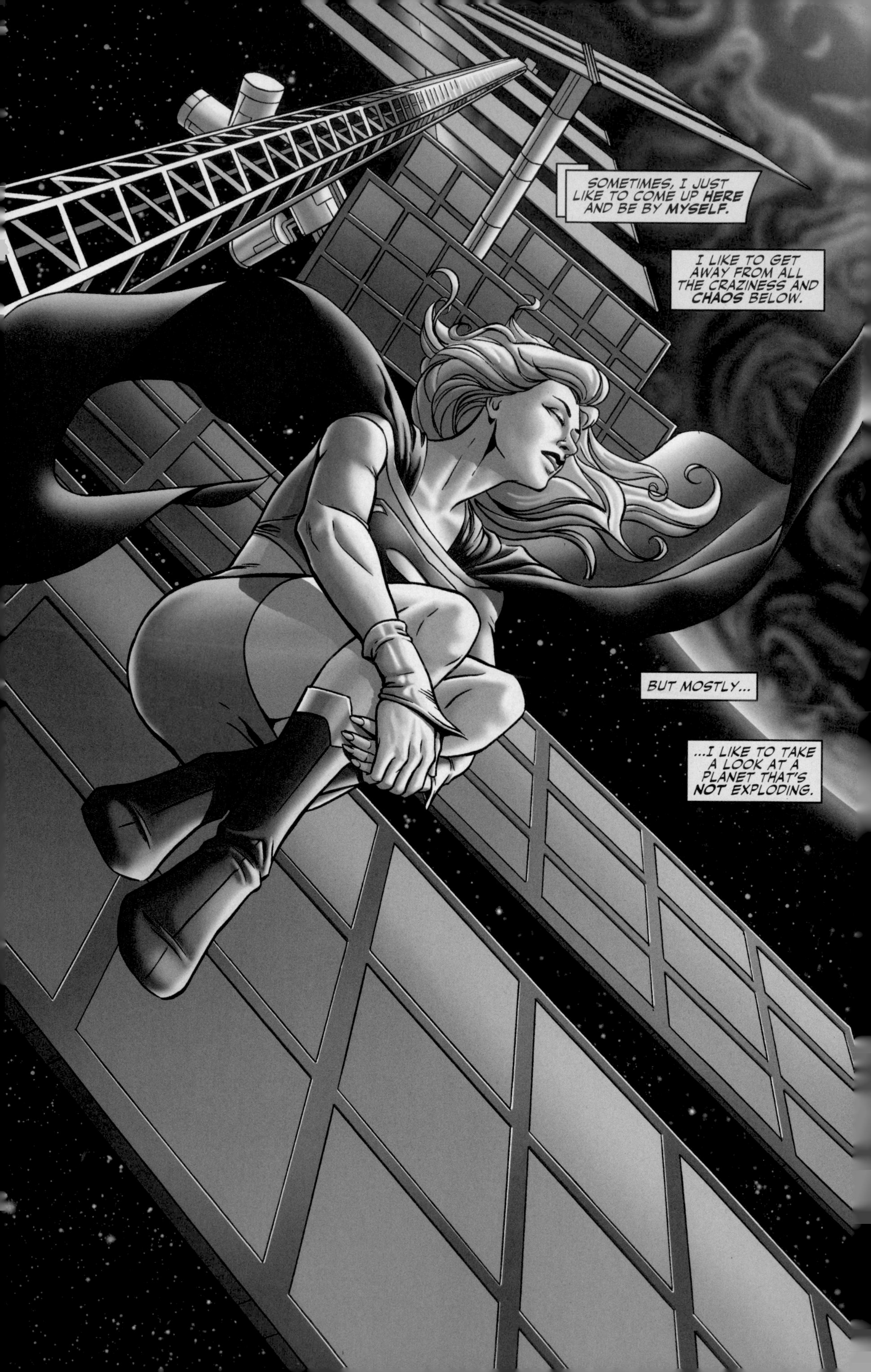
SOMETIMES, I JUST LIKE TO COME UP HERE AND BE BY MYSELF.
I LIKE TO GET AWAY FROM ALL THE CRAZINESS AND CHAOS BELOW.
BUT MOSTLY...
...I LIKE TO TAKE A LOOK AT A PLANET THAT'S NOT EXPLODING.

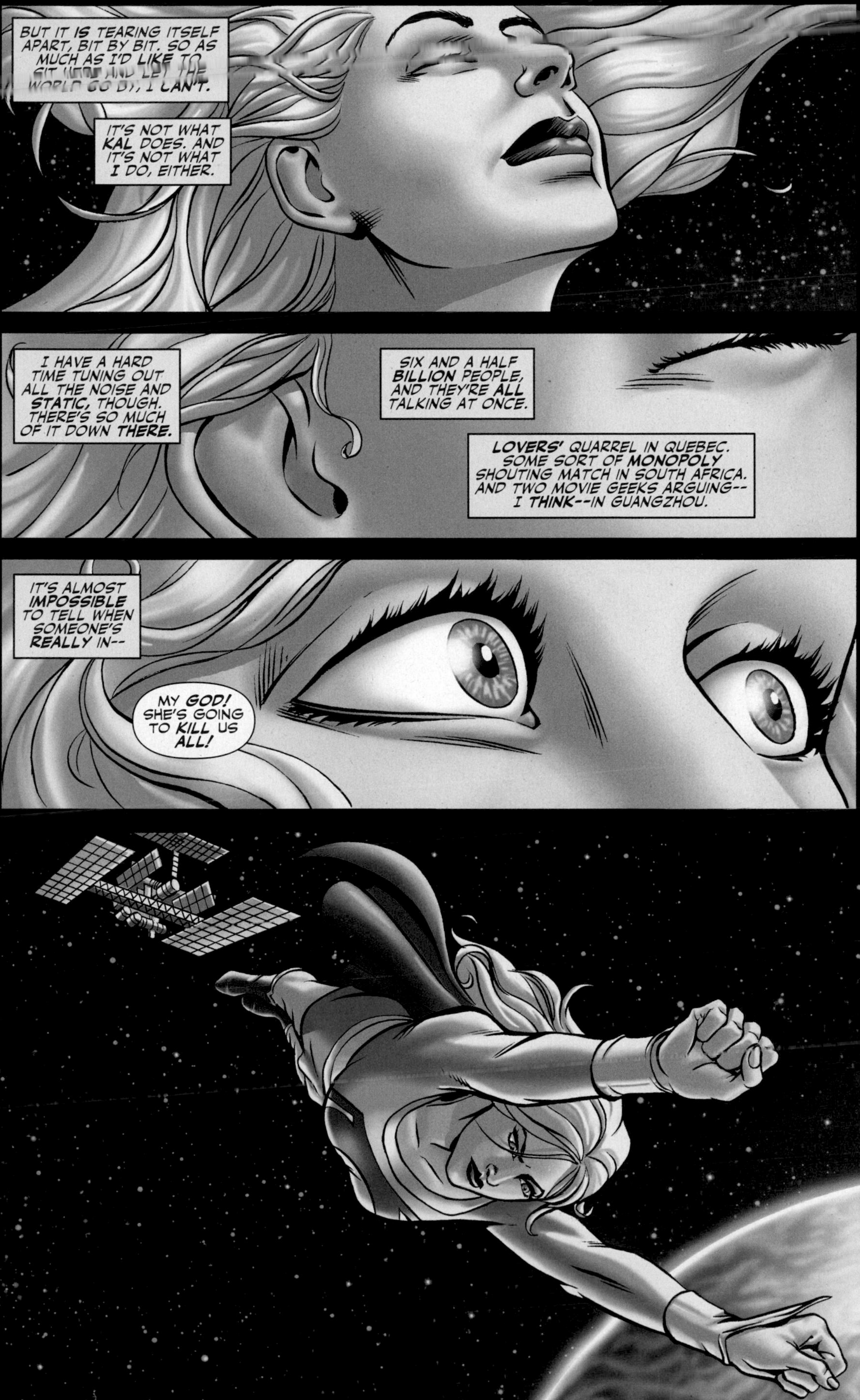

BUT IT IS TEARING ITSELF APART, BIT BY BIT. SO AS MUCH AS I'D LIKE TO SIT HERE AND LET THE WORLD GO BY, I CAN'T.
IT'S NOT WHAT KAL DOES. AND IT'S NOT WHAT I DO, EITHER.
I HAVE A HARD TIME TUNING OUT ALL THE NOISE AND STATIC, THOUGH. THERE'S SO MUCH OF IT DOWN THERE.
SIX AND A HALF BILLION PEOPLE, AND THEY'RE ALL TALKING AT ONCE.
LOVERS' QUARREL IN QUEBEC. SOME SORT OF MONOPOLY SHOUTING MATCH IN SOUTH AFRICA. AND TWO MOVIE GEEKS ARGUING-- I THINK--IN GUANGZHOU.
IT'S ALMOST IMPOSSIBLE TO TELL WHEN SOMEONE'S REALLY IN--
MY GOD! SHE'S GOING TO KILL US ALL!

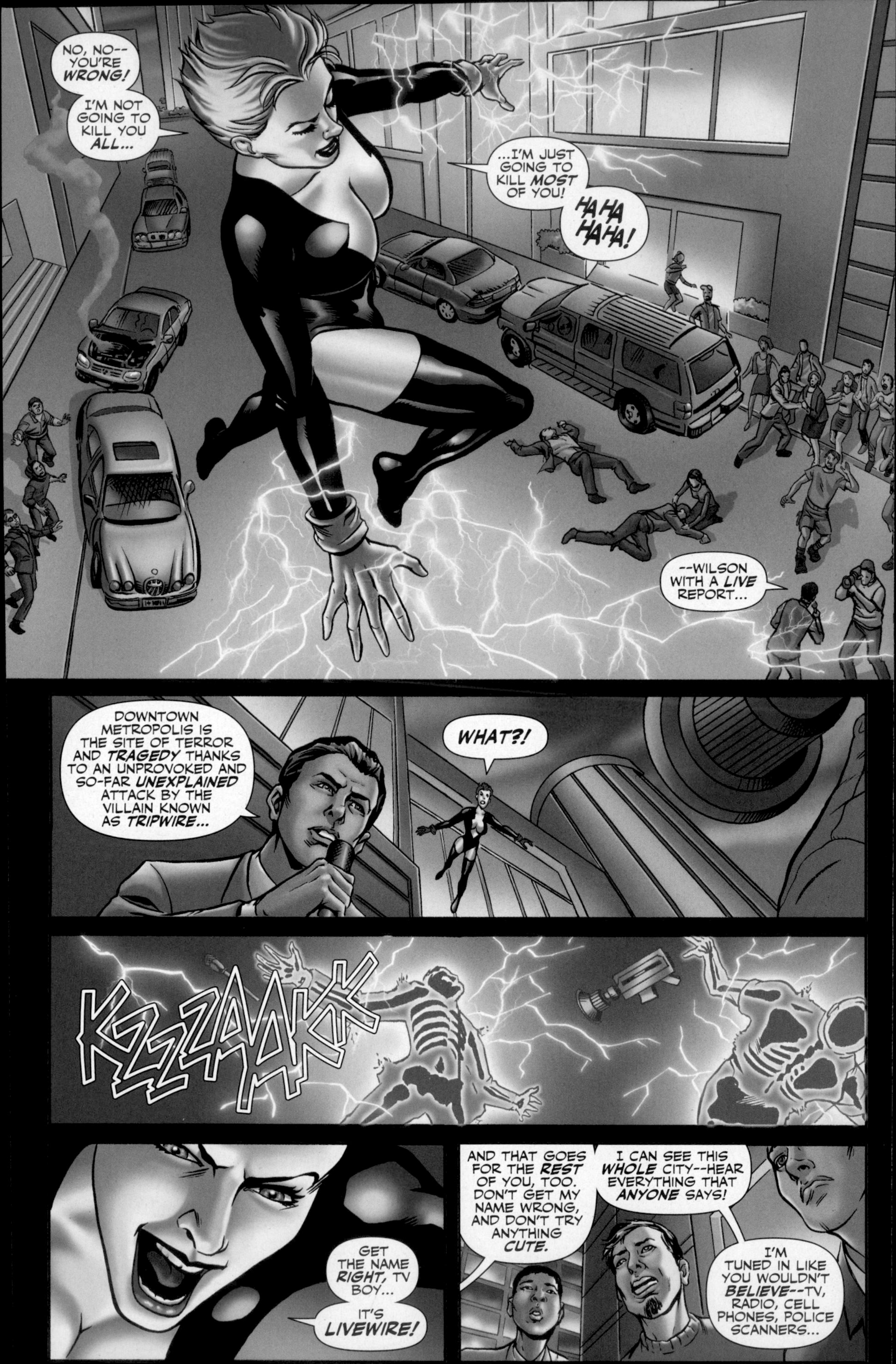
NO, NO-- YOU'RE WRONG!
I'M NOT GOING TO KILL YOU ALL...
...I'M JUST GOING TO KILL MOST OF YOU!
HA HA HA HA!
--WILSON WITH A LIVE REPORT...
DOWNTOWN METROPOLIS IS THE SITE OF TERROR AND TRAGEDY THANKS TO AN UNPROVOKED AND SO-FAR UNEXPLAINED ATTACK BY THE VILLAIN KNOWN AS TRIPWIRE...
WHAT?!
KZZZAAKK
GET THE NAME RIGHT, TV BOY...
IT'S LIVEWIRE!
AND THAT GOES FOR THE REST OF YOU, TOO. DON'T GET MY NAME WRONG, AND DON'T TRY ANYTHING CUTE.
I CAN SEE THIS WHOLE CITY--HEAR EVERYTHING THAT ANYONE SAYS!
I'M TUNED IN LIKE YOU WOULDN'T BELIEVE--TV, RADIO, CELL PHONES, POLICE SCANNERS...

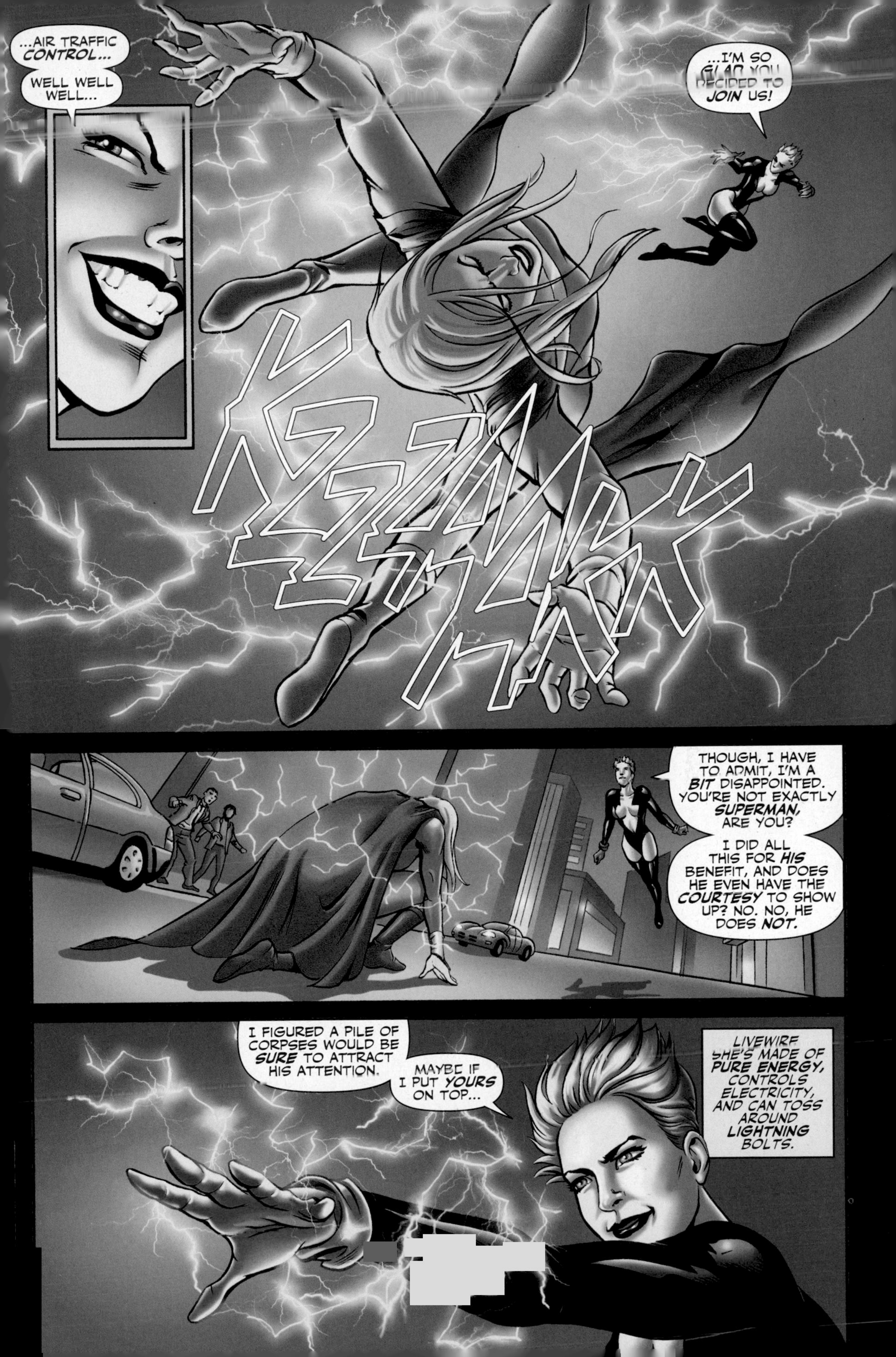
...AIR TRAFFIC CONTROL...
WELL WELL WELL...
...I'M SO GLAD YOU DECIDED TO JOIN US!
THOUGH, I HAVE TO ADMIT, I'M A BIT DISAPPOINTED. YOU'RE NOT EXACTLY SUPERMAN, ARE YOU?
I DID ALL THIS FOR HIS BENEFIT, AND DOES HE EVEN HAVE THE COURTESY TO SHOW UP? NO. NO, HE DOES NOT.
I FIGURED A PILE OF CORPSES WOULD BE SURE TO ATTRACT HIS ATTENTION.
MAYBE IF I PUT YOURS ON TOP...
LIVEWIRE. SHE'S MADE OF PURE ENERGY, CONTROLS ELECTRICITY, AND CAN TOSS AROUND LIGHTNING BOLTS.

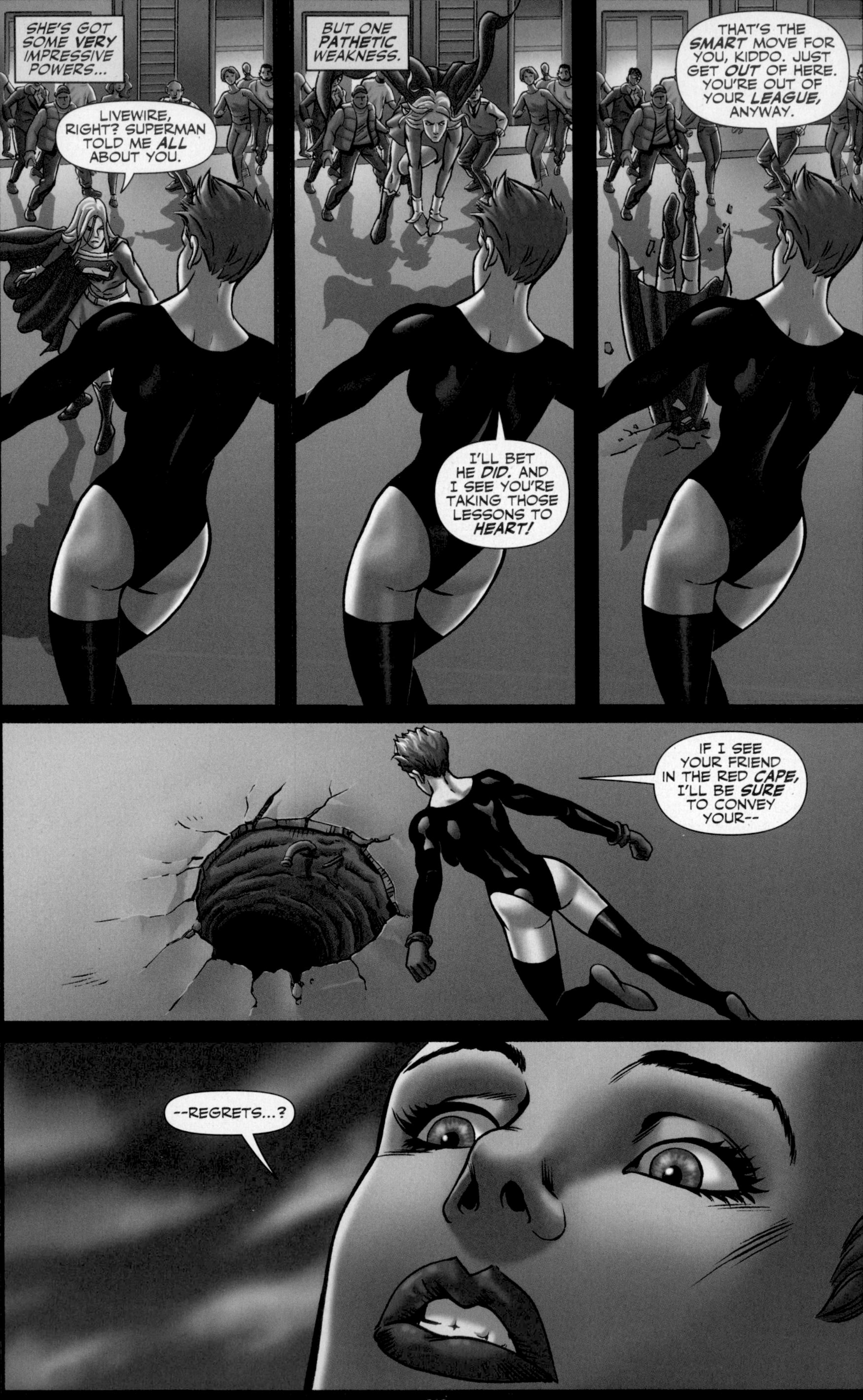
SHE'S GOT SOME VERY IMPRESSIVE POWERS...
LIVEWIRE, RIGHT? SUPERMAN TOLD ME ALL ABOUT YOU.
BUT ONE PATHETIC WEAKNESS.
I'LL BET HE DID. AND I SEE YOU'RE TAKING THOSE LESSONS TO HEART!
THAT'S THE SMART MOVE FOR YOU, KIDDO. JUST GET OUT OF HERE. YOU'RE OUT OF YOUR LEAGUE, ANYWAY.
IF I SEE YOUR FRIEND IN THE RED CAPE, I'LL BE SURE TO CONVEY YOUR--
--REGRETS...?

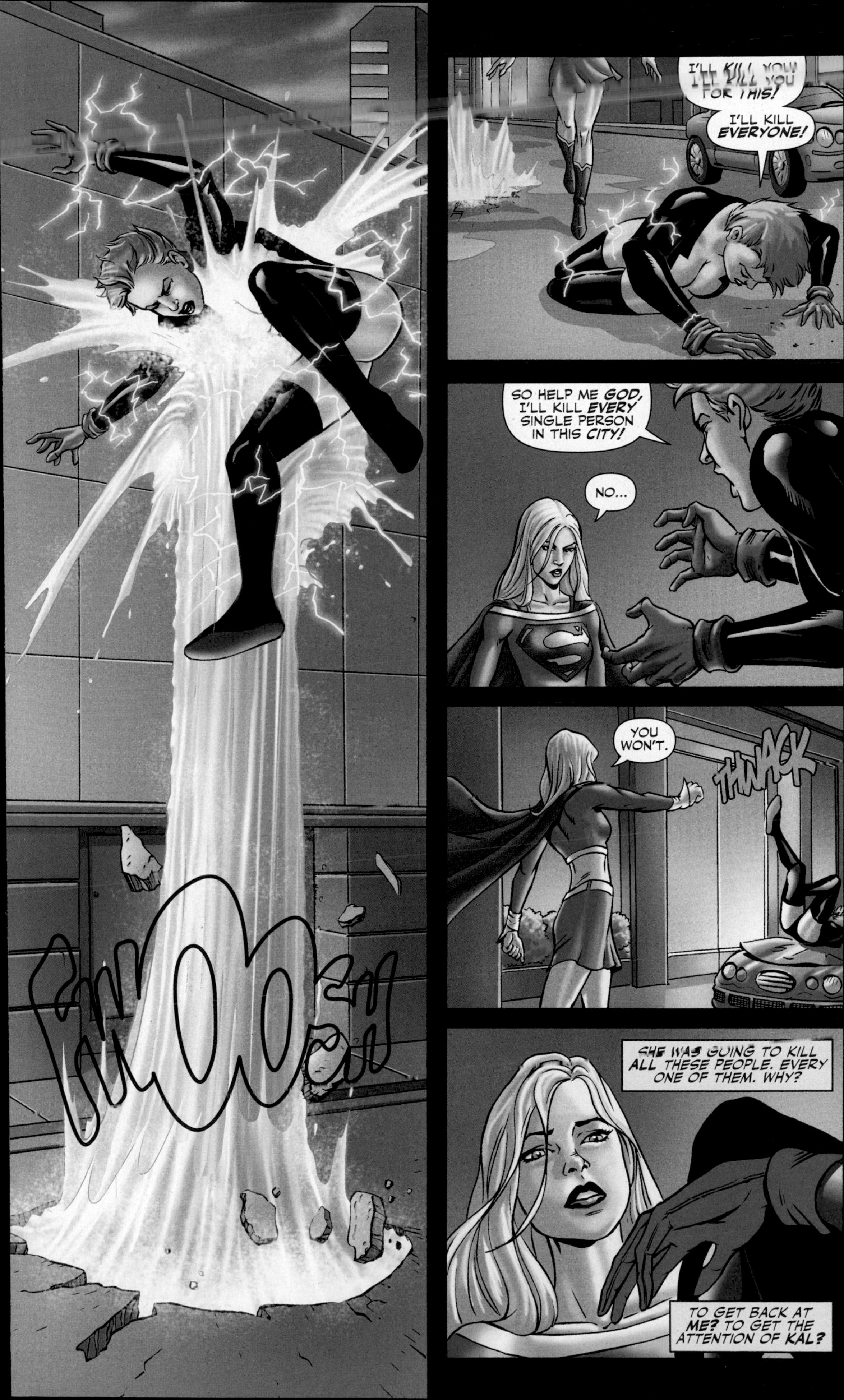

I'LL KILL YOU FOR THIS!
I'LL KILL EVERYONE!
SO HELP ME GOD, I'LL KILL EVERY SINGLE PERSON IN THIS CITY!
NO...
YOU WON'T.
THWACK
SHE WAS GOING TO KILL ALL THESE PEOPLE. EVERY ONE OF THEM. WHY?
TO GET BACK AT ME? TO GET THE ATTENTION OF KAL?

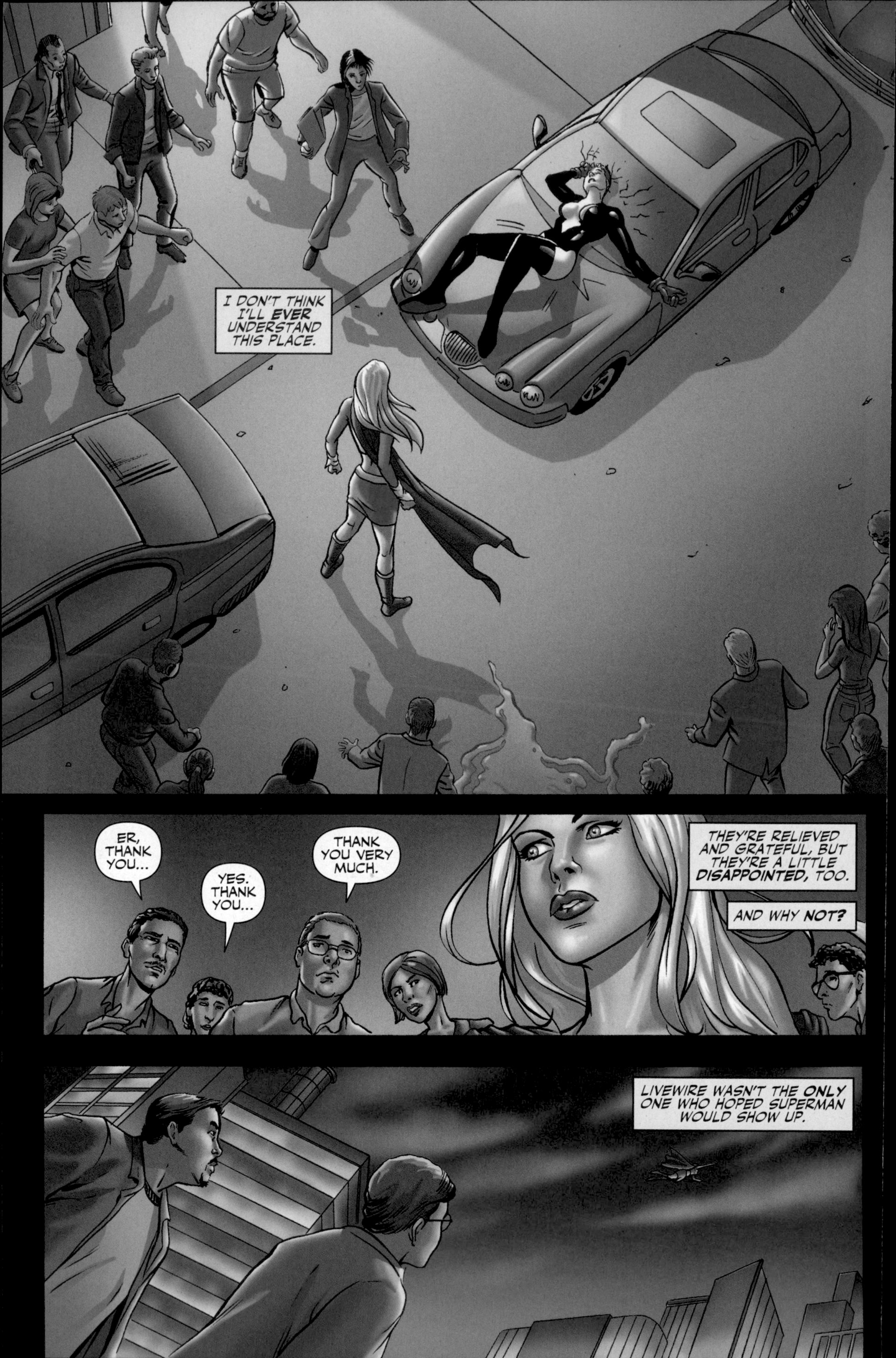

I DON'T THINK I'LL EVER UNDERSTAND THIS PLACE.
ER, THANK YOU...
YES. THANK YOU...
THANK YOU VERY MUCH.
THEY'RE RELIEVED AND GRATEFUL, BUT THEY'RE A LITTLE DISAPPOINTED, TOO.
AND WHY NOT?
LIVEWIRE WASN'T THE ONLY ONE WHO HOPED SUPERMAN WOULD SHOW UP.

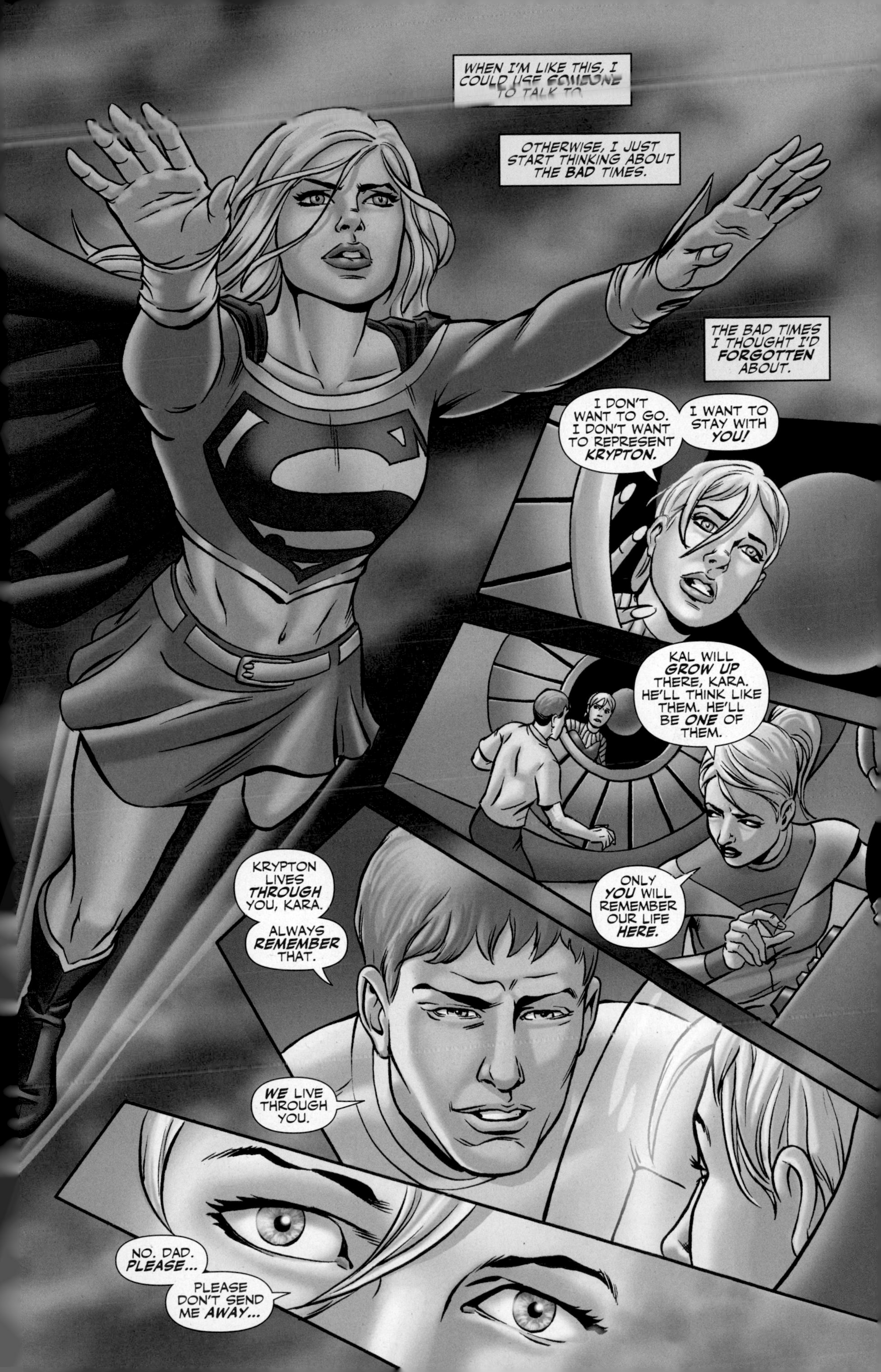
WHEN I'M LIKE THIS, I COULD USE SOMEONE TO TALK TO.
OTHERWISE, I JUST START THINKING ABOUT THE BAD TIMES.
THE BAD TIMES I THOUGHT I'D FORGOTTEN ABOUT.
I DON'T WANT TO GO. I DON'T WANT TO REPRESENT KRYPTON.
I WANT TO STAY WITH YOU!
KAL WILL GROW UP THERE, KARA. HE'LL THINK LIKE THEM. HE'LL BE ONE OF THEM.
ONLY YOU WILL REMEMBER OUR LIFE HERE.
KRYPTON LIVES THROUGH YOU, KARA.
ALWAYS REMEMBER THAT.
WE LIVE THROUGH YOU.
NO. DAD. PLEASE...
PLEASE DON'T SEND ME AWAY...

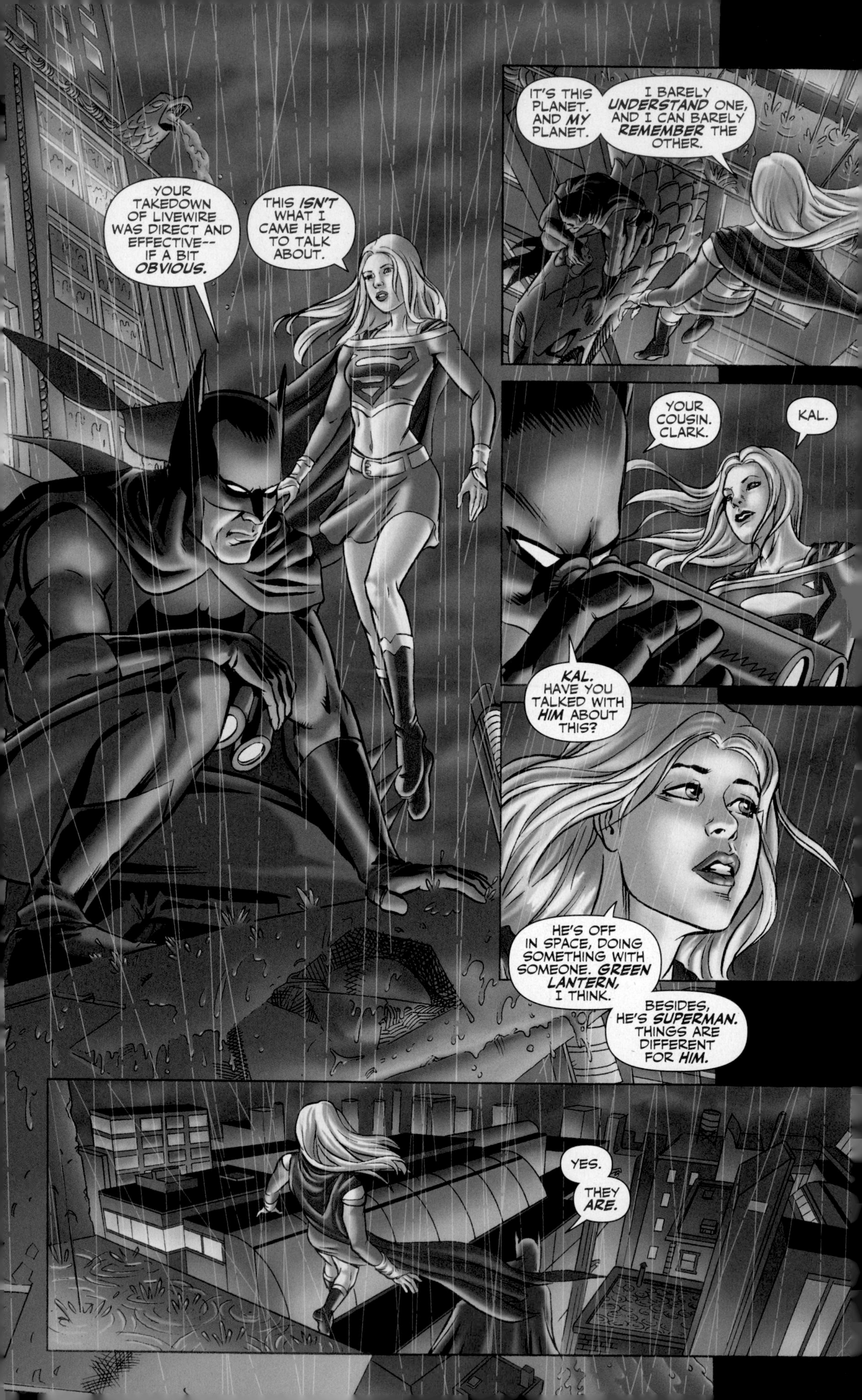
YOUR TAKEDOWN OF LIVEWIRE WAS DIRECT AND EFFECTIVE-- IF A BIT OBVIOUS.
THIS ISN'T WHAT I CAME HERE TO TALK ABOUT.
IT'S THIS PLANET. AND MY PLANET.
I BARELY UNDERSTAND ONE, AND I CAN BARELY REMEMBER THE OTHER.
YOUR COUSIN. CLARK.
KAL.
KAL. HAVE YOU TALKED WITH HIM ABOUT THIS?
HE'S OFF IN SPACE, DOING SOMETHING WITH SOMEONE. GREEN LANTERN, I THINK.
BESIDES, HE'S SUPERMAN. THINGS ARE DIFFERENT FOR HIM.
YES.
THEY ARE.

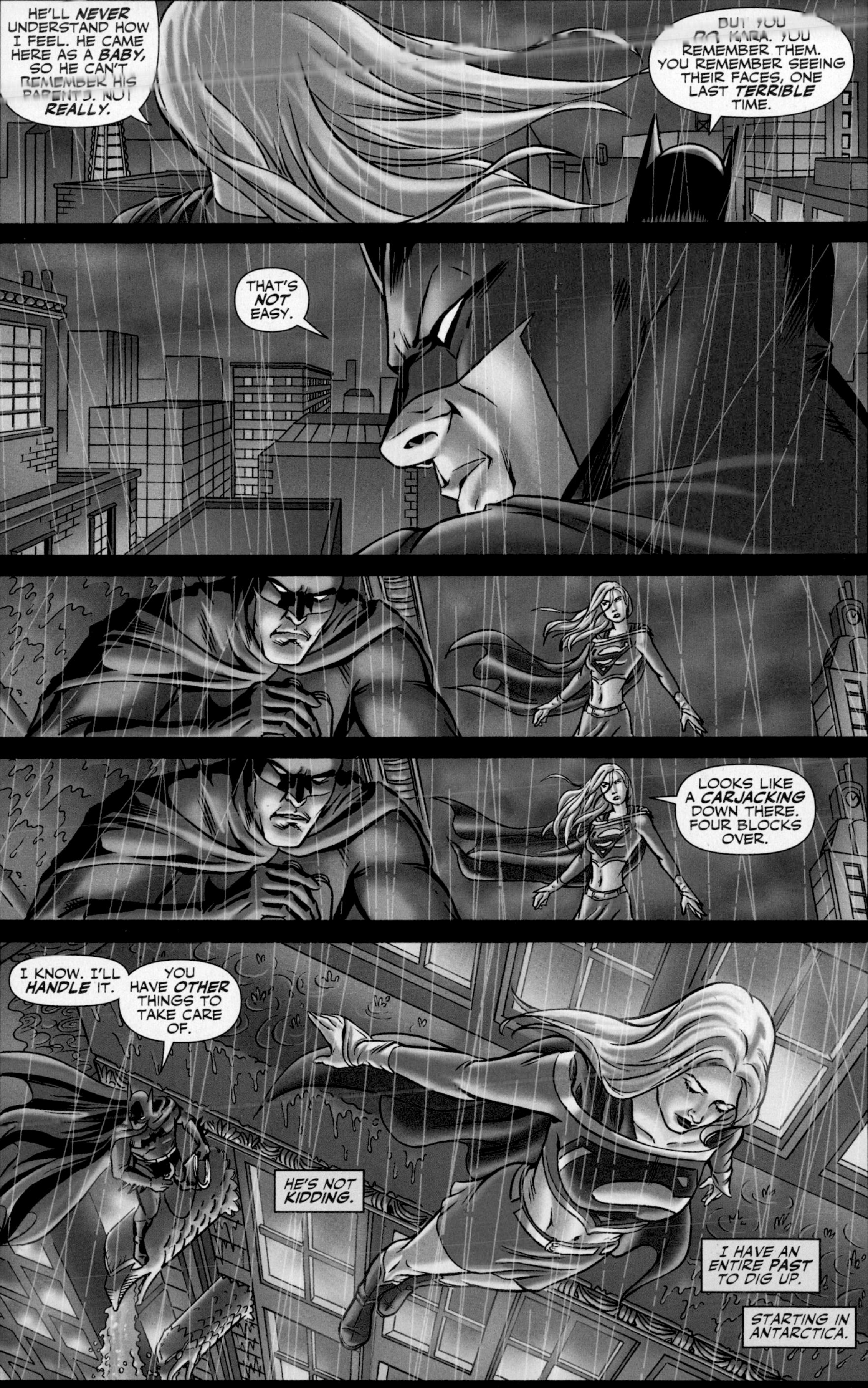
HE'LL NEVER UNDERSTAND HOW I FEEL. HE CAME HERE AS A BABY, SO HE CAN'T REMEMBER HIS PARENTS. NOT REALLY.
BUT YOU DO, KARA. YOU REMEMBER THEM. YOU REMEMBER SEEING THEIR FACES, ONE LAST TERRIBLE TIME.
THAT'S NOT EASY.
LOOKS LIKE A CARJACKING DOWN THERE. FOUR BLOCKS OVER.
I KNOW. I'LL HANDLE IT.
YOU HAVE OTHER THINGS TO TAKE CARE OF.
HE'S NOT KIDDING.
I HAVE AN ENTIRE PAST TO DIG UP.
STARTING IN ANTARCTICA.

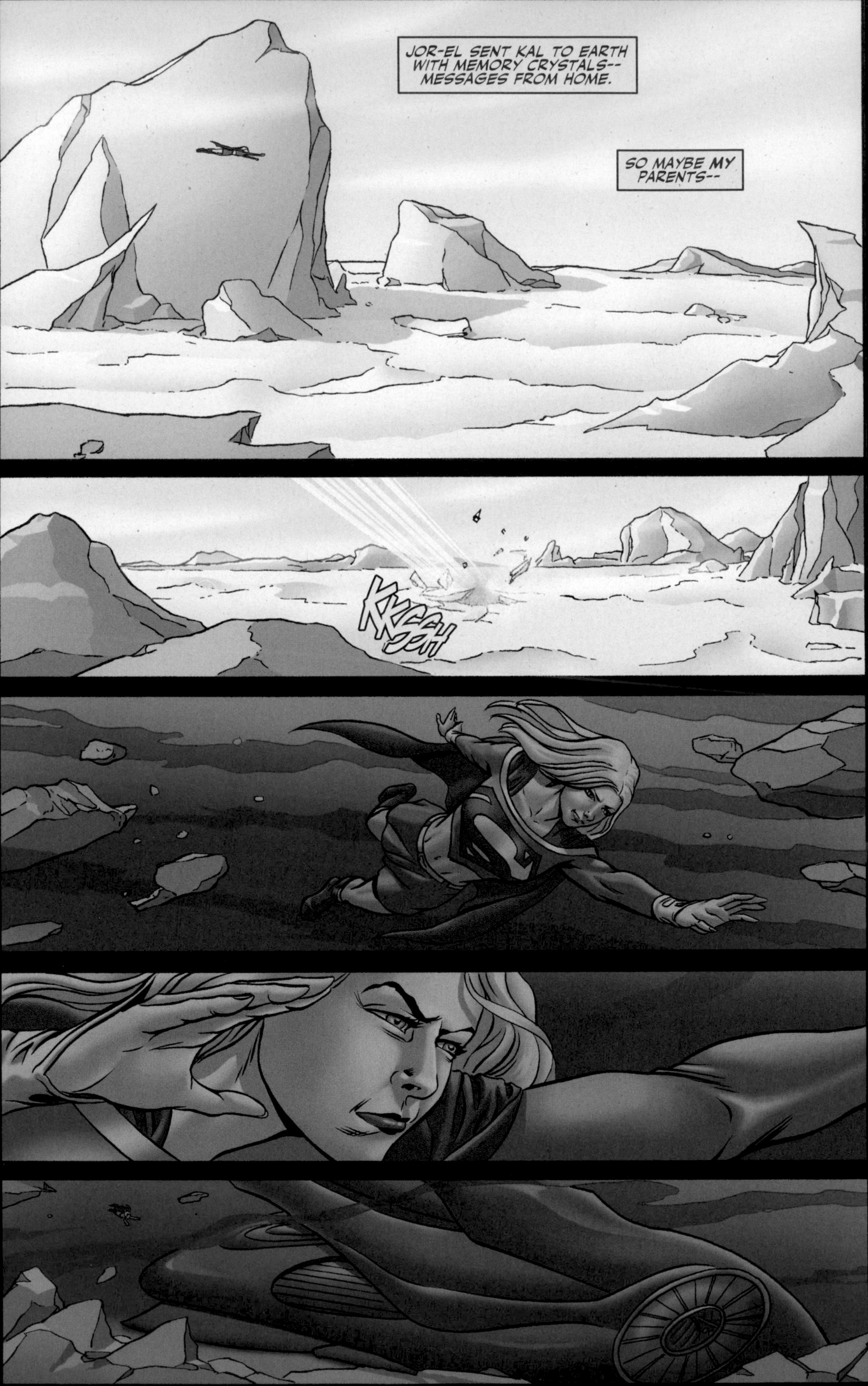
JOR-EL SENT KAL TO EARTH WITH MEMORY CRYSTALS-- MESSAGES FROM HOME.
SO MAYBE MY PARENTS--
KKSSH

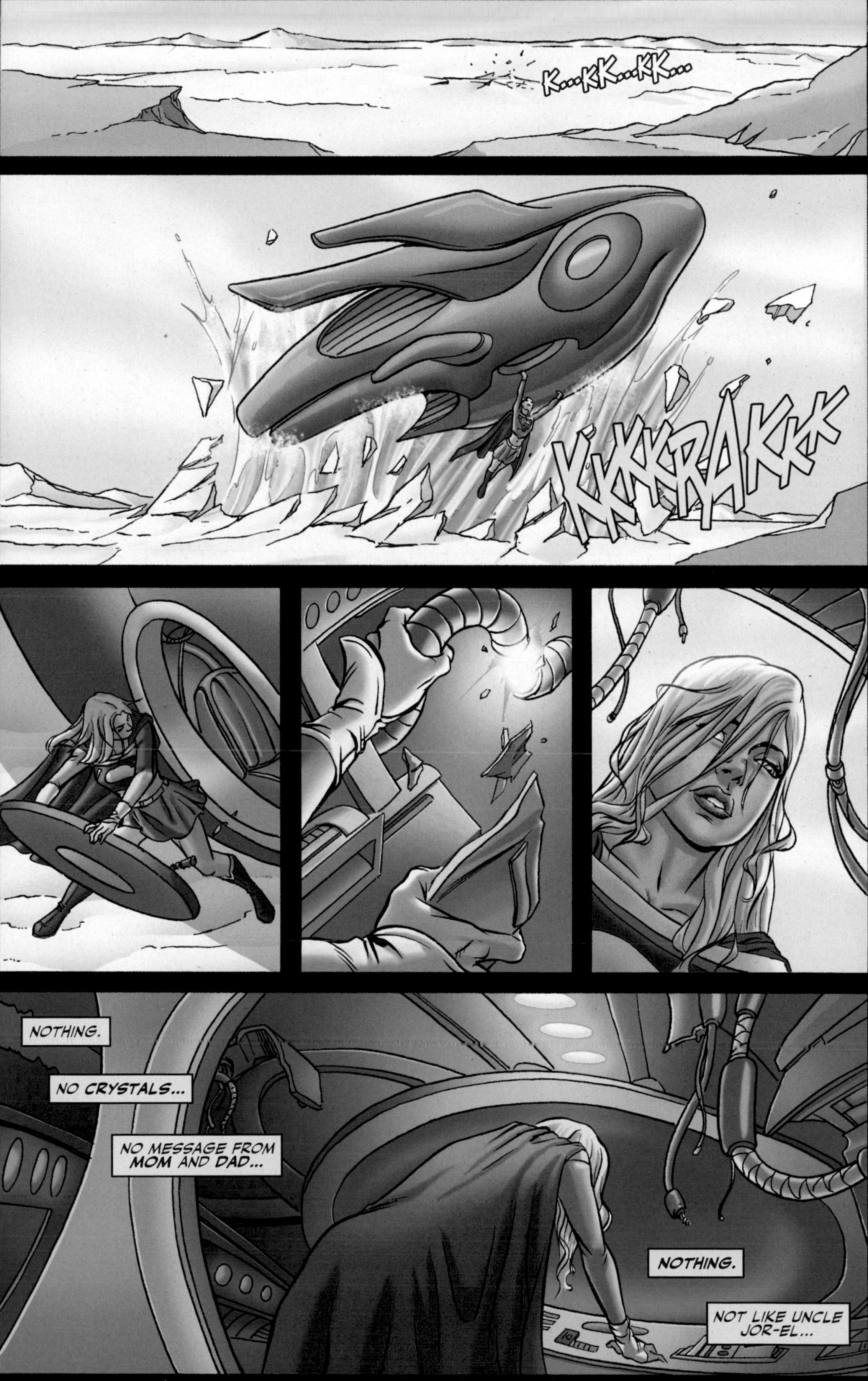
K...KK...KK...
KKKRAKKK
NOTHING.
NO CRYSTALS...
NO MESSAGE FROM MOM AND DAD...
NOTHING.
NOT LIKE UNCLE JOR-EL...

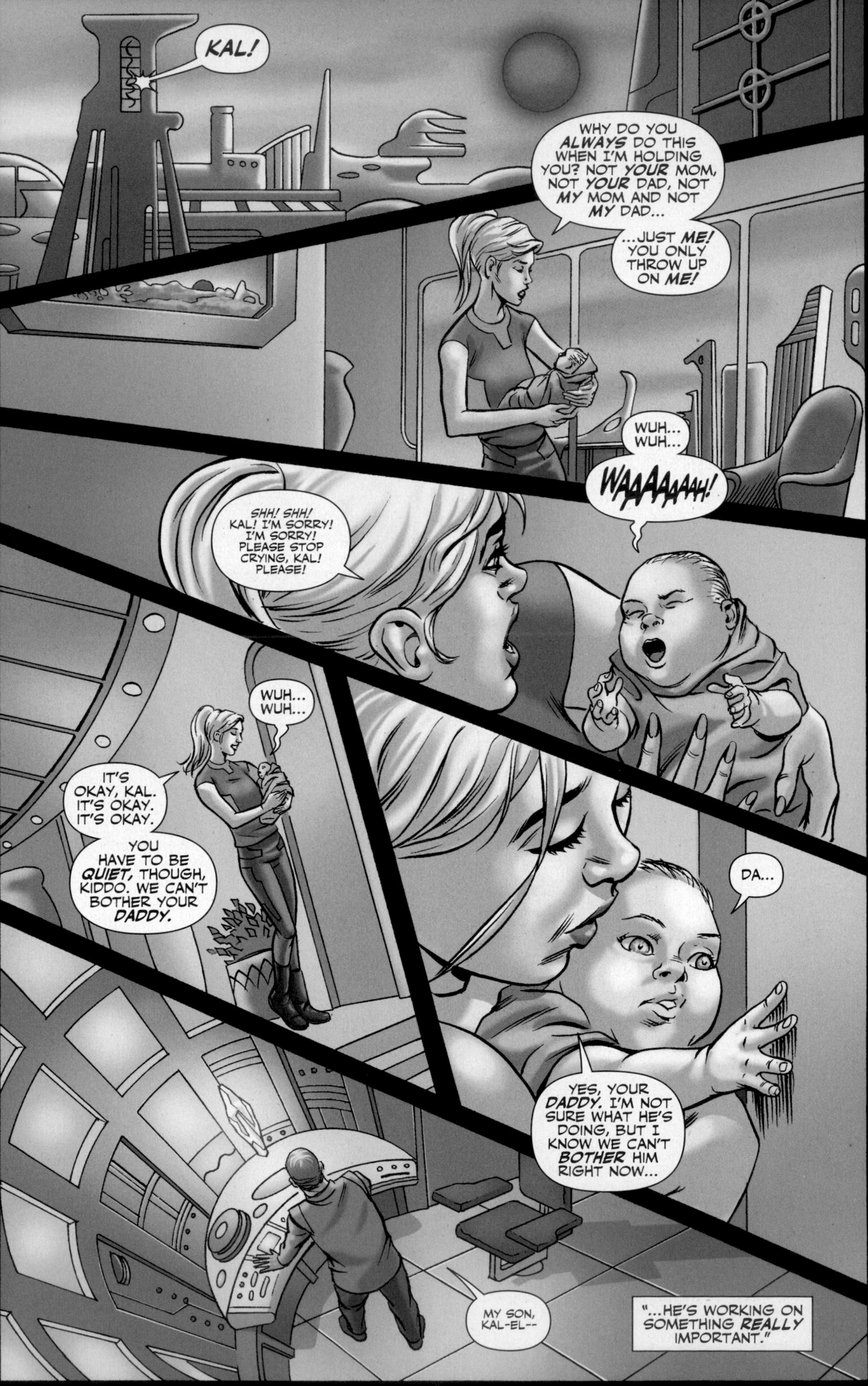
KAL!
WHY DO YOU ALWAYS DO THIS WHEN I'M HOLDING YOU? NOT YOUR MOM, NOT YOUR DAD, NOT MY MOM AND NOT MY DAD...
...JUST ME! YOU ONLY THROW UP ON ME!
WUH... WUH...
WAAAAAAAH!
SHH! SHH! KAL! I'M SORRY! I'M SORRY! PLEASE STOP CRYING, KAL! PLEASE!
WUH... WUH...
IT'S OKAY, KAL. IT'S OKAY. IT'S OKAY.
YOU HAVE TO BE QUIET, THOUGH, KIDDO. WE CAN'T BOTHER YOUR DADDY.
DA...
YES, YOUR DADDY. I'M NOT SURE WHAT HE'S DOING, BUT I KNOW WE CAN'T BOTHER HIM RIGHT NOW...
MY SON, KAL-EL--
"...HE'S WORKING ON SOMETHING REALLY IMPORTANT."

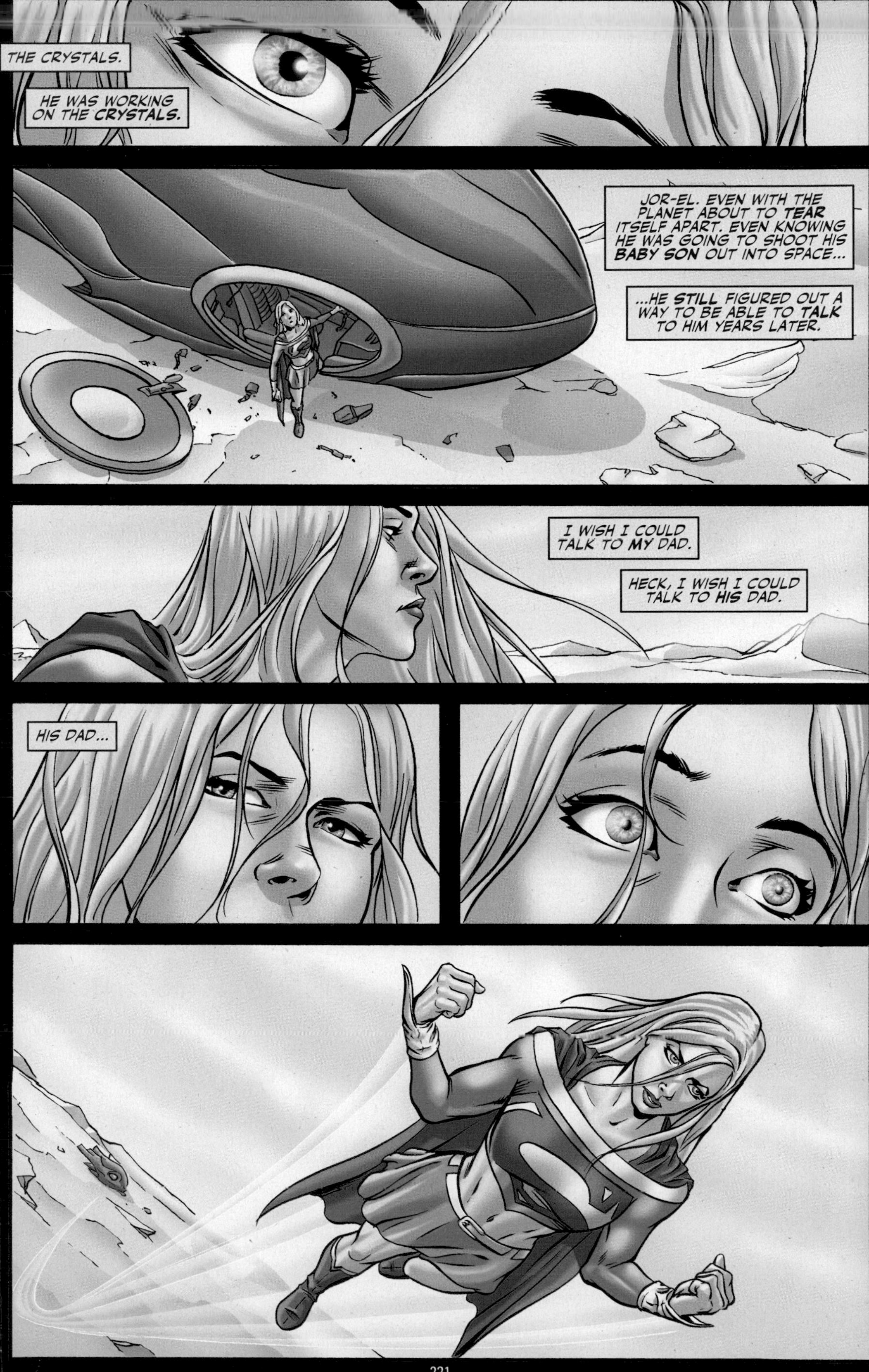
THE CRYSTALS.
HE WAS WORKING ON THE **CRYSTALS.**
JOR-EL. EVEN WITH THE PLANET ABOUT TO **TEAR** ITSELF APART. EVEN KNOWING HE WAS GOING TO SHOOT HIS **BABY SON** OUT INTO SPACE...
...HE **STILL** FIGURED OUT A WAY TO BE ABLE TO **TALK** TO HIM YEARS LATER.
I WISH I COULD TALK TO **MY** DAD.
HECK, I WISH I COULD TALK TO **HIS** DAD.
HIS DAD...

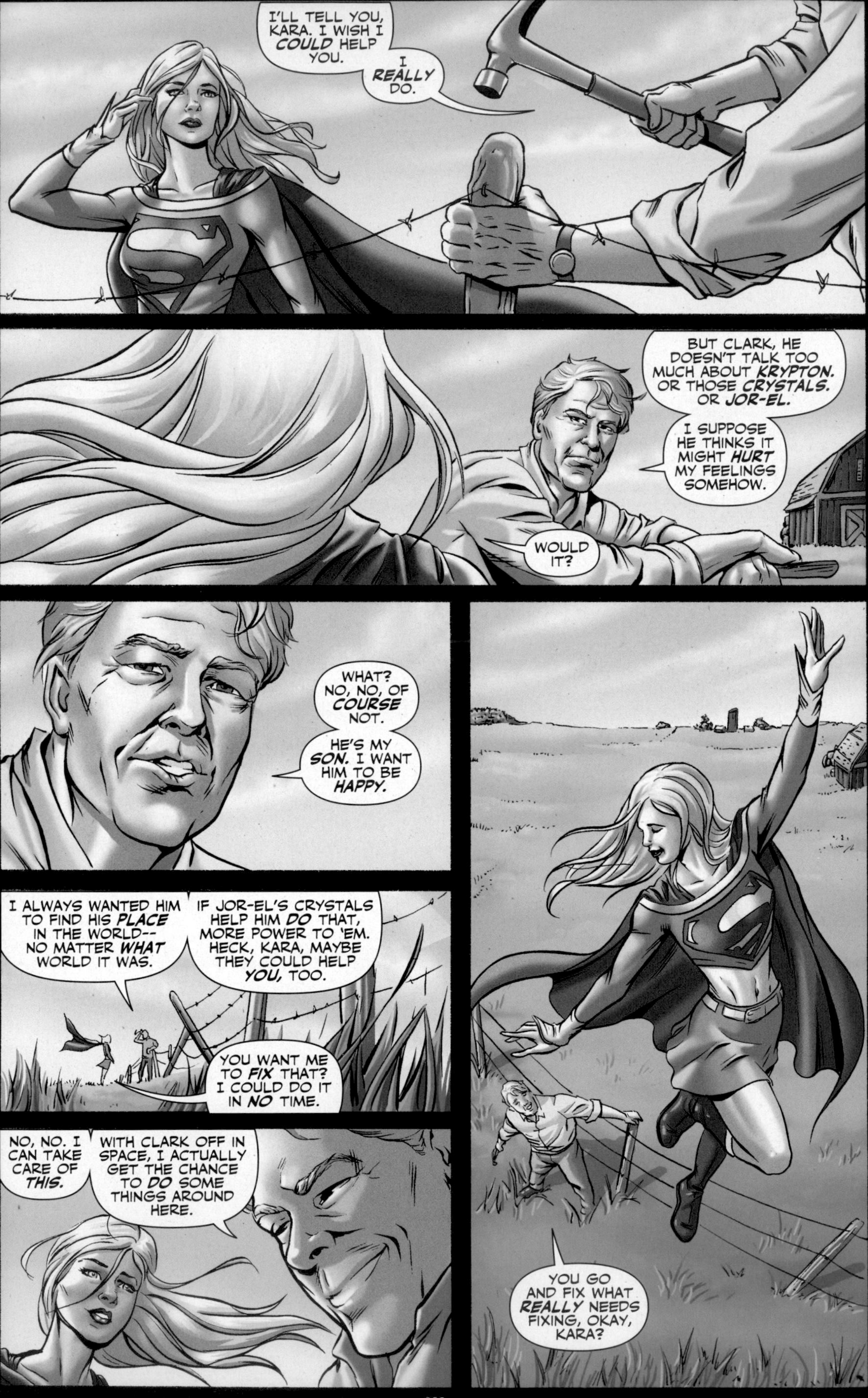

I'LL TELL YOU, KARA. I WISH I COULD HELP YOU.
I REALLY DO.
BUT CLARK, HE DOESN'T TALK TOO MUCH ABOUT KRYPTON. OR THOSE CRYSTALS. OR JOR-EL.
I SUPPOSE HE THINKS IT MIGHT HURT MY FEELINGS SOMEHOW.
WOULD IT?
WHAT? NO, NO, OF COURSE NOT.
HE'S MY SON. I WANT HIM TO BE HAPPY.
I ALWAYS WANTED HIM TO FIND HIS PLACE IN THE WORLD-- NO MATTER WHAT WORLD IT WAS.
IF JOR-EL'S CRYSTALS HELP HIM DO THAT, MORE POWER TO 'EM. HECK, KARA, MAYBE THEY COULD HELP YOU, TOO.
YOU WANT ME TO FIX THAT? I COULD DO IT IN NO TIME.
NO, NO. I CAN TAKE CARE OF THIS.
WITH CLARK OFF IN SPACE, I ACTUALLY GET THE CHANCE TO DO SOME THINGS AROUND HERE.
YOU GO AND FIX WHAT REALLY NEEDS FIXING, OKAY, KARA?

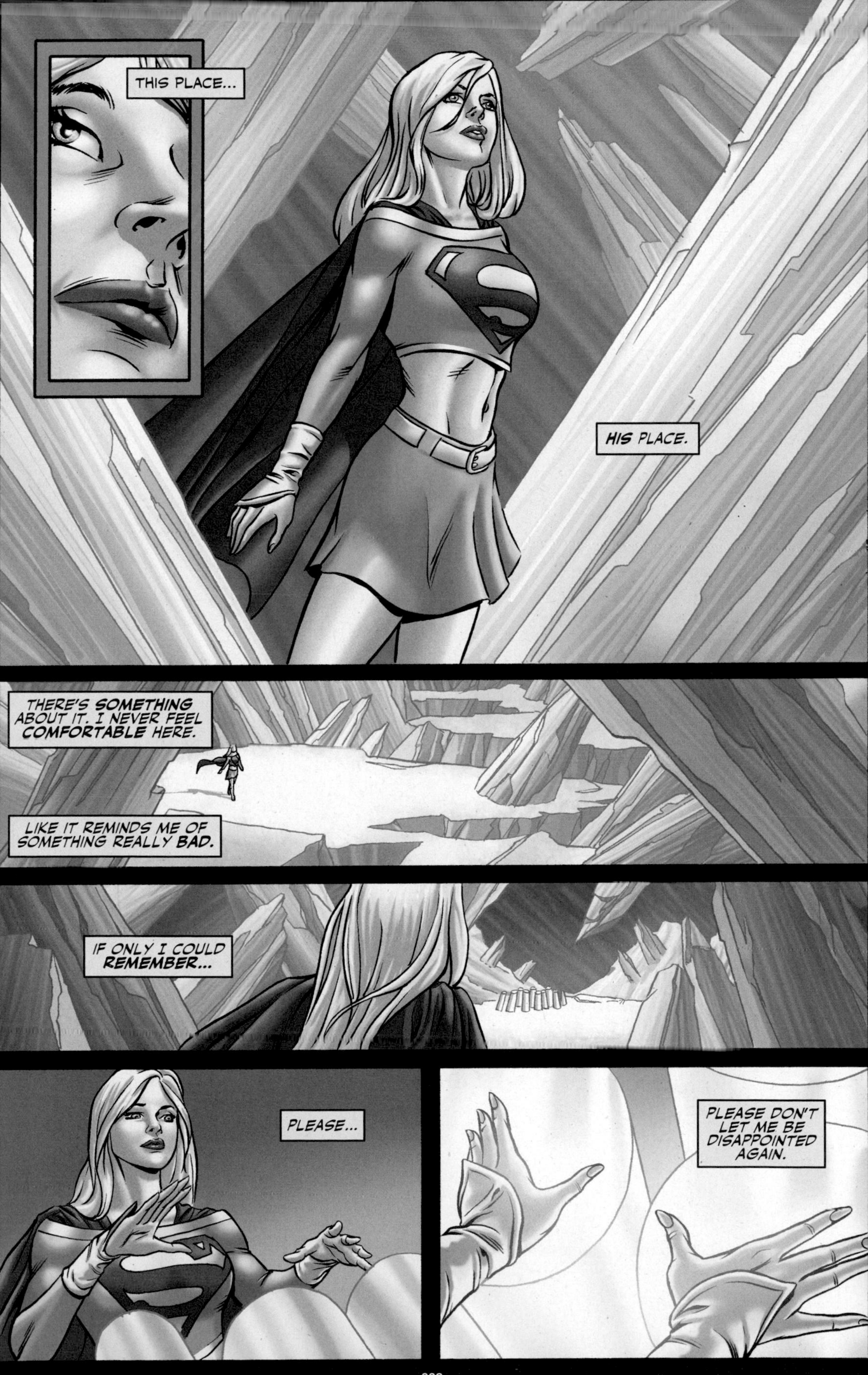
THIS PLACE...
HIS PLACE.
THERE'S SOMETHING ABOUT IT. I NEVER FEEL COMFORTABLE HERE.
LIKE IT REMINDS ME OF SOMETHING REALLY BAD.
IF ONLY I COULD REMEMBER...
PLEASE...
PLEASE DON'T LET ME BE DISAPPOINTED AGAIN.

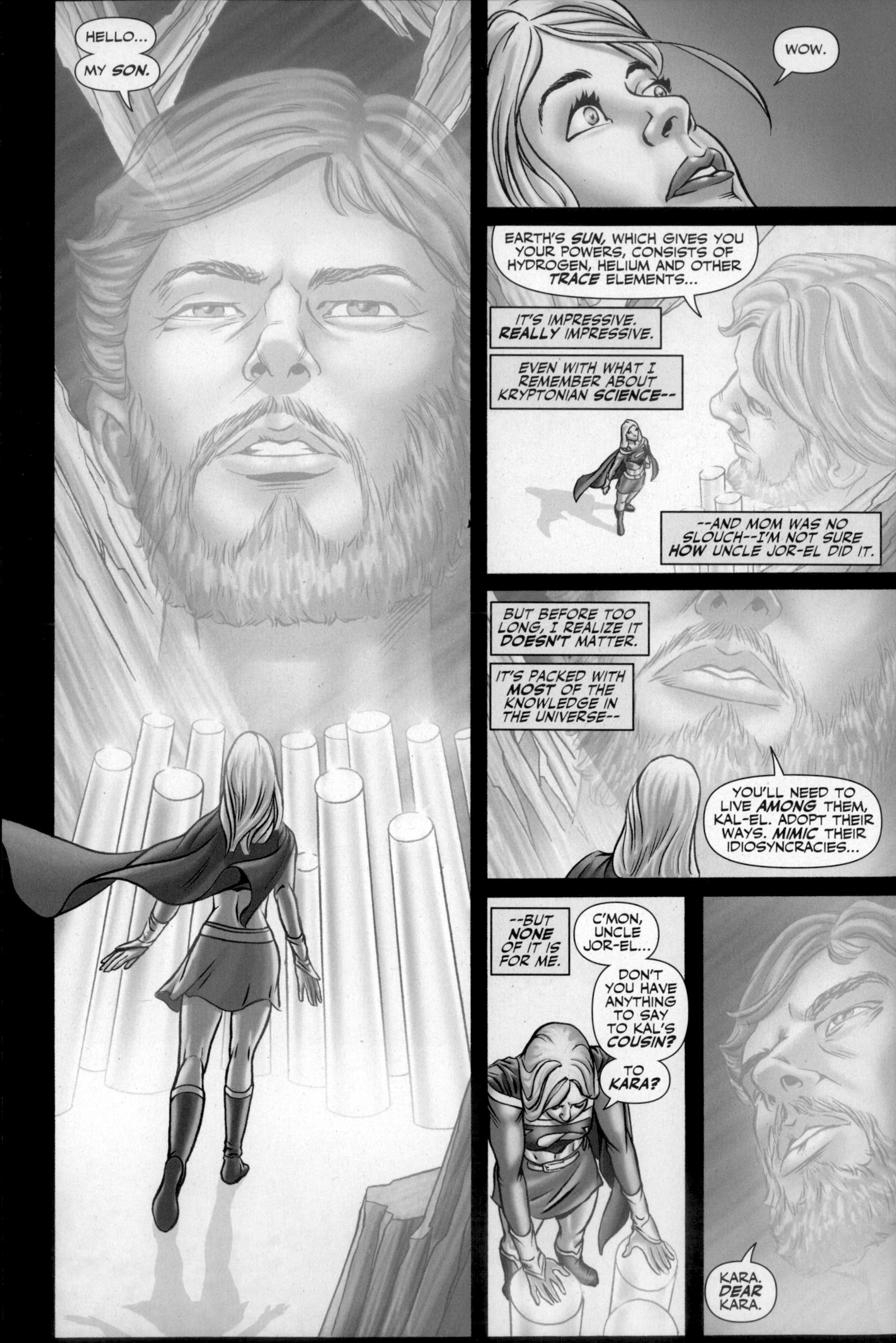
HELLO...
MY SON.
WOW.
EARTH'S SUN, WHICH GIVES YOU YOUR POWERS, CONSISTS OF HYDROGEN, HELIUM AND OTHER TRACE ELEMENTS...
IT'S IMPRESSIVE. REALLY IMPRESSIVE.
EVEN WITH WHAT I REMEMBER ABOUT KRYPTONIAN SCIENCE--
--AND MOM WAS NO SLOUCH--I'M NOT SURE HOW UNCLE JOR-EL DID IT.
BUT BEFORE TOO LONG, I REALIZE IT DOESN'T MATTER.
IT'S PACKED WITH MOST OF THE KNOWLEDGE IN THE UNIVERSE--
YOU'LL NEED TO LIVE AMONG THEM, KAL-EL. ADOPT THEIR WAYS. MIMIC THEIR IDIOSYNCRACIES...
--BUT NONE OF IT IS FOR ME.
C'MON, UNCLE JOR-EL...
DON'T YOU HAVE ANYTHING TO SAY TO KAL'S COUSIN?
TO KARA?
KARA. DEAR KARA.

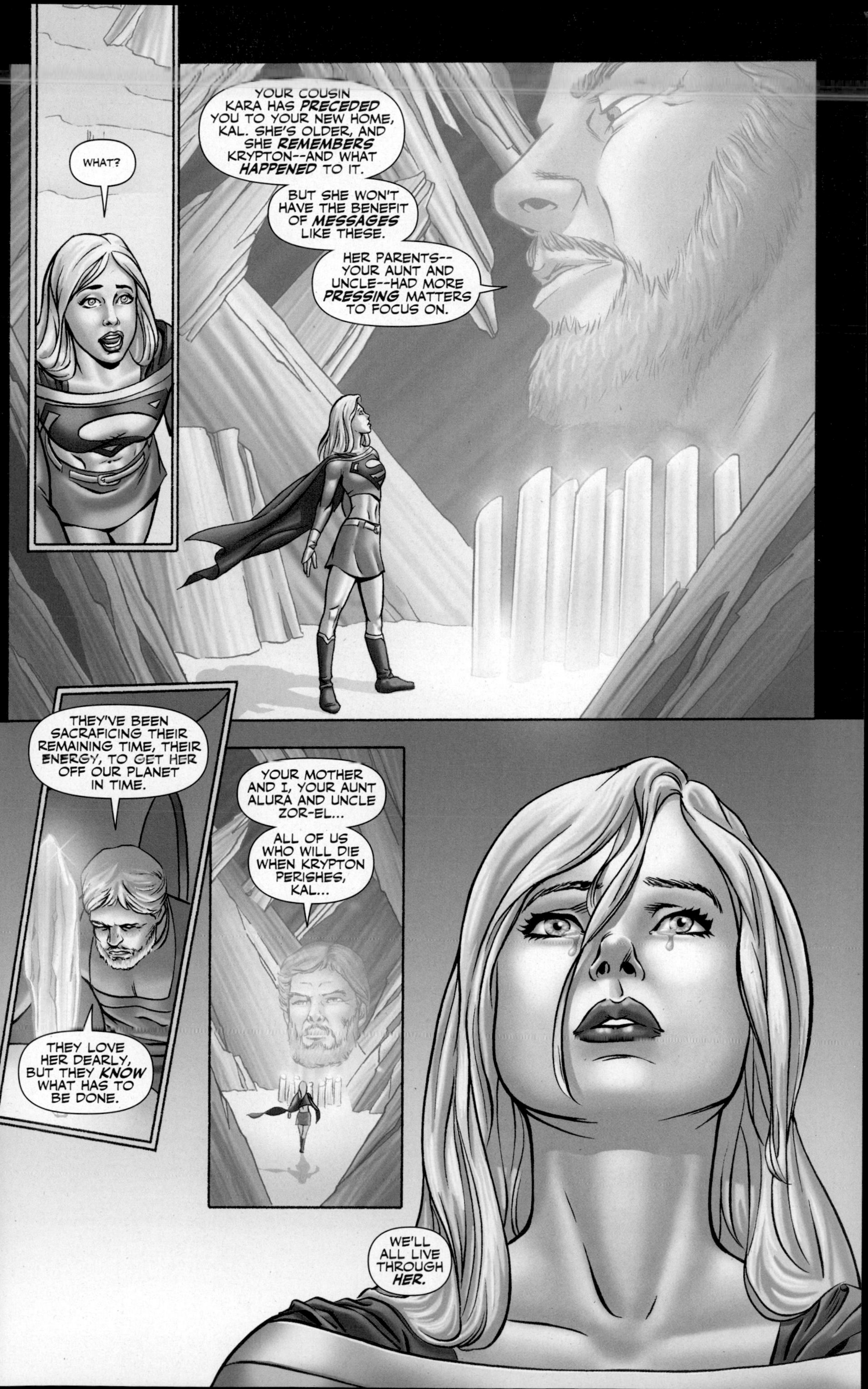
WHAT?
YOUR COUSIN KARA HAS PRECEDED YOU TO YOUR NEW HOME, KAL. SHE'S OLDER, AND SHE REMEMBERS KRYPTON--AND WHAT HAPPENED TO IT.
BUT SHE WON'T HAVE THE BENEFIT OF MESSAGES LIKE THESE.
HER PARENTS--YOUR AUNT AND UNCLE--HAD MORE PRESSING MATTERS TO FOCUS ON.
THEY'VE BEEN SACRAFICING THEIR REMAINING TIME, THEIR ENERGY, TO GET HER OFF OUR PLANET IN TIME.
THEY LOVE HER DEARLY, BUT THEY KNOW WHAT HAS TO BE DONE.
YOUR MOTHER AND I, YOUR AUNT ALURA AND UNCLE ZOR-EL...
ALL OF US WHO WILL DIE WHEN KRYPTON PERISHES, KAL...
WE'LL ALL LIVE THROUGH HER.

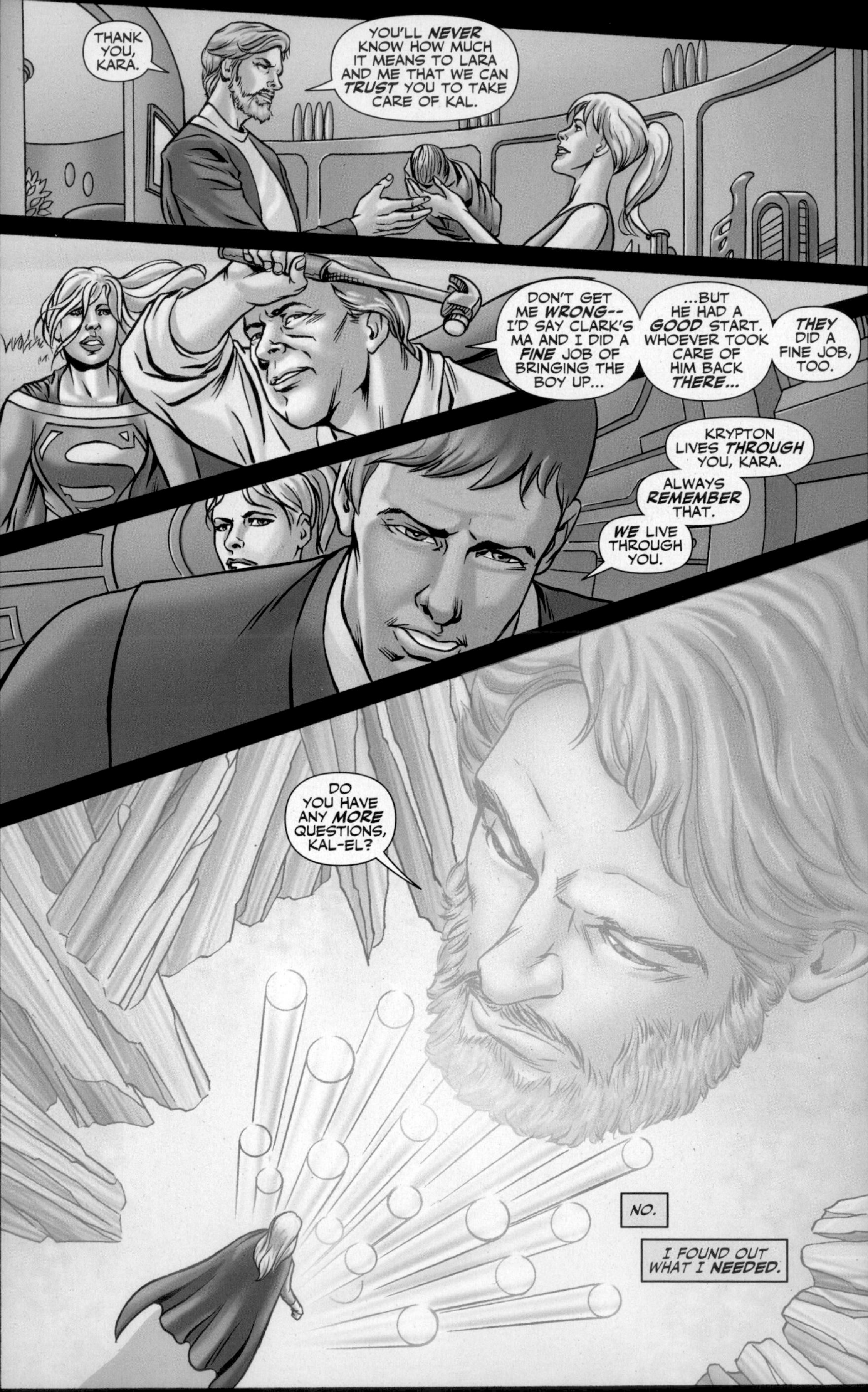
THANK YOU, KARA.
YOU'LL NEVER KNOW HOW MUCH IT MEANS TO LARA AND ME THAT WE CAN TRUST YOU TO TAKE CARE OF KAL.
DON'T GET ME WRONG-- I'D SAY CLARK'S MA AND I DID A FINE JOB OF BRINGING THE BOY UP...
...BUT HE HAD A GOOD START. WHOEVER TOOK CARE OF HIM BACK THERE...
THEY DID A FINE JOB, TOO.
KRYPTON LIVES THROUGH YOU, KARA.
ALWAYS REMEMBER THAT.
WE LIVE THROUGH YOU.
DO YOU HAVE ANY MORE QUESTIONS, KAL-EL?
NO.
I FOUND OUT WHAT I NEEDED.

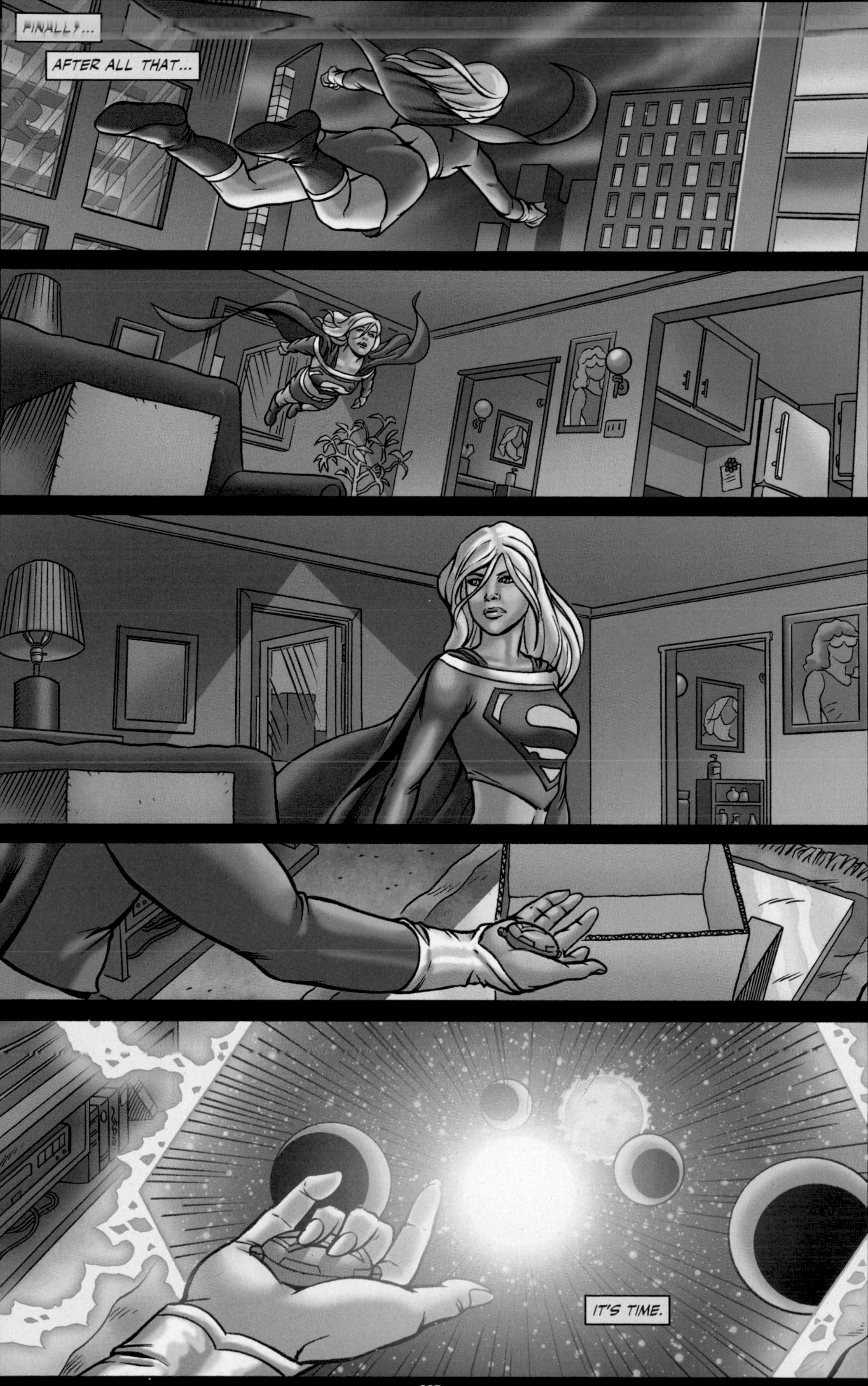
FINALLY...
AFTER ALL THAT...
IT'S TIME.

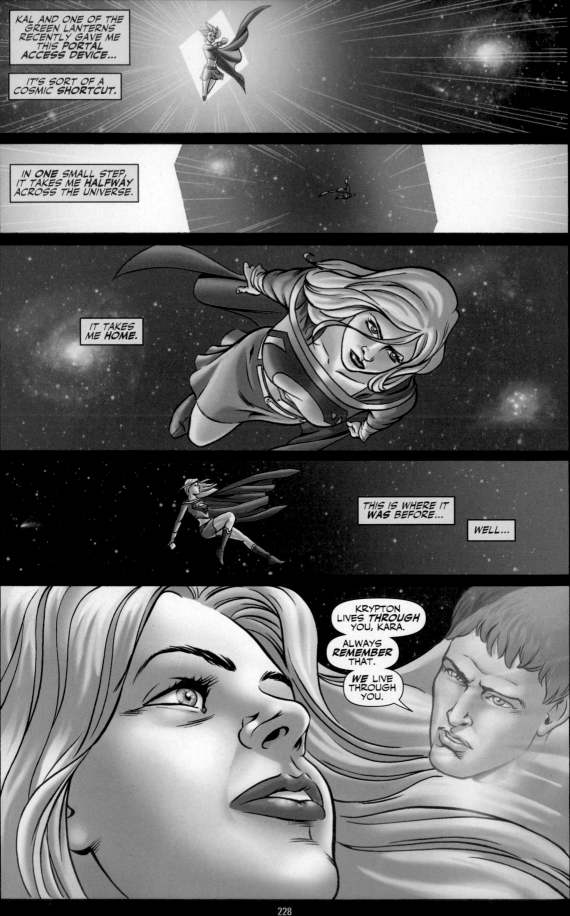

KAL AND ONE OF THE GREEN LANTERNS RECENTLY GAVE ME THIS PORTAL ACCESS DEVICE...

IT'S SORT OF A COSMIC SHORTCUT.

IN ONE SMALL STEP, IT TAKES ME HALFWAY ACROSS THE UNIVERSE.

IT TAKES ME HOME.

THIS IS WHERE IT WAS BEFORE...

WELL...

KRYPTON LIVES THROUGH YOU, KARA.

ALWAYS REMEMBER THAT.

WE LIVE THROUGH YOU.

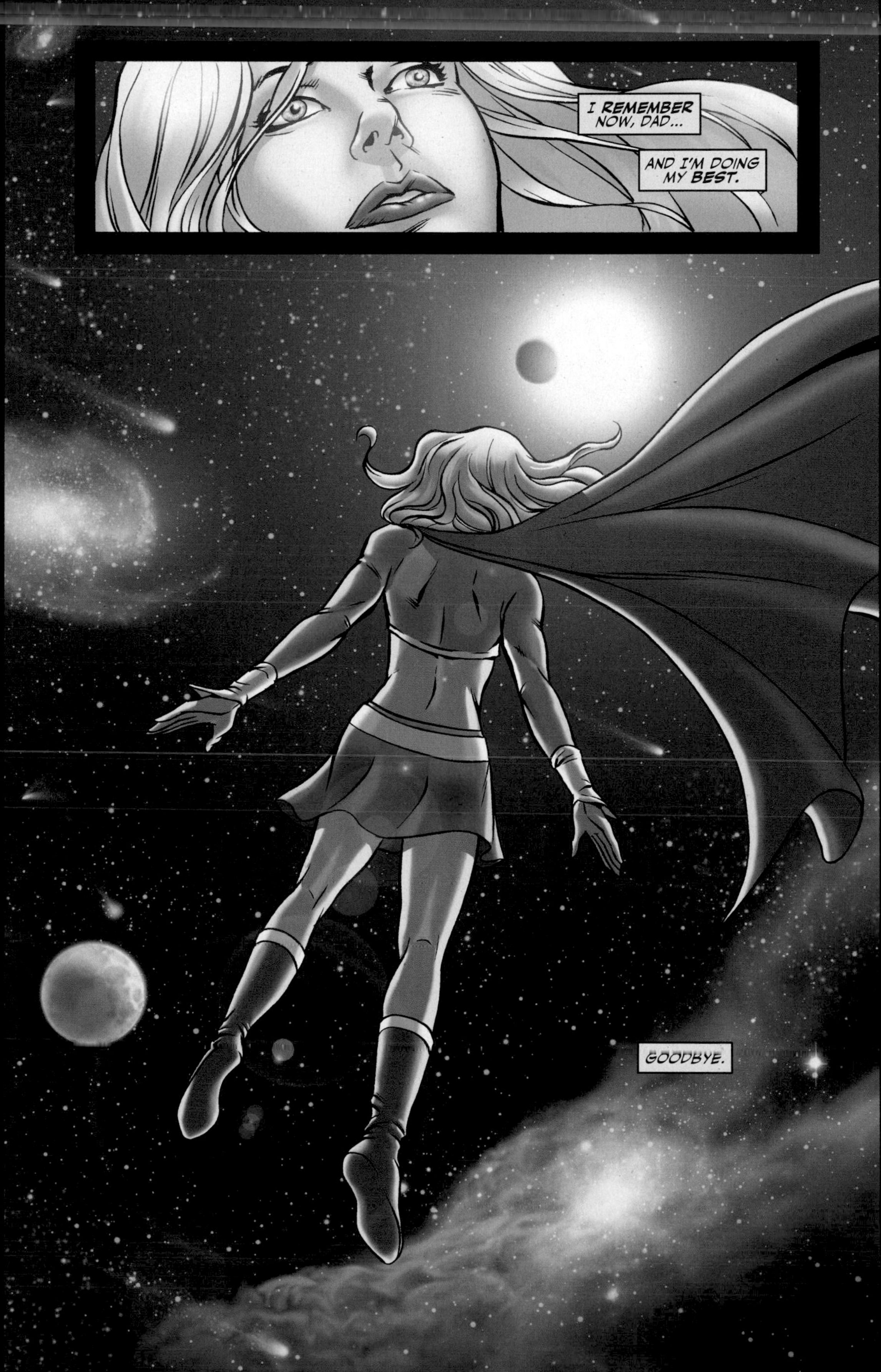
I REMEMBER NOW, DAD...
AND I'M DOING MY BEST.
GOODBYE.

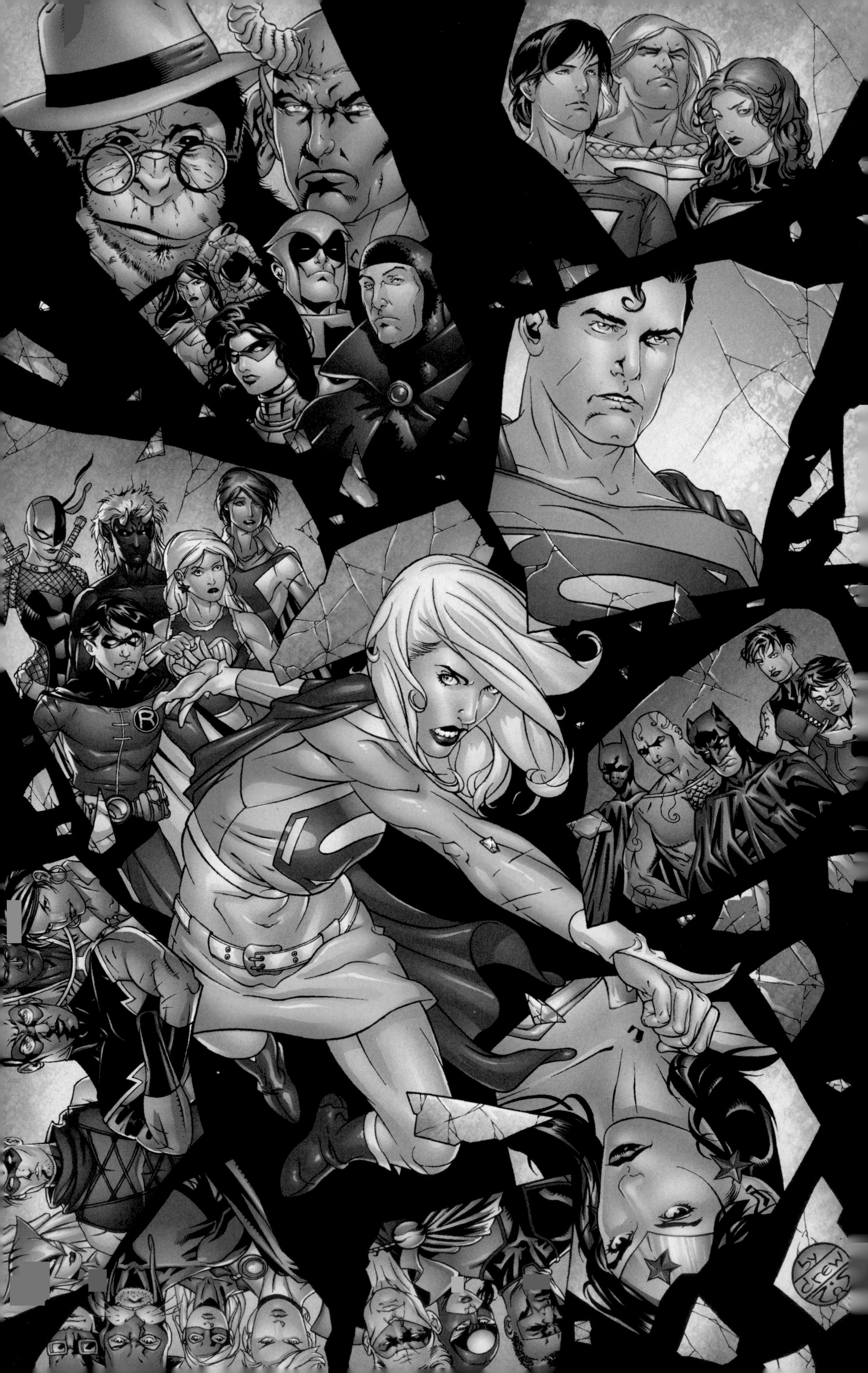

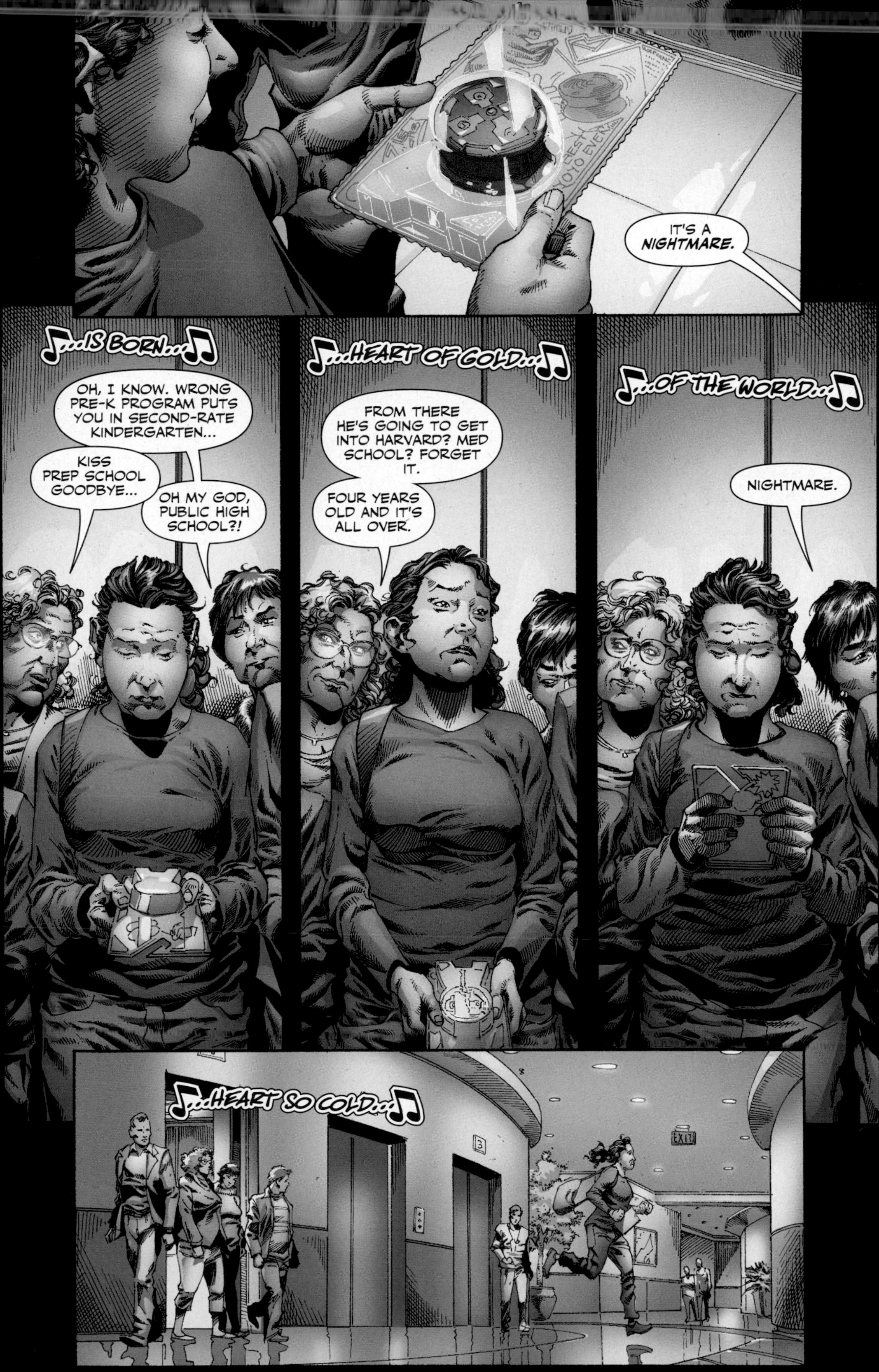
IT'S A NIGHTMARE.
♪...IS BORN...♪
OH, I KNOW. WRONG PRE-K PROGRAM PUTS YOU IN SECOND-RATE KINDERGARTEN...
KISS PREP SCHOOL GOODBYE...
OH MY GOD, PUBLIC HIGH SCHOOL?!
♪...HEART OF GOLD...♪
FROM THERE HE'S GOING TO GET INTO HARVARD? MED SCHOOL? FORGET IT.
FOUR YEARS OLD AND IT'S ALL OVER.
♪...OF THE WORLD...♪
NIGHTMARE.
♪...HEART SO COLD...♪
EXIT

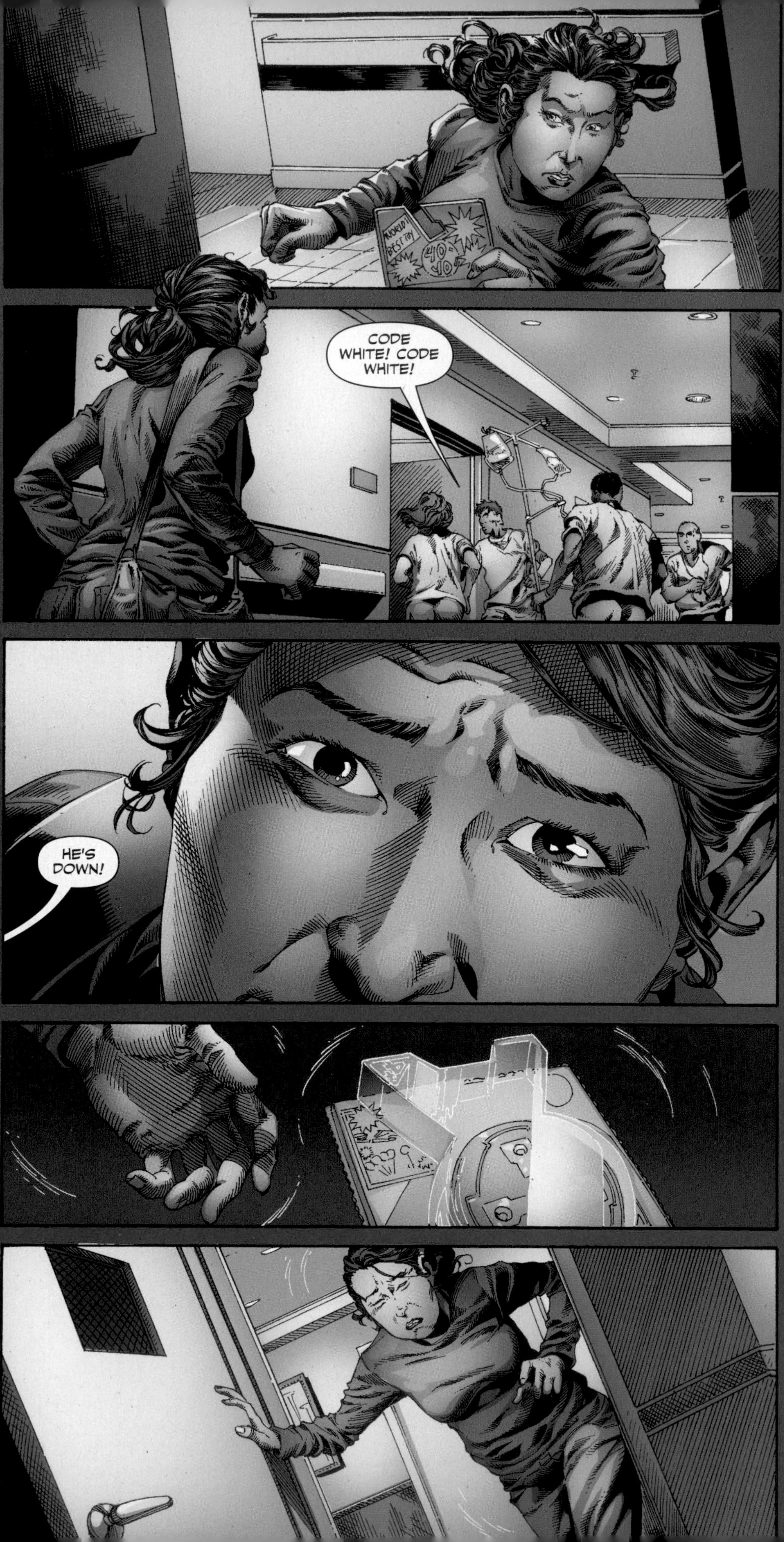
WORLD'S BEST TOY
40%
CODE WHITE! CODE WHITE!
HE'S DOWN!

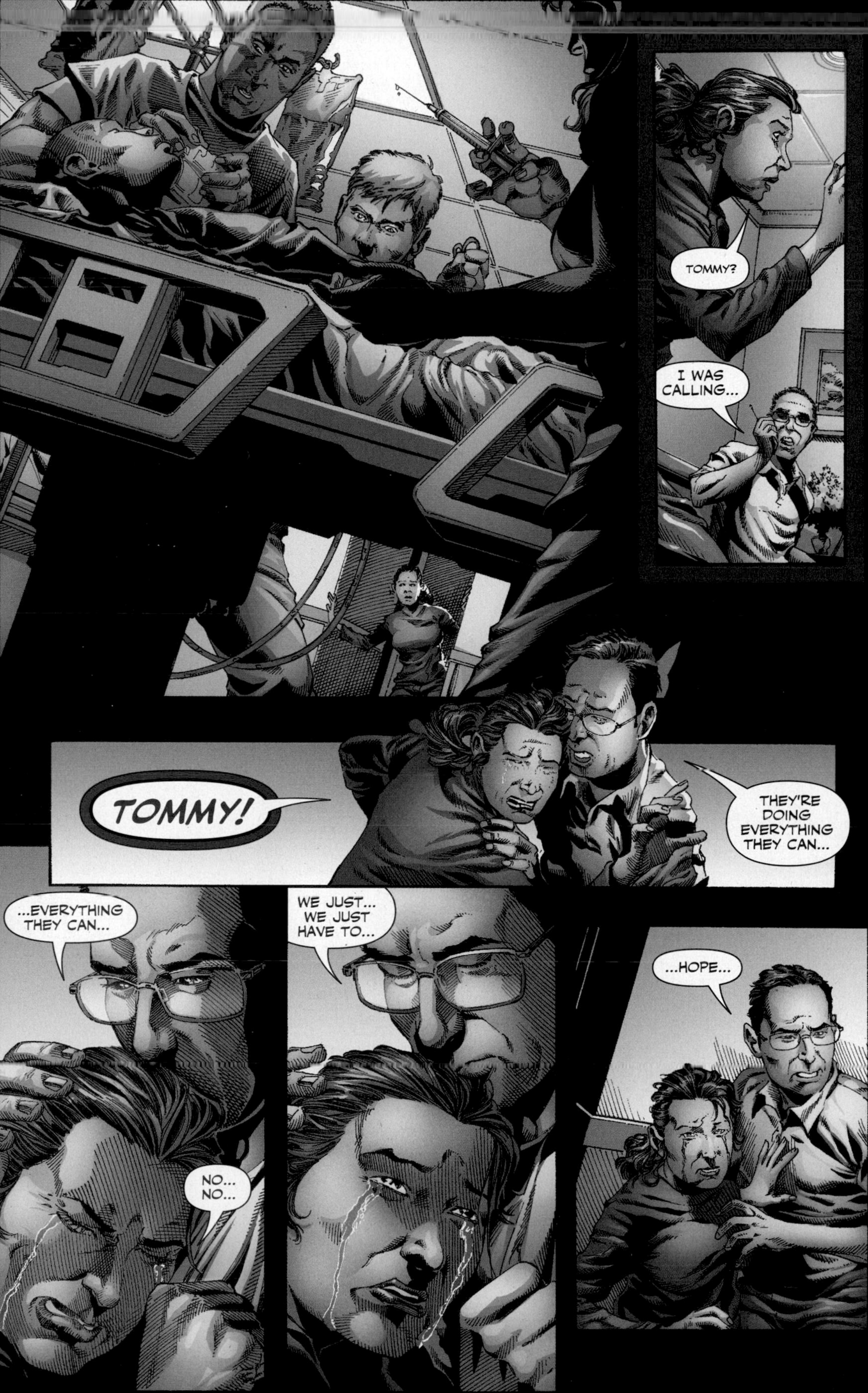
TOMMY?
I WAS CALLING...
TOMMY!
THEY'RE DOING EVERYTHING THEY CAN...
...EVERYTHING THEY CAN...
NO... NO...
WE JUST... WE JUST HAVE TO...
...HOPE...

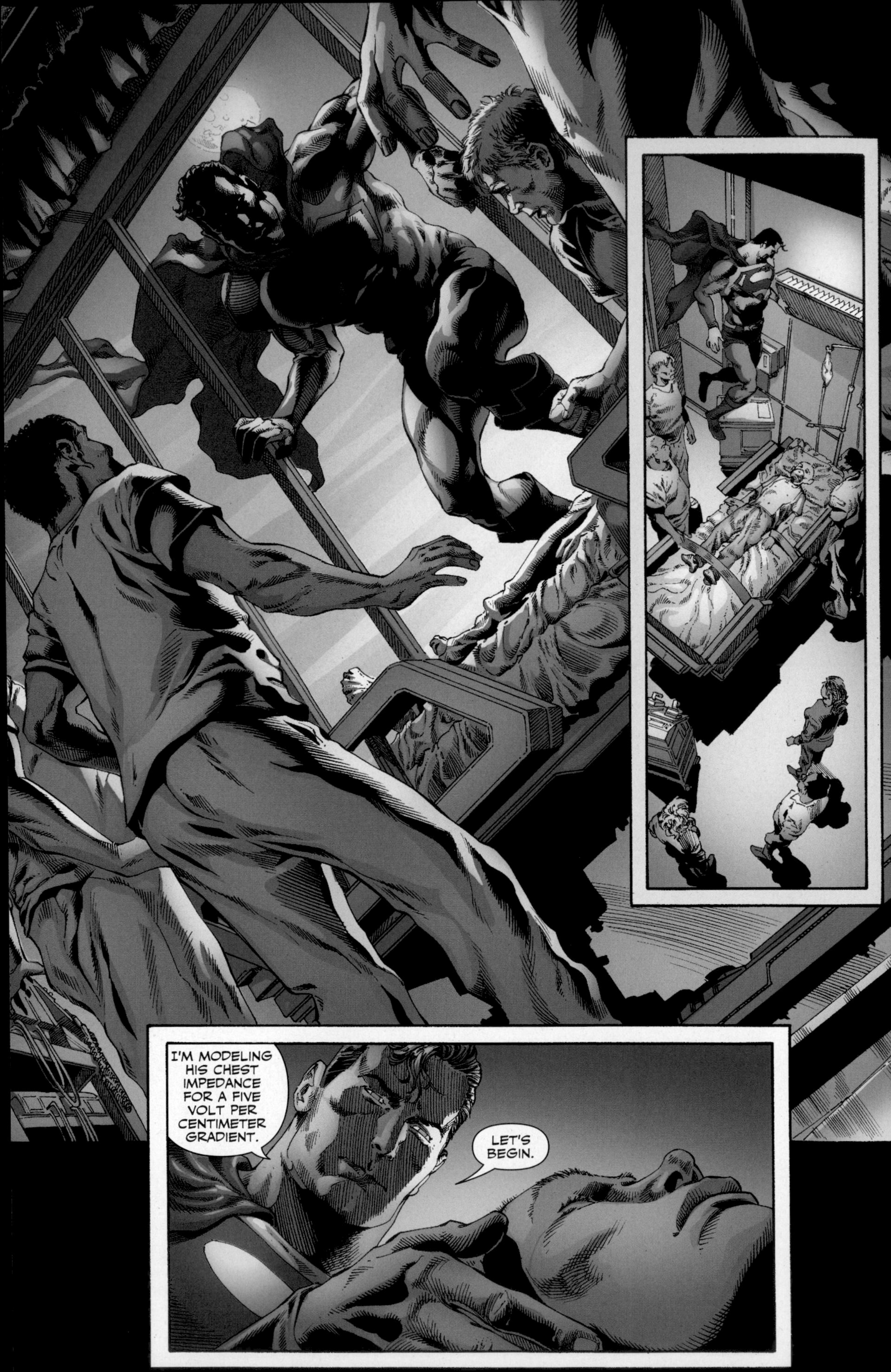
I'M MODELING HIS CHEST IMPEDANCE FOR A FIVE VOLT PER CENTIMETER GRADIENT.
LET'S BEGIN.

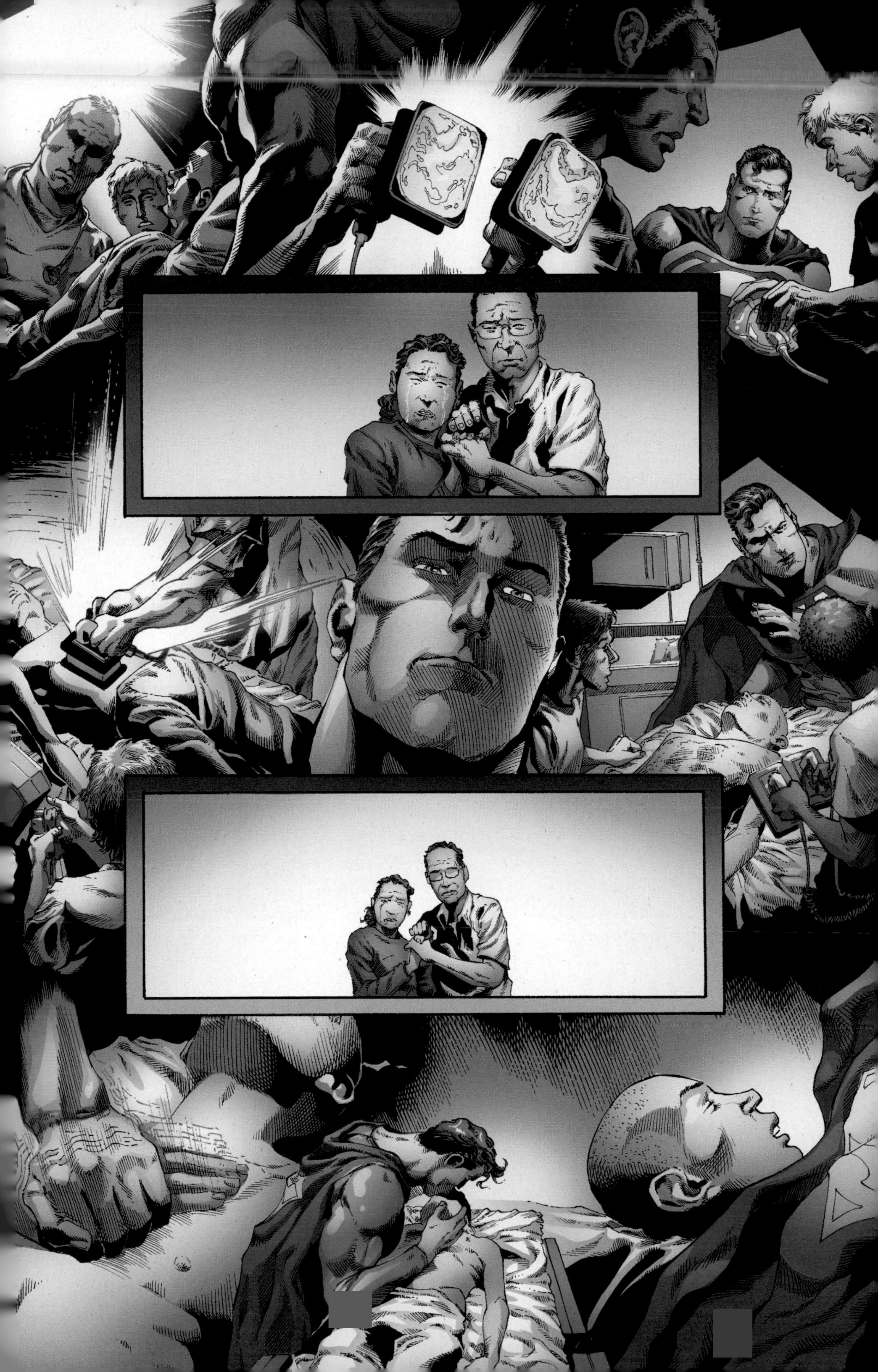

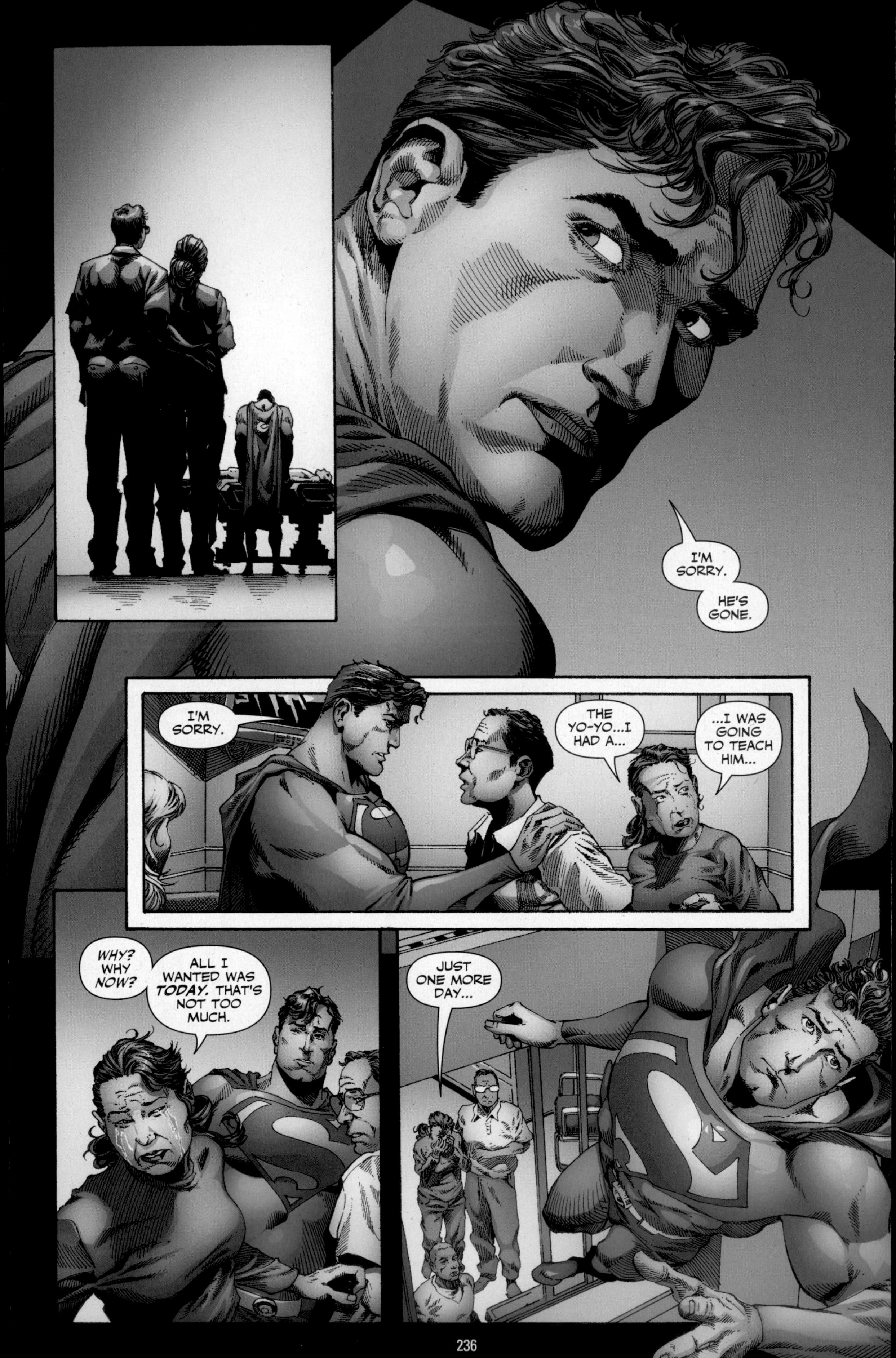
I'M SORRY.
HE'S GONE.
I'M SORRY.
THE YO-YO...I HAD A...
...I WAS GOING TO TEACH HIM...
WHY? WHY NOW?
ALL I WANTED WAS *TODAY.* THAT'S NOT TOO MUCH.
JUST ONE MORE DAY...

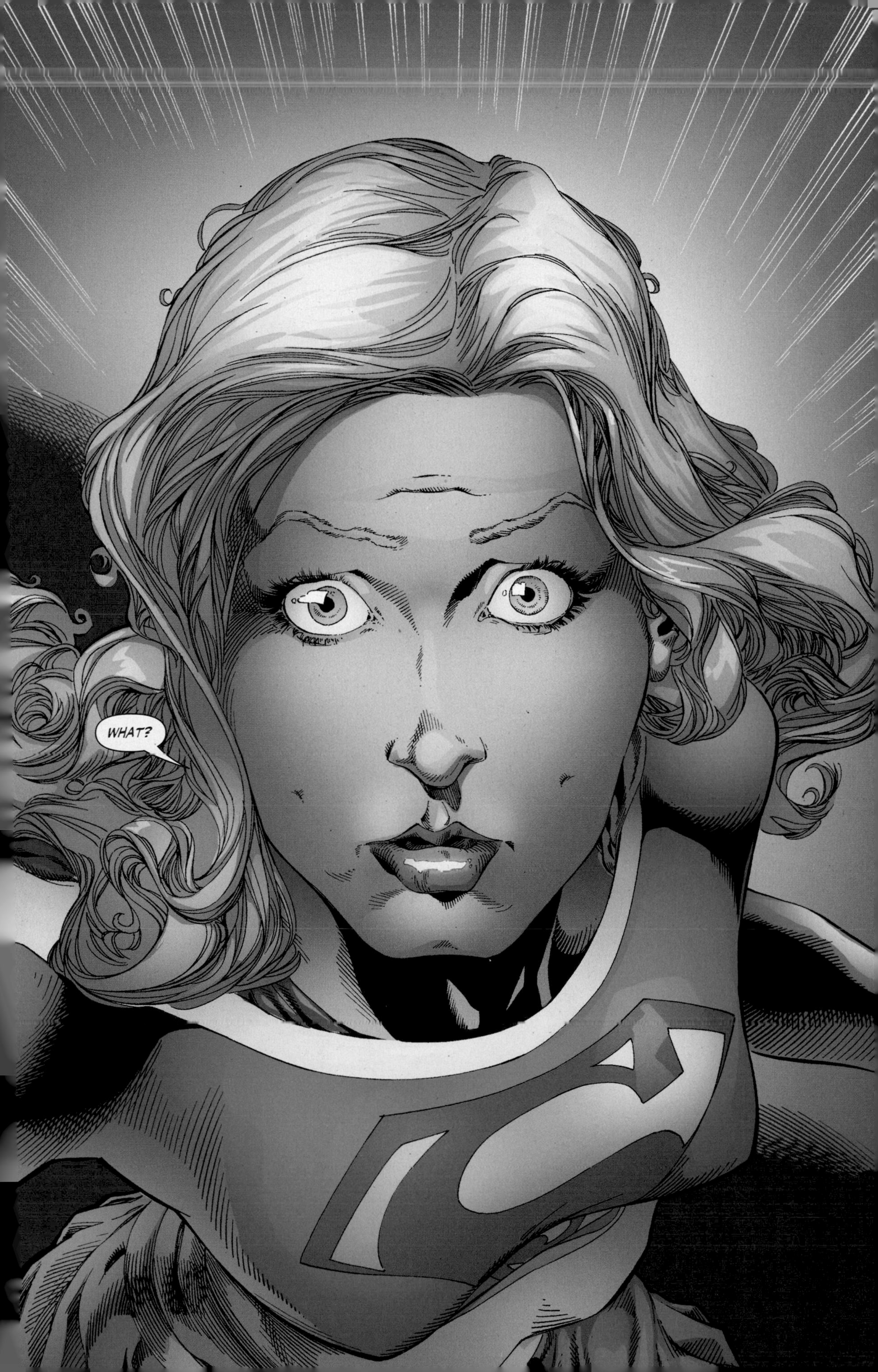
WHAT?

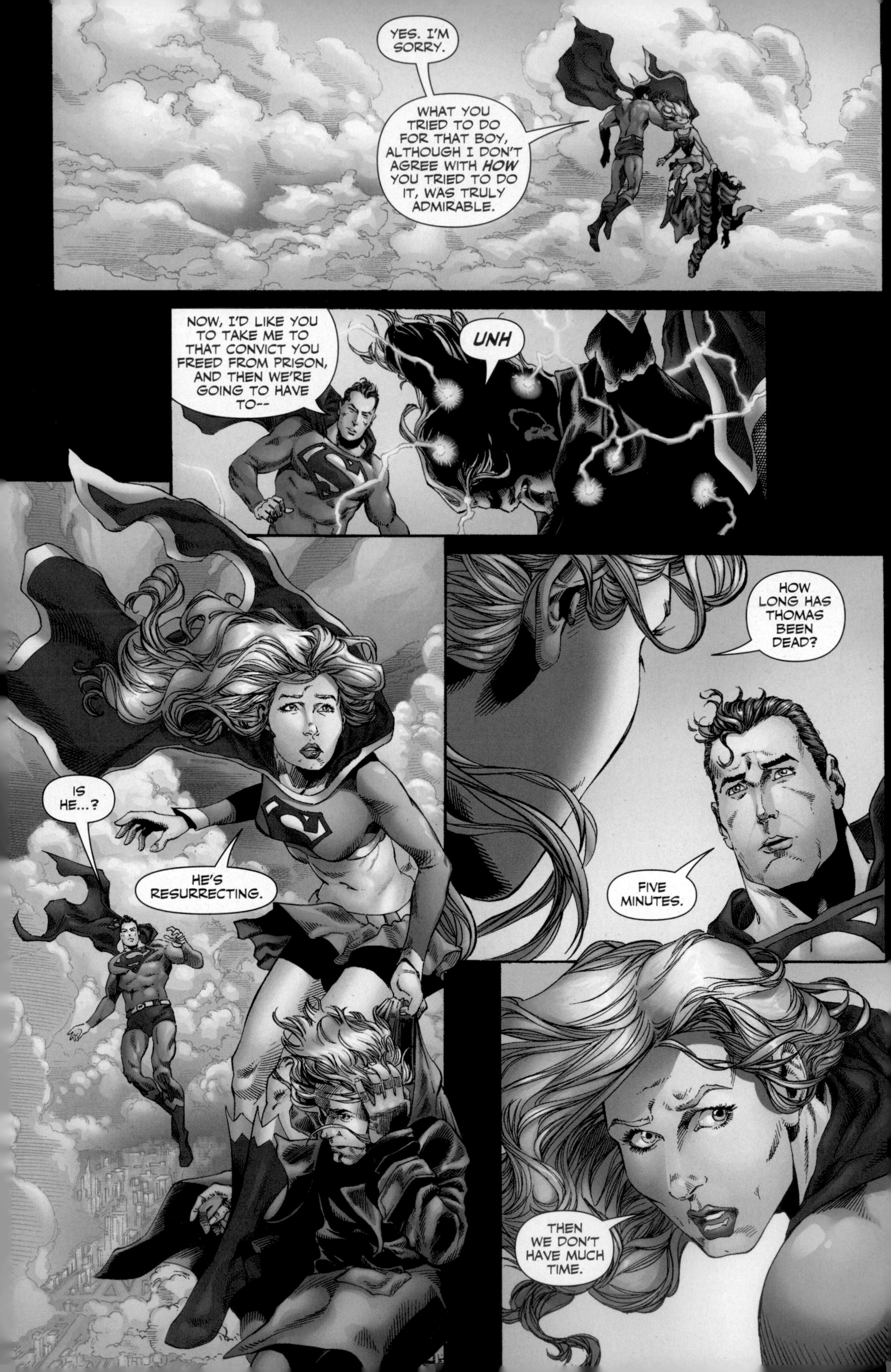
YES. I'M SORRY.
WHAT YOU TRIED TO DO FOR THAT BOY, ALTHOUGH I DON'T AGREE WITH *HOW* YOU TRIED TO DO IT, WAS TRULY ADMIRABLE.
NOW, I'D LIKE YOU TO TAKE ME TO THAT CONVICT YOU FREED FROM PRISON, AND THEN WE'RE GOING TO HAVE TO--
UNH
IS HE...?
HE'S RESURRECTING.
HOW LONG HAS THOMAS BEEN DEAD?
FIVE MINUTES.
THEN WE DON'T HAVE MUCH TIME.

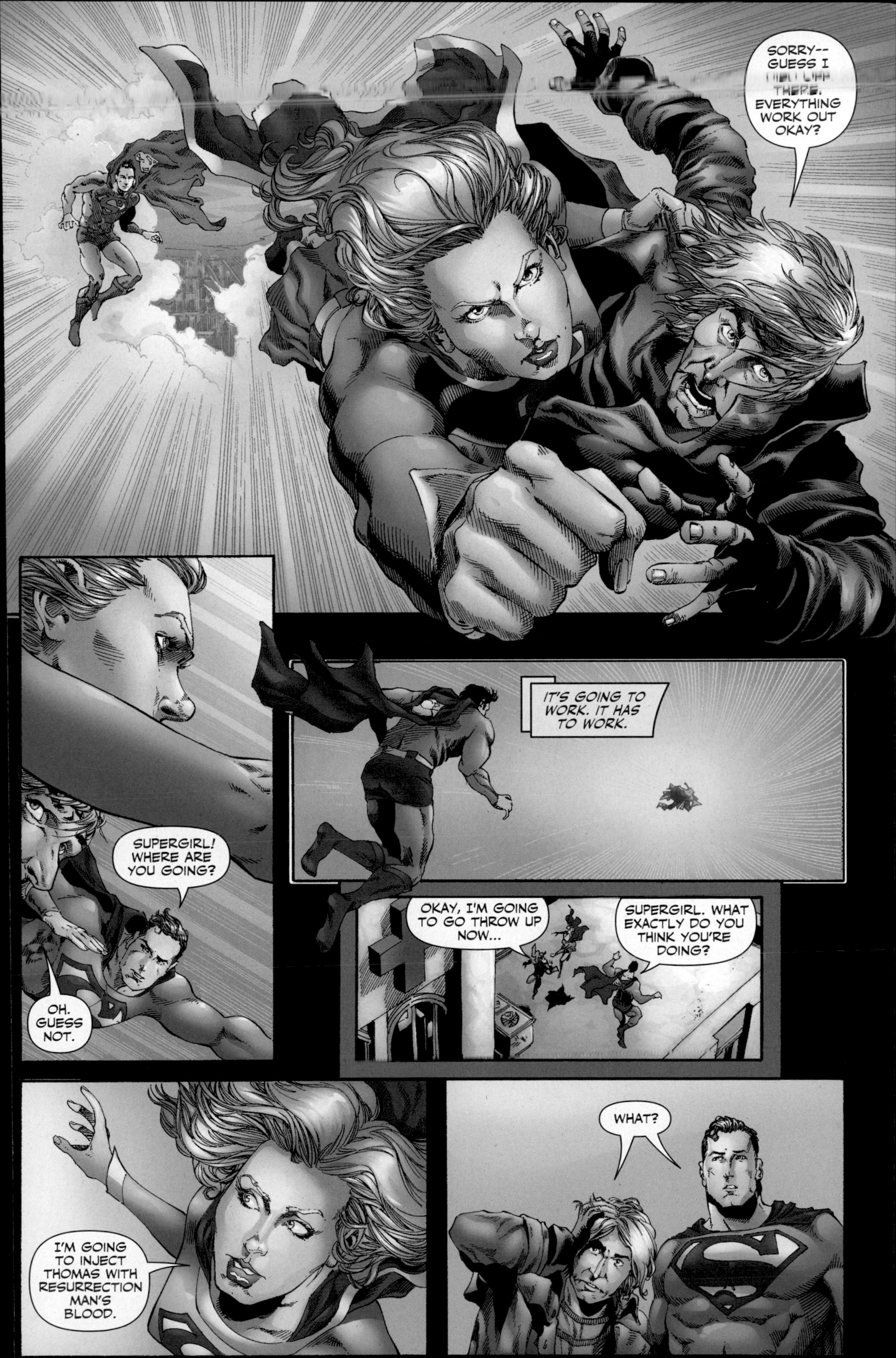
SORRY--
GUESS I
EVERYTHING
WORK OUT
OKAY?
IT'S GOING TO WORK. IT HAS TO WORK.
SUPERGIRL! WHERE ARE YOU GOING?
OH. GUESS NOT.
OKAY, I'M GOING TO GO THROW UP NOW...
SUPERGIRL. WHAT EXACTLY DO YOU THINK YOU'RE DOING?
I'M GOING TO INJECT THOMAS WITH RESURRECTION MAN'S BLOOD.
WHAT?

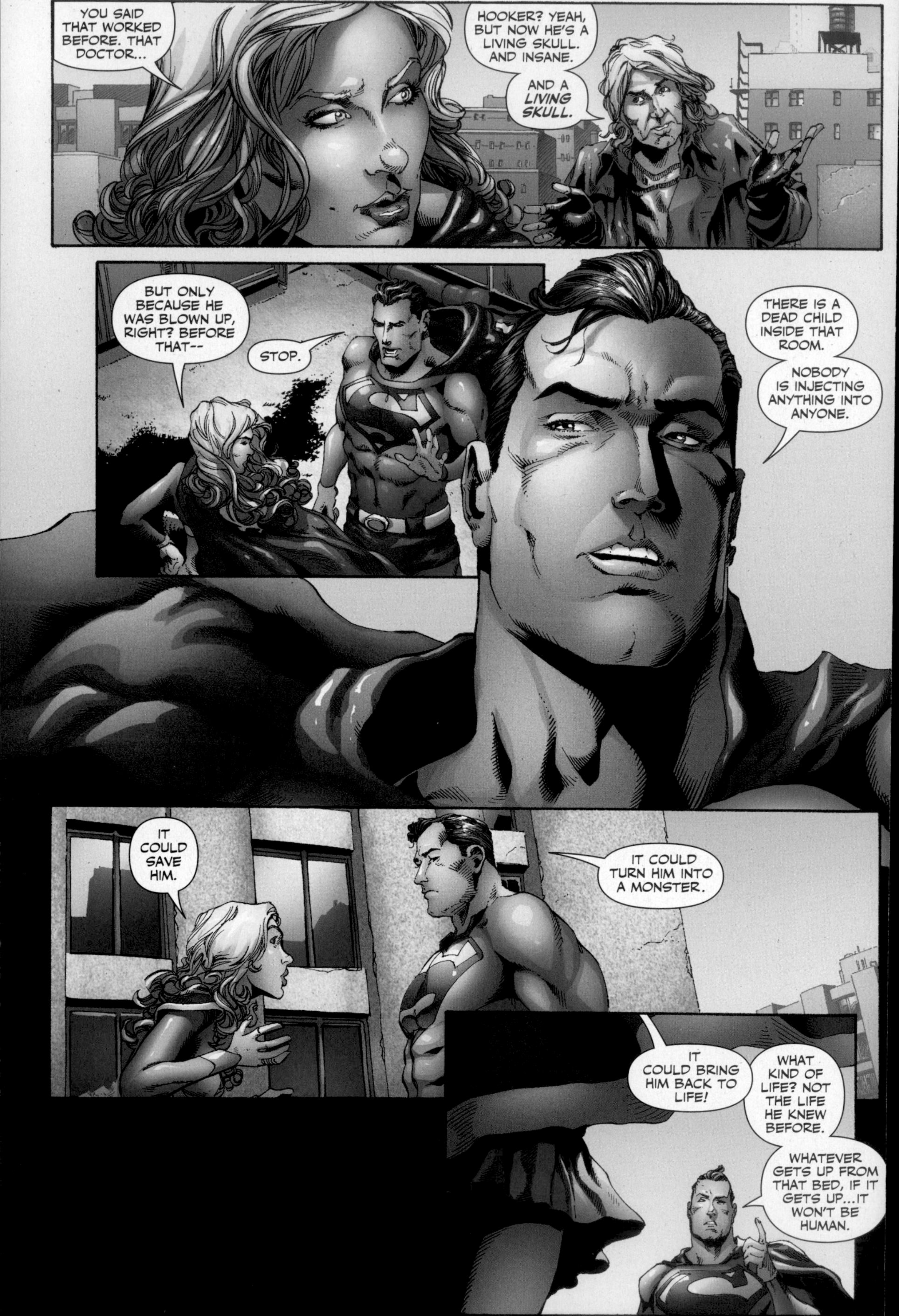
YOU SAID THAT WORKED BEFORE. THAT DOCTOR...
HOOKER? YEAH, BUT NOW HE'S A LIVING SKULL. AND INSANE.
AND A *LIVING SKULL*.
BUT ONLY BECAUSE HE WAS BLOWN UP, RIGHT? BEFORE THAT--
STOP.
THERE IS A DEAD CHILD INSIDE THAT ROOM.
NOBODY IS INJECTING ANYTHING INTO ANYONE.
IT COULD SAVE HIM.
IT COULD TURN HIM INTO A MONSTER.
IT COULD BRING HIM BACK TO LIFE!
WHAT KIND OF LIFE? NOT THE LIFE HE KNEW BEFORE.
WHATEVER GETS UP FROM THAT BED, IF IT GETS UP...IT WON'T BE HUMAN.

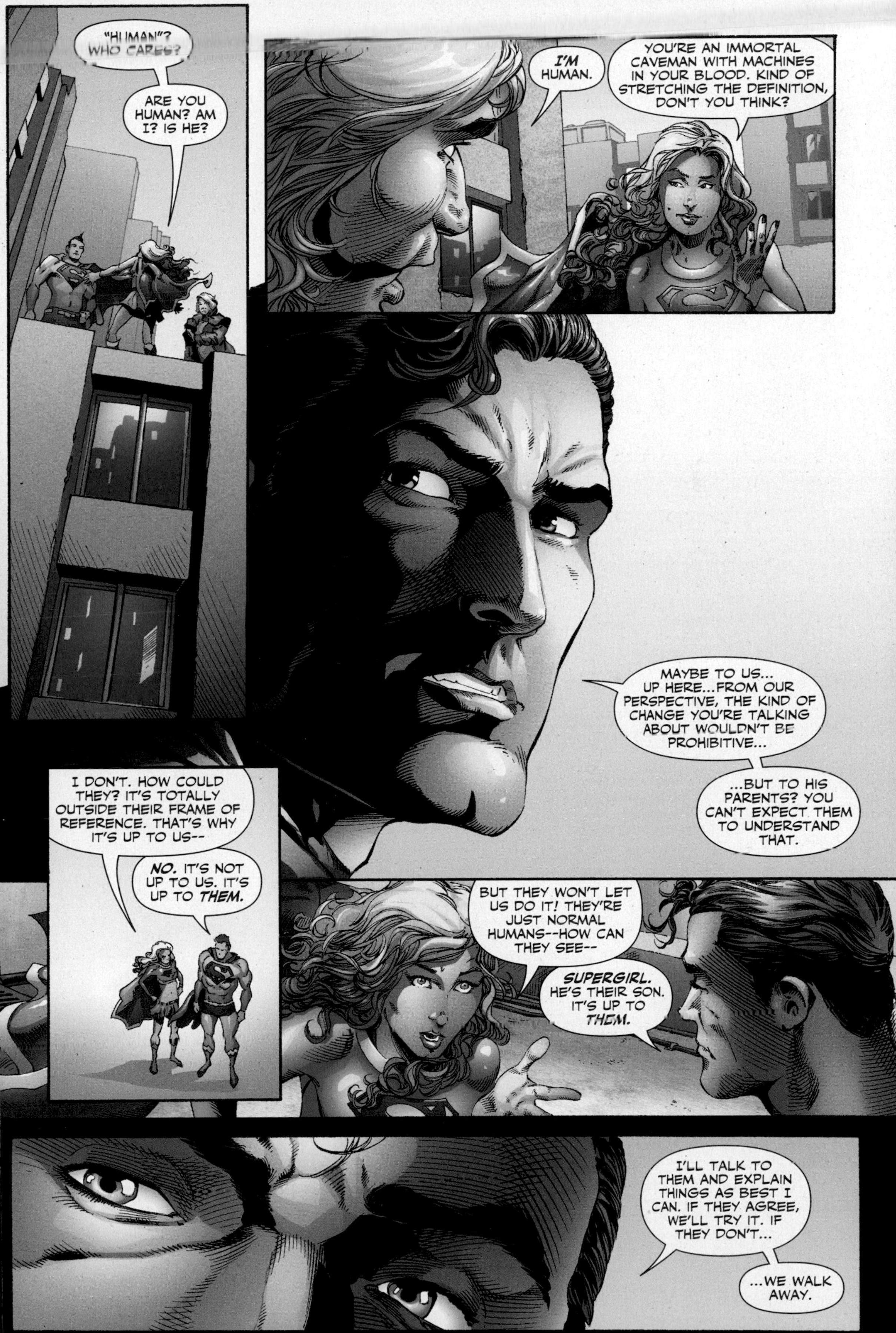
"HUMAN"? WHO CARES?
ARE YOU HUMAN? AM I? IS HE?
I'M HUMAN.
YOU'RE AN IMMORTAL CAVEMAN WITH MACHINES IN YOUR BLOOD. KIND OF STRETCHING THE DEFINITION, DON'T YOU THINK?
MAYBE TO US... UP HERE...FROM OUR PERSPECTIVE, THE KIND OF CHANGE YOU'RE TALKING ABOUT WOULDN'T BE PROHIBITIVE...
...BUT TO HIS PARENTS? YOU CAN'T EXPECT THEM TO UNDERSTAND THAT.
I DON'T. HOW COULD THEY? IT'S TOTALLY OUTSIDE THEIR FRAME OF REFERENCE. THAT'S WHY IT'S UP TO US--
NO. IT'S NOT UP TO US. IT'S UP TO THEM.
BUT THEY WON'T LET US DO IT! THEY'RE JUST NORMAL HUMANS--HOW CAN THEY SEE--
SUPERGIRL. HE'S THEIR SON. IT'S UP TO THEM.
I'LL TALK TO THEM AND EXPLAIN THINGS AS BEST I CAN. IF THEY AGREE, WE'LL TRY IT. IF THEY DON'T...
...WE WALK AWAY.

WHAT?

I KNOW, IT SOUNDS STRANGE...IT IS STRANGE...BUT WE HAVE REASON TO BELIEVE THAT WE MIGHT BE ABLE TO REVIVE YOUR SON.

PERHAPS.

BUT...BUT HE'S...ISN'T HE...?

IS THIS SOME KIND OF JOKE?

NO, NO, PLEASE... LET ME EXPLAIN...

THAT MAN OVER THERE-- INSIDE HIS BLOOD THERE ARE MICROSCOPIC MACHINES. THESE MACHINES

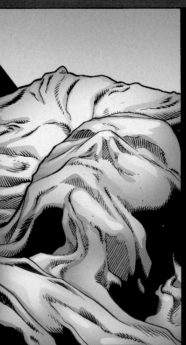

THEY WON'T LISTEN TO HIM. IT'S UP TO ME.

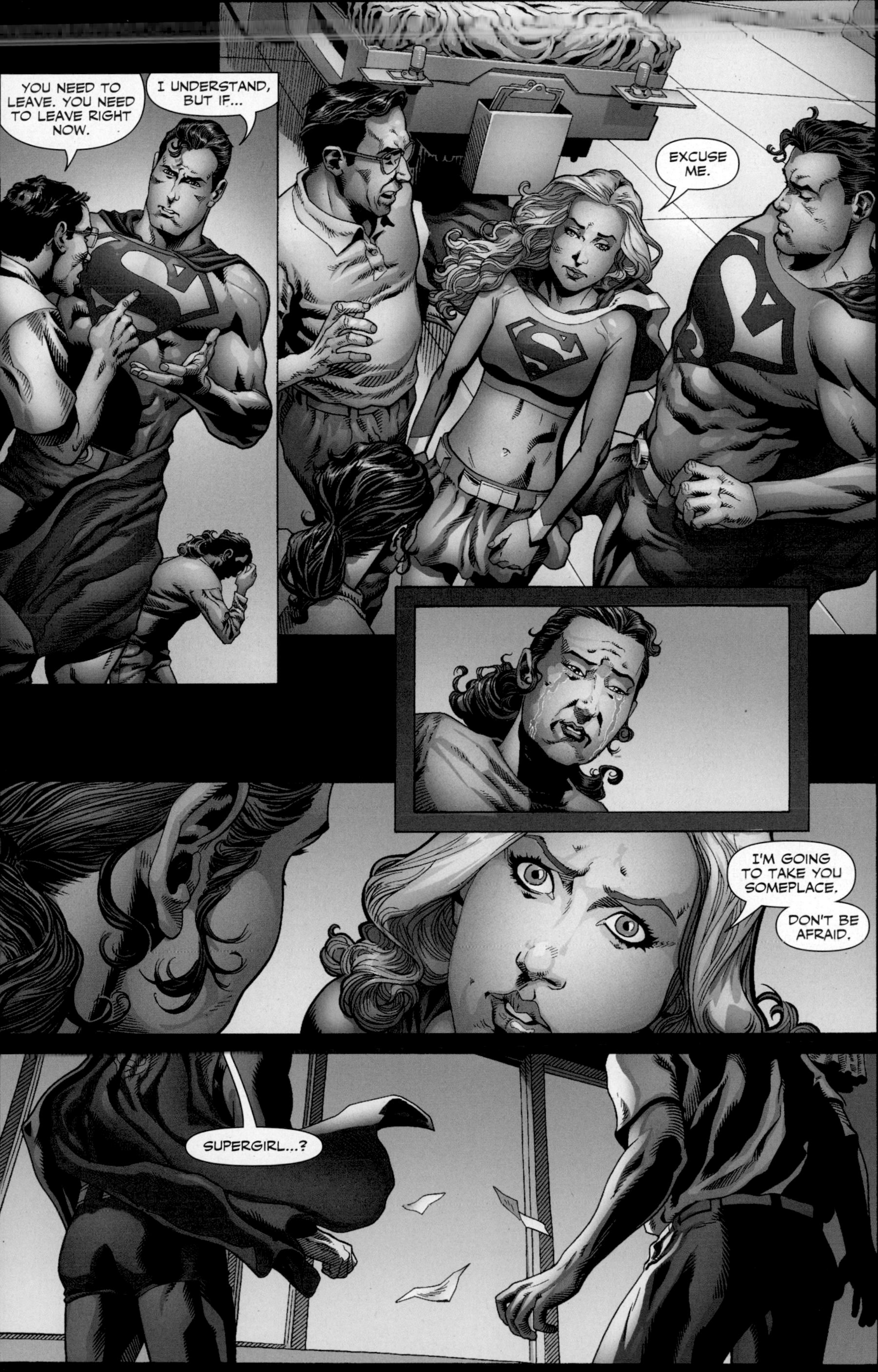
YOU NEED TO LEAVE. YOU NEED TO LEAVE RIGHT NOW.
I UNDERSTAND, BUT IF...
EXCUSE ME.
I'M GOING TO TAKE YOU SOMEPLACE.
DON'T BE AFRAID.
SUPERGIRL...?

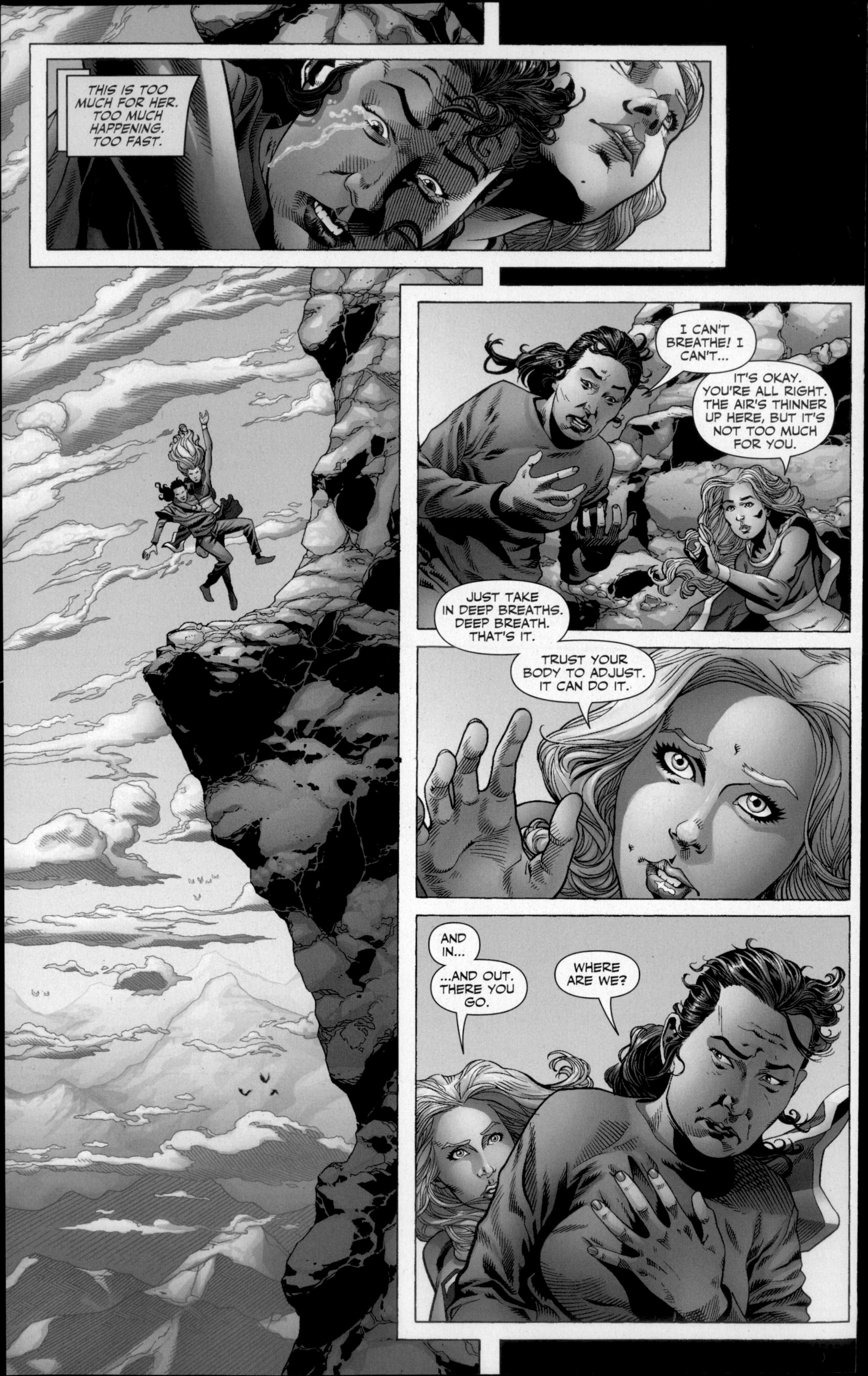
THIS IS TOO MUCH FOR HER. TOO MUCH HAPPENING. TOO FAST.
I CAN'T BREATHE! I CAN'T...
IT'S OKAY. YOU'RE ALL RIGHT. THE AIR'S THINNER UP HERE, BUT IT'S NOT TOO MUCH FOR YOU.
JUST TAKE IN DEEP BREATHS. DEEP BREATH. THAT'S IT.
TRUST YOUR BODY TO ADJUST. IT CAN DO IT.
AND IN...
...AND OUT. THERE YOU GO.
WHERE ARE WE?

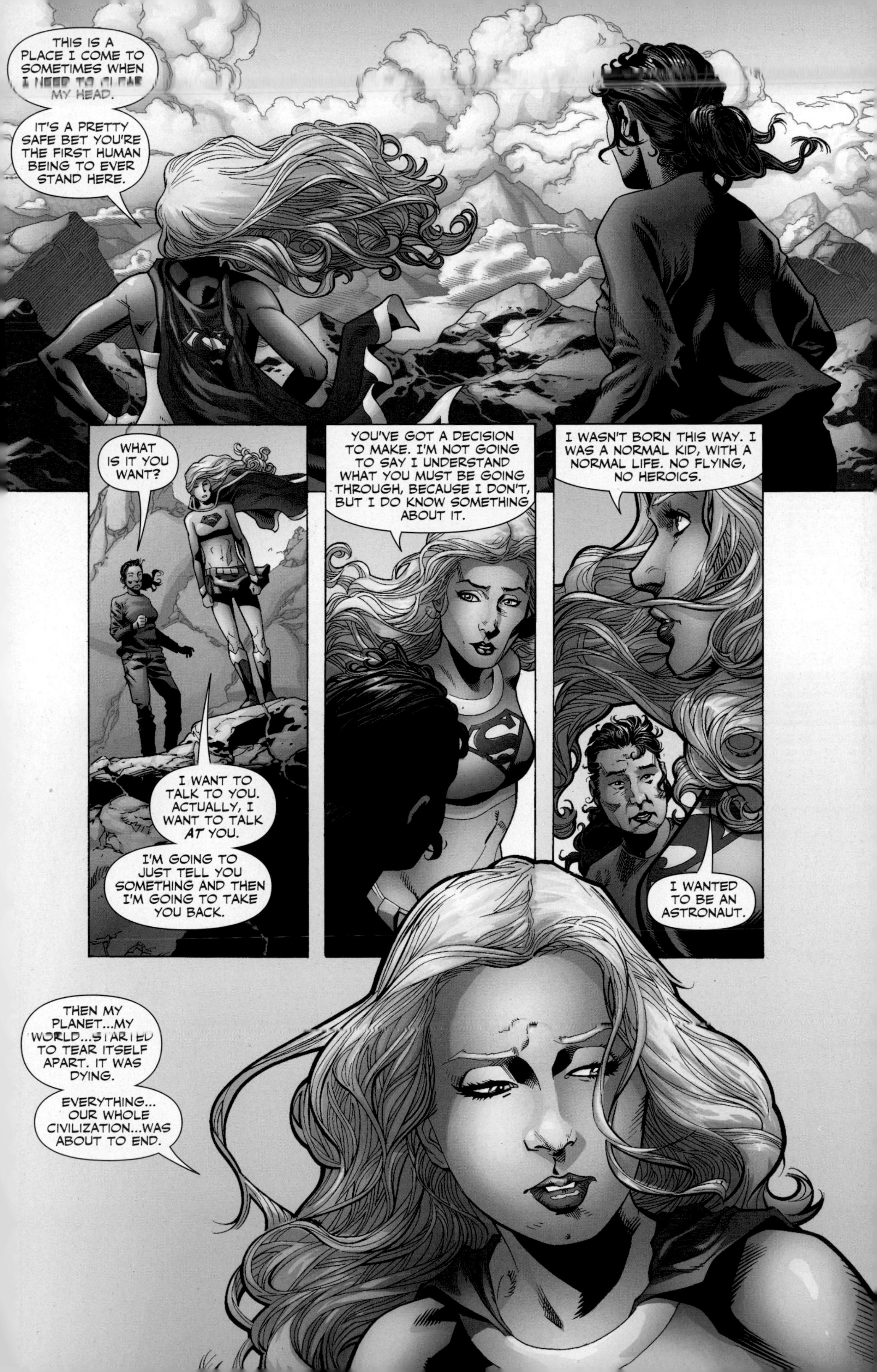

THIS IS A PLACE I COME TO SOMETIMES WHEN I NEED TO CLEAR MY HEAD.
IT'S A PRETTY SAFE BET YOU'RE THE FIRST HUMAN BEING TO EVER STAND HERE.
WHAT IS IT YOU WANT?
I WANT TO TALK TO YOU. ACTUALLY, I WANT TO TALK *AT* YOU.
I'M GOING TO JUST TELL YOU SOMETHING AND THEN I'M GOING TO TAKE YOU BACK.
YOU'VE GOT A DECISION TO MAKE. I'M NOT GOING TO SAY I UNDERSTAND WHAT YOU MUST BE GOING THROUGH, BECAUSE I DON'T, BUT I DO KNOW SOMETHING ABOUT IT.
I WASN'T BORN THIS WAY. I WAS A NORMAL KID, WITH A NORMAL LIFE. NO FLYING, NO HEROICS.
I WANTED TO BE AN ASTRONAUT.
THEN MY PLANET...MY WORLD...STARTED TO TEAR ITSELF APART. IT WAS DYING.
EVERYTHING... OUR WHOLE CIVILIZATION...WAS ABOUT TO END.

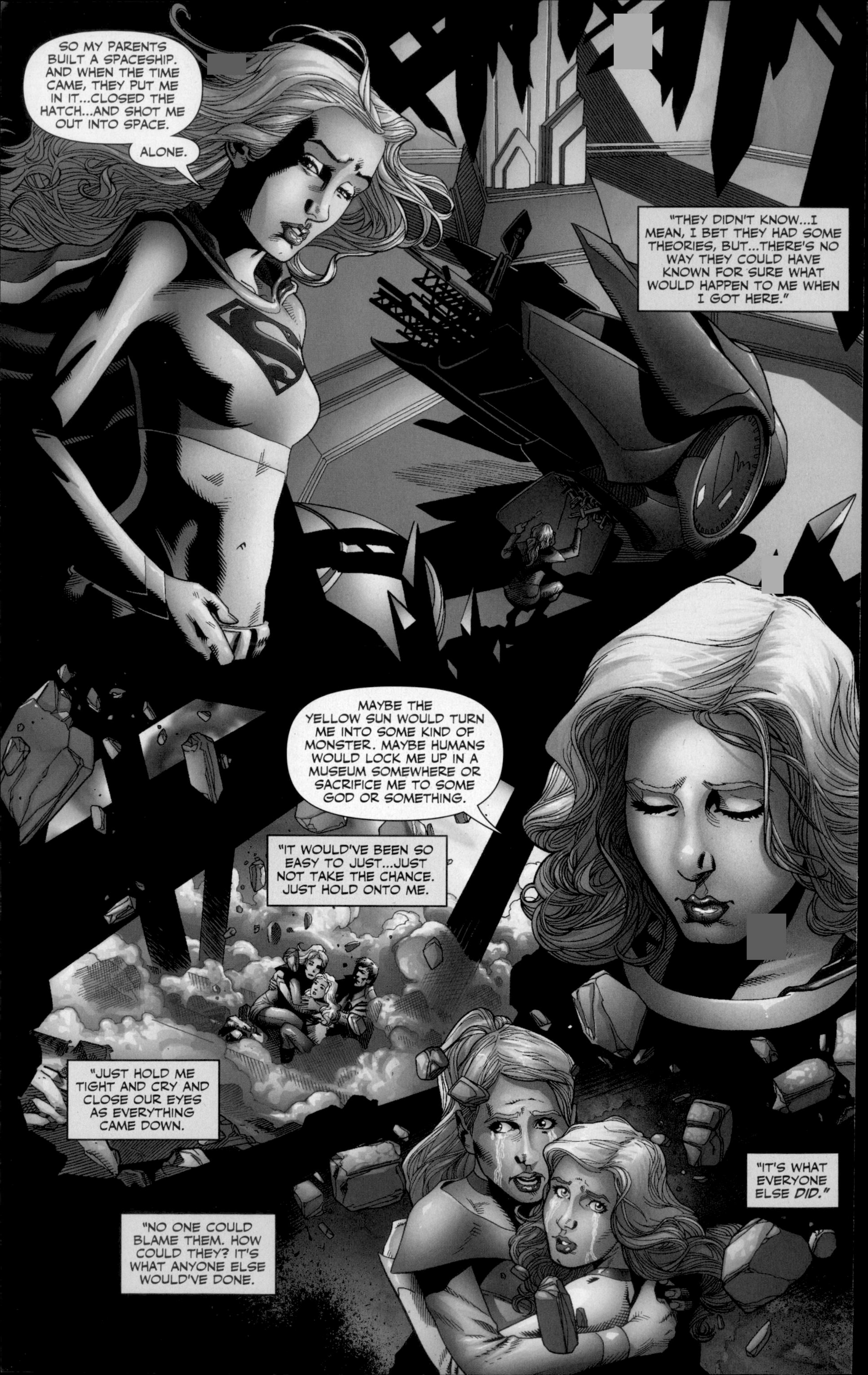
SO MY PARENTS BUILT A SPACESHIP. AND WHEN THE TIME CAME, THEY PUT ME IN IT...CLOSED THE HATCH...AND SHOT ME OUT INTO SPACE.
ALONE.
"THEY DIDN'T KNOW...I MEAN, I BET THEY HAD SOME THEORIES, BUT...THERE'S NO WAY THEY COULD HAVE KNOWN FOR SURE WHAT WOULD HAPPEN TO ME WHEN I GOT HERE."
MAYBE THE YELLOW SUN WOULD TURN ME INTO SOME KIND OF MONSTER. MAYBE HUMANS WOULD LOCK ME UP IN A MUSEUM SOMEWHERE OR SACRIFICE ME TO SOME GOD OR SOMETHING.
"IT WOULD'VE BEEN SO EASY TO JUST...JUST NOT TAKE THE CHANCE. JUST HOLD ONTO ME.
"JUST HOLD ME TIGHT AND CRY AND CLOSE OUR EYES AS EVERYTHING CAME DOWN.
"NO ONE COULD BLAME THEM. HOW COULD THEY? IT'S WHAT ANYONE ELSE WOULD'VE DONE.
"IT'S WHAT EVERYONE ELSE *DID*."

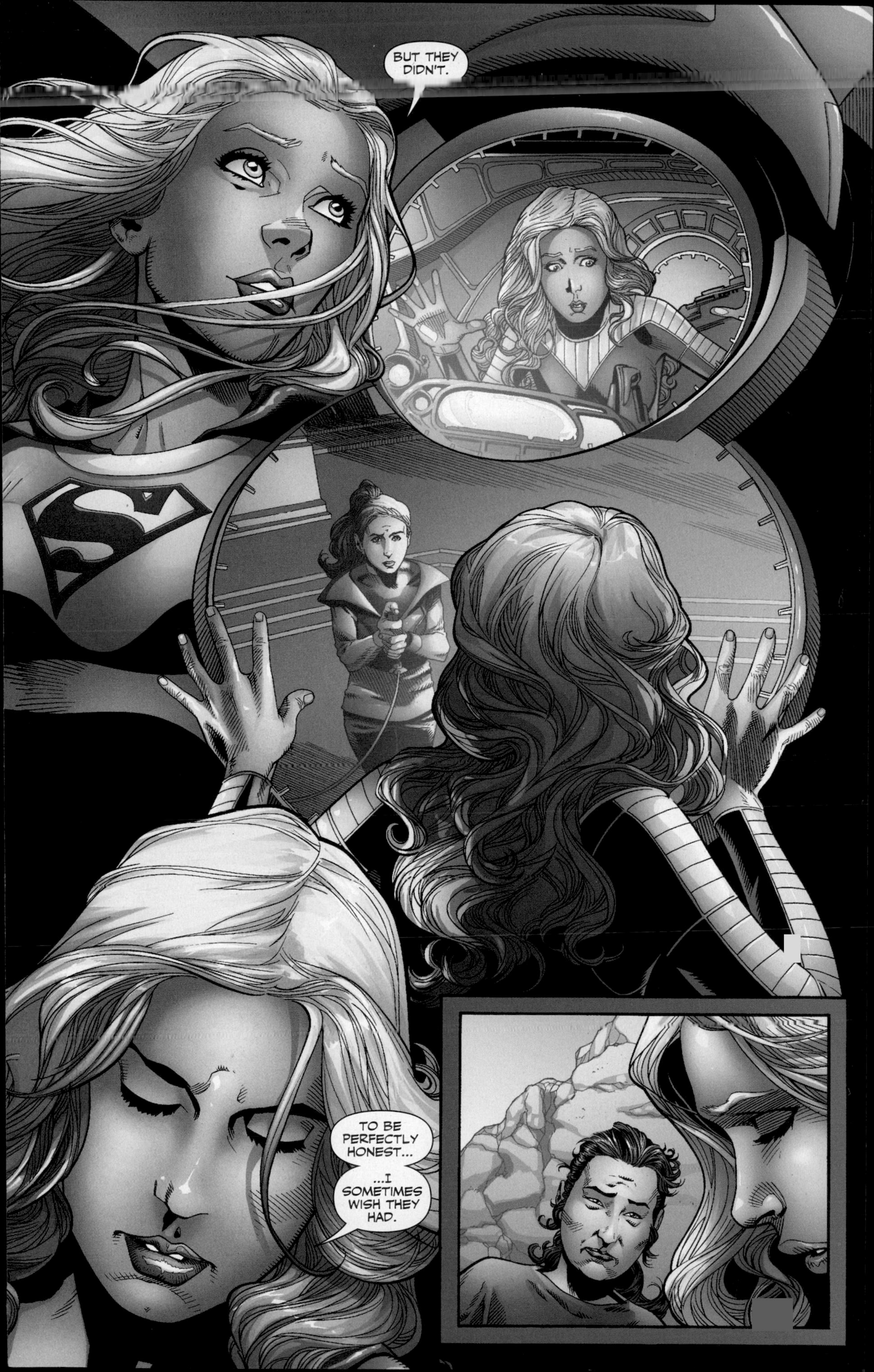
BUT THEY DIDN'T.
TO BE PERFECTLY HONEST...
...I SOMETIMES WISH THEY HAD.

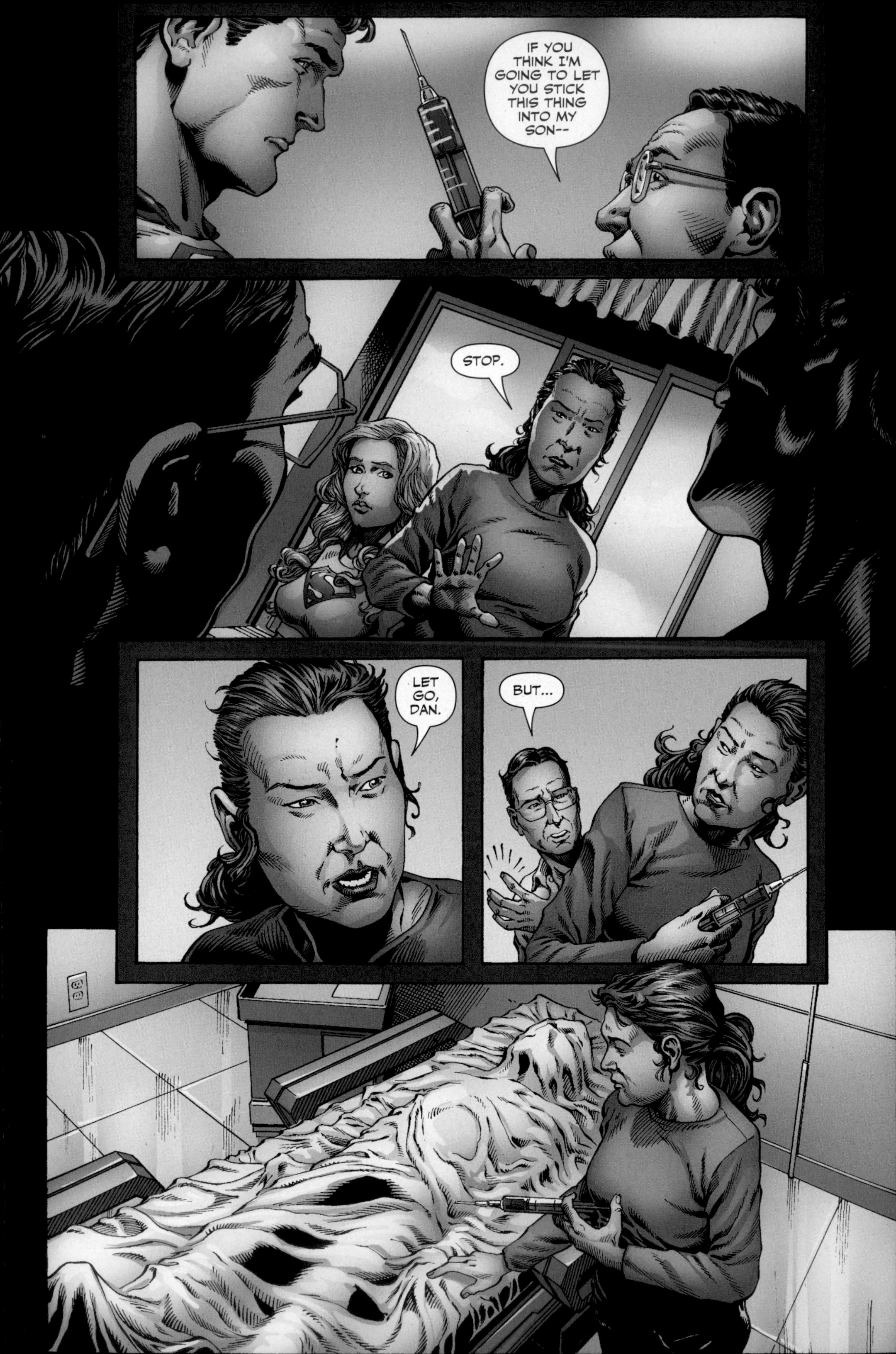
IF YOU THINK I'M GOING TO LET YOU STICK THIS THING INTO MY SON--
STOP.
LET GO, DAN.
BUT...

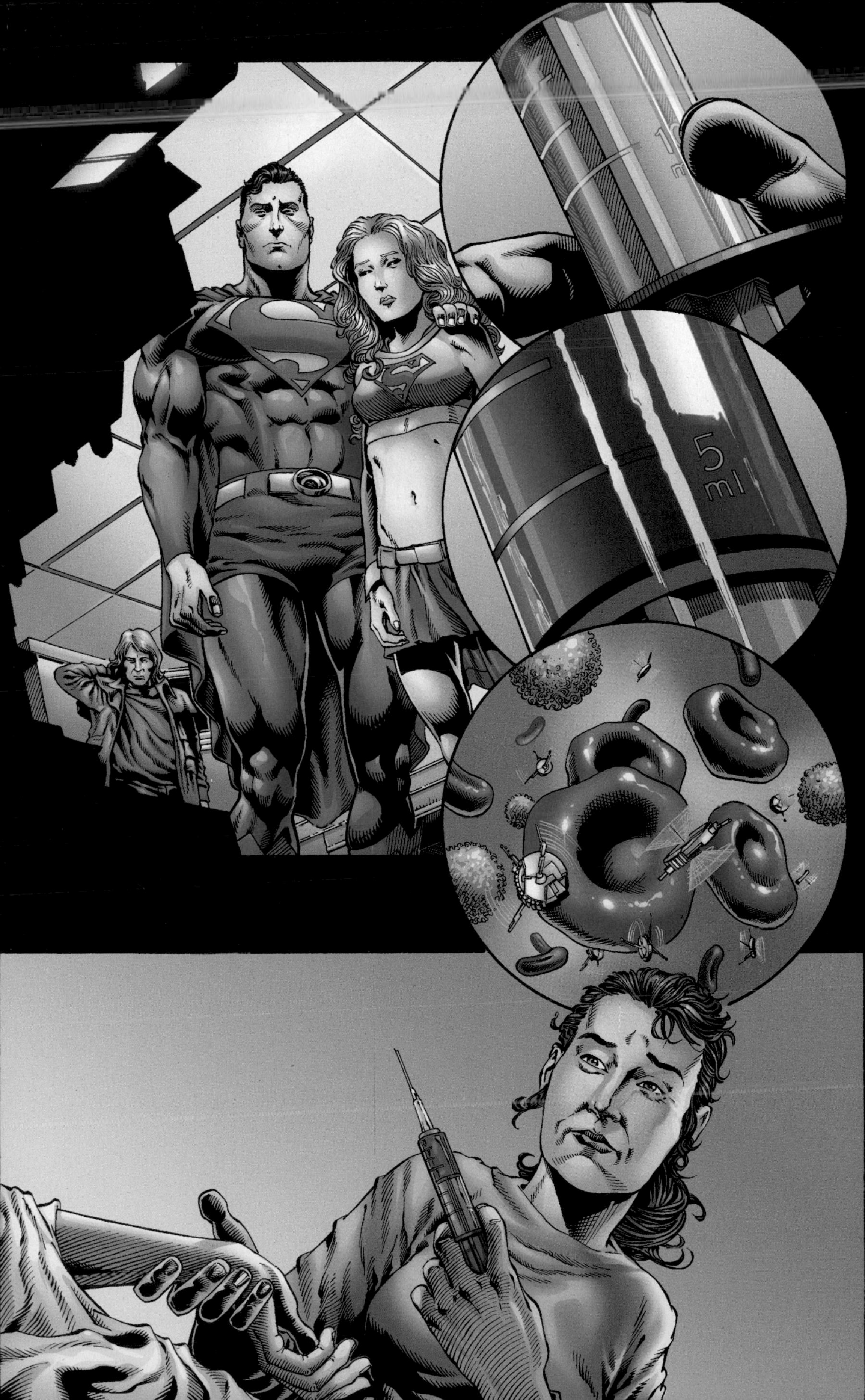
5 ml

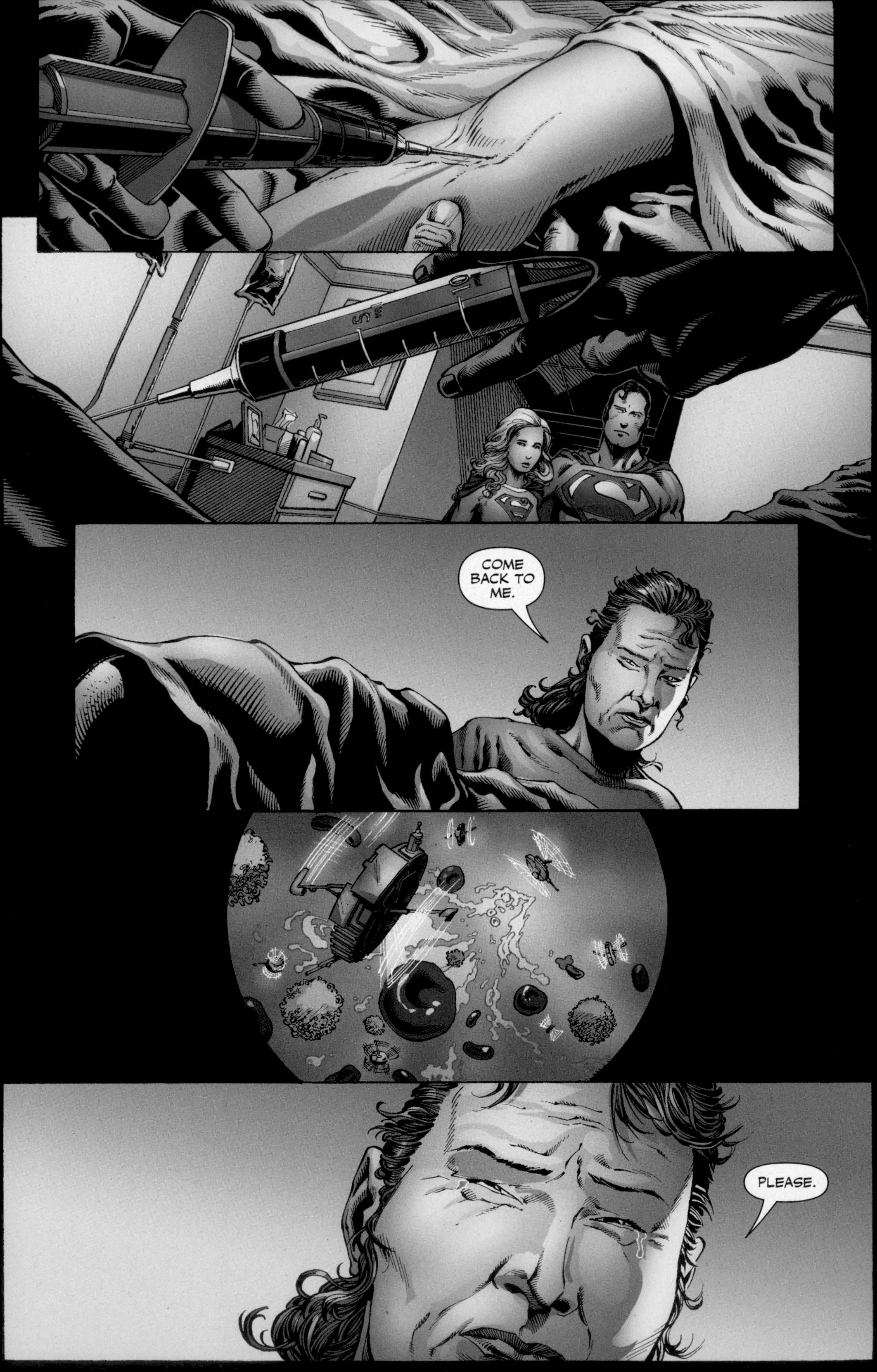
COME BACK TO ME.
PLEASE.

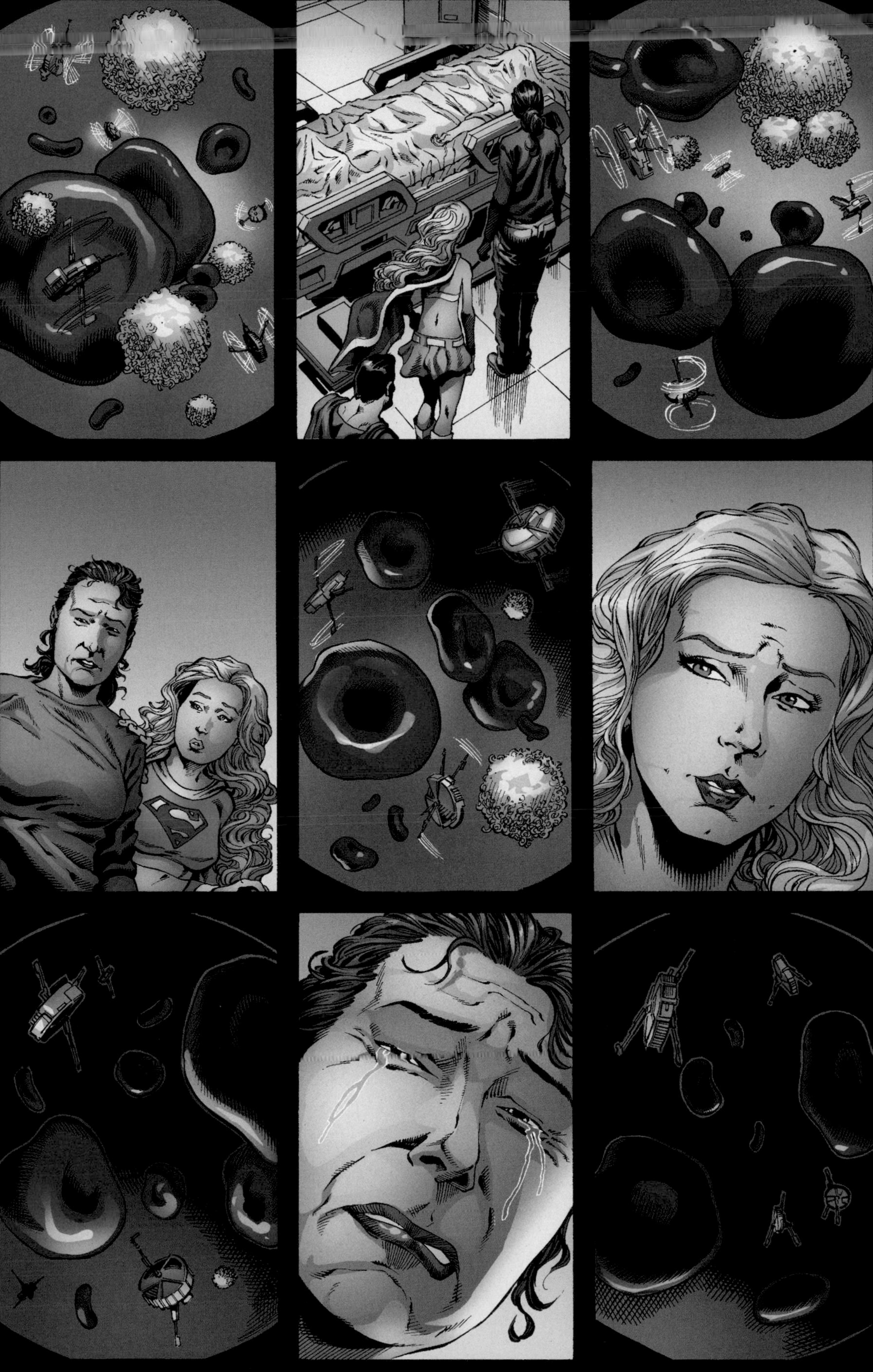

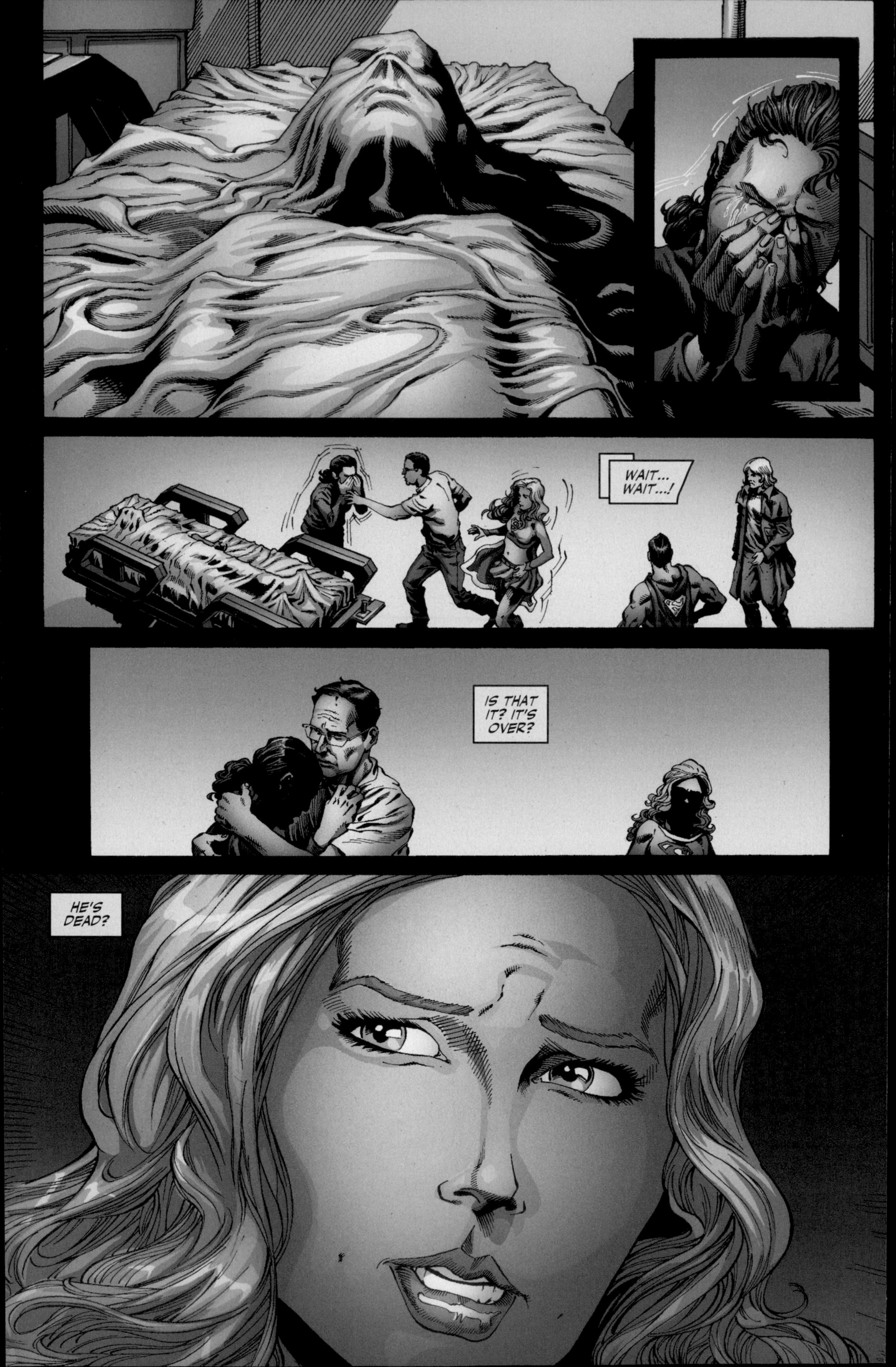
WAIT... WAIT...!
IS THAT IT? IT'S OVER?
HE'S DEAD?

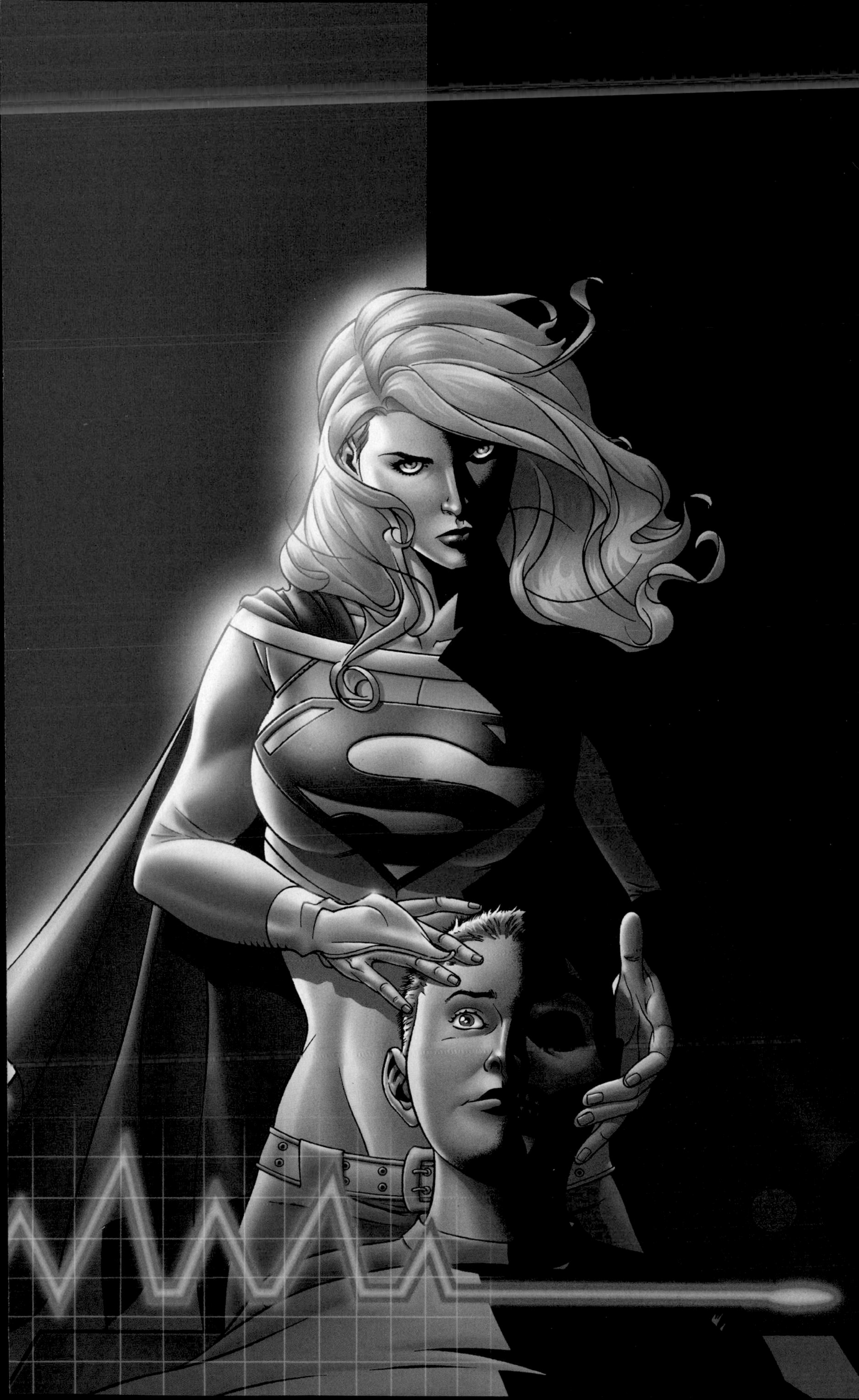

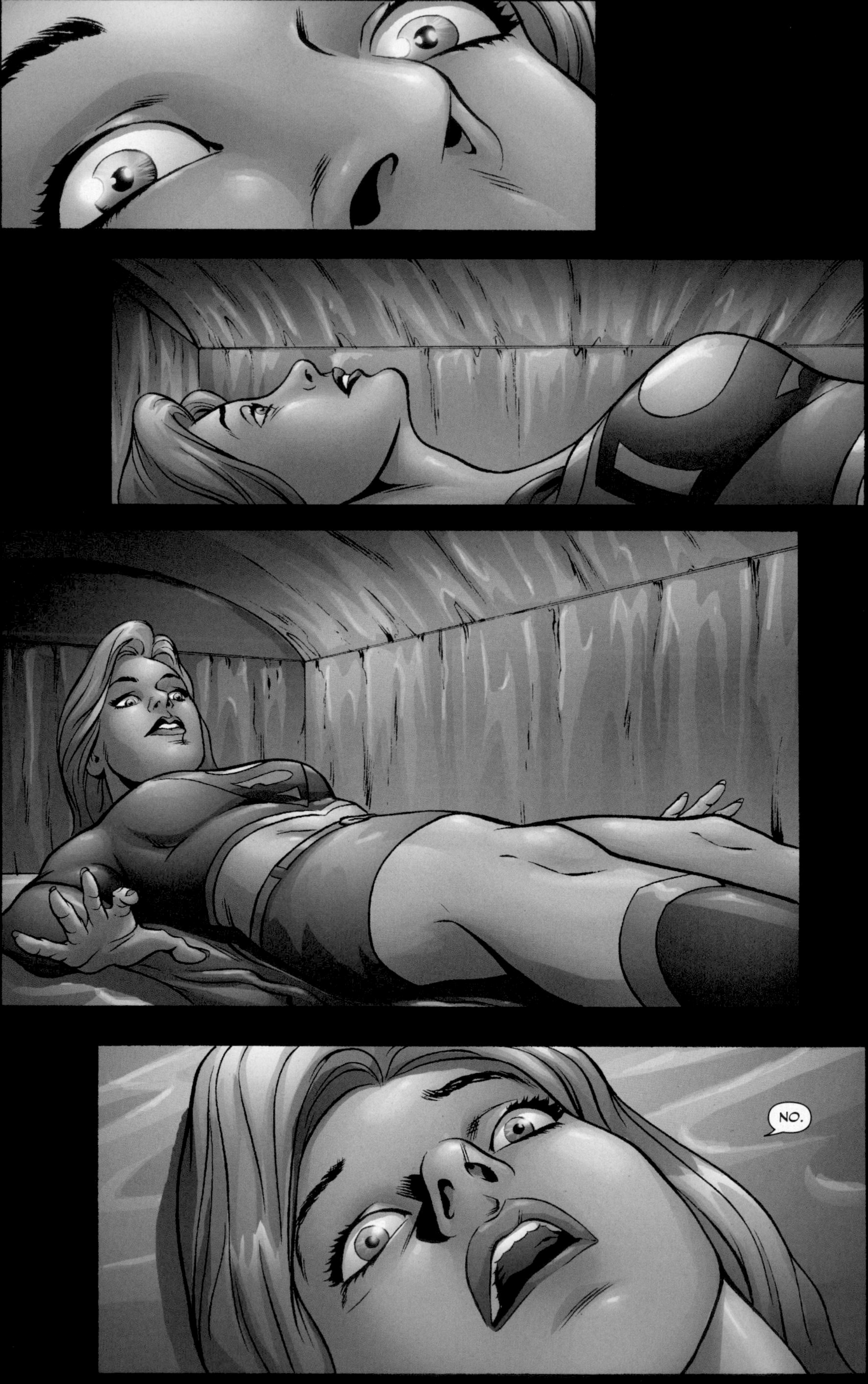
NO.

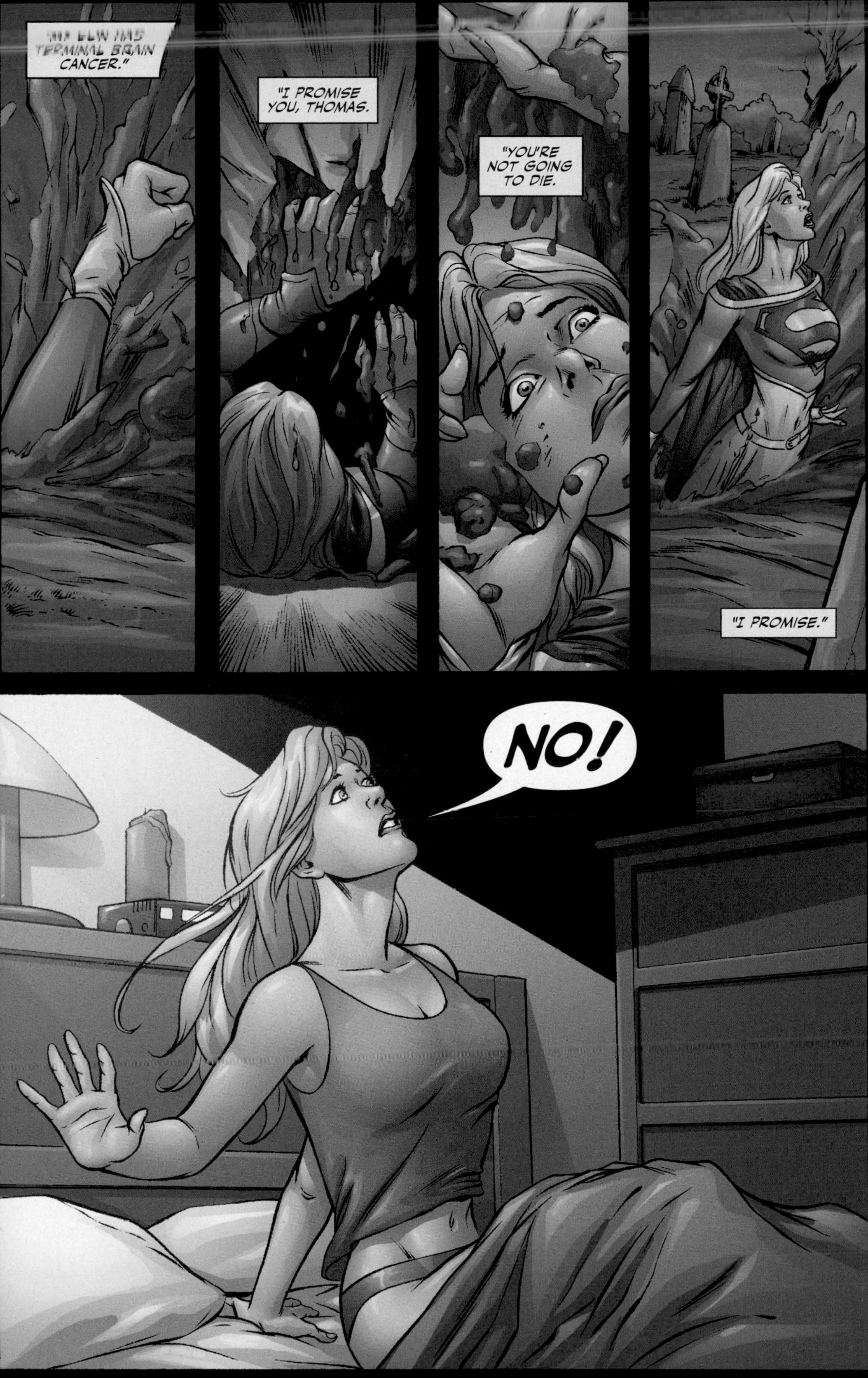
TERMINAL BRAIN CANCER."
"I PROMISE YOU, THOMAS.
"YOU'RE NOT GOING TO DIE.
"I PROMISE."
NO!

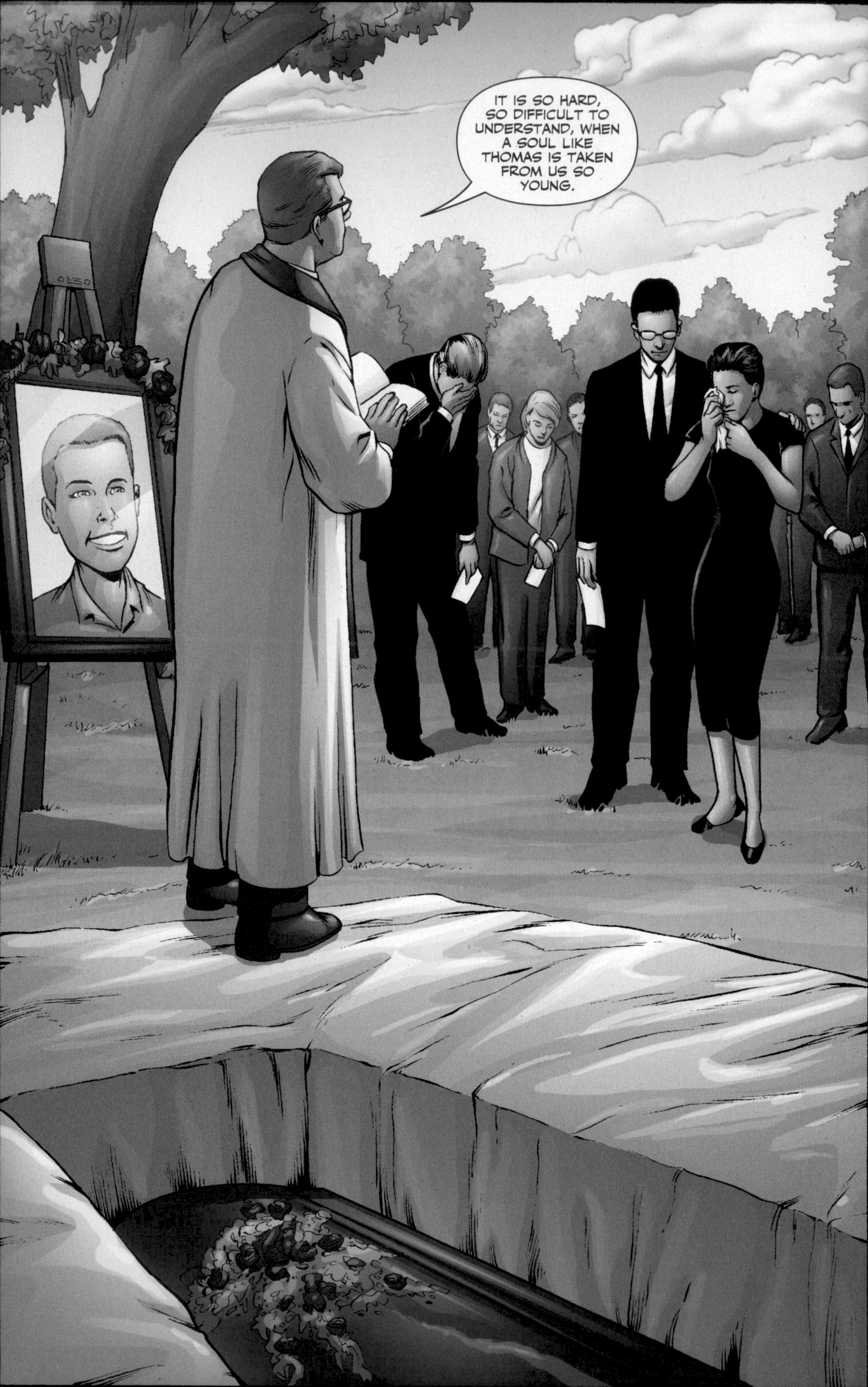
IT IS SO HARD, SO DIFFICULT TO UNDERSTAND, WHEN A SOUL LIKE THOMAS IS TAKEN FROM US SO YOUNG.

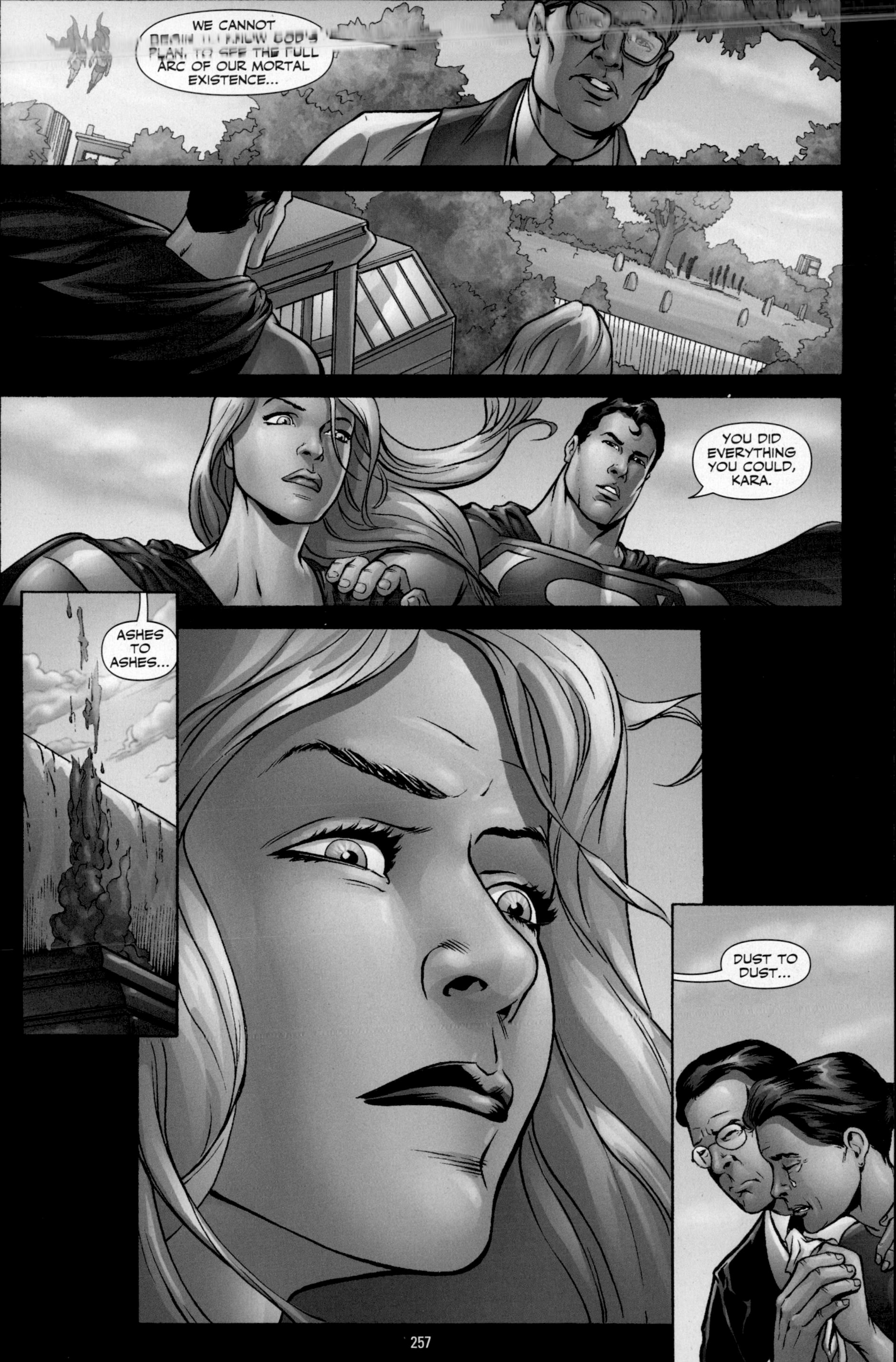
WE CANNOT BEGIN TO KNOW GOD'S PLAN, TO SEE THE FULL ARC OF OUR MORTAL EXISTENCE...
YOU DID EVERYTHING YOU COULD, KARA.
ASHES TO ASHES...
DUST TO DUST...

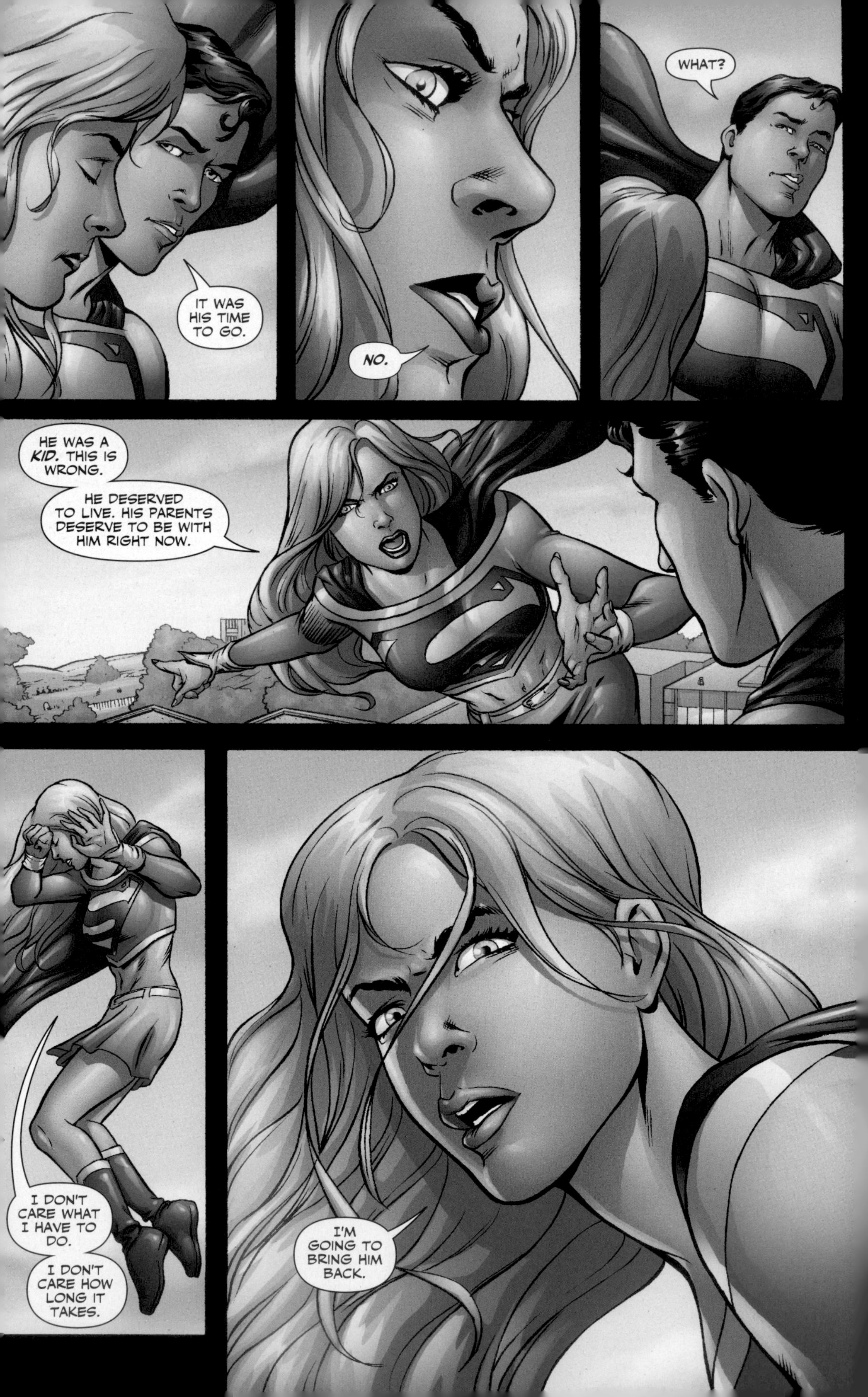
IT WAS HIS TIME TO GO.
NO.
WHAT?
HE WAS A KID. THIS IS WRONG.
HE DESERVED TO LIVE. HIS PARENTS DESERVE TO BE WITH HIM RIGHT NOW.
I DON'T CARE WHAT I HAVE TO DO.
I DON'T CARE HOW LONG IT TAKES.
I'M GOING TO BRING HIM BACK.

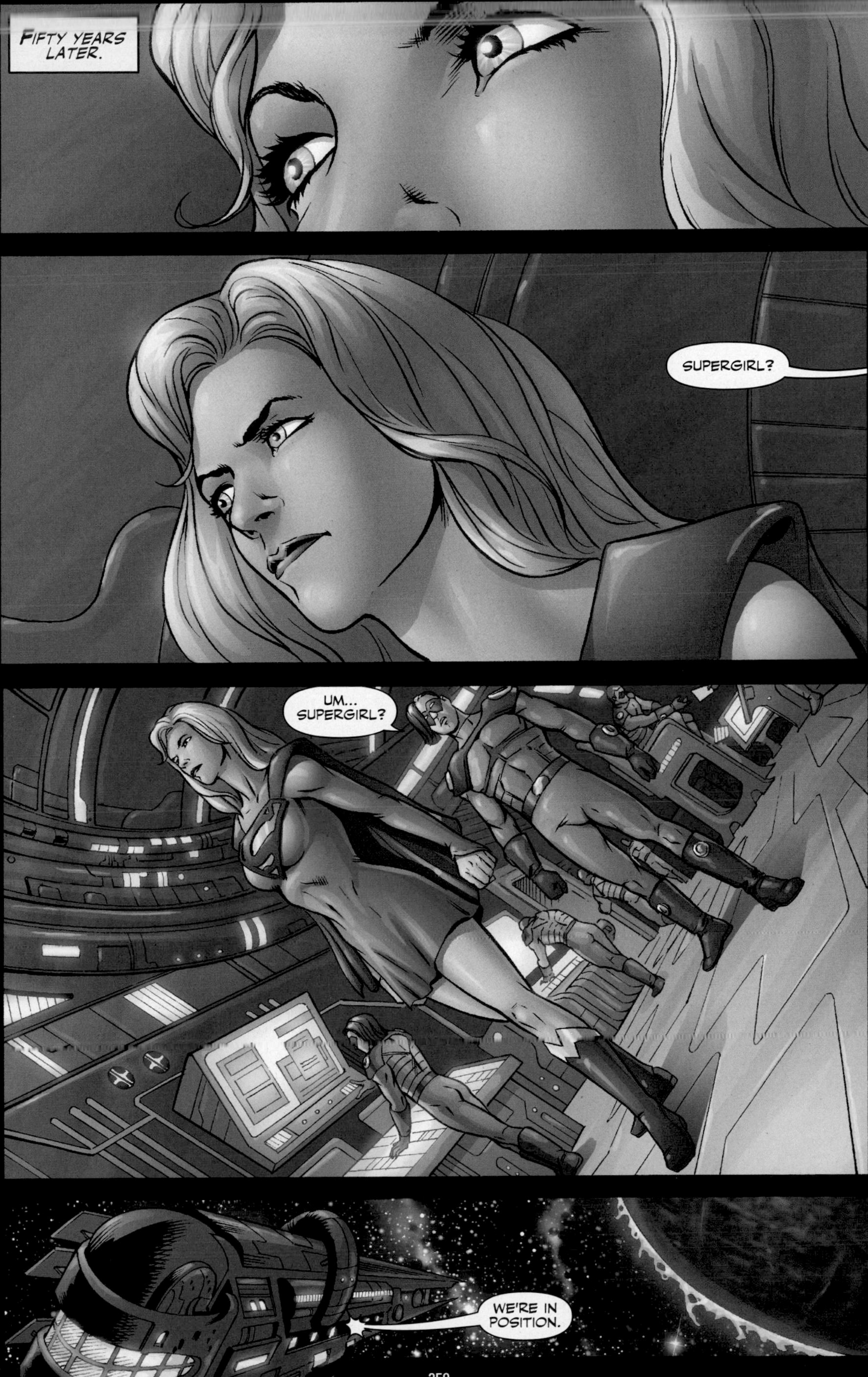
FIFTY YEARS LATER.
SUPERGIRL?
UM... SUPERGIRL?
WE'RE IN POSITION.

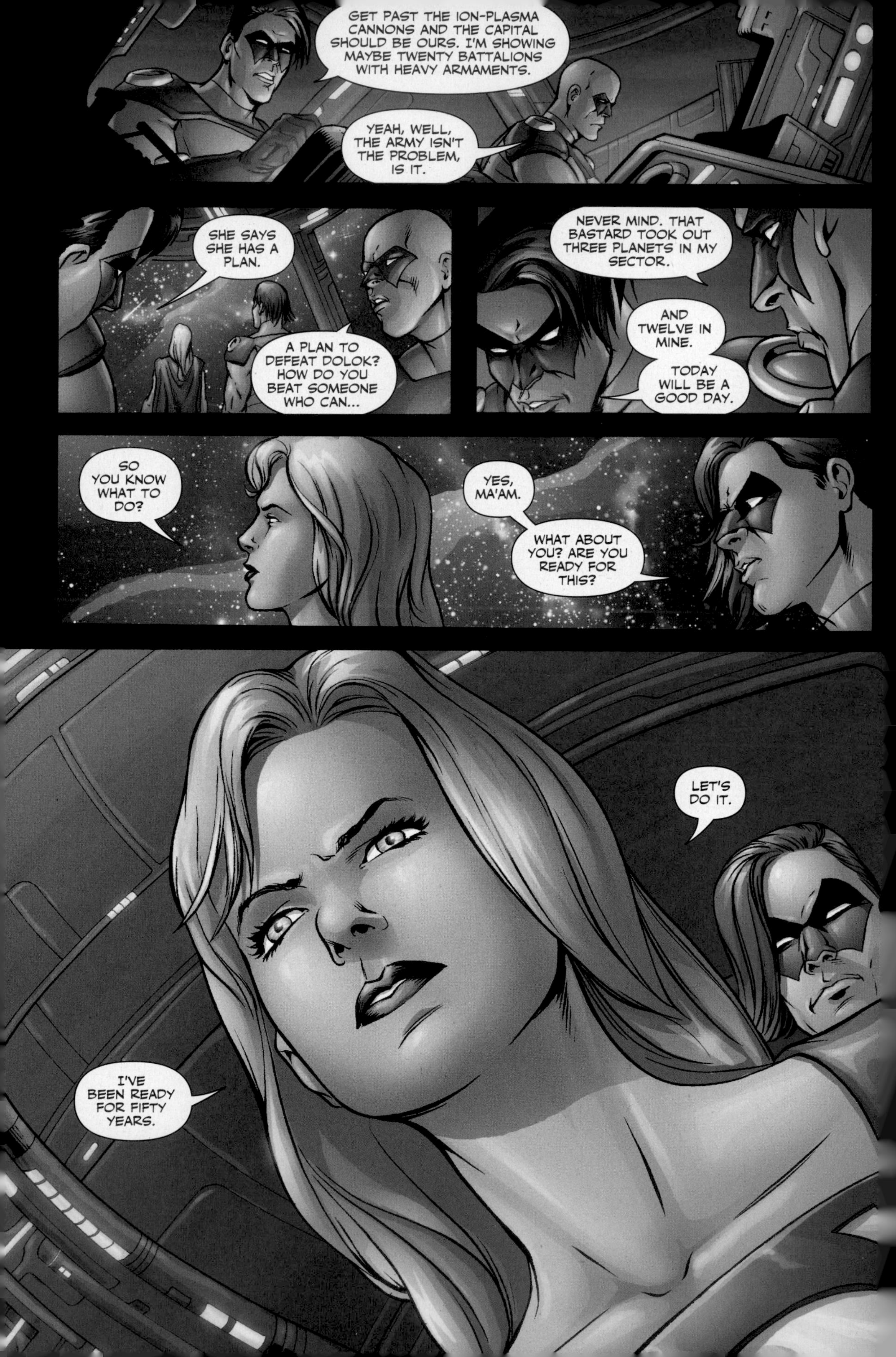
GET PAST THE ION-PLASMA CANNONS AND THE CAPITAL SHOULD BE OURS. I'M SHOWING MAYBE TWENTY BATTALIONS WITH HEAVY ARMAMENTS.
YEAH, WELL, THE ARMY ISN'T THE PROBLEM, IS IT.
SHE SAYS SHE HAS A PLAN.
A PLAN TO DEFEAT DOLOK? HOW DO YOU BEAT SOMEONE WHO CAN...
NEVER MIND. THAT BASTARD TOOK OUT THREE PLANETS IN MY SECTOR.
AND TWELVE IN MINE.
TODAY WILL BE A GOOD DAY.
SO YOU KNOW WHAT TO DO?
YES, MA'AM.
WHAT ABOUT YOU? ARE YOU READY FOR THIS?
LET'S DO IT.
I'VE BEEN READY FOR FIFTY YEARS.

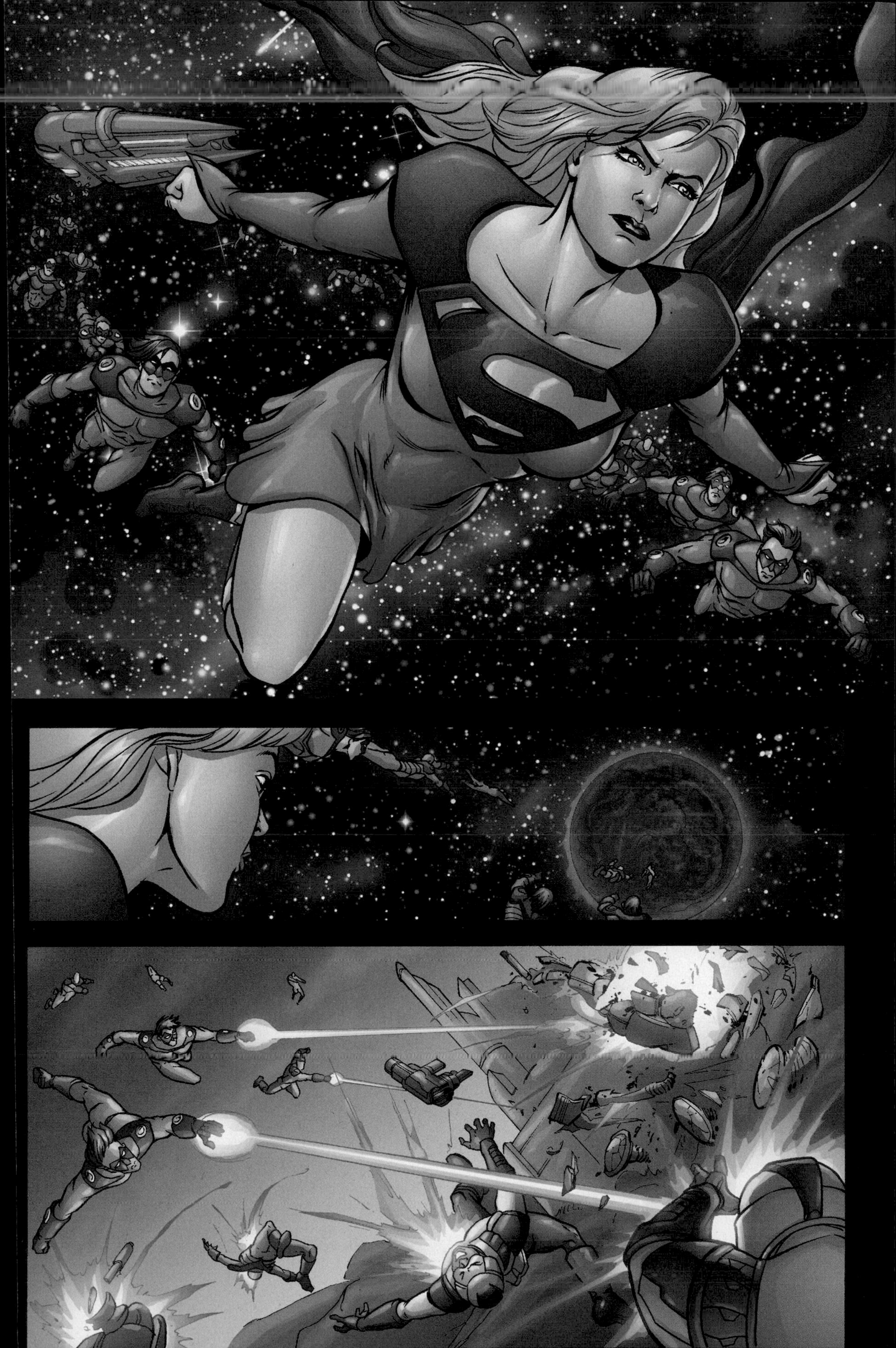

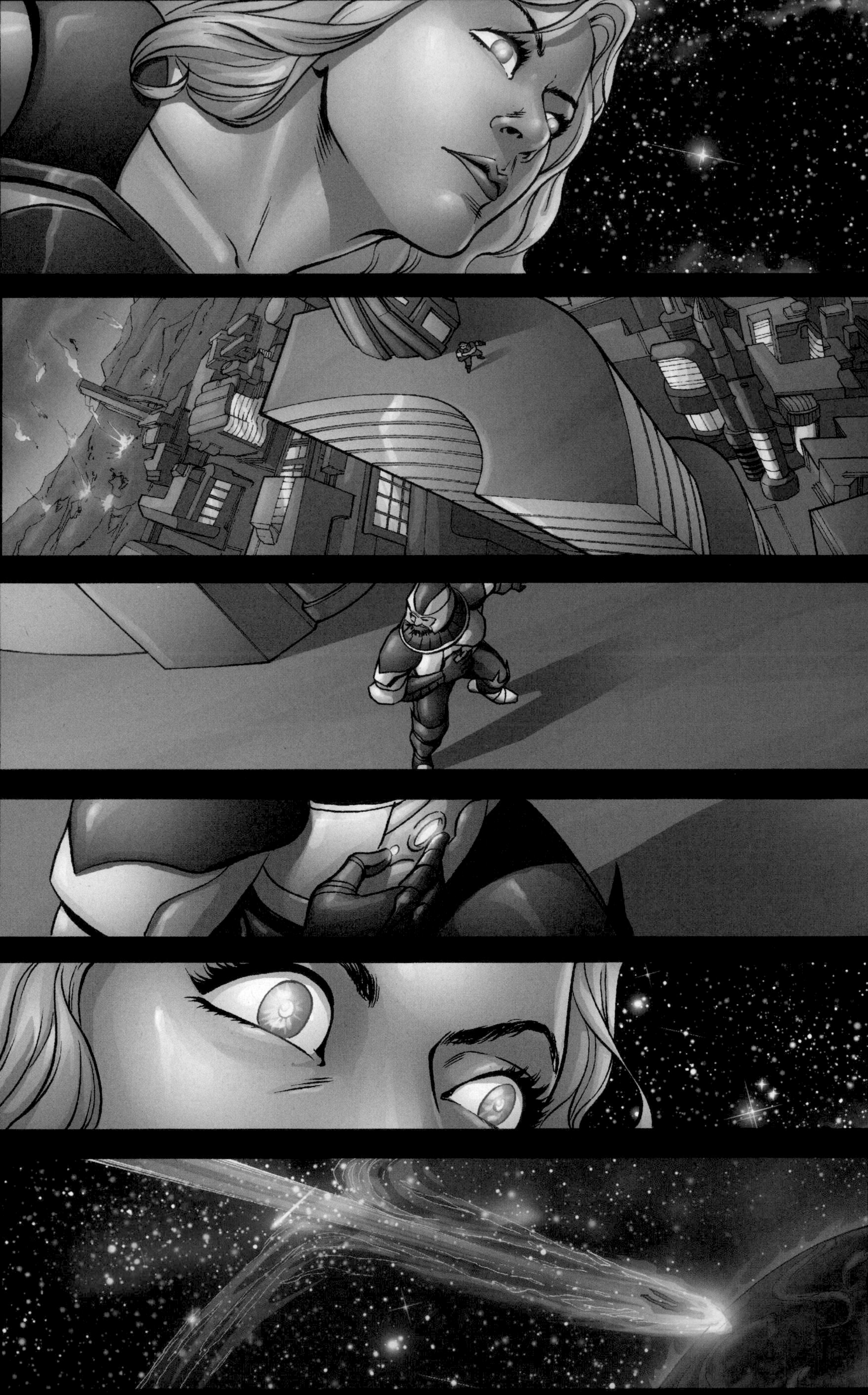

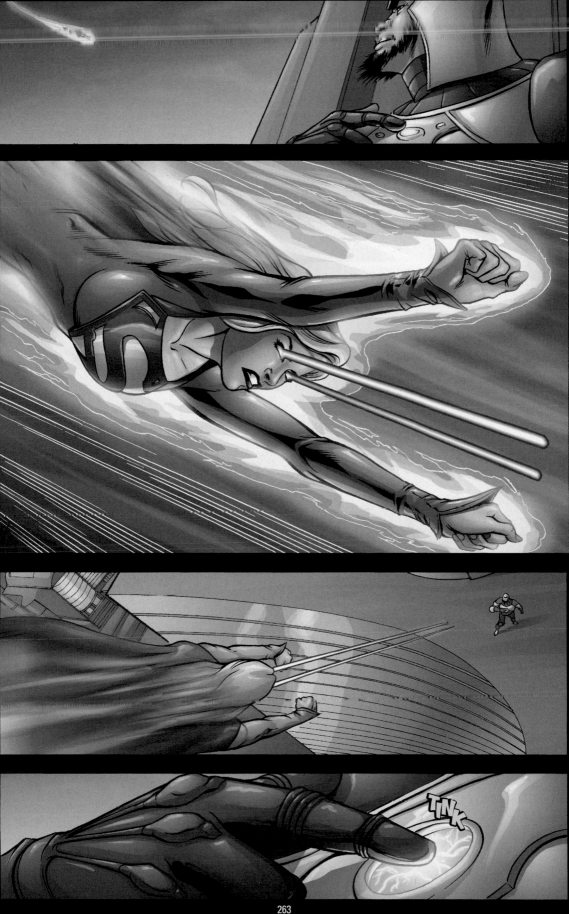

TINK

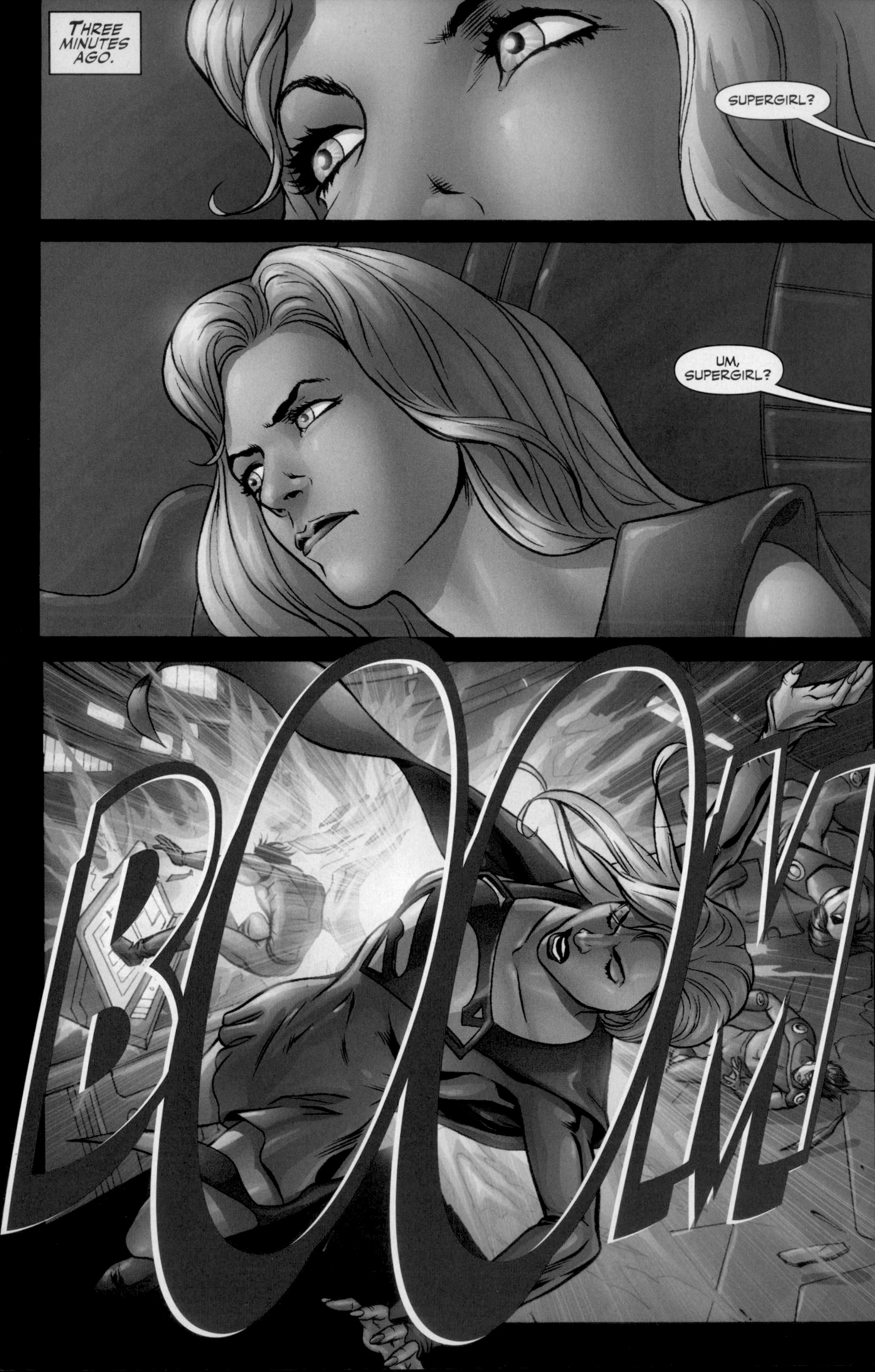
THREE MINUTES AGO.
SUPERGIRL?
UM, SUPERGIRL?
BOOM!

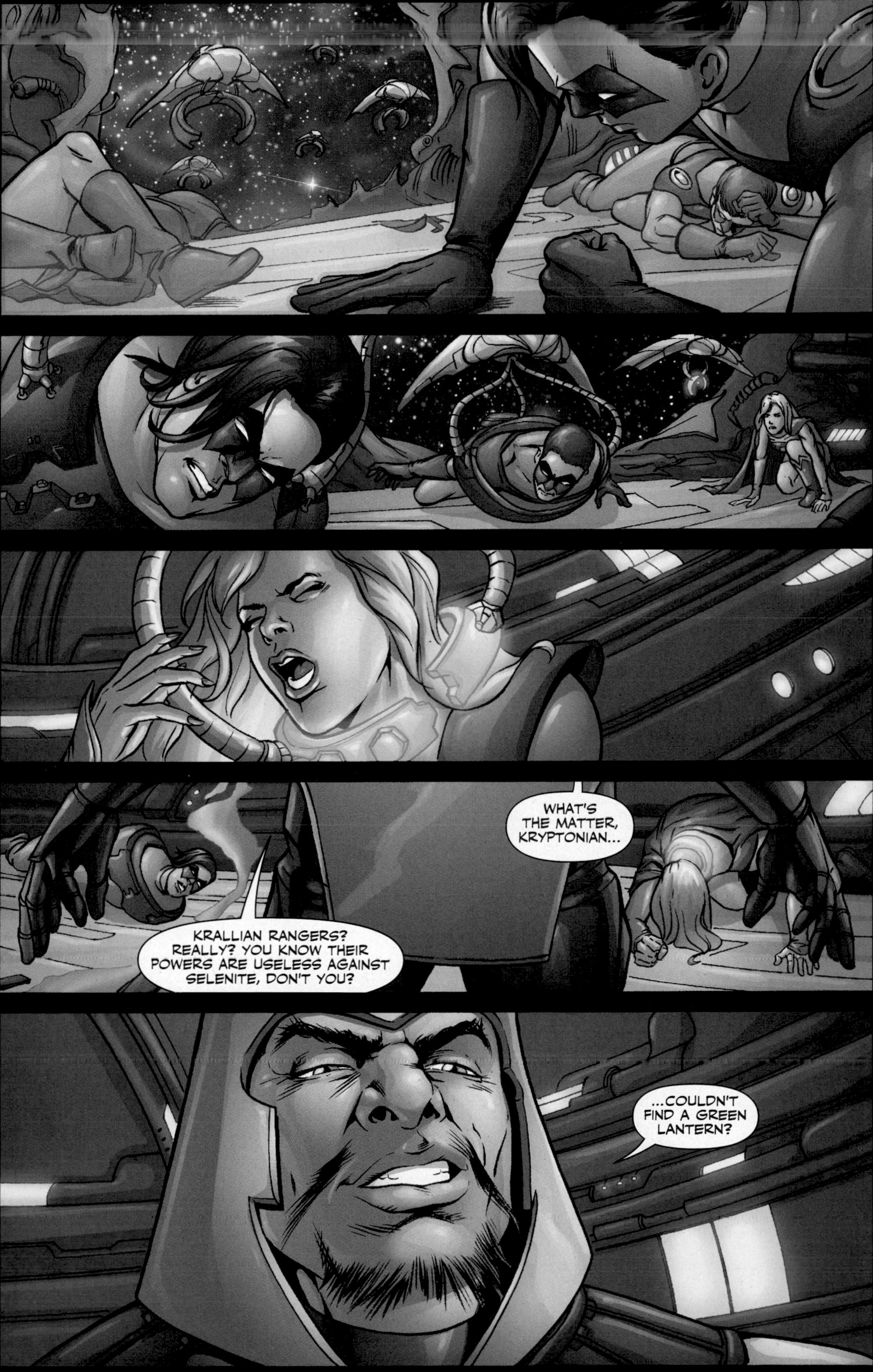
KRALLIAN RANGERS? REALLY? YOU KNOW THEIR POWERS ARE USELESS AGAINST SELENITE, DON'T YOU?
WHAT'S THE MATTER, KRYPTONIAN...
...COULDN'T FIND A GREEN LANTERN?

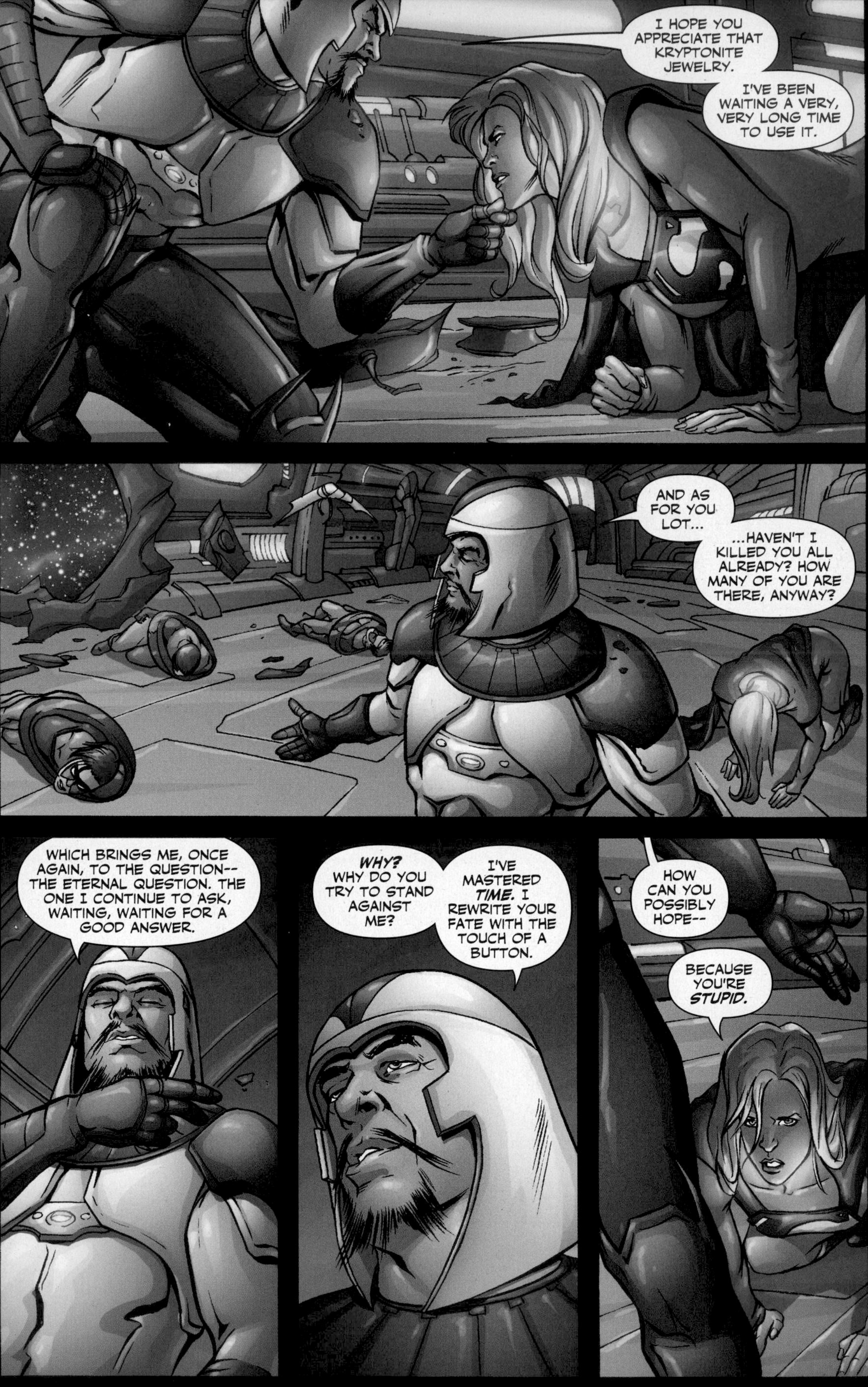
I HOPE YOU APPRECIATE THAT KRYPTONITE JEWELRY.
I'VE BEEN WAITING A VERY, VERY LONG TIME TO USE IT.
AND AS FOR YOU LOT...
...HAVEN'T I KILLED YOU ALL ALREADY? HOW MANY OF YOU ARE THERE, ANYWAY?
WHICH BRINGS ME, ONCE AGAIN, TO THE QUESTION-- THE ETERNAL QUESTION. THE ONE I CONTINUE TO ASK, WAITING, WAITING FOR A GOOD ANSWER.
WHY? WHY DO YOU TRY TO STAND AGAINST ME?
I'VE MASTERED TIME. I REWRITE YOUR FATE WITH THE TOUCH OF A BUTTON.
HOW CAN YOU POSSIBLY HOPE--
BECAUSE YOU'RE STUPID.

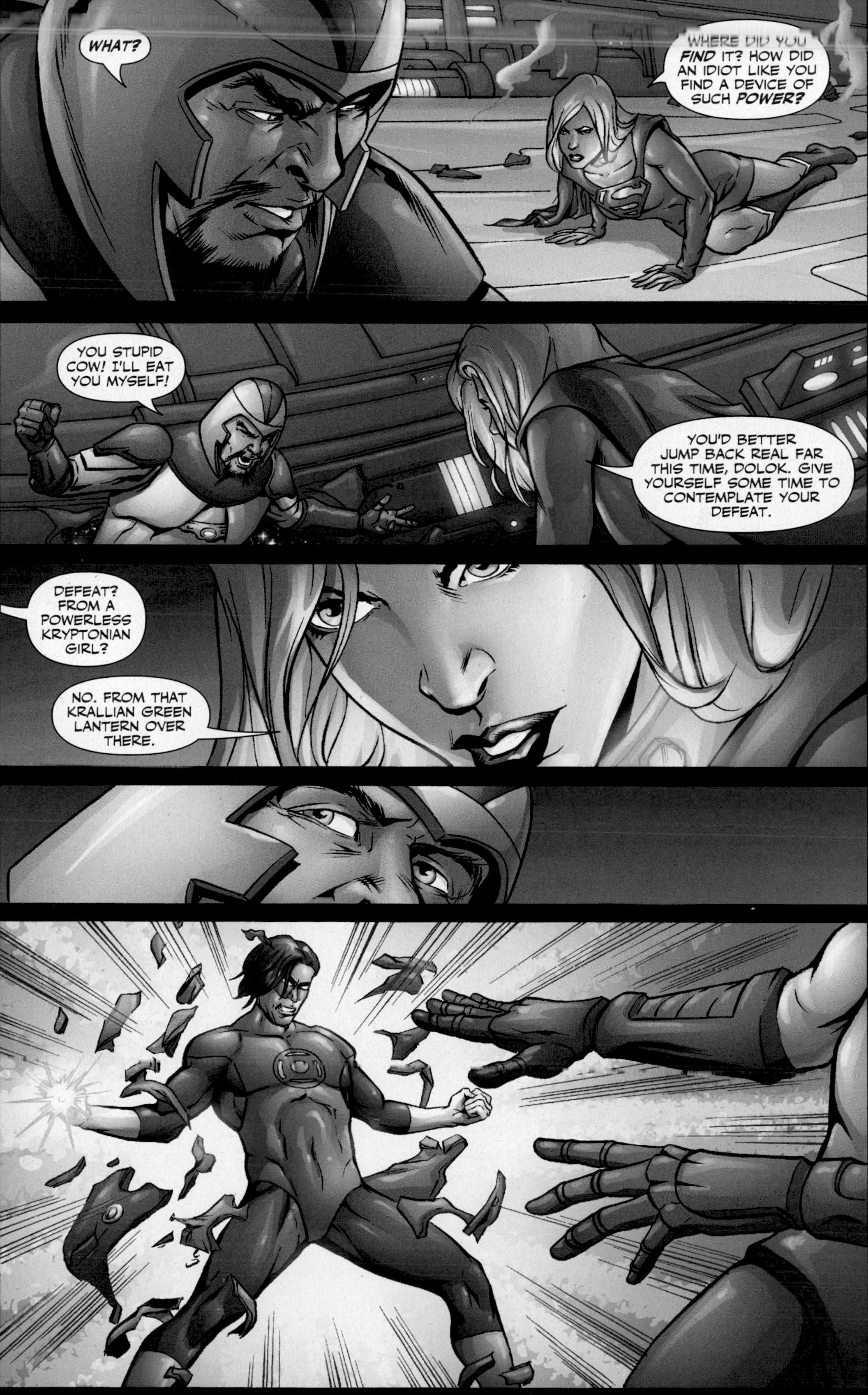
WHAT?
WHERE DID YOU FIND IT? HOW DID AN IDIOT LIKE YOU FIND A DEVICE OF SUCH POWER?
YOU STUPID COW! I'LL EAT YOU MYSELF!
YOU'D BETTER JUMP BACK REAL FAR THIS TIME, DOLOK. GIVE YOURSELF SOME TIME TO CONTEMPLATE YOUR DEFEAT.
DEFEAT? FROM A POWERLESS KRYPTONIAN GIRL?
NO. FROM THAT KRALLIAN GREEN LANTERN OVER THERE.

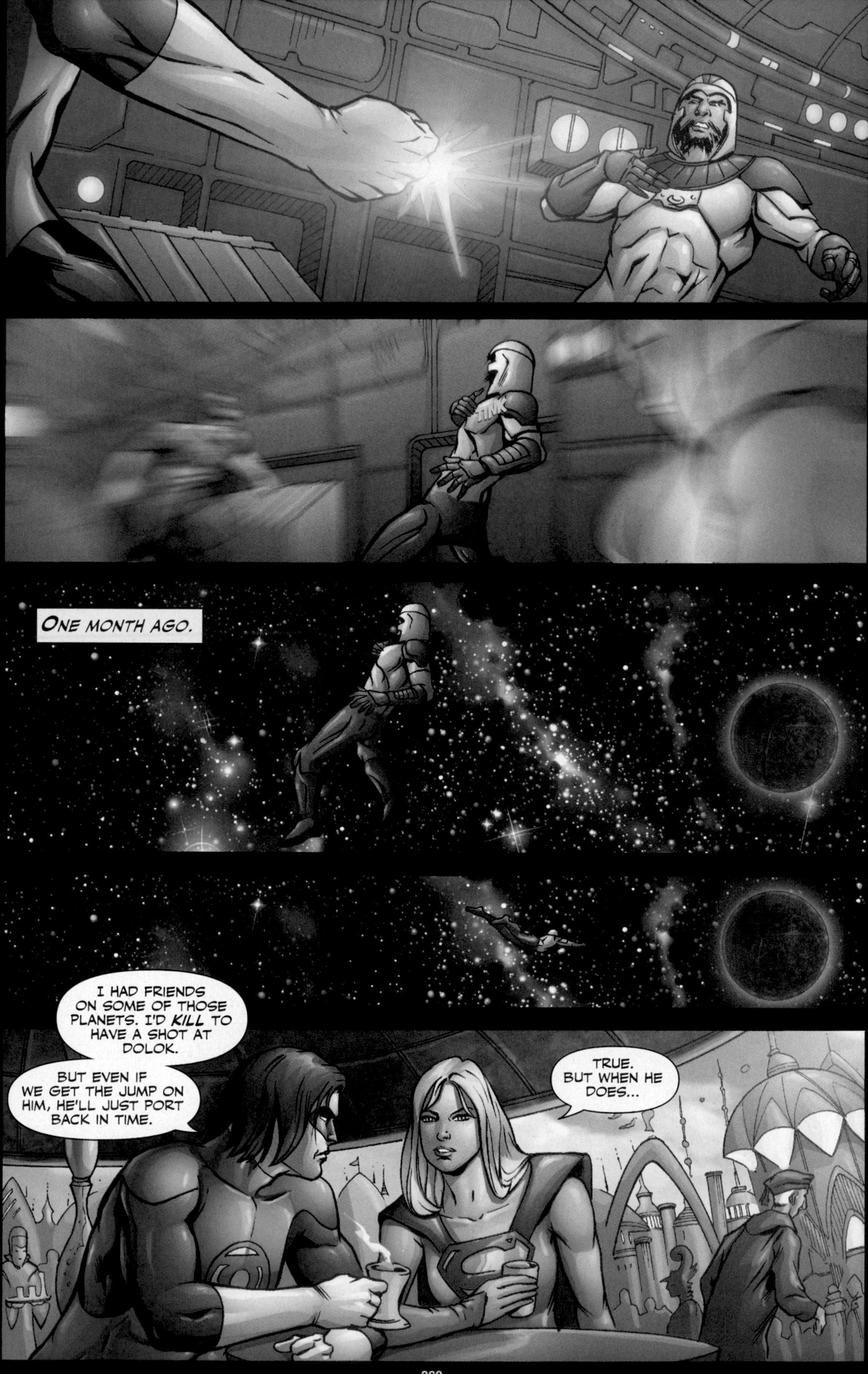
TINK
ONE MONTH AGO.
I HAD FRIENDS ON SOME OF THOSE PLANETS. I'D *KILL* TO HAVE A SHOT AT DOLOK.
BUT EVEN IF WE GET THE JUMP ON HIM, HE'LL JUST PORT BACK IN TIME.
TRUE. BUT WHEN HE DOES...

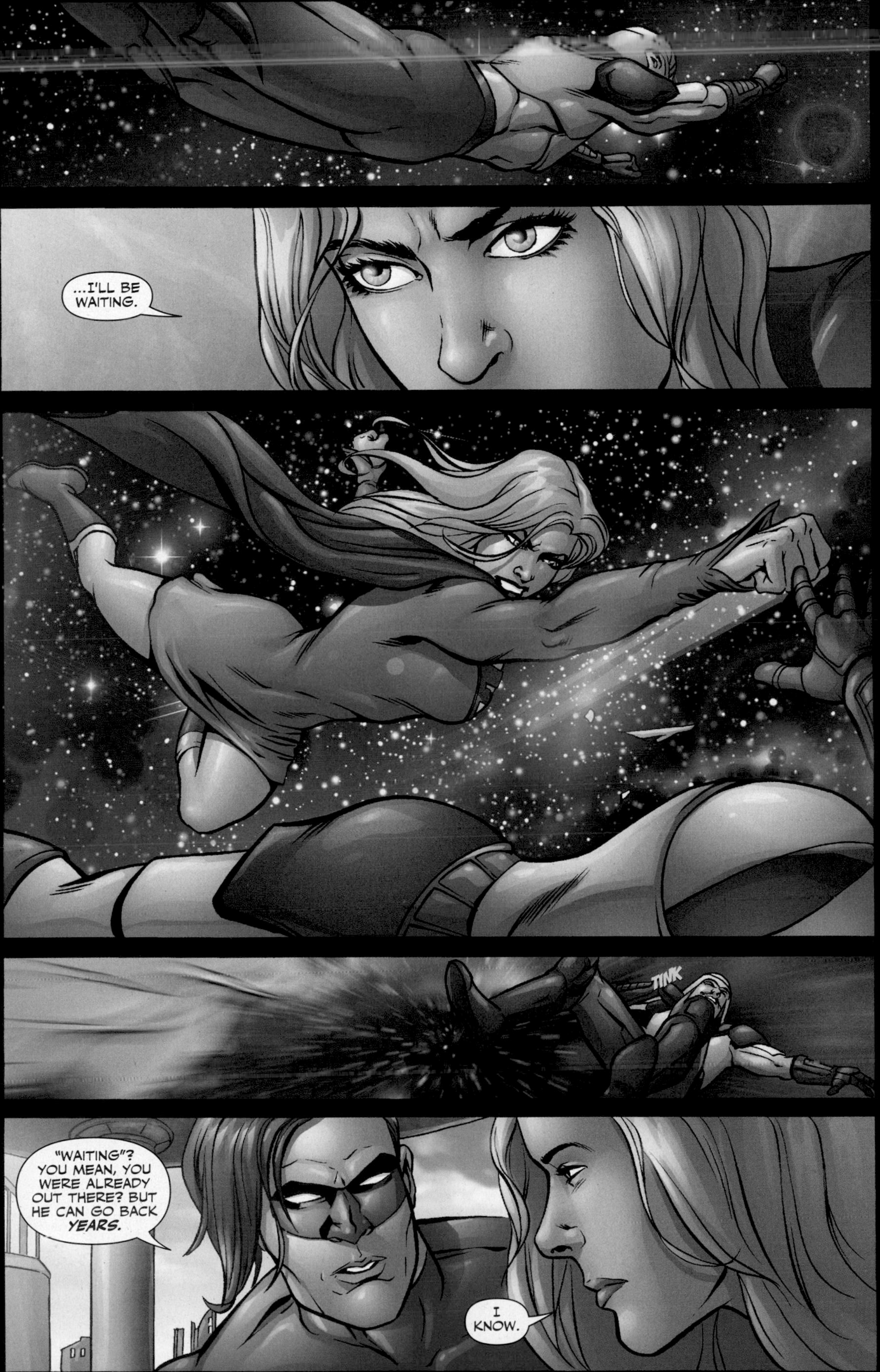
...I'LL BE WAITING.
TINK
"WAITING"? YOU MEAN, YOU WERE ALREADY OUT THERE? BUT HE CAN GO BACK *YEARS*.
I KNOW.

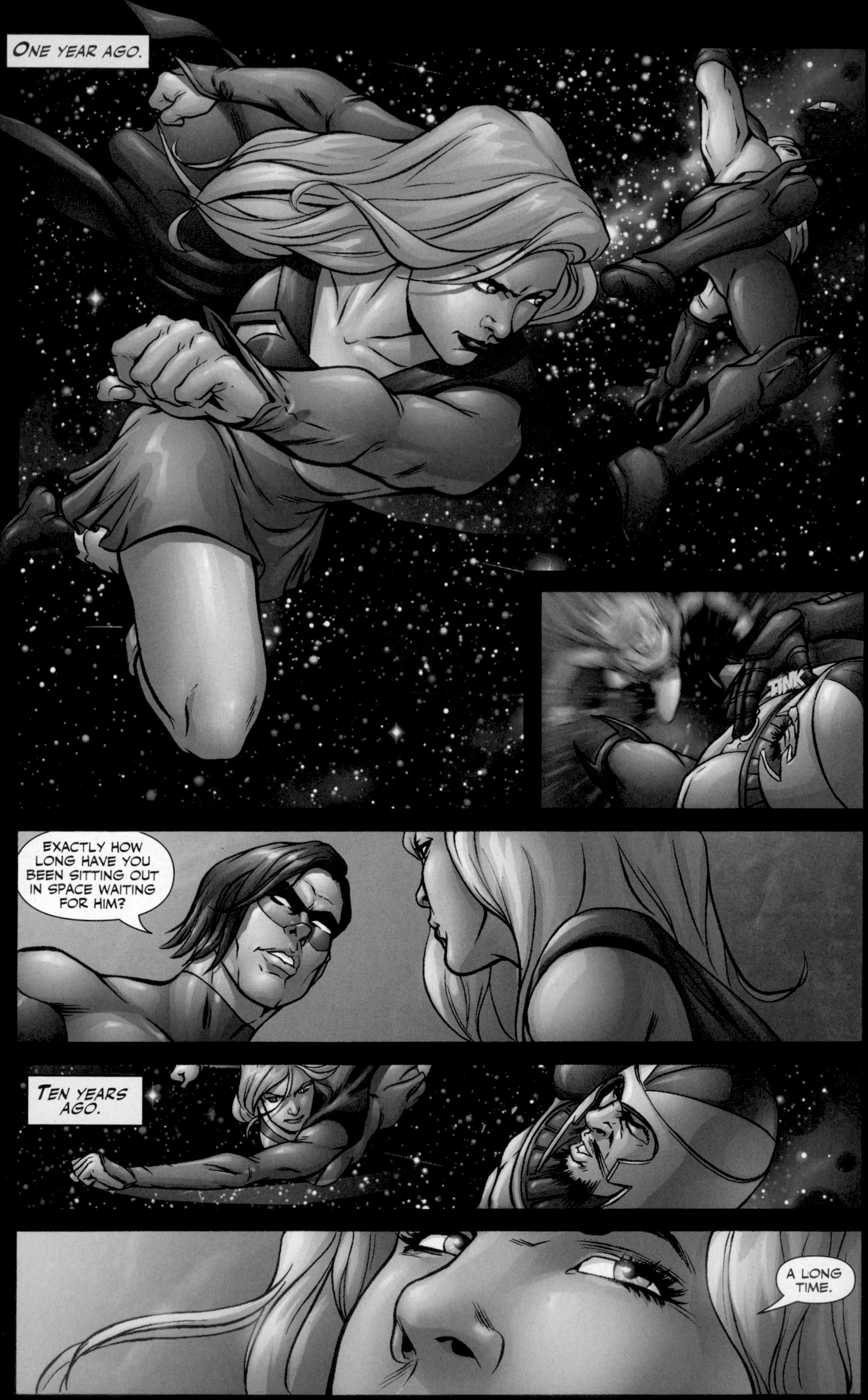

ONE YEAR AGO.
TINK
EXACTLY HOW LONG HAVE YOU BEEN SITTING OUT IN SPACE WAITING FOR HIM?
TEN YEARS AGO.
A LONG TIME.

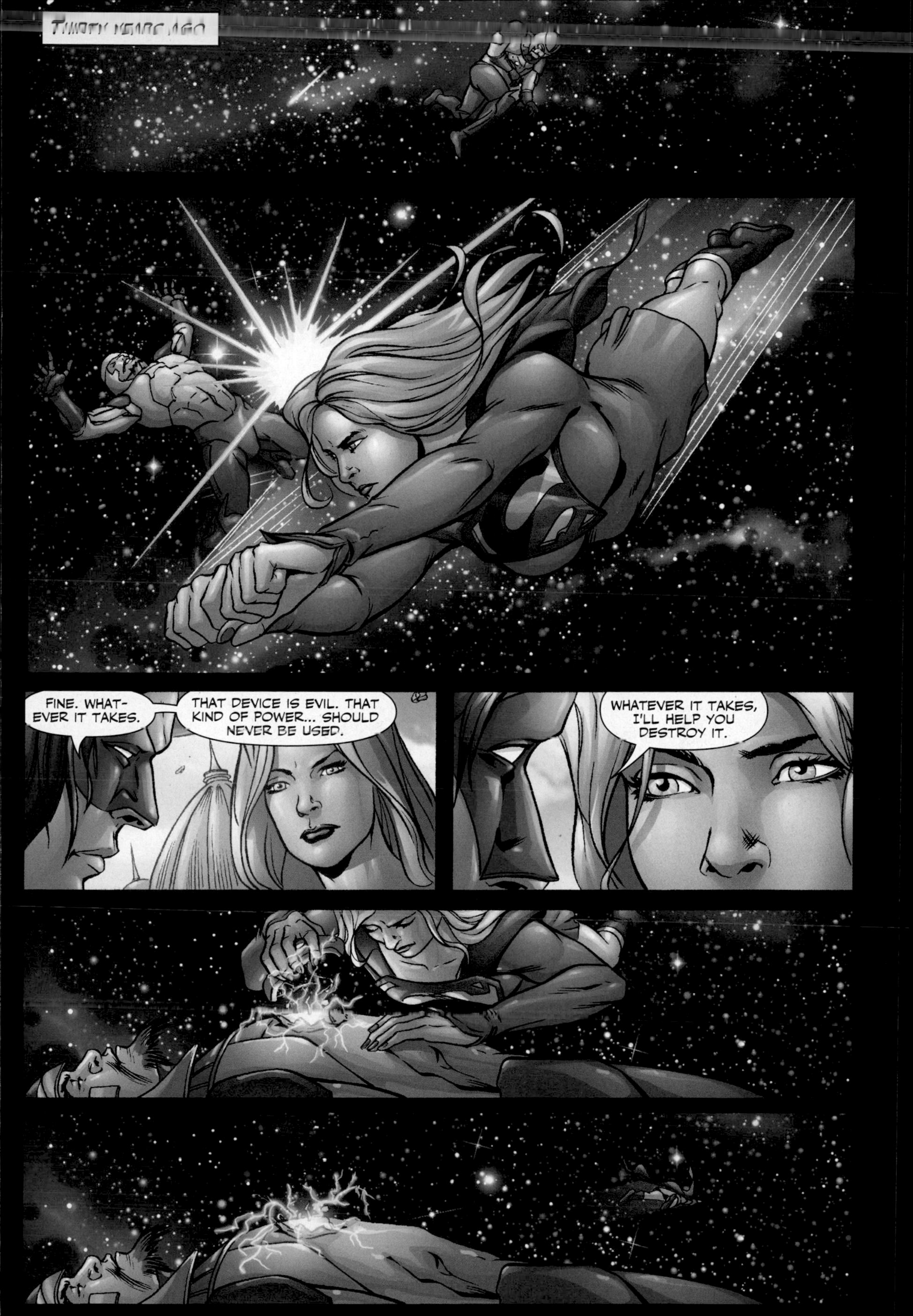

FINE. WHATEVER IT TAKES.
THAT DEVICE IS EVIL. THAT KIND OF POWER... SHOULD NEVER BE USED.
WHATEVER IT TAKES, I'LL HELP YOU DESTROY IT.

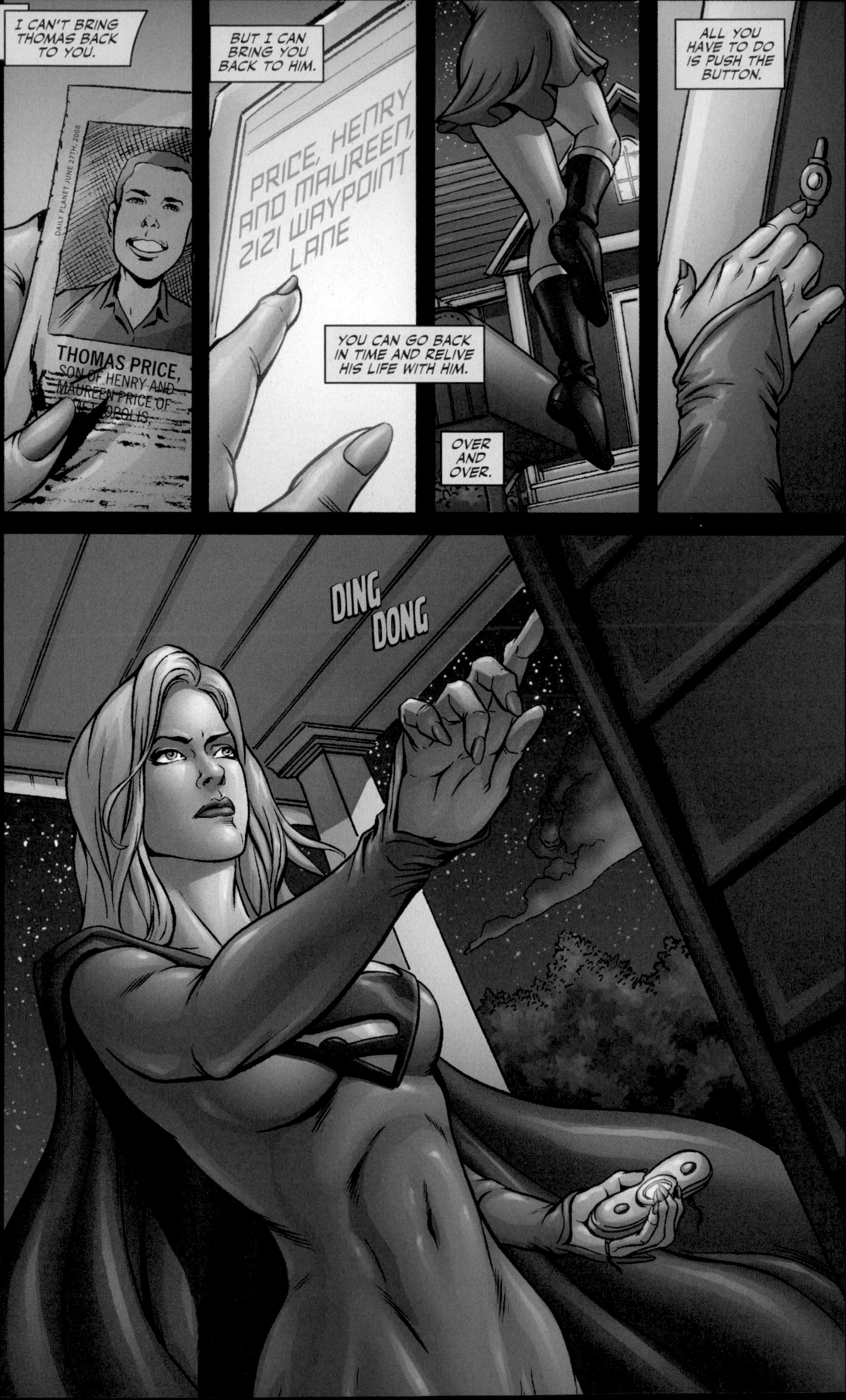
I CAN'T BRING THOMAS BACK TO YOU.
DAILY PLANET JUNE 27TH, 2008
THOMAS PRICE, SON OF HENRY AND MAUREEN PRICE OF METROPOLIS.
BUT I CAN BRING YOU BACK TO HIM.
PRICE, HENRY AND MAUREEN, 2121 WAYPOINT LANE
YOU CAN GO BACK IN TIME AND RELIVE HIS LIFE WITH HIM.
OVER AND OVER.
ALL YOU HAVE TO DO IS PUSH THE BUTTON.
DING DONG

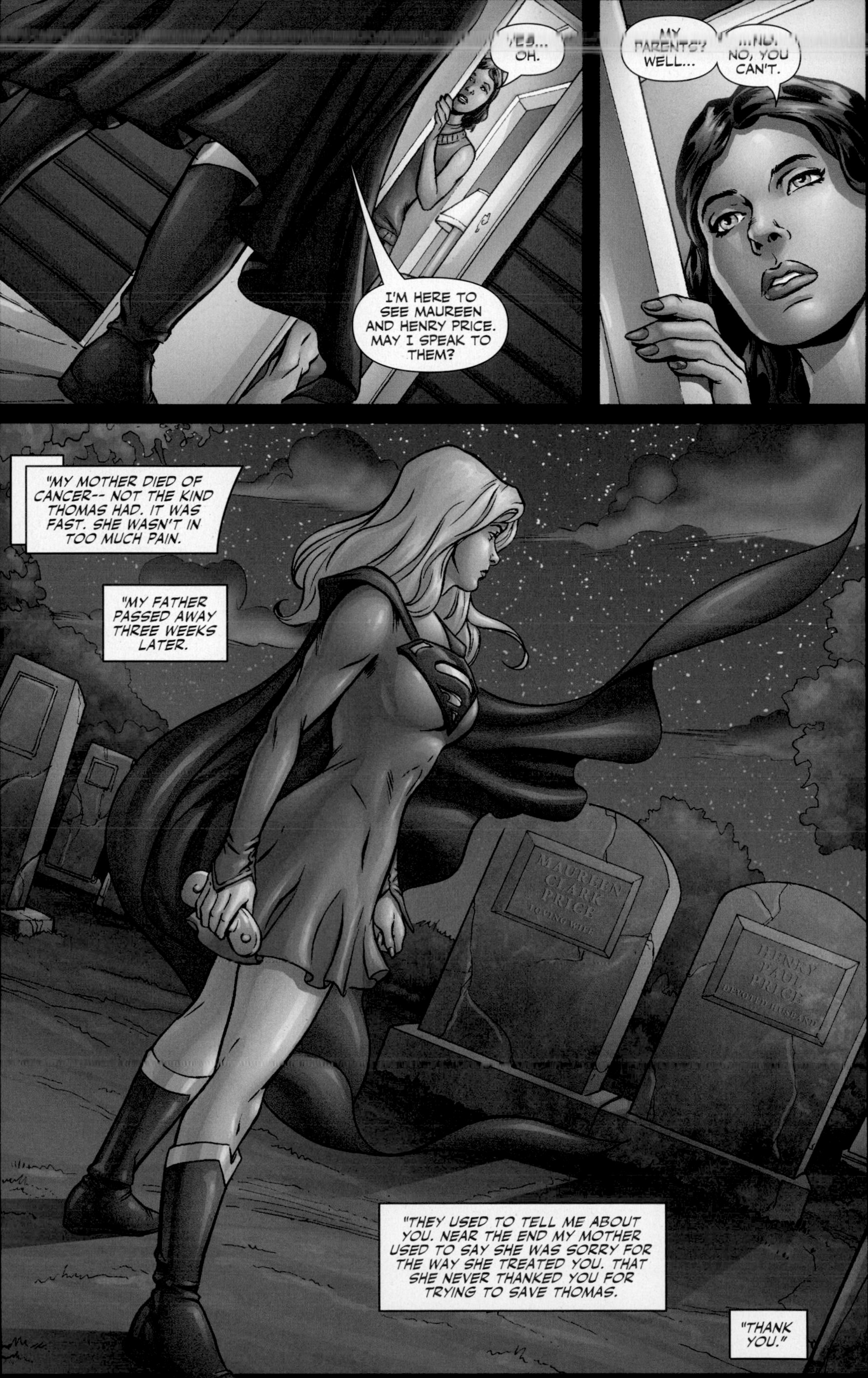
YES... OH.
I'M HERE TO SEE MAUREEN AND HENRY PRICE. MAY I SPEAK TO THEM?
MY PARENTS? WELL...
...NO. NO, YOU CAN'T.
"MY MOTHER DIED OF CANCER-- NOT THE KIND THOMAS HAD. IT WAS FAST. SHE WASN'T IN TOO MUCH PAIN.
"MY FATHER PASSED AWAY THREE WEEKS LATER.
MAUREEN CLARK PRICE LOVING WIFE
HENRY PAUL PRICE DEVOTED HUSBAND
"THEY USED TO TELL ME ABOUT YOU. NEAR THE END MY MOTHER USED TO SAY SHE WAS SORRY FOR THE WAY SHE TREATED YOU. THAT SHE NEVER THANKED YOU FOR TRYING TO SAVE THOMAS.
"THANK YOU."

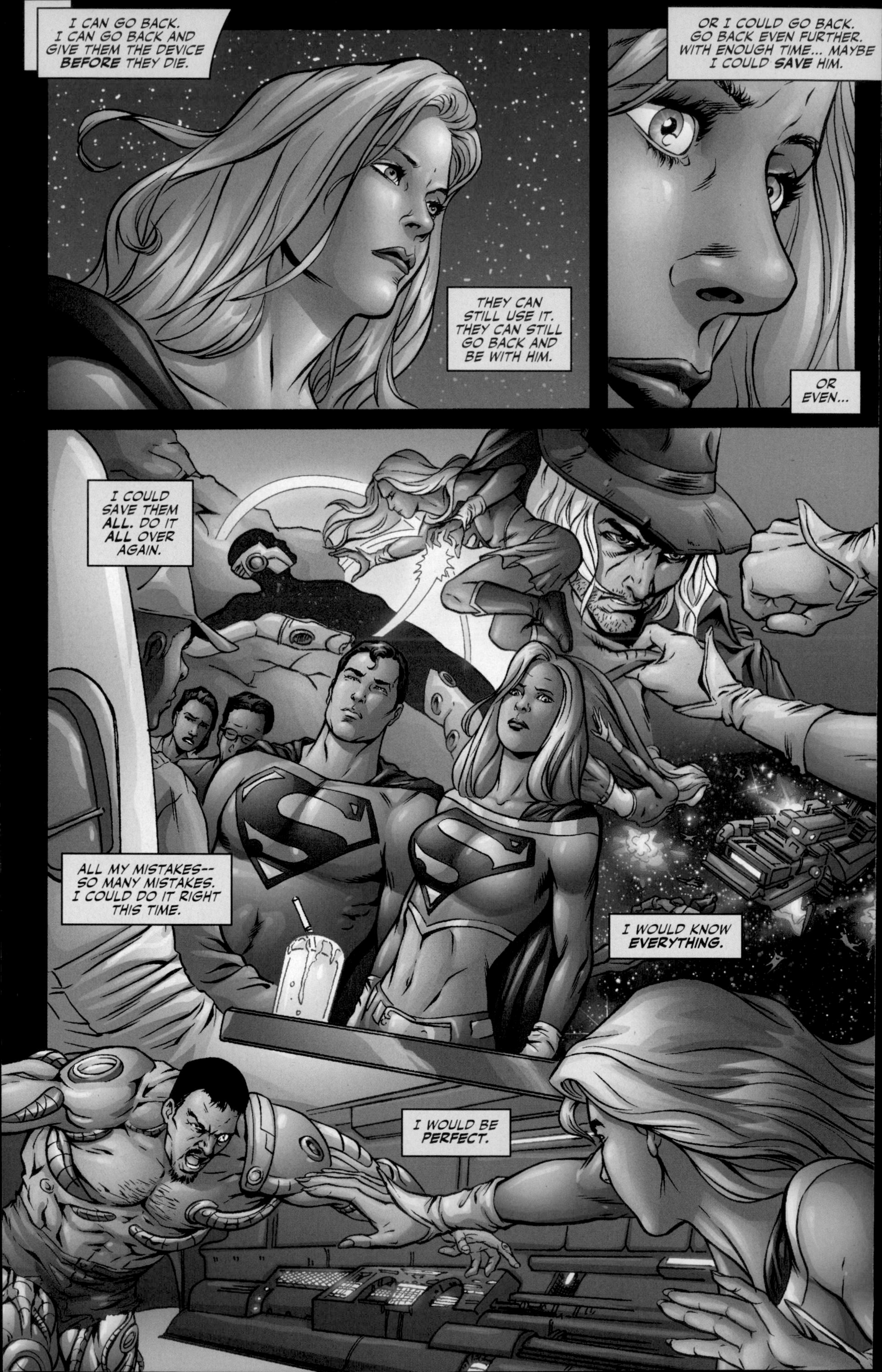
I CAN GO BACK. I CAN GO BACK AND GIVE THEM THE DEVICE BEFORE THEY DIE.
THEY CAN STILL USE IT. THEY CAN STILL GO BACK AND BE WITH HIM.
OR I COULD GO BACK. GO BACK EVEN FURTHER. WITH ENOUGH TIME... MAYBE I COULD SAVE HIM.
OR EVEN...
I COULD SAVE THEM ALL. DO IT ALL OVER AGAIN.
ALL MY MISTAKES-- SO MANY MISTAKES. I COULD DO IT RIGHT THIS TIME.
I WOULD KNOW EVERYTHING.
I WOULD BE PERFECT.

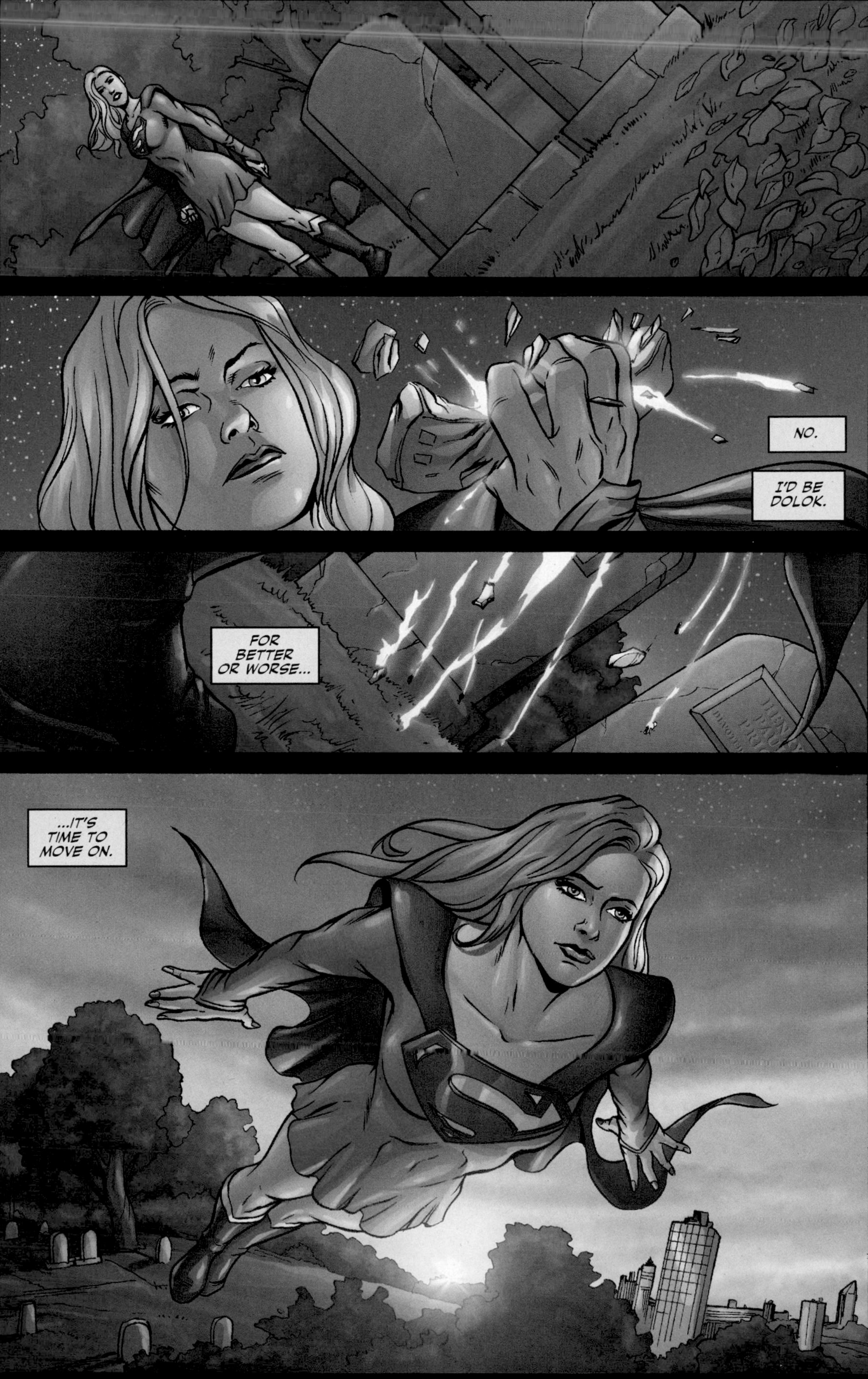
NO.
I'D BE DOLOK.
FOR BETTER OR WORSE...
...IT'S TIME TO MOVE ON.

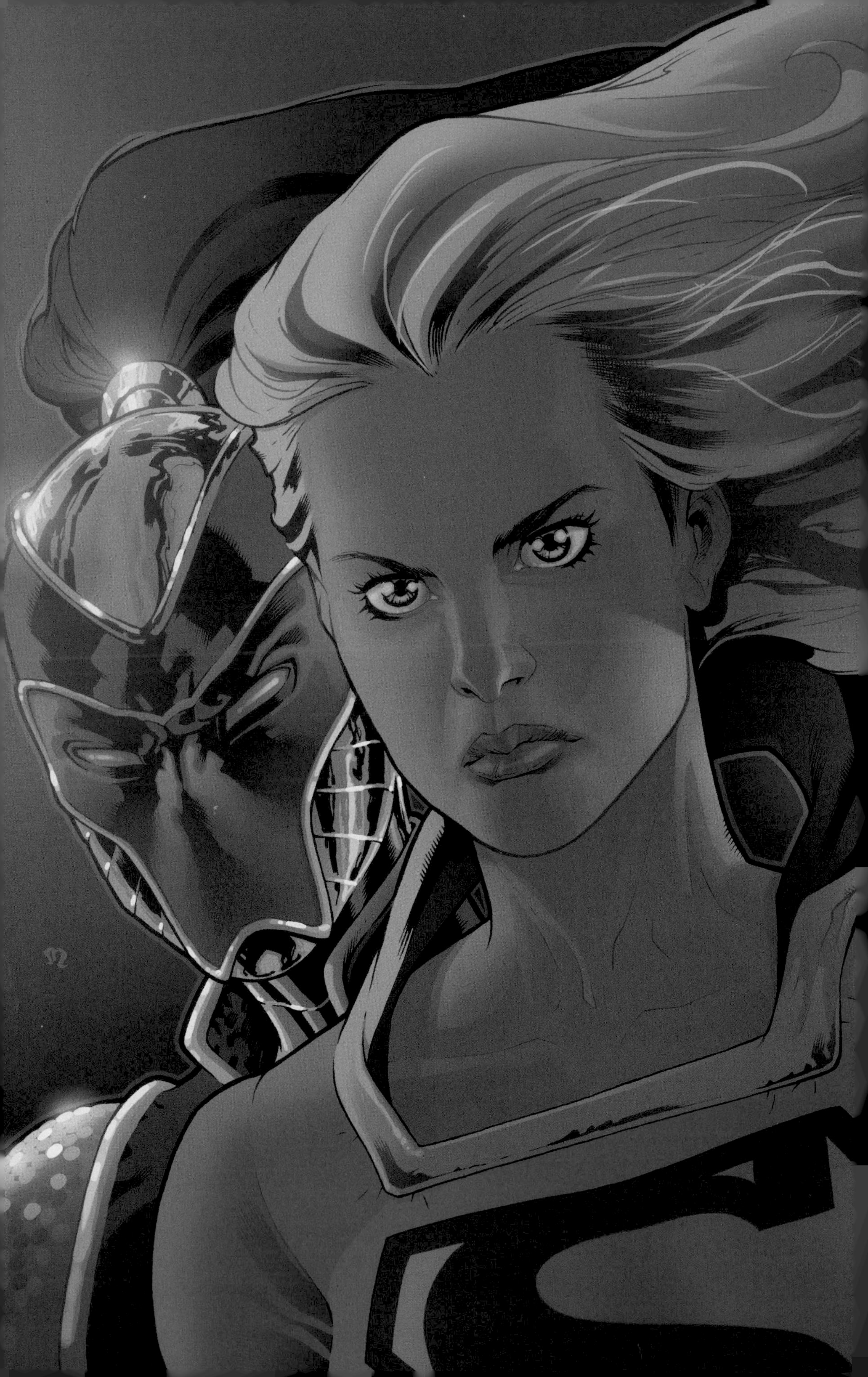

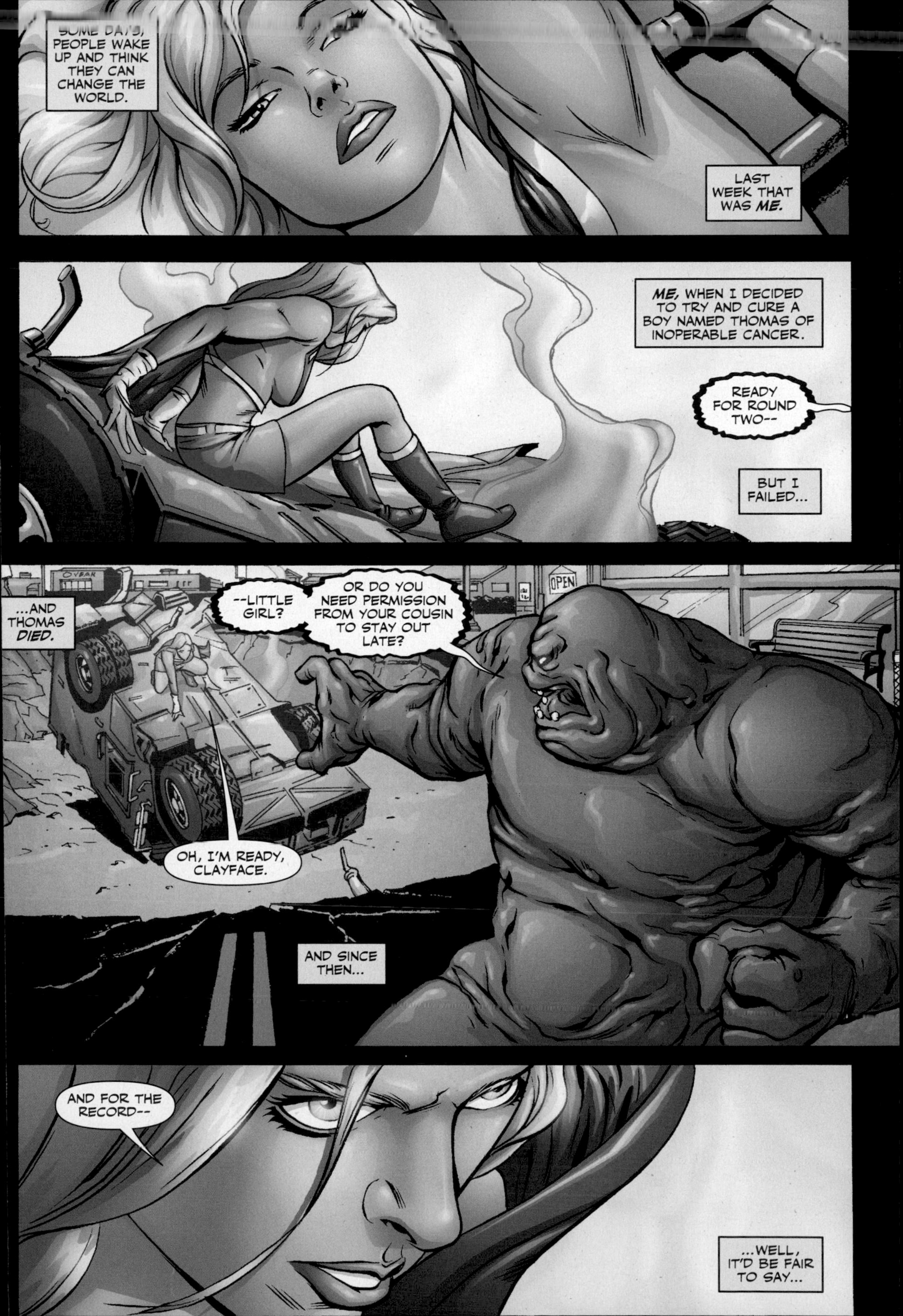
SOME DAYS, PEOPLE WAKE UP AND THINK THEY CAN CHANGE THE WORLD.
LAST WEEK THAT WAS ME.
ME, WHEN I DECIDED TO TRY AND CURE A BOY NAMED THOMAS OF INOPERABLE CANCER.
READY FOR ROUND TWO--
BUT I FAILED...
...AND THOMAS DIED.
--LITTLE GIRL?
OR DO YOU NEED PERMISSION FROM YOUR COUSIN TO STAY OUT LATE?
OPEN
OH, I'M READY, CLAYFACE.
AND SINCE THEN...
AND FOR THE RECORD--
...WELL, IT'D BE FAIR TO SAY...

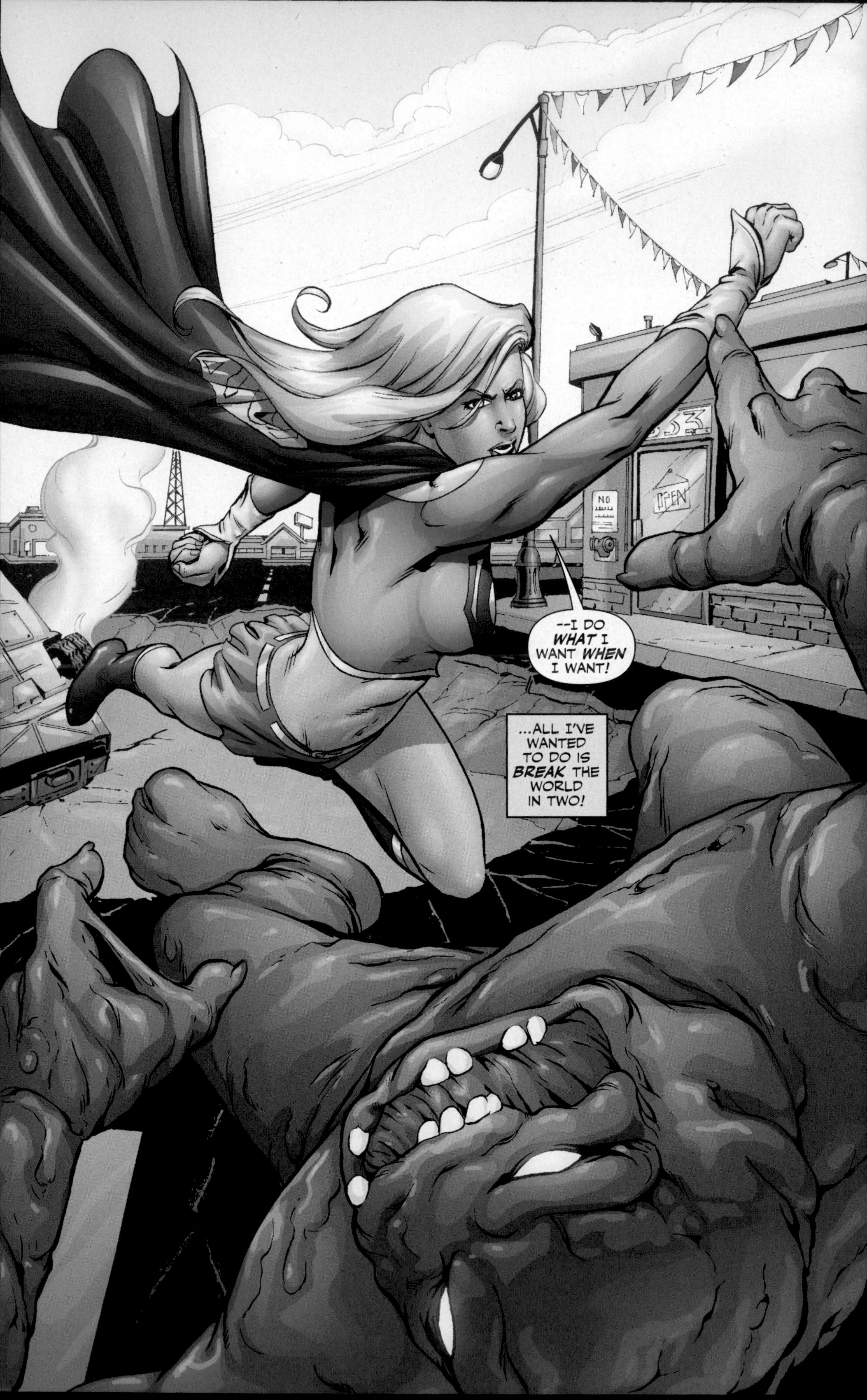
--I DO WHAT I WANT WHEN I WANT!
...ALL I'VE WANTED TO DO IS BREAK THE WORLD IN TWO!

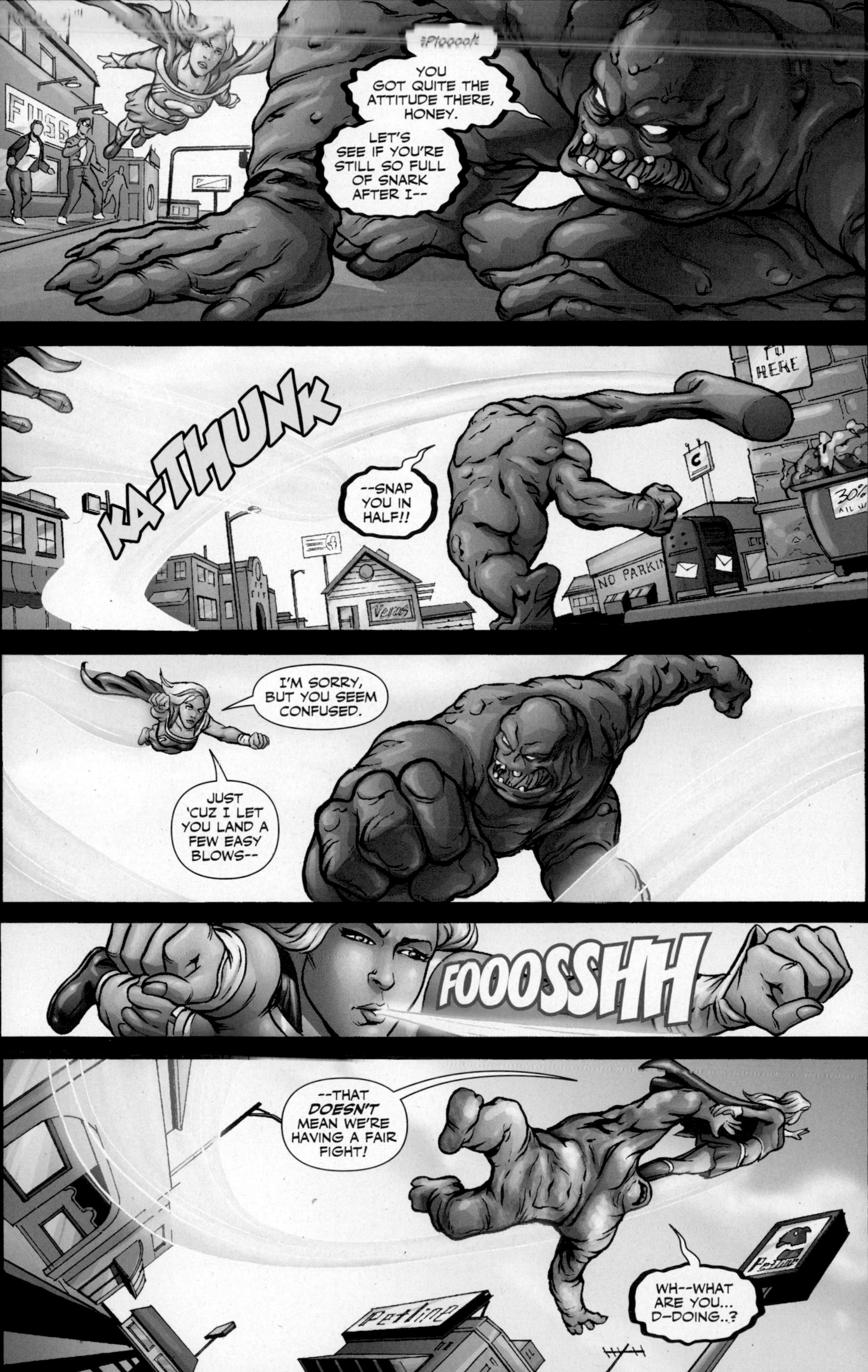
YOU GOT QUITE THE ATTITUDE THERE, HONEY.
LET'S SEE IF YOU'RE STILL SO FULL OF SNARK AFTER I--
KA-THUNK
--SNAP YOU IN HALF!!
I'M SORRY, BUT YOU SEEM CONFUSED.
JUST 'CUZ I LET YOU LAND A FEW EASY BLOWS--
FOOOSSHH
--THAT *DOESN'T* MEAN WE'RE HAVING A FAIR FIGHT!
WH--WHAT ARE YOU... D-DOING..?

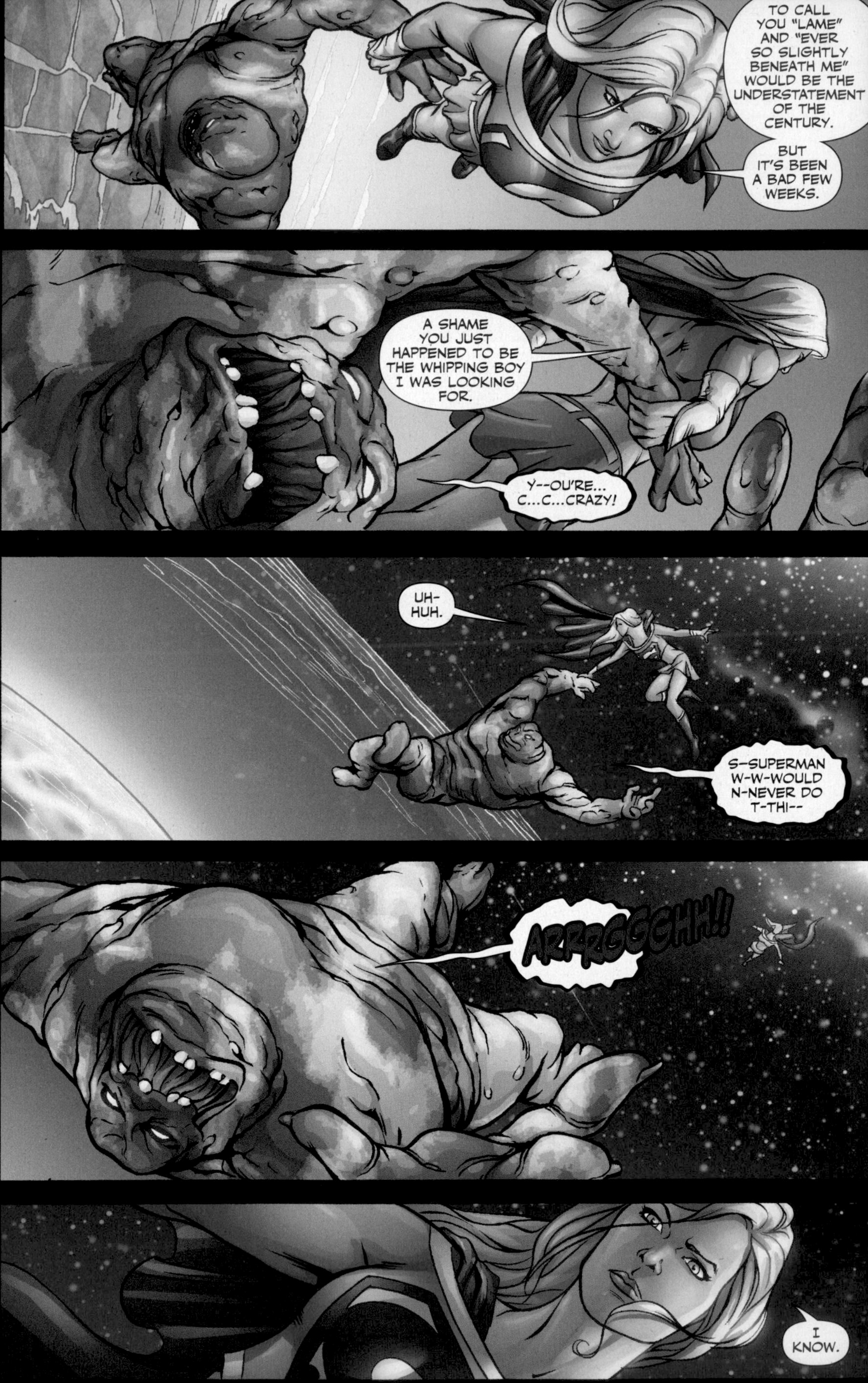

TO CALL YOU "LAME" AND "EVER SO SLIGHTLY BENEATH ME" WOULD BE THE UNDERSTATEMENT OF THE CENTURY.
BUT IT'S BEEN A BAD FEW WEEKS.
A SHAME YOU JUST HAPPENED TO BE THE WHIPPING BOY I WAS LOOKING FOR.
Y--OU'RE... C...C...CRAZY!
UH-HUH.
S-SUPERMAN W-W-WOULD N-NEVER DO T-THI--
ARRRGGGHHH!!
I KNOW.

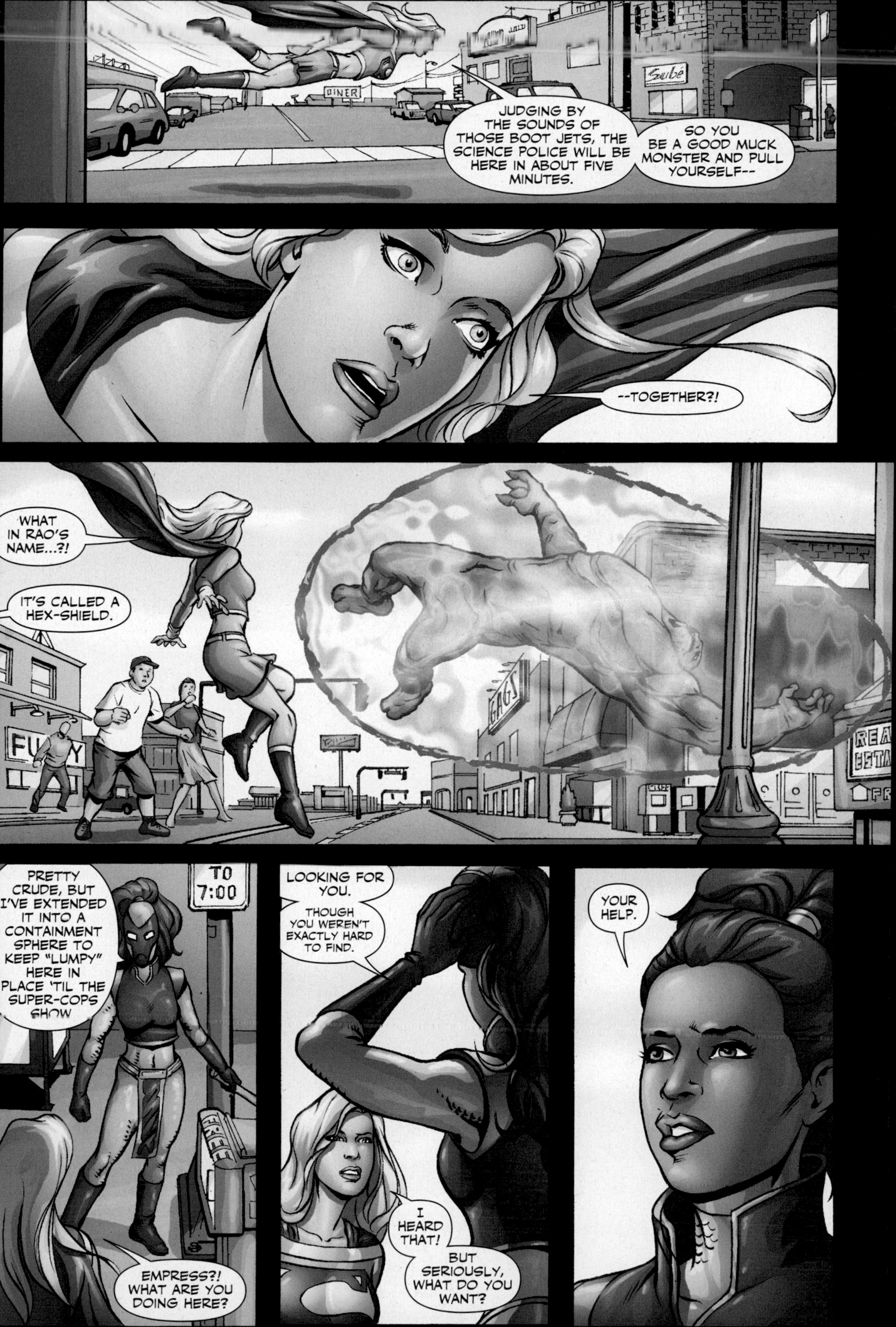
DINER
Subé
JUDGING BY THE SOUNDS OF THOSE BOOT JETS, THE SCIENCE POLICE WILL BE HERE IN ABOUT FIVE MINUTES.
SO YOU BE A GOOD MUCK MONSTER AND PULL YOURSELF--
--TOGETHER?!
WHAT IN RAO'S NAME...?!
IT'S CALLED A HEX-SHIELD.
GAGS
PRETTY CRUDE, BUT I'VE EXTENDED IT INTO A CONTAINMENT SPHERE TO KEEP "LUMPY" HERE IN PLACE 'TIL THE SUPER-COPS SHOW
TO 7:00
EMPRESS?! WHAT ARE YOU DOING HERE?
LOOKING FOR YOU.
THOUGH YOU WEREN'T EXACTLY HARD TO FIND.
I HEARD THAT!
BUT SERIOUSLY, WHAT DO YOU WANT?
YOUR HELP.

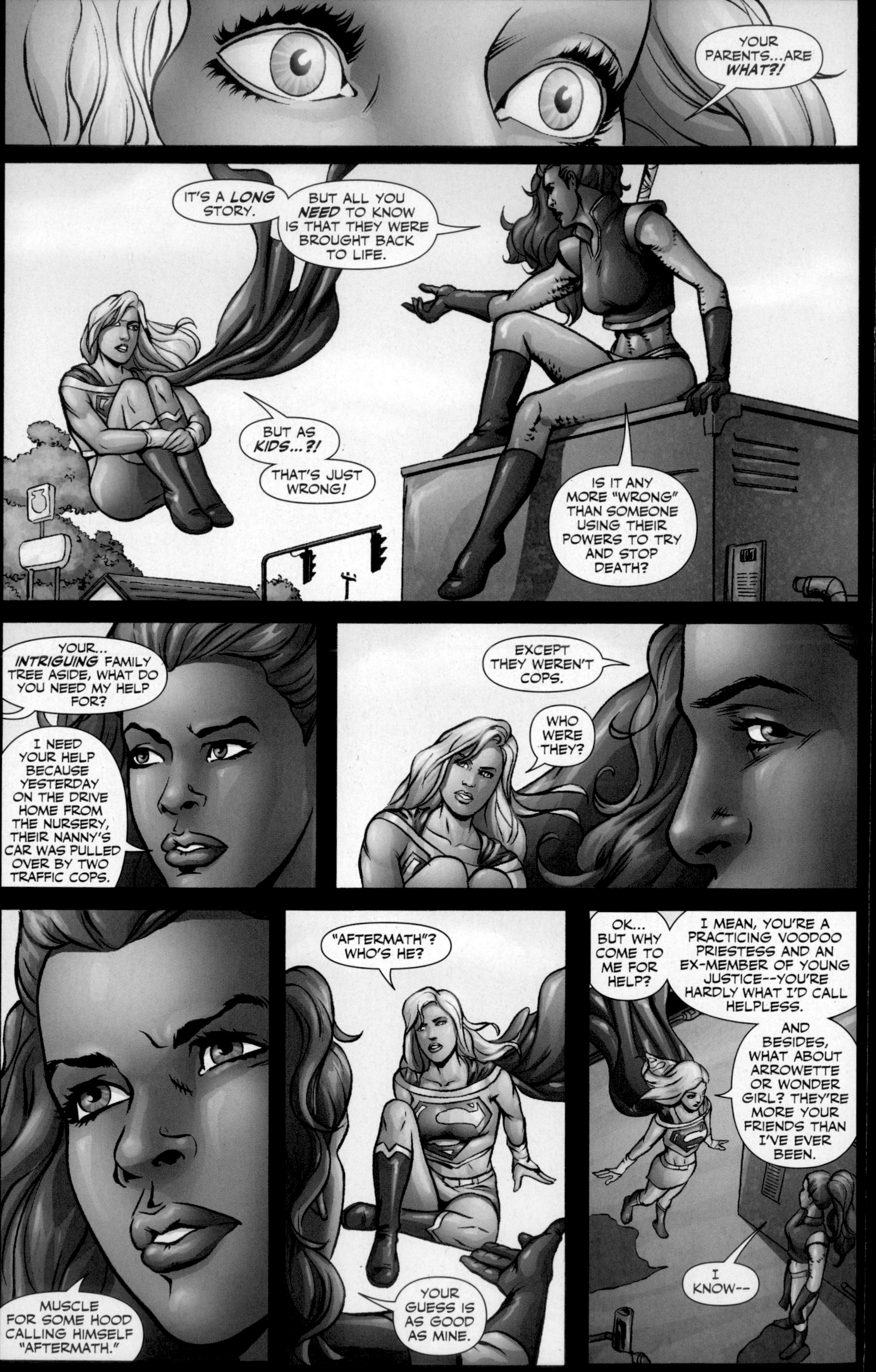
YOUR PARENTS...ARE WHAT?!
IT'S A LONG STORY.
BUT ALL YOU NEED TO KNOW IS THAT THEY WERE BROUGHT BACK TO LIFE.
BUT AS KIDS...?!
THAT'S JUST WRONG!
IS IT ANY MORE "WRONG" THAN SOMEONE USING THEIR POWERS TO TRY AND STOP DEATH?
YOUR... INTRIGUING FAMILY TREE ASIDE, WHAT DO YOU NEED MY HELP FOR?
I NEED YOUR HELP BECAUSE YESTERDAY ON THE DRIVE HOME FROM THE NURSERY, THEIR NANNY'S CAR WAS PULLED OVER BY TWO TRAFFIC COPS.
EXCEPT THEY WEREN'T COPS.
WHO WERE THEY?
MUSCLE FOR SOME HOOD CALLING HIMSELF "AFTERMATH."
"AFTERMATH"? WHO'S HE?
YOUR GUESS IS AS GOOD AS MINE.
OK... BUT WHY COME TO ME FOR HELP?
I MEAN, YOU'RE A PRACTICING VOODOO PRIESTESS AND AN EX-MEMBER OF YOUNG JUSTICE--YOU'RE HARDLY WHAT I'D CALL HELPLESS.
AND BESIDES, WHAT ABOUT ARROWETTE OR WONDER GIRL? THEY'RE MORE YOUR FRIENDS THAN I'VE EVER BEEN.
I KNOW--

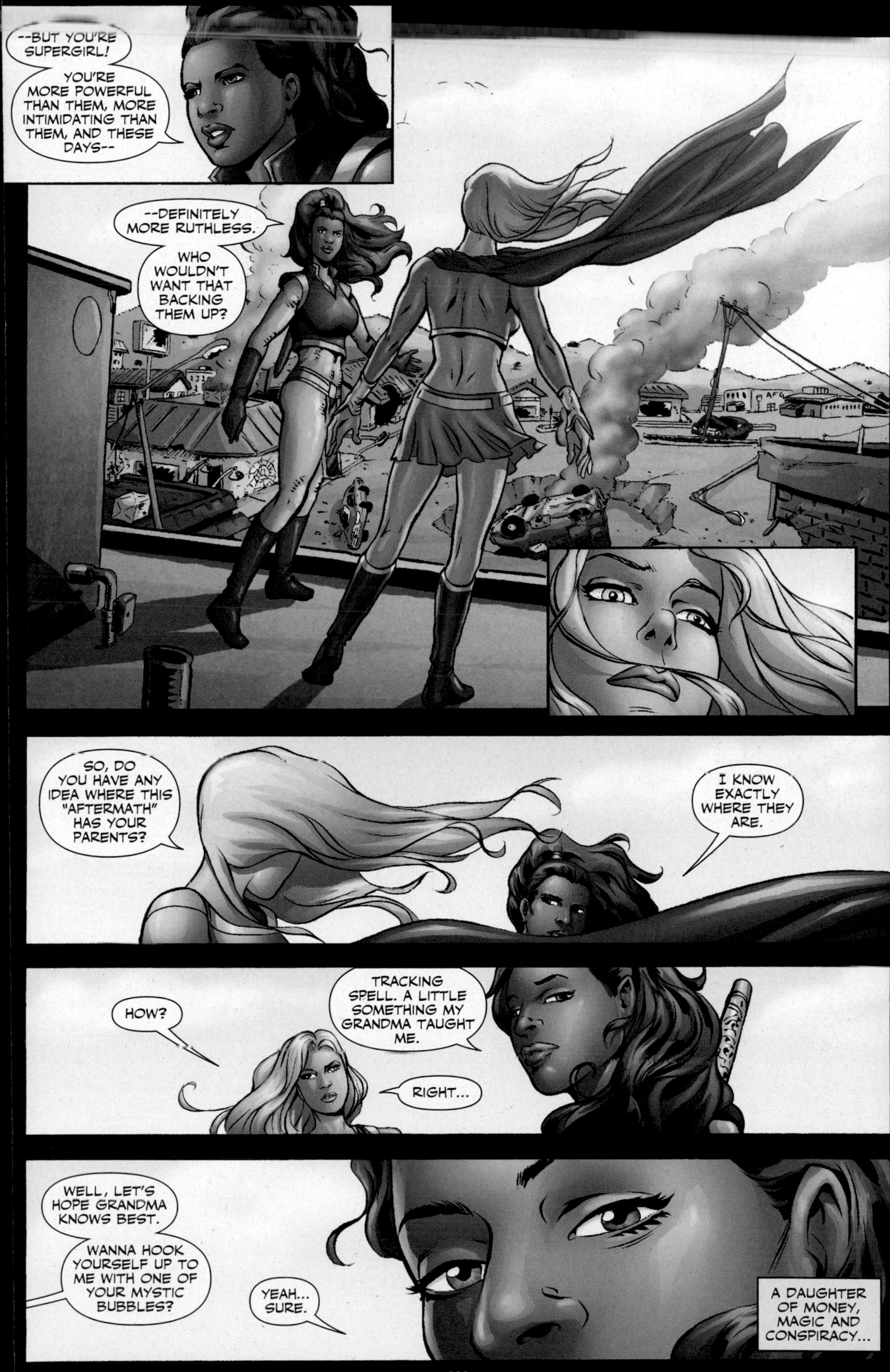
--BUT YOU'RE SUPERGIRL!
YOU'RE MORE POWERFUL THAN THEM, MORE INTIMIDATING THAN THEM, AND THESE DAYS--
--DEFINITELY MORE RUTHLESS.
WHO WOULDN'T WANT THAT BACKING THEM UP?
SO, DO YOU HAVE ANY IDEA WHERE THIS "AFTERMATH" HAS YOUR PARENTS?
I KNOW EXACTLY WHERE THEY ARE.
HOW?
TRACKING SPELL. A LITTLE SOMETHING MY GRANDMA TAUGHT ME.
RIGHT...
WELL, LET'S HOPE GRANDMA KNOWS BEST.
WANNA HOOK YOURSELF UP TO ME WITH ONE OF YOUR MYSTIC BUBBLES?
YEAH... SURE.
A DAUGHTER OF MONEY, MAGIC AND CONSPIRACY...

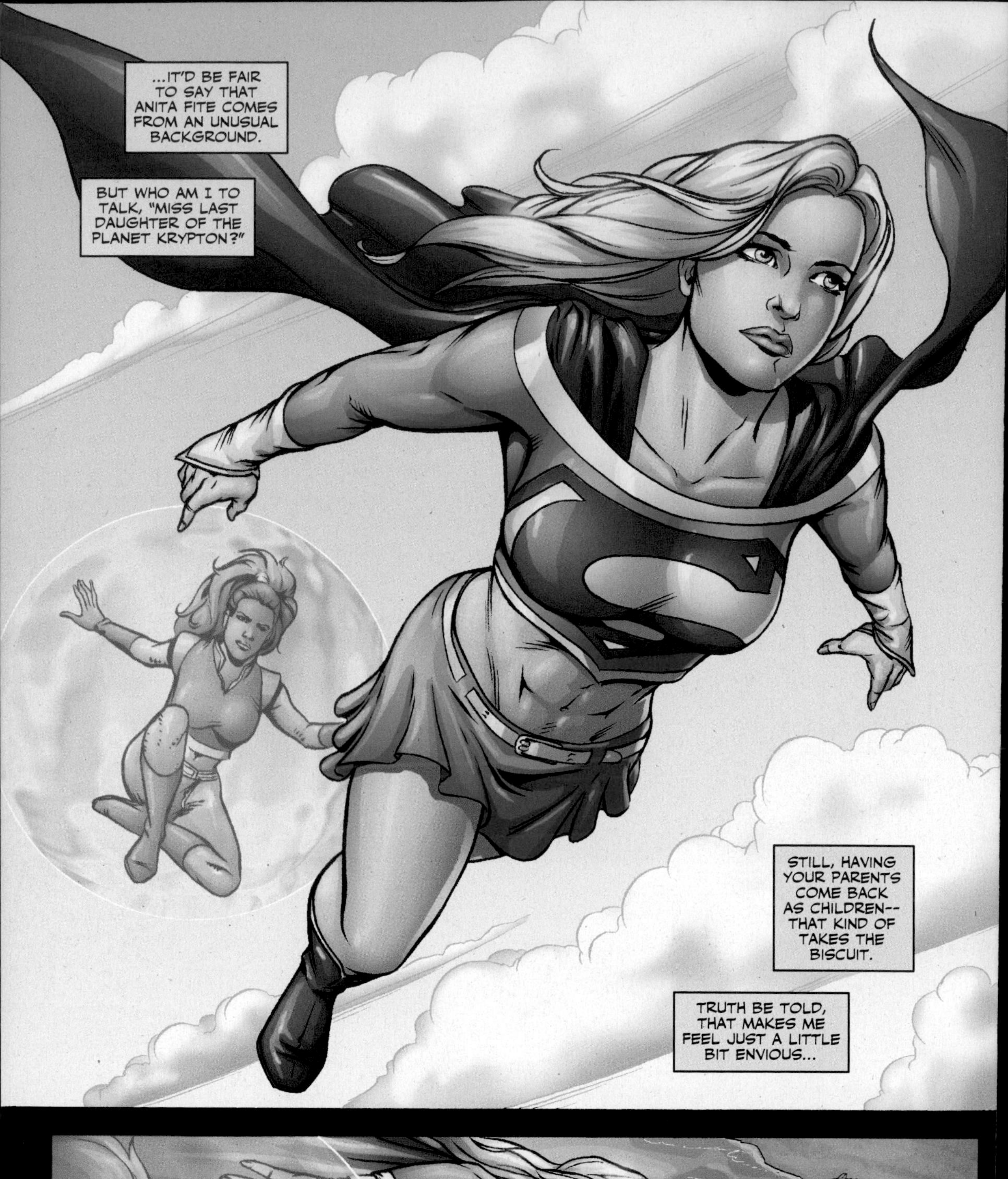
...IT'D BE FAIR TO SAY THAT ANITA FITE COMES FROM AN UNUSUAL BACKGROUND.
BUT WHO AM I TO TALK, "MISS LAST DAUGHTER OF THE PLANET KRYPTON?"
STILL, HAVING YOUR PARENTS COME BACK AS CHILDREN-- THAT KIND OF TAKES THE BISCUIT.
TRUTH BE TOLD, THAT MAKES ME FEEL JUST A LITTLE BIT ENVIOUS...
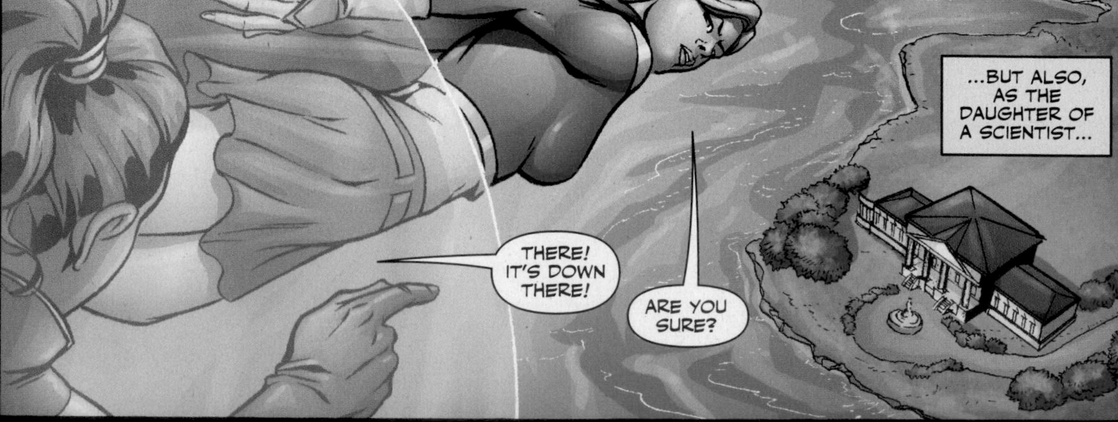
...BUT ALSO, AS THE DAUGHTER OF A SCIENTIST...
THERE! IT'S DOWN THERE!
ARE YOU SURE?

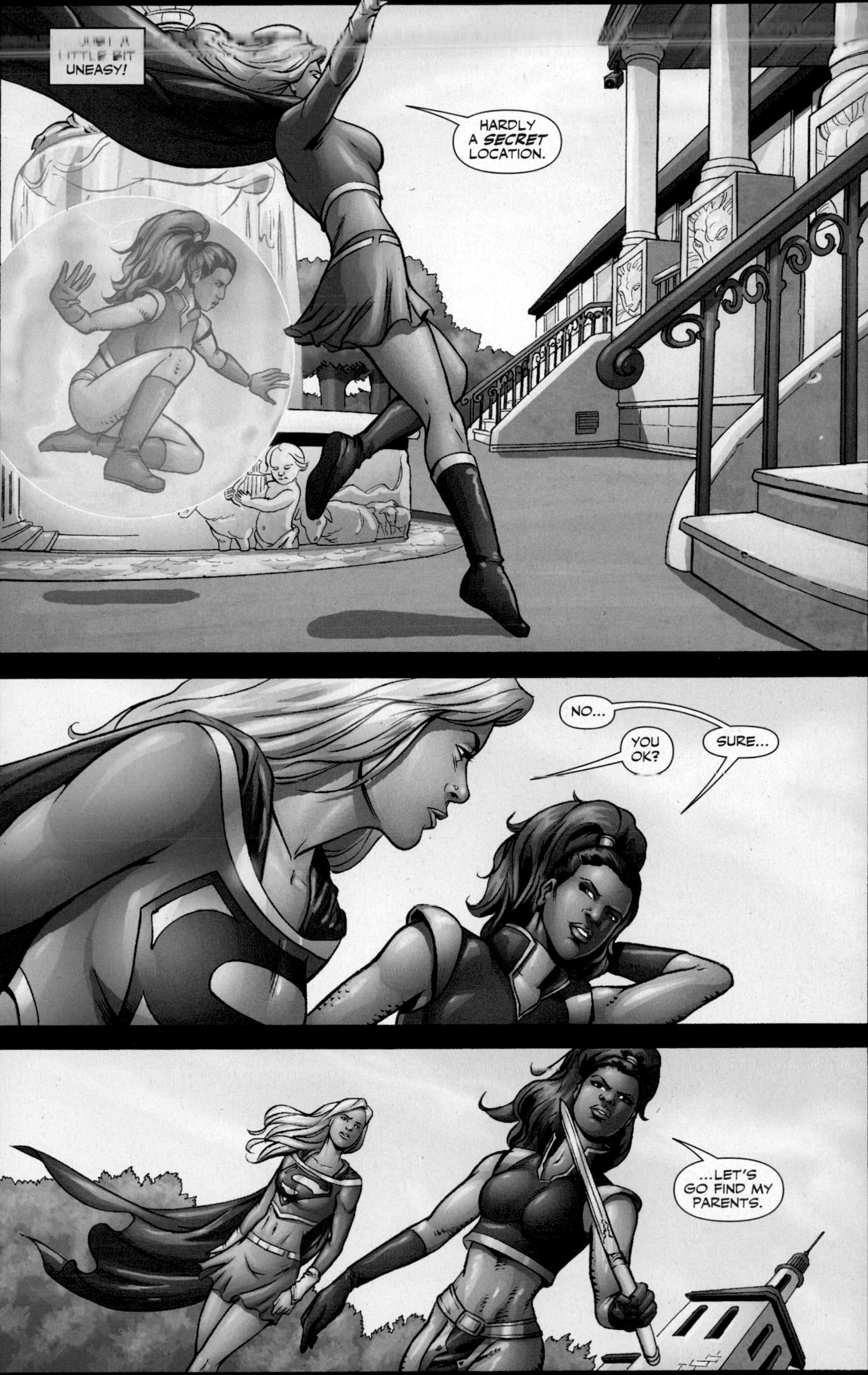
UNEASY!
HARDLY A SECRET LOCATION.
NO...
YOU OK?
SURE...
...LET'S GO FIND MY PARENTS.

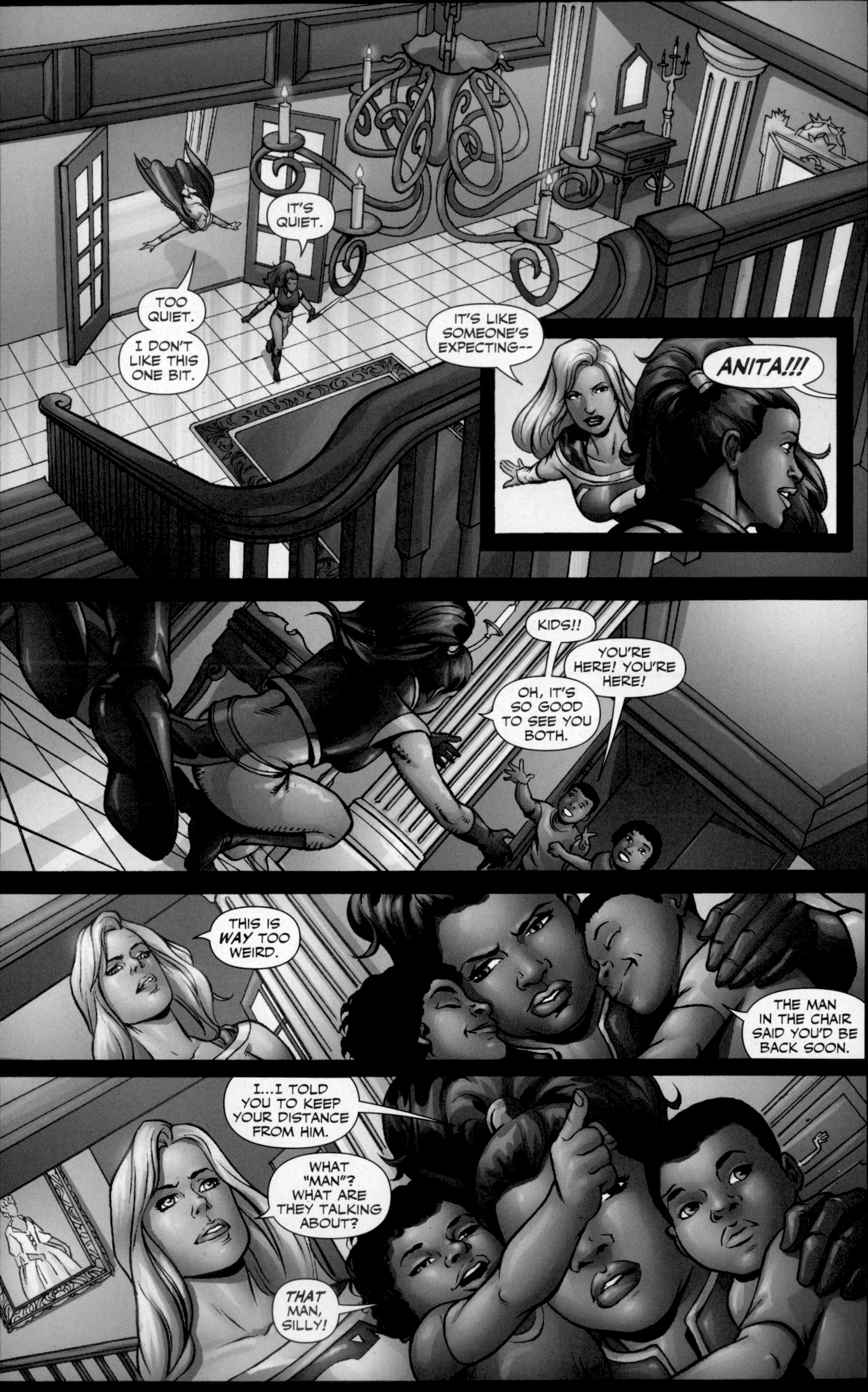
IT'S QUIET.
TOO QUIET.
I DON'T LIKE THIS ONE BIT.
IT'S LIKE SOMEONE'S EXPECTING--
ANITA!!!
KIDS!!
YOU'RE HERE! YOU'RE HERE!
OH, IT'S SO GOOD TO SEE YOU BOTH.
THIS IS WAY TOO WEIRD.
THE MAN IN THE CHAIR SAID YOU'D BE BACK SOON.
I...I TOLD YOU TO KEEP YOUR DISTANCE FROM HIM.
WHAT "MAN"? WHAT ARE THEY TALKING ABOUT?
THAT MAN, SILLY!

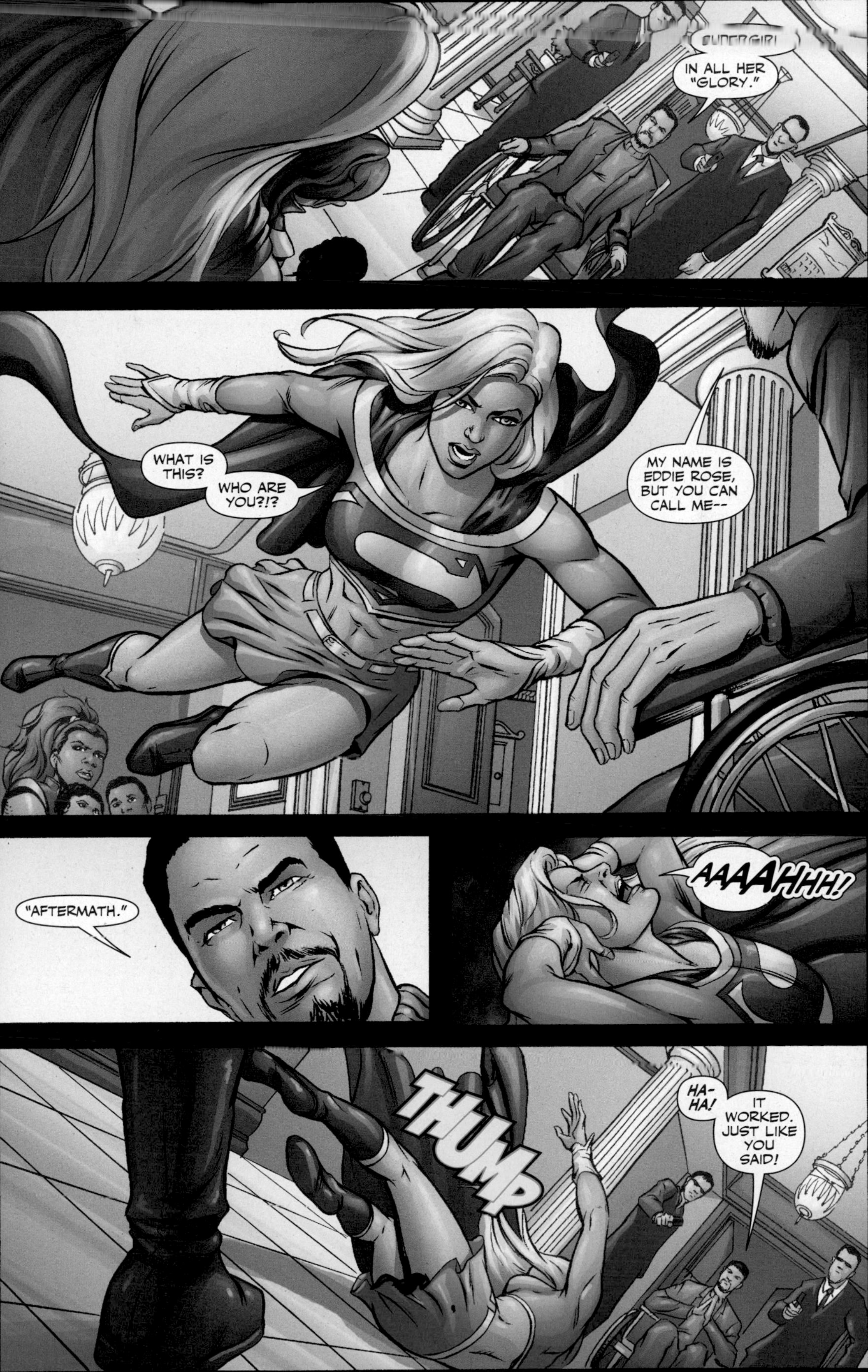
SUPERGIRL
IN ALL HER "GLORY."
WHAT IS THIS?
WHO ARE YOU?!?
MY NAME IS EDDIE ROSE, BUT YOU CAN CALL ME--
"AFTERMATH."
AAAAHHHH!
THUMP
HA-HA!
IT WORKED. JUST LIKE YOU SAID!

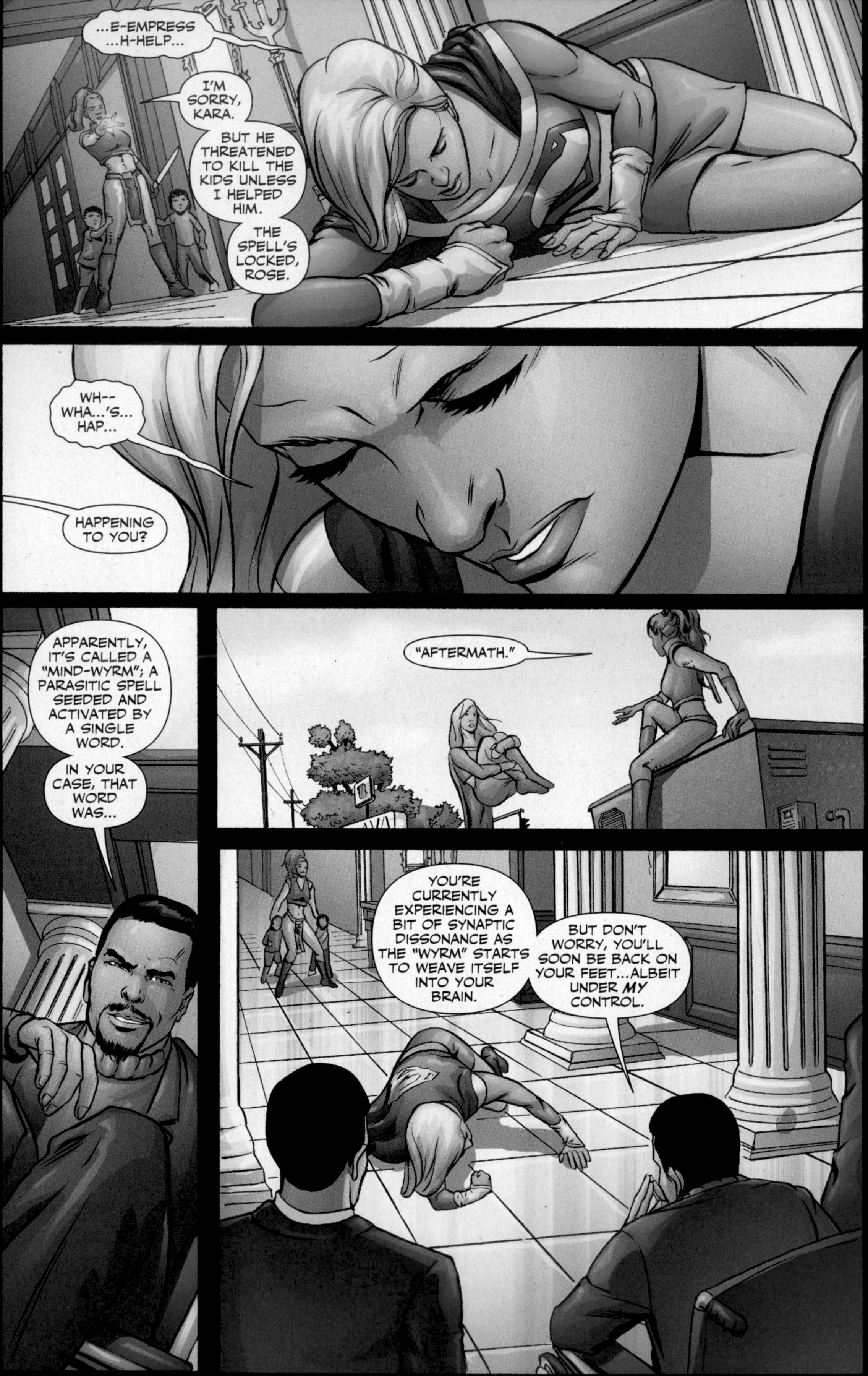
...E-EMPRESS ...H-HELP...
I'M SORRY, KARA.
BUT HE THREATENED TO KILL THE KIDS UNLESS I HELPED HIM.
THE SPELL'S LOCKED, ROSE.
WH-- WHA...'S... HAP...
HAPPENING TO YOU?
APPARENTLY, IT'S CALLED A "MIND-WYRM"; A PARASITIC SPELL SEEDED AND ACTIVATED BY A SINGLE WORD.
IN YOUR CASE, THAT WORD WAS...
"AFTERMATH."
YOU'RE CURRENTLY EXPERIENCING A BIT OF SYNAPTIC DISSONANCE AS THE "WYRM" STARTS TO WEAVE ITSELF INTO YOUR BRAIN.
BUT DON'T WORRY, YOU'LL SOON BE BACK ON YOUR FEET...ALBEIT UNDER *MY* CONTROL.

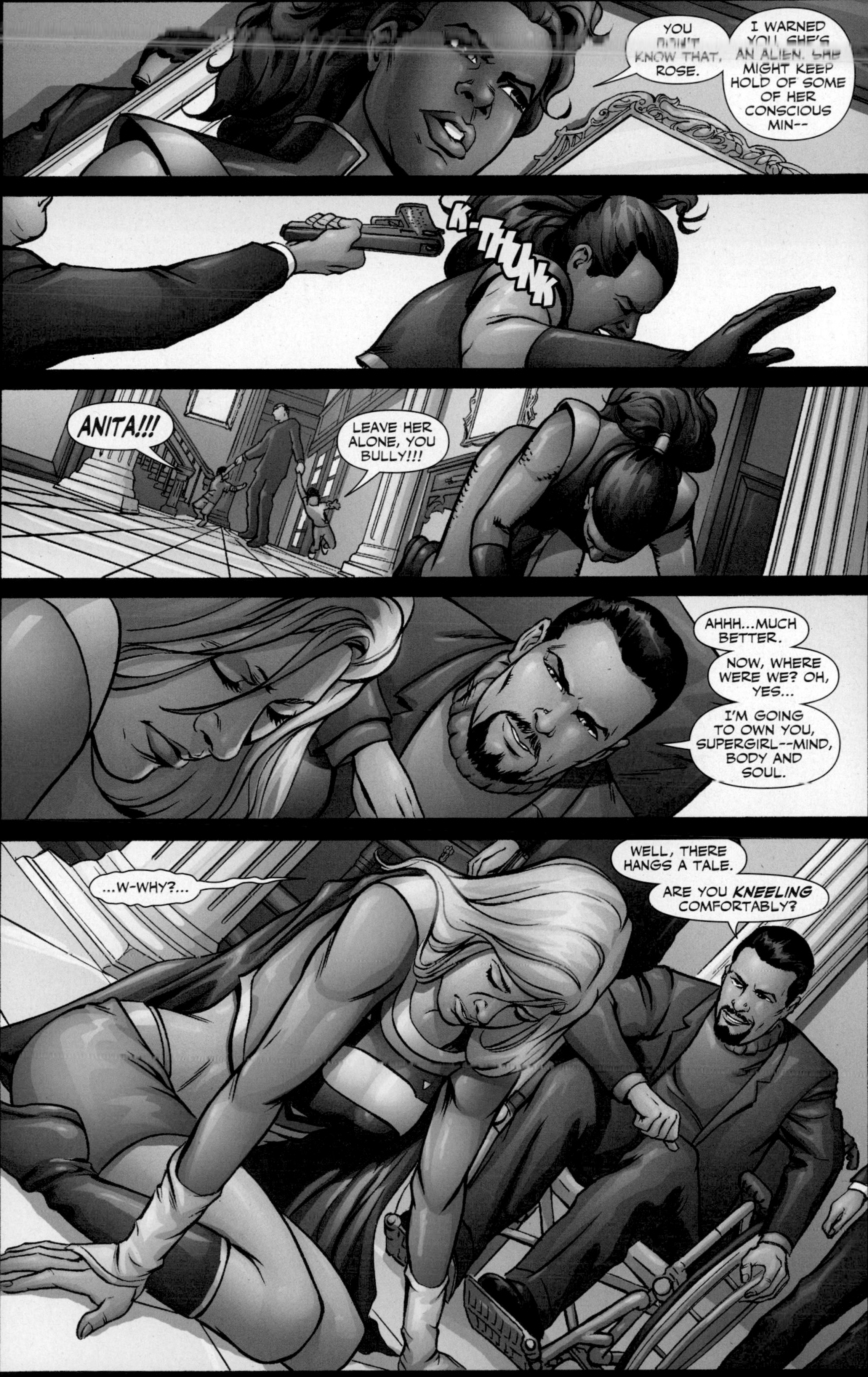
YOU DIDN'T KNOW THAT, ROSE.
I WARNED YOU, SHE'S AN ALIEN. SHE MIGHT KEEP HOLD OF SOME OF HER CONSCIOUS MIN--
K-THUNK
ANITA!!!
LEAVE HER ALONE, YOU BULLY!!!
AHHH...MUCH BETTER.
NOW, WHERE WERE WE? OH, YES...
I'M GOING TO OWN YOU, SUPERGIRL--MIND, BODY AND SOUL.
...W-WHY?...
WELL, THERE HANGS A TALE.
ARE YOU *KNEELING* COMFORTABLY?

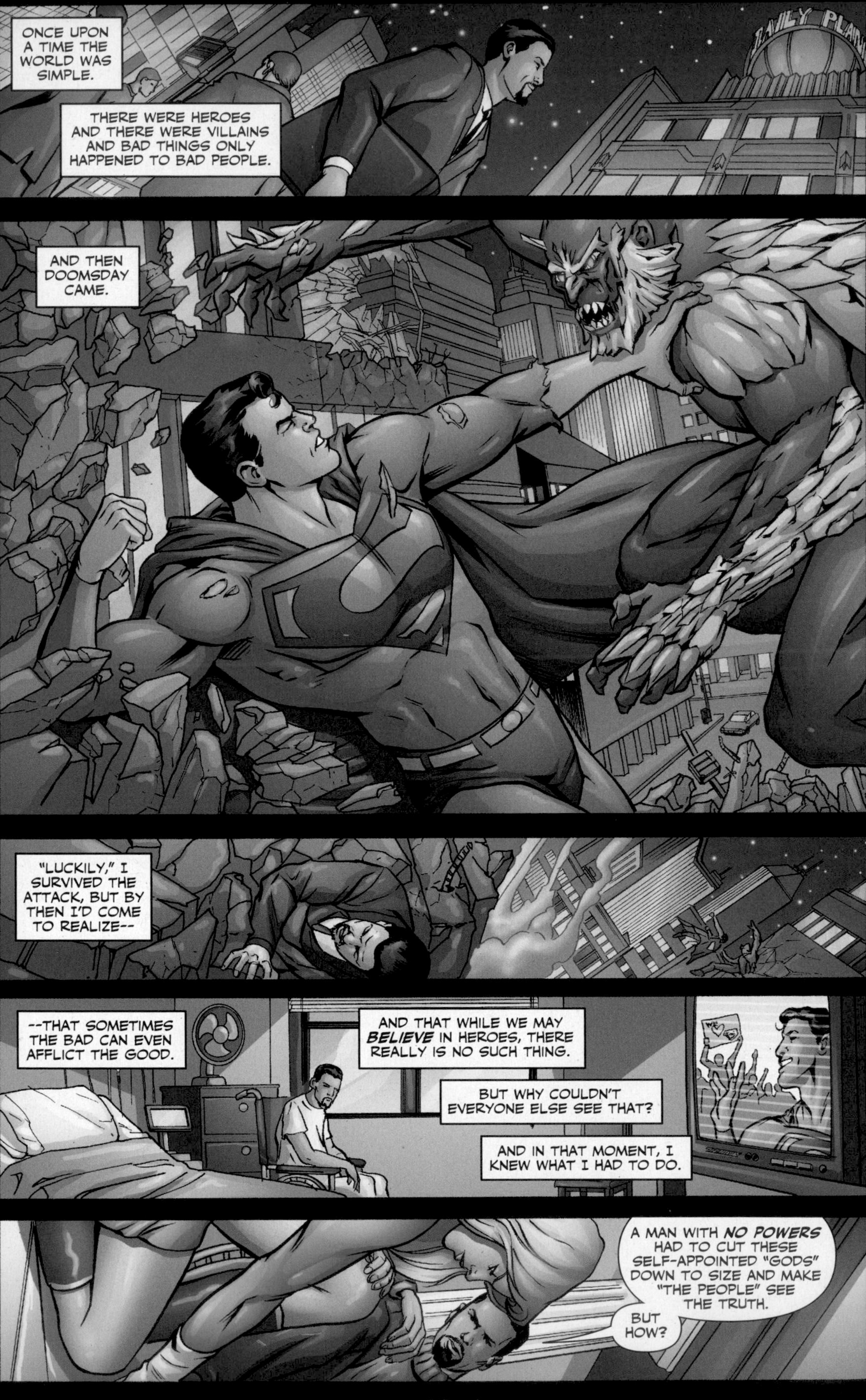
ONCE UPON A TIME THE WORLD WAS SIMPLE.
THERE WERE HEROES AND THERE WERE VILLAINS AND BAD THINGS ONLY HAPPENED TO BAD PEOPLE.
AND THEN DOOMSDAY CAME.
"LUCKILY," I SURVIVED THE ATTACK, BUT BY THEN I'D COME TO REALIZE--
--THAT SOMETIMES THE BAD CAN EVEN AFFLICT THE GOOD.
AND THAT WHILE WE MAY *BELIEVE* IN HEROES, THERE REALLY IS NO SUCH THING.
BUT WHY COULDN'T EVERYONE ELSE SEE THAT?
AND IN THAT MOMENT, I KNEW WHAT I HAD TO DO.
A MAN WITH *NO POWERS* HAD TO CUT THESE SELF-APPOINTED "GODS" DOWN TO SIZE AND MAKE "THE PEOPLE" SEE THE TRUTH.
BUT HOW?

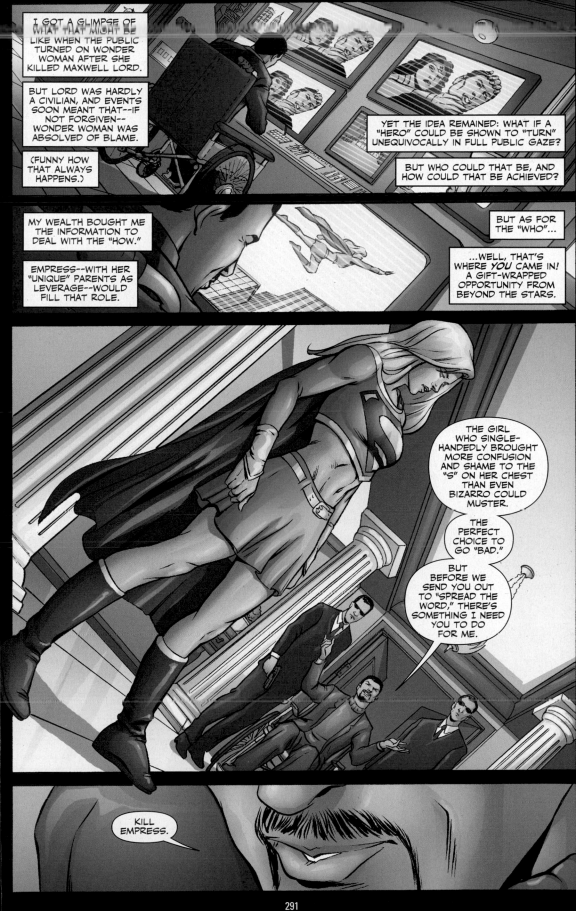

I GOT A GLIMPSE OF WHAT THAT MIGHT BE LIKE WHEN THE PUBLIC TURNED ON WONDER WOMAN AFTER SHE KILLED MAXWELL LORD.

BUT LORD WAS HARDLY A CIVILIAN, AND EVENTS SOON MEANT THAT--IF NOT FORGIVEN-- WONDER WOMAN WAS ABSOLVED OF BLAME.

(FUNNY HOW THAT ALWAYS HAPPENS.)

YET THE IDEA REMAINED: WHAT IF A "HERO" COULD BE SHOWN TO "TURN" UNEQUIVOCALLY IN FULL PUBLIC GAZE?

BUT WHO COULD THAT BE, AND HOW COULD THAT BE ACHIEVED?

MY WEALTH BOUGHT ME THE INFORMATION TO DEAL WITH THE "HOW."

EMPRESS--WITH HER "UNIQUE" PARENTS AS LEVERAGE--WOULD FILL THAT ROLE.

BUT AS FOR THE "WHO"...

...WELL, THAT'S WHERE YOU CAME IN! A GIFT-WRAPPED OPPORTUNITY FROM BEYOND THE STARS.

THE GIRL WHO SINGLE-HANDEDLY BROUGHT MORE CONFUSION AND SHAME TO THE "S" ON HER CHEST THAN EVEN BIZARRO COULD MUSTER.

THE PERFECT CHOICE TO GO "BAD."

BUT BEFORE WE SEND YOU OUT TO "SPREAD THE WORD," THERE'S SOMETHING I NEED YOU TO DO FOR ME.

KILL EMPRESS.

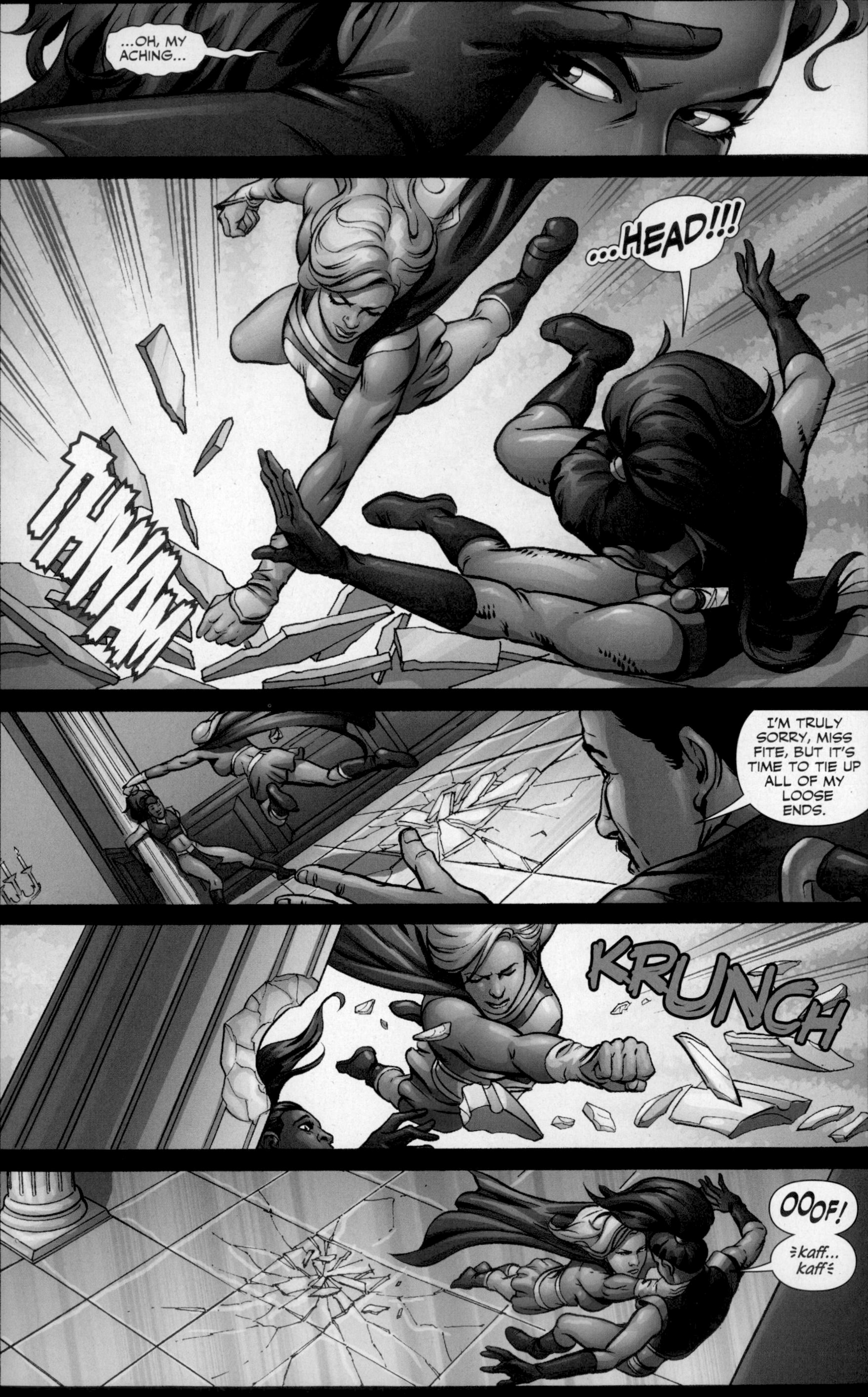
...OH, MY ACHING...
...HEAD!!!
THWAM
I'M TRULY SORRY, MISS FITE, BUT IT'S TIME TO TIE UP ALL OF MY LOOSE ENDS.
KRUNCH
OOOF!
kaff... kaff

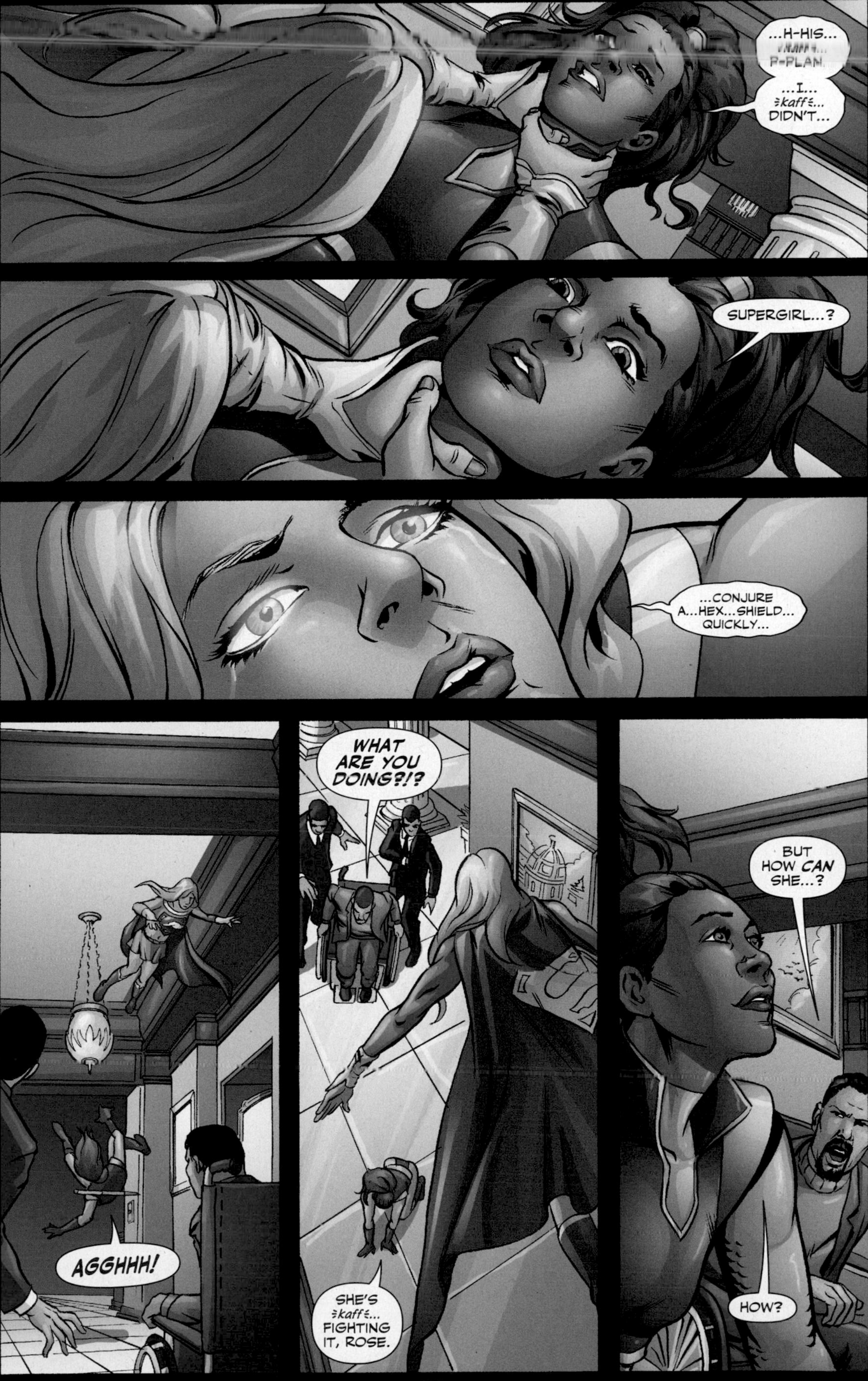
...H-HIS... kaff... P-PLAN.
...I... kaff... DIDN'T...
SUPERGIRL...?
...CONJURE A...HEX...SHIELD... QUICKLY...
AGGHHH!
WHAT ARE YOU DOING?!?
SHE'S kaff... FIGHTING IT, ROSE.
BUT HOW CAN SHE...?
HOW?

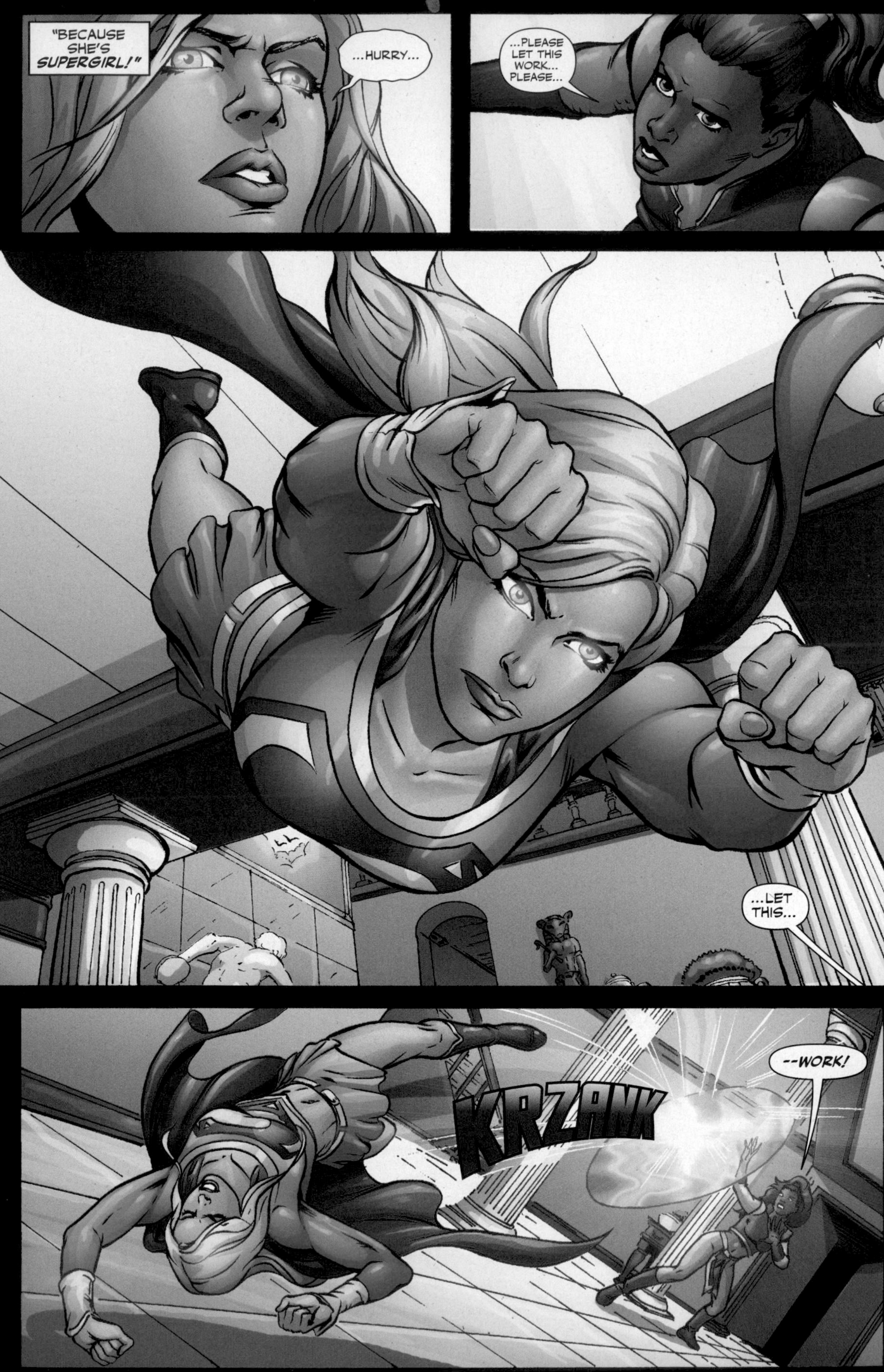
"BECAUSE SHE'S SUPERGIRL!"
...HURRY...
...PLEASE LET THIS WORK... PLEASE...
...LET THIS...
KRZANK
--WORK!

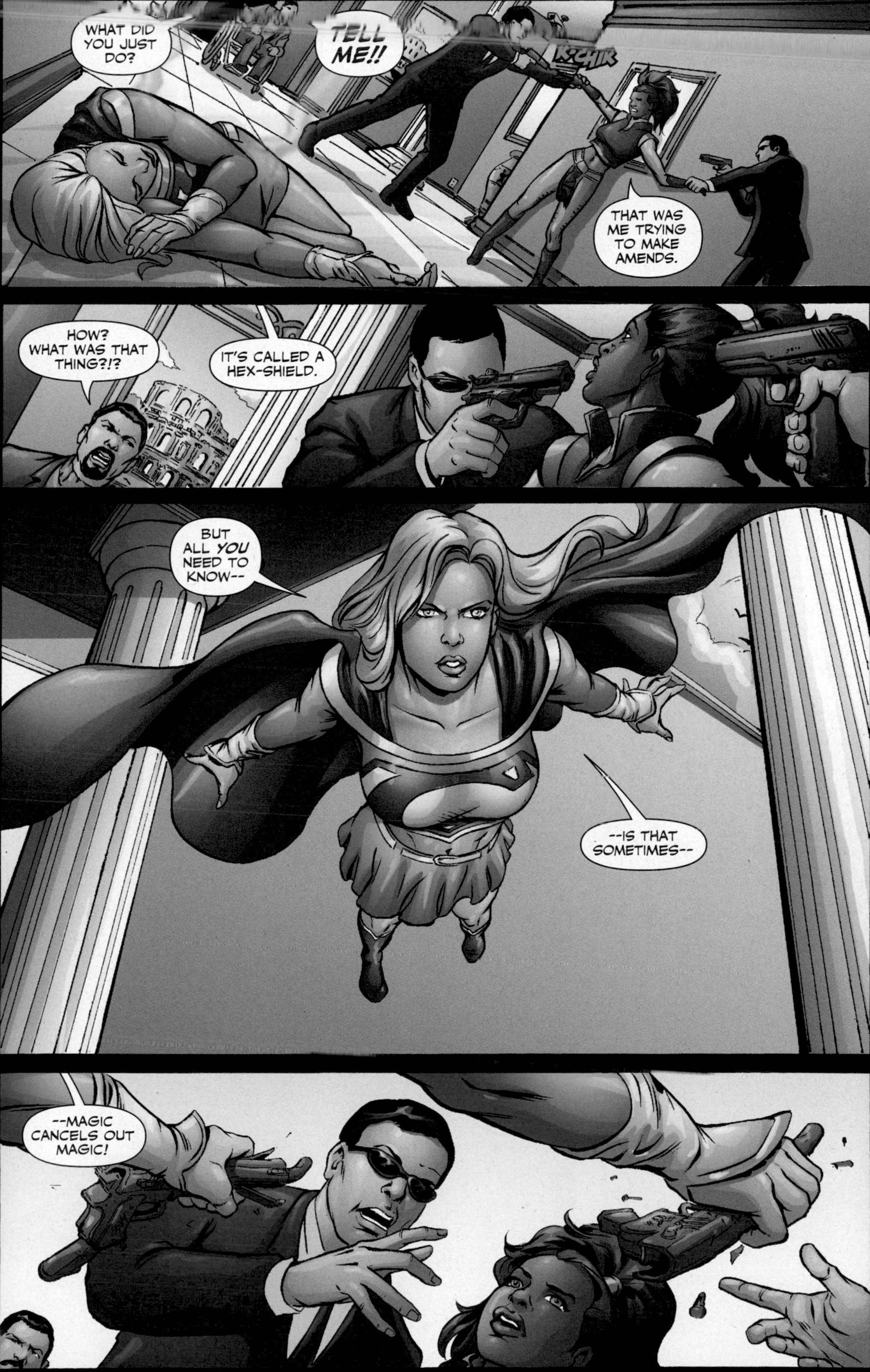
WHAT DID YOU JUST DO?
TELL ME!!
K-CHIK
THAT WAS ME TRYING TO MAKE AMENDS.
HOW? WHAT WAS THAT THING?!?
IT'S CALLED A HEX-SHIELD.
BUT ALL YOU NEED TO KNOW--
--IS THAT SOMETIMES--
--MAGIC CANCELS OUT MAGIC!

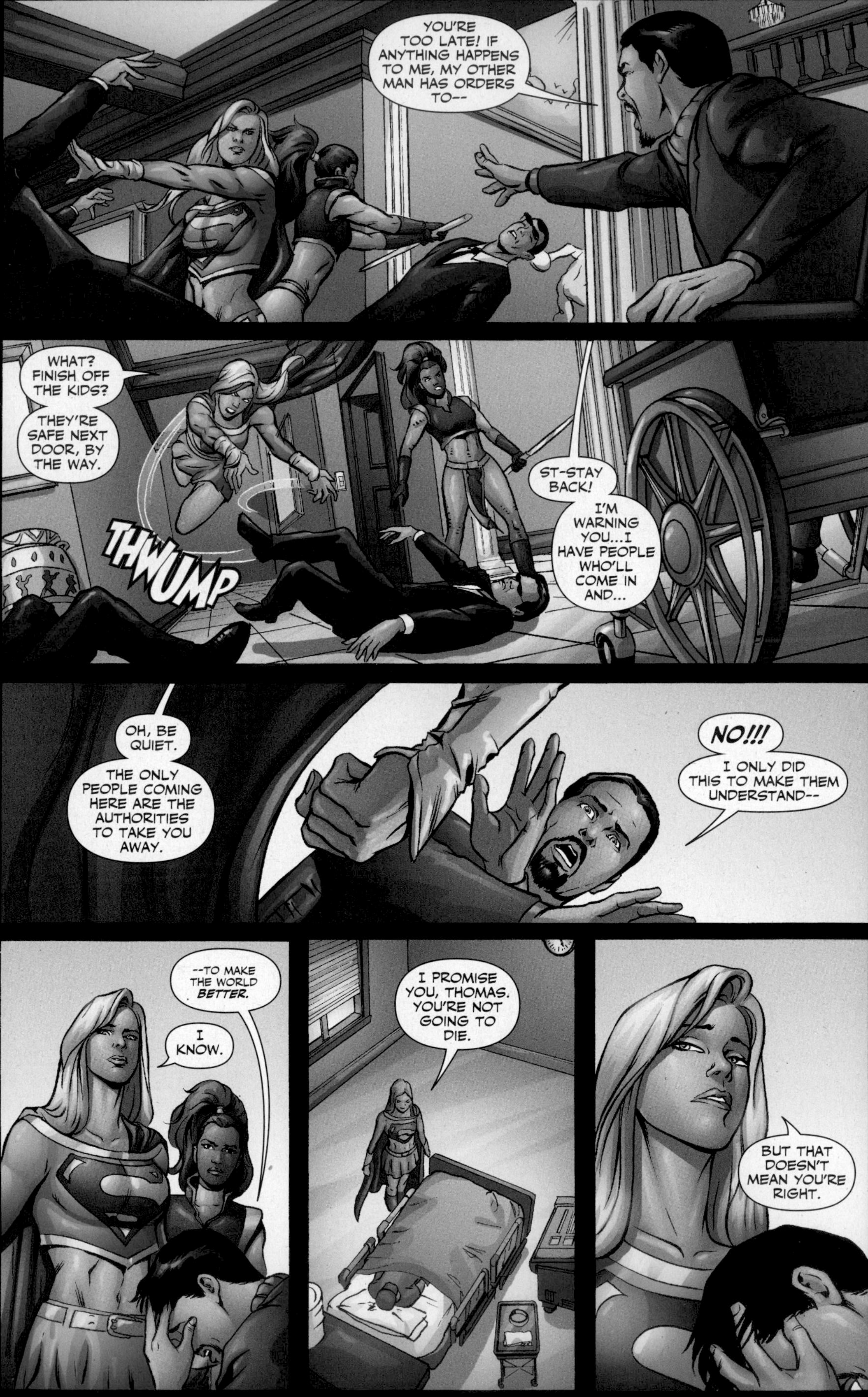
YOU'RE TOO LATE! IF ANYTHING HAPPENS TO ME, MY OTHER MAN HAS ORDERS TO--
WHAT? FINISH OFF THE KIDS?
THEY'RE SAFE NEXT DOOR, BY THE WAY.
THWUMP
ST-STAY BACK!
I'M WARNING YOU...I HAVE PEOPLE WHO'LL COME IN AND...
OH, BE QUIET.
THE ONLY PEOPLE COMING HERE ARE THE AUTHORITIES TO TAKE YOU AWAY.
NO!!!
I ONLY DID THIS TO MAKE THEM UNDERSTAND--
--TO MAKE THE WORLD *BETTER.*
I KNOW.
I PROMISE YOU, THOMAS. YOU'RE NOT GOING TO DIE.
BUT THAT DOESN'T MEAN YOU'RE RIGHT.

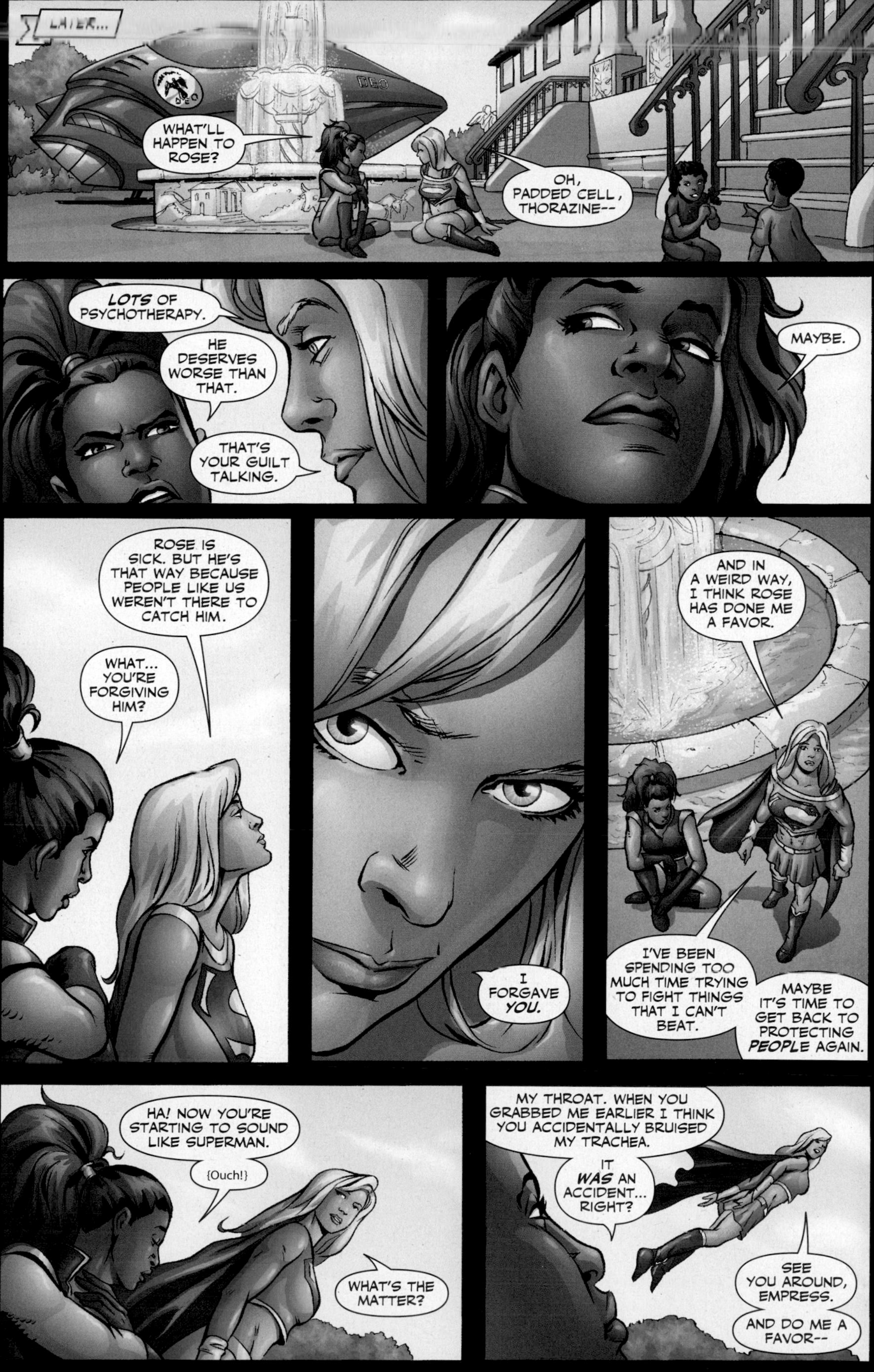
LATER...
WHAT'LL HAPPEN TO ROSE?
OH, PADDED CELL, THORAZINE--
LOTS OF PSYCHOTHERAPY.
HE DESERVES WORSE THAN THAT.
THAT'S YOUR GUILT TALKING.
MAYBE.
ROSE IS SICK. BUT HE'S THAT WAY BECAUSE PEOPLE LIKE US WEREN'T THERE TO CATCH HIM.
WHAT... YOU'RE FORGIVING HIM?
I FORGAVE YOU.
AND IN A WEIRD WAY, I THINK ROSE HAS DONE ME A FAVOR.
I'VE BEEN SPENDING TOO MUCH TIME TRYING TO FIGHT THINGS THAT I CAN'T BEAT.
MAYBE IT'S TIME TO GET BACK TO PROTECTING PEOPLE AGAIN.
HA! NOW YOU'RE STARTING TO SOUND LIKE SUPERMAN.
{Ouch!}
WHAT'S THE MATTER?
MY THROAT. WHEN YOU GRABBED ME EARLIER I THINK YOU ACCIDENTALLY BRUISED MY TRACHEA.
IT WAS AN ACCIDENT... RIGHT?
SEE YOU AROUND, EMPRESS.
AND DO ME A FAVOR--

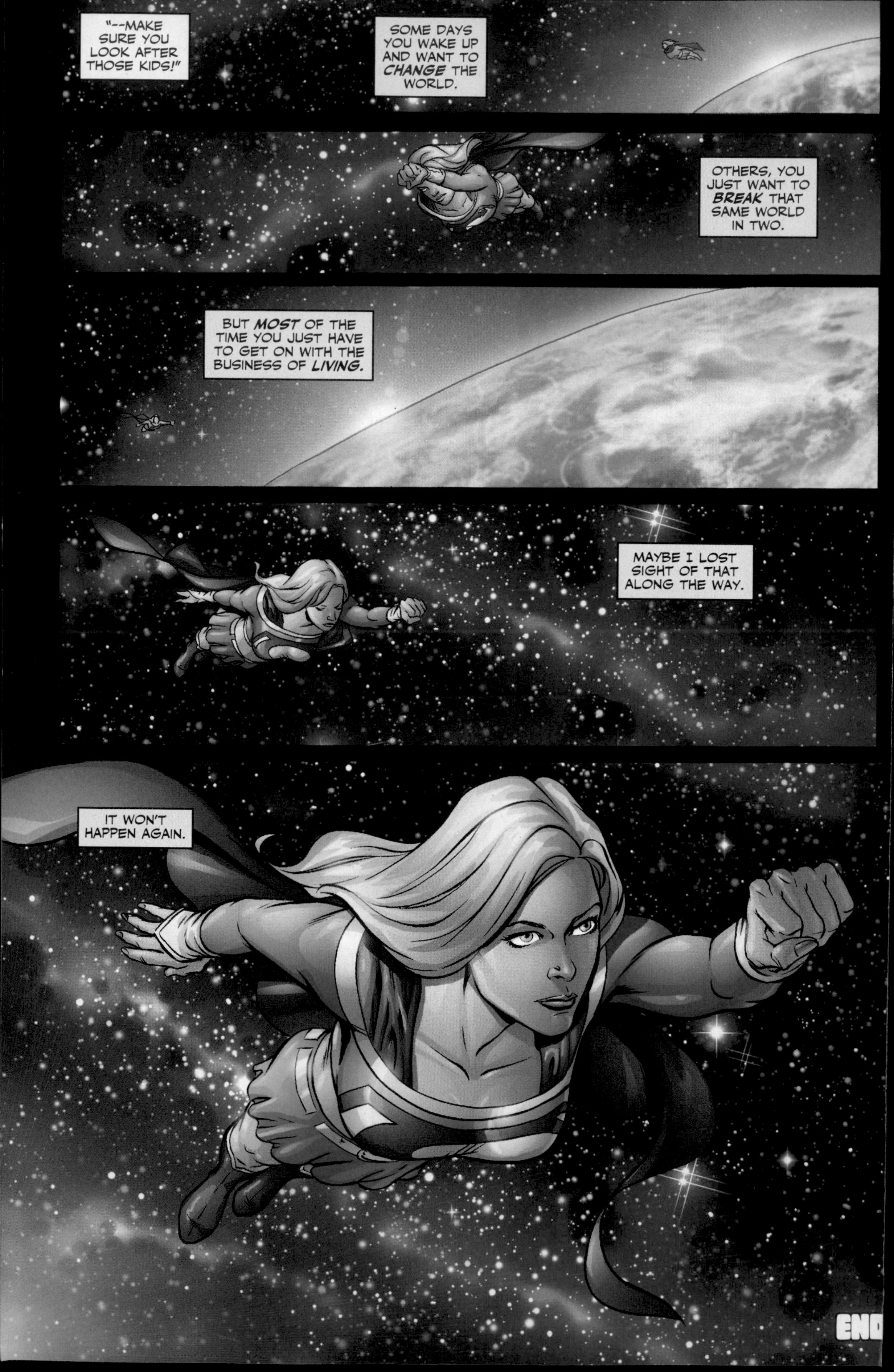
"--MAKE SURE YOU LOOK AFTER THOSE KIDS!"
SOME DAYS YOU WAKE UP AND WANT TO *CHANGE* THE WORLD.
OTHERS, YOU JUST WANT TO *BREAK* THAT SAME WORLD IN TWO.
BUT *MOST* OF THE TIME YOU JUST HAVE TO GET ON WITH THE BUSINESS OF *LIVING.*
MAYBE I LOST SIGHT OF THAT ALONG THE WAY.
IT WON'T HAPPEN AGAIN.
END

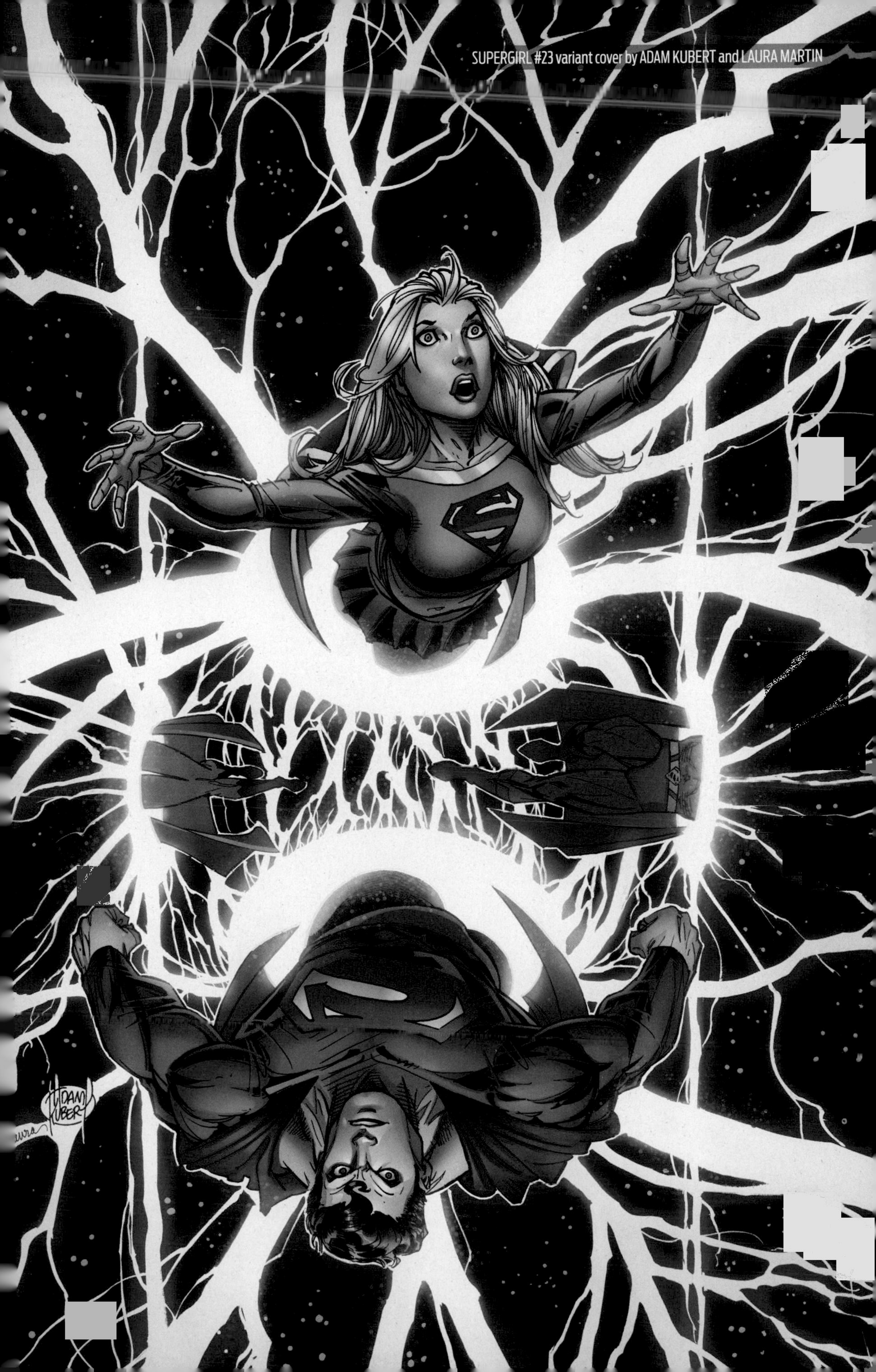

SUPERGIRL #23 variant cover by ADAM KUBERT and LAURA MARTIN

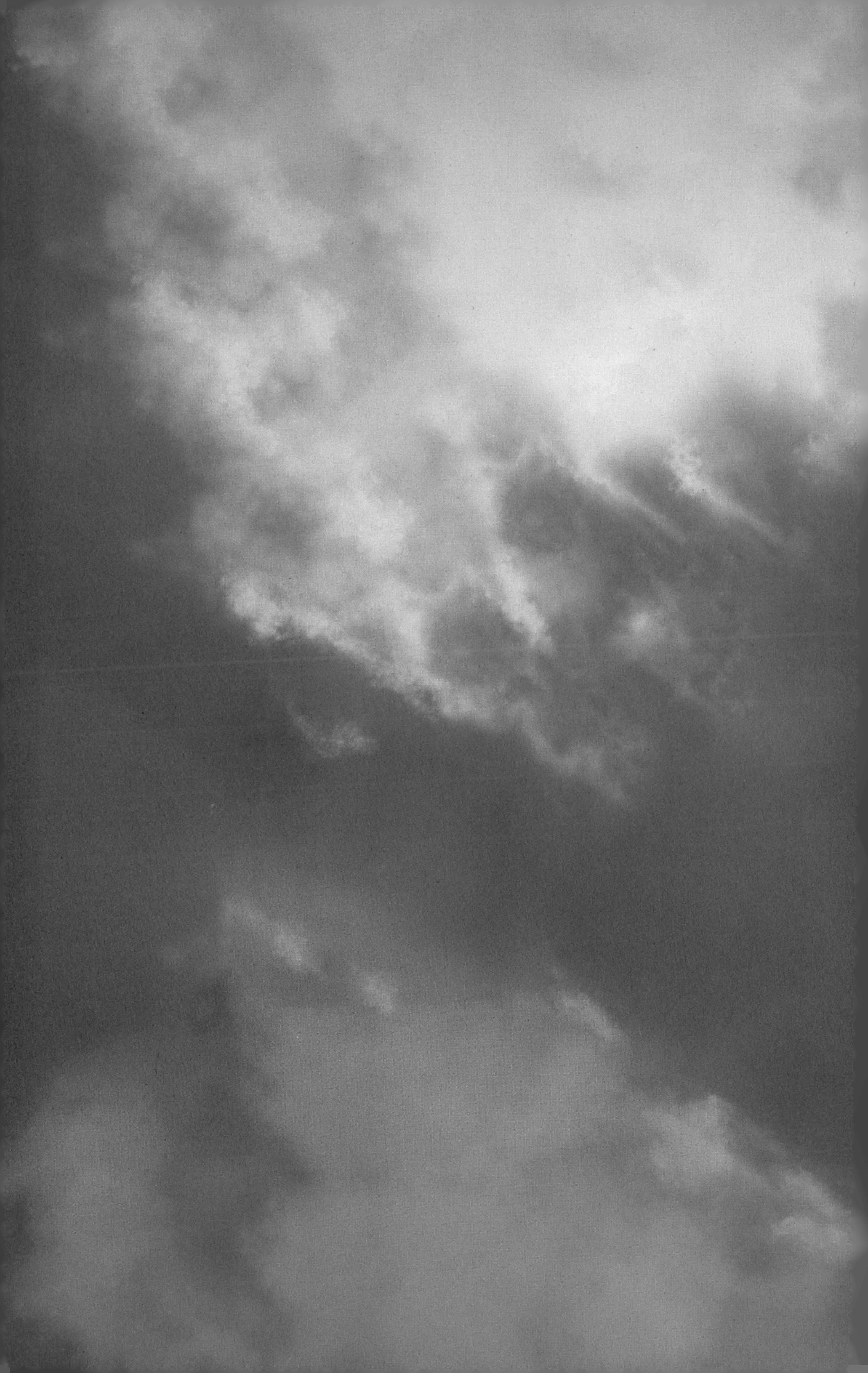

DC UNIVERSE REBIRTH

SUPERMAN

"That gorgeous spectacle is an undeniable part of Superman's appeal, but the family dynamics are what make it such an engaging read."
– A.V. CLUB

"Head and shoulders above the rest."
– NEWSARAMA

DC UNIVERSE REBIRTH
SUPERMAN
VOL. 1: SON OF SUPERMAN
PETER J. TOMASI with PATRICK GLEASON, DOUG MAHNKE & JORGE JIMENEZ

VOL.1 SON OF SUPERMAN
PETER J.TOMASI • PATRICK GLEASON • DOUG MAHNKE • JORGE JIMENEZ • MICK GRAY

**SUPERGIRL VOL. 1:
REIGN OF THE SUPERMEN**

**ACTION COMICS VOL. 1:
PATH OF DOOM**

**BATMAN VOL. 1:
I AM GOTHAM**

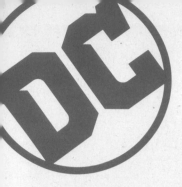

"Greg Rucka and company have created a compelling narrative for fans of the Amazing Amazon."– **NERDIST**

"(A) heartfelt and genuine take on Diana's origin."– **NEWSARAMA**

DC UNIVERSE REBIRTH

WONDER WOMAN

VOL. 1: THE LIES

GREG RUCKA
with LIAM SHARP

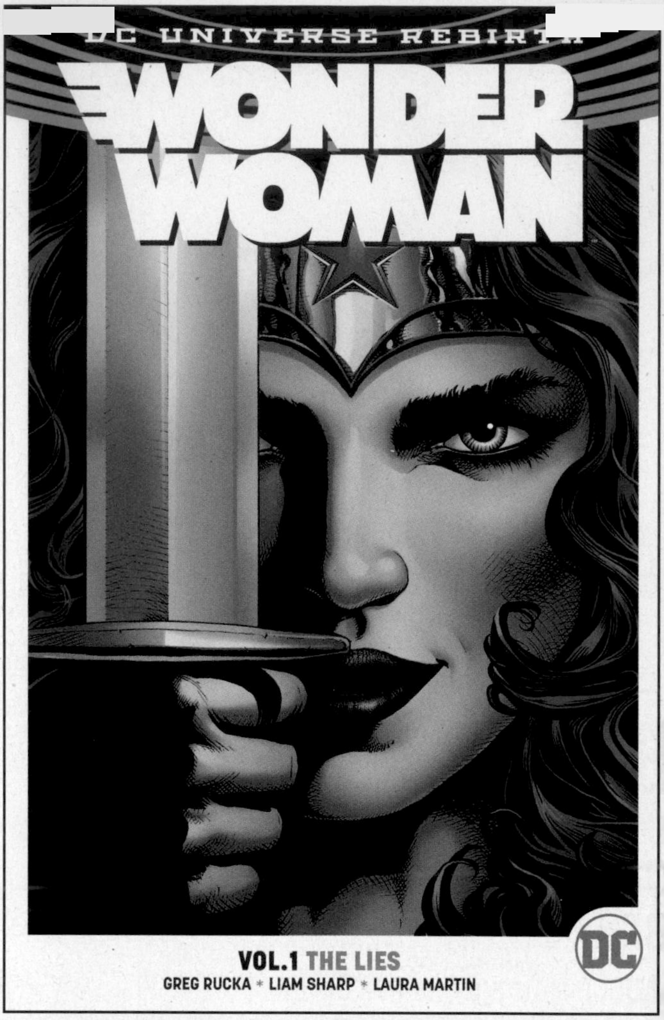
DC UNIVERSE REBIRTH
WONDER WOMAN
DC
VOL.1 THE LIES
GREG RUCKA • LIAM SHARP • LAURA MARTIN

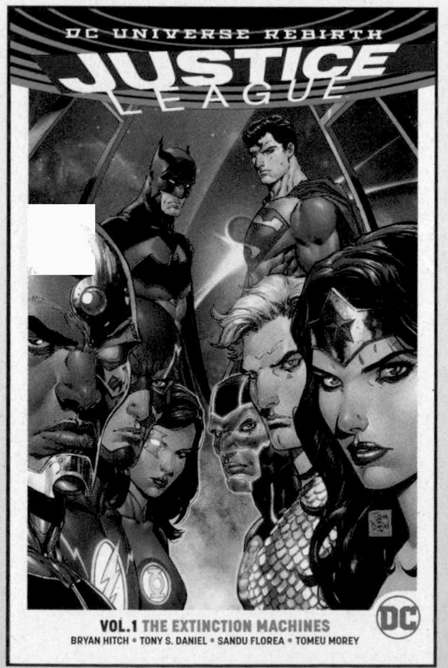
DC UNIVERSE REBIRTH
JUSTICE LEAGUE
DC
VOL.1 THE EXTINCTION MACHINES
BRYAN HITCH • TONY S. DANIEL • SANDU FLOREA • TOMEU MOREY

JUSTICE LEAGUE VOL. 1: THE EXTINCTION MACHINES

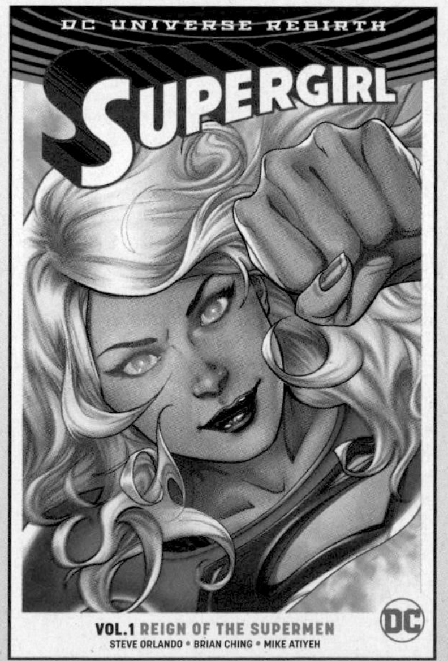
DC UNIVERSE REBIRTH
SUPERGIRL
DC
VOL.1 REIGN OF THE SUPERMEN
STEVE ORLANDO • BRIAN CHING • MIKE ATIYEH

SUPERGIRL VOL. 1: REIGN OF THE SUPERMEN

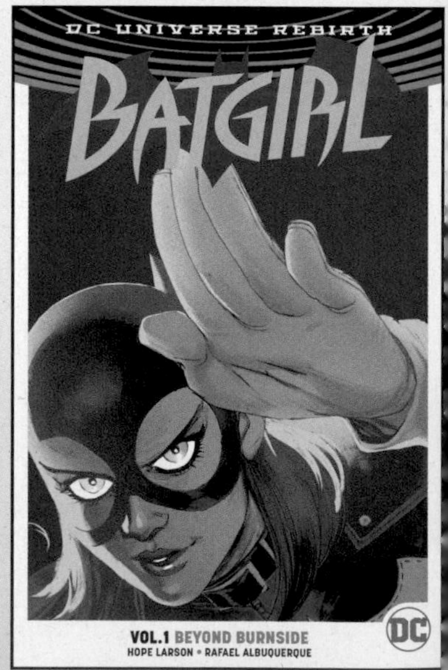
DC UNIVERSE REBIRTH
BATGIRL
DC
VOL.1 BEYOND BURNSIDE
HOPE LARSON • RAFAEL ALBUQUERQUE

BATGIRL VOL. 1: BEYOND BURNSIDE

Get more DC graphic novels wherever comics and books are sold!

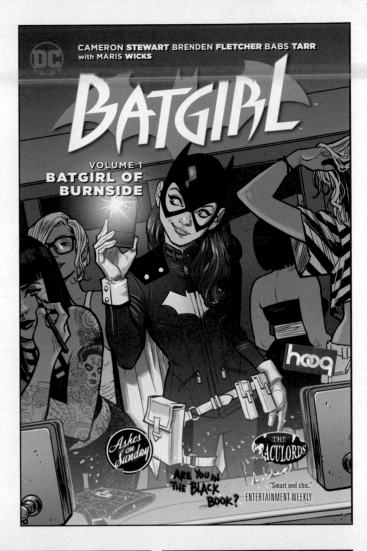